ACTS OF INQUIRY

A Guide to Reading, Research, and Writing at the University of Washington

WITH READINGS

A CUSTOM EDITION OF

From Inquiry to Academic Writing: A Practical Guide
By Stuart Greene and April Lidinsky

WITH ADDITIONAL CHAPTERS TAKEN FROM

The Well-Crafted Sentence: A Writer's Guide to Style
By Nora Bacon

The Academic Writer: A Brief Guide
By Lisa Ede

Writing Now: Shaping Words and Images
By Lee Odell and Susan M. Katz

ACTS OF INQUIRY

A Guide to Reading, Research, and Writing at the University of Washington

WITH READINGS

Edited by Allison Gross, Annie Dwyer,
David Holmberg, and Anis Bawarshi

Bedford/St. Martin's   BOSTON ■ NEW YORK

Cover design: Edmond Chang
Cover photographs: University of Washington and Edmond Chang

Acknowledgments

Jean Anyon. "The Economic Is Political." From *Radical Possibilities: Public Policy, Urban Education and a New Social Movement* by Jean Anyon. Copyright © 2005 by Taylor & Francis Group LLC. Reprinted by permission of Routledge, an imprint of Taylor & Francis Group.

Gloria Anzaldúa. "How to Tame a Wild Tongue." From *Borderlands/La Frontera: The New Mestiza*, by Gloria Anzaldúa. Copyright © 1987, 1999 by Gloria Anzaldua. Reprinted by permission of Aunt Lute Books.

James Baldwin. "If Black English Isn't a Language, Then Tell Me, What Is?" Originally published in the *New York Times*, July 29, 1979, Op-Ed. Copyright © 1979 by James Baldwin. Collected in *The Price of the Ticket*, published by St. Martin's. Reprinted by arrangement with the James Baldwin Estate.

John Berger. "Ways of Seeing." Chapter 1 from *Ways of Seeing* by John Berger. Copyright © 1972 by John Berger. Reprinted by permission of Viking Penguin, a division of Penguin Group (USA) Inc.

Acknowledgments and copyrights are continued at the back of the book on pages 735–36, which constitute an extension of the copyright page.

Preface

Welcome to the Expository Writing Program and to your composition course! Whether you are taking English 109/110, English 111, English 121, or English 131, we hope the course will help you not only to fulfill the University of Washington's composition ("C") requirement but also to continue to develop the critical reading, research, and writing skills that will allow you to succeed as a writer at the UW and beyond.

In offering a gateway to academic reading, research, and writing at the University of Washington, Expository Writing Program (EWP) courses are designed around a set of shared learning outcomes, which are printed immediately following this Preface. These outcomes articulate the need for students to develop and practice the skills and habits that are foundational to academic writing and at the same time prepare students to adapt these skills and habits for the varied demands of university-wide writing. In what follows, we will first explain what these outcomes mean for you as a student in this course, and we will then describe how this book is designed to support you in meeting these outcomes.

Research in writing development has demonstrated that writing is not a skill that is mastered once and for all. Instead, successful writers draw on and adapt writing strategies to participate meaningfully and effectively within various contexts. Because writing is intimately connected to how people in different contexts inquire, make meaning, get things done, and relate to one another, in order to write effectively, writers need to consider strategies that are appropriate to these contexts. For example, they need to consider what kinds of writing (genres) to use, how to organize their writing, what counts as evidence and how to present that evidence, what word choices to make, and so on. In the same way, students within a university are often called on to adapt their writing for different disciplines, learning to write effectively in history, biology, business, political science, sociology, geography, chemistry, and more, as they learn the conventions, expectations, and methods of inquiry of their major fields of study.

This composition course prepares you to write effectively for these different contexts by focusing on reading, research, writing, and revision as acts of inquiry. Although academic writing is varied and discipline specific, it does possess foundational features that can be identified, generalized, and learned. Among the hallmarks of academic writing are the ability to read and analyze complex texts critically, to apply methods and concepts for particular purposes, to use research to generate ideas as well as support them, and to make arguments based in claims, evidence, and analysis. Successful academic writers also recognize writing as a process of learning, and they make effective use of revision, peer review, and editing. This course will enable you to develop and practice these general skills and habits, as outlined in outcomes 2, 3, and 4. But because we want you to be able to build on and apply these skills and habits as you encounter different writing contexts and tasks throughout and beyond your college career, the course will also allow you to develop an awareness of the strategies that writers use in different writing contexts as articulated in outcome 1, so that you can effectively situate your writing skills and habits in these contexts.

Acts of Inquiry: A Guide to Reading, Research, and Writing at the University of Washington is designed to support you in meeting these course outcomes. It is meant to help you not only develop writing skills and habits that you can build on throughout your time at the UW but also situate these skills and habits in different contexts of inquiry. To that end, the book is divided into five parts, each of which provides strategies to guide you from understanding academic writing contexts and situating your inquiry within them (Part One), to reading and conducting research as ways to generate and support your inquiry (Part Two), to formulating and developing arguments as forms of inquiry (Part Three), to practicing strategies for drafting, revising, and editing your writing as processes of inquiry (Part Four). Part Five contains a wide range of readings that offer both methods and objects for inquiry. These five parts, which describe writing as a way of engaging with and working through ideas, reflect the acts of inquiry suggested in the book's title.

Part One introduces you to academic inquiry as a "conversation" that you can join through reading and writing. Chapters 1 and 2 describe what academic conversations are like and how you can situate your inquiry within different writing situations. In Part Two, you will have an opportunity to develop reading and research skills that will help you generate and support your inquiry. Chapters 3 and 4, which examine how reading and writing are interconnected, will teach you critical reading skills. They will teach you to pay attention not only to what a text is saying but also to *how* and *why* it is saying it — in short, to critically examine the choices that the writer of a text has made and the effects these choices have on readers. Chapters 5 and 6 provide strategies for conducting research, from finding and evaluating sources to doing field research. Chapter 7 will teach you how to analyze claims and arguments in what you are reading, so that you can then produce your own claims and arguments — the focus of Part Three. Part Three provides strategies for formulating and developing academic arguments: identifying issues and framing questions (Chapter 8), formulating and developing claims (Chapter 9), and providing evidence and documenting sources (Chapter 10). Part Four focuses on drafting, revising, and editing your writing. Chapter 11 provides strategies for appealing to your readers, while Chapters 12 to 15 offer guidance for drafting your essays: from considering larger organizational issues to crafting meaning at the sentence level. Chapter 16 provides strategies for revising and editing your writing throughout your writing process, from early to later to final drafts.

Part Five of the book includes readings on a variety of topics, written in different contexts, for different audiences, in different genres, using different media (print, visual, electronic, multimedia). Many of the readings are academic in nature, resembling the kinds of texts you will encounter as a student at the UW. Others — such as ads, editorials, speeches, cartoons, public art, photographs, magazine articles, and poems — are directed at and produced for different audiences. And other documents are overtly political, like the "Academic Bill of Rights," the U.S. Supreme Court opinions, and the Black Panther Party's "Ten Point Plan." Some of the readings can be used as *methods*, meaning they can provide techniques for analyzing a concept, idea, phenomenon, and the like. Some of the readings can be used as *objects*, meaning they can be analyzed for their arguments, how they function, what they do, and so on. And some of the readings can serve both purposes. Whether these texts are used as models for your own work, objects of analysis, or conceptual lenses for inquiry, they provide a range of work that will allow you to explore how arguments take different forms for different purposes in different genres and media. The readings, together with the tools for inquiry presented in Parts One through Four, should enable you to fulfill the outcome goals for your composition course as well as your own personal writing goals by helping you situate your inquiry within the different contexts you will encounter at the University of Washington and beyond.

Anis Bawarshi
Director, Expository Writing Program

Outcomes for Expository Writing Program Courses

1. **To Demonstrate an Awareness of the Strategies That Writers Use in Different Writing Contexts.**

   - The writing employs style, tone, and conventions appropriate to the demands of a particular genre and situation.
   - The writer is able to demonstrate the ability to write for different audiences and contexts, both within and outside the university classroom.
   - The writing has a clear understanding of its audience, and various aspects of the writing (mode of inquiry, content, structure, appeals, tone, sentences, and word choice) address and are strategically pitched to that audience.
   - The writer articulates and assesses the effects of his or her writing choices.

2. **To Read, Analyze, and Synthesize Complex Texts and Incorporate Multiple Kinds of Evidence Purposefully in Order to Generate and Support Writing.**

   - The writing demonstrates an understanding of the course texts as necessary for the purpose at hand.
   - Course texts are used in strategic, focused ways (e.g., summarized, cited, applied, challenged, re-contextualized) to support the goals of the writing.
   - The writing is intertextual, meaning that a "conversation" between texts and ideas is created in support of the writer's goals.
   - The writer is able to utilize multiple kinds of evidence gathered from various sources (primary and secondary — for example, library research, interviews, questionnaires, observations, cultural artifacts) in order to support writing goals.

- The writing demonstrates responsible use of the MLA (or other appropriate) system of documenting sources.

3. **To Produce Complex, Analytic, Persuasive Arguments That Matter in Academic Contexts.**

   - The argument is appropriately complex, based in a claim that emerges from and explores a line of inquiry.
   - The stakes of the argument, why what is being argued matters, are articulated and persuasive.
   - The argument involves analysis, which is the close scrutiny and examination of evidence and assumptions in support of a larger set of ideas.
   - The argument is persuasive, taking into consideration counter-claims and multiple points of view as it generates its own perspective and position.
   - The argument utilizes a clear organizational strategy and effective transitions that develop its line of inquiry.

4. **To Develop Flexible Strategies for Revising, Editing, and Proofreading Writing.**

   - The writing demonstrates substantial and successful revision.
   - The writing responds to substantive issues raised by the instructor and peers.
   - Errors of grammar, punctuation, and mechanics are proofread and edited so as not to interfere with reading and understanding the writing.

Table of Contents

Readings: Methods and Objects of Inquiry   335

Alternative Tables of Contents

Quantitative Research

Theoretical Analysis

THEMES FOR INQUIRY

Education

Language

Politics of Identity

Visual Representation

Media

REPRESENTING INQUIRY (GENRE, AUDIENCE, MODALITY)

Personal Essay

Academic Writing for Public Audiences

Scholarly Writing for Academic Audiences

Public Documents

Visual Argument

Declarations

Hybrid Genres

Poetry/Song

ACTS OF INQUIRY

A Guide to
Reading, Research,
and Writing at the
University of Washington

WITH READINGS

PART ONE

Situating Inquiry: Joining the Conversation

1

Habits of Mind of Academic Writers

A t the center of all academic writing is a curiosity about how the world works and a desire to understand it in its full complexity. To discover and make sense of that complexity, academic writers apply rigorous **habits of mind**, patterns of thought that lead them to question assumptions, explore alternatives, anticipate opposing arguments, compare experiences, and identify the causes and consequences of ideas and events. Habits of mind are especially important today, when we are bombarded with appeals to buy this or that product and with information that may or may not be true. For example, in "106 Science Claims and a Truckful of Baloney" (*The Best American Science and Nature Writing*, 2005), William Speed Weed illustrates the extent to which the claims of science vie for our attention alongside the claims of advertising. He notes that advertisers often package their claims as science, but wonders whether a box of Cheerios really can reduce cholesterol. As readers we have a responsibility to test the claims of both science and advertising in order to decide what to believe and act upon. Weed found that "very few of the 100 claims" he evaluated "proved completely true" and that "a good number were patently false." Testing the truth of claims — learning to consider information carefully and critically, and to weigh competing points of view before making our own judgments — gives us power over our own lives.

The habits of mind and practices valued by academic writers are probably ones you already share. You are behaving "academically" when you comparison shop, a process that entails learning about the product in magazines and on the Internet and then looking at the choices firsthand before you decide which one you will purchase. You employ these same habits of mind when you deliberate over casting a vote in an election. You

Taken from Stuart Greene and April Lidinsky, *From Inquiry to Academic Writing: A Practical Guide*, pp. 11–24 (Chapter 1, "Starting with Inquiry: Habits of Mind of Academic Writers").

inform yourself about the issues that are most pressing; you learn about the candidates' positions on these issues; you consider other arguments for and against both issues and candidates; and you weigh those arguments and your own understanding to determine which candidate you will support.

Fundamentally, academic habits of mind are analytical. When you consider a variety of factors — the quality and functionality of the item you plan to buy, how it meets your needs, how it compares to similar items before making a shopping choice, you are conducting an **analysis**. That is, you are pausing to examine the reasons why you should buy something, instead of simply handing over your cash and saying, "I want one of those." To a certain extent, analysis involves breaking something down into its various parts and reflecting on how the parts do or don't work together. For example, when you deliberate over your vote, you may consult one of those charts that newspapers often run around election time: A list of candidates appears across the top of the chart, and a list of issues appears on the side. You can scan the columns to see where each candidate stands on the issues, and you can scan the rows to see how the candidates compare on a particular issue. The newspaper editors have performed a preliminary analysis for you. They've asked, "Who are the candidates?" "What are the issues?" and "Where does each candidate stand on the issues?"; and they have presented the answers to you in a format that can help you make your decision. But you still have to perform your own analysis of the information before you cast your ballot. Suppose no candidate holds your position on every issue. Who do you vote for? Which issues are most important to you? Or suppose two candidates hold your position on every issue. Which one do you vote for? What characteristics or experience are you looking for in an elected official? And you may want to investigate further by visiting the candidates' Web sites or by talking with your friends to gather their thoughts on the election.

As you can see, analysis involves more than simply disassembling or dissecting something. It is a process of continually asking questions and looking for answers. Analysis reflects, in the best sense of the word, a *skeptical* habit of mind, an unwillingness to settle for obvious answers in the quest to understand why things are the way they are and how they might be different.

This book will help you develop the questioning, evaluating, and conversational skills you already have into strategies that will improve your ability to make careful, informed judgments about the often conflicting and confusing information you are confronted with every day in your classes, in the news, in advertising, in all of your interactions. With these strategies, you will be in a position to use your writing skills to create change where you feel it is most needed.

The first steps in developing these skills are to recognize the key academic habits of mind and then to refine your practice of them. We explore four key habits of mind in the rest of this chapter: (1) inquiring, (2) seeking and valuing complexity, (3) understanding that academic writing is a conversation, and (4) understanding that writing is a process.

ACADEMIC WRITERS MAKE INQUIRIES

Academic writers usually study a body of information so closely and from so many different perspectives that they can ask questions that may not occur to people who are just scanning the information. That is, academic writers learn to make **inquiries**. Every piece of academic writing begins with a question about the way the world works, and the best questions lead to rich, complex insights that others can learn from and build on. You will find that the ability to ask good questions is equally valuable in your daily life. Asking thoughtful questions about politics, popular culture, work, or anything else — questions like, How has violence become so commonplace in our schools? What exactly did that candidate mean by "Family values are values for all of us," anyway? What is lost and gained by bringing Tolkien's *Lord of the Rings* trilogy to the screen? What does it take to move ahead in this company? Are those practices ethical? — is the first step in understanding how the world works and how it can be changed.

Inquiry typically begins with **observation**, a careful noting of phenomena or behaviors that puzzle you or challenge your beliefs and values (in a text or in the real world), which prompts an attempt to understand them by **asking questions** (Why does this exist? Why is this happening? Do things have to be this way?) and **examining alternatives** (Maybe this doesn't need to exist. Maybe this could happen another way instead.). For example, Mark Edmundson, a professor of English at the University of Virginia, *observes* that his students seem to prefer classes they consider "fun" over those that push them to work hard. This prompts him to *ask* how the consumer culture — especially the entertainment culture — has altered the college experience. In his essay "On the Uses of a Liberal Education," he wonders what it means that colleges increasingly see students as customers they need to please with Club Med–style exercise facilities that look "like a retirement spread for the young" more than as minds to be educated. He further *asks* what will happen if we don't change course — if entertaining students and making them feel good about themselves continue to be higher priorities than challenging students to stretch themselves with difficult ideas. Finally, he considers alternatives to entertainment-style education and *examines those alternatives* to see what they would offer students.

In her reading on the American civil rights movement of the 1950s and 1960s, one of our students *observed* that the difficulties many immigrant groups experienced when they first arrived in the United States are not acknowledged as struggles for civil rights. This student of Asian descent *wondered why* the difficulties Asians faced in assimilating into American culture are not seen as analogous to the efforts of African Americans to gain civil rights (Why are things this way?). In doing so, she *asked* a number of relevant questions: What do we leave out when we tell stories about ourselves? Why reduce the struggle for civil rights to black-and-white terms? How can we represent the multiple struggles of people who have contributed to building our nation? Then she *examined alternatives* — different ways of presenting the history of a nation that prides itself on justice and the protection of its people's civil rights (Maybe this doesn't need to exist. Maybe this could happen another way.). The academic writing you will read — and write yourself — starts with questions and seeks to find rich answers.

Steps to Inquiry

1 **Observe.** Note phenomena or behaviors that puzzle you or challenge your beliefs and values.

2 **Ask questions.** Consider why things are the way they are.

3 **Examine alternatives.** Explore how things could be different.

A Practice Sequence: Inquiring

The activities below will help you practice the strategies of observing, asking questions, and examining alternatives.

1 Find an advertisement for a political campaign (you can find many political ads on the Internet), and write down anything about what you observe in the ad that puzzles you or that challenges your beliefs and values. Next, write down questions you might have (Do things have to be this way?). Finally, write down other ways you think the ad could persuade you to vote for this particular candidate (Maybe this could happen another way instead.).

2 Locate and analyze data about the students at your school. For example, you might research the available majors and determine which departments have the highest and lowest enrollments. (Some schools have fact books that can be accessed online; and typically the registrar maintains a database with this information.) Is there anything that puzzles you? Write down any questions you have (Why are things the way they are?). What alternative explanations can you provide to account for differences in the popularity of the subjects students major in?

3 Read the following passage about school choice that appeared on the Civil Rights Project Web site in 2002. The Civil Rights Project is a leading research center on civil rights, with a particular interest in education reform. Since its founding in 1996, the project has convened dozens of national conferences and roundtables; commissioned more than 400 new research and policy studies; and produced major reports on desegregation, student diversity, school discipline, special education, dropouts, and Title I programs.

After you read the passage, write down what puzzles you or challenges your beliefs and values. Next, write down any questions you might have. Finally, write down what you see as alternative ways to look at the problem the writer identifies. When you complete this exercise, share your responses with one of your classmates.

> School choice has been viewed as a remedy to improve the quality of local schools and empower inner-city and lower-income parents by offering parents the freedom to choose the kind of education their children would receive.
>
> In the realm of public school education, school choice has taken the form of magnet schools, charter schools, and other test-based or specially tracked schools. Parents and students have the option to choose schools other than neighborhood schools that generally have a similar racial, ethnic, and socio-economic makeup to their local area. Private school choice, on the other hand, is a measure that some states have adopted to give lower-income students the opportunity to attend private schools they otherwise could not afford. This comes in the form of a voucher that parents can use toward the cost of private or religious school tuition for their children.
>
> Though advocates of school choice claim that it is the best way to enable students in failing public schools to get a better education, the issue of school choice raises some troubling questions about the impacts of individual "choice" on a society that aims to provide all of its citizens with equal access to educational opportunities.
>
> Educators have found that choice programs are likely to increase the segregation of students by race, social class, and educational background. Greater choice in public education is also unlikely, on its own, to increase either the number of programs offered or the overall performance of schools.
>
> While school choice may allow such *informed* families and communities to make significant decisions about their children's education, it is important to understand that not all families are equally informed. Better-educated parents who are more likely to be involved closely with their children's schooling, for example, have consistently been prone to participate in choice programs. While those children in families that are aware of school options and have the means to actively choose them may benefit from a greater range of opportunities, those that are not aware of options will not. The lack of resources and information for families living in largely minority areas of high poverty means that not everyone will benefit equally from school choice. Those students that are able to make informed school decisions will leave those that are not in their neighborhood schools. Thus, school choice will further segregate schools along racial, ethnic, socio-economic, and educational backgrounds.

ACADEMIC WRITERS SEEK AND VALUE COMPLEXITY

Seeking and valuing complexity are what inquiry is all about. As you read academic arguments (for example, about school choice), observe how the media work to influence your opinions (for example, in political ads), or analyze data (for example, about major subjects), you will explore reasons why things are the way they are and how they might be different. When you do so, we encourage you not to settle for simple either/or reasons. Instead, look for multiple explanations.

When we rely on **binary thinking** — imagining there are only two sides to an issue — we tend to ignore information that does not fall tidily into one side or the other. Think of the sound-bite assertions you hear bandied about on talk shows on the pretext of "discussing" a hot-button issue like stem-cell research or abortion: "It's just wrong/right because it is!" Real-world questions — How has the Internet changed our sense of what it means to be an author? What are the global repercussions of fast food? How do we make sense of terrorism? — don't have easy for-or-against answers. Remember that an **issue** is a subject that can be explored and debated. Issue-based questions, then, need to be approached with a mind open to complex possibilities. (We say more about identifying issues and formulating issue-based questions in Chapter 8.)

If we take as an example the issue of terrorism, we would discover that scholars of religion, economics, ethics, and politics tend to ask very different questions about terrorism, and to propose very different approaches for addressing this worldwide problem. This doesn't mean that one approach is right and the others are wrong; it means that complex issues are likely to have multiple explanations, rather than a simple choice between A and B.

In her attempt to explain the popularity of the Harry Potter books and movies, Elizabeth Teare, a professor of English, provides a window on the steps we can take to examine the complexity of a topic. She begins her essay "Harry Potter and the Technology of Magic" with the observations that author J. K. Rowling is one of the ten most influential people in publishing, and that her books have "transformed both the technologies of reading and the way we understand those technologies." Motivated by a sense of curiosity, if not puzzlement, Teare formulates a guiding question: "What is it that makes these books — about a lonely boy whose first act on learning he is a wizard is to go shopping for a wand — not only an international phenomenon among children and parents and teachers but also a topic of compelling interest to literary, social, and cultural critics?" Notice that in doing so, she indicates that she will examine this question from the multiple perspectives of literary, social, and cultural critics. To find answers to this question, Teare explores a range of perspectives from a variety of sources, including publishers' Web sites, trade journals, academic studies, and works of fiction for young readers.

One of our students was curious about why a well-known musician, Eminem, was at once so widely popular and so bitterly reviled, a phenomenon he observed in discussions with friends and in reviews of Eminem's music. He set out to understand these conflicting responses by examining the differing perspectives of music critics, politicians, religious evangelists, and his peers; and then he formulated an issue-based question: "How can we explain Eminem's popularity given the ways people criticize Eminem personally and his music?" In looking at this issue, the student opened himself to complexity by resisting simple answers to his question about why Eminem and his music evoked such different and conflicting responses.

Steps to Seeking and Valuing Complexity

1 **Reflect on what you observe.** Clarify your initial interest in a phenomenon or behavior by focusing on its particular details. Then reflect on what is most interesting and least interesting to you about these details, and why.

2 **Examine issues from multiple points of view.** Imagine more than two sides to the issue, and recognize that there may well be other points of view too.

3 **Ask issue-based questions.** Try to put into words questions that will help you explore why things are the way they are.

A Practice Sequence: Seeking and Valuing Complexity

These activities build on the previous exercises we asked you to complete.

1 Look again at the political ad. Think about other perspectives that would complicate your understanding of how the ad might persuade voters.

2 Imagine other perspectives on the data you found on the students in your school. Let's say, for example, that you've looked at data on student majors. How did you explain the popularity of certain majors and the unpopularity of others? How do you think other students would explain these discrepancies? What explanations would faculty members offer?

3 Consider your responses to the excerpt on school choice that you shared with one of your classmates. In addition to the explanations each of you provided, what are some other ways you could look at the issue of school choice? What would parents argue? What about administrators? Teachers? Students?

ACADEMIC WRITERS SEE WRITING AS A CONVERSATION

Another habit of mind at the heart of academic writing is the understanding that ideas always build on and respond to other ideas, just as they do in the best kind of conversations. Of course, conversations in academic writing happen on the page; they are not spoken. Still, these conversations are quite similar to the conversations you have through e-mail and instant messaging: You are responding to something someone else has written (or said) and are writing back in anticipation of future responses. Academic writing also places a high value on the belief that good, thoughtful ideas come from conversations with others, *many* others. As your exposure to other viewpoints increases, as you take more and different points of view into consideration and build on them, your own ideas will develop more fully and fairly. You already know that to get a full picture of something, often you have to ask for multiple perspectives. When you want to find out what "really" happened at an event when your friends are telling you different stories, you listen to all of them and then evaluate the evidence to draw conclusions you can stand behind — just as academic writers do.

Theologian Martin Marty starts a conversation about hospitality in his book *When Faiths Collide* (2004). *Hospitality* is a word he uses to describe a human behavior that has the potential to bring about real understanding among people who do not share a common faith or culture. As Marty points out, finding common ground is an especially important and timely concern "in a world where strangers meet strangers with gunfire, barrier walls, spiritually land-mined paths, and the spirit of revenge." He believes that people need opportunities to share their stories, their values, and their beliefs; in doing so, they feel less threatened by ideas they do not understand or identify with.

Yet Marty anticipates the possibility that the notion of hospitality will be met with skepticism or incomprehension by those who find the term "dainty." After all, he observes, that there are hospitality suites and hospitality industries suggests current usage of the term is different from historical usage, particularly in the Bible. To counter the incredulity or incomprehension of those who do not immediately understand his use of the term *hospitality*, Marty gives his readers entré to a conversation with other scholars who understand the complexity and power of the kind of hospitality shown by people who welcome a stranger into their world. The stranger he has in mind may simply be the person who moves in next door; but that person could also be an immigrant, an exile, or a refugee. Marty brings another scholar, Darrell Fasching, into the conversation to explain that hospitality entails welcoming "the stranger . . . [which] inevitably involves us in a sympathetic passing over into the other's life and stories" (cited in Marty, p. 132). And John Koenig, another scholar Marty cites, traces the biblical sources of the term in an effort to show the value of understanding those we fear. That understanding, Marty argues, might lead to peace among warring factions. The conversation Marty begins on the page helps us see that his views on bringing about peace have their source in other people's ideas. In turn, the fact that he draws on multiple sources gives strength to Marty's argument.

The characteristics that make for effective oral conversation are also in play in effective academic conversation: empathy, respect, and a willingness to exchange and revise ideas. **Empathy** is the ability to understand the perspectives that shape what people think, believe, and value. To express both empathy and respect for the positions of all people involved in the conversation, academic writers try to understand the conditions under which each opinion might be true and then to represent the strengths of that position accurately. For example, imagine that your firm commitment to protecting the environment is challenged by those who see the value of developing land rich with oil and other resources. In challenging their position, it would serve you well to understand their motives, both economic (lower gas prices, new jobs that will create a demand for new houses) and political (less dependence on foreign oil). If you can demonstrate your knowledge of these factors, those committed to developing resources in protected areas will listen to you. To convey empathy and respect while presenting your own point of view, you might introduce your argument by saying:

> Although it is important to develop untapped resources in remote areas of the United States both to lower gas prices and create new jobs, and to eliminate our dependence on other countries' resources, it is in everyone's interest to use alternative sources of power and protect our natural resources.

As you demonstrate your knowledge and a sense of shared values, you could also describe the conditions under which you might change your own position.

People engaging in productive conversation try to create change by listening and responding to one another rather than dominating one another. Instead of trying to win an argument, they focus on reaching a mutual understanding. This does not mean that effective communicators do not take strong positions; more often than not they do. However, they are more likely to achieve their goals by persuading others instead of ignoring them and their points of view. Similarly, writers come to every issue with an agenda. But they realize that they may have to compromise on certain points to carry those that mean the most to them. More important, they understand that their perceptions and opinions may be flawed or limited, and they are willing to revise them when valid new perspectives are introduced.

In an academic community, ideas develop through give-and-take, through a conversation that builds on what has come before and grows stronger from multiple perspectives. You will find this dynamic at work in your classes, when you discuss your ideas: You will build on other people's insights, and they will build on yours. As a habit of mind, paying attention to academic conversations can improve the thinking and writing you do in every class you take.

Steps to Joining an Academic Conversation

1 **Be receptive to the ideas of others.** Listen carefully and empathetically to what others have to say.

2 **Be respectful of the ideas of others.** When you refer to the opinions of others, be respectful.

3 **Engage with the ideas of others.** Try to understand how people have arrived at their feelings and beliefs.

4 **Be flexible in your thinking about the ideas of others.** Be willing to exchange ideas and to revise your own opinions.

A Practice Sequence: Joining an Academic Conversation

The following excerpt is taken from Thomas Patterson's *The Vanishing Voter* (2002), an examination of voter apathy. Read the excerpt and then complete the exercises that follow.

> Does a diminished appetite for voting affect the health of American politics? Is society harmed when the voting rate is low or in decline? As the *Chicago Tribune* said in an editorial, it may be "humiliating" that the United States, the oldest continuous democracy, has nearly the lowest voting rate in the world. But does it have any practical significance? . . .
>
> The increasing number of nonvoters could be a danger to democracy. Although high participation by itself does not trigger radical change, a flood of new voters into the electorate could possibly do it. It's difficult to imagine a crisis big and divisive enough to prompt millions of new voters to suddenly flock to the polls, especially in light of Americans' aversion to political extremism. Nevertheless, citizens who are outside the electorate are less attached to the existing system. As the sociologist Seymour Martin Lipset observed, a society of nonvoters "is potentially more explosive than one in which most citizens are *regularly* involved in activities which give them some sense of participation in decisions which affect their lives."
>
> Voting can strengthen citizenship in other ways, too. When people vote, they are more attentive to politics and are better informed about issues affecting them. Voting also deepens community involvement, as the philosopher John Stuart Mill theorized a century ago. Studies indicate that voters are more active in community affairs than nonvoters are. Of course, this association says more about the type of person who votes as opposed to the effect of voting. But recent evidence, as Harvard University's Robert Putnam notes, "suggests that the act of voting itself encourages volunteering and other forms of government citizenship."

1 In this excerpt, Patterson presents two arguments: that increasing voter apathy is a danger to democracy and that voting strengthens citizenship. With which of these arguments do you sympathize more? Why? Can you imagine reasons that another person might not agree with you? Write them down. Now do the same exercise with the argument you find less compelling.

2 Your instructor will divide the class into four groups and assign each group a position — pro or con — on one of Patterson's arguments. Brainstorm with the members of your group to come up with examples or reasons why your group's position is valid. Make a list of those examples or reasons, and be prepared to present them to the class.

3 Your instructor will now break up the groups into new groups, each with at least one representative of the original groups. In turn with the other members of your new group, take a few moments to articulate your position and the reasons for it. Remember to be civil and as persuasive as possible.

4 Finally, with the other members of your new group, talk about the merits of the various points of view. Try to find common ground ("I understand what you are saying; in fact, it's not unlike the point I was making about . . ."). The point of this discussion is not to pronounce a winner (who made the best case for his or her perspective) but to explore common ground, exchange and revise ideas, and imagine compromises.

ACADEMIC WRITERS UNDERSTAND THAT WRITING IS A PROCESS

Academic writing is a process of defining issues, formulating questions, and developing sound arguments. This view of writing counters a number of popular myths: that writing depends on inspiration, that writing should happen quickly, that learning to write in one context prepares you to write in other contexts, and that revision is the same as editing. The writing process addresses these myths. First, choosing an idea that matters to you is one way to make your writing matter. And, there's a better chance that writing you care about will contribute in a meaningful way to the conversation going on about a given issue in the academic community. Second, writers who invest time in developing and revising their ideas will improve both the quality of their ideas and their language — their ability to be specific and express complexity.

There are three main stages to the writing process: collecting information, drafting, and revising. We introduce them here and expand on them throughout this book.

▪ Collect Information and Material

Always begin the process of writing an essay by collecting *in writing* the material — the information, ideas, and evidence — from which you will shape your own argument. Once you have read and marked the pages of a text, you have begun the process of building your own argument. The important point here is that you start to put your ideas on paper. Good writing comes from returning to your ideas on your own and with your classmates, reconsidering them, and revising them as your thinking develops. This is not something you can do with any specificity unless you have written down your ideas. The box below shows the steps for gathering information from your reading, the first stage in the process of writing an academic essay. (In Chapter 3, these steps are illustrated and discussed in more detail.)

Steps to Collecting Information and Material

1 **Mark your texts as you read.** Note key terms; ask questions in the margins; indicate connections to other texts.

2 **List quotations you find interesting and provocative.** You might even write short notes to yourself about what you find significant about the quotes.

3 **List your own ideas in response to the reading or readings.** Include what you've observed about the way the author or authors make their arguments.

4 **Sketch out the similarities and differences among the authors whose work you plan to use in your essay.** Where would they agree or disagree? How would each respond to the others' arguments and evidence?

▪ Draft, and Draft Again

The next stage in the writing process begins when you are ready to think about your focus and how to arrange the ideas you have gathered in the collecting stage. Writers often find that writing a first draft is an act of discovery, that their ultimate focus emerges during this initial drafting process. Sometimes it is only at the end of a four-page draft that a writer says, "Aha! This is what I really want to talk about in this essay!" Later revisions of an essay, then, are not simply editing or cleaning up the grammar of a first draft. Instead, they truly involve *re*vision, seeing the first draft again to establish the clearest possible argument and the most persuasive evidence. This means that you do not have to stick with the way a draft turns out the first time. You can — and must! — be willing to rewrite a substantial amount of a first draft if the focus of the argument changes, or if in the process of writing new ideas emerge that enrich the essay. This is why it's important not to agonize over wording in a first draft: It's difficult to toss out a paragraph you've sweated over for hours. Use the first draft to get your ideas down on paper so that you and your peers can discuss what you see there, with the knowledge that you (like your peers) will need to stay open to the possibility of changing an aspect of your focus or argument.

Steps to Drafting

1 **Look through the materials** you have collected to see what interests you most and what you have the most to say about.

2 **Identify what is at issue,** what is open to dispute.

3 **Formulate a question** that your essay will respond to.

4 **Select the material you will include,** and decide what is outside your focus.

5 **Consider the types of readers** who might be most interested in what you have to say.

6 **Gather more material** once you've decided on your purpose — what you want to teach your readers.

7 **Formulate a working thesis** that conveys the point you want to make.

8 **Consider possible arguments** against your position and your response to them.

■ Revise Significantly

The final stage, revising, might involve several different drafts as you continue to sharpen your insights and the organization of what you have written. As we discuss in Chapter 16, you and your peers will be reading one another's drafts, offering feedback as you move from the larger issues to the smaller ones. It should be clear by now that academic writing is done in a community of thinkers: That is, people read other people's drafts and make suggestions for further clarification, further development of ideas, and sometimes further research. This is quite different from simply editing someone's writing for grammatical errors and typos. Instead, drafting and revising with real readers, as we discuss in Chapter 10, allow you to participate in the collaborative spirit of the academy, in which knowledge making is a group activity that comes out of the conversation of ideas. Importantly, this process approach to writing in the company of real readers mirrors the conversation of ideas carried on in the pages of academic books and journals.

Steps to Revising

1 Draft and revise the introduction and conclusion.

2 Clarify any obscure or confusing passages your peers have pointed out.

3 Provide details and textual evidence where your peers have asked for new or more information.

4 Check to be sure you have included opposing points of view and have addressed them fairly.

5 Consider reorganization.

6 Check to be sure every paragraph contributes clearly to your thesis or main claim, and that you have included signposts along the way, phrases that help a reader understand your purpose ("Here I turn to an example from current movies to show how this issue is alive and well in pop culture").

7 Consider using strategies you have found effective in other reading you have done for class (repeating words or phrases for effect, asking rhetorical questions, varying your sentence length).

The four academic habits of mind we have discussed throughout this chapter — making inquiries, seeking and valuing complexity, understanding writing as a conversation, and understanding writing as a process — are fundamental patterns of thought you will need to cultivate as an academic writer. The core skills we discuss through the rest of the book build on these habits of mind.

2

Understanding Writing Situations

ANALYZING TEXTUAL CONVENTIONS

When you analyze your rhetorical situation, you ask commonsense questions about your writing purpose and situation. As you do so, you draw on your previous experiences as a writer, reader, speaker, and listener. No one had to teach you, for instance, that a letter applying for a job should be written differently than an instant message asking a friend to drop by for pizza. Your social and cultural understanding of job-hunting would automatically cause you to write a formal letter. You make similar judgments as a reader. When you glance through your mail, tossing aside ads while eagerly searching for a letter about a financial aid package, your actions are the result of a rhetorical judgment you're making about the nature and value of these texts.

Whether you are reading or writing, you draw on your previous experiences to make judgments about a text's purpose, subject matter, and form. For familiar kinds of texts, these judgments occur almost automatically. In less familiar situations, you may have to work to understand the form and purpose of a text. I recently received a letter from a former student, Monica Molina, who now works at a community health center, where one of her responsibilities is to write grant proposals. In her letter, she commented:

> It took quite a while before I could feel comfortable even thinking about trying to write my first grant proposal. Most of the ones at our center run 50 to 100 pages and seem so intimidating — full of strange subheadings, technical language, complicated explanations. I had to force myself to calm down and get into them. First I read some recent proposals, trying to figure out how they worked. Luckily, my boss is friendly and supportive, so she sat down with

---

Taken from Lisa Ede, *The Academic Writer: A Brief Guide*, pp. 59–74 (Chapter 3, "Analyzing Rhetorical Situations").

me and talked about her experiences writing proposals. We looked at some proposals together, and she told me about how proposals are reviewed by agencies. Now we're working together on my first proposal. I'm still nervous, but I'm beginning to feel more comfortable.

Students entering a new discipline may be puzzled by unfamiliar language or writing styles. And like Monica, those entering new professions often must learn new forms of writing.

Writers who wish to participate in a new community must strive to understand its reading and writing practices — to learn how to enter its conversation, as the rhetorician Kenneth Burke might say. After all, the forms of writing that characterize different communities reflect important shared assumptions and practices. These shared assumptions and practices — sometimes referred to as textual conventions — represent agreements between writers and readers about how to construct and interpret texts. As such, they are an important component of any rhetorical situation.

The term *textual convention* may be new to you, but you can understand it easily if you think about other uses of the word *convention*. For example, social conventions are implicit agreements among the members of a community or culture about how to act in particular situations. At one time in the United States, for example, it was acceptable for persons who chewed tobacco to spit tobacco juice into spittoons in restaurants and hotel lobbies. This particular social convention has changed over time and is no longer acceptable.

If social conventions represent agreements among individuals about how to act, textual conventions represent similar agreements about how to write and read texts. Just as we often take our own social conventions for granted, so too do we take for granted those textual conventions most familiar to us as readers and writers. When we begin an e-mail or letter to our parents by writing "Dear Mom and Dad," for instance, we don't stop to wonder if this greeting is appropriate; we know from our experience as writers and readers that it is. E-mail is so informal that some writers don't even use this salutation but jump right into their message. If they're rhetorically savvy, those composing e-mails will recognize that when they're writing a work- or school-related e-mail to a superior or teacher, they should include both a salutation and a clear statement of their subject.

Textual conventions are dynamic, changing over time as the assumptions, values, and practices of writers and readers change. Consider some of the textual conventions of e-mail and other online writing. Emoticons, for instance — symbols such as :-) to indicate happiness, :-(to indicate sadness, or :-O to indicate shock or surprise — were developed by online writers to express the kind of emotion often conveyed in face-to-face communication by voice, gesture, and facial expression. Not all who use e-mail use emoticons, and those who do use them know they're more appropriate in some situations than others. But as a textual convention, emoticons clearly respond to the needs of online writers and readers.

■ Seeing Textual Conventions in Use

Whether you are entering a community of online writers or a new academic or professional community, analyzing your rhetorical situation will enable you to communicate effectively. Because textual conventions play such a critical role in communication between writers and readers, they are an important component of the rhetorical situation. When you think about the kind of writing that you are being asked to do, you are thinking in part about the textual conventions that may limit your options as a writer in a specific situation. Textual conventions bring constraints, but they also increase the likelihood that readers will respond appropriately to your ideas.

The relationship between textual conventions and medium can be critical. Students organizing a protest against increased tuition would hardly write a long analytical essay on this topic. Their goal is to encourage as many students as possible to participate in the protest, so they would be more likely to create an attention-getting flyer that they could inexpensively and quickly create and distribute. After the protest march, they might draft a letter to the editor to summarize the speakers' most important points. They might also set up a blog to post announcements and to encourage student participation.

Some textual conventions are specific. Personal letters typically begin with a greeting and end with a signature. Lab reports usually include the following elements: title page, abstract, introduction, experimental design and methods, results, discussion, and references. Someone writing a lab report can deviate from these textual conventions, but doing so runs the risk of confusing or irritating readers. The medium you choose to compose in can also influence textual conventions. When you communicate through e-mail, you are presented with a predetermined form, with headings that say "To," "Cc," "Bcc," and "Subject."

Other textual conventions are much more general. Consider, for instance, the conventions of an academic essay, which are listed in the box at the top of page 20.

To see how textual conventions operate, let's consider just one of the conventions of an effective essay: It uses an introduction to establish its subject or main idea. This convention is learned early, for many young children introduce stories with the words *Once upon a time*. Most writers and readers understand why an essay needs an introduction. No one likes to be thrown into the middle of a discussion without any idea of the subject. Still, writers aren't always certain about what constitutes the best introduction for a specific essay.

■ Comparing and Contrasting Textual Conventions

Let's look at three articles by linguist Deborah Tannen to see how one writer tackles the problem of creating an effective and appropriate introduction. Each article is based on Tannen's research into the limitations of

---

Characteristics of an Effective Academic Essay

- An effective essay is well organized and well developed. It establishes its subj ect or main idea in the introduction, develops that idea in a coherent manner in the body, and summarizes or completes the discussion in the conclusion.

- An effective essay is logical. It supports its main points with well-chosen evidence, illustrations, and details.

- An effective essay is clear and readable. It uses words, sentences, and paragraphs that are carefully crafted, appropriate for the writer's purpose and subject, and free of errors of usage, grammar, and punctuation.

These statements summarize some of the most general conventions that govern academic essays. Because these statements apply to so many different kinds of writing, you may not know just what they mean in specific situations and in your own writing.

---

what she describes as America's "argument culture," a subject she investigated in her book *The Argument Culture: Stopping America's War of Words*. Tannen is not only a prolific and best-selling writer — she has published 21 books and over 100 articles — but she writes for unusually diverse audiences. If you visit her homepage at <www.georgetown.edu/faculty/tannend/>, you'll notice the following categories for her publications: books, academic publications, general audience publications, and creative writing (poetry, short stories, essays, and plays).

The first article excerpted here — "For Argument's Sake: Why Do We Feel Compelled to Fight about Everything?" (pp. 21–22) — appeared in the Sunday edition of the *Washington Post*, a major newspaper with a large national distribution. The second article — "Agonism in the Academy: Surviving Higher Learning's Argument Culture" (pp. 23–24) — appeared in the *Chronicle of Higher Education*. This weekly newspaper is read by faculty, staff, and administrators in community colleges, four-year colleges, and universities. The final section of each issue of the *Chronicle* concludes with a one-page opinion column. Tannen's article appeared as such a column. The final article excerpted here — "Agonism in Academic Discourse" (pp. 25–26) — was published in the *Journal of Pragmatics*, a British scholarly publication for people who are interested in such topics as pragmatics (the study of language as it is used in a social context), semantics, language acquisition, and so on. Those who read this journal work in academic disciplines such as linguistics, sociology, psychology, anthropology, and philosophy. (Note that the article follows the British style of punctuation.)

For Argument's Sake

Why Do We Feel Compelled to Fight About Everything?

By DEBORAH TANNEN

I was waiting to go on a television talk show a few years ago for a discussion about how men and women communicate, when a man walked in wearing a shirt and tie and a floor-length skirt, the top of which was brushed by his waist-length red hair. He politely introduced himself and told me that he'd read and liked my book *You Just Don't Understand,* which had just been published. Then he added, "When I get out there, I'm going to attack you. But don't take it personally. That's why they invite me on, so that's what I'm going to do."

We went on the set and the show began. I had hardly managed to finish a sentence or two before the man threw his arms out in gestures of anger, and began shrieking — briefly hurling accusations at me, and then railing at length against women. The strangest thing about his hysterical outburst was how the studio audience reacted: They turned vicious — not attacking me (I hadn't said anything substantive yet) or him (who wants to tangle with someone who screams at you?) but the other guests: women who had come to talk about problems they had communicating with their spouses.

My antagonist was nothing more than a dependable provocateur, brought on to ensure a lively

show. The incident has stayed with me not because it was typical of the talk shows I have appeared on — it wasn't, I'm happy to say — but because it exemplifies the ritual nature of much of the opposition that pervades our public dialogue.

Everywhere we turn, there is evidence that, in public discourse, we prize contentiousness and aggression more than cooperation and conciliation. Headlines blare about the Starr Wars, the Mommy Wars, the Baby Wars, the Mammography Wars;

everything is posed in terms of battles and duels, winners and losers, conflicts and disputes. Biographies have metamorphosed into demonographies whose authors don't just portray their subjects warts and all, but set out to dig up as much dirt as possible, as if the story of a person's life is contained in the warts, only the warts, and nothing but the warts.

It's all part of what I call the argument culture, which rests on the assumption that opposition is the best way to get anything done: The best way to discuss an idea is to set up a debate. The best way to cover news is to find people who express the most extreme views and present them as "both sides." The best way to begin an essay is to attack someone. The best way to show you're really thoughtful is to criticize. The best way to settle disputes is to litigate them.

It is the automatic nature of this response that I am calling into question. This is not to say that passionate opposition and strong verbal attacks are never appropriate. In the words of the Yugoslavian-born poet Charles Simic, "There are moments in life when true invective is called for, when it becomes an absolute necessity, out of a deep sense of justice, to denounce, mock, vituperate, lash out, in the strongest possible language." What I'm questioning is the ubiquity, the knee-jerk nature of approaching almost any issue, problem or public person in an adversarial way.

Smashing heads does not open minds. In this as in so many things, results are also causes, looping back and entrapping us. The pervasiveness of warlike formats and language grows out of, but also gives rise to, an ethic of aggression: We come to value aggressive tactics for their own sake — for the sake of argument. Compromise becomes a dirty word, and we often feel guilty if we are conciliatory rather than confrontational — even if we achieve the result we're seeking.

Here's one example. A woman called another talk show on which I was a guest. She told the following story: "I was in a place where a man was smoking, and there was a no-smoking sign. Instead of saying 'You aren't

allowed to smoke in here. Put that out!' I said, 'I'm awfully sorry, but I have asthma, so your smoking makes it hard for me to breathe. Would you mind terribly not smoking?' When I said this, the man was extremely polite and solicitous, and he put his cigarette out, and I said, 'Oh, thank you, thank you!' as if he'd done a wonderful thing for me. Why did I do that?"

I think this woman expected me — the communications expert — to say she needs assertiveness training to confront smokers in a more aggressive manner. Instead, I told her that her approach was just fine. If she had tried to alter his behavior by reminding him of the rules, he might well have rebelled: "Who made you the enforcer? Mind your own business!" She had given the smoker a face-saving way of doing what she wanted, one that allowed him to feel chivalrous rather than chastised. This was kinder to him, but it was also kinder to herself, since it was more likely to lead to the result she desired.

Another caller disagreed with me, saying the first caller's style was "self-abasing." I persisted: There was nothing necessarily destructive about the way the woman handled the smoker. The mistake the second caller was making — a mistake many of us make — was to confuse ritual self-effacement with the literal kind. All human relations require us to find ways to get what we want from others without seeming to dominate them.

The opinions expressed by the two callers encapsulate the ethic of aggression that has us by our throats, particularly in public arenas such as politics and law.

Issues are routinely approached by having two sides stake out opposing positions and do battle. This sometimes drives people to take positions that are more adversarial than they feel — and can get in the way of reaching a possible resolution. I have experienced this firsthand.

For my book about the workplace, "Talking from 9 to 5," I spent time in companies, shadowing people, interviewing them and having individuals tape conversations when I wasn't there. Most companies were happy to proceed on a verbal agreement setting forth certain ground rules: Individuals would control the taping, identifying names would be changed, I would show them what I wrote about their company and change or delete anything they did not approve. I also signed confidentiality agreements promising not to reveal anything I learned about the company's business.

Some companies, however, referred the matter to their attorneys so a contract could be written. In no case where attorneys became involved — mine as well as theirs — could we reach an agreement on working together.

Negotiations with one company stand out. Having agreed on the procedures and safeguards, we expected to have a contract signed in a matter of weeks. But six months later, after thousands of dollars in legal fees and untold hours of everyone's time, the negotiations reached a dead end. The company's lawyer was demanding veto power over my entire book; it meant the company could (if it chose) prevent me from publishing the book even if I used no more than a handful of examples from this

Agonism in the Academy: Surviving Higher Learning's Argument Culture

By Deborah Tannen

A READING GROUP that I belong to, composed of professors, recently discussed a memoir by an academic. I came to the group's meeting full of anticipation, eager to examine the insights I'd gained from the book and to be enlightened by those that had intrigued my fellow group members. As the meeting began, one member announced that she hadn't read the book; four, including me, said they'd read and enjoyed it; and one said she hadn't liked it because she does not like academic memoirs. She energetically criticized the book. "It's written in two voices," she said, "and the voices don't interrogate each other."

Quickly, two other members joined her critique, their point of view becoming a chorus. They sounded smarter, seeing faults that the rest of us had missed, making us look naive. We credulous three tried in vain to get the group talking about what we had found interesting or important in the book, but our suggestions were dull compared to the game of critique.

I left the meeting disappointed because I had learned nothing new about the book or its subject. All I had learned about was the acumen of the critics. I was especially struck by the fact that one of the most talkative and influential critics was the member who had not read the book. Her unfamiliarity with the work had not hindered her, because the critics had focused more on what they saw as faults of the genre than on faults of the particular book.

The turn that the discussion had taken reminded me of the subject of my most recent book, *The*

Argument Culture. The phenomenon I'd observed at the book-group meeting was an example of what the cultural linguist Walter Ong calls "agonism," which he defines in *Fighting for Life* as "programmed contentiousness" or "ceremonial combat." Agonism does not refer to disagreement, conflict, or vigorous dispute. It refers to retualized opposition — for instance, a debate in which the contestants are assigned opposing positions and one party wins, rather than an argument that arises naturally when two parties disagree.

In *The Argument Culture*, I explored the role and effects of agonism in three domains of public discourse: journalism, politics, and the law. But the domain in which I first identified the phenomenon and began thinking about it is the academic world. I remain convinced that agonism is endemic in academe — and bad for it.

The way we train our students, conduct our classes and our research, and exchange ideas at meetings and in print are all driven by our ideological assumption that intellectual inquiry is a metaphorical battle. Following from that is a second assumption, that the best way to demonstrate intellectual prowess is to criticize, find fault, and attack.

Many aspects of our academic lives can be described as agonistic. For example, in our scholarly papers, most of us follow a conventional framework that requires us to position our work in opposition to someone else's, which we prove wrong. The framework tempts — almost requires — us to oversimplify or even misrepresent others' positions; cite the weakest example to make a generally resonable work appear less so; and ignore facts that supports others' views, citing only evidence that supports our own positions.

The way we train our students frequently reflects the battle metaphor as well. We assign scholarly work for them to read, then invite them to tear it apart. That is helpful to an extent, but it often means that they don't learn to do the harder work of integrating ideas, or of considering the work's historical and disciplinary context. Moreover,

it fosters in students a stance of arrogance and narrow-mindedness, qualities that do not serve the fundamental goals of education.

In the classroom, if students are engaged in heated debate, we believe that education is taking place. But in a 1993 article in *The History Teacher*, Patricia Rosof, who teaches at Hunter College High School in New York City, advises us to look more closely at what's really happening. If we do, she says, we will probably find that only a few students are participating; some other students may be paying attention, but many may be turned off. Furthermore, the students who are arguing generally simplify the points they are making or disputing. To win the argument, they ignore complexity and nuance. The refuse to concede a point raised by their opponents, even if they can see that it is valid, because such a concession would weaken their position. Nobody tries to synthesize the various views, because that would look indecisive, or weak.

If the class engages in discussion rather than debate — adding such intellectual activities as exploring ideas, uncovering nuances, comparing and contrasting different interpretations of a work — more students take part, and more of them gain a deeper, and more accurate, understanding of the material. Most important, the students learn a stance of respect and open-minded inquiry.

Academic rewards — good grades and good jobs — typically go to students and scholars who learn to tear down others' work, not to those who learn to build on the work of their colleagues. In *The Argument Culture*, I cited a study in which communications researchers Karen Tracy and Sheryl Baratz ex-

amined weekly colloquia attended by faculty members and graduate students at a large university. As the authors reported in a 1993 article in *Communication Monographs*, although most people said the purpose of the colloquia was to "trade ideas" and "learn things," faculty members in fact were judging the students' competence based on their participation in the colloquia. And the professors didn't admire students who asked "a nice little supportive question," as one put it — they valued "tough and challenging questions."

One problem with the agonistic culture of graduate training is that potential scholars who are not comfortable with that kind of interaction are likely to drop out. As a result, many talented and creative minds are lost to academe. And, with fewer colleagues who prefer different approaches, those who remain are more likely to egg each other on to even grater adversarial heights. Some scholars who do stay in acaceme are reluctant to present their work at conferences or submit it for publication because of their reluctance to take part in adversarial discourse. The cumulative effect is that nearly everyone feels vulnerable and defensive, and thus less willing to suggest new ideas, offer new perspectives, or question received wisdom.

Although scholarly attacks are ritual — prescribed by the conventions of academe — the emotions propelling them can be real. Jane Tompkins, a literary critic who has written about the genre of the western in modern fiction and film, has compared scholarly exchanges to shootouts. In a 1988 article in *The Georgia Review*, she noted that her own career took off when she published an essay that "began with a

ELSEVIER

Journal of Pragmatics 34 (2002) 1651–1669

journal of
PRAGMATICS

www.elsevier.com/locate/pragma

Agonism in academic discourse[☆]

Deborah Tannen

Linguistics Department, Georgetown University, Box 571051, Washington DC 20057-1051, USA

Abstract

The pervasiveness of agonism, that is, ritualized adversativeness, in contemporary western academic discourse is the source of both obfuscation of knowledge and personal suffering in academia. Framing academic discourse as a metaphorical battle leads to a variety of negative consequences, many of which have ethical as well as personal dimensions. Among these consequences is a widespread assumption that critical dialogue is synonymous with negative critique, at the expense of other types of 'critical thinking'. Another is the requirement that scholars search for weaknesses in others' work at the expense of seeking strengths, understanding the roots of theoretical differences, or integrating disparate but related ideas. Agonism also encourages the conceptualization of complex and subtle work as falling into two simplified warring camps. Finally, it leads to the exclusion or marginalization of those who lack a taste for agonistic interchange. Alternative approaches to intellectual interchange need not entirely replace agonistic ones but should be accommodated alongside them. © 2002 Elsevier Science B.V. All rights reserved.

Keywords: Academic discourse; Agonism; Disagreement; Ritualized opposition; Exclusion

☆ Varying versions of this paper were delivered at the Georgetown Linguistics Society 1995, Washington, DC; Georgetown University Round Table on Languages and Linguistics 1999, Washington, D.C.; Pragma99, Tel Aviv, Israel, August 1999; and as the Hayward Keniston Lecture, University of Michigan, October 27, 1999. A briefer account, written for a more general audience, appears as "Agonism in the Academy: Surviving Higher Learning's Argument Culture", The Chronicle of Higher Education March 31, 2000, B7-8. Some sections of the present paper are based on material that appears in my book The Argument Culture; most, however, is new. I would like to thank Elizabeth Eisenstein, Shari Kendall, Joseph P. Newhouse, and Keli Yerian for leading me to sources that I cite here. For thoughtful comments on an earlier draft, I am grateful to A.L. Becker, Paul Friedrich, Susan Gal, Heidi Hamilton, Natalie Schilling-Estes, Ron Scollon, Malcah Yaeger-Dror, and three anonymous reviewers. This contribution is dedicated to the memory of Suzanne Fleischman, whose death which occurred while I was working on the paper cast a shadow of sadness, and whose own work, like her article cited here, made such an enormous contribution to restoring the person of the scholar to scholarship.

E-mail address: tannend@georgetown.edu (D. Tannen).

1652   *D. Tannen / Journal of Pragmatics 34 (2002) 1651–1669*

1. Introduction and overview

In doing discourse analysis, we use discourse to do our analysis, yet we seldom examine the discourse we use. There are, of course, important exceptions, such as Tracy (1997) on departmental colloquia, Fleischman (1998) on the erasure of the personal in academic writing, Goffman (1981) on "The Lecture", Herring (1996) on e-mail lists, Chafe and Danielewicz (1987) who include "academic speaking" and "academic writing" in their comparison of spoken and written language, and Swales' (1990) study of academic writing as well as his recent examination of the physical and interactional contexts that give rise to it (1998). Perhaps most closely related to my topic is Hunston (1993), who examines oppositional argumentation in biology, history, and sociolinguistics articles (two each), and concludes that the less empirical disciplines are more 'argumentative'. Here I turn my attention to an aspect of academic discourse that, as far I know, has not previously been examined: what I call "agonism".

Ong (1981: 24), from whom I borrow the term, defines agonism as "programmed contentiousness", "ceremonial combat". I use the term to refer not to conflict, disagreement, or disputes per se, but rather to *ritualized* adversativeness. In academic discourse, this means conventionalized oppositional formats that result from an underlying ideology by which intellectual interchange is conceptualized as a metaphorical battle. In a recent book (Tannen, 1998), I explore the role and effects of agonism in three domains of public discourse: journalism, politics, and law. Here I turn to the discourse domain in which I first identified the phenomenon and began thinking about it: the academy.

My goal is to uncover agonistic elements in academic discourse and to examine their effects on our pursuit of knowledge and on the community of scholars engaged in that pursuit. In arguing that an ideology of agonism provides a usually unquestioned foundation for much of our oral and written interchange, I focus on exposing the destructive aspects of this ideology and its attendant practices. I do not, however, call for an end to agonism — a goal that would be unrealistic even if it were desirable, which I am not sure it is. Rather, I argue for a broadening of our modes of inquiry, so that agonism is, one might say, demoted from its place of ascendancy, and for a re-keying or 'toning down' of the more extreme incarnations of agonism in academic discourse.

In what follows, I begin by sketching my own early interest in agonism in conversational discourse. Then I briefly present some historical background, tracing the seeds of agonism in academic discourse to classical Greek philosophy and the medieval university. Against this backdrop, I move to examining agonistic elements as well as the cultural and ideological assumptions that underlie them in academic discourse: both spoken (at conferences, in classrooms, and in intellectual discussions) and written (in grant proposals, journal articles, books, and reviews of all of these). I demonstrate some unfortunate consequences of the agonistic character of these discourse types, both for the pursuit of knowledge and for the community of scholars and others who hope to gain from our knowledge. I then suggest that the existence and perpetuation of agonistic elements in academic discourse depends on

By glancing at the first pages of Tannen's three articles, you'll notice some striking differences among them. The first page of "For Argument's Sake: Why Do We Feel Compelled to Fight about Everything?" (p. 21), has a good deal of white space and large illustrations. These illustrations, along with the title of the article, help draw readers into Tannen's text. After all, the *Washington Post* is a large multi-section newspaper, and the Sunday edition is much larger than the daily edition. If Tannen and her editors hope to capture readers' interest, they must draw their attention in a dramatic way.

The incident that Tannen describes at the start of her article is certainly dramatic. She recalls her encounter with a strangely dressed man with waist-long red hair who, like her, is waiting to appear on a television show. After he praises her book *You Just Don't Understand*, the man announces that "When I get out there, I'm going to attack you. But don't take it personally. That's why they invite me on, so that's what I'm going to do." After describing the rest of this incident and reflecting on her antagonist, Tannen moves to the major assertion of her article: "Everywhere we turn, there is evidence that, in public discourse, we prize contentiousness and aggression more than cooperation and conciliation." The rest of her article provides examples of a widespread argument culture in America and suggests some of that culture's limitations.

The second article, from the *Chronicle of Higher Education* (p. 23), is more visually dense than the first — though it does have some white space and a drawing of stylized boxers at the bottom of the first page. Rather than using an attention-getting title, in this article Tannen uses the scholarly term *agonism* to identify her subject. She does appeal to her readers' interests, however, with her subtitle, "Surviving Higher Learning's Argument Culture." Most readers would be aware that the academy can be a difficult and argumentative place, so they would appreciate knowing how best to survive in such a climate.

In the *Chronicle* article, as in the first article, Tannen begins by recounting an incident that suggests a culture of argument. Since her readers are educators, she focuses on an experience they might share — participating in a reading group whose members find it easier to criticize than praise a book (even when they haven't read it). After reflecting on this incident, she mentions her recently published book *The Argument Culture* and clarifies what she means by agonism. After briefly describing her book, she sets out the thesis of her article: "The way we train our students, conduct our classes and our research, and exchange ideas at meetings and in print are all driven by our ideological assumption that intellectual inquiry is a metaphorical battle. Following from that is a second assumption, that the best way to demonstrate intellectual prowess is to criticize, find fault, and attack." In the remainder of this article, Tannen provides evidence to support her assertions, considers some of the negative consequences of agonism in the academy, and (in a brief closing paragraph) affirms the benefits of changing the culture of the academy. If the latter would happen, Tannen argues, academics "would learn more from each other, be heard more clearly by others, attract more varied talents to the scholarly life, and restore a measure of humanity to ourselves, our endeavor, and the academic world we inhabit."

An important difference between the *Washington Post* article and the *Chronicle of Higher Education* article involves the examples and evidence that Tannen provides. In the *Post* article, Tannen focuses on examples that a broad range of readers can identify with, such as a phone call to a call-in talk show, the adversarial nature of the legal process, and the ritual attacks on politicians that often appear in the popular press. However, in the *Chronicle* article, she provides a limited range of examples that involve academic life. She also supports her position by citing other scholars whose research supports her position. In these and other ways, Tannen adjusts her argument to address her particular rhetorical situation.

Tannen's third article (p. 25) appeared in the *Journal of Pragmatics*, a specialized publication that has the most cramped and least inviting first page. Rather than using an attention-getting title, Tannen simply announces her subject: "Agonism in Academic Discourse." The article begins with a full page of prefatory material: the article title, the author's name and university address, an abstract, keywords, and a lengthy footnote that mentions previous versions of the article and makes extensive acknowledgments of people who assisted Tannen in writing it.

The article itself is divided into sections with numbered headings. The first section, "Introduction and overview," begins with a dense and heavily referenced discussion of the fact that "In doing discourse analysis, we [scholars] use discourse to do our analysis, yet we seldom examine the discourse we use." After acknowledging exceptions to this statement, Tannen stakes out a major claim for her article: "Here I turn my attention to an aspect of academic discourse that, as far [as] I know, has not previously been examined: what I call 'agonism.'" (Because originality is highly prized in the academy, Tannen's claim that her subject "has not previously been examined" is particularly strong.) After providing further information about this term, Tannen establishes the framework for her article: "My goal is to uncover agonistic elements in academic discourse and to examine their effects on our pursuit of knowledge and on the community of scholars engaged in that pursuit." Unlike the *Post* and *Chronicle* articles, which are relatively brief, Tannen's article in the *Journal of Pragmatics* is eighteen densely argued pages long. In subsequent sections, she covers such topics as the roots of agonism in ancient Greek and medieval church discourse. Clearly, Tannen expects much more of readers of this scholarly article than she does of readers of the previous two articles. She assumes that readers will be familiar with the many references she cites or will at least appreciate their inclusion. She also assumes that readers will have considerable prior knowledge of her topic and will care deeply about it.

Analyzing the first few pages of each article supplies important clues about these three publications and about Tannen's expectations about their readers. In the less specialized publications, Tannen tries hard to interest readers in her subject. The publishers of those periodicals also seem to pay more attention to visual images and design elements like white space. People who read the *Washington Post*, the most general and least specialized of these publications, often don't have a clear purpose when they read. They purchase newspapers to learn about recent news and to keep up with recent intellectual, cultural, economic, and political developments. Even a person who spends a couple of hours reading the Sunday paper might well pass over Tannen's article. Consequently, a writer like Tannen will attempt to gain these readers' attention — and so will the editors who commission illustrations and design the visual look of the text.

Subscribers to the weekly *Chronicle of Higher Education* represent a more specialized — though still diverse — readership. They either work in or are interested in higher education. One reader might be a faculty member in the humanities; such a reader might well be interested in Tannen's essay. But other readers might work in admissions, financial aid, or athletics. For these readers, the term *agonism* might be unfamiliar. Moreover, just as readers skim daily newspapers like the *Washington Post*, so too do many readers skim the *Chronicle*. As a consequence, even though the readership of the *Chronicle* is less diverse than that of the *Post*, Tannen uses a similar introductory strategy for each article: a catchy title or subtitle, and an interesting opening anecdote.

Tannen faces a different rhetorical situation in addressing readers of the scholarly *Journal of Pragmatics*. If readers of the *Post* and the *Chronicle* read — or skim — these publications to keep current, subscribers to the *Journal of Pragmatics* read this journal to keep up with advances in their field. These readers undoubtedly subscribe to many professional publications. They don't have the time to read every article, so they skim the tables of contents, noting articles that affect their own research or have broad significance for their field. The prefatory material in Tannen's third article matters very much to them; they can review the abstract to determine not only *if* but also *how* they will read the article. Some will read only an article's abstract, others will skim the major points, and others will read the article with great care, returning to it as they conduct their own research. Readers of the *Journal of Pragmatics* wouldn't want an engaging introduction like the ones Tannen includes in the *Post* and the *Chronicle* articles. Instead, they want a straightforward, concise approach. They value clear, specific headings and scholarly citations over inviting titles, illustrations, and opening anecdotes.

Although these three articles are grounded in the same research project, they differ dramatically in structure, tone, language, and approach to readers. Textual conventions play an important role in these differences. As shared agreements about the construction and interpretation of texts, textual conventions enable readers and writers to communicate successfully in different rhetorical situations.

UNDERSTANDING THE CONVENTIONS OF ACADEMIC WRITING

Some textual conventions are easy to identify. After reading just a few lab reports, for example, you recognize that this form of writing adheres to a set format. Other textual conventions are less easy to discern and to understand. When you join a new community of writers and readers, as you do when you enter college, you need to understand the demands of the writing you are expected to complete. Look again, for instance, at the Characteristics of an Effective Academic Essay on p. 20. When you first read these characteristics, they probably made sense to you. Of course, essays should be well organized, well developed, and logical.

When you begin work on an essay for history, sociology, or economics, however, you may find it difficult to determine how to embody these characteristics in your own writing. You might wonder what will make your analysis of the economic impact of divorce on the modern family logical or illogical. What do economists consider to be appropriate evidence, illustrations, and details? And does your economics teacher value the same kind of logic, evidence, and details as your American literature teacher?

■ Using Textual Conventions

You already know enough about rhetoric and the rhetorical situation to realize that there can be no one-size-fits-all approach to every academic writing situation.

What can you do when you are unfamiliar with the textual conventions of academic writing in general or of a particular discipline? A rhetorical approach suggests that one solution is to read examples of the kind of writing you wish to do. Discussing these models with an insider — your teacher, perhaps, or an advanced student in the field — can help you understand why these conventions work for such readers and writers. Forming a study group or meeting with a tutor can also increase your rhetorical sensitivity to your teachers' expectations and the conventions of academic writing.

Finally, a rhetorical approach to communication encourages you to think strategically about writing — whether personal, professional, or academic — and to respond creatively to the challenges of each situation. As a writer, you have much to consider: your own goals as a writer, the nature of your subject and writing task, the expectations of your readers, the textual conventions your particular situation requires or allows, the medium in which to express your ideas. The rhetorical sensitivity that you have already developed can help you respond appropriately to these and other concerns. But you can also draw on other resources — on textual examples and on discussions with teachers, tutors, and other students. As a writer, you are not alone. By reaching out to other writers, in person or by reading their work, you can become a fully participating member of the academic community.

PART TWO

Reading and Research as Acts of Inquiry

3

Reading as a Writer, Writing as a Reader

Reading for class and then writing an essay might seem to be separate tasks, but reading is actually the first step in the writing process. In this chapter we present the small steps and specific practices that will help you read more effectively and move from reading to writing strategies as you compose your own college essays. These steps and practices will lead you to understand a writer's purpose in responding to a situation, the motivation for asserting a claim in an essay and entering a particular conversation with a particular audience.

READING AS AN ACT OF COMPOSING: ANNOTATING

Leaving your mark on the page — **annotating** — is your first act of composing. When you mark up the pages of a text, you are reading critically, engaging with the ideas of others, questioning and testing those ideas, and inquiring into their significance. **Critical reading** is sometimes called *active reading* to distinguish it from memorization, when you just read for the main idea so that you can "spit it back out on a test." When you read actively and critically, you bring your knowledge, experiences, and interests to a text, so that you can respond to the writer, continuing the conversation the writer has begun.

Experienced college readers don't try to memorize a text or assume they must understand it completely before they respond to it. Instead they read strategically, looking for the writer's claims, for the writer's key ideas

---

Taken from Stuart Greene and April Lidinsky, *From Inquiry to Academic Writing: A Practical Guide*, pp. 25–46 (Chapter 2, "From Reading as a Writer to Writing as a Reader").

and terms, and for connections with key ideas and terms in other texts they have read. They also read to discern what conversation the writer has entered, and how the writer's own argument is connected to those he or she makes reference to.

When you annotate a text, your notes in the margins might address the following questions:

- What arguments is this author responding to?
- Is the issue relevant or significant?
- How do I know that what the author says is true?
- Is the author's evidence legitimate? Sufficient?
- Can I think of an exception to the author's argument?
- What would the counterarguments be?

Good readers ask the same kinds of questions of every text they read, considering not just *what* a writer says (the content), but *how* he or she says it given the writer's purpose and audience.

The marks you leave on a page might indicate your own ideas and questions, patterns you see emerging, links to other texts, even your gut response to the writer's argument — agreement, disgust, enthusiasm, confusion. They reveal your own thought processes as you read and signal that you are entering the conversation. In effect, they are traces of your own responding voice.

Developing your own system of marking or annotating pages can help you feel confident when you sit down with a new reading for your classes. Based on our students' experiences, we offer this practical tip: Although wide-tipped highlighters have their place in some classes, it is more useful to read with a pen or pencil in your hand, so that you can do more than draw a bar of color through words or sentences you find important. Experienced readers write their responses to a text in the margins, using personal codes (boxing key words, for example), writing out definitions of words they have looked up, drawing lines to connect ideas on facing pages, or writing notes to themselves ("Connect this to Scholes on video texts"; "Hirsch would disagree big time — see his ideas on memorization in primary grades"; "You call THIS evidence?!"). These notes will help you get started on your own writing assignments, and you cannot make them with a highlighter.

Marking or annotating your readings benefits you twice. First, it is easier to participate in class discussions if you have already noted passages that are important, confusing, or linked to specific passages in other texts you have read. It's a sure way to avoid that sinking feeling you get when you return to pages you read the night before but now can't remember at all. Second, by marking key ideas in a text, noting your ideas about them, and making connections to key ideas in other texts, you have begun the process of writing an essay. When you start writing the first draft of your essay, you can quote the passages you have already marked and explain what you find significant about them based on the notes you have already made to yourself. You can make the connections to other texts in the paragraphs of your own essay that you have already begun to make on the pages of your textbook. If you mark your texts effectively, you'll never be at a loss when you sit down to write the first draft of an essay.

Let's take a look at how one of our students marked several paragraphs of Douglas Massey and Nancy Denton's *American Apartheid: Segregation and the Making of the Underclass* (1993). In the excerpt below, the student underlines what she believes is important information and begins to create an outline of the authors' main points.

1. racist attitudes	The spatial isolation of black Americans was achieved by *1*
2. private behaviors	a conjunction of <u>racist attitudes</u>, <u>private behaviors</u>, and
3. & institutional practices	<u>institutional practices</u> that disenfranchised blacks from
lead to <u>ghettos</u> (authors' claim?)	urban housing markets and led to the creation of the <u>ghetto</u>.
Ghetto = multi-story, high-density housing projects. Post-1950	Discrimination in employment exacerbated black poverty and limited the economic potential for integration, and black residential mobility was systematically blocked by pervasive
I remember this happening where I grew up, but I didn't know the government was responsible. Is this what happened in There Are No Children Here?	discrimination and white avoidance of neighborhoods containing blacks. <u>The walls of the ghetto were buttressed after 1950</u> by government programs that promoted slum clearance and <u>relocated displaced ghetto residents into multi-story, high-density housing projects</u>.

In theory, this self-reinforcing cycle of prejudice,   *2* discrimination, and segregation was broken during the 1960s by a growing rejection of racist sentiments by whites and a series of court decisions and federal laws that banned discrimination in public life. (1) <u>The Civil Rights Act of 1964 outlawed racial discrimination in employment</u>, (2) the <u>Fair Housing Act of 1968 banned discrimination in housing</u>, and

Authors say situation of "spatial isolation" remains despite court decisions. Does it?

(3) the *Gautreaux* and *Shannon* <u>court decisions prohibited public authorities from placing housing projects</u> exclusively in black neighborhoods. Despite these changes, however, the <u>nation's largest black communities remained as segregated as ever in 1980</u>. Indeed, many urban areas displayed a pattern of intense racial isolation that could only be described as <u>hypersegregation</u>.

Although the racial climate of the United States   *3* improved outwardly during the 1970s, <u>racism still restricted the residential freedom of black Americans</u>; it just did so in

Subtler racism, not on public record.

less blatant ways. In the aftermath of the civil rights revolution, few whites voiced openly racist sentiments; realtors no longer refused outright to rent or sell to blacks; and few

Lack of enforcement
of Civil Rights Act?
Fair Housing Act?
Gautreaux and
Shannon? Why?
Why not?

local governments went on record to oppose public housing projects because they would contain blacks. This lack of overt racism, however, did not mean that prejudice and discrimination had ended.

Notice that this student underlines information that helps her understand the argument the authors make. In her annotations, she numbers the three key factors (racist attitudes, private behaviors, and institutional practices) that influenced the formation of ghettos in the United States. She also identifies the situation that motivates the authors' analysis: the extent to which "the spatial isolation of black Americans" still exists despite laws and court decisions designed to end residential segregation. And she makes connections to her own experience and to another book she has read. By understanding the authors' arguments and making these connections, she begins the writing process. She also sets the stage for her own research, for examining the authors' claim that residential segregation still exists.

A Practice Sequence: Annotating

1 Take a few minutes to read and mark what you find significant in the paragraph below from Massey and Denton's *American Apartheid*. Notice how many different kinds of marks you make (circling, boxing, underlining, asking questions, noting your responses and connections to other texts you've read, and the like).

> Economic arguments can be invoked to explain why levels of black-white segregation changed so little during the 1970s. After decades of steady improvement, black economic progress stalled in 1973, bringing about a rise in black poverty and an increase in income inequality. As the black income distribution bifurcated, middle-class families experienced downward mobility and fewer households possessed the socioeconomic resources necessary to sustain residential mobility and, hence, integration. If the economic progress of the 1950s and 1960s had been sustained into the 1970s, segregation levels might have fallen more significantly. William Clark estimates that 30%–70% of racial segregation is attributable to economic factors, which, together with urban structure and neighborhood preferences, "bear much of the explanatory weight for present residential patterns."

2 Now, move into a small group with three or four other students and compare your annotated texts. What do you make of the similarities and differences you see? What strategies can you borrow from one another?

READING AS A WRITER: ANALYZING A TEXT RHETORICALLY

When you identify a writer's purpose for responding to a situation by composing an essay that puts forth claims meant to sway a particular audience, you are performing **rhetorical analysis** — separating out the parts of an argument to better understand how the argument works as a whole. We discuss each of these elements — situation, purpose, claims, and audience — as we analyze the following preface from E. D. Hirsch's book *Cultural Literacy: What Every American Needs to Know* (1987). Formerly a professor of English, Hirsch has long been interested in educational reform. That interest developed from his (and others') perception that today's students do not know as much as students did in the past. Although he wrote this book more than twenty years ago, many observers still believe that the contemporary problems of illiteracy and poverty can be traced to a lack of cultural literacy. Read the preface. You may want to mark it up with your own questions and responses, and then consider them in light of our analysis (following the preface) of Hirsch's rhetorical situation, purpose, claims, and audience.

ABOUT THE READING

E. D. Hirsch Jr., a retired English professor, is the author of many acclaimed books, including *The Schools We Need and Why We Don't Have Them* (1996) and *The Knowledge Deficit* (2006). His book *Cultural Literacy* was a best seller in 1987 and had a profound effect on the focus of education in the late 1980s and 1990s.

E. D. HIRSCH JR.

Preface to *Cultural Literacy*

Rousseau points out the facility with which children lend themselves to our false methods: . . . "The apparent ease with which children learn is their ruin."
—JOHN DEWEY

There is no matter what children should learn first, any more than what leg you should put into your breeches first. Sir, you may stand disputing which is best to put in first, but in the meantime your backside is bare. Sir, while you stand considering which of two things you should teach your child first, another boy has learn't 'em both.
—SAMUEL JOHNSON

To be culturally literate is to possess the basic information needed to thrive in the modern world. The breadth of that information is great, extending over the major domains of human activity from sports   *1* to science. It is by no means confined to "culture" narrowly understood as an acquaintance with the arts. Nor is it confined to one social class. Quite the contrary. Cultural literacy constitutes the only sure avenue of opportunity for disadvantaged children, the only reliable way of combating the social determinism that now condemns them to remain in the same social and educational condition as their parents. That children from poor and illiterate homes tend to remain poor and illiterate is an unacceptable failure of our schools, one which has occurred not because our teachers are inept but chiefly because they are compelled to teach a fragmented curriculum based on faulty educational theories. Some say that our schools by themselves are powerless to change the cycle of poverty and illiteracy. I do not agree. They *can* break the cycle, but only if they themselves break fundamentally with some of the theories and practices that education professors and school administrators have followed over the past fifty years.

Although the chief beneficiaries of the educational reforms advocated in this book will be disadvantaged children, these same reforms will also enhance the literacy of children from middle-class homes. The educational goal advocated is that of mature literacy for *all* our citizens. 2

The connection between mature literacy and cultural literacy may already be familiar to those who have closely followed recent discussions of education. Shortly after the publication of my essay "Cultural Literacy," Dr. William Bennett, then chairman of the National Endowment for the Humanities and subsequently secretary of education in President Ronald Reagan's second administration, championed its ideas. This endorsement from an influential person of conservative views gave my ideas some currency, but such an endorsement was not likely to recommend the concept to liberal thinkers, and in fact the idea of cultural literacy has been attacked by some liberals on the assumption that I must be advocating a list of great books that every child in the land should be forced to read. 3

But those who examine the Appendix to this book will be able to judge for themselves how thoroughly mistaken such an assumption is. Very few specific titles appear on the list, and they usually appear as words, not works, because they represent writings that culturally literate people have read about but haven't read. *Das Kapital* is a good example. Cultural literacy is represented not by a *prescriptive* list of books but rather by a *descriptive* list of the information actually possessed by literate Americans. My aim in this book is to contribute to making that information the possession of all Americans. 4

The importance of such widely shared information can best be understood if I explain briefly how the idea of cultural literacy relates to currently prevailing theories of education. The theories that have dominated American education for the past fifty years stem ultimately from 5

Jean Jacques Rousseau, who believed that we should encourage the natural development of young children and not impose adult ideas upon them before they can truly understand them. Rousseau's conception of education as a process of natural development was an abstract generalization meant to apply to all children in any time or place: to French children of the eighteenth century or to Japanese or American children of the twentieth century. He thought that a child's intellectual and social skills would develop naturally without regard to the specific content of education. His content-neutral conception of educational development has long been triumphant in American schools of education and has long dominated the "developmental," content-neutral curricula of our elementary schools.

In the first decades of this century, Rousseau's ideas powerfully influenced the educational conceptions of John Dewey, the writer who has the most deeply affected modern American educational theory and practice. Dewey's clearest and, in his time, most widely read book on education, *Schools of Tomorrow*, acknowledges Rousseau as the chief source of his educational principles. The first chapter of Dewey's book carries the telling title "Education as Natural Development" and is sprinkled with quotations from Rousseau. In it Dewey strongly seconds Rousseau's opposition to the mere accumulation of information. ₆

> Development emphasizes the need of intimate and extensive personal acquaintance with a small number of typical situations with a view to mastering the way of dealing with the problems of experience, not the piling up of information.

Believing that a few direct experiences would suffice to develop the skills that children require, Dewey assumed that early education need not be tied to specific content. He mistook a half-truth for the whole. He placed too much faith in children's ability to learn general skills from a few typical experiences and too hastily rejected "the piling up of information." Only by piling up specific, communally shared information can children learn to participate in complex cooperative activities with other members of their community. ₇

This old truth, recently rediscovered, requires a countervailing theory of education that once again stresses the importance of specific information in early and late schooling. The corrective theory might be described as an anthropological theory of education, because it is based on the anthropological observation that all human communities are founded upon specific shared information. Americans are different from Germans, who in turn are different from Japanese, because each group possesses specifically different cultural knowledge. In an anthropological perspective, the basic goal of education in a human community is acculturation, the transmission to children of the specific information shared by the adults of the group or polis. ₈

Plato, that other great educational theorist, believed that the specific contents transmitted to children are by far the most important elements of education. In *The Republic* he makes Socrates ask rhetorically, "Shall we carelessly allow children to hear any casual tales which may be devised by casual persons, and to receive into their minds ideas for the most part the very opposite of those which we shall wish them to have when they are grown up?" Plato offered good reasons for being concerned with the specific contents of schooling, one of them ethical: "For great is the issue at stake, greater than appears — whether a person is to be good or bad." *9*

Time has shown that there is much truth in the durable educational theories of both Rousseau and Plato. But even the greatest thinkers, being human, see mainly in one direction at a time, and no thinkers, however profound, can foresee the future implications of their ideas when they are translated into social policy. The great test of social ideas is the crucible of history, which, after a time, usually discloses a one-sidedness in the best of human generalizations. History, not superior wisdom, shows us that neither the content-neutral curriculum of Rousseau and Dewey nor the narrowly specified curriculum of Plato is adequate to the needs of a modern nation. *10*

Plato rightly believed that it is natural for children to learn an adult culture, but too confidently assumed that philosophy could devise the one best culture. (Nonetheless, we should concede to Plato that within our culture we have an obligation to choose and promote our best traditions.) On the other side, Rousseau and Dewey wrongly believed that adult culture is "unnatural" to young children. Rousseau, Dewey, and their present-day disciples have not shown an adequate appreciation of the need for transmission of specific cultural information. *11*

In contrast to the theories of Plato and Rousseau, an anthropological theory of education accepts the naturalness as well as the relativity of human cultures. It deems it neither wrong nor unnatural to teach young children adult information before they fully understand it. The anthropological view stresses the universal fact that a human group must have effective communications to function effectively, that effective communications require shared culture, and that shared culture requires transmission of specific information to children. Literacy, an essential aim of education in the modern world, is no autonomous, empty skill but depends upon literate culture. Like any other aspect of acculturation, literacy requires the early and continued transmission of specific information. Dewey was deeply mistaken to disdain "accumulating information in the form of symbols." Only by accumulating shared symbols, and the shared information that the symbols represent, can we learn to communicate effectively with one another in our national community. *12*

■ Identify the Situation

The **situation** is what motivates you to write. Suppose you want to respond to the government's attempts to limit music downloads from the Internet. The *situation* is that the music industry has long believed it has been losing sales of CDs and other music products because of downloading, so industry leaders lobbied lawmakers in Washington, D.C., and persuaded them to restrict people's ability to take what the industry argues is its property. Discovering the range of perspectives here — for instance, of the music industry and its lobbyists, of legislators, of copyright lawyers, of consumer groups, of consumers who download music — will take some research, which is why we call writing a form of inquiry — it often begins with learning to identify the situation. Learning to identify the situation in a piece of writing, the conversations and issues that motivated the author to respond in writing, will help you figure out how to respond in your own writing.

To understand what motivated Hirsch to write, we need look no further than the situation he identifies in the first paragraph of the preface: "the social determinism that now condemns [disadvantaged children] to remain in the same social and educational condition as their parents." Hirsch wants to make sure his readers are aware of the problem so that they will be motivated to read his argument (and take action). He presents as an urgent problem the situation of disadvantaged children, an indication of what is at stake for the writer and for the readers of the argument. For Hirsch, this situation needs to change.

The urgency of a writer's argument is not always triggered by a single situation; often it is multifaceted. Again in the first paragraph, Hirsch identifies a second concern when he states that poverty and illiteracy reflect "an unacceptable failure of our schools, one which has occurred not because our teachers are inept but chiefly because they are compelled to teach a fragmented curriculum based on faulty educational theories." When he introduces a second problem, Hirsch helps us see the interconnected and complex nature of the situations authors confront in academic writing.

■ Identify the Writer's Purpose

The **purpose** for writing an essay may be to respond to a particular situation; it also can be what a writer is trying to accomplish. Specifically, what does the writer want readers to do? Does the writer want us to think about an issue, to change our opinions? Does the writer want to make us aware of a problem that we may not have recognized? Does the writer advocate for some type of change? Or is some combination of all three at work?

Hirsch's overall purpose is to promote educational reforms that will produce a higher degree of literacy for all citizens. He begins his argument with a broad statement about the importance of cultural literacy: "Cultural literacy constitutes the only sure avenue of opportunity for disadvantaged children, the only reliable way of combating the social determinism that now condemns them to remain in the same social and educational condition as their parents" (para. 1). As his argument unfolds, his purpose continues to unfold as well. He identifies the schools as a source of the problem and suggests how they must change to promote literacy:

> Some say that our schools by themselves are powerless to change the cycle of poverty and illiteracy. I do not agree. They *can* break the cycle, but only if they themselves break fundamentally with some of the theories and practices that education professors and school administrators have followed over the past fifty years. (para. 1)

The "educational goal," Hirsch says at the end of paragraph 2, is "mature literacy for *all* our citizens." To reach that goal, he insists, education must break with the past. In paragraphs 5 through 11, he cites the influence of Jean-Jacques Rousseau, John Dewey, and Plato, tracing what he sees as the educational legacies of the past. Finally, in the last paragraph of the excerpt, Hirsch describes an "anthropological view, . . . the universal fact that a human group must have effective communications to function effectively, that effective communications require shared culture, and that shared culture requires transmission of specific information to children." It is here, Hirsch argues, in the "transmission of specific information" to children, that schools must do a better job.

■ Identify the Writer's Claims

Claims are assertions that authors must justify and support with evidence and good reasons. The **thesis**, or **main claim**, is the controlling idea that crystallizes a writer's main point, helping readers track the idea as it develops throughout the essay. A writer's purpose clearly influences the way he or she crafts the main claim of an argument, the way he or she presents all assertions and evidence.

Hirsch's main claim is that "cultural literacy constitutes the only sure avenue of opportunity for disadvantaged children, the only reliable way of combating the social determinism that now condemns them to remain in the same social and educational condition as their parents" (para. 1). Notice that his thesis also points to a solution: making cultural literacy the core of public school curricula. Here we distinguish the main claim, or thesis, from the other claims or assertions that Hirsch makes. For example, at the very outset, Hirsch states that "to be culturally literate is to possess the basic information needed to thrive in the modern world." Although this is an assertion that requires support, it is a **minor claim**; it does not shape what Hirsch writes in the remainder of his essay. His main claim, or thesis, is really his call for reform.

■ Identify the Writer's Audience

A writer's language can help us identify his or her **audience**, the readers whose opinions and actions the writer hopes to influence or change. In

Hirsch's text, words and phrases like *social determinism, cycle of poverty and illiteracy, educational reforms, prescriptive,* and *anthropological* indicate that Hirsch believes his audience is well educated. References to Plato, Socrates, Rousseau, and Dewey also indicate the level of knowledge Hirsch expects of his readers. Finally, the way the preface unfolds suggests that Hirsch is writing for an audience that is familiar with a certain **genre**, or type, of writing: the formal argument. Notice how the author begins with a statement of the situation and then asserts his position. The very fact that he includes a preface speaks to the formality of his argument. Hirsch's language, his references, the structure of the document, all suggest that he is very much in conversation with people who are experienced and well-educated readers.

More specifically, the audience Hirsch invokes is made up of people who are concerned about illiteracy in the United States and the kind of social determinism that appears to condemn the educationally disadvantaged to poverty. Hirsch also acknowledges directly "those who have closely followed recent discussions of education," including the conservative William Bennett and liberal thinkers who might be provoked by Bennett's advocacy of Hirsch's ideas (para. 3). Moreover, he appears to assume his readers have achieved "mature literacy," even if they are not actually "culturally literate." He is writing for an audience that not only is well educated but also is deeply interested in issues of education as they relate to social policy.

Steps to Analyzing a Text Rhetorically

1 **Identify the situation.** What motivates the writer to write?

2 **Identify the writer's purpose.** What does the writer want readers to do or think about?

3 **Identify the writer's claims.** What is the writer's main claim? What minor claims does he or she make?

4 **Identify the writer's audience.** What do you know about the writer's audience? What does the writer's language imply about the readers? What about the writer's references? The structure of the essay?

A Practice Sequence: Reading Rhetorically

This exercise asks you to work your way through a series of paragraphs, identifying in turn the key elements of rhetorical analysis: situation, purpose, claim, and audience.

1 Begin by identifying the situation. Read the following passage from a student essay titled "Overcoming Social Stratification in

America." As you read, identify the specific words and phrases that suggest the situation that motivated the writer to compose the essay. Then describe the situation in one or two sentences.

> The social stratification encompassing American society today has placed African Americans and other minority groups at a disadvantage: Limited social mobility is preventing them from achieving higher social status. In his article "What Every American Needs to Know," E. D. Hirsch suggests that minority groups are disadvantaged as a result of a major decline in communication among Americans caused by the current educational system's failure to teach "cultural literacy." Hirsch contends that cultural literacy acts as a social equalizer, creating an American identity based on shared knowledge among all individuals independent of their social stratum. However, Hirsch's theory ignores race's inherent ability to define all social constructions in America. JanMohamed and Lloyd, in their article "Toward a Theory of Minority Discourse: What Is to Be Done?" propose that a schism separating minorities from the majority has been evolving since the colonial period. E. B. Higginbotham alludes to the effect of this deep separation and a broad antagonism toward the majority, claiming they have turned the idea of race into what she calls in her article "African-American Women's History and the Metalanguage of Race," a "metalanguage." Because of race, Hirsch's notion of cultural literacy has little relevance to attempts to eradicate social stratification in America. For minorities to achieve higher status, they must overcome the metalanguage, which has turned the term *minority* into a reference to a person of inferior political status instead of a group of people comprising a smaller population in society.

2 Identify the writer's purpose. Read the passage below from a student essay titled "Education Today: From Cultural Literacy to Multicultural Contact." What words and phrases suggest the student's purpose for writing? In a few sentences, describe the writer's purpose.

> The telephone as we know it today was invented exactly 125 years ago. The first wireless telephone was first used some 45 years later. The development of the Internet took place in the late sixties. Today, handheld devices can transmit real-time video via satellite. These and other technological advances have allowed the world to expand at an ever-increasing pace. Nowadays, the world is a place of continuous progress, a constantly changing environment in which adaptation is the only key to success. While some sectors of society were able to perform a smooth transition from the national to the global level of thinking, others had a more difficult time. One particular component that failed to adapt properly is the educational system. The emphasis on test taking and short-term memorization, which was introduced during the early 1900s, is outdated but still maintained in the teaching style today. I propose that education should be more multifaceted.

3 Identify the writer's claim. Read the passage below from a student essay titled " 'Writing' the Wrong: The Dilemma of the Minority Author." Identify and write down the writer's main claim, or thesis.

> Literature, because of its ability to convey a set of values and ideals to a particular audience, has been a significant medium for shaping revolutionary events in America. For minority authors of various ethnic backgrounds, literature is a means by which they can encourage an end to the subordination of minority groups. Yet the goal of minority literature goes beyond achieving reform. Minority authors also hope to convey a piece of their own unique identity through the text that fills their pages. Unfortunately, however, because of the marginalization of minority texts by Western culture, many minority authors have found it difficult to achieve the twofold purpose of their writing. To move their works toward the forefront of society and so disseminate their message of societal reform to a larger audience that includes European Americans, minority authors have found that they must risk a portion of their own unique identity. An unwillingness to do so, in fact, can leave them powerless to effect any form of societal revolution that could end the overshadowing of minorities by the dominant culture. Although it is unfortunate that minority authors must initially sacrifice a piece of their identity to reach a larger audience, doing so gives them "insider" status and thus greater influence on societal change.

4 Identify the writer's audience. Read the following excerpt from "The Problems and Dangers of Assimilatory Policies." Admittedly, the essay was written in response to a classroom assignment, so the student's instructor and classmates would be part of the writer's audience. But what sort of generalizations can you make about the audience that would read this essay outside the classroom environment?

> American society considers itself to be in an age of enlightenment. Racism has been denounced, and cultural colorblindness in all things is encouraged. Economic opportunities are available for everyone, and equal consideration before the law is provided for each citizen. American society considers itself the embodiment of liberty, equality, and justice for all.
>
> In a society like the one described, it follows that one's background and culture [do] not have any influence on one's socioeconomic status; theoretically, the two should be completely disconnected. Yet, as we all know, this is not the case. The people of the highest status in America are almost uniformly white males. Sadly, America, the place of equality and liberty, is still very much a stratified society, not only by socioeconomic class/status, but minority cultures much more often fill the ranks of the lower classes. Fortunately for those of minority cultures, the country's policymakers now accept, at least in

speech, the basic equality and potential of all cultures to rise out of poverty; unfortunately, they still refuse to recognize the validity of differences in these cultures from what they, the policymakers, view as American.

5 Share your analysis. Working with two or three of your classmates, come to a consensus on the (1) situation, (2) purpose, (3) main claim, and (4) audience of the excerpts. Then choose a spokesperson to report your group's thoughts to the rest of the class.

WRITING AS A READER: COMPOSING A RHETORICAL ANALYSIS

One of our favorite exercises is to ask our students to choose a single paragraph from a text they have read and to write a rhetorical analysis of it. Once you are able to identify how writers make their arguments, you are better able to make use of their strategies in your own writing. You may be amazed by how much you can say or write about a single paragraph in an essay once you begin to consider such factors as purpose and audience.

For example, one of our students wrote a rhetorical analysis of the third paragraph of Ada María Isasi-Díaz's essay "Hispanic in America: Starting Points." Here is the paragraph from Isasi-Díaz's work:

> A preliminary note about terminology. What to call ourselves is an issue hotly debated in some segments of our communities. I use the term "Hispanic" because the majority of the communities I deal with include themselves in that term, though each and every one of us refers to ourselves according to our country of origin: Cubans, Puerto Ricans, Mexican Americans, etc. What I do wish to emphasize is that "Latina/o" does not have a more politicized or radical connotation than "Hispanic" among the majority of our communities. In my experience it is most often those outside our communities who insist on giving Latina/o such a connotation. The contrary, however, is true of the appellation "Chicana/o," which does indicate a certain consciousness and political stance different from but not necessarily contrary to those who call themselves Mexican Americans.

Now here is the student's analysis of the paragraph, which she wrote after she read Isasi-Díaz's whole essay and identified (1) the situation that Isasi-Díaz responded to, (2) her purpose, (3) her claim, and (4) her intended audience (through the use of language). Our annotations highlight some of the rhetorical strategies the student made use of in her analysis.

The student focuses on the author's language as a way to grasp the situation.

Isasi-Díaz is obviously concerned about the words she uses to set out her argument: She begins this early paragraph with "a preliminary note about terminology." She wants us to know that there is an argument about the label *Hispanic* within Hispanic communities, and she uses *our* repeatedly in this paragraph to remind us that she is part of those communities. She assumes that we might be outside those communities and that we need this terminology clarified (in my case, she's right!). Isasi-Díaz uses personal experience to show us that she knows what she is talking about: "In my experience it is most often those outside our communities who insist . . ." She walks us through the different terms (*Latina/o, Chicana/o, Mexican American*) and offers not exactly definitions but connotations, telling us which label indicates what kind of political position. I like the way she wants to clear up all these different terms, and I think I might try in my own essay to have a paragraph early on that clarifies the definitions and connotations of the key words I am using.

The student notes that the author uses personal experience as evidence.

The student also considers how what she reads might apply to her own writing. The student identifies those parts of the essay that could affect readers, using her own response as an example.

It is interesting that Isasi-Díaz makes a big deal of being inside her communities, and blames those "outside" her communities for "insist[ing]" on giving what she sees as the wrong connotation to words. As an outsider myself, this might have turned me off a bit, but she does make clear that there is a wide range of experiences (suggested by her long list of countries of origin) and opinions within "our communities" (the fact that *communities* is plural rather than singular suggests this, too), so she is doing something more complicated than "us versus them" here. It makes me think of Gloria Anzaldúa's essay, where she also shows how many different perspectives are embedded in the very words a person uses, particularly on the border between Mexico and the United States. It also reminded me of Mary Louise Pratt's idea of "transculturation," where people struggle to retain and adapt their cultural identities in "contact zones."

The student makes a connection to other essays she has read.

■ Write a Rhetorical Analysis of a Paragraph

Now we'd like you to try the same exercise. First, read the excerpt from Ada María Isasi-Díaz's essay that follows. As you read, underline where the writer makes the following points explicit:

- The situation to which she is responding
- The purpose of her essay
- Her main claim, or thesis
- Words and phrases that suggest who she believes is her audience

---

┌─ ABOUT THE READING ───

Ada María Isasi-Díaz is a professor of theology and ethics at the Theological
School, Drew University. A political refugee from Cuba, she came to the
United States in 1960 and entered an Ursuline convent. She later spent
three years as a missionary in Lima, Peru, where she worked with the poor
and the oppressed, joining them in their struggle for justice. In her
book *Mujerista Theology* (1996), she provides what she calls a comprehensive introduction to Hispanic feminist theology, which seeks to create a
valid voice for Latinas and challenges theological understandings, church
teachings, and religious practices that oppress Latinas. "Hispanic in
America: Starting Points" was originally published in the May 13, 1991,
issue of *Christianity in Crisis*.

ADA MARÍA ISASI-DÍAZ

Hispanic in America: Starting Points

The twenty-first century is rapidly approaching and with it comes a   1
definitive increase in the Hispanic population of the United States.
We will soon be the most numerous ethnic "minority" — a minority
that seems greatly problematic because a significant number of us,
some of us would say the majority, behave differently from other immigrant groups in the United States.

Our unwillingness to jump into the melting pot; our insistence on   2
maintaining our own language; our ongoing links with our countries of
origin — due mostly to their geographic proximity and to the continuous
flow of more Hispanics into the United States; and the fact that the
largest groups of Hispanics, Mexican Americans and Puerto Ricans are
geographically and politically an integral part of this country: These
factors, among others, make us different. And the acceptance of that
difference, which does not make us better or worse than other groups
but simply different, has to be the starting point for understanding us.
What follows is a kind of working paper, a guide toward reaching that
starting point.

A preliminary note about terminology. What to call ourselves is an   3
issue hotly debated in some segments of our communities. I use the term
"Hispanic" because the majority of the communities I deal with include
themselves in that term, though each and every one of us refers to
ourselves according to our country of origin: Cubans, Puerto Ricans,
Mexican Americans, etc. What I do wish to emphasize is that "Latina/o"
does not have a more politicized or radical connotation than "Hispanic"
among the majority of our communities. In my experience it is most often
those outside our communities who insist on giving Latina/o such a

connotation. The contrary, however, is true of the appellation "Chicana/o," which does indicate a certain consciousness and political stance different from but not necessarily contrary to those who call themselves Mexican Americans.

The way Hispanics participate in this society has to do not only with us, but also with U.S. history, economics, politics, and society. Hispanics are in this country to begin with mostly because of U.S. policies and interests. Great numbers of Mexican Americans never moved to the United States. Instead, the border crossed *them* in 1846 when Mexico had to give up today's Southwest in the Treaty of Guadalupe-Hidalgo. The spoils of the Spanish American War at the end of the nineteenth century included Puerto Rico, where the United States had both military and economic interests. Without having any say, that nation was annexed by the United States.

Cuba suffered a somewhat similar fate. The United States sent troops to Cuba in the midst of its War of Independence against Spain. When Spain surrendered, the United States occupied Cuba as a military protectorate. And though Cuba became a free republic in 1902, the United States continued to maintain economic control and repeatedly intervened in Cuba's political affairs. It was, therefore, only reasonable that when Cubans had to leave their country, they felt they could and should find refuge here. The United States government accepted the Cuban refugees of the Castro regime, giving them economic aid and passing a special law making it easy for them to become residents and citizens.

As for more recent Hispanic immigrants, what can be said in a few lines about the constant manipulation by the United States of the economies and political processes of the different countries of Central America? The United States, therefore, has the moral responsibility to accept Salvadorans, Guatemalans, Hondurans, and other Central Americans who have to leave their countries because of political persecution or hunger. In short, the reasons Hispanics are in the United States are different from those of the earlier European immigrants, and the responsibility the United States has for our being here is vastly greater.

In spite of this difference, many people believe we Hispanics could have become as successful as the European immigrants. So why haven't we? For one thing, by the time Hispanics grew in numbers in the United States, the economy was no longer labor-intensive. Hispanics have lacked not "a strong back and a willingness to work," but the opportunity to capitalize on them. Then, unlike the European immigrants who went west and were able to buy land, Hispanics arrived here after homesteading had passed. But a more fundamental reason exists: racism. Hispanics are considered a nonwhite race, regardless of the fact that many of us are of the white race. Our ethnic difference has been officially construed as a racial difference: In government, businesses, and school forms, "Hispanic" is one of the choices under the category *race*.

No possibility exists of understanding Hispanics and being in dialogue   *8*
with us unless the short exposition presented is studied and analyzed.
The starting point for all dialogue is a profound respect for the other, and
respect cannot flourish if the other is not known. A commitment to study
the history of Hispanics in the United States — from the perspective of
Hispanics and not only from the perspective presented in the standard
textbooks of American history — must be the starting point in any
attempt to understand Hispanics.

A second obstacle to dialogue is the prevalent insistence in this coun-   *9*
try that one American Way of Life exists, and it is the best way of life for
everybody in the world. The melting pot concept has provided a framework in which assimilation is a must, and plurality of cultures an impossibility. Hispanic culture is not seen as an enrichment but as a threat. Few
understand that Hispanic culture provides for us, as other cultures do for
other peoples, guidelines for conduct and relationships, a system of values, and institutions and power structures that allow us to function at our
best. Our culture has been formed and will continue to be shaped by the
historical happenings and the constant actions of our communities —
communities in the United States that are influenced by what happens
here as well as in our countries of origin.

It is only within our own culture that Hispanics can acquire a sense of   *10*
belonging, of security, of dignity, and of participation. The ongoing
attempts to minimize or to make our culture disappear will only create
problems for the United States. They engender a low sense of identity that
can lead us to nonhealthy extremes in our search for some self-esteem.
For us, language is the main means of identification here in the United
States. To speak Spanish, in public as well as in private, is a political act, a
means of asserting who we are, an important way of struggling against
assimilation. The different state laws that forbid speaking Spanish in official situations, or militate against bilingual education, function as an
oppressive internal colonialism that ends up hurting U.S. society.

A Practice Sequence: Rhetorically Analyzing a Paragraph

1 Review your annotations and write a paragraph in which you
describe the rhetorical situation and the writer's purpose, main
claim, and audience.

2 Now write an analysis of a paragraph in Isasi-Díaz's essay. Choose
a substantial paragraph (not paragraph 3!) that you find especially
interesting either for what the author writes or how she writes it.
Using quotations from the text, write a one-page essay in which
you consider the situation Isasi-Díaz is responding to, her purpose
as a writer, or her audience.

■ Write a Rhetorical Analysis of an Essay

By now you should be developing a strong sense of what is involved in analyzing a paragraph rhetorically. You should be ready to take the next steps: performing a rhetorical analysis of a complete text and then sharing your analysis and the strategies you've learned with your classmates.

Read the next text, "Cultural Baggage" by Barbara Ehrenreich, annotating it to help you identify her situation, purpose, thesis, and audience. As you read, also make a separate set of annotations — possibly with a different color pen or pencil, circled, or keyed with asterisks — in which you comment on or evaluate the effectiveness of her essay. What do you like or dislike about it? Why? Does Ehrenreich persuade you to accept her point of view? What impressions do you have of her as a person? Would you like to be in a conversation with her?

ABOUT THE READING

Barbara Ehrenreich is a social critic, activist, and political essayist. Her book *Nickel and Dimed: On (Not) Getting By in America* (2001) describes her attempt to live on low-wage jobs; it became a national best seller in the United States. Her most recent book, *Bait and Switch: The (Futile) Pursuit of the American Dream* (2005), explores the shadowy world of the white-collar unemployed. Ehrenreich has also written for *Mother Jones, The Atlantic, Ms., The New Republic, In These Times,* Salon.com, and other publications. "Cultural Baggage" was originally published in the *New York Times Magazine* in 1992.

BARBARA EHRENREICH

Cultural Baggage

An acquaintance was telling me about the joys of rediscovering her *1* ethnic and religious heritage. "I know exactly what my ancestors were doing 2,000 years ago," she said, eyes gleaming with enthusiasm, "and *I can do the same things now.*" Then she leaned forward and inquired politely, "And what is your ethnic background, if I may ask?"

"None," I said, that being the first word in line to get out of my mouth. *2* Well, not "none," I backtracked. Scottish, English, Irish — that was something, I supposed. Too much Irish to qualify as a WASP; too much of the hated English to warrant a "Kiss Me, I'm Irish" button; plus there are a number of dead ends in the family tree due to adoptions, missing records, failing memories and the like. I was blushing by this time. Did "none" mean I was rejecting my heritage out of Anglo-Celtic self-hate? Or was I revealing a hidden ethnic chauvinism in which the Britannically derived serve as a kind of neutral standard compared with the ethnic "others"?

Throughout the 1960s and 70s, I watched one group after another — 3 African Americans, Latinos, Native Americans — stand up and proudly reclaim their roots while I just sank back ever deeper into my seat. All this excitement over ethnicity stemmed, I uneasily sensed, from a past in which *their* ancestors had been trampled upon by *my* ancestors, or at least by people who looked very much like them. In addition, it had begun to seem almost un-American not to have some sort of hyphen at hand, linking one to more venerable times and locales.

But the truth is, I was raised with none. We'd eaten ethnic foods in my 4 childhood home, but these were all borrowed, like the pasties, or Cornish meat pies, my father had picked up from his fellow miners in Butte, Montana. If my mother had one rule, it was militant ecumenism in all manners of food and experience. "Try new things," she would say, meaning anything from sweetbreads to clams, with an emphasis on the "new."

As a child, I briefly nourished a craving for tradition and roots. 5 I immersed myself in the works of Sir Walter Scott. I pretended to believe that the bagpipe was a musical instrument. I was fascinated to learn from a grandmother that we were descended from certain Highland clans and longed for a pleated skirt in one of their distinctive tartans.

But in *Ivanhoe*, it was the dark-eyed "Jewess" Rebecca I identified 6 with, not the flaxen-haired bimbo Rowena. As for clans: Why not call them "tribes," those bands of half-clad peasants and warriors whose idea of cuisine was stuffed sheep gut washed down with whiskey? And then there was the sting of Disraeli's remark — which I came across in my early teens — to the effect that his ancestors had been leading orderly, literate lives when my ancestors were still rampaging through the Highlands daubing themselves with blue paint.

Motherhood put the screws on me, ethnicity-wise. I had hoped that by 7 marrying a man of Eastern European Jewish ancestry I would acquire for my descendants the ethnic genes that my own forebears so sadly lacked. At one point, I even subjected the children to a seder of my own design, including a little talk about the flight from Egypt and its relevance to modern social issues. But the kids insisted on buttering their matzos and snickering through my talk. "Give me a break, Mom," the older one said. "You don't even believe in God."

After the tiny pagans had been put to bed, I sat down to brood over 8 Elijah's wine. What had I been thinking? The kids knew that their Jewish grandparents were secular folks who didn't hold seders themselves. And if ethnicity eluded me, how could I expect it to take root in my children, who are not only Scottish English Irish, but Hungarian Polish Russian to boot?

But, then, on the fumes of Manischewitz, a great insight took form in 9 my mind. It was true, as the kids said, that I didn't "believe in God." But

EHRENREICH | CULTURAL BAGGAGE **53**

this could be taken as something very different from an accusation — a reminder of a genuine heritage. My parents had not believed in God either, nor had my grandparents or any other progenitors going back to the great-great level. They had become disillusioned with Christianity generations ago — just as, on the in-law side, my children's other ancestors had shaken their Orthodox Judaism. This insight did not exactly furnish me with an "identity," but it was at least something to work with: We are the kind of people, I realized — whatever our distant ancestors' religions — who do *not* believe, who do not carry on traditions, who do not do things just because someone has done them before.

The epiphany went on: I recalled that my mother never introduced a procedure for cooking or cleaning by telling me, "Grandma did it this way." What did Grandma know, living in the days before vacuum cleaners and disposable toilet mops? In my parents' general view, new things were better than old, and the very fact that some ritual had been performed in the past was a good reason for abandoning it now. Because what was the past, as our forebears knew it? Nothing but poverty, superstition and grief. "Think for yourself," Dad used to say. "Always ask why."

In fact, this may have been the ideal cultural heritage for my particular ethnic strain — bounced as it was from the Highlands of Scotland across the sea, out to the Rockies, down into the mines and finally spewed out into high-tech, suburban America. What better philosophy, for a race of migrants, than "Think for yourself"? What better maxim, for a people whose whole world was rudely inverted every thirty years or so, than "Try new things"?

The more tradition-minded, the newly enthusiastic celebrants of Purim and Kwanzaa and Solstice, may see little point to survival if the survivors carry no cultural freight — religion, for example, or ethnic tradition. To which I would say that skepticism, curiosity and wide-eyed ecumenical tolerance are also worthy elements of the human tradition and are at least as old as such notions as "Serbian" or "Croatian," "Scottish" or "Jewish." I make no claims for my personal line of progenitors except that they remained loyal to the values that may have induced all of our ancestors, long, long ago, to climb down from the trees and make their way into the open plains.

A few weeks ago, I cleared my throat and asked the children, now mostly grown and fearsomely smart, whether they felt any stirrings of ethnic or religious identity, etc., which might have been, ahem, insufficiently nourished at home. "None," they said, adding firmly, "and the world would be a better place if nobody else did, either." My chest swelled with pride, as would my mother's, to know that the race of "none" marches on.

A Practice Sequence: Rhetorically Analyzing an Essay

1 Write a brief rhetorical analysis of Barbara Ehrenreich's essay, referring to your notes and citing passages where she indicates her situation, purpose, main claim, and audience.

2 An option for group work: As a class, divide into three or more groups. Each group should answer the following questions in response to their reading of Ehrenreich's essay "Cultural Baggage":

Group 1: Identify the situation(s) motivating Ehrenreich to write. Then evaluate: How well does her argument function as a conversation with other authors who have written on the same topic?

Group 2: Analyze the audience's identity, perspectives, and conventional expectations. Then evaluate: How well does the argument function as a conversation with the audience?

Group 3: Analyze the writer's purpose. Then evaluate: Do you believe Ehrenreich achieves her purpose in this essay? Why or why not?

Then, as a class, share your observations:

- To what extent does the author's ability as a conversationalist — that is, her ability to enter into a conversation with other authors and her audience — affect your evaluation of whether she achieves her purpose in this essay?

- If you were to meet this writer, what suggestions or advice would you give her for making her argument more persuasive?

■ ■ ■

Much if not all of the writing you do in college will be based on what you have read. This is the case, for example, when you summarize a philosopher's theory, analyze the significance of an experiment in psychology, or, perhaps, synthesize different and conflicting points of view in making an argument about race and academic achievement in sociology. As we maintain throughout this book, writing and reading are inextricably linked to each other. Good academic writers are also good critical readers: They leave their mark on what they read, identifying issues, making judgments about the truth of what writers tell them, and evaluating the adequacy of the evidence in support of an argument. This is where writing and inquiry begin: understanding our own position relative to the scholarly conversations that we want to enter. Moreover, critical readers try to understand the strategies that writers use to persuade them to agree with them. At times, these are strategies that we can adapt in advancing our arguments. In the next chapter, we provide some strategies for identifying and evaluating the adequacy of a writer's claims.

4

Rhetorical Analysis

A rhetorical analysis is relentlessly functional. Because it is based on a view of language as a medium of communication and not a system of representation, it assumes that speakers and writers have intentions or designs on readers and hearers, and it seeks to identify the verbal means typically used to achieve those intentions or designs. In the paradigmatic rhetorical situation, a speaker addresses an audience and attempts to persuade its members to understand the speaker's position, to adopt the speaker's perspective, to believe what the speaker believes, and to act as the speaker recommends. And this speaker and audience always face each other in a particular setting and moment in time: Pericles delivers a funeral oration to the assembled citizens of Athens after the battle of Marathon; Elizabeth Cady Stanton addresses the supporters of suffrage gathered at Seneca Falls to celebrate the 4th of July, 1876; President Richard Nixon delivers an inaugural address when sworn into office in January 1969. A speaker in such a particular setting selects among the "available means" to persuade, including what is physically present as well all what can be verbally constructed (Kennedy 36). Because the means of inducement can be sensory as well as verbal, a rhetorical analysis can also examine nonverbal means of persuasion such as the lighting or music used to create a mood in the audience or the film technique used to predispose viewers to an interpretation.

Although the study of sensory and symbolic inducement is also part of a rhetorical approach, we limit this discussion to persuasive appeals constructed in language. Limiting ourselves to language, we also turn to the written and published texts that preserve it, and in so doing we risk losing the essential situatedness of the rhetorical act. Nevertheless, a rhetorical

Taken from Jeanne Fahnestock and Marie Secor, "Rhetorical Analysis," in *Discourse Studies in Composition*, ed. Ellen Barton and Gail Stygall (Cresskill, NJ: Hampton Press: 2002), pp. 177–94, 196–200.

analysis, whether of a written or a spoken text, must always factor into account the speaker, audience, context, and "moment" of a text as explanatory principles for the linguistic and strategic choices identified. It may also work backward from the rhetor's (speaker's or writer's) choices to the situation that could have produced the text. Thus, rhetorical analysis is inevitably situational as well as functional.

Rhetorical analysis also aims to elucidate the argument of a text. Because it assumes that humans communicate with purposes, the rhetorical perspective acknowledges no "innocent" exchanges, no free-floating natural language. Even "hello" can have the minimum phatic purpose of channel opening, as communication experts call it, and even casual chit-chat negotiates common ground and mutual nonaggression. Traditionally, however, rhetoric has focused on higher end persuasion, on full and formal argumentation of the kind produced by rhetors who are conscious of what they want to persuade an audience about and who have therefore formulated their points into explicit propositions and supporting arguments.

As we talk about rhetorical *analysis*, however, it is important to remember that rhetoric, the art of how to use language to persuade, developed in antiquity as a heuristic rather than a hermeneutic art. Rhetoric was not originally a theory of interpretation or a methodology for analysis; it was a theory — or at least a list of things to try — for constructing an effective speech. Early rhetorics are how-to manuals or, in the teaching of Antiphon and Isocrates, they might skip the instructions and offer samples. Adopting this productive art for the purpose of analyzing someone else's text requires some shifts in perspective and an awareness of the situation, function, and argument of one's own analytical discourse.

OVERVIEW: THE ELEMENTS OF RHETORICAL ANALYSIS

Over the centuries, the advice offered in rhetorics on how to construct an effective text has accumulated at what might be called different levels of generality. Some advice concerned global issues such as the choice of genre and, consequent on that choice, a determination of the required parts and their arrangement. Rhetorical treatises also specified how smaller units of text could be constructed, such as appeals based on the speaker's character, on the nature of the audience, on the issue addressed, and on individual lines of argument. Finally, rhetorical manuals also offered very detailed advice about sentence construction and word choice to produce the various effects desired. The following overview of the basic elements of a rhetorical analysis moves from the level of the whole text to the level of sentence and word choice.

At the highest level is consideration of what might be called the abstract genre of an argument (*genera dicendi*), whether it is forensic, epideictic, or deliberative. Each of these three types had its real prototype and its own characteristics resulting from the needs of its situation. The forensic speech occurred in an adversarial setting (such as a courtroom) and involved a contest over whether or not a past action (a crime) was committed as charged; the deliberative speech occurred in the legislative assembly where future courses of action were spoken for or against; and the epideictic speech was delivered on occasions of public celebration or mourning where the present beliefs and values of the audience were constructed or reinforced. All three of these genres, however, were assumed to require roughly the same parts: an introduction, narration (or overview of the case), description of the parts to come, arguments for the speaker's position, refutation of those against, and a closing peroration.

Needless to say, the prototypical situations of forensic, epideictic, and deliberative discourse still exist, and the advice for constructing speeches to fit them offered in texts such as Aristotle's *Rhetoric* or Cicero's *De Inventione* can still be applied to contemporary instances. More challenging for the analyst, however, is discovering ways in which these basic genres persist in mutated forms (e.g., the scientific research report is essentially a forensic speech) and the ways in which they blend (e.g., an epideictic performance such as a graduation speech can be used to address an ongoing deliberative debate).

In addition to the three general speech types, rhetorical treatises over the centuries also identified many other genres and provided advice on their key features and construction. Some of these genres developed from the pedagogical traditions that grew up around training in rhetoric itself. For example, Quintilian and later pedagogues described a series of brief compositional exercises, called the progymnasmata, that students wrote to practice their rhetorical skills (see Matsen, Rollinson, and Sousa 251–88). Because the ability to describe vividly a heinous murder or the sack of a city were skills a good rhetor needed, exercises in description alone were practiced and a "literary" genre was born. Other genres explained in rhetorical manuals were culturally important; thus in the 12th century, many letter-writing manuals appeared, detailing the essential parts of a letter and providing examples. Such genre-based manuals differ little from a 20th-century representative of the type like Edward Huth's *How to Write and Publish Papers in the Medical Sciences* or from business and technical writing textbooks that show students how to write resumés or lab reports. They reflect the importance of a genre in a particular time and culture as, in Carolyn Miller's terms, a formalized response to a recurring rhetorical situation.

In any genre, however, Aristotelian rhetoric recommended an awareness of three kinds of appeals, those stemming from the character of the speaker (ethos), those from the nature of the audience (pathos), and those from the material of the case itself (logos). The combining of these appeals represents the extent to which Aristotle saw rhetoric as a bridge between the separate arts of poetics, where the passions are manipulated, and dialectic, where the best probable case is constructed in an exchange of questions and answers. Although the potential appeals, out of which the actual appeals are constructed, can be treated as given — the speaker has a prior reputation and the audience certain predispositions that must be worked with — 20th-century interpretive rhetoric has emphasized the ways in which the appeals themselves textually construct the author and audience. Hence, some of the most stylistically sensitive analyses of how readers' roles are produced by language choices can be found in the work of reader-response critics. But whether dealing with givens or textual constructions, rhetorical analysis informed by the three appeals will ask the following questions: How is the speaker of this text being constructed? How is the audience constructed? How is the argument constructed? And how do these three aspects either reinforce or interfere with each other?

Hellenistic rhetoric added another set of questions that applied to all three speech genres but that primarily concerned the case argued for. Rhetors preparing a speech were told to identify or to negotiate with their adversary the precise issue under debate. In a forensic setting, where determining the issue of a criminal trial can have dramatic consequences, they were given three possible general types of issue: Did the debate turn on an issue of fact (*an sit*), or one of definition (*quid sit*), or one of quality or value (*quale sit*)? In modern courtroom terms: Did the defendant kill the victim? If that is admitted, was it self-defense or murder in the first, second, or third degree? If murder in the first degree, was it aggravated or mitigated? This ancient taxonomy of issues, called the *stases*, has been revised in the 20th century (see Fahnestock and Secor) into other hier-archical series of basic questions (e.g., fact, definition, cause, value, and policy). But more important than the particular taxonomy is the move of issue identification itself. Any analysis of an argument will identify its overall point, but there is a difference between an analysis based on a par-ticular claim and one that also considers the *type* of issue at stake in a claim. Identifying type directs attention to the *prima facie* elements for such a case (see Fulkerson). In a how-to manual like Cicero's *De Inventione*, the rhetor learns about the required elements needed to argue claims at different stases. So when rhetorical theory is used as a hermeneutic rather than a heuristic, issue identification directs the analyst to question what parts of a *prima facie* case in a particular stasis are present or absent in a particular situation.

Along with an understanding of the overall situation, genre, types of appeal, and stasis, rhetoric also offered its students an array of potential lines of argument to choose from, the so-called *topoi*, topics or places. These topoi were offered in open-ended lists like the famous group of 28 common topics in II.23 of Aristotle's *Rhetoric*. Because such lists lack a certain economy or theoretical elegance, it is easy to overlook the radical epistemology they imply — no less than the claim that there are certain semantic and syntactic manipulations that at least western minds (but probably any minds) can use as sources of compelling arguments. To take just the first of the 28, Aristotle recommends that an arguer look at the key terms in a case and see if they have opposites. If they do, a premise plausible for most audiences can be built by pairing opposites with opposites. Aristotle's example looks obvious ("to be temperate is a good thing, for to lack self-control is harmful" [Kennedy 190–91]), but such argument "kernels" can be powerfully persuasive. Topics can be general (useful in all kinds of arguments) or quite specific to particular genres or fields. Thus, topical analysis, depending on its purpose, can look at either widely appealing moves or those fitting the assumptions of particular groups.

At the more specific level of sentence construction and word choice, rhetoricians offered advice on language choices or "style." They passed on the four criteria for language use that still inform most drafting and editing decisions and most of the advice that composition teachers offer students: Language should be correct (grammatical), perspicuous (clear to its intended audience), appropriate (fitting the occasion), and vivid or capable of sticking in a listener's memory. Also under style, rhetoricians long held to a doctrine of levels — low, middle, and high — roughly conforming to the degree of formality in language situations. Low corresponds most closely to what we would call a colloquial style, typical of informal conversation with intimates. A middle style is a serviceable common denominator (although it may incorporate elements from both high and low), a style we would now associate with most journalism. A high style is appropriate to formal occasions and purposes (like legal documents or institutional mission statements) and to ceremonial occasions where the performative dimension of language demands certain formulaic choices to accomplish rituals like ship launching and marriage. Modern language analysts use the cognate notions of "register" or "lexical field," the complex of words and phrasing appropriate to a given occupational group (air traffic controllers) or to recurring social situations (mall rats meeting other mall rats).

Finally, under the canon of style, rhetorical manuals specify scores of precise linguistic devices under the general rubric of figures of speech. For most of rhetorical history, this category was divided into three subcategories: tropes, which involve word and phrase choice (e.g., simile); figures of speech, which concern syntactic patterns (e.g., antithesis); and figures of thought, which construct the potential interactional dynamics of a text (e.g., rhetorical question). Perhaps no part of the analytical legacy of rhetoric has been more distorted in the hands of contemporary poststructuralists, whose appropriations of rhetoric ignore virtually every level of analysis save that of the *tropes*, a term whose meaning either contracts to be synonymous with metaphor or expands to label any frequently repeated term or image. The figures that reappear today in accessible books like Arthur Quinn's *Figures of Speech: 60 Ways to Turn a Phrase* represent only a selection of the figures detailed in classical and early modern sources. As rich as the tradition of rhetorical stylistics is, a rhetorical analysis of style need not limit itself to the classical tradition; contemporary linguistics has addressed the ideational consequences of less remarkable linguistic choices, like ordinary predication and the choice of agents.

Although the preceding paragraphs describe the basic constituents of rhetorical analysis learned from classical rhetorical theory, many theorists, especially those reviving rhetoric after World War II, have elaborated specific elements of it, adding new terms and emphases. Burke, for example, revises the traditional understanding of the speaker-audience relationship by describing the process of "identification," in essence an overlapping of ethos and pathos so that the audience does not merely construct an image of the speaker and of itself, but comes away with a notion that audience and speaker are "consubstantial," sharing the same substance, deeply connected with one another as members of the same group or tribe with identical natures and interests. A speaker who constructs this sense of identification in an audience, to the point of appearing to speak for them, is likely to be powerful, sometimes dangerously so. However, not all speaker-audience appeals employ this formula; a "letter to the editor" of a newspaper from a Nobel laureate appeals from an ethos of authority rather than one of identification. But by articulating the power of overlapping appeals to ethos and pathos, Burke adds an important concept that elaborates on the classical rhetorical paradigm.

Certainly, the most innovative post–World War II project of rhetorical recovery, one that takes seriously the relationship between dialectic and rhetoric, is *The New Rhetoric* of Perelman and Olbrechts-Tyteca. Although consistent with the classical paradigm, this work reconfigures the topics, the sources from which arguments are drawn, revising the architecture and terms for kinds of arguments and providing a way to understand knowledge-forming arguments as well as political, legal, and ceremonial ones. Among its many contributions to the terminology of rhetorical analysis, one deserves singling out here: the idea of a "dissociation" as an argumentative move (411–50). Arguers "dissociate" when they are faced with anomalies in a category or when they face conflicting imperatives. They take a formerly unified concept, field, or practice and separate out the part that no longer seems to fit, an action usually signaled by various linguistic acts of renaming.

Given the variety of texts and schools that fit under the rubric "rhetoric," it is useful to stipulate here four basic characteristics of a rhetorical analysis informed by but not necessarily limited to the classical paradigm.

1. Rhetorical analysis pays attention to the who, when, where, and probable why of a text. These elements are taken to govern its genre, stasis, and language choices. If they are not recoverable independently, they can, to some extent, be reconstructed from the text based on contextual knowledge. If, for instance, we did not know the circumstances surrounding the Gettysburg Address, if it were recovered as an anonymous fragment on the

back of an envelope, it would still be possible, based on its content and idiom, to argue for its identification as a 19th-century funeral oration.

2. Rhetorical analysis uses an identifiable vocabulary drawn from the rhetorical tradition and/or from a particular school or theorist. It is possible to combine, more or less comfortably, the terminologies of different theorists. For example, a Burkean analysis based on the pentad (which considers five questions: act, scene, agent, agency, purpose) actually works in the tradition of the *De Inventione*, where arguers are advised on how to put together arguments in criminal trials (who did what to whom, when, where, and by what means). But differences in terminology often make the underlying similarities difficult to see, and the formulations of different theorists vary in explanatory power.

3. Rhetorical analysis identifies language choices that serve the rhetor's ostensible purpose or perhaps, depending on the interpreter, his or her unconscious or subverted purposes. Thus, even deconstructionist analyses assume a functional rationale: language choices have an effect, even if that effect is destabilizing or subverting a text's ostensible purposes. Questions of intention do arise in rhetorical analysis — intentions may be complex, multiple, incompletely articulated, assumed, or confused — but texts are always assumed to have designs and effects on readers.

4. Rhetorical analysis seeks to uncover the argument of a text. Here perhaps is the feature that most distinguishes it from other methods of analysis. Some systems may be sensitive to linguistic choices, but they are fairly sentence-bound and do not always address the relationship of small-scale choices to larger argumentative units. They lack the vocabulary for analyzing linguistic moves that may operate over several phrases, sentences, or even paragraphs such as arguments by analogy, *a fortiori* arguments, arguments by division, and so on. Other systems of analysis may be quite sensitive to the interplay of contextual factors as they affect word and sentence choice, but often at the expense of engagement with its argument.

CASE STUDY: STANLEY FISH'S BID INTO THE SOKAL/*SOCIAL TEXT* CONTROVERSY

A rhetorical analysis, using rhetoric as a hermeneutic not a heuristic, usually begins by characterizing the rhetor, genre, audience, subject, and occasion of a text. These constituents are often recoverable from external sources such as the facts of publication or, in the case of speeches, eyewitness accounts of the delivery. But if these basics are not so recoverable, clues in the text can be used to reconstruct them. Of course, how these constituents are identified is very much a matter of interpretation, and as arguers themselves, rhetorical analysts will select and highlight those features that serve their own claims and attitudes. When the subject is contemporary, as is the case selected here for study, interpreters can draw on common knowledge shared with the audience of the analysis; when historical pieces are involved, more elaborate and potentially controversial reconstructions of context are required.

Once the basic features of a rhetorical situation are identified or reconstructed, a rhetorical analysis can proceed in many different ways. It can follow the arrangement of the analyzed text closely, characterizing the multiple effects sequentially encountered by the audience. Or it can be organized according to any of the systems of division offered in rhetoric such as by genre features (good for mixed modes), by appeals, by lines of argument, by small-scale devices such as figures of speech. Our analysis is organized by the three traditional appeals. After characterizing the basic rhetorical situation of the text under scrutiny (author, subject, place of publication, genre — some features of audience are postponed), we discuss separately the lines of argument or logos (keeping to sequence in that section), the projection of the author's character or ethos, and the manipulation of the audience or pathos. Our organizational strategy falsifies the actual interactive effect of the appeals, but it allows, we hope, a better demonstration of the kind of evidence used in a rhetorical analysis.

Our rhetor here is Stanley Fish, and the text we are considering, reproduced in the appendix, appeared May 21, 1996, on the op-ed page of *The New York Times*, a forum for argued positions on diverse contemporary issues. Because titles and openings in the genre of the op-ed piece must identify the subject matter and the issue that is at stake, Fish uses his first paragraph to declare his subject: New York University physicist Alan Sokal ("Transgressing") wrote a postmodernist/cultural studies critique of quantum mechanics that the editors of the journal *Social Text* accepted and published; he then revealed that his piece was a parody in a subsequent article in *Lingua Franca* (Sokal, "A Physicist"). According to Sokal, the *Social Text* piece was filled with factual errors, and yet the editors apparently accepted it without scholarly review. Readers of Fish's op-ed piece may have been aware of Sokal's double publications, which were described in the *Times* itself three days earlier, but Fish's editorial helped to turn Sokal's parody into an academic *cause celebre* rather than just a clever hoax known to a few.

Fish's simultaneous identification of his subject and bid for his readers' attention are, however, more than a conventional opening. From classical manuals on, rhetors, especially those in the courtroom where the reconstruction of a particular crime was at issue, have been advised to recapitulate events so as to serve their cause. Fish's reconstruction casts the editors of *Social Text* as innocent victims: when they "accepted" Sokal's piece they "could not have anticipated" that he would later pronounce it a "hoax." Even the use of an initial subordinate clause, deemphasizing the action of accepting, suggests their passive role as dupes. It was, however, precisely Sokal's point that if they had done their jobs as responsible scholarly editors, they should have known from the start that his piece was an error-filled parody. So — as rhetorical critics might expect because they interpret discourse through the lens of argument — Fish's beginning is no "mere" exposition of the Sokal controversy, but an opening salvo in a hotly contested skirmish.

Another element in the rhetorical situation of a written text is its place of publication. Why *The New York Times*? As a "national" newspaper, with a circulation of about 1.6 million and a readership concentrated in but not limited to New York, the *Times* occasionally takes note of academic controversies; coverage in this forum suggests that this issue has national importance. But there is also a local New York angle to this story, appropriate to the predominantly East Coast readership of the paper. Alan Sokal is a physics professor at New York University; Andrew Ross and Stanley Aronowitz, editors of *Social Text*, are faculty members at other New York universities; and *Lingua Franca*, the journal that published Sokal's revelation of his "gotcha," is also based in New York. So, in addition to its presumed general interest, this issue has local appeal, a tie-in emphasized by Fish's mention of Sokal's academic affiliation in the opening paragraph.

Another part of the situation of a rhetorical text, determined primarily by its place of publication or means of dissemination, is its genre. Having to conform to a well-established genre constrains a speaker or writer, opening up some means of persuasion and closing off others. Length is one obvious constraint. Although there is some room for variation, editors insist and readers expect an editorial to appear on a single page along with three or four others. Fish's 38 column inches constitute a generously sized editorial for the *Times* op-ed page, but Fish still had considerably less space to create his argument than we have to analyze it. An op-ed piece's revealing title, usually bestowed by the editors, is another constraint. For newspaper readers, who are essentially captured browsers, the title must announce the topic and even the claim in very few words. The title here, "Professor Sokal's Bad Joke," makes it clear that Fish judges Sokal's parody negatively; it therefore precludes the arrangement strategy of postponing the disclosure of his true opinion. Because postponement is recommended when the rhetor faces a hostile audience, immediate disclosure of one's stance presumes a predisposed or at least neutral audience.

As a piece in a certain rhetorical genre, Fish's text can be categorized as a forensic argument. It resembles a courtroom speech by a defense attorney, with the editors of *Social Text* cast as the defendants, Fish's clients, and Sokal as the prosecutor (an appropriate categorization given Fish's joint appointment at the time in Duke University's law school and in its English department). Like any lawyer, Fish understands that the best defense is often a strong offense, especially an attack on the character and motives of the prosecution. Thus, his overall forensic strategy is a reversal that will turn the prosecutor into the defendant: "This means that it is Alan Sokal, not his targets, who threatens to undermine the intellectual standards he vows to protect." We can almost visualize an accusing finger pointing to Sokal as a result of Fish's use of an anticipatory subject in this accusation: "This means that it is Alan Sokal." With Sokal cast as the defendant, the editorial will attack his character in its closing argument. He and not the editors of *Social Text* is the betrayer of the standards of science and academic cooperation.

APPEALS TO LOGOS

Having identified the rhetorical type of argument here, we can turn to an analysis based on the three appeals, beginning with the appeal to logos. Literary scholars are familiar with analyses that uncover appeals to ethos and pathos, but appeals to logos, to types and lines of argument, are less obvious to those untrained in rhetoric or forensics. Yet these constitute the material substance of the case and deserve the most attention, although they are inextricably connected with the other two appeals, as we will point out.

Fish's overall argument strategy unfolds at the stasis of definition. In order to refute Sokal's characterization of what "sociologists of science" believe and do, he seeks to define what they "really" believe and do. This strategy uses direct statements about what the sociology of science is and about what science is, as well as statements about what both are not. Fish's definitions lead to his construction of a deeper issue: that the "facts" of science are both "real" and "socially constructed." Thus, Fish tries to have it both ways by constructing a position that incorporates both Sokal's supposed claim that nature is real and the sociologists' supposed claim that nature is an artifact. He is undoing an antithesis when he characterizes the sociologists' position as follows: "What sociologists of science say is that of course the world is real and independent of our observations but that accounts of the world are produced by observers and are therefore relative to their capacities, education, training, etc." These innocent scholars "just maintain and demonstrate that the nature of scientific procedure is a question continually debated in its own precincts." "Why then," Fish asks, "does Professor Sokal attack them?" Because, he answers, Sokal mistakenly thinks that "socially constructed" means "not real," "whereas for workers in the field 'socially constructed' is a compliment paid to a fact or a procedure that has emerged from the welter of disciplinary competition into real and productive life where it can be cited, invoked and perhaps challenged." Fish's definitions here can be accused of disingenuousness or even misrepresentation; few familiar with the work of sociologists of science think that they "just" pay compliments to scientists or praise the reigning scientific orthodoxy. But his interpretation may go unchallenged by *New York Times* readers unfamiliar with the disciplinary scholarship.

Identifying Fish's strategy as definition indicates his tactics only in a rough way. More precisely, how is this strategy delivered by his linguistic choices? The following brief analysis suggests his linguistic technique for delivering this appeal. In Paragraph 3, Fish accuses Sokal of misrepresenting the beliefs of the *Social Text* editors and the social constructionist school they represent: "The truth is that none of his targets would ever make such statements." "Truth," "none," and "ever" — these words are deliberate universalizers for Fish's opinion. All the sentences in the following two paragraphs, where Fish offers his definition of what sociologists of science actually say and do, use the linking verb "is" and no modal qualifiers at all — no "might's," "could be's," or "perhaps's." Note the following constructions: "What sociologists of science say is . . . ," "Distinguishing fact from fiction is . . . ," "Consequently the history of science is. . . ." Another "zone" of sentences using predominantly linking verbs, the markers of categorization, occurs after the baseball analogy where Fish defines what science really "is" and what scientists really "do." These verb choices in definition statements, along with the absence of modals and adverbial modification, also contribute to what we call Fish's magisterial tone, a feature of his distinctive ethos.

Fish's definition argument also depends somewhat on a conflation of categories that is signaled by some term shifting. In Paragraph 4, Fish characterizes and defends sociologists of science ("what sociologists of science say is that"). But in Paragraphs 5 and 6, the subject of characterization actually changes to a different discipline, "history of science" and then to "those who concern themselves with this history." At the end of Paragraph 6, we are back with the "sociologists of science," who are trying to get the "complex and rich" story of science right. Although casual readers might be unaware of the distinction, most historians of science would distinguish themselves from sociologists of science, who work primarily with the contemporary scientific scene, a natural site of attention for those engaged in cultural critique.

After claiming that the enterprise he is defending actually honors scientists, Fish then uses another argumentative tactic, an analogy (and characteristic of Fish a baseball analogy) that he both sets up and defends against his own attack. Fish's baseball analogy is not a separate line of argument; rather, it allows him some curious moves within his broader strategy of arguing from definition. Paragraph 11 presumably shows how real facts of nature are involved in baseball, and Paragraph 12 presumably shows how scientists submit to decisions from their peers rather than from nature (a characterization that Sokal would by no means accept). These points presumably support again the claim of the essential mixture of the "real" and the "socially constructed." On the other side of this reciprocal contamination, Fish unites the two halves of his analogy in strong identity statements: "Both science and baseball then are" and "both will be." The third version of this bracketing, however, suddenly shifts to separating these two as though someone could confuse them ("Baseball and science may be both social constructions, but not all social constructions are the same.") He then heavily enumerates differences and directly admonishes the reader, "Even if two activities are alike social constructions, if you want to

take the measure of either, it is the differences you must keep in mind."
Why end an analogy with contrasts? Why such sententiousness?

The undermining of his own analogy with the sage advice to keep the differences in mind allows Fish to return to Sokal himself, who, he says, has violated this maxim: "This is what Professor Sokal does not do, and this is his second mistake." Because Sokal neither compared baseball and science nor claimed that science (or anything else) was socially constructed, it makes no sense to accuse him of having failed to keep in mind the differences among socially constructed phenomena. But Fish's argument is essentially as follows: "Baseball and science are both socially constructed and real, but not all socially constructed activities are alike, and science and the sociology of science are completely distinct." Although Fish may be trying for the appearance of consecutive logic here, in a linked chain of points, there is none. At best, he has managed a transition that allows him to charge Sokal with yet another erroneous belief: "He thinks that sociology is in competition with mainstream science — wants either to replace or debunk it — and he doesn't understand that it is a distinct enterprise, with objects of study, criteria, procedures and goals of its own."

In the line of argument that begins in Paragraph 16, which develops claims about the separation of science and the sociology of science, Fish uses a topic that *The New Rhetoric* would call a quasi-logical argument, one that mimics deductive rigor. Readers might visualize science and the sociology of science as two separate circles in a Venn diagram, floating further and further apart. It is unlikely that Sokal would disagree with the claim that the sociology of science is a unique discipline. But the sentence structure suggests that Fish's observation about the distinctness of science and the sociology of science is intended to answer the charge, attributed to Sokal, that the sociology of science wants to debunk or replace science. If we remove the content from the sentence the implication of its structure becomes clear: "He thinks X and he doesn't understand Y. Presumably if he understood Y he wouldn't think X." But it is perfectly plausible to agree that science and the sociology of science are distinct enterprises and still believe that the one wants to replace or debunk the other.

Having once claimed the unproblematic separation, Fish continues to draw out arguments from this quasi-logical division: Sociologists of science aren't trying to do science, he says, but to explain it, so they cannot be criticized for not helping find a cure for AIDS or any other social problem, because they never set that as a goal. Fish's final argument here "is a simple one," meaning one whose self-evidence cannot be questioned. This "simple" point leads to another staple line of argument, a consequence argument based on the claim that the sociology of science poses no threat to science: "A research project that takes the practice of science as an object of study is not a threat to that practice because, committed as it is to its own goals and protocols, it doesn't reach into, and therefore doesn't pose a danger to, the goals and protocols it studies." In other words, the sociology of science is a consequence-less, a harmless discipline. (But, again, the point of Sokal's hoax was not that the sociology of science was threatening, but that it does not have among its "goals and protocols" reputable disciplinary standards.) Extrapolating from his separation of science and sociology of science, Fish argues that a self-contained discipline is in danger only from insiders, a move that allows him now to charge Sokal as an insider threatening science. One might reply that because Sokal was not putting forth a scientific hoax, he cannot be accused of threatening science, but Fish here seems to evoke a more general point about the dependence of coordinated activities, even in different disciplines, on "trust." Thus, Fish's last point, contrary to his earlier distinctions, implies a high degree of similarity between science and sociology of science after all.

APPEALS TO ETHOS

Rhetoricians since Aristotle have acknowledged that an important factor in the credibility of an argument is the character of the arguer. Readers of *The New York Times* might ask themselves, "Who is Stanley Fish that we should listen to him, let alone believe him?" Those familiar with Fish's other writings know that he has often assumed the role of "public intellectual," someone whose academic reputation allows him to speak to a wider public on issues concerning universities and scholarly matters. However, Fish has an additional professional interest in this controversy, one candidly identified in the biographical blurb accompanying the editorial: He is identified as the "executive director of the Duke University Press, which publishes the journal *Social Text*." This information is external to what Fish writes in his column; he does not mention this source of his interest in the issue. Thus, in addition to his academic reputation, known to some readers, his position with the press, as revealed in the blurb, constitutes another element of "extrinsic ethos."

In addition to his external reputation and his possible loss of credibility with the revelation of his self-interest, Fish's intrinsic ethos, his persona, is constructed by verbal choices within the text. Although rhetorical manuals do not specify what linguistic features carry textual ethos, among salient features would be the presence of self-reference and word choices that suggest expertise or level of education. One pattern of choice we have already noted is Fish's tendency to use unqualified or absolute statements. His is not a voice or view that leaves room for a nuanced position: Sokal is wrong, period, and as the argument progresses we will learn that he is a bad person too.

In addition to the explicit lines of argument drawn from definition, analogy, and consequence that we have discussed, Fish also "argues," that is, attempts to induce confidence in himself and his views through his language choices. Consider first how Fish's level or register shifting contributes to his distinctive voice. For example, he mixes vocabulary from a formal, scholarly register with informal or colloquial terms: "Distinguishing fact from fiction is surely the business of science, but the means of doing so are not perspicuous in nature — for if they were, there would be no work to be done." The term "business" as used here and the phrases "work to be done" and "fact from fiction" are less formal. More formal — that is, less conversational — are the choices "surely" and "the means of doing so." But the most striking word choice in the sentence, "perspicuous," is an unusual if not arcane usage. Fish apparently uses this word in the sense of "clear" or "easy to understand," but because "perspicuous" and its noun form "perspicuity" are usually applied to language (indeed, perspicuity is one of the four virtues of style in rhetoric), the application to "nature" is a self-conscious stretch. The word itself suggests the notion of nature as a text to be read with interpretive differences, a notion that comes from the disciplinary camp of the sociologists of science. Notice too the register shifts within the sentence, from low at the beginning and end to high in the middle: The overall impression is of accessibility, but there is a marked formality amidst the casual. Fish's choices seem to say, "I can communicate on your level, but I'm doing so from above."

Fish's strategic use of Latinate terms also contributes to an overall sententiousness in his voice, creating a tone of someone precise but somewhat irritated. Other markers of this tone include the "Exactly!" (an exasperated "gotcha") that opens Paragraph 3, the "Perhaps a humble example" in Paragraph 8 (one might question the disingenuous modifier), and the slightly condescending, very instructional "My point finally is a simple one" in Paragraph 19.

APPEALS TO PATHOS

Although Aristotle complains in the *Rhetoric* about the "warping" of judges by appeals outside the case at issue (Kennedy 30), he admits that working on an audience's emotional attitudes contributes forcefully to persuasion, and he produces in Book II the first systematic account in the western tradition of the emotions and their triggers. Fish's response to Sokal seems to offer little potential for overt emotionality, but indirect emotional appeals abound. Consider that, in crude terms, it is Fish's goal to cast Sokal as the villain of the story. He does so directly, as explained above, by working him into the defendant's chair. But even before that move, Fish has already cast a shadow over Sokal by using primarily negative words to describe him and his actions, as the following inventory indicates: *hoax, gloated, prank, deception, conjures, attack, mistakes, doesn't understand, right and wrong, wrong, his targets, threatens to undermine, boasts, deception, carefully packaged his deception so as not to be detected, pretended to be himself.* Such word choices, although spread over the piece, incline the audience to judge Sokal's enterprise and his character negatively.

Although the usual understanding of pathos conflates it with appeals to an audience's emotions, it is best understood as any appeal that constructs the audience's identity and state of mind. Fish's audience here presents him with problems, because except for a few academics, most *Times* readers can have little stake in this abstruse controversy. Imagine the difference if Fish had been addressing an audience of MLA members. For them he could exploit the traditional science/humanities antithesis, build on their likely affiliation with cultural studies, and create a sense of offense in the group so constructed. Moreover, he could legitimately identify with this audience and, by showing himself offended, model the offense that they, identifying with him in a Burkean sense, would feel. Instead, Fish writes to an audience of spectators distant from the two forces pitted against each other in this controversy, so direct appeals to the audience are not salient in this argument.

But if direct appeals and overt audience construction are lacking, audience accommodation is not. By audience accommodation we mean all attempts to fit the material to the audience's background and interests. The most obvious ploy is the use of the baseball analogy, which is especially resonant for but not limited to the *Times'* predominantly New York, urban, male, upper middle-class audience. There is also a certain cultural symbiosis between baseball commentary and intellectuals, a connection we owe to the popular writing on baseball by pundits like George Will and Doris Kearns Goodwin and to the crossover case of Bartlett Giamatti, once president of Yale and commissioner of baseball. Fish's working out of the baseball analogy uses the stylistic figure of *hypophora*, which underscores the assumption of the accessibility of this example for the audience. The speaker both asks a question and answers it on behalf of the audience, as Fish does in Paragraph 8, where he obligingly answers "yes" or "no" to his own questions, taking on two normally divided roles. Paragraph 10 uses another stylistic device, the *prosopopoeia*. Here the speaker mimics absent voices, allowing them to speak in the text. The voice is attributed not to a known person but to a hypothetical reader who objects to the analogy ("Sure the facts of baseball . . .") by arguing that, unlike baseball, science concerns facts that preexist humans and that cannot change by majority vote. After conceding the reasonableness of this objection, Fish answers that there are physical facts involved in baseball (hence, the distance of the pitcher's mound from the plate) and that science does have something resembling a voting system on results in the shape of peer review. The audience accommodation continues in the sudden use of the chummy pronoun "we" in Paragraph 11: "shape in which we have the game and the shapes in which we couldn't." Thus, after the questioning of the analogy by a representative reader, speaker and audience are joined again by sharing the "humble" baseball analogy. But, not surprisingly, the scientists become an excluded "they" in the immediately following example. It's "us" versus "them."

This entire mid-section of the argument — the analogy, the challenge to it, the answer — not only serves audience accommodation by creating a certain involvement, but it also serves the construction of Fish's ethos as a regular guy who listens to others and adapts. Of course, this reasonableness is highly artificial because Fish is dealing not with an actual objection raised by a reader or opponent but with a fabricated objection to a fabricated analogy. Nevertheless, the appearance of answering an interlocutor, of engaging in dialogue, is the essential gesture of a reasonable arguer, counteracting the stance of the pontificator, the dispenser of absolute definitions displayed elsewhere in the text.

This analysis of Fish's text by no means exhausts what could be said about his Sokal editorial from a rhetorical perspective, nor does it pretend to describe its every feature systematically. Rather, it emphasizes particular features that arguably reveal how this text functions, how it delivers one rhetor's views on a certain subject for a certain audience at a certain time. Of course a rhetorical analysis such as this is itself not conducted without intentions, usually an intention to critique a rhetorical performance and ultimately to praise or blame. Thus, a rhetorical analysis is also an argument that can be assessed for its effectiveness with its audience. Although pointing out the artifice of someone else's discourse is often taken merely as a trumping gesture, rhetorical analysis can have a significant role to play in education. First, the careful teasing out of the arguments along with the emotional and ethical appeals of a text is useful because it can help us think through our positions on any given issue. Second, by understanding how others have crafted effective or ineffective arguments, we can acquire models for presenting our own views on issues we care about to audiences we want to move.

APPENDIX

Professor Sokal's Bad Joke
New York Times, 21 May 1996

When the editors of *Social Text* accepted an essay purporting to link developments in quantum mechanics with the formulations of postmodern thought, they could not have anticipated that on the day of its publication the author, Alan Sokal, a physicist at New York University, would be announcing the pages of another journal, *Lingua Franca*, that the whole thing had been an elaborate hoax.   *1*

He had made it all up, he said, and gloated that his "prank" proved that sociologists and humanists who spoke of science as a "social construction" didn't know what they were talking about. Acknowledging the   *2*

ethical issues raised by his deception, Professor Sokal declared it justified by the importance of the truths he was defending from postmod-
ernist attack: "There is a real world; its properties are not merely social
constructions; facts and evidence do matter. What sane person would
contend otherwise?" [pt 2, "Revelation"].

Exactly! Professor Sokal's question should alert us to the improbability   *3*
of the scenario he conjures up: Scholars with impeccable credentials
making statements no sane person could credit. The truth is that none of
his targets would ever make such statements.

What sociologists of science say is that of course the world is real and   *4*
independent of our observations but that accounts of the world are produced by observers and are therefore relative to their capacities, education, training, etc. It is not the world or its properties but the vocabularies
in whose terms we know them that are socially constructed — fashioned
by human beings — which is why our understanding of those properties
is continually changing.

Distinguishing fact from fiction is surely the business of science, but   *5*
the means of doing so are not perspicuous in nature — for if they were,
there would be no work to be done. Consequently, the history of science is
a record of controversies about what counts as evidence and how facts
are to be established.

Those who concern themselves with this history neither dispute the   *6*
accomplishments of science nor deny the existence or power of scientific
procedure. They just maintain and demonstrate that the nature of scientific procedure is a question continually debated in its own precincts.
What results is an incredibly complex and rich story, full of honor for scientists, and this is the story sociologists of science are trying to tell and
get right.

Why then does Professor Sokal attack them? The answer lies in two   *7*
misunderstandings. First, Professor Sokal takes "socially constructed" to
mean "not real," whereas for workers in the field "socially constructed" is
a compliment paid to a fact or a procedure that has emerged from the
welter of disciplinary competition into a real and productive life where it
can be cited, invoked and perhaps challenged. It is no contradiction to say
that something is socially constructed and also real.

Perhaps a humble example from the world of baseball will help make   *8*
the point. Consider the following little catechism:

Are there balls and strikes in the world? Yes.

Are there balls and strikes in nature (if by nature you understand
physical reality independent from human actors)? No.

Are balls and strikes socially constructed? Yes.

Are balls and strikes real? Yes.

Do some people get $3.5 million either for producing balls and
strikes or for preventing their production? Yes.

So balls and strikes are both socially constructed and real, socially constructed and consequential. The facts about balls and strikes are also real but they can change, as they would, for example, if baseball's rule makers were to vote tomorrow that from now on it's four strikes and you're out.   *9*

But that's just the point, someone might object. "Sure the facts of baseball, a human institution that didn't exist until the 19th century, are socially constructed. But scientists are concerned with facts that were there before anyone looked through a microscope. And besides, even if scientific accounts of facts can change, they don't change by majority vote."   *10*

This appears to make sense, but the distinction between baseball and science is not finally so firm. On the baseball side, the social construction of the game assumes and depends on a set of established scientific facts. That is why the pitcher's mound is not 400 feet from the plate. Both the shape in which we have the game and the shapes in which we couldn't have it are strongly related to the world's properties.   *11*

On the science side, although scientists don't take formal votes to decide what facts will be considered credible, neither do they present their competing accounts to nature and receive from her an immediate and legible verdict. Rather they hazard hypotheses that are then tested by other workers in the field in the context of evidentiary rules, which may themselves be altered in the process. Verdicts are then given by publications and research centers whose judgments and monies will determine they way the game goes for a while.   *12*

Both science and baseball then are mixtures of adventuresome inventiveness and reliance on established norms and mechanisms of validation, and the facts yielded by both will be social constructions and be real.   *13*

Baseball and science may be both social constructions, but not all social constructions are the same. First, there is the difference in purpose — to refine physical skills and entertain, on the one hand, and to solve problems of a theoretical and practical kind, on the other. From this difference flow all the other differences, in the nature of the skills involved, the quality of the attention required, the measurements of accomplishment, the system of reward, and on and on.   *14*

Even if two activities are alike social constructions, if you want to take the measure of either, it is the differences you must keep in mind.   *15*

This is what Professor Sokal does not do, and this is his second mistake. He thinks that the sociology of science is in competition with mainstream science — wants either to replace it or debunk it — and he doesn't understand that it is a distinct enterprise, with objects of study, criteria, procedures and goals all of its own.   *16*

Sociologists of science aren't trying to do science; they are trying to come up with a rich and powerful explanation of what it means to do it. Their question is, "What are the conditions that make scientific accomplishments possible?" and answers to that question are not intended to be either substitutes for scientific work or arguments against it.   *17*

When Professor Sokal declares that "theorizing about 'the social con-   *18*
struction of reality' won't help us find an effective treatment for AIDS," he
is at once right and wrong. He is right that sociologists will never do the
job assigned properly to scientists. He is wrong to imply that the failure of
the sociology of science to do something it never set out to do is a mark
against it.

My point is finally a simple one: A research project that takes the prac-   *19*
tice of science as an object of study is not a threat to that practice because, committed as it is to its own goals and protocols, it doesn't reach
into, and therefore doesn't pose a danger to, the goals and protocols it
studies. Just as the criteria of an enterprise will be internal to its own history, so will the threat to its integrity be internal, posed not by presumptuous outsiders but by insiders who decide not to play by the rules or to
put the rules in the service of a devious purpose.

This means that it is Alan Sokal, not his targets, who threatens to   *20*
undermine the intellectual standards he vows to protect. Remember, science is above all a communal effort. No scientist (and for that matter, no
sociologist or literary critic) begins his task by inventing new the facts
he will assume, the models he will regard as exemplary, and the standards
he tries to be faithful to.

They are all given by the tradition of inquiry he has joined, and for the   *21*
most part he must take them on faith, and he must take on faith, too, the
reports offered to him by colleagues, all of whom are in the same position, unable to start from scratch and therefore dependent on the information they receive from fellow researchers. (Indeed, some professional
physicists who take Professor Sokal on faith report finding his arguments
plausible.)

The large word for all this it "trust," and in his *A Social History of Truth*,   *22*
Steven Shapin poses the relevant (rhetorical) question: "How could coordinated activity of any kind be possible if people could not rely upon others' undertakings?"

Alan Sokal put forward his own undertakings as reliable, and he took   *23*
care, as he boasts, to surround his deception with all the marks of
authenticity, including dozens of "real" footnotes and an introductory
section that enlists a roster of the century's greatest scientists in support of a line of argument he says he never believed in. He carefully
packaged his deception so as not to be detected except by someone who
began with a deep and corrosive attitude of suspicion that may now be
in full flower in the offices of learned journals because of what he has
done.

In a 1989 report published in The Proceedings of the National Acad-   *24*
emy of Science, fraud is said to go "beyond error to erode the foundation
of trust on which science is built." That is Professor Sokal's legacy, one
likely to be longer lasting than the brief fame he now enjoys for having
successfully pretended to be himself.

REFERENCES

Burke, Kenneth. *A Grammar of Motives*. Berkeley: University of California Press, [1945] 1969.

Fahnestock, Jeanne and Marie Secor. "Toward a Modern Version of Stasis Theory." *Oldspeak/Newspeak*. Ed. Charles W. Knuepper. Arlington, TX: The Rhetoric Society of America and NCTE, 1985. 179–93.

Fish, Stanley. "Professor Sokal's Bad Joke." *New York Times* (21 May 1996): A26.

Fulkerson, Richard. *Teaching the Argument in Writing*. Urbana, IL: NCTE, 1996.

Huth, Edward. *How to Write and Publish Papers in the Medical Sciences*. Philadelphia: ISI Press, 1982.

Kennedy, George A. Trans. *Aristotle On Rhetoric: A Theory of Civic Discourse*. New York: Oxford University Press, 1991.

Matsen, Patricia P., Philip Rollinson, and Marion Sousa. *Readings from Classical Rhetoric*. Carbondale: Southern Illinois University Press, 1990.

Miller, Carolyn. "Genre as Social Action." *Quarterly Journal of Speech* 70 (1984): 151–67.

Perelman, Chaim and Lucie Olbrechts-Tyteca. *The New Rhetoric: A Treatise on Argumentation*. Trans. J. Wilkinsons and P. Weaver. Notre Dame, IN: University of Notre Dame Press, 1969.

Quinn, Arthur. *Figures of Speech: 60 Ways to Turn a Phrase*. Salt Lake City, UT: Gibbs, 1982.

Quintilian. *Institutio Oratoria*. 4 vols. Trans. H. E. Butler. Cambridge, MA: Harvard University Press [Loeb Classical Library], 1921.

Sokal, Alan. "A Physicist Experiments with Cultural Studies." *Lingua Franca* (May/June 1996): 62–64.

———. "Transgressing the Boundaries: Toward a Transformative Hermeneutics of Quantum Gravity." *Social Text* 14.1–2 (1996): 217–52.

5

Finding and Evaluating Sources

I n this chapter, we look at strategies for expanding the base of sources you work with to support your argument. The habits and skills of close reading and analysis that we have discussed and that you have practiced are essential for evaluating the sources you find. Once you find sources, you will need to assess the claims the writers make, the extent to which they provide evidence in support of those claims, and the recency, relevance, accuracy, and reliability of the evidence. The specific strategies we discuss here are those you will use to find and evaluate the sources you find in your library's electronic catalog or on the Internet. These strategies are core skills for developing a researched academic argument. They are also essential to avoid being overwhelmed by the torrent of information unleashed at the click of a computer mouse.

Finding sources is not difficult; finding and identifying good sources is challenging. You know how simple it is to look up a subject in an encyclopedia or to use a search engine like Google or Yahoo! to discover basic information on a subject or topic. Unfortunately, this kind of research will only take you so far. What if the information you find doesn't really address your question? True, we have emphasized the importance of thinking about an issue from multiple perspectives — and finding multiple perspectives is easy when you search the Internet. But how do you know whether a perspective is authoritative or trustworthy or even legitimate? Without knowing how to find and identify good sources, you can waste a lot of time reading material that will not contribute to your essay. Our goal is to help you use your time wisely to collect the sources you need to support your argument.

Taken from Stuart Greene and April Lidinsky, *From Inquiry to Academic Writing: A Practical Guide*, pp. 105–24 (Chapter 6, "From Finding to Evaluating Sources").

IDENTIFYING SOURCES

We assume that by the time you visit the library or log on to the Internet to find sources, you are not flying blind. At the very least, you will have chosen a topic to explore (something in general you want to write about), possibly identified an issue (a question or problem about the topic that is arguable), and perhaps even have a working thesis (a main claim that you want to test against other sources) in mind. Let's say you are already interested in the topic of mad cow disease. Perhaps you have identified an issue: Is mad cow disease a significant threat in the United States given the massive scale of factory farming? And maybe you have drafted a working thesis: "Although factory farming is rightly criticized for its often unsanitary practices and lapses in quality control, the danger of an epidemic of mad cow disease in the United States is minimal." The closer you are to having a working thesis, the more purposeful your research will be. With the working thesis above, instead of trying to sift through hundreds of articles about mad cow disease, you can probably home in on materials that examine mad cow disease in relation to epidemiology and agribusiness.

Once you start expanding your research, however, even a working thesis is just a place to begin. As you digest all the perspectives your research yields, you may discover that your thesis, issue, and perhaps even interest in the topic will shift significantly. Maybe you'll end up writing about factory farming rather than mad cow disease. This kind of shift happens more often than you may think. What is important is to follow what interests you and to keep in mind what is going to matter to your readers.

■ Consult Experts Who Can Guide Your Research

Before you embark on a systematic hunt for sources, you may want to consult with experts who can help guide your research. The following experts are nearer to hand and more approachable than you may think.

Your Writing Instructor.   Your first and best expert is likely to be your writing instructor, who can help you define the limits of your research and the kinds of sources that would prove most helpful. Your writing instructor can probably advise you on whether your topic is too broad or too narrow, help you identify your issue, and perhaps even point you to specific reference works or readings you should consult. He or she can also help you figure out whether you should concentrate mainly on popular or scholarly sources (for more about popular and scholarly sources, see pp. 81–82).

Librarians at Your Campus or Local Library.   In all likelihood, there is no better repository of research material than your campus or local library, and no better guide to those resources than the librarians who work there. Their job is to help you find what you need (although it's up to you to make the most of what you find). Librarians can give you a map or tour of the library, and provide you with booklets or other handouts that instruct you in the specific resources available and their uses. They can explain the catalog system and reference system. And, time allowing, most librarians are willing to give you personal help in finding and using specific sources, from books and journals to indexes and databases.

Experts in Other Fields.   Perhaps the idea for your paper originated outside your writing course, in response to a reading assigned in, say, your psychology or economics course. If so, you may want to discuss your topic or issue with the instructor in that course, who can probably point you to other readings or journals you should consult. If your topic originated outside the classroom, you can still seek out an expert in the appropriate field. If so, you may want to read the advice on interviewing in Chapter 6.

Manuals, Handbooks, and Dedicated Web Sites.   These exist in abundance, for general research as well as for discipline-specific research. They are especially helpful in identifying a wide range of authoritative search tools and resources, although they also offer practical advice on how to use and cite them. Indeed, your writing instructor may assign one of these manuals or handbooks, or recommend a Web site, at the beginning of the course. If not, he or she can probably point you to the one that is best suited to your research.

■ Develop a Working Knowledge of Standard Sources

As you start your hunt for sources, it helps to know broadly what kinds of sources are available and what they can help you accomplish. Table 5.1 lists a number of the resources you are likely to rely on when you are looking for material, the purpose and limitations of each type of resource, and some well-known examples. Although it may not help you pinpoint specific resources that are most appropriate for your research, the table does provide a basis for finding sources in any discipline. And familiarizing yourself with the types of resources here should make your conversations with the experts more productive.

■ Distinguish Between Primary and Secondary Sources

As you define the research task before you, you will need to understand the difference between primary and secondary sources, and figure out which you will need to answer your question. Your instructor may specify which he or she prefers, but chances are you will have to make the decision yourself. A **primary source** is a firsthand, or eyewitness, account, the kind of account you find in letters or newspapers or research reports in which

TABLE 5.1   Standard Types of Sources for Doing Research

Source	Type of Information	Purpose	Limitations	Examples
Abstract	Brief summary of a text and the bibliographic information needed to locate the complete text	To help researchers decide whether or not they want to read the entire source		*Biological Abstracts* *Historical Abstracts* *New Testament Abstracts* *Reference Sources in History: An Introductory Guide*
Bibliography	List of works, usually by subject and author, with full publication information	For an overview of what has been published in a field and who the principal researchers in the field are	Difficult to distinguish the best sources and the most prominent researchers	Bibliography of the History of Art *MLA International Bibliography*
Biography	Story of an individual's life and the historical, cultural, or social context in which he or she lived	For background on a person of importance	Lengthy and reflects the author's bias	Biography and Genealogy Master Index Biography Resource Center Biography .com Literature Resource Center *Oxford Dictionary of National Biography*
Book review	Description and usually an evaluation of a recently published book	To help readers stay current with research and thought in their field and to evaluate scholarship	Reflects the reviewer's bias	ALA *Booklist* *Book Review Digest* Book Review Index *Books in Print* with Book Reviews on Disc

Source	Type of Information	Purpose	Limitations	Examples
Database, index	Large collection of citations and abstracts from books, journals, and digests, often updated daily	To give researchers access to a wide range of current sources	Lacks evaluative information	Education Resources Information Center (ERIC) Humanities International Index Index to Scientific & Technical Proceedings United Nations Bibliographic Information System
Data, statistics	Measurements derived from studies or surveys	To help researchers identify important trends (e.g., in voting, housing, residential segregation)	Requires a great deal of scrutiny and interpretation	American FactFinder American National Election Studies Current Index to Statistics Current Population Survey *Statistical Abstract of the United States*
Dictionary	Alphabetical list of words and their definitions	To explain key terms and how they are used		*Merriam-Webster's Collegiate Dictionary* *Oxford English Dictionary*
Encyclopedia	Concise articles about people, places, concepts, and things	A starting point for very basic information	Lack of in-depth information	*The CQ Researcher* Encyclopedia Brittanica Online *Information Please Almanac*

(*continued on next page*)

TABLE 5.1   *(continued)*

SOURCE	TYPE OF INFORMATION	PURPOSE	LIMITATIONS	EXAMPLES
				McGraw-Hill Encyclopedia of Science & Technology
Internet search engine	Web site that locates online information by keyword or search term	For quickly locating a broad array of current resources	Reliability of information open to question	Google Yahoo!
Newspaper, other news sources	Up-to-date information	To locate timely information	May reflect reporter's or medium's bias	America's Historical Newspapers
				LexisNexis Academic
				Newspaper Source
				ProQuest Historical Newspapers
				World News Connection
Thesaurus	Alphabetical list of words and their synonyms	For alternative search terms		*Roget's II: The New Thesaurus*

the researcher explains his or her impressions of a particular phenomenon. For example, "Hidden Lessons" found on page 117, the Sadkers' study of gender bias in schools, is a primary source. The authors report their own experiences of the phenomenon in the classroom. A **secondary source** is an analysis of information reported in a primary source. For example, even though it may cite the Sadkers' primary research, an essay that analyzes the Sadkers' findings along with other studies of gender dynamics in the classroom would be considered a secondary source.

If you were exploring issues of language diversity and the English-only movement, you would draw on both primary and secondary sources. You would be interested in researchers' firsthand (primary) accounts of language learning and use by diverse learners for examples of the challenges nonnative speakers face in learning a standard language. And you would also want to know from secondary sources what others think about whether national unity and individuality can and should coexist in communities and homes as well as in schools. You will find that you are often expected to use both primary and secondary sources in your research.

■ Distinguish Between Popular and Scholarly Sources

To determine the type of information to use, you also need to decide whether you should look for popular or scholarly books and articles. **Popular sources** of information — newspapers like *USA Today* and *The Chronicle of Higher Education,* and large-circulation magazines like *Newsweek* and *Field & Stream* — are written for a general audience. This is not to say that popular sources cannot be specialized: *The Chronicle of Higher Education* is read mostly by academics; *Field & Stream,* by people who love the outdoors. But they are written so that any educated reader can understand them. **Scholarly sources**, by contrast, are written for experts in a particular field. *The New England Journal of Medicine* may be read by people who are not physicians, but they are not the journal's primary audience. In a manner of speaking, these readers are eavesdropping on the journal's conversation of ideas; they are not expected to contribute to it (and in fact would be hard pressed to do so). The articles in scholarly journals undergo **peer review**. That is, they do not get published until they have been carefully evaluated by the author's peers, other experts in the academic conversation being conducted in the journal. Reviewers may comment at length about an article's level of research and writing, and an author may have to revise an article several times before it sees print. And if the reviewers cannot reach a consensus that the research makes an important contribution to the academic conversation, the article will not be published.

When you begin your research, you may find that popular sources provide helpful information about a topic or issue — the results of a national poll, for example. Later, however, you will want to use scholarly sources to advance your argument. You can see from Table 5.2 that popular magazines and scholarly journals can be distinguished by a number of characteristics. Does the source contain advertisements? If so, what kinds of advertisements? For commercial products? Or for academic events and resources? How do the advertisements appear? If you find ads and glossy pictures and illustrations, you are probably looking at a popular magazine. This is in contrast to the tables, charts, and diagrams you are likely to find in an education, psychology, or microbiology journal. Given your experience with rhetorical analyses, you should also be able to determine the makeup of your audience — specialists or nonspecialists — and the level of language you need to use in your writing.

TABLE 5.2 Popular Magazines Versus Scholarly Journals

CRITERIA	POPULAR MAGAZINES	SCHOLARLY JOURNALS
Advertisements	Numerous full-page color ads	Few if any ads
Appearance	Eye-catching; glossy; pictures and illustrations	Plain; black-and-white graphics, tables, charts, and diagrams
Audience	General	Professors, researchers, and college students
Author	Journalists	Professionals in an academic field or discipline
Bibliography	Occasional and brief	Extensive bibliography at the end of each article; footnotes and other documentation
Content	General articles to inform, update, or introduce a contemporary issue	Research projects, methodology, and theory
Examples	*Newsweek, National Review, PC World, Psychology Today*	*International Journal of Applied Engineering Research, New England Journal of Medicine*
Language	Nontechnical, simple vocabulary	Specialized vocabulary
Publisher	Commercial publisher	Professional organization, university, research institute, or scholarly press

SOURCE: Adapted from materials at the Hessburg Library, University of Notre Dame.

Again, as you define your task for yourself, it is important to consider why you would use one source or another. Do you want facts? Opinions? News reports? Research studies? Analyses? Personal reflections? The extent to which the information can help you make your argument will serve as your basis for determining whether or not a source of information is of value.

Steps to Identifying Sources

1 **Consult experts who can guide your research.** Talk to people who can help you formulate issues and questions.

2 **Develop a working knowledge of standard sources.** Identify the different kinds of information that different types of sources provide.

3 **Distinguish between primary and secondary sources.** Decide what type of information can best help you answer your research question.

4 **Distinguish between popular and scholarly sources.** Determine what kind of information will persuade your readers.

A Practice Sequence: Identifying Sources

We would now like you to practice using some of the strategies we have discussed so far: talking with experts, deciding what sources of information you should use, and determining what types of information can best help you develop your paper and persuade your readers. We assume you have chosen a topic for your paper, identified an issue, and perhaps formulated a working thesis. If not, think back to some of the topics mentioned in earlier chapters. Have any of them piqued your interest? If not, here are five very broad topics you might work with:

- The civil rights movement
- The media and gender
- Global health
- Science and religion
- Immigration

Once you've decided on a topic, talk to experts and decide which types of sources you should use: primary or secondary, popular or scholarly. Consult with your classmates to evaluate the strengths and weaknesses of different sources of information and the appropriateness of using different types of information. Here are the steps to follow:

1 Talk to a librarian about the sources you might use to get information about your topic (for example, databases, abstracts, or bibliographies). Be sure to take notes.

2 Talk to an expert who can provide you with some ideas about current issues in the field of interest. Be sure to take detailed notes.

3 Decide whether you should use primary or secondary sources. What type of information would help you develop your argument?

4 Decide whether you should use popular or scholarly sources. What type of information would your readers find compelling?

SEARCHING FOR SOURCES

Once you've decided on the types of sources you want to use — primary or secondary, popular or scholarly — you can take steps to locate the information you need. You might begin with a tour of your university or local library, so that you know where the library keeps newspapers, government documents, books, journals, and other sources of information. Notice where the reference desk is: This is where you should head to ask a librarian for help if you get stuck. You also want to find a computer where you can log on to your library's catalog to start your search. Once you have located your sources in the library, you can begin to look through them for the information you need.

You may be tempted to rely on the Internet and a search engine like Google or Yahoo! But keep in mind that the information you retrieve from the Internet may not be trustworthy: Anyone can post his or her thoughts on a Web site. Of course, you can also find excellent scholarly sources on the Internet. (For example, Johns Hopkins University Press manages Project MUSE, a collection of 300-plus academic journals that can be accessed online through institutional subscription.) School libraries also offer efficient access to government records and other sources essential to scholarly writing.

Let's say you are about to start researching a paper on language diversity and the English-only movement. When you log on to the library's site, you find a menu of choices: Catalog, Electronic Resources, Virtual Reference Desk, and Services & Collections. (The wording may vary slightly from library to library, but the means of locating information will be the same.) When you click on Catalog, another menu of search choices appears: Keyword, Title, Author, and Subject (Figure 5.1). The hunt is on.

FIGURE 5.1   Menu of Basic Search Strategies

■ Perform a Keyword Search

A **keyword** is essentially your topic: It defines the topic of your search. To run a keyword search, you can look up information by author, title, or subject. You would search by author to locate all the works a particular author has written on a subject. So, for example, if you know that Paul Lang is an expert on the consequences of the English-only movement, you might begin with an author search. You can use the title search to locate all works with a key word or phrase in the title. The search results are likely to include a number of irrelevant titles, but you should end up with a list of authors, titles, and subject headings to guide another search.

A search by subject is particularly helpful as you begin your research, while you are still formulating your thesis. You want to start by thinking of as many words as possible that relate to your topic. (A thesaurus can help you come up with different words you can use in a keyword search.) Suppose you type in the phrase "English only." A number of different sources appear on the screen, but the most promising is Paul Lang's book *The English Language Debate: One Nation, One Language*? You click on this record, and another screen appears with some valuable pieces of information, including the call number (which tells you where in the library you can find the book) and an indication that the book has a bibliography, something you can make use of once you find the book (Figure 5.2). Notice that the subject listings — *Language policy, English language – Political aspects, English-only movement, Bilingual education* — also give

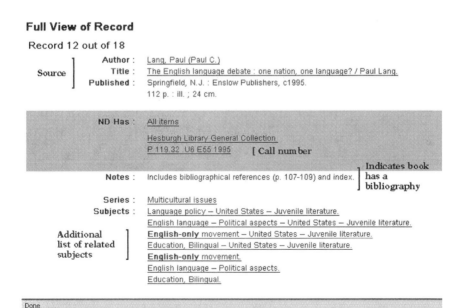

Full View of Record

Record 12 out of 18

Source {
Author : Lang, Paul (Paul C.)
Title : The English language debate : one nation, one language? / Paul Lang.
Published : Springfield, N.J. : Enslow Publishers, c1995.
112 p. : ill. ; 24 cm.

ND Has : All items

Hesburgh Library General Collection
P 119.32 .U6 E55 1995 [Call number

Notes : Includes bibliographical references (p. 107-109) and index. } Indicates book has a bibliography

Series : Multicultural issues
Subjects : Language policy – United States – Juvenile literature.
English language – Political aspects – United States – Juvenile literature.
Additional list of related subjects {
English-only movement – United States – Juvenile literature.
Education, Bilingual – United States – Juvenile literature.
English-only movement.
English language – Political aspects.
Education, Bilingual.

Done

FIGURE 5.2 Full-View Bibliographic Entry

you additional keywords to use in finding relevant information. The lesson here is that it is important to generate keywords to get initial information and then to look at that information carefully for more keywords and to determine if the source has a bibliography. Even if this particular source isn't relevant, it may lead you to other sources that are.

■ Try Browsing

Browse is a headings search; it appears in the menu of choices in Figure 5.1 as "Subject begins with . . ." This type of search allows you to scroll through an alphabetical index. Some of the indexes available are the Author Index, the Title Index, and the Library of Congress Subject Headings, a subject index. Browse

- displays an alphabetical list of entries;
- shows the number of records for each entry;
- indicates whether or not there are cross-references for each entry.

What appears in the window is "Browse List: Choose a field, enter a phrase and click the 'go' button." Figure 5.3 shows the results of a preliminary browse when the words "English-only" are entered. Notice that a list of headings or titles appears on the screen. This is not a list of books, and not all of the entries are relevant. But you can use the list to determine which headings are relevant to your topic, issue, or question.

For your paper on the English-only movement, the first two headings seem relevant: *English-only debate* and *English-only movement*. A further

Browse List: Subjects

No. of Recs	Entry
	English one-act plays - [LC Authority Record] See: One-act plays, English
	English-only debate - [LC Authority Record] See: English-only movement
4	English-only movement - [LC Authority Record]
1	English-only movement – California – Case studies
1	English-only movement – Colorado
4	English-only movement – United States
1	English-only movement – United States – Juvenile literature
	English-only question - [LC Authority Record] See: English-only movement
1	English – Ontario – Correspondence
1	English oration

FIGURE 5.3   Preliminary Browse of "English-only" Subject Heading

click would reveal the title of a relevant book and a new list of subject headings (Figure 5.4) that differs from those of your initial search. This list gives you a new bibliography from which you can gather new leads and a list of subject headings to investigate.

We suggest that you do a keyword search first and then a browse search to home in on a subject. Especially when you don't know the exact subject, you can do a quick keyword search, retrieve many sets of results, and then begin looking at the subjects that correspond to each title. Once you find a subject that fits your needs, you can click on the direct subject (found in each bibliographic record) and execute a new search that will yield more-relevant results.

■ Perform a Journal or Newspaper Title Search

Finally, you can search by journal or newspaper title. For this kind of search, you will need exact information. You can take the name of a journal, magazine, or newspaper cited in your keyword or browse search. The journal or newspaper title search will tell you if your library subscribes to the publication and in what format — print, microform or -film, or electronic.

Suppose you want to continue your search in the *New York Times* for information on the English-only movement by searching for articles in the *New York Times*. You would run a basic search under the category "Periodicals": "Periodical Title begins with. . . ." That would give you access to a limited number of articles that focused on the debate surrounding the English-only movement. To find more recent articles, you could go to the *New York Times* Web site (nytimes.com) where you could find many potentially useful listings. Recent newspaper articles will lack the depth and complexity of more scholarly studies, but they are undeniably useful in helping you establish the timeliness and relevance of your research. To see the full text of the articles, you must subscribe or pay a nominal fee,

#	Year	Author	Title
1 ☐	2006	United States.	English as the official language : hearing before the Subcommittee on Education Reform of the Co <Book> Click for ONLINE ACCESS (Text version:) Documents Center Owned: 1 Checked Out: 0 Display full record
2 ☐	1996	United States.	S. 356—Language of Government Act of 1995 : hearings before the Committee on Governmental Affai <Book> Documents Center Display full record
3 ☐	1996	United States.	Hearing on English as the common language : hearing before the Subcommittee on Early Childhood, <Book> Documents Center Display full record
4 ☐	1995	United States.	Hearing on English as a common language : hearing before the Subcommittee on Early Childhood, Yo <Book> Documents Center Display full record

Done

FIGURE 5.4   Results of Browsing Deeper: A New List of Sources

although you can usually preview the articles because the Web site will include a few sentences describing the content of each article.

Steps to Searching for Sources

1 **Perform a keyword search.** Choose a word or phrase that best describes your topic.

2 **Try browsing.** Search an alphabetical list by subject.

3 **Perform a journal or newspaper title search.** Find relevant citations by identifying the exact title of a journal or newspaper, or by subject.

A Practice Sequence: Searching for Sources

If you tried the practice sequence on identifying sources (p. 83), explore your topic further by practicing the types of searches discussed in this section: a keyword search; a browse; and a journal or newspaper title search (or a subject search).

EVALUATING LIBRARY SOURCES

The information you collect can and will vary in terms of its relevance and overall quality. You will want to evaluate this information as systematically as possible to be sure that you are using the most appropriate sources to develop your argument. Once you have obtained at least some of the sources you located by searching your library's catalog, you should evaluate the material as you read it. In particular, you want to evaluate the following information for each article or book:

- the author's background and credentials (What is the author's educational background? What has he or she written about in the past? Is this person an expert in the field?)
- the writer's purpose
- the topic of discussion
- the audience the writer invokes and whether you are a member of that audience
- the nature of the conversation (How have others addressed the problem?)
- what the author identifies as a misinterpretation or a gap in knowledge, or an argument that needs modifying

- what the author's own view is
- how the author supports his or her argument (that is, with primary or secondary sources, with facts or opinions)
- the accuracy of the author's evidence (can you find similar information elsewhere?)

If your topic is current and relevant, chances are your searches are going to turn up a large number of possible sources. How do you go about choosing which sources to rely on in your writing? Of course, if time were not an issue, you would read them all from start to finish. But in the real world, assignments come with due dates. To decide whether a library source merits a close reading and evaluation, begin by skimming each book or article. **Skimming** — briefly examining the material to get a sense of the information it offers — involves four steps:

1. Read the introductory sections.
2. Examine the table of contents and index.
3. Check the notes and bibliographic references.
4. Skim deeper.

■ Read the Introductory Sections

Turn to the introductory sections of the text first. Many authors use a preface or introduction to explain the themes they focus on in a book. An **abstract** serves a similar purpose, but article abstracts are usually only 250 words long. In the introductory sections, writers typically describe the issue that motivated them to write, whether or not they believe the work corrects a misconception, fills a gap, or builds on and extends the research of others. For example, in the preface to her book *Learning and Not Learning English: Latino Students in American Schools* (2001), Guadalupe Valdés explains that even after two years of language instruction, many students remain at a low level of language competence. In this passage, Valdés makes clear the purpose of her work:

> This book examines the learning of English in American schools by immigrant children. It focuses on the realities that such youngsters face in trying to acquire English in settings in which they interact exclusively with other non-English-speaking youngsters the entire school day. It is designed to fill a gap in the existing literature on non-English-background youngsters by offering a glimpse of the challenges and difficulties faced by four middle-school students enrolled in the United States for the first time when they were 12 or 13 years old. It is my purpose here to use these youngsters' lives and experiences as a lens through which to examine the policy and instructional dilemmas that now surround the education of immigrant children in this country. (p. 2)

If you were looking for sources for a paper on the English-only movement, in particular the consequences of that movement for young students, you might very well find Valdés's words compelling and decide the book is worth a closer reading.

■ Examine the Table of Contents and Index

After reading the introductory sections, it is useful to analyze the table of contents to see how much emphasis the writer gives to topics that are relevant to your own research. For example, the table of contents to *Learning and Not Learning English* includes several headings that may relate to your interest: "Educating English-Language Learners," "Challenges and Realities," "Implications for Policy and Practice," and the "Politics of Teaching English." You also should turn to the back of the book to examine the **index**, an alphabetical list of the important and likely to be repeated concepts in a book, and the page numbers on which they appear. An index also would include the names of authors cited in the book. In the index to Valdés's book, you would find references to "English-language abilities and instruction" with specific page numbers where you can read what the author has to say on this subject. You would also find references to "English-only instruction," "equal educational opportunities," and "sheltered instruction."

■ Check the Notes and Bibliographic References

Especially in the initial stages of writing, you should look closely at writers' notes and bibliographies to discern who they feel are the important voices in the field. Frequent citation of a particular researcher's work may indicate that the individual is considered to be an expert in the field you are studying. Notes usually provide brief references to people, concepts, or context; the bibliography includes a long list of related works. Mining Valdés's bibliography, you would find such titles as "Perspectives on Official English," "Language Policy in Schools," "Not Only English," "Language and Power," and "The Cultural Politics of English."

■ Skim Deeper

Skimming a book or article entails briefly looking over the elements we have discussed so far: the preface or abstract, the table of contents and the index, and the notes and bibliography. Skimming also can mean reading chapter titles, headings, and the first sentence of each paragraph to determine the relevance of a book or article.

Skimming the first chapter of *Learning and Not Learning English*, several topic sentences reveal the writer's purpose:

> "In this book, then, I examine and describe different expressions that both learning and not-learning English took among four youngsters."
>
> "In the chapters that follow . . ."
>
> "What I hope to suggest . . ."

These are the types of phrases you should look for to get a sense of what the writer is trying to accomplish and whether the writer's work will be of use to you.

If after you've taken these steps, a source still seems promising, you should read it closely, from start to finish, to determine how effectively it can help you answer your research question. Keep in mind all you've learned about critical reading. Those skills are what you'll rely on most as you work through the texts and choose the ones you should use in your paper. Remember the steps of rhetorical analysis: identifying the writer's situation, purpose, claims, and audience. And remember how to identify claims and evaluate the reasons used to support the claims: Is the evidence recent, relevant, accurate, and reliable?

Steps to Evaluating Library Sources

1 **Read the introductory section(s).** Get an overview of the researcher's argument.

2 **Examine the table of contents and index.** Consider the most relevant chapters to your topic and the list of relevant subjects.

3 **Check the notes and bibliographic references.** Identify the authors a researcher refers to (do the names come up in many different books?) and the titles of both books and articles.

4 **Skim deeper.** Read chapter titles and headings and topic sentences to determine the relevance of what you are reading for your own research.

A Practice Sequence: Evaluating Library Sources

For this exercise, we would like you to choose a specific book or article to examine in order to practice these strategies. If you are far along on your own research, use a book or article you have identified as potentially useful.

1 Read the introductory section(s). What issue is the author responding to? What is the writer's purpose? To correct a misconception? To fill a gap? To build on or extend the work of others?

2 Examine the table of contents and index. What key words or phrases are related to your own research? Which topics does the author focus on? Are you intending to give these topics similar emphasis? (Will you give more or less?)

3 Check the notes and bibliographic references. Make a list of the sources you think you want to look up for your own research. Do certain sources seem more important than others?

4 Skim deeper. What is the writer's focus? Is that focus relevant to your own topic, issue, question, or working thesis?

EVALUATING INTERNET SOURCES

Without question, the World Wide Web has revolutionized how research is conducted. It has been a particular boon to experienced researchers who have a clear sense of what they are looking for, giving them access to more information more quickly than ever before. But the Internet is rife with pitfalls for inexperienced researchers. That is, sites that appear accurate and reliable may prove not to be. The sources you find on the Internet outside your school library's catalog pose problems because anyone can post anything he or she wants. Unfortunately, there is no way to monitor the accuracy of what is published on the Internet. Although Internet sources can be useful, particularly because they are current, you must take steps to evaluate them before using information from them.

■ Evaluate the Author of the Site

If an author's name appears on a Web site, ask: Who is this person? What is this person's background? Can I contact this person?

One of our students googled "English only" and clicked on the first result, "Language Policy — English Only Movement," which eventually led her to James Crawford's Language Policy Web Site & Emporium. On the site, Crawford explains that he is "a writer and lecturer — formerly the Washington editor of *Education Week* — who specializes in the politics of language."* He notes that "since 1985, I have been reporting on the English Only movement, English Plus, bilingual education, Native American language revitalization, and language rights in the U.S.A." Between 2004 and 2006, he served as executive director of the National Association for Bilingual Education. Perhaps most important, Crawford has authored four books and a number of articles, and has testified before Congress on "Official English Legislation." From this biographical sketch, the student inferred that Crawford is credentialed to write about the English-only movement.

Less certain, however, are the credentials of the writer who penned an article titled "Should the National Anthem Be Sung in English Only?" which appeared on another Web site our student visited. Why? Because the writer's name never appears on the site. An anonymous posting is the first clue that you want to move on to a more legitimate source of information.

■ Evaluate the Organization That Supports the Site

You have probably noticed that Internet addresses usually end in with a suffix: .edu, .gov, .org, or .com. The .edu suffix means the site is associated

---

Education Week has been published since 1981 by Editorial Projects in Education, a nonprofit organization that was founded with the help of a Carnegie grant. The publication covers issues related to primary and secondary education. If you are not familiar with a publication and are uncertain about its legitimacy, you can always ask your instructor, a librarian, or another expert to vouch for its reliability.

with a university or college, which gives it credibility. The same holds true for .gov, which indicates a government agency. Both types of sites have a regulatory body that oversees their content. The suffix .org indicates a nonprofit organization; .com, a commercial organization. You will need to approach these Web sites with a degree of skepticism because you cannot be sure that they are as carefully monitored by a credentialed regulatory body. (In fact, even .edu sites may turn out to be postings by a student at a college or university.)

Our student was intrigued by James Crawford's site because he appears to be a credible source on the English-only movement. She was less sure about the reference to the Institute for Language and Education Policy. Is the institute a regulatory body that oversees what appears on the site? How long has the institute existed? Who belongs to the institute? Who sits on its board of directors? As a critical thinker, the student had to ask these questions.

■ Evaluate the Purpose of the Site

Information is never objective, so whenever you evaluate a book, an article, or a Web site, you should consider the point of view the writer or sponsor is taking. It's especially important to ask if there is a particular bias among members of the group that sponsors the site. Can you tell what the sponsors of the site advocate? Are they hoping to sell or promote a product, or to influence opinion?

Not all Web sites provide easy answers to these questions. However, James Crawford's Language Policy Web Site & Emporium is quite explicit. In fact, Crawford writes that "the site is designed to encourage discussion of language policy issues, expose misguided school 'reforms,'" and, among other goals, "promote [his] own publications." (Notice "Emporium" in the name of the site.) He is candid about his self-interest, which does raise a question about his degree of objectivity.

What about a site like Wikipedia ("The Free Encyclopedia")? The site appears to exist to convey basic information. Although the popularity of Wikipedia recommends it as a basic resource, you should approach the site with caution because it is not clear whether and how information posted on the site is regulated. It is prudent to confirm information from Wikipedia by checking on sites that are regulated more transparently rather than take Wikipedia as an authoritative source.

■ Evaluate the Information on the Site

In addition to assessing the purpose of a Web site like Wikipedia, you need to evaluate the extent to which the information is recent, accurate, and consistent with information you find in print sources and clearly regulated sites. For example, clicking on "The modern English-only movement" on Wikipedia takes you to a timeline of sorts with a number of links to other sites. But again, what is the source of this information? What is included?

What is left out? You should check further into some of these links, reading the sources cited and keeping in mind the four criteria for evaluating a claim — recency, relevance, accuracy, and reliability. Because you cannot be certain that Internet sources are reviewed or monitored, you need to be scrupulous about examining the claims they make: How much and what kind of evidence supports the writer's (or site's) argument? Can you offer counterarguments?

In the last analysis, it comes down to whether the information you find stands up to the criteria you've learned to apply as a critical reader and writer. If not, move on to other sources. In a Web-based world of information, there is no shortage of material, but you have to train yourself not to settle for the information that is most readily available if it is clearly not credible.

Steps to Evaluating Internet Sources

1 **Evaluate the author of the site.** Determine whether or not the author is an expert.

2 **Evaluate the organization that supports the site.** Find out what the organization stands for and the extent of its credibility.

3 **Evaluate the purpose of the site.** What interests are represented on the site? What is the site trying to do? Provide access to legitimate statistics and information? Advance an argument? Spread propaganda?

4 **Evaluate the information on the site.** Identify the type of information on the site and the extent to which the information is recent, relevant, accurate, and reliable.

A Practice Sequence: Evaluating Internet Sources

For this exercise, we would like you to work in groups on a common topic. The class can choose its own topic or use one of the topics we suggest on page 83. Then google the topic and agree on a Web site to analyze:

> *Group 1:* Evaluate the author of the site.
>
> *Group 2:* Evaluate the organization that supports the site.
>
> *Group 3:* Evaluate the purpose of the site.
>
> *Group 4:* Evaluate the information on the site.

Next, each group should share its evaluation. The goal is to determine the extent to which you believe you could use the information on this site in writing an academic essay.

6

Conducting Field Research

In some situations, it will be important to bolster your library or Internet research with field research. Internet and library research often involve looking at information from secondary sources — material created by people who were not witnesses to the events they describe. Field research, on the other hand, requires you to conduct firsthand research using primary sources involving people or situations connected to your research topic. You may need to do field research if you want data that does not yet exist in another form — information about a hot issue on your campus or the habits of its current students, for example, or about local people or practices in a community today.

This chapter presents guidelines to help you conduct the type of primary field research you may be asked to do for an English class. You will find information here about three common methods of gathering primary research data: interviews, observations, and surveys.

CONDUCTING INTERVIEWS

Interviews can be extremely useful sources of information and opinions, especially in the early stages of an investigation. You can use interviews to accomplish the following tasks.

- Gather new information on a topic, based on a person's firsthand experience or expertise
- Identify varying opinions or perspectives on a topic
- Gather interesting and relevant quotes to add to your project

Taken from Lee Odell and Susan M. Katz, *Writing Now: Shaping Words and Images*, pp. 589–607 (Chapter 11, "Conducting Field Research").

- Gather anecdotal evidence to support your position on a topic
- Get suggestions and advice on additional sources of information to pursue

■ Setting Up the Interview

You will have to make a number of decisions before you can conduct the interview.

Decide who would be the most appropriate person or people to interview.   This choice will depend on your audience and purpose. For a research report on a disease, such as mononucleosis, you might want to interview a doctor who is an expert in diagnosing and treating the disease as well as a patient who has had it. For a project on an environmental issue, such as the effects of recycling programs on a particular community, you might want to interview a town official, an environmental activist, and a local resident. You also need to decide how many people to interview. Is the topic extremely controversial? If the answer is yes, you cannot simply present one point of view — you will need to interview at least two people who have differing perspectives. Even for a profile, you will probably want to interview not only the person being profiled but also some of that person's friends, colleagues, and family members who can offer additional insight into your subject's life or work.

Figure out how you are going to approach each person you want to interview.   Do you already know this person? If not, do you know someone who does and who would be willing to make the initial contact for you? Do you think this person would be willing to talk to you? Keep in mind that most people — even busy professionals — are happy to talk about themselves and their work and are often enthusiastic about helping students (as long as those students sound motivated and polite). Before you contact each person to schedule the interview, be sure to think about exactly what you want to say and how you want to say it. You might even consider preparing a script requesting an interview, but be sure to rehearse it so that you do not have to read it awkwardly over the phone. (See the box on Requesting an Interview on page 97 for tips on what to include in your script.)

Decide whether you will be able to conduct the interview in a face-to-face setting.   You will get the most information from this type of interview because people communicate a great deal through facial expressions, gestures, and body language; thus you can more fully "read" a person's responses when you are talking face-to-face. You can also learn a lot by observing a person's home or office (if the interview takes place there), and then you can add descriptive, personality-revealing details of setting.

Requesting an Interview

It is often helpful to prepare exactly what you are going to say before you contact a potential interview subject. If you use a script for requesting an interview, try to include the following types of information.

- Your name and why you are calling ("Hi, my name is Dan George, and I'm writing a research report on campus safety for my English class at North Carolina State University.")

- Any connection you have to this person and what you want from him or her ("My instructor, Professor Fetzer, suggested that you might be willing to talk to me about the new call-box system that has been installed on campus this year.")

- A specific suggestion about how long the interview will take ("I would like to talk with you for about thirty minutes.")

- A few alternative dates and times, as well as a suggestion for where the interview might take place ("I could meet with you at your office any time next Tuesday or Thursday morning or after 3:00 p.m. next Wednesday.")

- A specific request for an appointment ("Would you be able to meet with me at one of those times next week?")

- A sincere thank-you at the end, and a repetition of the date, time, and meeting place that you have both agreed on ("Thank you for your help with my project. I look forward to talking with you at 4 o'clock next Wednesday afternoon at your office.")

If such a meeting is impossible or impractical, consider conducting the interview over the telephone. You can still establish rapport with your interviewee and can learn a lot from his or her tone of voice, general attitude toward you and the topic, and the pauses in the conversation. If all else fails, you can conduct the interview by e-mail, sending questions that the interviewee will respond to in a reply message, or by using instant messaging. Recognize, however, that with an electronic interview you will lose a great deal of the richness of human communication.

■ Preparing for the Interview

Before you go to the interview, you will want to do some preparation. Be sure to build in ample time to set up, prepare for, conduct, and analyze your interview. Contact your interviewee well in advance of the actual date when you want to conduct the interview. This allows for the possibility of a last-minute cancellation or postponement. You will also need to allow time in your schedule for follow-up phone calls or e-mails if you find that you need to clarify a point or ask another question. Other preparations include the following.

Prepare a list of questions that elicit meaningful answers.   This list should be relevant to your topic and appropriate for the person you are interviewing. Avoid writing questions in such a way that you tell the person what you want (or expect) to hear.

Avoid questions that can be answered by a simple yes or no or with a brief factual response.   Ask open-ended questions that inspire answers full of details, opinions, anecdotes, and analysis. Try asking the interviewee to describe, explain, or simply tell you about something.

Practice your interview questions with a friend or family member so that you feel comfortable.   Audio- or video-record yourself asking the questions and then play back the recording to hear how you sound (or look).

Decide whether you are going to record the interview or just take notes.   If you record the interview, take notes as a backup because recording devices can malfunction, and some people can be hard to understand on the recording. If you use a recording device, be sure to get the permission of the person you are interviewing, even if you are recording a phone interview.

Consider taking one or more photographs of the interview.   Depending on the type of research project, you may want to add the visual impact of a well-chosen photo — either of the interviewee or of a setting or object that is important to that person. Again, be sure to ask permission before taking any photographs.

The day before the interview, call or e-mail to confirm the appointment.   If you have decided to take photographs or tape-record the interview, now is the time to ask permission. If the person says no, be gracious and agreeable.

Make sure that all equipment is in working order.   If you are recording the interview, be sure your recorder is working properly and that you have extra batteries. Also make sure to have good note-taking equipment — a pad, notebook, or laptop computer, as well as several sharpened pencils or working pens. If you plan to take photographs, make sure that your camera works.

Exercise: Interview Questions

Why are the following questions inappropriate for an interview? Rewrite them in a way that requests the same type of information while eliciting a meaningful response.

- Whose bright idea was it to have the clock tower chime all night long?
- Don't you agree that the dorms need to be renovated?
- Why doesn't someone solve the parking problem on campus?
- Doesn't it bother you that your medical research involves killing innocent animals?

Now read the next group of interview questions. Rewrite these questions so they are phrased to solicit more detailed, informative answers instead of one-word answers.

- Do you like your job?
- Was it hard to be a working mother during the 1960s?
- Was your first job out of college meaningful?
- Did you find the transition from a small town to a big city difficult?

■ Conducting the Interview

Everyone has his or her own style of conducting an interview, but here are a few tips that can help you in any interview situation.

On the day of the interview, arrive on time, dressed appropriately, with all the equipment and writing tools you need.   If you have to wait, be patient. If the person originally gave you permission to record the interview or take photographs, ask again before turning on the tape recorder or taking out your camera.

During the interview, speak slowly and clearly and try to establish friendly eye contact.   Resist the temptation to look down at your notes the whole time.

Write down not only what the interviewee says but also descriptive details.   Notes about his or her appearance, voice, body language, gestures, or setting might enliven your report.

Remember that your list of prepared questions is just a starting point.   Be flexible, and allow the interview to move in a new direction if necessary (without going completely off course).

Keep within the time limits you agreed on in your initial request for an interview.   If you run out of time and the person does not invite you to stay longer, ask if you may call or e-mail in a few days to complete the interview.

Ask for permission to call or e-mail if any additional questions arise. You may find in the writing of your report that you need to contact the interview subject again to clarify a particular point.

Say a sincere thank-you before you leave.   If you make a positive impression, your interview subject will likely be receptive to any follow-up queries that you might have.

■ Writing Up the Interview

Once the interview is over, it is easy to relax and think that the hard part is done. However, while the interview is still fresh in your mind, it is important to take several additional steps.

Write up your notes as soon as possible.   If you do this within an hour or two, you will remember a lot of details that would otherwise become fuzzy.

Write down your own thoughts about the interview in addition to fleshing out your notes about what the interviewee said.   For example, did the person seem knowledgeable and insightful? Did he or she demonstrate any strong opinions or reactions to your questions or to the general topic? Did the person say or do anything to indicate a particular bias? If so, does that bias seem strong enough to affect his or her credibility as a source for your research project, or is the bias something you could simply point out in your project?

Reflect on what you learned during the interview, and write down your response to what the interviewee said.   Looking back at the interview, do you think you asked the right questions? Did you stick too rigidly to your script? Is there a point you should have pursued more aggressively or a fact you still don't understand? If so, consider calling or e-mailing with a follow-up question.

Send a thank-you note after the interview, particularly if it took place at the person's home or lasted a long time.   In your note, offer to send copies of any photographs you took (or perhaps even your finished research project).

Using Data

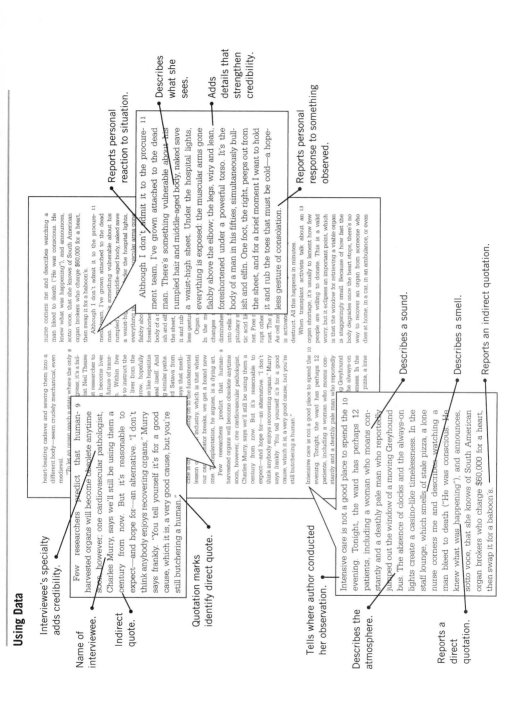

Annotations:

- Interviewee's specialty adds credibility.
- Name of interviewee.
- Indirect quote.
- Quotation marks identify direct quote.
- Tells where author conducted her observation.
- Describes the atmosphere.
- Reports a direct quotation.
- Reports personal reaction to situation.
- Describes what she sees.
- Adds details that strengthen credibility.
- Reports personal response to something observed.
- Describes a sound.
- Describes a smell.
- Reports an indirect quotation.

Few researchers predict that human-harvested organs will become obsolete anytime soon, however; one cardiovascular pathologist, Charles Murry, says we'll still be using them a century from now. But it's reasonable to expect—and hope for—an alternative. "I don't think anybody enjoys recovering organs," Murry says frankly. "You tell yourself it's for a good cause, which it is, a very good cause, but you're still butchering a human."

Intensive care is not a good place to spend the [10] evening. Tonight, the ward has perhaps 12 patients, including a woman who moans constantly and a deathly pale man who reportedly jumped out the window of a moving Greyhound bus. The absence of clocks and the always-on lights create a casino-like timelessness. In the staff lounge, which smells of stale pizza, a lone nurse corners me and describes watching a man bleed to death ("He was conscious. He knew what was happening"), and announces, sotto voce, that she knows of South American organ brokers who charge $60,000 for a heart, then swap it for a baboon's.

Although I don't admit it to the procure-[11] ment team, I've grown attached to the dead man. There's something vulnerable about his rumpled hair and middle-aged body, naked save a waist-high sheet. Under the hospital lights, everything is exposed: the muscular arms gone flabby above the elbow; the legs, wiry and lean, foreshortened under a powerful torso. It's the body of a man in his fifties, simultaneously bullish and elfin. One foot, the right, peeps out from the sheet, and for a brief moment I want to hold it and rub the toes that must be cold—a hopeless gesture of consolation.

When transplant activists talk about an [13] organ shortage, it's usually to lament how few people are willing to donate. This is a valid worry, but it eclipses an important point, which is that the window for retrieving a viable organ is staggeringly small. Because of how fast the body degrades once the heart stops, there's no way to recover an organ from someone who dies at home, in a car, in an ambulance, or even

■ Integrating Data Effectively

Information that you gather through your research, whether interviews, observations, surveys, or other forms of research, must be integrated into your written text. The example on page 101 shows how one author used interviews along with observation to gather data about organ transplants, which she then integrated into a report of her personal experience. Notice how she identifies the sources of her information, uses both direct and indirect quotes, and includes lots of detail about what she saw and heard — and even what she could smell. She also reports on her personal reaction to the environment and the people she interviewed and observed.

MAKING OBSERVATIONS

Before reading this chapter, you probably already knew that interviews and surveys are frequently used as research strategies, but you may not have realized that it is also possible to conduct research by simply observing the behaviors of others. In fact, observations can be a useful way to accomplish the following research tasks.

- See how people behave in their natural environment
- Collect data without influencing the participants
- Gather anecdotal evidence (see box on p. 103) that will make your research report more realistic
- Generate questions and ideas that can be investigated further through interviews and surveys
- Verify the information gained through interviews or surveys
- Collect data without relying on the interpretation, memory, accuracy, or honesty of interviewees or survey participants
- Gain a great deal of information about specific groups or situations, often in a short amount of time

Although some researchers and reporters make their observations fairly quickly, other researchers, such as anthropologists, conduct very detailed, long-term observations of groups of people. For example, many researchers visit remote parts of the world to live with and observe aboriginal peoples and then report on their observations. Many issues of *National Geographic* contain reports based largely on observation. This type of study is done with the permission of the people being observed and may involve years of field research. It also requires years of training.

However, it is possible to conduct some types of observation in a short amount of time, without any formal training, and often without asking for permission. For example, if you are researching the number of people who try to drive the wrong way down a poorly marked one-way street, you can stand on the corner of the street and keep track of how many people make

Anecdotal Evidence

An *anecdote* is a little story; thus, anecdotal evidence uses a story or stories to prove a point. Often anecdotal evidence comes from your own experience, but it can also come from observations. An anecdote makes a great opening paragraph because a story is a good hook to get the reader interested in your topic. You can also intersperse anecdotes throughout a report to support specific points. A memorable anecdote may even work well as a conclusion. The following is an example of an anecdote that you might use in an opening for a research paper about Lyme disease.

> The recurring low-grade fever that had plagued me for three months indicated that something was wrong. But despite repeated trips to the doctor, the fever's cause remained a mystery. I was surprised when a new doctor suggested that I get tested for Lyme disease. Even more surprising is that my eventual diagnosis was just one of twenty new confirmed cases of the disease this month in our county.

the attempt during a certain period without asking anyone's permission to do so. But if you want to observe the number of people who order salads in a particular fast-food restaurant at lunchtime, you will need to ask the manager for permission to sit at a table and take notes.

In another type of observational research, you might want to watch a specific person or group of people over an extended period. For example, you might be interested in writing a report on students' attentiveness in large lecture courses at your college. To do this, you would need permission to attend several different lecture courses. Then you would sit quietly and observe the students, lecturer, and classroom (or lecture hall) setting, taking notes about your observations of details such as those in the example on the next page.

In your report, you might present a chart or table summarizing some of this information. You might also want to make sketches to show how certain physical and environmental features affect students' attentiveness.

▪ Planning the Observation

As with any research project, the most important steps are in the planning stage. Your first step is to figure out what you want to accomplish by conducting an observation. What research question(s) do you hope to answer? What will you need to observe to get your answer(s)? How much time will be required? You then need to decide exactly what you want to focus on. For example, an observation for a report on food preferences might involve sitting in a fast-food restaurant for several hours and keeping track

Observation Notes

Course: American History 101

Number of Students: 43

Classroom description: Large auditorium. Professor lectures from a "stage" with students seated in rising rows of chairs, a third of which are empty. Lighting is dim and room is overheated. Good acoustics.

Technology: PowerPoint slides displayed on a large dropdown screen. A white board had a notice that the reading assignment for the next session had been changed. The notice stayed up throughout the class period.

Student behavior:

- took notes actively   ~~HHt~~ ~~HHt~~ ~~HHt~~ |||
- read from laptop |||
- texted messages on their cell phones   ~~HHt~~ ||
- dozed or slept ||
- appeared to listen but didn't take notes   ~~HHt~~
- arrived late ||
- left early and didn't return |
- asked questions   0
- stayed after class to speak to professor |||

Professor's behavior: Lectured throughout with no time for discussion or Q & A. Used slides effectively, but otherwise read from a prepared lecture with little deviation from it.

General impression: Most students seemed to be paying attention, but there was little engagement between them and their instructor except at the end of class when a few students went up to talk to the professor about an upcoming assignment.

---

of the kinds of food people order. Do you want to answer questions about the number of people who order salads? French fries? Diet versus regular soft drinks? If so, you would need some kind of chart to keep track of all the orders; and because most fast-food restaurants offer a lot of variety, you would probably need to group your observations into broad categories. These categories would vary according to the research questions. For example, if you were interested only in salads versus burgers, you could have three categories: Salads, Burgers, Other. During the observation, you would record the total number of people who order anything so that you could say, "X percent of all customers ordered . . ." or "X out of Y customers ordered. . . ."

Once you have established the focus of your observation, you will need to make decisions about the following.

Select an appropriate site for your observation.   If you choose a public site (such as a city park), you probably will not have to ask permission. If the site you choose is private (such as a shopping mall or store), you must get permission from an authority to conduct the observation. When asking, be sure to say who you are, what you plan to observe and why, when you want to conduct the observation, and how long you will be there.

Make a visit to the site beforehand to get a sense of the available space.
Will you be able to sit down and use a table to take notes? How obvious will you be to those you are observing? Is there adequate lighting for note taking, or should you bring a pen light (for example, at a theater)? If you plan to plug in a piece of equipment, are there electrical outlets?

Decide how you will record your observations.   Depending on the site, you might use a laptop computer, an audio or video recorder, a notebook, or preformatted data charts to log in your observations. If you want to videotape, photograph, or electronically record someone's words and actions, you must get that person's permission.

■ Conducting the Observation

Once you have a plan in place, you are ready to begin your observation. Here are some suggestions for getting the most out of gathering data through observation.

Arrive early with all your tools and equipment.   Make sure that you have everything you need with you and that your equipment is in working order (pens, sharpened pencils, notebook or pad, camera, tape recorder, and so on).

If the site is private, immediately announce yourself to the person who gave you permission, and restate your project and purpose.   If the person who originally granted you permission is not there, give that person's name and title to the person who is on site, explaining that your original contact approved your observation.

Find a position where you can observe without interfering with other people.   Try to be unobtrusive — it may help to think of yourself as a spy or plainclothes detective trying to blend into the scene.

Take notes on everything you see or hear.   Put quotation marks around any direct quotes so you can remember later which words are your own and which ones are someone else's. Take notes about the people, place, and actions you observe (making sketches or taking photographs if you plan to include visuals) and your own thoughts and feelings.

■ Reviewing Your Observational Notes

As with interviews, you want to gather your thoughts about your observation as soon as possible after you have completed your observation. Review your notes carefully as follows.

Read through your notes and add any other ideas that occur to you. Now is the time to flesh out your observations by writing down your thoughts about what the observation revealed, as well as additional details about the people, setting, and actions — things you may have been too busy to record as they were happening.

Clarify what you meant by any abbreviations that you may have used to speed up your note taking. Do this as soon as possible — preferably within an hour or two of the observation — while your memory is still fresh.

Decide if you need to conduct additional observations. If your observation did not adequately answer your research question, you may need to conduct one or more additional observations. Think carefully about what you still need. Should you return to the same place at a different time or day, or would it be better to try a different site? Do you need to collect more of the same type of information, or should you focus on a slightly different research question?

■ Analyzing and Presenting the Data

You will probably have gathered a great deal of information. Don't feel overwhelmed; use your research question to guide your analysis. What did you see that might help answer your question(s)? Use the following suggestions to help you figure out what to do with all the data.

Read through your notes carefully to find any patterns. Use a highlighter or colored pen to mark patterns or particular observations that provide evidence to support the claims you plan to make in your report. Pay attention to the exceptions — the information you gathered that does not fit the pattern — to see if it sheds an interesting light on the topic. For example, if in fact you observed that more men than women ordered cheeseburgers, you might want to take a look at the women who did order cheeseburgers: Did they have any characteristics in common?

If you conducted observations at more than one site, check to see if the data from the different sites were consistent. If not, can you draw any conclusions about the differences? For example, if you conducted observations at several fast-food restaurants, you might have observed significant variations in the physical settings, types of food ordered, hours of operation, or employee-customer interactions. In analyzing the data, you might suggest possible causes or effects of these differences. Here are some other questions to consider as you analyze your data.

- What did I observe that I expected to see?
- What did I observe that surprised me?
- Did I observe anything that upset or angered me?
- How did my observation support or amplify what I learned through my other research (including interviews and surveys)?
- Did my observation contradict any of my other sources?
- As a result of my observation, do I need to conduct additional research?

Think about how to incorporate your observational research into your project.   Observational research can be used as the centerpiece of your research, as support for aspect of your argument, or for detail. How you plan to use it will dictate the form it takes in your paper. Will you present the data as anecdotal evidence or in a more formal way? How will you use this data in conjunction with the information you gathered from other sources? Will the results of your observation provide backup for your other research or represent a major element of your project?

CONDUCTING SURVEYS

Surveys (sometimes called questionnaires) typically consist of a series of questions that can be asked and answered in writing, in person, or over the phone. Surveys are used all the time by marketing consultants who want information about the public's response to new products and services. Those surveys are scientifically designed and conducted, and they lead to quantitative results — the kind that are often trumpeted in ads with claims such as "Four out of five dentists surveyed recommend product X." (See the box on page 108 for a discussion of the differences between quantitative and qualitative data.) A survey that you conduct for this course will probably not allow you to make generalizations about large groups of people because you will not have the time or the resources to develop a scientifically valid survey that collects a large number of responses. However, the answers to the questions in a simple survey can help you generate information for localized populations about topics such as the following.

- The prevalence of a particular practice ("How many people in this class have e-mailed the instructor about an assignment?")
- Varying points of view ("What do people in this dorm think of the food in the dining hall?")
- Preferences for particular products ("What brand of running shoes are preferred by men between the ages of eighteen and twenty-five?")

Quantitative and Qualitative Data

Quantitative data is any data that can be reported in numbers. Quantitative data that answers these questions may be helpful in your research.

- How many? ("Nine out of ten participants in the study showed improvement on this medication.")
- How much? ("Thirty percent of the precipitation fell as sleet before turning to rain.")
- How likely? ("Forty percent of all marriages in the United States are likely to end in divorce.")

Quantitative data deals in generalizations; it clusters facts together and counts them. Most people have a lot of confidence in quantitative data, which typically comes from surveys or experiments.

Qualitative data is descriptive and specific. It can give a more vivid picture of how people think, feel, or behave than quantitative data. Consider these statements that use qualitative data.

- "Every Friday, employees were allowed to wear casual clothes to work, which may have contributed to more casual behavior, such as less formality in meetings, no strict adherence to specified break times, and more personal conversations in the hallways."
- "Aleksandr R. Luria, a Soviet psychologist, found that illiterate peasants gave colors metaphorical names such as 'liver' or 'apple' instead of brown or red."
- "Cuna women wear intricate beaded bracelets on their arms and legs, bright shirts with elaborately appliquéd designs, and gold hoops in their noses."

While qualitative data is not generalizable, it can add the type of detail that makes writing more interesting or more believable. Qualitative data typically comes from interviews, open-ended survey questions, and observations.

- The beliefs of a particular group with regard to a particular topic ("Is the electoral college an appropriate mechanism for electing the president of the United States?")
- The feelings of a particular group ("How do first-year students feel about being away from home?")

If you were going to write a report on the type of food that college students purchase at fast-food restaurants, you might create a survey such as the example on page 109 to gather primary data. The student creating this survey used the online tool SurveyMonkey to organize and distribute her survey.

Sample Survey Created Using SurveyMonkey

Fast Food Preferences

Exit this survey >>

1. Questions

Thank you for agreeing to participate in this survey of fast food preferences. Please submit your responses to me by March 1. I appreciate your help!

1. At a fast-food restaurant, I am likely to order (check all that apply):

- [ ] hamburger
- [ ] chicken nuggets
- [ ] regular soda
- [ ] cheeseburger
- [ ] taco
- [ ] diet soda
- [ ] salad
- [ ] French fries
- [ ] chicken sandwich
- [ ] milkshake

Other (please specify)

2. Using the following scale, rate the different reasons you eat fast food.

1 = very important   2 = somewhat important   3 = not at all important

	1	2	3
convenience	○	○	○
low cost	○	○	○
taste	○	○	○
variety of offerings	○	○	○
familiarity with menu	○	○	○
fast service	○	○	○
drive-through access	○	○	○

3. Which fast food restaurants do you go to the most?

4. Describe a typical meal that you would order at a fast food restaurant.

5. Are there any menu items that you would like to see added to the typical fast food menu? please describe.

6. Why do you eat off campus?

Done >>

> ### Exercise: Sources Using Surveys
>
> Look through newspapers and popular magazines such as *Time* for examples of information derived from a survey. How was this material incorporated into the article? Did the inclusion of this material help to make the writer's main point more compelling? Why or why not?

■ Planning the Survey

As with interviews, there are many steps you have to take and decisions you have to make before you can conduct your research.

Figure out the characteristics of the people you want to survey.   These characteristics will vary according to your audience and purpose. For a report requested by the Dean of Advising on the reasons students drop out of your college, you will need to find people who have dropped out. For a workshop for instructors on the advantages and disadvantages of lecture-based courses versus discussion-based courses, you will need to survey students who have taken both types of courses. There may be other considerations, too: Are you writing about a topic that has a particular geographical limitation? Are you writing about a topic that has a gender, race, or age limitation?

Decide how many people need to complete the survey.   For statistically significant studies, there are scientific ways to determine the number of participants (respondents) needed. However, for your purposes, you will probably be able to survey a relatively small population as a representative sample. For the purposes of a writing course, you can probably get credible information if you survey at least twenty-five participants.

Decide whether the participants can remain anonymous.   If you are asking questions about a sensitive topic (such as sexuality, weight, drug or alcohol use, depression, or domestic violence), you will get a more honest response if you can guarantee that you will not reveal the identity of any participants. To do so, you must come up with a way to gather, store, and code the survey data so that no one can possibly know any of the respondents' names. Keep in mind that even if the respondents remain anonymous, you may still want them to identify their age, gender, race, ethnicity, or other characteristics. Also keep in mind that, theoretically, surveys conducted in person or over the phone can be anonymous in the sense that names and other identifying information will not be connected to the data. As a practical matter, however, participants usually will not feel that their survey responses are truly anonymous if, for example, they are your own classmates or relatives.

Decide whether you want to conduct the survey in writing, in person, or over the phone. Each method has advantages and disadvantages. One advantage of a written survey is that participants usually answer more honestly when they are not speaking directly with the researcher. However, you may have a better chance of getting people to answer the survey (and not forget to submit their responses to you) if you sit down with them in person or ask your questions over the phone. Another option is to create a Web-based survey that participants can view and submit online. Check with your instructor to see if your school has a free Web-based application for creating a survey.

Determine how to find and convince people to participate. Do any of your friends or relatives have the appropriate characteristics? Do you belong to a group that would allow you to survey its members? Would classmates or students who live in your dorm be suitable respondents? Once you've identified a target group for your survey, you will need to tell prospective participants why you need this information and what you plan to do with it. For a survey that you will mail or e-mail, write a cover letter supplying this information, asking people to complete the survey and giving them a deadline or due date. You might also want to assure them that the survey is brief and will not take too much of their time.

Develop a system for respondents to return surveys. Include postage-paid, self-addressed envelopes for the return of completed print surveys. If you ask respondents to complete a questionnaire online, you have the added benefit of cutting and pasting material from individual surveys into your analysis. If you can guarantee their anonymity, include that information in the cover letter or message.

Calculate how much time you can expect the participants to spend responding to the survey. This will help you decide how many questions you need to write. Many people are willing to take a few minutes to complete a survey, but very few will respond if they think it will take more than fifteen or twenty minutes.

■ Writing the Survey Questions

Writing a survey that elicits useful responses is challenging. It is usually a good idea to ask both closed and open-ended questions, as described in the box on page 113. In addition, the following suggestions will help you as you write your survey.

Avoid asking two questions at the same time. Asking a question such as "Do you think you eat a healthy diet and get enough exercise?" will cause a problem because respondents might have a different answer for each part or neglect to answer one part.

Avoid asking leading questions.   If your question gives a hint about what you think the answer might be, your respondents may tell you what they think you want to hear. For example, if you ask whether they eat "junk food," the word "junk" has a negative connotation, so even if they do eat junk food, they may not admit it.

Ask questions in a neutral and nonjudgmental way.   Avoid emotionally loaded terms that might indicate your own feelings about what is the correct answer.

Ask key questions in two different ways — in different parts of the survey — and then check to see if the participant answered both versions consistently.   For example, suppose you wanted to find out about students' eating habits. You might ask a series of questions about the types of food they eat regularly. In one section of the survey, you might have checklist questions such as the first item in the sample survey on page 109. Then, in a later section of the survey, you might ask an open-ended question such as question 4 on the sample survey and compare the two answers to see if the respondent answered consistently. Keep in mind that when you write two versions of the same question, you need to make sure that you really are teasing out inconsistencies. For example, if you worded the open-ended question to ask people to describe a typical meal that they eat off campus, you would be introducing a new, confounding element — because students might eat off-campus meals at a variety of places other than fast-food restaurants.

Keep your questions fairly simple.   Make sure they do not require expertise beyond participants' level. For example, asking how many calories they consume in a fast-food meal would be problematic because most people know too little about the caloric content of foods to give a correct answer.

Avoid questions that are vague, ambiguous, or open to different interpretations.   For example, if you want respondents to indicate how often they engage in a certain activity, such as eating at a fast-food restaurant, it would be better to provide a range of specific numbers of visits per week or month rather than subjective choices such as often, sometimes, and rarely.

Phrase questions carefully to avoid sexist language or unwarranted assumptions.   Don't introduce any biases about respondents' gender, race, ethnicity, marital status, sexual orientation, and so on.

Think about the survey's design.   Use a typeface and layout that are attractive and legible; include ample white space. Be sure respondents have enough space to write out the responses to open-ended questions.

Closed and Open-Ended Questions

Closed questions ask participants to choose an answer from a set of fixed choices. Common types of closed questions include the following.

- Multiple-choice questions
- Checklist questions ("Put a checkmark next to the modes of communication that you use most frequently.")
- Ranking questions ("Using this scale, rank how often you engage in the following list of leisure activities. 1 = never, 2 = rarely, 3 = sometimes, 4 = often, 5 = very often")
- *True/false* and *yes/no* questions

Open-ended questions ask participants to explain or describe something in their own words or to provide a specific factual response. Typically, open-ended questions require a short answer. Here are some examples.

- "How old were you when you first tried alcohol?"
- "List the different ways in which you practice a green lifestyle."
- "What qualities were most important to you in deciding which car to buy?"

Closed questions are easiest for participants to answer and for you to analyze, but if a respondent is frustrated by the choices, misinterprets the question, or rushes through the survey, you may not get accurate or nuanced answers. Open-ended questions often elicit more thoughtful responses and can provide information that you never considered when you designed the survey. When designing a survey, it is usually best to include both closed and open-ended questions.

■ Testing the Survey

Whether you plan to conduct your survey in writing or on the phone, once you have drafted all your questions you should test the survey with friends or family members who will not be participating.

- Ask testers to identify any confusing or difficult questions.
- Make sure that the time needed to complete the survey is realistic and easily achievable (usually no more than twenty minutes).
- Consider whether the test survey results indicate a problem with particular questions — for example, leading, biased, or easily misinterpreted questions.
- Revise any questions that have caused or revealed problems.

■ Conducting the Survey

After revising problematic questions, you are ready to conduct the survey. Regardless of your distribution method, make sure to ask participants to complete the survey and return it to you by a specific date.

- **Distribute the survey in person.** For example, you might hand it out in the dining hall. If you choose to distribute the survey in person, be sure you have a mechanism for collecting surveys, such as a collection box or a return envelope.

- **Mail it to participants.** You will get the best response rate with mailed surveys if you include a stamped, self-addressed return envelope.

- **Distribute the survey electronically via e-mail or by using a Web site.** In addition to using e-mail, there are many free, easy-to-use survey Web sites that you can use with tools for distributing and collating your survey.

■ Analyzing and Presenting the Results

Your method of analysis and presentation will vary depending on the type of data you gathered.

For multiple-choice, checklist, and ranking questions, simply tally the results.   Count how many participants gave each possible answer. For the checklist question about fast food on page 109, you would count the number of people who reported that they order hamburgers, salads, and so on. For yes/no and true/false questions, just count the total number of each answer. A computer application such as Excel can help you add up the data, calculate percentages, and so on.

Refer to the quantitative data — the things you have counted — in percentages or in actual numbers.   Put the data results in numbers that your reader will understand. You might say "Fifty percent of all participants order hamburgers or cheeseburgers in fast-food restaurants, whereas only 8 percent order salads" or "Only 2 out of 25 participants reported ordering salads in fast-food restaurants."

Break down data more specifically if you note significant differences based on specific criteria.   Trends may emerge that you had not asked about but that are relevant. For example, if you asked participants to give their gender, age, or other characteristics, you might be able to say something like "Only women order salads."

For open-ended questions, read all the responses to see how many types of answers were given.   Create a list of all the different types of responses and then record the number of times each response occurs. It is often helpful to cluster the answers into categories. For example, if you asked twenty-five students "Why do you eat off campus?" you might organize the answers around these recurring categories.

1. better food
2. shorter lines
3. takes less time
4. can eat anytime
5. costs less
6. better variety
7. to eat with friends
8. fresher salads
9. quieter
10. less crowded

You could cluster these responses further into categories such as *Quality of food* (#1, 6, 8), *Convenience* (#2, 3, 4), and *Environment* (#9, 10). You may find that some of the responses do not fit neatly into any recurring category (for example, "to eat with friends"). While you should note this information, it may be statistically insignificant or too off track to use in your final analysis.

If you cluster the data from open-ended questions, you can quantify it and present it the same way you present other quantitative data. For example, using the data from the question above, you can calculate the percentage of respondents who eat off campus for convenience.

Incorporate the survey results into your research project.   Determine whether you will present the data visually — for example, in pie charts or bar graphs. (If you used a spreadsheet, you can also have it generate graphic elements based on that data.) Most important, you must come up with a way to summarize your results, making generalizations and drawing conclusions about what the survey revealed. You must present not only the data but also your interpretation of that data in relationship to your topic and research questions. Use quotes from open-ended questions to add credibility and detail to your report. If relevant, explain how your survey results compare or contrast with the information you found in other sources.

Decide what to do with incomplete and invalid surveys.   It is likely that you will not be able to use every returned survey. Some participants might not take the survey seriously — for example, they may write an implausible or flippant response to an open-ended question. Other participants might not complete the entire survey. Use your judgment to decide whether to include these results. If a participant made inappropriate responses, you will probably decide to discard that survey. However, if the participant simply failed to respond to certain questions, you can still use the data provided. When you write up your research, include information about the total number of surveys and how many were not fully completed.

7

Identifying Claims and Analyzing Arguments

A **claim** is an assertion of fact or belief that needs to be supported with **evidence** — the information that backs up a claim. A main claim, or thesis, summarizes the writer's position on a situation and answers the question(s) the writer addresses. It also encompasses all of the minor claims and their supporting evidence that the writer makes throughout the argument. As readers, we need to identify a writer's main claim because it helps us organize our own understanding of the writer's argument. It acts as a signpost that tells us, "This is what the essay is about," "This is what I want you to pay attention to," and "This is how I want you to think, change, or act." When you evaluate a claim, whether it is an argument's main claim or a minor claim, it is helpful to identify the type of claim it is: a claim of fact, a claim of value, or a claim of policy. You also need to evaluate the reasons for and the evidence that supports the claim. Because academic argument should acknowledge multiple points of view, you also should be prepared to identify what, if any, concessions a writer offers his or her readers, and what counterarguments he or she anticipates from others in the conversation.

IDENTIFYING TYPES OF CLAIMS

To illustrate how to identify a writer's claims, let's take a look at a text by educators Myra and David Sadker that examines gender bias in schools. The text is followed by our analyses of the types of claims (fact, value, and policy) and then, in the next section, of the nature of the arguments (evidence, concessions, and counterarguments) the authors present.

Taken from Stuart Greene and April Lidinsky, *From Inquiry to Academic Writing: A Practical Guide*, pp. 47–64 (Chapter 3, "From Identifying Claims to Analyzing Arguments").

ABOUT THE READING

Myra Sadker was a professor of education at American University until 1995, the year she died. Dr. Sadker coauthored *Sexism in School and Society*, the first book on gender bias in America's schools in 1973, and became a leading advocate for equal educational opportunities.

David Sadker is a professor at American University and has taught at the elementary, middle school, and high school levels. David Sadker and his late wife earned a national reputation for their groundbreaking work in confronting gender bias and sexual harassment. "Hidden Lessons" is an excerpt from their book *Failing at Fairness: How Our Schools Cheat Girls* (1994).

MYRA SADKER AND DAVID SADKER

Hidden Lessons

Sitting in the same classroom, reading the same textbook, listening to the same teacher, boys and girls receive very different educations. From grade school through graduate school female students are more likely to be invisible members of classrooms. Teachers interact with males more frequently, ask them better questions, and give them more precise and helpful feedback. Over the course of years the uneven distribution of teacher time, energy, attention, and talent, with boys getting the lion's share, takes its toll on girls. Since gender bias is not a noisy problem, most people are unaware of the secret sexist lessons and the quiet losses they engender. 1

Girls are the majority of our nation's schoolchildren, yet they are second-class educational citizens. The problems they face — loss of self-esteem, decline in achievement, and elimination of career options — are at the heart of the educational process. Until educational sexism is eradicated, more than half our children will be shortchanged and their gifts lost to society. 2

Award-winning author Susan Faludi discovered that backlash "is most powerful when it goes private, when it lodges inside a woman's mind and turns her vision inward, until she imagines the pressure is all in her head, until she begins to enforce the backlash too — on herself."* Psychological backlash internalized by adult women is a frightening concept, but what is even more terrifying is a curriculum of sexist school lessons becoming secret mind games played against female children, our daughters, and tomorrow's women. 3

---

*Editor's note: Journalist Faludi's book *Backlash: The Undeclared War Against American Women* (1991) was a response to the antifeminist backlash against the women's movement.

After almost two decades of research grants and thousands of hours of   *4*
classroom observation, we remain amazed at the stubborn persistence of
these hidden sexist lessons. When we began our investigation of gender
bias, we looked first in the classrooms of one of Washington, D.C.'s elite
and expensive private schools. Uncertain of exactly what to look for, we
wrote nothing down; we just observed. The classroom was a whirlwind of
activity so fast paced we could easily miss the quick but vital phrase or
gesture, the insidious incident, the tiny inequity that held a world of
meaning. As we watched, we had to push ourselves beyond the blind
spots of socialization and gradually focus on the nature of the interaction
between teacher and student. On the second day we saw our first example
of sexism, a quick, jarring flash within the hectic pace of the school day:

> Two second-graders are kneeling beside a large box. They whisper excitedly
> to each other as they pull out wooden blocks, colored balls, counting sticks.
> So absorbed are these two small children in examining and sorting the
> materials, they are visibly startled by the teacher's impatient voice as she
> hovers over them. "Ann! Julia! Get your cottonpickin' hands out of the math
> box. Move over so the boys can get in there and do their work."

Isolated here on the page of a book, this incident is not difficult to inter-   *5*
pret. It becomes even more disturbing if you think of it with the teacher
making a racial distinction. Picture Ann and Julia as African American
children moved away so white children can gain access to the math materials. If Ann and Julia's parents had observed this exchange, they might
justifiably wonder whether their tuition dollars were well spent. But few
parents actually watch teachers in action, and fewer still have learned to
interpret the meaning behind fast-paced classroom events.

The incident unsettles, but it must be considered within the context of   *6*
numerous interactions this harried teacher had that day. While she talked
to the two girls, she was also keeping a wary eye on fourteen other active
children. Unless you actually shadowed the teacher, stood right next to
her as we did, you might not have seen or heard the event. After all, it
lasted only a few seconds.

It took us almost a year to develop an observation system that would   *7*
register the hundreds of daily classroom interactions, teasing out the gender bias embedded in them. Trained raters coded classrooms in math,
reading, English, and social studies. They observed students from different racial and ethnic backgrounds. They saw lessons taught by women
and by men, by teachers of different races. In short, they analyzed America's classrooms. By the end of the year we had thousands of observation
sheets, and after another year of statistical analysis, we discovered a syntax of sexism so elusive that most teachers and students were completely
unaware of its influence.

Recently a producer of NBC's *Dateline* contacted us to learn more about   *8*
our discovery that girls don't receive their fair share of education. Jane
Pauley, the show's anchorwoman, wanted to visit classrooms, capture

these covert sexist lessons on videotape, and expose them before a television audience. The task was to extricate sound bites of sexism from a fifth-grade classroom where the teacher, chosen to be the subject of the exposé, was aware she was being scrutinized for sex bias.

Dateline had been taping in her class for two days when we received a concerned phone call. "This is a fair teacher," the producer said. "How can we show sexism on our show when there's no gender bias in this teacher's class?" We drove to the NBC studio in Washington, D.C., and found two *Dateline* staffers, intelligent women concerned about fair treatment in school, sitting on the floor in a darkened room staring at the videotape of a fifth-grade class. "We've been playing this over and over. The teacher is terrific. There's no bias in her teaching. Come watch."

After about twenty minutes of viewing, we realized it was a case of déjà vu: The episodal sexist themes and recurring incidents were all too familiar. The teacher was terrific, but she was more effective for half of the students than she was for the other. She was, in fact, a classic example of the hundreds of skillful well-intentioned professionals we have seen who inadvertently teach boys better than girls.

We had forgotten how difficult it was to recognize subtle sexism before you learn how to look. It was as if the *Dateline* staff members were wearing blinders. We halted the tape, pointed out the sexist behaviors, related them to incidents in our research, and played the tape again. There is a classic "aha!" effect in education when people finally "get it." Once the hidden lessons of unconscious bias are understood, classrooms never look the same again to the trained observer.

Much of the unintentional gender bias in that fifth-grade class could not be shown in the short time allowed by television, but the sound bites of sexism were also there. *Dateline* chose to show a segregated math group: boys sitting on the teacher's right side and girls on her left. After giving the math book to a girl to hold open at the page of examples, the teacher turned her back to the girls and focused on the boys, teaching them actively and directly. Occasionally she turned to the girls' side, but only to read the examples in the book. This teacher, although aware that she was being observed for sexism, had unwittingly transformed the girls into passive spectators, an audience for the boys. All but one, that is: The girl holding the math book had become a prop.

Dateline also showed a lively discussion in the school library. With both girls' hands and boys' hands waving for attention, the librarian chose boy after boy to speak. In one interaction she peered through the forest of girls' hands waving directly in front of her to acknowledge the raised hand of a boy in the back of the room. Startled by the teacher's attention, the boy muttered, "I was just stretching."

The next day we discussed the show with future teachers, our students at the American University. They were bewildered. "Those teachers really were sexist. They didn't mean to be, but they were. How could that

9

10

11

12

13

14

happen — with the cameras and everyone watching?" When we took those students into classrooms to discover the hidden lessons for themselves, they began to understand. It is difficult to detect sexism unless you know precisely how to observe. And if a lifetime of socialization makes it difficult to spot gender bias even when you're looking for it, how much harder it is to avoid the traps when you are the one doing the teaching.

■ Identify Claims of Fact

Claims of fact are assertions (or arguments) that a condition has existed, exists, or will exist. Claims of fact are made by individuals who believe that something is true; but claims are never simply facts, and some claims are more objective, and so easier to verify, than others. For example, "It's raining in Boston today" is a "factual" claim of fact; it's easily verified. But consider the argument some make that the steel and automotive industries in the United States have depleted our natural resources and left us at a crisis point. This is an assertion that a condition exists. A careful reader must examine the basis for this kind of claim: Are we truly facing a crisis? And if so, are the steel and automotive industries truly responsible? A number of politicians counter this claim of fact by insisting that if the government would harness the vast natural resources in Alaska, there would be no "crisis." This is also a claim of fact, in this case an assertion that a condition will exist in the future. Again, it is based on evidence, evidence gathered from various sources that indicates sufficient resources in Alaska to keep up with our increasing demands for resources and to allay a potential crisis.

Our point is that most claims of fact are debatable. They may be based on factual information, but they are not necessarily true. Most claims of fact present **interpretations** of evidence derived from **inferences**. That is, a writer will examine evidence (for example, about the quantity of natural resources in Alaska and the rate that industries harness those resources and process them into goods), draw a conclusion based on reasoning (an inference), and offer an explanation based on that conclusion (an interpretation). So, for example, an academic writer will study the evidence on the quantity of natural resources in Alaska and the rate that industries harness those resources and process them into goods; only after the writer makes an informed decision on whether Alaska's resources are sufficient to keep pace with the demand for them will he or she take a position on the issue.

In the first paragraph of their essay, the Sadkers make the claims of fact that female students are "more likely to be invisible members of classrooms," and that teachers interact differently with female students than they do with male students. The careful reader will want to see how the Sadkers support these claims of fact throughout the essay. Can they convincingly present their argument about "the secret sexist lessons and the quiet losses they engender" in the paragraphs that follow?

■ Identify Claims of Value

A claim of fact is different from a **claim of value**, which expresses an evaluation of a condition that has existed, exists, or will exist. Is a condition good or bad? Is it important or inconsequential? An argument that developing the wilderness in Alaska would irreversibly mar the beauty of the land indicates that the writer values the beauty of the land over the possible benefits of development. A claim of value presents a judgment, which is sometimes signaled by a value-laden word like *ugly, beautiful,* or *immoral,* but may also be conveyed more subtly by the writer's tone and attitude.

Sadker and Sadker make a claim of value when they suggest that a "majority of our nation's schoolchildren" have become "second-class educational citizens" and point out that the consequences of treating girls differently from boys in school has resulted in a "loss of self-esteem, decline in achievement, and elimination of career options" for girls (para. 2). Of course, the critical reader's task is to question these evaluations: Does gender bias in the classroom affect self-esteem, achievement, and career options? Both of these statements are minor claims, but they make assertions that require support. After all, how do the Sadkers know these things? Whether or not readers are persuaded by these claims depends on the evidence or reasons that the authors use to support them. We discuss the nature of evidence and what constitutes "good reasons" later in this chapter.

■ Identify Claims of Policy

A **claim of policy** is an argument for what should be the case; it is a call for change. Two recent controversies on college campuses center on claims of policy. One has activists arguing that universities and colleges should have a policy that all workers on campus earn a living wage. The other has activists arguing that universities and colleges should have a policy that prevents them from investing in countries where the government ignores human rights. Claims of policy are often signaled by words like *should* and *must*: "For public universities to live up to their democratic mission, they *must* provide all their workers with a living wage." Myra and David Sadker make a claim of policy when they assert that "educational sexism" must be eradicated; otherwise, they point out, "more than half our children will be shortchanged and their gifts lost to society" (para. 2).

Not all writers make their claims as explicitly as the Sadkers do; nor does every argument include all three types of claims. But you should be able to identify the three different types of claims. Moreover, you should keep in mind what the situation is and what kind of argument can best address what you see as a problem. Ask yourself: Does the situation involve a question of fact? Does the situation involve a question of value? Does the situation require a change in policy? Or is some combination at work?

Steps to Identifying Claims

1 **Ask:** Does the argument assert that a condition has existed, exists, or will exist? If so, it's a claim of fact.

2 **Ask:** Does the argument express an evaluation of a condition that has existed, exists, or will exist? If so, it's a claim of value.

3 **Ask:** Does the argument call for change, and is it directed at some future action? If so, it's a claim of policy.

A Practice Sequence: Identifying Claims

What follows is a series of claims. Identify each one as a claim of fact, value, or policy. Be prepared to justify your categorizations.

1 Taxing the use of fossil fuels will end the energy crisis.

2 We should reform the welfare system to ensure that people who receive support from the government also work.

3 Images of violence in the media create a culture of violence in schools.

4 The increase in homelessness is a deplorable situation that contradicts the whole idea of democracy.

5 Distributing property taxes is the one sure way to end poverty and illiteracy.

6 Individual votes don't really count.

7 Despite the 20 percent increase in the number of females in the workforce over the past forty years, women are still not treated equitably.

8 Affirmative action is a policy that has outlived its usefulness.

9 There are a disproportionate number of black males in American prisons.

10 The media are biased, which means we cannot count on newspapers or television news for the truth.

ANALYZING ARGUMENTS

Analyzing an argument involves identifying the writer's main and minor claims and then examining (1) the reasons and evidence given in support of each claim, (2) the writer's concessions, and (3) the writer's attempts to handle counterarguments.

■ Analyze the Reasons Used to Support a Claim

Stating a claim is one thing; supporting that claim is another. As a critical reader, you need to evaluate whether a writer has provided *good reasons* to support his or her position. Specifically, you will need to decide whether the support for a claim is recent, relevant, reliable, and accurate. As a writer, you will need to use the same criteria when you support your claims.

Is the source recent?   Knowledgeable readers of your written arguments not only will be aware of classic studies that you should cite as "intellectual touchstones"; they will also expect you to cite recent evidence, evidence published within five years of when you are writing. Of course, older research can be valuable. For example, in a paper about molecular biology, you might very well cite James Watson and Francis Crick's groundbreaking 1953 study in which they describe the structure of DNA. That study is an intellectual touchstone that changed the life sciences in a fundamental way, much as Einstein's theory of relativity changed how physicists think about the universe. Or if you were writing about educational reform, you might very well mention Hirsch's 1987 book *Cultural Literacy*. Hirsch's book did not change the way people think about curricular reform as profoundly as Watson and Crick's study changed the way scientists think about biology, but his term *cultural literacy* continues to serve as useful shorthand for a particular way of thinking about curricular reform that remains influential to this day.

Although citing Hirsch is an effective way to suggest you have studied the history of an educational problem, it will not convince your readers that there is a crisis in education today. To establish that, you would need to use as evidence studies published over the past few years to show, for example, that there has been a steady decline in test scores since Hirsch wrote his book. And you would need to support your claim that curricular reform is the one sure way to bring an end to illiteracy and poverty with data that are much more current than those available to Hirsch in the 1980s. No one would accept the judgment that our schools are in crisis if your most recent citation is more than twenty years old.

Is the source relevant?   Evidence that is relevant must have real bearing on your issue and also depends greatly on what your readers expect. Suppose two of your friends complain that they were unable to sell their condominiums for the price they asked. You can claim there is a crisis in the housing market, but your argument won't convince most readers if your only evidence is personal anecdote. Such anecdotal evidence may alert you to a possible topic and help you connect with your readers, but you will need to test the **relevance** of your friends' experience — Is it pertinent? Is it typical of a larger situation or condition? — if you want your readers to take your argument seriously. At the very least, you should scan real estate listings to see what the asking prices are for properties comparable to your friends' properties. By comparing listings, you are defining the grounds for your argument. If your friends are disappointed that their one-bedroom condominiums sold for less than a three-bedroom condominium with deeded parking in the same neighborhood, it may will be that their expectations were too high. If you aren't comparing like things, your argument is going to be seriously flawed. If your friends' definition of what constitutes a "reasonable price" differs dramatically from everyone else's, their experience is probably irrelevant to the larger question of whether the local housing market is depressed.

Is the source reliable?   You also need to evaluate whether the data you are using to support your argument are reliable. After all, some researchers present findings based on a very small sample of people that can also be rather selective. For example, a researcher might argue that 67 percent of the people he cited believe that school and residential integration are important concerns. But how many people did this person interview? More important, who responded to the researcher's questions? A reliable claim cannot be based on a few of the researcher's friends.

Let's return to the real estate example. You have confirmed that your friends listed their condominiums at prices that were not out of line with the market. Now what? You need to seek out reliable sources to continue testing your argument. For example, you might search the real estate or business section of your local newspaper to see if there are any recent stories about a softening of the market; and you might talk with several local real estate agents to get their opinions on the subject. In consulting your local newspapers and local agents, you are looking for **authoritative sources** against which to test your anecdotal evidence — the confirmation of experts who report on, study, evaluate, and have an informed opinion on local real estate. Local real estate agents are a source of **expert testimony**, firsthand confirmation of the information you have discovered. You would probably not want to rely on the testimony of a single real estate agent, who may have a bias; instead, talk with several agents to see if a consensus emerges.

Is the source accurate?   To determine the accuracy of a study that you want to use to support your argument, you have to do a little digging to find out who else has made a similar claim. For instance, if you want to cite authoritative research that compares the dropout rate for white students with the rate for students of color, you could look at research conducted by the Civil Rights Project. Of course, you don't need to stop your search there. You could also check the resources available through the National Center for Education Statistics. You want to show your readers that you have done a relatively thorough search to make your argument as persuasive as possible.

The accuracy of **statistics** — factual information presented numerically or graphically (for example, in a pie or bar chart) — is difficult to verify. To a certain extent, then, their veracity has to be taken on faith. Often the best you can do is assure yourself that the source of your statistical information is authoritative and reliable — government and major research universities generally are "safe" sources — and that whoever is interpreting the statistical information is not distorting it. Returning again to our real estate example, let's say you've read a newspaper article that cites statistical information about the condition of the local real estate market (for example, the average price of property and volume of sales this year in comparison to last year). Presumably the author of the article is an expert, but he or she may be interpreting rather than simply reporting on the statistics. To reassure yourself one way or the other, you may want to check the sources of the author's statistics — go right to your source's sources — which a responsible author will cite. That will allow you to look over the raw data and come to your own conclusions. A further step you could take would be to discuss the article with other experts — local real estate agents — to find out what they think of the article and the information it presents.

Now, let's go back to Myra and David Sadker's essay. How do they develop their assertion that girls are treated differently from boys in classrooms from "grade school through graduate school"? First, they tell us (in paragraph 4) that they have been conducting research continuously for "almost two decades" and that they have accumulated "thousands of hours of classroom observation." This information suggests that their research is both recent and relevant. But are their studies reliable and accurate? That their research meets the reliability criterion is confirmed by the grants they received over the years: Granting institutions (experts) have assessed their work and determined that it deserved to be funded. Grants confer authority on research. In addition, the Sadkers explain that they observed and refined their analyses over time to achieve accuracy: "As we watched, we had to push ourselves beyond the blind spots of socialization and gradually focus on the nature of the interaction between teacher and student."

In paragraph 7, the authors provide more evidence that the observations that support their claim are accurate. Not only have they observed many instances of gender bias in classrooms, so have trained "raters." The raters add objectivity to the findings because they did not share the Sadkers' interest in drawing a specific conclusion about whether gender bias exists in classrooms. Also the raters observed a wide cross-section of students and teachers from "different racial and ethnic backgrounds." At the end of their study, the Sadkers had collected thousands of pieces of data and could feel quite confident about their conclusion — that they had "discovered a syntax of sexism so elusive that most teachers and students were completely unaware of its influence."

■ Identify Concessions

Part of the strategy of developing a main claim supported with good reasons is to offer a **concession**, an acknowledgment that readers may not agree with every point the writer is making. A concession is a writer's way of saying, "Okay, I can see that there may be another way of looking at the issue or another way to interpret the evidence used to support the argument I am making." For example, you may not want your energy costs to go up, but after examining the reasons why it may be necessary to increase taxes on gasoline — to lower usage and conserve fossil fuels — you might concede that a tax increase on gasoline could be useful. The willingness to make concessions is valued in academic writing because it acknowledges both complexity and the importance of multiple perspectives. It also acknowledges the fact that information can always be interpreted in different ways.

The Sadkers make a concession when they acknowledge in the last paragraph of the excerpt that "it is difficult to detect sexism unless you know precisely how to observe." And, they explain, "if a lifetime of socialization makes it difficult to spot gender bias even when you're looking for it, how much harder it is to avoid the traps when you are the one doing the teaching." Notice that these concessions do not weaken their argument. The authors' evidence appears overwhelmingly to support their thesis. The lesson here is that conceding a point in your argument shows that you have acknowledged there are other ways of seeing things, other interpretations. This is an important part of what it means to enter a conversation of ideas.

Often a writer will signal a concession with a variation of the phrase "It is true that . . ." (for example, "I agree with X that Y is an important factor to consider" or "Some studies have convincingly shown that . . ."). Generally, the writer will then go on to address the concession, explaining how it needs to be modified or abandoned in the light of new evidence or the writer's perspective on the issue.

■ Identify Counterarguments

As the term suggests, a **counterargument** is an argument raised in response to another argument. You want to be aware of and acknowledge what your readers may object to in your argument. Anticipating readers' objections is an important part of developing a conversational argument. For example, if you were arguing in support of universal health care, you would have to acknowledge that the approach departs dramatically from the traditional role the federal government has played in providing health insurance. That is, most people's access to health insurance has depended on their individual ability to afford and purchase this kind of insurance. You would have to anticipate how readers would respond to your proposal, especially readers who do not feel that the federal government should ever play a role in what has heretofore been an individual responsibility. Anticipating readers' objections demonstrates that you understand the complexity of the issue and are willing at least to entertain different and conflicting opinions.

In the excerpt from "Hidden Lessons," the Sadkers describe the initial response of *Dateline* staffers to what they observed in the classroom they were videotaping: "This is a fair teacher. . . . [T]here's no gender bias in this teacher's class." Two women whom the Sadkers describe as "intelligent" and "concerned about fair treatment in school" agreed: "We've been playing this over and over. The teacher is terrific. There's no bias in her teaching. Come watch" (para. 9).

Notice the Sadkers' acknowledgment that even intelligent, concerned people may not see the problems that the Sadkers spent more than twenty years studying. In addressing the counterargument — that sexism does not exist — the authors are both empathetic to and respectful of what any reasonable person might or might not see. This is in keeping with what we would call a conversational argument: that writers listen to different points of view, that they respect arguments that diverge from their own, and that they be willing to exchange ideas and revise their own points of view.

In an argument that is more conversational than confrontational, writers often establish areas of common ground, both to convey to readers that they are understood and to acknowledge the conditions under which readers' views are valid. Writers do this by making concessions and anticipating and responding to counterarguments. This conversational approach is what many people call a **Rogerian approach to argument**, based on psychologist Carl Rogers's approach to psychotherapy. The objective of a Rogerian strategy is to reduce listeners' sense of threat so that they are open to alternatives. For academic writers, it involves four steps:

1. Conveying to readers that they are understood
2. Acknowledging conditions under which readers' views are valid
3. Helping readers see that the writer shares common ground with them
4. Creating mutually acceptable solutions to agreed-on problems

The structure of an argument, according to the Rogerian approach, grows out of the give-and-take of conversation between two people and the topic under discussion. In a written conversation, the give-and-take of face-to-face conversation takes the form of anticipating readers' counterarguments and uses language that is both empathetic and respectful to put the readers at ease.

Steps to Analyzing an Argument

1 **Identify the type of claim.** A claim of fact? Value? Policy?

2 **Analyze the reasons used to support the claim.** Are they recent? Relevant? Reliable? Accurate?

3 **Identify concessions.** Is there another argument that even the author acknowledges is legitimate?

4 **Identify counterarguments.** What arguments contradict or challenge the author's position?

■ Analyze a Sample Student Argument

Read the excerpt from a student essay that follows with pen or pencil in hand, noting the writer's claims, reasons, concessions, and responses to counterarguments. The essay is an example of a **researched argument**: The writer uses evidence to advance an argument that contributes to the ongoing conversation about an issue. The author, Ryan Metheny, was writing at a time when anti-immigrant attitudes in the United States were running high. In this essay, which was selected from a pool of exceptional student essays to be published in a campus magazine that was required reading for all first-year students at his school, Metheny addresses what he sees as a fundamental tension between democratic principles of equality and the exclusionary nature of the English-only movement. Specifically, he responds to the marginalization of Ebonics (also known as African American Vernacular English) in schools. His purpose is to make policymakers and educators aware of the problem. He also explains to a broader audience the ways in which race and power, not grammatical correctness, determine which language practices gain legitimacy and which do not.

Metheny 1

Ryan Metheny
Professor Klein
English 1020
May 16, 20--

The Problems and Dangers of Assimilatory Policies

1 American society considers itself to be in an age of enlightenment. Racism has been denounced and cultural colorblindness in all things is encouraged. Economic opportunities are available for everyone, and equal consideration before the law is provided for each citizen. American society considers itself the embodiment of liberty, equality, and justice for all.

2 In a society such as the one described, it follows that one's background and culture do not have any influence on one's socioeconomic status; theoretically, the two should be completely disconnected. Yet, as we all know, this is not the case. The people of the highest status in America are almost uniformly white males. Sadly, America, the place of equality and liberty, is still very much a

Metheny 2

stratified society, not only by socioeconomic class/status, but because minority cultures much more often fill the ranks of the lower classes. Fortunately for those of minority cultures, the country's policymakers now accept, at least in speech, the basic equality and potential of all cultures to rise out of poverty; unfortunately, they still refuse to recognize the validity of differences in these cultures from what they, the policymakers, view as American (Labov i–iii).

3

The most obvious example of this is the stubborn grasp the country holds on what it calls "standard English" — the dialect used by the intellectual and social elite of America. Standard English is considered to be the one and only conduit through which people of status exchange information — and therefore the one and only conduit through which power can be attained. It is seen as the American method of communication. Historically, the various groups that come to America have had to adopt this method as their own in order to receive their piece of the American socioeconomic pie — and, indeed, many groups have — Germans, Irish, Italians. These groups, however, are white. Assimilation for non-white groups has been agonizingly slow, especially for historically oppressed peoples such as African Americans (Smitherman 167–200). We consider adoption of standard English to be the price one pays for entrance into the all-inclusive society. But, of course, this is not only contradictory (an inclusive society should accept all cultural differences as valid), but it is also an unfair policy for non-white groups. We have set up standard English as the holy grail of communication. If we wish to avoid hypocrisy, we should live up to the virtues of inclusiveness we claim to have.

4

Implementation of more inclusiveness should begin by decreasing our fervor in support of standard English. The reasons for this are many. On the technical, linguistic level, standard English should certainly not be esteemed so highly because it is a superior language — it is not. Standard English is just as flexible and changing as any other language. It is ironic that the cultural dialects that many minorities utilize, such as Ebonics, have a heavy hand in changing the standard English that we demand they adopt. Even the slaves brought to America, the lowest of the low socioeconomically during the period in which they were enslaved, had a heavy hand in changing American standard English. Joseph Holloway and Winifred

Metheny 3

Voss pointed out in 1993 that nearly 200 place names in nine Southern states are of African origin. They also [point] out the African origins of many other terms now used in standard English — even the beloved name "Bambi" of Walt Disney's cartoon has its origins in the Bantu word "mubambi," a word which means "one who lies down in order to hide" (Holloway and Voss 57, 227–229). This flexibility of standard English seems to point toward another hypocrisy of America — we play down the importance of the non-standard Ebonics dialect, while accepting parts of that dialect as our own. Certainly this suggests that standard English is not inherently more "civilized" than other dialects.

Conversely, is Ebonics then not accepted because it is inherently "uncivilized"? No. Ebonics can be just as expressive and meaningful, if not more so, than standard English (Smitherman 167–200). Ebonics as a language fosters important verbal reasoning and logical skills, just as any language does. Its nuances of grammar and intonation are highly communicative combinations of English vocabulary and grammar with African mechanics. Anyone who has ever heard a bout of the "dozens" will readily admit that Ebonics can indeed be a fast-paced, inventive dialect that requires quick thinking. The ability to express an impromptu "yo mama" joke on the spur of the moment is a kind of genius all its own. Such verbal skills should not be discouraged. To do so invalidates the experiences of African Americans. A people's experiences cannot be denied, especially in the land of equality and justice. If Ebonics remains unrecognized despite its clear validity as a mode of communication, and despite standard English's lack of any kind of superiority to it, what ideologies are truly behind its continuing lack of recognition? Actually, the lack of recognition of Ebonics may well be rooted in mere class-related bigotry (Smitherman). The upper class views such a mode of speech as unintelligent, a mockery of the "true" language. What such a view is in fact indicative of is not only a blatant case of ethnocentrism . . . but also a feeling of superiority that native standard English speakers feel over the lower classes. This sense of superiority fuels the demand that speakers of other dialects and languages adopt standard English in order to join the successful mainstream. Such an attitude supports the dominance of the upper classes. This must surely be considered wrong in a land

5

where every person, regardless of income and status, is equal before
the law.

Ebonics is not inferior: oppression of Ebonics could well be a case   6
of bigotry. Therefore, acceptance of Ebonics as a valid form of communication should be strongly considered. To implement such an acceptance, we must begin with the schools, for that is where society first
exerts influence upon the individual. So far, any kind of acceptance
here has been rare, and when present, it has often been implemented
inappropriately. Baugh pointed out in 1999 several cases in which
Ebonics and Ebonics-related problems were not addressed appropriately. In one case, two native Ebonics speakers were placed in special
education based on verbal aptitude tests given in standard English — a
dialect they were not familiar with. In another case, a math teacher
gave his inner-city students word problems that he thought were being
culturally sensitive, but which in fact could be considered racist. One
problem asked, "If you were a pimp and had knocked up seven hos, and
had twenty-three hos total, how many hos would still need to be
knocked up?" while another asked, "If you had a half-pound of heroin,
and want to make twenty percent more profit, how much cut would you
need?" These are extreme examples, true, but they illustrate the lack of
success that many educators have had when it comes to addressing the
problems inherent in educating Ebonics speakers.

Such problems are further frustrated by the aforementioned   7
stratified nature of American society. Baugh illustrates this using a
graph in which five theoretical socioeconomic groups, and their
corresponding dialects, are arrayed vertically from upper to lower
classes. The children in the uppermost group are capable of going
even higher socioeconomically than their parents, shown by a line
slanting up, or slightly lower, shown by a line slanting down. The
next group down is similarly capable of a certain amount of increase
or decrease in status.

This graph shows two things: first, that each socioeconomic   8
group is normally only capable of a certain range of change in status;
and second, that there is very little overlap in range between groups.
This implies that the lower classes most minorities are still a part of
cannot advance their status very quickly in succeeding generations.
Baugh goes on to claim that this is due to the manner in which

Metheny 5

children are educated from a very early age, both in schools and at home. Inner-city schools are often poorly funded and fail to teach their students adequately. Similarly, the home life of poorer students often does not foster learning in important ways, such as the reading of parents to children at an early age. Which is not to say, of course, that Ebonics as a language does not support learning — rather, low socioeconomic status often does not support learning. Ebonics speakers, since they more often fill lower socioeconomic groups, are often at an unfair disadvantage when compared to native standard English speakers.

As the inclusive society, we must address this economic unfairness. Arguments in favor of using standard English as the only valid form of communication in the United States have not done this. E. D. Hirsch argues that cultural literacy focused around a single standard dialect is necessary for a society to operate efficiently. Complementing Hirsch's ideas, Richard Rodriguez argues that knowing the "public language" is needed for one to have a public identity. These scholars make logical points in support of the efficiency of having one language per society. Efficiency, however, should not come at the expense of the marginalization of economically disadvantaged nonstandard English speakers. Standard English proponents have no solution to the problem of assimilation other than telling the marginalized to bite the bullet and join the mainstream, so to speak. What ever happened to equality and inclusiveness? Assimilation should not even be necessary — rather, differences should be accepted. Pragmatists may respond that joining the mainstream is vital in order to advance economically, whether doing so at the expense of one's identity is right or not. Of course, in the current state of American society, they are largely correct. I propose, however, that living up to reasonable standards of inclusiveness as a country will correct the join-the-mainstream-or-fail dilemma. We should not simply accept the hard reality, but rather work to change.

9

Metheny 6

Works Cited

Baugh, John. *Out of the Mouths of Slaves: African American Language and Educational Malpractice.* Austin: University of Texas Press, 1999. 1–39. Print.

Hirsch, E. D. *Cultural Literacy: What Every American Needs to Know.* New York: Vintage Books, 1988. 1–32. Print.

Holloway, Joseph E., and Winifred K. Voss. *The African Heritage of American English.* Bloomington: Indiana University Press, 1993. Print.

Labov, William. Foreword. *Out of the Mouths of Slaves: African American Language and Educational Malpractice.* By John Baugh. Austin: University of Texas Press, 1999. i–iii. Print.

Rodriguez, Richard. *Hunger of Memory: The Education of Richard Rodriguez.* New York: Bantam Books, 1983. Print.

Smitherman, Geneva. *Talkin and Testifyin: The Language of Black America.* Detroit: Wayne State University Press, 1977. 167–200. Print.

A Practice Sequence: Analyzing an Argument

Now that you have annotated Ryan Metheny's essay, we would like you to work in four groups to consider the strategies this writer uses to advance his argument. That is, analyze the way the writer states his main claim and develops his argument in drawing the conclusions he does.

Group 1: What type of claim does Metheny make? What reasons does he use to support his argument?

Group 2: To what extent are you persuaded by the reasons the writer gives to support his argument that Ebonics should be given legitimacy? Point to specific words and phrases you found persuasive.

Group 3: How effective is the writer in anticipating his readers' responses? Does he make any concessions to readers or anticipate possible counterarguments?

Group 4: Make an outline in which you include your own counterargument to this writer's position.

PART THREE

Argument as an Act of Inquiry

8

Identifying Issues and Forming Questions

R emember that inquiry is central to the process of composing. As you read and begin to write an essay, you will find that the real work of writing is figuring out the answers to the following questions:

- What have these authors been talking about?
- What are the relevant concerns of those whose work I have been reading?
- What are the situations motivating these people to write?
- What frames do these writers use to construct their arguments?
- Who will be interested in reading what I have to say?
- How can I connect with readers who may be both sympathetic and antagonistic toward my argument?
- What is at stake in my own argument? (What if things change? What if things stay the same?) For whom?
- What kinds of evidence might persuade my readers?
- What objections are my readers likely to raise?

To answer these questions, you must read in the role of writer, with an eye toward *identifying an issue* (an idea or statement that is open to dispute) that compels you to respond in writing, *understanding the situation* (the factors that give rise to the issue and shape your response), and *formulating a question* (what you intend to answer in response to the issue). In Table 8.1, we identify a series of situations and one of the issues and questions that derive from each of them. Notice that the question you ask is a tool that defines the area of inquiry as you read; it also can help you

Taken from Stuart Greene and April Lidinsky, *From Inquiry to Academic Writing: A Practical Guide*, pp. 65–82 (Chapter 4, "From Identifying Issues to Forming Questions").

TABLE 8.1   A Series of Situations with Related Issues and Questions

SITUATION	ISSUE	QUESTION
Congress plans to pass legislation that prohibits music downloads.	You feel that this piece of legislation would challenge your freedom as a consumer.	To what extent can Congress pass legislation that compromises the freedoms of individual consumers?
Different state legislatures are passing legislation to prevent Spanish-speaking students from using their own language in schools.	Your understanding of research on learning contradicts the idea that students should be prevented from using their own language in the process of learning a new language.	Under what conditions should students be allowed to use their own language while they learn English?
A manufacturing company has plans to move to your city with the promise of creating new jobs in a period of high unemployment.	You feel that this company will compromise the quality of life for the surrounding community because the manufacturing process will pollute the air.	What would persuade the city to prevent this company from moving in even though the company will provide much-needed jobs?
Your school has made an agreement with a local company to supply vending machines that sell drinks and food. The school plans to use its share of the profit to improve the library and purchase a new scoreboard for the football field.	You see that the school has much to gain from this arrangement, but you also know that obesity is a growing problem at the school.	Is there another way for the school to generate needed revenue without putting students' health at risk?
An increasing number of homeless people are seeking shelter on your college campus.	Campus security has stepped up its efforts to remove the homeless even though the shelters off campus are overcrowded.	How can you persuade the school to shelter the homeless and to provide funds to support the needs of the homeless in your city?

formulate your working thesis, the statement that answers your question. (We say more about developing a thesis in Chapter 9.) In this chapter, in addition to further discussing the importance of situation, we look at how you can identify issues and formulate questions to guide your reading and writing.

IDENTIFYING ISSUES

Below we present several steps to identifying an issue. You don't have to follow them in this particular order, of course; in fact, you may find yourself going back and forth among them as you try to bring an issue into focus. Keep in mind that issues do not simply exist in the world well formed. Instead, writers construct what they see as issues from the situations they observe. For example, consider legislation to limit music downloads from the Internet. If this kind of law conflicts with your own practices and sense of freedom, you may have begun to identify an issue: the clash of values over what constitutes fair use and what does not. Be aware that others may not understand your issue, and that in your writing you will have to explain carefully what is at stake.

■ Draw on Your Personal Experience

Writing begins with critical reading, identifying what is at issue for *you*. After all, the issue typically is what motivates people to write. You may have been taught that formal writing is objective, that you must keep a dispassionate distance from your subject, and that you should not use *I* in a college-level paper. The fact is, however, that our personal experiences influence how we read, what we pay attention to, and what inferences we draw. It makes sense, then, to begin with you — where you are and what you think and believe. We all use personal experience to make arguments in our everyday lives, to urge the people around us to act or think in certain ways. In an academic context, the challenge is to use personal experience to argue a point, to illustrate something, or to illuminate a connection between theories and the sense we make of our daily experience. You don't want simply to tell your story; but you do want your story to strengthen your argument.

In his book *Cultural Literacy*, E. D. Hirsch personalizes his interest in reversing the cycle of illiteracy in America's cities. To establish the nature of the problem in the situation he describes, he cites research showing that student performance on standardized tests in the United States is falling. But he also reflects on his own teaching in the 1970s, when he first perceived "the widening knowledge gap [that] caused me to recognize the connection between specific background knowledge and mature literacy." And he injects anecdotal evidence from conversations with his son, a teacher. Those stories heighten readers' awareness that school-aged children do not know much about literature, history, or government. (For example, his son mentions a student who challenged his claim that Latin is a "dead language" by demanding, "What do they speak in Latin America?") Hirsch's use of his son's testimony makes him vulnerable to criticism, as readers might question whether Hirsch can legitimately use his son's experience to make generalizations about education. But in fact, Hirsch is using personal testimony — his own and his son's — to augment and put a human face on the research he cites. He presents his issue, that schools must teach cultural literacy, both as something personal and as something with which we should all be concerned. The personal note helps readers see Hirsch as someone who has long been concerned with education and who has even raised a son who is an educator.

In "Dyes and Dolls: Multicultural Barbie and the Merchandising of Difference," author Ann duCille reveals how a personal experience drives her argument about the cultural significance of children's toys. She explains that although Barbie as icon seems harmless, her own examination reveals that "toys and games play crucial roles in helping children determine what is valuable in and around them." The questions she raises not only grow out of her statement of the issue, but also motivate the concerns she addresses in her essay: "More than simple instruments of pleasure and amusement, toys and games play crucial roles in helping children determine what is valuable in and around them." The issue she seizes on is the role toys play in shaping cultural attitudes; but her personal stake in the issue — what may have attracted her to it in the first place — was her own experience playing with dolls that did not reflect her ethnicity.

■ Identify What Is Open to Dispute

We have said that an issue is something that is open to dispute. Sometimes the way to clarify an issue is to think of it as a fundamental tension between two or more conflicting points of view. If you can identify conflicting points of view, an issue may become clear. Consider E. D. Hirsch, who believes that the best approach to educational reform (the subject he writes about) is to change the curriculum in schools. His position: A curriculum based on cultural literacy is the one sure way to reverse the cycle of poverty and illiteracy in urban areas. What is the issue? Hirsch's issue emerges in the presence of an alternative position. Jonathan Kozol, a social activist who has written extensively about educational reform, believes that policymakers need to address reform by providing the necessary resources that all students need to learn. Kozol points out how students in many inner-city schools are reading textbooks that were published twenty years ago, and that the dilapidated conditions in these schools — windows that won't close, for example — make it impossible for students to learn. In tension are two different views of the reform that can reverse illiteracy: Hirsch's view that educational reform should occur through curricular changes, and Kozol's view that educational reform demands socioeconomic resources.

■ Resist Binary Thinking

As you begin to define what is at issue, try to tease out complexities that may not be immediately apparent. That is, try to resist the either/or mind-set that signals binary thinking. Looking at what Hirsch and Kozol have to say, it would be easy to characterize the problems facing our schools as either curricular or socioeconomic. But it may be that the real issue combines these arguments with a third or even a fourth, that neither curricular nor socioeconomic changes by themselves can resolve the problems with American schools.

After reading essays by both Hirsch and Kozol, one of our students pointed out that both Hirsch's focus on curriculum and Kozol's socioeconomic focus ignore another concern. She went on to describe her school experience in racial terms. In the excerpt below, notice how this writer uses personal experience (in a new school, she is not treated as she had expected to be treated) to formulate an issue.

> Moving to Tallahassee from Colorado Springs, Colorado, I was immediately struck by the differences apparent in local home life, school life, and community unity, or lack thereof. Ripped from my sheltered world at a small Catholic school characterized by racial harmony, I, both bewildered and unprepared, was thrown into a large public school where outward prejudice from classmates and teachers and "race wars" were common and tolerated. . . .
>
> In a school where students and teachers had the power and free reign to abuse anyone different from them, I was constantly abused. As the only black student in English honors, I was commonly belittled in front of my "peers" by my all-knowing teacher. If I developed courage enough to ask a question, I was always answered with the use of improper grammar and such words as "ain't" as my teacher attempted to simplify the material to "my level" and to give me what he called "a little learning." After discussing several subjects he often turned to me, singling me out of a sea of white faces, and asked, "Do *you* understand, Mila?" When asking my opinion of a subject, he frequently questioned, "What do *your* people think about this?" Although he insisted on including such subjects as Martin Luther King's "I Have a Dream" speech in the curriculum, the speech's themes of tolerance and equity did not accompany his lesson.

Through her reading, this student discovered that few prominent scholars have confronted the issue of racism in schools directly. Although she grants that curricular reform and increased funding may be necessary to improve education, she argues that scholars also need to address race in their studies of teaching and learning.

Our point in using this example is to emphasize that issues may be more complex than you first think they are. For this student, the issue wasn't one of two positions — reform the curriculum or provide more funding. Instead it combined a number of different positions, including race ("prejudice" and "race wars") and the relationship between student and teacher ("Do *you* understand, Mila?") in a classroom. In this passage, the writer uses her experience to challenge binary thinking. Like the student writer, you should examine issues from different perspectives, avoiding either/or propositions that oversimplify the world.

■ Build On and Extend the Ideas of Others

Academic writing builds on and even extends the ideas of others. As an academic writer, you will find that by extending other people's ideas, you will extend your own. You may begin in a familiar place; but as you read more and pursue connections to other readings, you may well end up at an unexpected destination. For example, one of our students was troubled when he read Melissa Stormont-Spurgin's description of homeless children. The student uses details from her work (giving credit, of course) in his own:

> The children . . . went to school after less than three hours of sleep. They wore the same wrinkled clothes that they had worn the day before. What will their teachers think when they fall asleep in class? How will they get food for lunch? What will their peers think? What could these homeless children talk about with their peers? They have had to grow up too fast. Their worries are not the same as other children's worries. They are worried about their next meal and where they will seek shelter. Their needs, however, are the same. They need a home and all of the securities that come with it. They also need an education (Stormont-Spurgin 156).

Initially the student was troubled by his own access to quality schools, and the contrast between his life and the lives of the children Stormont-Spurgin describes. Initially, then, his issue was the fundamental tension between his own privileged status, something he had taken for granted, and the struggle that homeless children face every day. However, as he read further and grew to understand homelessness as a concern in a number of studies, he connected his personal response to a larger conversation about democracy, fairness, and education:

> Melissa Stormont-Spurgin, an author of several articles on educational studies, addresses a very real and important, yet avoided issue in education today. Statistics show that a very high percentage of children who are born into homeless families will remain homeless, or in poverty, for the rest of their lives. How can this be, if everyone actually does have the same educational opportunities? There must be significant educational disadvantages for children without homes. In a democratic society, I feel that we must pay close attention to these disadvantages and do everything in our power to replace them with equality.

Ultimately, the student refined his sense of what was at issue: *Although all people should have access to public education in a democratic society, not everyone has the opportunity to attend quality schools in order to achieve personal success.* In turn, his definition of the issue began to shape his argument:

> Parents, teachers, homeless shelters and the citizens of the United States who fund [homeless] shelters must address the educational needs of homeless children, while steering them away from any more financial or psychological struggles. Without this emphasis on education, the current trend upward in the number of homeless families will inevitably continue in the future of American society.

The student has shifted away from a personal issue — the difference between his status and that of homeless children — to an issue of clashing values: the principle of egalitarian democracy on the one hand and the social reality of citizens in a democracy living in abject poverty on the other. When he started to read about homeless children, he could not have made the claim he ends up making, that policymakers must make education a basic human right. This student offers us an important lesson about the role of inquiry and the value of resisting easy answers. He has built on and extended his own ideas — and the ideas of others — after repeating the process of reading, raising questions, writing, and seeing problems a number of times.

■ Read to Discover a Writer's Frame

A more specialized strategy of building on and extending the ideas of others involves reading to discover a writer's **frame**, the perspective through which a writer presents his or her arguments. Writers want us to see the world a certain way, so they frame their arguments much the same way photographers and artists frame their pictures. For example, if you were to take a picture of friends in front of the football stadium on campus, you would focus on what you would most like to remember — your friends' faces — blurring the images of the people walking behind your friends. Setting up the picture, or framing it, might require using light and shade to make some details stand out more than others. Writers do the same with language.

E. D. Hirsch uses the term *cultural literacy* to frame his argument for curricular reform. For Hirsch, the term is a benchmark, a standard: People who are culturally literate are familiar with the body of information that every educated citizen should know. Hirsch's implication, of course, is that people who are not culturally literate are not well educated. But that is not necessarily true. In fact, a number of educators insist that literacy is simply a means to an end — reading to complete an assignment, for example, or to understand the ramifications of a decision — not an end in itself. By defining and using *cultural literacy* as the goal of education, Hirsch is framing his argument; he is bringing his ideas into focus.

When writers use framing strategies, they also call attention to the specific conversations that set up the situation for their arguments. Framing often entails quoting specific theories and ideas from other authors, and then using those quotations as a perspective, or lens, through which to examine other material. In his memoir *Hunger of Memory: The Education of Richard Rodriguez* (1982), Richard Rodriguez uses this method to examine his situation as a nonnative speaker of English desperate to enter the mainstream culture, even if it means sacrificing his identity as the son of Mexican immigrants. Reflecting on his life as a student, Rodriguez comes across Richard Hoggart's book *The Uses of Literacy* (1957). Hoggart's description of "the scholarship boy" presents a lens through which Rodriguez can see his own experience. Hoggart writes:

> With his family, the boy has the intense pleasure of intimacy, the family's consolation in feeling public alienation. Lavish emotions texture home life.

Then, at school, the instruction bids him to trust lonely reason primarily. Immediate needs set the pace of his parents' lives. From his mother and father the boy learns to trust spontaneity and nonrational ways of knowing. *Then*, at school, there is mental calm. Teachers emphasize the value of a reflectiveness that opens a space between thinking and immediate action.

Years of schooling must pass before the boy will be able to sketch the cultural differences in his day as abstractly as this. But he senses those differences early. Perhaps as early as the night he brings home an assignment from school and finds the house too noisy for study. He has to be more and more alone, if he is going to "get on." He will have, probably unconsciously, to oppose the ethos of the hearth, the intense gregariousness of the working-class family group. . . . The boy has to cut himself off mentally, so as to do his homework, as well as he can.

Here is Rodriguez's response to Hoggart's description of the scholarship boy:

For weeks I read, speed-read, books by modern educational theorists, only to find infrequent and slight mention of students like me. . . . Then one day, leafing through Richard Hoggart's *The Uses of Literacy*, I found, in his description of the scholarship boy, myself. For the first time I realized that there were other students like me, and so I was able to frame the meaning of my academic success, its consequent price — the loss.

Notice how Rodriguez introduces ideas from Hoggart "to frame" his own ideas: "I found, in his description of the scholarship boy, myself. For the first time I realized that there were other students like me, and so I was able to frame the meaning of my academic success, its consequent price — the loss." Hoggart's scholarship boy enables Rodriguez to revisit his own experience with a new perspective. Hoggart's words and idea advance Rodriguez's understanding of the problem he identifies in his life: his inability to find solace at home and within his working-class roots. Hoggart's discription of the scholarship boy's moving between cultural extremes — spontaneity at home and reflection at school — helps Rodriguez bring his own youthful discontent into focus.

Rodriguez's response to Hoggart's text shows how another writer's lens can help frame an issue. If you were using Hoggart's term *scholarship boy* as a lens through which to clarify an issue in education, you might ask how the term illuminates new aspects of another writer's examples or your own. And then you might ask, "To what extent does Hirsch's cultural literacy throw a more positive light on what Rodriguez and Hoggart describe?" or "How do my experiences challenge, extend, or complicate the scholarship-boy concept?"

■ Consider the Constraints of the Situation

In identifying an issue, you have to understand the situation that gives rise to the issue, including the contexts in which it is raised and debated. One of the contexts is the audience. In thinking about your issue, you must consider the extent to which your potential readers are involved in the dialogue you want to enter, and what they know and need to know. In a sense, audience functions as both context and **constraint**, a factor that narrows the choices you can make in responding to an issue. An understanding of your potential readers will help you choose the depth of the discussion; it will also determine the kind of evidence you can present and the language you can use.

Another constraint on your response to an issue is the form that response takes. For example, if you decide to make an issue of government-imposed limits on the music you can download from the Internet, your response in writing might take the form of an editorial or a letter to a legislator. In this situation, length is an obvious constraint: Newspapers limit the word count of editorials, and the best letters to legislators tend to be brief and very selective about the evidence they cite. A few personal examples and a few statistics may be all you can include to support your claim about the issue. By contrast, if you were making your case in an academic journal, a very different set of constraints would apply. You would have more space for illustrations and support, for example.

Finally, the situation itself can function as a major constraint. For instance, suppose your topic is the decline of educational standards. It's difficult to imagine any writer making the case for accelerating that decline or any audience being receptive to any argument that a decline in standards is a good thing.

Steps to Identifying Issues

1 **Draw on your personal experience.** Start with your own sense of what's important, what puzzles you, or what you are curious about. (Then build your argument by moving on to other sources to support your point of view.)

2 **Identify what is open to dispute.** Identify a phenomenon or some idea in a written argument that challenges what you think or believe.

3 **Resist binary thinking.** Think about the issue from multiple perspectives.

4 **Build on and extend the ideas of others.** As you read, be open to new ways of looking at the issue. The issue you finally write about may be very different from what you set out to write about.

5 **Read to discover a writer's frame.** What theories or ideas shape the writer's focus? How can these theories or ideas help you frame your argument?

6 **Consider the constraints of the situation.** Craft your argument to meet the needs of and constraints imposed by your audience and form.

▪ Identify Issues in an Essay

Consider the situation of writer Anna Quindlen, who in 1992 published an editorial in the *New York Times* addressing the issue of homelessness. At the time, New Yorkers seemed to have accepted homelessness as something that could be studied but not remedied. As you read Quindlen's "No Place Like Home," note the words and phrases Quindlen uses to identify both the situation and her audience. Is her main claim one of fact, value, or policy? Finally, answer the questions that follow the essay to see if you can discern how Quindlen locates, defines, and advances her issue.

ABOUT THE READING

Anna Quindlen is the best-selling author of novels (including *Blessings, Black and Blue, One True Thing,* and *Object Lessons*) and nonfiction books (including *A Short Guide to a Happy Life, Living Out Loud, Thinking Out Loud,* and *How Reading Changed My Life*). She has also written children's books (including *The Tree That Came to Stay* and *Happily Ever After*). She won the Pulitzer Prize in 1992 for her *New York Times* column, "Public & Private." Since 1999 she has been writing a biweekly column for *Newsweek*.

ANNA QUINDLEN

No Place Like Home

Homeless is like the government wanting you locked up
And the people in America do not like you.
They look at you and say Beast!
I wish the people would help the homeless
And stop their talking.

—FRANK S. RICE, *The Rio Times*

The building is beautiful, white and beige and oak, the colors of yuppies. The rehab of the Rio came in $700,000 under budget, two months ahead of schedule. The tenants say they will not mess it up, no, no, no. "When you don't have a place and you get a good place, the last thing you want to do is lose it," said one man who slept in shelters for seven years, seven years during which time you might have gotten married, or lost a loved one, or struck it rich, but all this guy did was live on the streets. 1

Mayor David Dinkins has announced that he will study parts of the study he commissioned from a commission on the homeless, the newest in a long line of studies. 2

One study, done in 1981, was called "Private Lives, Public Spaces." It was researched by Ellen Baxter, who now runs the nonprofit company 3 that has brought us the Rio and four other buildings that provide permanent housing for the homeless in Washington Heights.

Another study, done in 1987, was called "A Shelter Is Not a Home" and   *4*
was produced by the Manhattan Borough President David Dinkins, who now runs the City of New York. At the time, the Koch administration said it would study Mr. Dinkins's study, which must have taught Mr. Dinkins something.

Robert Hayes, one of the founding fathers of the movement to help the   *5*
homeless, once told me there were three answers to the problem: housing, housing, housing. It was an overly simplistic answer, and it was essentially correct.

Despite our obsessions with pathology and addiction, Ms. Baxter has   *6*
renovated one apartment building after another and filled them with people. At the Rio, what was once a burnt-out eyesore is now, with its curving facade and bright lobby, the handsomest building on the block; what were once armory transients with dirt etched in the creases of hands and face are now tenants. The building needed people; the people needed a home. The city provided the rehab money; Columbia University provides social service support.

Some of the tenants need to spend time in drug treatment and some go   *7*
to Alcoholics Anonymous and some of them lapse into pretty pronounced fugue states from time to time. So what? How would you behave if you'd lived on the streets for seven years? What is better: to leave them out there while we lament the emptying of the mental hospitals and the demise of jobs? Or to provide a roof over their heads and then get them psychiatric care and job training?

What is better: to spend nearly $20,000 each year to have them   *8*
sleep on cots at night and wander the streets by day? Or to make a one-time investment of $38,000 a unit, as they did in the single rooms with kitchens and baths in the Rio, for permanent homes for people who will pay rent from their future wages or from entitlement benefits?

Years ago I became cynical enough to envision a game plan in which   *9*
politicians, tussling over government stuff like demonstration projects and agency jurisdiction and commission studies, ignored this problem until it went away.

And, in a sense, it has. We have become so accustomed to people sleep-   *10*
ing on sidewalks and in subway stations that recumbent bodies have become small landmarks in our neighborhoods. Mary Brosnahan, executive director of the Coalition for the Homeless, says she was stunned, talking to students, at their assumption that people always had and always would be living on the streets. My children call by pet names — "the man with the cup," "the lady with the falling-down pants" — the homeless people around their school.

And when a problem becomes that rooted in our everyday perceptions,   *11*
it is understood to be without solution. Nonprofit groups like the one that

renovated the Rio prove that this is not so. The cots in the armory are poison; drug programs and job training are icing. A place to shut the door, to sleep without one eye open, to be warm, to be safe — that's the cake. There's no place like home. You didn't need a study to figure that out, did you?

For Analysis and Discussion

1. Can you find evidence of Quindlen's personal responses and experiences?
2. What phenomenon has challenged what Quindlen thinks and believes about homelessness? How has she made it into an issue?
3. Where does she indicate that she has considered the issue from multiple perspectives and is placing her ideas in conversation with those of others?
4. What sort of lens does Quindlen seem to be using to frame her argument?
5. What constraints seem to be in play in the essay?

A Practice Sequence: Identifying Issues

This sequence of activities will give you practice in identifying and clarifying issues based on your own choice of reading and collaboration with your classmates.

1 Draw on your personal experience. Reflect on your own responses to what you have been reading in this or in other classes, or issues that writers have posed in the media. What concerns you most? Choose a story that supports or challenges the claims people are making in what you have read or listened to. What questions do you have? Make some notes in response to these questions, explaining your personal stake in the issues and questions you formulate.

2 Identify what is open to dispute. Take what you have written and formulate your ideas as an issue, using the structure we used in our example of Hirsch's and Kozol's competing arguments:

- Part 1: Your view of a given topic
- Part 2: At least one view that is in tension with your own

If you need to, read further to understand what others have to say about this issue.

3 Resist binary thinking. Share your statement of the issue with one or more peers and ask them if they see other ways to formulate the issue that you may not have thought about. What objections, if any, do they make to your statement in part 1? Write these objections down in part 2 so that you begin to look at the issue from multiple perspectives.

4 Build on and extend the ideas of others. Now that you have formulated an issue from different perspectives, explaining your personal stake in the issue, connect what you think to a broader conversation in what you are reading. Then try making a claim using this structure: "Although some people would argue _____, I think that _____."

5 Read to discover a writer's frame. As an experiment in trying out multiple perspectives, revise the claim you make in exercise 4 by introducing the frame, or lens, through which you want readers to understand your argument. You can employ the same sentence structure. For example, here is a claim framed in terms of race: "Although people should have access to public education, recent policies have exacerbated racial inequalities in public schools." In contrast, here is a claim that focuses on economics: "Although people should have access to public education, the unequal distribution of tax money has created what some would call an 'economy of education.'" The lens may come from reading you have done in other courses or from conversations with your classmates, and you may want to attribute the lens to a particular author or classmate: "Although some people would argue_____, I use E. D. Hirsch's notion of cultural literacy to show_____."

6 Consider the constraints of the situation. Building on these exercises, develop an argument in the form of an editorial for your local newspaper. This means that you will need to limit your argument to about 250 words. You also will need to consider the extent to which your potential readers are involved in the conversation. What do they know? What do they need to know? What kind of evidence do you need to use to persuade readers?

FORMULATING ISSUE-BASED QUESTIONS

When you identify an issue, you need to understand it in the context of its situation. Ideally, the situation and the issue will be both recent and relevant, which will make your task of connecting to your audience that much easier when you write about the issue. For example, the student writer who was concerned about long-standing issues of homelessness and lack of educational opportunity connected to his readers by citing recent statistics and giving the problem of homelessness a face: "The children . . . went to school after less than three hours of sleep. They wore the same wrinkled clothes that they had worn the day before." If your issue does not immediately meet the criteria of timeliness and relevance, you will need to take that into consideration as you continue your reading and research. Ask yourself: What is on people's minds these days? What do they need to know about? Think about why the issue matters to you, and imagine why it might matter to others. By the time you write, you should be prepared to make the issue relevant for your readers.

In addition to understanding the situation and defining the issue that you feel is most timely and relevant, you can formulate an **issue-based question** to help you think through your subject. This question should be specific enough to guide your inquiry into what others have written. An issue-based question should help you

- clarify what you know about the issue and what you still need to learn.
- clearly guide your inquiry.
- organize your inquiry.
- develop an argument — a more complex task than simply collecting information by asking how, why, should, or the extent to which something is true or not.
- consider who your audience is.
- determine what resources you have so that you can ask a question that you have the resources to answer.

A good question develops out of an issue, some fundamental tension that you identify within a conversation. For Anna Quindlen in "No Place Like Home," the tension exists between what she sees as an unacceptable situation in New York and the city's ongoing failure to do something about it. Implicit is a question of how she can change people's attitudes, especially those of city leaders, who seem willing to "spend nearly $20,000 each year to have [homeless people] sleep on cots at night and wander the streets by day" rather than "make a one-time investment of $38,000 a unit" for housing. By identifying what is at issue, you should begin to understand for whom it is an issue — for whom you are answering the question. In turn, the answer to your question will help you craft your thesis.

In the following paragraphs, we trace the steps one of our students took to formulate an issue-based question on the broad topic of language diversity. Although we present the steps in sequence, be aware that they are guidelines only: The steps often overlap, and there is a good deal of room for rethinking and refining along the way.

■ Refine Your Topic

Generally speaking, a **topic** is the subject you want to write about. For example, homelessness, tests, and violence are all topics. So are urban homelessness, standardized tests, and video game violence. And so are homelessness in New York City, aptitude tests versus achievement tests, and mayhem in the video game Grand Theft Auto. As our list suggests, even a specific topic needs refining into an issue before it can be explored effectively in writing.

The topic our student wanted to focus on was language diversity, a subject her linguistics class had been discussing. She was fascinated by the extraordinary range of languages spoken in the United States, not just by immigrant groups but by native speakers whose dialects and varieties of English are considered nonstandard. She herself had relatives for whom English was not a first language. She began refining her topic by putting her thoughts into words:

> I want to describe the experience of being raised in a home where non-Standard English is spoken.
>
> I'd like to know the benefits and liabilities of growing up bilingual.
>
> I am curious to know what it's like to live in a community of nonnative speakers of English while trying to make a living in a country where the dominant language is English.

Although she had yet to identify an issue, her attempts to articulate what interested her about the topic were moving her toward the situation of people in the United States who don't speak Standard English or don't have English as their first language.

■ Explain Your Interest in the Topic

At this point, the student encountered E. D. Hirsch's *Cultural Literacy* in her reading, which had both a provocative and a clarifying effect on her thinking. She began to build on and extend Hirsch's ideas. Reacting to Hirsch's assumption that students should acquire the same base of knowledge and write in Standard Written English, her first, somewhat mischievous thought was, "I wonder what Hirsch would think about cultural literacy being taught in a bilingual classroom?" But then her thinking took another turn, and she began to contemplate the effect of Hirsch's cultural-literacy agenda on speakers whose English is not standard or for whom English is not a first language. She used a demographic fact that she had learned in her linguistics class in her explanation of her interest in the topic: "I'm curious about the consequences of limiting language diversity when the presence of ethnic minorities in our educational system is growing."

■ Identify an Issue

The more she thought about Hirsch's ideas, and the more she read about language diversity, the more concerned our student grew. It seemed to her that Hirsch's interest in producing students who all share the same base of knowledge and all write in Standard Written English was in tension with her sense that this kind of approach places a burden on people whose first language is not English. That tension clarified the issue for her. In identifying the issue, she wrote:

> Hirsch's book actually sets some priorities, most notably through his list of words and phrases that form the foundations of what it means to be "American." However, this list certainly overlooks several crucial influences in American culture. Most oversights generally come at the expense of the minority populations.

These two concerns — with inclusion and with exclusion — helped focus the student's inquiry.

■ Formulate Your Topic as a Question

To further define her inquiry, the student formulated her topic as a question that pointed toward an argument: "To what extent can E. D. Hirsch's notion of 'cultural literacy' coexist with our country's principles of democracy and inclusion?" Notice that her choice of the phrase *To what extent* implies that both goals do not go hand in hand. If she had asked, "Can common culture coexist with pluralism?" her phrasing would imply that a yes or no answer would suffice, possibly foreclosing avenues of inquiry and certainly ignoring the complexity of the issue.

Instead, despite her misgivings about the implications of Hirsch's agenda, the student suspended judgment, opening the way to genuine inquiry. She acknowledged the usefulness and value of sharing a common language and conceded that Hirsch's points were well taken. She wrote:

> Some sort of unification is necessary. Language, . . . on the most fundamental level of human interaction, demands some compromise and chosen guidelines. . . . How can we learn from one another if we cannot even say hello to each other?

Suspending judgment led her to recognize the complexity of the issue, and her willingness to examine the issue from different perspectives indicated the empathy that is a central component of developing a conversational argument.

■ Acknowledge Your Audience

This student's question ("To what extent can E. D. Hirsch's notion of 'cultural literacy' coexist with our country's principles of democracy and inclusion?") also acknowledged an audience. By invoking cultural literacy, she assumed an audience of readers who are familiar with Hirsch's ideas, probably including policymakers and educational administrators. In gesturing toward democracy, she cast her net very wide: Most Americans probably admire the "principles of democracy." But in specifying inclusion as a democratic principle, she wisely linked all Americans who believe in democratic principles, including the parents of schoolchildren, with all people who have reason to feel excluded by Hirsch's ideas, especially non-native speakers of English, among them immigrants from Mexico and speakers of African American Vernacular English. Thus this student was acknowledging an audience of policymakers, administrators, parents (both mainstream and marginalized), and those who knew about and perhaps supported cultural literacy.

Steps to Formulating an Issue-Based Question

1 **Refine your topic.** Examine your topic from different perspectives. For example, what are the causes of homelessness? What are its consequences?

2 **Explain your interest in the topic.** Explore the source of your interest in this topic and what you want to learn.

3 **Identify an issue.** Consider what is open to dispute.

4 **Formulate your topic as a question.** Use your question to focus your inquiry.

5 **Acknowledge your audience.** Reflect on what readers may know about the issue, why they may be interested, and what you would like to teach them.

A Practice Sequence: Formulating an Issue-Based Question

As you start developing your own issue-based question, it might be useful to practice a five-step process that begins with a topic, a word or phrase that describes the focus of your interests. Here, apply the process to the one-word topic homelessness.

1 Expand your topic into a phrase. "I am interested in the *consequences* of homelessness," "I want to *describe* what it means to be homeless," or "I am interested in discussing the *cause* of homelessness."

2 Explain your interest in this topic. "I am interested in the consequences of homelessness because it challenges democratic principles of fairness."

3 Identify an issue. "The persistence of homelessness contradicts my belief in social justice."

4 Formulate your topic as a question. "To what extent can we allow homelessness to persist in a democratic nation that prides itself on providing equal opportunity to all?"

5 Acknowledge your audience. "I am interested in the consequences of homelessness because I want people who believe in democracy to understand that we need to work harder to make sure that everyone has access to food, shelter, and employment."

The answer to the question you formulate in step 4 should lead to an assertion, your main claim, or *thesis*. For example, you could state your main claim this way: "Although homelessness persists as a widespread problem in our nation, we must develop policies that eliminate homelessness, ensuring that everyone has access to food, shelter, and employment. This is especially important in a democracy that embraces social justice and equality."

The thesis introduces a problem and makes an assertion that you will need to support: "We must develop policies that eliminate homelessness, ensuring that everyone has access to food, shelter, and employment." What is at issue? Not everyone would agree that policies must be implemented to solve the problem. In fact, many would argue that homelessness is an individual problem, that individuals must take responsibility for lifting themselves out of poverty, homelessness, and unemployment. Of course, you would need to read quite a bit to reach this final stage of formulating your thesis.

Try using the five-step process we describe above to formulate your own topic as a question, or try formulating the following topics as questions:

- Downloading music
- Violence in video games
- Gender and employment
- The popularity of a cultural phenomenon (a book, a film, a performer, an icon)
- Standardized tests
- Civil rights
- Town-gown relationships
- Media and representation
- Government and religion
- Affirmative action

9

Formulating and Developing a Claim

Academic writing explores complex issues that grow out of relevant, timely conversations in which something is at stake. An academic writer reads as a writer to understand the issues, situations, and questions that lead other writers to make claims. Readers expect academic writers to take a clear, specific, logical stand on an issue, and they evaluate how writers support their claims and anticipate counterarguments. The logical stand is the **thesis**, an assertion that academic writers make at the beginning of what they write and then support with evidence throughout their essay. The illustrations and examples that a writer includes must relate to and support the thesis. Thus, a thesis encompasses all of the information writers use to further their arguments; it is not simply a single assertion at the beginning of an essay.

One of our students aptly described the thesis using the metaphor of a shish kebab: The thesis penetrates every paragraph, holding the paragraphs together, just as a skewer penetrates and holds the ingredients of a shish kebab together. Moreover, the thesis serves as a signpost throughout an essay, reminding readers what the argument is and why the writer has included evidence — examples, illustrations, quotations — relevant to that argument.

An academic thesis

- makes an assertion that is clearly defined, focused, and supported.
- reflects an awareness of the conversation from which the writer has taken up the issue.
- is placed at the beginning of the essay.

Taken from Stuart Greene and April Lidinsky, *From Inquiry to Academic Writing: A Practical Guide*, pp. 83–99, 103–04 (Chapter 5, "From Formulating to Developing a Thesis").

- penetrates every paragraph like the skewer in a shish kebab.
- acknowledges points of view that differ from the writer's own, reflecting the complexity of the issue.
- demonstrates an awareness of the readers' assumptions and anticipates possible counterarguments.
- conveys a significant fresh perspective.

It is a myth is that writers first come up with a thesis and then write their essays. The reality is that writers use issue-based questions to read, learn, and develop a thesis throughout the process of writing. Through revising and discussing their ideas, writers hone their thesis, making sure that it threads through every paragraph of the final draft. The position writers ultimately take in writing — their thesis — comes at the end of the writing process, after not one draft but many.

WORKING VERSUS DEFINITIVE THESES

Writers are continually challenged by the need to establish their purpose and to make a clear and specific assertion of it. To reach that assertion, you must first engage in a prolonged process of inquiry, aided by a well-formulated question. The question serves as a tool for inquiry that will help you formulate your **working thesis**, your first attempt at an assertion of your position. A working thesis is valuable in the early stages of writing because it helps you read selectively, in the same way that your issue-based question guides your inquiry. Reading raises questions, helping you see what you know and need to know, and challenging you to read on. Never accept your working thesis as your final position. Instead, continue testing your assertion as you read and write, and modify your working thesis as necessary. A more definitive thesis will come once you are satisfied that you have examined the issue from multiple perspectives.

For example, one of our students wanted to study representations of femininity in the media. In particular, she focused on why the Barbie doll has become an icon of femininity despite what many cultural critics consider Barbie's "outrageous and ultimately unattainable physical characteristics." Our student's working thesis suggested she would develop an argument about the need for change:

> The harmful implications of ongoing exposure to these unattainable ideals, such as low self-esteem, eating disorders, unhealthy body image, and acceptance of violence, make urgent the need for change.

The student assumed that her research would lead her to argue that Barbie's unattainable proportions have a damaging effect on women's self-image and that something needs to be done about it. However, as she read scholarly research to support her tentative thesis, she realized that a more compelling project would be less Barbie-centric. Instead, she chose to examine the broader phenomenon of how the idea of femininity is created and reinforced by society. That is, her personal interest in Barbie was supplanted by her discoveries about cultural norms of beauty and the power they have to influence self-perception and behavior. In her final draft, this was her definitive thesis:

> Although evidence may be provided to argue that gender is an innate characteristic, I will show that it is actually the result of one's actions, which are then labeled *masculine* or *feminine* according to society's definitions of ideal gender. Furthermore, I will discuss the communication of such definitions through the media, specifically in music videos, on TV, and in magazines, and the harmful implications of being exposed to these ideals.

Instead of arguing for change, the student chose to show her readers how they were being manipulated, leaving it to them to decide what actions they might want to take.

DEVELOPING A WORKING THESIS: THREE MODELS

What are some ways to develop a working thesis? We suggest three models that may help you organize the information you gather in response to the question guiding your inquiry.

■ The Correcting-Misinterpretations Model

This model is used to correct writers whose arguments you believe have misconstrued one or more important aspects of an issue. The thesis typically takes the form of a factual claim. Consider this example and the words we have underlined:

> <u>Although scholars have addressed curriculum</u> to explain low achievement in schools, <u>they have failed to fully appreciate the impact of limited resources</u> to fund up-to-date textbooks, quality teachers, and computers. Therefore, reform in schools must focus on economic need as well as curriculum.

The clause beginning with "Although" lays out the assumption that many scholars make, that curriculum explains low educational achievement; the clause beginning with "they have failed" identifies the error those scholars have made by ignoring the economic reasons for low achievement in schools. Notice that the structure of the sentence reinforces the author's position. He offers the faulty assumption in a subordinate clause, reserving the main clause for his own position. The two clauses also reinforce that there are conflicting opinions here. One more thing: Although it is a common myth that a thesis must be phrased in a single sentence, this example shows that a thesis can be written in two (or more) sentences.

■ The Filling-the-Gap Model

The gap model points to what other writers may have overlooked or ignored in discussing a given issue. The gap model typically makes a claim of value. Consider this student's argument that discussions of cultural diversity in the United States are often framed in terms of black and white. Our underlining indicates the gap the writer has identified:

> If America is truly a "melting pot" of cultures, as it is often called, then <u>why is it that stories and events seem only to be in black and white? Why is it that when history courses are taught about the period of the civil rights movement, only the memoirs of African Americans are read</u>, like those of Melba Pattillo Beals and Ida Mae Holland? Where are <u>the works of Maxine Hong Kingston,</u> who tells the story of alienation and segregation in schools through the eyes of a Chinese child? African Americans were denied the right to vote, and many other citizenship rights; but Chinese Americans were denied even the opportunity to become citizens. I am not diminishing the issue of discrimination against African Americans, nor belittling the struggles they went through. <u>I simply want to call attention to discrimination against other minority groups and their often-overlooked struggles to achieve equality.</u>

In the student's thesis, the gap in people's knowledge stems from their limited understanding of history — that many minority groups were denied their rights.

A variation on the gap model also occurs when a writer suggests that although something might appear to be the case, a closer look reveals something different. For example: "Although it would *appear* that women and people of color have achieved equality in the workplace, their paychecks suggest that this is not true." One of our students examined two poems by the same author that appeared to contradict each other. She noticed a gap others had not seen:

> In both "The Albatross" and "Beauty," Charles Baudelaire chooses to explore the plight of the poet. Interestingly, despite their common author, the two poems' portrayals of the poet's struggles appear contradictory. "The Albatross" seems to give a somewhat sympathetic glimpse into the exile of the

poet — the "winged voyager" so awkward in the ordinary world. "Beauty" takes what appears to be a less forgiving stance: The poet here is docile, simply a mirror. Although both pieces depict the poet's struggles, a closer examination demonstrates how the portrayals differ.

In stating her thesis, the student indicates that although readers might expect Baudelaire's images of poets to be similar, a closer examination of his words would prove them wrong.

■ The Modifying-What-Others-Have-Said Model

The modification model of thesis writing is premised on the possibility of mutual understanding. For example, in proposing a change in policy, one student asserts:

Although scholars have claimed that the only sure way to reverse the cycle of homelessness in America is to provide an adequate education, we need to build on this work, providing school-to-work programs that ensure graduates have access to employment.

Here the writer seeks to modify other writers' claims, suggesting that education alone does not solve the problem of homelessness; the challenge he sets for himself is to understand the complexity of the problem by building on and extending the ideas of others. In effect, he is in a constructive conversation with those whose work he wants to build on, helping readers see that he shares common ground with the other writers and hopes to find a mutually acceptable solution to the agreed-on problem.

Steps to Formulating a Working Thesis: Three Models

1 **Misinterpretations model:** "Although many scholars have argued about X and Y, a careful examination suggests Z."

2 **Gap model:** "Although scholars have noted X and Y, they have missed the importance of Z."

3 **Modification model:** "Although I agree with the X and Y ideas of other writers, it is important to extend/refine/limit their ideas with Z."

A Practice Sequence: Identifying Types of Theses

Below is a series of working theses. Read each one and then identify the model — misinterpretations, gap, or modification — it represents.

1 A number of studies indicate that violence on television has a detrimental effect on adolescent behavior. However, few researchers have examined key environmental factors like peer pressure, music, and home life. In fact, I would argue that many researchers have oversimplified the problem.

2 Although research indicates that an increasing number of African American and Hispanic students are dropping out of high school, researchers have failed to fully grasp the reasons why this has occurred.

3 I want to argue that studies supporting single-sex education are relatively sound. However, we don't really know the long-term effects of single-sex education, particularly on young women's career paths.

4 Although recent studies of voting patterns in the United States indicate that young people between the ages of 18 and 24 are apathetic, I want to suggest that not all of the reasons these studies provide are valid.

5 Indeed, it's not surprising that students are majoring in fields that will enable them to get a job after graduation. But students may not be as pragmatic as we think. Many students choose majors because they feel that learning is an important end in itself.

6 Although good teachers are essential to learning, we cannot ignore the roles that race and class play in students' access to a quality education.

7 It is clear that cities need to clean up the dilapidated housing projects that were built over half a century ago; but few, if any, studies have examined the effects of doing so on the life chances of those people who are being displaced.

8 In addition to its efforts to advance the cause of social justice in the new global economy, the university must make a commitment to ending poverty on the edge of campus.

9 Although the writer offers evidence to explain the sources of illiteracy in America, he overstates his case when he ignores other factors, among them history, culture, and economic well-being. Therefore, I will argue that we place the discussion in a broader context.

10 More and more policymakers argue that English should be the national language in the United States. Although I agree that English is important, we should not limit people's right to maintain their own linguistic and cultural identity.

ESTABLISHING A CONTEXT FOR A THESIS

In addition to defining the purpose and focus of an essay, a thesis must set up a **context** for the writer's claim. The process of establishing a background for understanding an issue typically involves four steps:

1. Establish that the topic of conversation, the issue, is current and relevant — that it is on people's minds or should be.

2. Briefly summarize what others have said to show that you are familiar with the topic or issue.

3. Explain what you see as the problem — a misinterpretation, gap, or a modification that needs to be made in how others have addressed the topic or issue — perhaps by raising the questions you believe need to be answered.

4. State your thesis, suggesting that your view on the issue may present readers with something new to think about as it builds on and extends what others have argued.

You need not follow these steps in this order as long as your readers come away from the first part of your essay knowing why you are discussing a given issue and what your argument is.

We trace these four steps below in our analysis of the opening paragraphs of one of our student's essays. She was writing in response to what many call the English-only movement. Specifically, she responds to the effects of Proposition 227 in California, a piece of legislation that prevents non-English-speaking students from using their first language in school. Our discussion of how she provides a context for her thesis follows the excerpt.

Nuestra Clase 1

Jenny Eck
Professor Walters
English 200
March 18, 20--

Nuestra Clase: Making the Classroom a Welcoming Place
for English Language Learners

    With the Latino population growing exponentially and Spanish   *1*
quickly becoming one of the most widely spoken languages in the
United States, the question arises of how the American educational
system is meeting the needs of a growing Hispanic population. What
does our educational system do to address the needs of students
whose primary language is not English?

Nuestra Clase 2

2

In 1998, the state of California passed Proposition 227, which prohibited bilingual instruction in public schools. Ron Unz, a former Republican gubernatorial candidate and software developer, launched the initiative under the name "English for the Children." Unz argued that the initiative would help Latinos and other recent immigrants free themselves from bilingual education, which he avowed would hinder the ability of immigrants to assimilate into American culture (Stritikus, 2002). Supporters of Proposition 227 assert that bilingual education has failed English language learners (ELLs) because it does not adequately equip them with the English language skills essential to success in school. Eradicating bilingual education, they believe, will help students learn English more effectively and consequently achieve more in their educational careers.

3

Since its passage, Proposition 227 has been hotly debated. Many researchers claim that its strictures have stunted the education of Spanish-speaking students (Halcón, 2001; Stritikus, 2002). Many studies have indicated the harmful effects of what Gutiérrez and her colleagues describe as "backlash pedagogy" (Gutiérrez, Asato, Santos & Gotanda, 2002), which prohibits the use of students' complete linguistic, sociocultural, and academic repertoire. In essence, they claim that Proposition 227's backlash pedagogy, in attempting to emphasize "colorblindness" in education, has instead eradicated differences that are crucial to students' efforts to become educated. They argue that by devaluing these differences, the educational system devalues the very students it is attempting to help.

4

A sociocultural theory of learning, with its emphasis on the significant impact that factors such as language, culture, family, and community have on a student's potential for educational success (Halcón, 2001), calls attention to growing concerns that schools may not be meeting the needs of ELLs. Russian psychologist Lev Vygotsky (1978) introduced this viewpoint to educators when he proposed that development and learning are firmly embedded in and influenced by society and culture. With Vygotsky's theory in mind, other researchers have embraced the idea that the failure of minority students is more often than not a systematic failure, rather than an individual failure (Trueba, 1989). Sociocultural theory posits that learning needs to be understood not only in the broader context of the sociocultural lives

Nuestra Clase 3

of students, teachers, and schools, but also in their sociopolitical lives. A sociocultural context takes a student's culture, race, religion, language, family, community, and other similar factors into consideration, while a sociopolitical context takes into account the inherent ideologies and prejudices that exist in society today. In order for teaching to be effective, both sociocultural and sociopolitical factors must be identified and addressed.

Many educators seem to dismiss sociocultural and sociopolitical factors, perhaps not realizing that by ignoring these factors, they are inadvertently privileging the students in their classrooms for whom English is a first language (Larson, 2003). Such a dismissive attitude does not reckon with other studies that have shown how important it is for English language learners to explore and express their bilingual/bicultural identities (McCarthey, García, López-Velásquez, Lin & Guo, 2004). Some of these other studies have even proposed that schooling acts as a "subtractive process" for minority students, not only denying them opportunities to express their identities, but also divesting them of important social and cultural resources, which ultimately leaves them vulnerable to academic failure (Valenzuela, 1999). These other studies convincingly show that sociocultural factors are essential to the educational success of English language learners. Therefore, although many educators believe they know the best way to teach these students, I will argue that the educational system, by not taking into account factors that sociocultural theory emphasizes, has mostly failed to create classrooms that embrace cultural differences, and by so doing has failed to create optimal conditions for teaching and learning.

5

Nuestra Clase 9

References

Gutiérrez, K., Asato, J., Santos, M., & Gotanda, N. (2002). Backlash pedagogy: Language and culture and the politics of reform. *The review of education, pedagogy, and cultural studies, 24*(4), 335–351.

Nuestra Clase 10

Halcón, J. J. (2001). Mainstream ideology and literacy instructions for Spanish-speaking children. In M. Reyes & J. J. Halcón (Eds.), *The best for our children: Critical perspectives on literacy for Latino students* (pp. 65–77). New York, NY: Teacher's College Press.

Larson, J. (2003). Negotiating race in classroom research: Tensions and possibilities. In S. Greene & D. Abt-Perkins (Eds.), *Making race visible: Literacy research for cultural understanding* (pp. 89–106). New York, NY: Teacher's College Press.

McCarthey, S. J., López-Velásquez, A. M., García, G. E., Lin, S., & Guo, Y. (2004). Understanding writing contexts for English language learners. *Research in the teaching of English, 38*(4), 351–394.

Stritikus, T. (2002). *Immigrant children and the politics of English-only: Views from the classroom.* New York, NY: LFB Scholarly Publishing LLC.

Trueba, H. T. (1989). *Raising silent voices: Educating the linguistic minorities for the 21st century.* Cambridge, MA: Newbury House.

Valenzuela, A. (1999). *Subtractive schooling: U.S. Mexican youth and the politics of caring.* Albany, NY: State University of New York Press.

Vygotsky, L. S. (1978). *Thought and language.* Cambridge, MA: MIT Press.

■ Establish That the Issue Is Current and Relevant

Ideally, you should convey to readers that the issue you are discussing is both current (what's on people's minds) and relevant (of sufficient importance to have generated some discussion and written conversation). In the first sentence, Eck tells readers of a trend she feels they need to be aware of, the dramatic growth of the Hispanic population in the United States. Her issue is what the schools are doing to meet the needs of a growing population of students "whose primary language is not English." At the beginning of the third paragraph, she signals the relevance of the issue when she observes that the passage of Proposition 227 has been "hotly debated."

■ Briefly Present What Others Have Said

It is important to introduce who has said what in the conversation you are entering. After all, you are interrupting that conversation to make your contribution, and those who are already in that conversation expect you to have done your homework and acknowledge those who have already made important contributions. (For more on presenting the ideas of others, see Chapter 10.)

In the second paragraph, Eck sets the stage for her review with a brief history of Proposition 227. Here she describes what was at issue for supporters of the law and what they hoped the law would accomplish. Starting with paragraph 3, Eck acknowledges the researchers who have participated in the debate surrounding Proposition 227 and reviews a number of studies that challenge the premises on which Proposition 227 rested. Notice that she introduces the frame of sociocultural theory to help her readers see that denying students the use of their native language in the classroom is a problem.

By pointing out the ways that researchers on language learning challenge the assumptions underlying the English-only movement, Eck is doing more than listing sources. She is establishing that a problem, or issue, exists. Moreover, her review gives readers intellectual touchstones, the scholars who need to be cited in any academic conversation about bilingual education. A review is not a catchall for anyone writing on a topic; instead, it should reflect a writer's selection of the most relevant participants in the conversation. Eck's choice of sources, and how she presents them, conveys that she is knowledgeable about her subject. (Of course, it is her readers' responsibility to read further to determine whether she has reviewed the most relevant work and has presented the ideas of others accurately. If she has, readers will trust her whether or not they end up agreeing with her on the issue.)

■ Explain What You See as the Problem

If a review indicates a problem, as Eck's review does, the problem can often be couched in terms of the models we discussed earlier: misinterpretations, gap, or modification. In paragraph 5, Eck identifies what she concludes is a misunderstanding of how students learn a new language. She suggests that the misunderstanding stems from a gap in knowledge (notice our underlining):

> Many educators seem to dismiss sociocultural and sociopolitical factors, perhaps not realizing that by ignoring these factors, they are inadvertently privileging the students in their classrooms for whom English is a first language (Larson, 2003). Such a dismissive attitude does not reckon with other studies that have shown how important it is for English language learners to explore and express their bilingual/bicultural identities (McCarthey, García, López-Velásquez, Lin & Guo, 2004). Some of these other studies have even proposed that schooling acts as a "subtractive process" for minority students, not only denying them opportunities to express their identities, but also divesting them of important social and

cultural resources, which ultimately leaves them vulnerable to academic failure (Valenzuela, 1999).

While Eck concedes that efforts to understand the problems of language learning have been extensive and multifaceted, her review of the research culminates with her assertion that ignoring students' language practices could have devastating results — that educators, by denying students "important social and cultural resources," may be leaving those students "vulnerable to academic failure."

■ State Your Thesis

An effective thesis statement helps readers see the reasoning behind the author's claim; it also signals what readers should look for in the remainder of the essay. Eck closes paragraph 5 with a statement that speaks to both the purpose and the substance of her writing:

> Therefore, although many educators believe they know the best way to teach [ELL] students, I will argue that the educational system, by not taking into account factors that sociocultural theory emphasizes, has mostly failed to create classrooms that embrace cultural differences, and by so doing has failed to create optimal conditions for teaching and learning.

In your own writing, you can make use of the strategies that Eck uses in her essay. Words like *although* and *though* can set up problem statements: "Although [though] some people think that nonnative speakers of English can best learn English by not using their first language, the issue is more complex than most people realize." Words like *but, however,* and *yet* can serve the same purpose: "One might argue that nonnative speakers of English can best learn English by not using their first language; but [however, yet] the issue is more complex than most people realize."

Steps to Establishing a Context for a Thesis

1 **Establish that the issue is current and relevant.** Point out the extent to which others have recognized the problem, issue, or question that you are writing about.

2 **Briefly review what others have said.** Explain how others have addressed the problem, issue, or question you are focusing on.

3 **Explain what you see as the problem.** Identify what is open to dispute.

4 **State your thesis.** Help readers see your purpose and how you intend to achieve it — by correcting a misconception, filling a gap, or modifying a claim others have accepted.

▪ Analyze the Context of a Thesis

In "Protean Shapes in Literacy Events," cultural anthropologist and linguist Shirley Brice Heath argues that communities of practice shape the ways in which people use reading and writing. Heath points out the problem of holding up a standard of literacy from one community to measure the extent to which another community is or is not literate. Her essay, originally published in 1982, is addressed to a community of scholars who study literacy. As you read the excerpt that follows, you will likely find yourself puzzled by Heath's vocabulary and possibly even excluded from the conversation at times. Our point in reprinting this excerpt is not to initiate you into Heath's academic community but to show, through our annotations, how Heath has applied the strategies we have been discussing in this chapter. As you read, feel free to make your own annotations, and then try to answer the questions — which may involve some careful rereading — that we pose after the excerpt. In particular, watch for signpost words (*but, few, little, however*) that signal the ideas the writer is challenging.

SHIRLEY BRICE HEATH

From Protean Shapes in Literacy Events: Ever-Shifting Oral and Literate Traditions

The first sentence establishes that the issue that interests Heath has been discussed for more than a few years, helping us see the continuing relevance of the area of study.

From the sentence that begins "Much of this research" to the end of the paragraph, Heath reviews some of the relevant literature and points to a problem: that previous work has seen literate and oral cultures as somehow opposed to one another. The author gives us more than a list of sources.

Since the mid-1970s, anthropologists, linguists, historians, and psychologists have turned with new tools of analysis to the study of oral and literate societies. They have used discourse analysis, econometrics, theories of schemata and frames, and proposals of developmental performance to consider the possible links between oral and written language, and between literacy and its individual and societal consequences. Much of this research is predicated on a dichotomous view of oral and literate traditions, usually attributed to researchers active in the 1960s. Repeatedly, Goody and Watt (1963), Ong (1967), Goody (1968), and Havelock (1963) are cited as having suggested a dichotomous view of oral and literate societies and as having asserted certain cognitive, social, and linguistic effects of literacy on both the society and the individual. Survey research tracing the invention and diffusion of writing systems across numerous societies (Kroeber, 1948) and positing the effects of the spread of literacy on social and individual

1

memory (Goody and Watt, 1963; Havelock, 1963, 1976) is cited as supporting a contrastive view of oral and literate social groups. Research which examined oral performance in particular groups is said to support the notion that as members of a society increasingly participate in literacy, they lose habits associated with the oral tradition (Lord, 1965).

In short, existing scholarship makes it easy to interpret a picture which depicts societies existing along a continuum of development from an oral tradition to a literate one, with some societies having a restricted literacy, and others having reached a full development of literacy (Goody, 1968:11). One also finds in this research specific characterizations of oral and written language associated with these traditions.

In the first sentence in this paragraph, Heath suggests that a close reading would raise some important unanswered questions about the relationship between orality and literacy.

But a close reading of these scholars, especially Goody (1968) and Goody and Watt (1963), leaves some room for questioning such a picture of consistent and universal processes or products—individual or societal—of literacy. Goody pointed out that in any traditional society, factors such as secrecy, religious ideology, limited social mobility, lack of access to writing materials and alphabetic scripts could lead to restricted literacy. Furthermore, Goody warned that the advent of a writing system did not amount to technological determinism or to sufficient cause of certain changes in either the individual or the society. Goody went on to propose exploring the concrete context of written communication (1968:4) to determine how the potentialities of literacy developed in traditional societies. He brought together a collection of essays based on the ethnography of literacy in traditional societies to illustrate the wide variety of ways in which *traditional,* i.e., pre-industrial but not necessarily pre-literate, societies played out their uses of oral and literate traditions.

The previous paragraph sets up the problem and the gap that Heath believes her research — indicated in the first two sentences of this paragraph — should address.

Few researchers in the 1970s have, however, heeded Goody's warning about the possible wide-ranging effects of societal and cultural factors on literacy and its uses. In particular, little attention has been given in *modern* complex industrial societies to the social and cultural correlates of literacy or to the work experiences adults have which may affect the

2

3

4

maintenance and retention of literacy skills acquired in formal schooling. The public media today give much attention to the decline of literacy skills as measured in school settings and the failure of students to acquire certain levels of literacy. However, the media pay little attention to occasions for literacy retention—to the actual uses of literacy in work settings, daily interactions in religious, economic, and legal institutions, and family habits of socializing the young into uses of literacy. In the clamor over the need to increase the teaching of basic skills, there is much emphasis on the positive effects extensive and critical reading can have on improving oral language. Yet there are scarcely any data comparing the forms and functions of oral language with those of written language produced and used by members of social groups within a complex society. One of the most appropriate sources of data for informing discussions of these issues is that which Goody proposed for traditional societies: the concrete context of written communication. Where, when, how, for whom, and with what results are individuals in different social groups of today's highly industrialized society using reading and writing skills? How have the potentialities of the literacy skills learned in school developed in the lives of today's adults? Does modern society contain certain conditions which restrict literacy just as some traditional societies do? If so, what are these factors, and are groups with restricted literacy denied benefits widely attributed to full literacy, such as upward socioeconomic mobility, the development of logical reasoning, and access to the information necessary to make well-informed political judgments?

The underlined sentence indicates the gap: The media focus on one set of concerns when they should be attending to a very different set of issues.

Heath elaborates on what she sees as a troubling gap between what educators know and what they need to know.

In the last four sentences of the excerpt, Heath raises the questions that she wants readers to consider and that guide her own research.

For Analysis and Discussion

1. What specific places can you point to in the selection that illustrate what is at issue for Heath?
2. How does Heath use her review to set up her argument?
3. What specific words and phrases does Heath use to establish what she sees as the problem? Is she correcting misinterpretations, filling a gap, or modifying what others have said?

4. What would you say is Heath's thesis? What specifics can you point to in the text to support your answer?

5. What would you say are the arguments Heath wants you to avoid? Again, what specific details can you point to in the text to support your answer?

A Practice Sequence: Building a Thesis

We would like you to practice some of the strategies we have covered in this chapter. If you have already started working on an essay, exercises 1 through 4 present an opportunity to take stock of your progress, a chance to sort through what you've discovered, identify what you still need to discover, and move toward refining your thesis. Jot down your answer to each of the questions below and make lists of what you know and what you need to learn.

1 Have you established that your issue is current and relevant, that it is or should be on people's minds? What information would you need to do so?

2 Can you summarize briefly what others have said in the past to show that you are familiar with how others have addressed the issue? List some of the key texts you have read and the key points they make.

3 Have you identified any misunderstandings or gaps in how others have addressed the issue? Describe them. Do you have any ideas or information that would address these misunderstandings or help fill these gaps? Where might you find the information you need? Can you think of any sources you should reread to learn more? (For example, have you looked at the works cited or bibliographies in the texts you've already read?)

4 At this point, what is your take on the issue? Try drafting a working thesis statement that will present readers with something new to think about, building on and extending what others have argued. In drafting your thesis statement, try out the three models discussed in this chapter and see if one is an especially good fit:

- *Misinterpretations model*: "Although many scholars have argued about X and Y, a careful examination suggests Z."
- *Gap model*: "Although scholars have noted X and Y, they have missed the importance of Z."
- *Modification model*: "Although I agree with X and Y ideas of other writers, it is important to extend/refine/limit their ideas with Z."

5 If you haven't chosen a topic yet, try a group exercise. Sit down with a few of your classmates and choose one of the following topics to brainstorm about as a group. Choose a topic that every-one in the group finds interesting, and work through exercises 1 through 4 in this practice sequence. Here are some suggestions:

- The moral obligation to vote
- The causes or consequences of poverty
- The limits of academic freedom
- Equity in education
- The popularity of _____
- The causes or consequences of teen violence
- Gender stereotypes in the media
- Linguistic diversity
- On the uses of a liberal education
- Journalism and truth

We cannot overstate the role your working thesis statement plays in helping you organize your evidence, illustrations, and quotations from other texts. Remember that the writing you do should begin with reading, identifying issues, formulating questions, and reading again before you try to state your thesis. Accept that you may have to write a few drafts of your essay before you actually decide on your thesis. An academic thesis state-ment is complex: It must help readers understand what is at issue, what the writer thinks is true, and what will follow in the essay itself. In this way, the thesis statement is as important for you as a writer as it is for your readers. Readers need signposts to grasp the meaning of what you write, to follow your ideas through every paragraph, and to understand how every paragraph contributes to your argument. The ability to write a good thesis statement is essential to persuading your readers to see your issue through fresh eyes — through your eyes as a writer.

10

Summarizing and Documenting Sources

When you start to use sources to build your argument, there are certain strategies for working with the words and ideas of others that you will need to learn. Often you can quote the words of an author directly; but just as often you will restate and condense the arguments of others (paraphrasing and summarizing) or make comparisons to the ideas of others in the process of developing your own argument (synthesizing). We walk you through these more challenging strategies in this chapter. We also briefly discuss plagiarism and ways to avoid it. Finally, we provide some guidelines for quoting, citing, and documenting sources in your writing.

SUMMARIES, PARAPHRASES, AND QUOTATIONS

In contrast to quotations, which involve using another writer's exact words, paraphrases and summaries are both restatements of another writer's ideas in your own words. The key difference: A paraphrase is usually about the same length as the original passage; a summary generally condenses a significantly longer text, conveying the argument not only of a few sentences, but also of entire paragraphs, essays, or books. In your own writing, you might paraphrase a few sentences or even a few paragraphs, but you certainly would not paraphrase a whole essay (much less a whole book). In constructing your arguments, however, you will often have to summarize the main points of the lengthy texts with which you are in conversation.

Taken from Stuart Greene and April Lidinsky, *From Inquiry to Academic Writing: A Practical Guide*, pp. 125–57, 165–66 (Chapter 7, "From Summarizing to Documenting Sources").

Both paraphrasing and summarizing are means to inquiry. That is, the act of recasting someone else's words or ideas into your own language, to suit your argument and reach your readers, forces you to think critically: What does this passage really mean? What is most important about it for my argument? How can I best present it to my readers? It requires making choices, not least of which is the best way to present the information — through paraphrase, summary, or direct quotation. In general, the following rules apply:

- *Paraphrase* when all the information in the passage is important, but the language may be difficult for your readers to understand.

- *Summarize* when you need to present only the key ideas of a passage (or essay or book) to advance your argument.

- *Quote* when the passage is so effective — so clear, so concise, so authoritative, so memorable — that you would find it difficult to improve on.

WRITING A PARAPHRASE

A **paraphrase** is a restatement of all the information in a passage in your own words, using your own sentence structure and composed with your own audience in mind to advance your argument. When you paraphrase a passage, start by identifying key words and phrases and substituting synonyms for them. A dictionary or thesaurus can help, but you may also have to reread what led up to the passage to remind yourself of the context. For example, did the writer define terms earlier that he or she uses in the passage and now expects you to know? Continue by experimenting with word order and sentence structure, combining and recombining phrases to convey what the writer says without replicating his or her style, in the best sequence for your readers. As you shuffle words and phrases, you should begin arriving at a much better understanding of what the writer is saying. By thinking critically, then, you are clarifying the passage for yourself as much as for your readers.

Let's look at a paraphrase of a passage from science fiction writer and scholar James Gunn's essay "Harry Potter as Schooldays Novel"*:

ORIGINAL PASSAGE

The situation and portrayal of Harry as an ordinary child with an extraordinary talent make him interesting. He elicits our sympathy at every turn. He plays a Cinderella-like role as the abused child of mean-spirited foster parents who favor other, less-worthy children, and also fits another fantasy role, that

---

*Gunn's essay appears in *Mapping the World of Harry Potter: An Unauthorized Exploration of the Bestselling Fantasy Series of All Time,* edited by Mercedes Lackey (Dallas: BenBella, 2006), p. 145.

of changeling. Millions of children have nursed the notion that they cannot be the offspring of such unremarkable parents; in the Harry Potter books, the metaphor is often literal truth.

PARAPHRASE

According to James Gunn, the circumstances and depiction of Harry Potter as a normal boy with special abilities captivate us by playing on our empathy. Gunn observes that, like Cinderella, Harry is scorned by his guardians, who treat him far worse than they treat his less-admirable peers. And like another fairy-tale figure, the changeling, Harry embodies the fantasies of children who refuse to believe that they were born of their undistinguished parents (146).

In this paraphrase, synonyms have replaced main words (*circumstances and depiction* for "situation and portrayal," *guardians* for "foster parents"), and the structure of the original sentences has been rearranged. But the paraphrase is about the same length as the original and says essentially the same things as Gunn's original.

Now, compare the paraphrase with this summary:

SUMMARY

James Gunn observes that Harry Potter's character is compelling because readers empathize with Harry's fairy tale–like plight as an orphan whose gifts are ignored by his foster parents (144–45).

The summary condenses the passage, conveying Gunn's main point without restating the details. Notice how both the paraphrase and the summary indicate that the ideas are James Gunn's, not the writer's — "According to James Gunn," "James Gunn observes" — and signal, with page references, where Gunn's ideas end. *It is essential that you acknowledge your sources*, a subject we come back to in our discussion of plagiarism on page 197. The point we want to make here is that borrowing from the work of others is not always intentional. Many students stumble into plagiarism, especially when they are attempting to paraphrase. Remember that it's not enough to change the words in a paraphrase; you also must change the structure of the sentences. The only sure way to protect yourself is to cite your source.

You may be wondering: If paraphrasing is so tricky, why bother? What does it add? I can see how the summary of Gunn's paragraph presents information more concisely and efficiently than the original, but the paraphrase doesn't seem to be all that different from the source, and doesn't seem to add anything to it. Why not simply quote the original or summarize it? Good questions. The answer is that you paraphrase when the ideas in a passage are important but are conveyed in language your readers may have difficulty understanding. When academics write for their peers, they draw on the specialized vocabulary of their disciplines to make their arguments. By paraphrasing, you may be helping your readers, providing a translation of sorts for those who do not speak the language.

Consider this paragraph by George Lipsitz from his academic book *Time Passages: Collective Memory and American Popular Culture*, 1990), and compare the paraphrase that follows it:

ORIGINAL PASSAGE

The transformations in behavior and collective memory fueled by the contradictions of the nineteenth century have passed through three major stages in the United States. The first involved the establishment and codification of commercialized leisure from the invention of the telegraph to the 1890s. The second involved the transition from Victorian to consumer-hedonist values between 1890 and 1945. The third and most important stage, from World War II to the present, involved extraordinary expansion in both the distribution of consumer purchasing power and in both the reach and scope of electronic mass media. The dislocations of urban renewal, suburbanization, and deindustrialization accelerated the demise of tradition in America, while the worldwide pace of change undermined stability elsewhere. The period from World War II to the present marks the final triumph of commercialized leisure, and with it an augmented crisis over the loss of connection to the past.

PARAPHRASE

Historian George Lipsitz argues that Americans' sense of the past is rooted in cultural changes dating from the 1800s, and has evolved through three stages. In the first stage, technological innovations of the nineteenth century gave rise to widespread commercial entertainment. In the second stage, dating from the 1890s to about 1945, attitudes toward the consumption of goods and services changed. Since 1945, in the third stage, increased consumer spending and the growth of the mass media have led to a crisis in which Americans find themselves cut off from their traditions and the memories that give meaning to them (12).

Notice that the paraphrase is not a word-for-word translation of the original. Instead, the writer has made choices that resulted in a slightly briefer and more accessible restatement of Lipsitz's thinking. (Although this paraphrase is shorter than the original passage, a paraphrase can also be a little longer than the original if extra words are needed to help readers understand the original.) Notice too that several specialized terms and phrases from the original passage — "the codification of commercialized leisure," "the transition from Victorian to consumer-hedonist values," "the dislocations of urban renewal, suburbanization, and deindustrialization" — have disappeared. The writer not only looked up these terms and phrases in the dictionary, but also reread the several pages that preceded the original passage to understand what Lipsitz meant by them. The paraphrase is not an improvement on the original passage — in fact, historians would probably prefer what Lipsitz wrote — but it may help readers who do not share Lipsitz's expertise understand his point without distorting his argument.

Now compare this summary to the paraphrase:

SUMMARY

Historian George Lipsitz argues that technological, social, and economic changes dating from the nineteenth century have culminated in what he calls a "crisis over the loss of connection to the past," in which Americans find themselves cut off from the memories of their traditions (12).

Which is better, the paraphrase or the summary? Neither is better or worse in and of itself. Their correctness and appropriateness depend on how the restatements are used in a given argument. That is, the decision to paraphrase or summarize depends entirely on the information you need to convey. Would the details in the paraphrase strengthen your argument? Or is a summary sufficient? In this case, if you plan to focus your argument on the causes of America's loss of cultural memory (the rise of commercial entertainment, changes in spending habits, globalization), then a paraphrase might be more helpful. But if you plan to define *loss of cultural memory,* then a summary may provide enough context for the next stage of your argument.

Steps to Writing a Paraphrase

1 **Decide whether to paraphrase.** If your readers don't need all the information in the passage, consider summarizing it or presenting the key points as part of a summary of a longer passage. If a passage is clear, concise, and memorable as originally written, consider quoting instead of paraphrasing. Otherwise, and especially if the original was written for an academic audience, you may want to paraphrase the original to make its substance more accessible to your readers.

2 **Understand the passage.** Start by identifying key words, phrases, and ideas. If necessary, reread the pages leading up to the passage, to place it in context.

3 **Draft your paraphrase.** Replace key words and phrases with synonyms and alternative phrases (possibly gleaned from the context provided by the surrounding text). Experiment with word order and sentence structure until the paraphrase captures your understanding of the passage, in your own language, for your readers.

4 **Acknowledge your source.** That's the only sure way to protect yourself from a charge of plagiarism.

A Practice Sequence: Paraphrasing

1 In one of the sources you've located in your research, find a sentence of some length and complexity, and paraphrase it. Share the original and your paraphrase of it with a classmate, and discuss the effectiveness of your restatement. Is the meaning clear to your reader? Is the paraphrase written in your own language, using your own sentence structure?

2 Repeat the activity using a short paragraph from the same source. You and your classmate may want to attempt to paraphrase the same paragraph and then compare results. What differences do you detect?

WRITING A SUMMARY

As you have seen, a **summary** condenses a body of information, presenting the key ideas and acknowledging their source. Summarizing is not an active way to make an argument, but summaries do provide a common ground of information for readers so that you can make your argument more effectively. You can summarize a paragraph, several paragraphs, an essay, a chapter in a book, or even an entire book, depending on the use you plan to make of the information in your argument.

We suggest a method of summarizing that involves (1) describing the author's key claims, (2) selecting examples to illustrate the author's argument, (3) presenting the gist of the author's argument, and (4) contextualizing what you summarize. We demonstrate these steps following the excerpt from "Debating the Civil Rights Movement: The View from the Nation," by Steven F. Lawson. Read Lawson's essay, and then follow along as we write a summary of it.

ABOUT THE READING

A professor of history at Rutgers University, Steven F. Lawson's main area of research is the history of the civil rights movement, especially the expansion of black voting rights and black politics. His major publications include *Black Ballots: Voting Rights in the South, 1944–1969* (1976); *In Pursuit of Power: Southern Blacks and Electoral Politics, 1965–1982* (1985); and *Running for Freedom: Civil Rights and Black Politics in America Since 1941* (1990). The following excerpt is from *Debating the Civil Rights Movement: 1945–1968,* where it appeared with Charles Payne's essay (see p. 186) in 1998.

STEVEN F. LAWSON

From Debating the Civil Rights Movement: The View from the Nation

The federal government played an indispensable role in shaping the   *1*
fortunes of the civil rights revolution. It is impossible to understand
how Blacks achieved first-class citizenship rights in the South without
concentrating on what national leaders in Washington, D.C., did to
influence the course of events leading to the extension of racial equality.
Powerful presidents, congressional lawmakers, and members of the
Supreme Court provided the legal instruments to challenge racial segregation and disfranchisement. Without their crucial support, the struggle
against white supremacy in the South still would have taken place but
would have lacked the power and authority to defeat state governments
intent on keeping Blacks in subservient positions.

Along with national officials, the fate of the civil rights movement   *2*
depended on the presence of national organizations. Groups such as the
National Association for the Advancement of Colored People (NAACP),
founded in 1901, drew on financial resources and legal talent from all
over the country to press the case for equal rights in Congress and the
courts. In similar fashion, Dr. Martin Luther King, Jr., and the Southern
Christian Leadership Conference (SCLC), established in the mid-1950s,
focused their attention on spotlighting white southern racism before a
national audience to mobilize support for their side. Even if white Americans outside the South had wanted to ignore the plight of southern
Blacks, NAACP lawyers and lobbyists, SCLC protesters, and their like-
minded allies made that choice impossible. They could do what Black
residents of local communities could not do alone: turn the civil rights
struggle into a national cause for concern and prod the federal government into throwing its considerable power to overturn the entrenched
system of white domination that had prevailed for centuries in the South.

Historical accounts that center on the national state in Washington   *3*
and the operations of national organizations take on a particular narrative. The story begins with World War II, which stimulated Black protests
against racism, and winds its way through the presidencies of Franklin D.
Roosevelt, Harry S. Truman, Dwight D. Eisenhower, John F. Kennedy,
and Lyndon B. Johnson. This period witnessed significant presidential
executive orders promulgating desegregation in the military and in
housing, five pieces of pioneering civil rights legislation, and landmark
Supreme Court rulings toppling segregationist practices and extending the right to vote. The familiar geographical signposts of civil rights
demonstrations — Montgomery, Birmingham, Selma, Albany, Little Rock
— derive their greatest importance as places that molded the critical
national debate on ending racial discrimination.

Overall, a nuanced account of the Black freedom struggle requires an *4* interconnected approach. A balanced portrayal acknowledges that Black activists had important internal resources at their disposal, derived from religious, economic, educational, and civic institutions, with which to make their demands. But it does not belittle African American creativity and determination to conclude that given existing power relationships heavily favoring whites, southern Blacks could not possibly eliminate racial inequality without outside federal assistance. Furthermore, Washington officials had to protect African Americans from intimidation and violence to allow them to carry out their challenges to discrimination. Without this room for maneuvering, civil rights advocates would encounter insurmountable hurdles in confronting white power.

At the same time, the federal government could shape the direction of *5* the struggle by choosing whether and when to respond to Black protest and by deciding on whom to bestow its support within Black communities. Although united around the struggle against white supremacy, African Americans were not monolithic in their outlook and held various shades of opinion on how best to combat racial bias. By allocating precious resources and conferring recognition on particular elements within local Black communities, national leaders could accelerate or slow down the pace of racial change.

■ Describe the Key Claims of the Text

As you read through a text with an eye to summarizing it, you want to recognize how the author develops his or her argument. You can do this by "chunking," grouping related material together into the argument's key claims. Here are two strategies to try:

Pay attention to the beginnings and endings of paragraphs. Often, underlining the first and last sentences of paragraphs will alert you to the shape and direction of an author's argument. For example, consider the first and last sentences of Lawson's opening paragraphs:

> *Paragraph 1:* The federal government played an indispensable role in shaping the fortunes of the civil rights revolution. . . . Without their crucial support, the struggle against white supremacy in the South still would have taken place but would have lacked the power and authority to defeat state governments intent on keeping Blacks in subservient positions.

> *Paragraph 2:* Along with national officials, the fate of the civil rights movement depended on the presence of national organizations. . . . They could do what Black residents of local communities could not do alone: turn the civil rights struggle into a national cause for concern and prod the federal government into throwing its considerable power to overturn the entrenched system of white domination that had prevailed for centuries in the South.

Right away you can see that Lawson has introduced a topic in each paragraph — the federal government in the first, and national civil rights organizations in the second — and has indicated a connection between them. How will Lawson elaborate on this connection? What major points does he seem to be developing?

Notice the author's point of view and use of transitions.   Another strategy for identifying major points is to pay attention to descriptive words and transitions. Notice the words Lawson uses to describe how the federal government advanced the cause of civil rights: *indispensable, significant, pioneering, landmark,* and *precious.* His word choices suggest an aspect of Lawson's point of view: that he highly values government action. Once you identify an author's point of view, you will start noticing contrasts and oppositions in the argument — instances where the words are less positive, or neutral, or even negative — which often are signaled by how the writer uses transitions.

For example, Lawson begins his fourth paragraph with two neutral-sounding sentences: "Overall, a nuanced account of the Black freedom struggle requires an interconnected approach. A balanced portrayal acknowledges that Black activists had important internal resources . . . with which to make their demands." However, in the next two sentences (the sentences that begin with the transition words *But* and *Furthermore*) Lawson signals that he is not neutral on what he believes was most important to the "Black freedom struggle": help from federal institutions.

These strategies can help you recognize the main points of an essay and describe them in a few sentences. For example, you could describe the key claims of Lawson's essay this way:

1. The civil rights movement would have failed without the support of the federal government.
2. Certainly the activism of national organizations with a local presence in the South was vital to making the struggle for civil rights a national cause.
3. But the primary importance of local activism was providing the executive, legislative, and judicial branches of the federal government with choices of where best to throw the weight of their support for racial equality in the nation.

■ Select Examples to Illustrate the Author's Argument

A summary should be succinct, which means you should limit the number of examples or illustrations you use. As you distill the major points of the argument, try to choose one or two examples to illustrate each major point. Here are the examples you might use to support Lawson's main points:

1. The civil rights movement would have failed without the support of the federal government. *Examples of federal support: Desegregation in*

the military and in housing; Supreme Court rulings toppling segrega-tionist practices and extending the right to vote (para. 3).

2. Certainly the activism of national organizations with a local presence in the South was vital to making the struggle for civil rights a national cause. *Examples of activism: NAACP drew on nationwide resources to press the case for equal rights; SCLC spotlighted white southern racism* (para. 2).

3. But the primary importance of local activism was providing the executive, legislative, and judicial branches of the federal government with choices of where best to throw the weight of their support for racial equality in the nation. *Examples of events prompting federal support: Local struggles in Montgomery, Birmingham, Selma, Albany, and Little Rock* (para. 3).

A single concrete example may be sufficient to clarify the point you want to make about an author's argument. In his five paragraphs, Lawson cites numerous examples to support his argument, but the most concrete, specific instance of federal involvement appears in paragraph 3, where he cites the series of presidential orders that mandated desegregation. This one example may be sufficient for the purposes of a summary of Lawson's passage.

■ Present the Gist of the Author's Argument

When you present the **gist of an argument**, you are expressing the author's central idea in a sentence or two. The gist of an argument is not the same thing as the author's thesis statement; it is your formulation of the author's main idea, written with the needs of your own argument in mind. Certainly you need to understand the author's thesis when you formulate the gist. Lawson's first sentence — "The federal government played an indispensable role in shaping the fortunes of the civil rights movement" — is his thesis statement: It clearly expresses his central idea. But in formulating the gist of his argument, you want to do more than paraphrase Lawson. You want to use his position to support your own. For example, suppose you want to expand on how the three branches of the federal government each played an important role in the civil rights movement. You would want to mention each branch when you describe the gist of Lawson's argument:

GIST

In his essay, "Debating the Civil Rights Movement: The View from the Nation," Steven Lawson argues that actions taken by the president, Congress, and the Supreme Court were all vital to advancing the struggle for civil rights.

Notice that this gist could not have been written based only on Lawson's thesis statement. It reflects a knowledge of Lawson's major points and his examples (of executive orders, legislation, and judicial rulings).

■ Contextualize What You Summarize

Your summary should help readers understand the context of the conversation:

- Who is the author?
- What is the author's expertise?
- What is the title of the work?
- Where did the work appear?
- What was the occasion of the work's publication? What prompted the author to write the work?
- What are the issues?
- Who else is taking part in the conversation, and what are their perspectives on the issues?

Again, because a summary must be concise, you must make decisions about how much of the conversation your readers need to know. If your assignment is to practice summarizing, it may be sufficient to include only information about the author and the source. However, if you are using the summary to build your own argument, you may need to provide more context. Your practice summary of Lawson's essay should mention that he is an historian and should cite the title of and page references to his essay. Depending on what else your argument needs, you may want to mention that this piece appeared as one of two essays, each of which sets the stage for a series of primary documents focusing on the roots of the civil rights movement. You also may want to include information about Lawson's audience (historians, other academics, policymakers, general readers); publication information (publisher, date); and what led to the work's publication. Was it published in response to another essay or book, or to commemorate an important event?

We compiled our notes on Lawson's essay (key claims, examples, gist, context) in a worksheet (Figure 10.1). All of our notes in the worksheet constitute a type of prewriting, our preparation for writing the summary. Creating a worksheet like this can help you track your thoughts as you plan to write a summary.

FIGURE 10.1 Worksheet for Writing a Summary			
KEY CLAIMS (BY PARAGRAPH)	**EXAMPLES** (BY KEY CLAIM)	**GIST**	**CONTEXT**
1. The civil rights movement would have failed without the support of the federal government.	Desegregation in the military and in housing; Supreme Court rulings toppling segregationist practices and extending the right to vote (para. 3).	In his essay, "Debating the Civil Rights Movement: The View from the Nation," Steven Lawson argues that actions taken by the president, Congress, and the Supreme Court were all vital to advancing the struggle for civil rights.	Lawson is a historian. His essay "Debating the Civil Rights Movement: The View from the Nation" appeared in *Debating the Civil Rights Movement*, 1945–1968 by Lawson and Charles Payne (Lanham, MD: Rowman & Littlefield, 1998). Lawson's essay runs from pages 3 to 42; under consideration are his opening paragraphs on pages 3 to 5.
2. Certainly the activism of national organizations with a local presence in the South was vital to making the struggle for civil rights a national cause.	NAACP drew on nationwide resources to press the case for equal rights; SCLC spotlighted white southern racism (para. 2).		
3. But the primary importance of local activism was providing the executive, legislative, and judicial branches of the federal government with choices of where best to throw the weight of their support for racial equality in the nation.	Local struggles in Montgomery, Birmingham, Selma, Albany, and Little Rock (para. 3).		

Here is our summary of Lawson's essay:

The gist of Lawson's argument, with supporting examples.

In his essay "Debating the Civil Rights Movement: The View from the Nation," historian Steven Lawson argues that actions taken by the president, Congress, and the Supreme Court were all vital to advancing the struggle for civil rights. Lawson's emphasis on the role the federal government played in the civil rights movement comes at a time when other historians are challenging that thinking.

Sentence places Lawson's argument in context, explaining the larger conversation.

Many of these historians believe that the success of the movement rested on activists' participation in the struggle to create change and achieve equality. Although Lawson

Lawson's main point.

recognizes the value of black activism in the South, he also makes clear that desegregation could only have occurred as a result of the federal government's intervention (3–5).

Steps to Writing a Summary

1 **Describe the key claims of the text.** To understand the shape and direction of the argument, study how paragraphs begin and end, and pay attention to the author's point of view and use of transitions. Then combine what you have learned into a few sentences describing the key claims.

2 **Select examples to illustrate the author's argument.** Find one or two examples to support each key claim. You may need only one example when you write your summary.

3 **Present the gist of the author's argument.** Describe the author's central idea in your own language with an eye to where you expect your argument to go.

4 **Contextualize what you summarize.** Cue your readers into the conversation. Who is the author? Where and when did the text appear? Why was the author writing? Who else is in the conversation?

A Practice Sequence: Summarizing

1 Summarize a text that you have been studying for research or for one of your other classes. You may want to limit yourself to an excerpt of just a few paragraphs or a few pages. Follow the four steps we've described, using a summary worksheet for notes, and write a summary of the text. Then share the excerpt and your summary of it with two of your peers. Be prepared to justify your choices in composing the summary. Do your peers agree that your summary captures what is important in the original?

2 With a classmate, choose a brief text of about three pages. Each of you use the method we describe above to write a summary of the text. Exchange your summaries and worksheets, and discuss the effectiveness of your summaries. Each of you should be prepared to discuss your choice of key claims and examples and your wording of the gist. Did you set forth the context effectively?

SYNTHESIS VERSUS SUMMARY

A **synthesis** is a discussion that forges connections between the arguments of two or more authors. Like a summary, a synthesis requires you to understand the key claims of each author's argument, including his or her use of supporting examples and evidence. Also like a summary, a synthesis requires you to present a central idea, a *gist*, to your readers. But in contrast to a summary, which explains the context of a source, a synthesis creates a context for your own argument. That is, when you write a synthesis comparing two or more sources, you demonstrate that you are aware of the larger conversation about the issue, and begin to claim your own place in that conversation. Most academic arguments begin with a synthesis that sets the stage for the argument that follows. By comparing what others have written on a given issue, writers position themselves in relation to what has come before them, acknowledging the contributions of their predecessors as they advance their own points of view.

Like a summary, a synthesis requires analysis: You have to break down arguments and categorize their parts to see how they work together. In our summary of Lawson's passage (p. 184), the parts we looked at were the key claims, the examples and evidence that supported them, the central idea (conveyed in the gist), and the context. But in a synthesis, your main purpose is not simply to report what another author has said. Rather, you must think critically about how multiple points of view intersect on your issue, and decide what those intersections mean.

Comparing different points of view prompts you to ask why they differ. It also makes you more aware of *counterarguments* — passages where claims conflict ("writer X says this, but writer Y asserts just the opposite") or at least differ ("writer X interprets this information this way, while writer Y sees it differently"). And it starts you formulating your own counterarguments: "Neither X nor Y has taken this into account. What if they had?"

Keep in mind that the purpose of a synthesis is not merely to list the similarities and differences you find in different sources, nor to assert your agreement with one source as opposed to others. Instead, it sets up your argument. Once you discover connections between texts, you have to decide what those connections mean to you and your readers. What bearing do they have on your own thinking? How can you make use of them in your argument?

WRITING A SYNTHESIS

To compose an effective synthesis, you must (1) make connections between ideas in different texts, (2) decide what those connections mean, and (3) formulate the gist of what you've read, much like you did when you wrote a summary. The difference is that in a synthesis, your gist should be a succinct statement that brings into focus not the central idea of one text but the relationship among different ideas in multiple texts.

To help you grasp the strategies of writing a synthesis, read the essays below by historians Charles Payne and Ronald Takaki which, like Steven Lawson's essay, deal with race in America. You will see that we have annotated the Payne and Takaki readings not only to comment on their ideas, but also to connect their ideas with those of Lawson. Annotating your texts in this manner is a useful first step in writing a synthesis.

Following the Payne and Takaki selections, we explain how annotating contributes to writing a synthesis. Then we show how you can use a worksheet to organize your thinking on the way to formulating the gist of your synthesis. Finally, we present our own synthesis based on the texts of Lawson, Payne, and Takaki.

┌─ **ABOUT THE READING** ──────────────────────────────

Charles Payne is a professor of history and African American studies at Duke University, where his current research focuses on urban education, the civil rights movement, social change, and social inequality. He is the principal investigator in an ethnographic study of the most improved low-income schools in Chicago. The following selection on the civil rights movement appears with Steven Lawson's essay in *Debating the Civil Rights Movement, 1945–1968.*

└──

CHARLES PAYNE

From Debating the Civil Rights Movement: The View from the Trenches

Point of paragraph seems to be that the language used to describe the civil rights movement distorts the actual goals and results of the movement. Is this Payne's main claim?

The [civil rights] movement continues to exercise a considerable hold on the American imagination. Our understanding of social change, our conceptions of leadership, our understanding of the possibilities of interracial cooperation are all affected by how we remember the movement. Even much of the language that we use to discuss social issues derives from movement days. We think of the movement as a movement for "civil rights" and against "segregation."   1

Even those seemingly innocuous terms carry their own historical baggage.

"Segregation" became the accepted way to describe the South's racial system among both Blacks and whites. In its denotative meaning, suggesting separation between Blacks and whites, it is not a very accurate term to describe that system. The system involved plenty of integration; it just had to be on terms acceptable to white people. Indeed, the agricultural economy of the early-twentieth-century South probably afforded a good deal more interracial contact than the modern urban ghetto. "White supremacy" is a more accurate description of what the system was about. "Segregation" is the way apologists for the South liked to think of it. It implies, "We're not doing anything to Black people: we just want to keep them separate from us." It was the most innocent face one could put on that system. When we use the term as a summary term for what was going on in the South, we are unconsciously adopting the preferred euphemism of nineteenth-century white supremacist leadership.

If "segregation" is a poor way to describe the problem, "integration" may not tell us much about the solution. It is not at all clear what proportion of the Black population was interested in "integration" as a general goal. African Americans have wanted access to the privileges that white people have enjoyed and have been interested in integration as a possible avenue to those privileges, but that view is different from seeing integration as important in and of itself. Even in the 1950s, it was clear that school integration, while it would potentially put more resources into the education of Black children, also potentially meant the loss of thousands of teaching jobs for Black teachers and the destruction of schools to which Black communities often felt deeply attached, however resource-poor they were. There was also something potentially demeaning in the idea that Black children had to be sitting next to white children to learn. The first Black children to integrate the schools in a given community often found

Margin notes:

Supports the claim that "movement" language hides or distorts reality.

Payne talks about African Americans' preferring "privileges" and "resources" to "integration."

Integration might lead to fewer resources — what's gained economically on the one hand would be lost on the other.

themselves in a strange position, especially if they were teenagers. While some Black people thought of them as endangering themselves for the greater good of the community, others saw them as turning their backs on that community and what it had to offer. It is probably safest to say that only a segment of the Black community had anything like an ideological commitment to "integration," while most Black people were willing to give it a try to see if it really did lead to a better life.

Is this "segment" the activists Lawson refers to? Are Lawson and Payne on the same page about the black community's not being "monolithic" (Lawson, para. 5) in its approach to civil rights?

We might also ask how "civil rights" came to be commonly used as a summary term for the struggle of African Americans. In the late 1960s, after several civil rights bills had been passed, a certain part of white America seemed not to understand why Black Americans were still angry about their collective status. "You have your civil rights. Now what's the problem?" In part, the problem was that "civil rights" was always a narrow way to conceptualize the larger struggle. For African Americans, the struggle has always been about forging a decent place for themselves within this society, which has been understood to involve the thorny issues of economic participation and self-assertion as well as civil rights. Indeed, in the 1940s, Gunnar Myrdal had demonstrated that economic issues were the ones that Black Americans ranked first in priority. At the 1963 March on Washington — which was initially conceived as a march for jobs — [the Student Nonviolent Coordinating Committee's] John Lewis wanted to point out that SNCC was not sure it could support what became the Civil Rights Act of 1964 partly because it did not have an economic component: 4

Lawson, by contrast, emphasizes that civil rights were vital to the struggle for equality.

Payne's examples suggest that economic equality, not legal rights, is what the civil rights movement was about.

> What is in the bill that will protect the homeless and starving people of this nation? What is there in this bill to insure the equality of a maid who earns $5.00 a week in the home of a family whose income is $100,000 a year?

One hypothesis, of course, would be that "civil rights" becomes so popular precisely because it is so narrow, precisely because it does not suggest that distribution of privilege is a part of the problem.   5

Payne's main point — that the language of civil rights is limited because it ignores economic factors.

ABOUT THE READING

Ronald Takaki is a professor of ethnic studies at the University of California, Berkeley. An adviser to the ethnic studies PhD program, he was instrumental in establishing Berkeley's American cultures graduation requirement. Takaki is a prolific writer with several award-winning books to his credit, including *A Pro-Slavery Crusade* (1971), a study of the South's ideological defense of slavery; *Violence in the Black Imagination* (1972), an examination of nineteenth-century black novelists; the Pulitzer Prize–nominated *Strangers from a Different Shore: A History of Asian Americans* (1989); and *A Different Mirror: A History of Multicultural America* (1993). The essay that follows is from a collection he edited, *Debating Diversity: Clashing Perspectives on Race and Ethnicity in America* (2002), and is his response to the Los Angeles riots of April 29, 1992.

RONALD TAKAKI

Policies: Strategies and Solutions

What dream? Civil rights? Economic equality?

What happens, asked black poet Langston Hughes, to a "dream deferred?" Does it "dry up like a raisin in the sun," or "does it explode?" An answer was hurled at America during the bloody and destructive 1992 Los Angeles race riot. On April 29, a California jury announced its not-guilty verdict in the trial of four white police officers charged with beating Rodney King, an African American who had been stopped for a traffic violation. Videotaped images of King being brutally clubbed had been repeatedly beamed across the country. The jury's shocking decision ignited an explosion of fury and violence in the inner city of Los Angeles. During the days of rage, scores of people were killed, over 2,000 injured, 12,000 arrested, and almost a billion dollars in property destroyed.

Business Week links the riots to economic inequality.

"It took a brutal beating, an unexpected jury verdict, and the sudden rampage of rioting, looting, and indiscriminate violence to bring this crisis [of urban America] back to the forefront," *Business Week* reported. "Racism surely explains some of the carnage in Los Angeles. But the day-to-day living conditions with which many of America's urban poor must contend is an equally compelling story — a tale of economic injustice." This usually conservative

The dream is not only deferred; it seems to be moving further away!

magazine pointed out that "the poverty rate, which fell as low as 11 percent in the 1970s, moved higher in the Reagan years and jumped during the last couple of years. Last year [1991], an estimated 36 million people — or about 14.7 percent of the total population — were living in poverty."

More recent examples of economic inequality than Payne's. Decades after the civil rights movement, economic inequality remains an issue.

The explosion unshrouded the terrible conditions and the anger of poor African Americans trapped in inner cities. "South Central Los Angeles is a Third World country," declared Krashaun Scott, a former member of the Los Angeles Crips gang. "There's a South Central in every city, in every state." Describing the desperate conditions in his community, he continued: "What we got is inadequate housing and inferior education. I wish someone would tell me the difference between Guatemala and South Central." This comparison graphically illustrated the squalor and poverty present within one of America's wealthiest and most modern cities. A gang member known as Bone commented that the recent violence was "not a riot — it was a class struggle. When Rodney King asked, 'Can we get along?' it ain't just about Rodney King. He was the lighter and it blew up."

3

More examples of increasing economic inequality.

What exploded was anguish born of despair. Plants and factories had been moved out of central Los Angeles into the suburbs, as well as across the border into Mexico and overseas to countries like South Korea. The Firestone factory, which had employed many of the parents of these young blacks, was boarded up, like a tomb. In terms of manufacturing jobs, South Central Los Angeles had become a wasteland. Many young black men and women nervously peered down the corridor of their futures and saw no possibility of full-time employment paying above minimum wage, or any jobs at all. The unemployment rate in this area was 59 percent — higher than the national rate during the Great Depression.

4

"Once again, young blacks are taking to the streets to express their outrage at perceived injustice," *Newsweek* reported, "and once again, whites are fearful that The Fire Next Time will consume them." But

5

this time, the magazine noticed, the situation was different from the 1965 Watts riot: "The nation is rapidly moving toward a multiethnic future in which Asians, Hispanics, Caribbean islanders, and many other immigrant groups compose a diverse and changing social mosaic that cannot be described by the old vocabulary of race relations in America." The terms "black" and "white," *Newsweek* concluded, no longer "depict the American social reality."

At the street level, African American community organizer Ted Watkins observed: "This riot was deeper and more dangerous. More ethnic groups were involved." Watkins had witnessed the Watts fury; since then, he had watched the influx of Hispanics and Koreans into South Central Los Angeles. Shortly after the terrible turmoil, social critic Richard Rodriguez reflected on the significance of these changes: "The Rodney King riots were appropriately multiracial in this multicultural capital of America. We cannot settle for black and white conclusions when one of the most important conflicts the riots revealed was the tension between Koreans and African Americans." He also noted that "the majority of looters who were arrested . . . turned out to be Hispanic."

Out of the ashes emerged a more complex awareness of our society's racial crisis. "I think good will come of [the riot]," stated Janet Harris, a chaplain at Central Juvenile Hall. "People need to take off their rose-colored glasses," she added, "and take a hard look at what they've been doing. They've been living in invisible cages. And they've shut out that world. And maybe the world came crashing in on them and now people will be moved to do something." A black minister called for cross-cultural understanding between African Americans and Korean Americans: "If we could appreciate and affirm each other's histories, there wouldn't be generalizations and stigmatizations, and we could see that we have more in common." The fires of the riot illuminated the harsh reality of class inequality. "At first I didn't notice," a Korean shopkeeper said, "but I slowly realized the

In a multiethnic America, do Payne's and Lawson's focus on black-and-white civil rights still apply?

Another comment on the new multicultural — black versus white — reality.

Like Payne, Takaki emphasizes the importance of economic factors — rich versus poor.

looters were very poor. The riot happened because of the gap between rich and poor." Executive director of the Asian Pacific American Legal Center, Steward Kwoh direly predicted that "the economic polarization between the 'haves' and 'have nots' would be the main ingredient for future calamities."

During the 1992 calamity, Rodney King pleaded: "We all can get along. I mean, we're stuck here for a while. Let's try to work it out." But we find ourselves wondering, how can we get along and how can we work it out? Is "the Negro today," as Irving Kristol contends, "like the immigrant yesterday," or do "race and class" intersect in the black community? Should there be limits on immigration from Mexico, or are these immigrants scapegoats for our nation's problems? What should we do and not do about crime? What should be the future of affirmative action? Have American blacks, Nathan Glazer admits, turned out to be "not like the immigrants of yesterday"?

8

■ Make Connections Between Different Texts

The texts by Lawson, Payne, and Takaki all deal with race in America, but race is such a large topic that you cannot assume that connections are going to leap off the page at you. In fact, each text deals with a main issue that does not immediately connect with those of the others:

- Lawson emphasizes the importance of federal actions for advancing the cause of civil rights.
- Payne contends that the terms we use to talk about the civil rights movement distort its goals and accomplishments.
- Takaki writes about the 1992 Los Angeles riots, arguing that desperate economic circumstances led to an outburst of multicultural violence.

But closer reading does suggest connections. Both Lawson and Payne are writing about the civil rights movement. They seem to agree that civil rights activists were a crucial minority in the black community, but they seem to disagree on the importance of legislation versus economic factors.

Notice how our annotations call out these connections: "Payne talks about African Americans' preferring 'privileges' and 'resources' to 'integration.'" "Are Lawson and Payne on the same page about the black community's not being 'monolithic' . . . in its approach to civil rights?" "Lawson, by contrast, emphasizes that civil rights were vital to the struggle for equality." "Payne's examples suggest that economic equality, not legal rights, is what the civil rights movement was about."

Turning to Takaki, we notice that he is also writing about economic inequality and race, but in the 1990s, not the 1950s and 1960s: "More recent examples of economic inequality than Payne's. Decades after the civil rights movement, economic inequality remains an issue." But Takaki adds another factor: economic inequality in an increasingly multicultural America. Our comment: "In a multiethnic America, do Payne's and Lawson's focus on black-and-white civil rights still apply?"

With these annotations, we are starting to think critically about the ideas in the essays, speculating about what they mean. Notice, however, that not all of the annotations make connections. Some try to get at the gist of the arguments: "Is this Payne's main claim?" Some note examples: "More examples of increasing economic inequality." Some offer impromptu opinions and reactions: "The dream is not only deferred; it seems to be moving further away!" You should not expect every annotation to contribute to your synthesis. Instead, use them to record your responses and spur your thinking too.

■ Decide What Those Connections Mean

Having annotated the selections, we filled out the worksheet in Figure 10.2, making notes in the grid to help us see the three texts in relation to one another. Our worksheet included columns for

- author and source information,
- the gist of each author's arguments,
- supporting examples and illustrations,
- counterarguments,
- our own thoughts.

A worksheet like this one can help you concentrate on similarities and differences in the texts to determine what the connections between texts mean. Of course, you can design your own worksheet as well, tailoring it to your needs and preferences. If you want to take very detailed notes about your authors and sources, for example, you may want to have separate columns for each.

Once you start noticing connections, including points of agreement and disagreement, you can start identifying counterarguments in the readings — for example, Payne countering Lawson's position that equality can be legislated. Identifying counterarguments gives you a sense of what is at issue for each author. And determining what the authors think in relation to one another can help you realize what may be at issue for you. Suppose you are struck by Payne's argument that the term *civil rights* obscures an

FIGURE 10.2   Worksheet for Writing a Synthesis

AUTHOR AND SOURCE	GIST OF ARGUMENT	EXAMPLES/ ILLUSTRATIONS	COUNTER-ARGUMENTS	WHAT I THINK
Historian Steven F. Lawson, from "Debating the Civil Rights Movement: The View from the Nation"	Actions taken by the president, Congress, and the Supreme Court were all vital to advancing the struggle for civil rights.	The executive orders, the legislation, and the court decisions that promoted desegregation	Desegregation cannot be legislated. The struggle was not simply about civil rights; it also was about achieving economic equality.	I'm not convinced by Lawson's argument.
Historian Charles Payne, from "Debating the Civil Rights Movement: The View from the Trenches"	By granting African Americans their civil rights, the Supreme Court did not — and could not — guarantee access to economic equality.	Continued inequalities between rich and poor	The executive orders, legislation, and Court rulings that promoted desegregation indicate that there was some attempt to achieve equality.	An interesting argument, but I'm not sure Payne took the best approach by working with definitions.
Ethnic historian Ronald Takaki, "Policies: Strategies and Solutions"	Economic inequality persists in urban areas where ethnic minorities live in poverty and squalor.	Inadequate housing, schools, and employment	Racial equality has been legislated; so poverty is an individual problem, not a systemic one.	The multiethnic connection makes me want to look into his issue more deeply.

equally important issue in African Americans' struggle for equality: economic equality. Suppose you connect Payne's point about economic inequality with Takaki's more-recent examples of racial inequality in the areas of housing, education, and employment. Turning these ideas around in your mind, you may decide that race-based economic inequality in a multicultural society is a topic you want to explore and develop.

■ Formulate the Gist of What You've Read

Remember that your gist should bring into focus the relationship among different ideas in multiple texts. Looking at the information juxtaposed on the worksheet, you can begin to construct the gist of your synthesis:

- The first writer, Lawson, believes that the civil rights movement owes its success to the federal government.
- The second writer, Payne, believes that blacks' struggle for economic equality was not addressed by the actions of the federal government.
- The third writer, Takaki, seems to support Payne when he claims that poverty still exists for African Americans. But he broadens the issue of economic inequality, extending it to people of different racial backgrounds.

How do you formulate this information into a gist? You can use a transition word (we've used *although*) to connect the ideas these authors bring together while conveying their differences (Lawson's emphasis on civil rights versus Payne and Takaki's emphasis on economic inequality). Thus a gist about these essays might read:

GIST OF A SYNTHESIS

Although historian Steven Lawson argues that the federal government played a crucial role in extending civil rights to African Americans, other scholars, among them Charles Payne and Ronald Takaki, point out that the focus on civil rights ignored the devastating economic inequality that persists among people of color today.

Having drafted this gist, we returned to our notes on the worksheet and complete the synthesis, presenting examples and using transitions to signal the relationships among the texts and their ideas. It's a good idea in a synthesis to use at least one illustration from each author's text to support the point you want to make, and to use transition words and phrases to lead your readers through the larger argument you want to make.

Here is our brief synthesis of the three texts:

The gist of our synthesis. "Although" signals that Lawson's argument is qualified or countered later in the sentence.

Although historian Steven Lawson argues that the federal government played a crucial role in extending civil rights to African Americans, other scholars, among them Charles Payne and Ronald Takaki, point out that the focus on civil rights ignored the devastating economic inequality that persists among people of color today. Indeed, Lawson illustrates the extent to which presidents, lawmakers, and judges brought an end to legal segregation, but he largely ignores the economic component of racial discrimination. Unfortunately, integration is still what Langston Hughes would call a "dream deferred" (quoted in Takaki). A historian, Charles Payne also observes that by granting

Transition: Lawson claims one thing, but ignores something else.

African Americans their civil rights, the federal government
did not — and could not — guarantee their access to economic equality. Ronald Takaki, an ethnic historian, <u>supports</u>
<u>Payne's argument, demonstrating through a number of</u>
<u>examples that economic inequality persists in urban areas</u>
<u>where ethnic minorities live in poverty and squalor.</u> Takaki
also makes the important point that the problem of
economic inequality is no longer a black-white problem, as it
was during the civil rights movement. Today's multiracial
<u>society complicates our understanding of the problem of</u>
<u>inequality and of a possible solution.</u>

Example that backs up the gist: Both Payne and Takaki argue that the negative effects of economic inequality outweigh the positive effects of civil rights protections.

Sets up argument to follow

Writing a synthesis, like writing a summary, is principally a strategy
for framing your own argument. In writing a synthesis, you are conveying
to your readers how various points of view in a conversation intersect and
diverge. The larger point of this exercise is to find your own issue — your
own position in the conversation — and make your argument for it.

Steps to Writing a Synthesis

1 **Make connections between different texts**. Annotate the texts
you are working with with an eye to comparing them. As you
would for a summary, note major points in the texts, choose relevant examples, and formulate the gist of each text.

2 **Decide what those connections mean**. Fill out a worksheet to
compare your notes on the different texts, track counterarguments,
and record your thoughts. Decide what the similarities and differences mean to you and what they might mean to your readers.

3 **Formulate the gist of what you've read**. Identify an overarching
idea that brings together the ideas you've noted, and write a synthesis that forges connections and makes use of the examples you've
noted. Use transitions to signal the direction of your synthesis.

A Practice Sequence: Writing a Synthesis

1 Choose at least three texts you expect to work with in your
researched argument, read them closely, and fill out a synthesis
worksheet to organize your information about them. With the
worksheet in hand, write down any similarities and differences
you find. Are the ideas weighted in one direction or the other, as
they are in our readings? On what points do the authors agree?
Formulate the gist of the works, and then write the synthesis,

incorporating examples and using transitions to signal the relationships among ideas and authors. Does the synthesis suggest the direction of your argument?

2 As a class, choose three or more texts to synthesize. Then break up into small groups, each group working with the same texts. Within each group, work through the steps in synthesizing. One person in each group should take notes in a format like our worksheet. After you complete the worksheet, identify similarities and differences among the ideas. Are they weighted in one direction or the other? Are there points of agreement among the authors? Your answers to these questions should help you formulate the gist of the synthesis. After you formulate the gist, share what you've written with the other groups. Be sure to explain how you arrived at the gist you formulated. Did each group construct the same gist? What was similar? What was different?

AVOIDING PLAGIARISM

Whether you paraphrase, summarize, or synthesize, it is essential that you acknowledge your sources. Academic writing requires you to use and document sources appropriately, making clear to readers the boundaries between your words and ideas and those of other writers. Setting boundaries can be a challenge because so much of academic writing involves interweaving the ideas of others into your own argument. Still, no matter how difficult, you must acknowledge your sources. It's only fair. Imagine how you would feel if you were reading a text and discovered that the writer had incorporated a passage from one of your papers, something you slaved over, without giving you credit. You would see yourself as a victim of plagiarism, and you would be justified in feeling very angry indeed.

In fact, **plagiarism** — the unacknowledged use of another's work, passed off as one's own — is a most serious breach of academic integrity, and colleges and universities deal with it severely. If you are caught plagiarizing in your work for a class, you can expect to fail that class and may even be expelled from your college or university. Furthermore, although a failing grade on a paper or in a course, honestly come by, is unlikely to deter an employer from hiring you, the stigma of plagiarism can come back to haunt you when you apply for a job. Any violation of the principles set forth in Table 10.1 could have serious consequences for your academic and professional career.

Even if you know what plagiarism is and wouldn't think about doing it, you can still plagiarize unintentionally. Again, paraphrasing can be especially tricky: Attempting to restate a passage without using the original words and sentence structure is, to a certain extent, an invitation to

TABLE 10.1   Principles Governing Plagiarism

1. All written work submitted for any purpose is accepted as your own work. This means it must not have been written even in part by another person.

2. The wording of any written work you submit is assumed to be your own. This means you must not submit work that has been copied, wholly or partially, from a book, article, essay, newspaper, another student's paper or notebook, or any other source. Another writer's phrases, sentences, or paragraphs can be included only if they are presented as quotations and the source acknowledged.

3. The ideas expressed in a paper or report are assumed to originate with you, the writer. Written work that paraphrases a source without acknowledgment must not be submitted for credit. Ideas from the work of others can be incorporated in your work as starting points, governing issues, illustrations, and the like, but in every instance the source must be cited.

4. Remember that any online materials you use to gather information for a paper are also governed by the rules for avoiding plagiarism. You need to learn to cite electronic sources as well as printed and other sources.

5. You may correct and revise your writing with the aid of reference books. You also may discuss your writing with your peers in a writing group or with peer tutors at your campus writing center. However, you may not submit writing that has been revised substantially by another person.

---

plagiarism. If you remember that your paper is *your* argument, and understand that any paraphrasing, summarizing, or synthesizing should reflect *your* voice and style, you will be less likely to have problems with plagiarism. Your paper should sound like you. And, again, the surest way to protect yourself is to cite your sources.

Steps to Avoiding Plagiarism

1 **Always cite the source.** Signal that you are paraphrasing, summarizing, or synthesizing by identifying your source at the outset — "According to James Gunn," "Steven Lawson argues," "Charles Payne and Ronald Takaki . . . point out." And if possible, indicate the end of the paraphrase, summary, or synthesis with relevant page references to the source. If you cite a source several times in your paper, don't assume your first citation has you covered; acknowledge the source as often as you use it.

2 **Provide a full citation in your bibliography.** It's not enough to cite a source in your paper; you must also provide a full citation for every source you use in the list of sources at the end of your paper.

INTEGRATING QUOTATIONS INTO YOUR WRITING

When you integrate quotations into your writing, bear in mind a piece of advice we've given you about writing the rest of your paper: Take your readers by the hand and lead them step-by-step. When you quote other authors to develop your argument — using their words to support your thinking or to address a counterargument — discuss and analyze the words you quote, showing readers how the specific language of each quotation contributes to the larger point you are making in your essay. When you integrate quotations, then, there are three basic things you want to do: (1) Take an active stance, (2) explain the quotations, and (3) attach short quotations to your own sentences.

■ Take an Active Stance

Critical reading demands that you adopt an active stance toward what you read — that you raise questions in response to a text that is telling you not only what the author thinks but also what you should think. You should be no less active when you are using other authors' texts to develop your own argument. Certainly taking an active stance when you are quoting means knowing when to quote. Don't use a quote when a paraphrase or summary can convey the information from a source more effectively and efficiently. (Don't forget to acknowledge your source!) More important, however, it means you have to make fair and wise decisions about what and how much you should quote to make your researched argument:

- It's not fair (or wise) to quote selectively — choosing only passages that support your argument — when you know you are distorting or misrepresenting the argument of the writer you are quoting. Ideally, you want to demonstrate that you understand the writer's argument and that you want to make evenhanded use of it in your own argument, whether you agree or disagree, in whole or in part, with what the other writer has written.

- It's not wise (or fair to yourself) to flesh out your paper with an overwhelming number of quotations that could make readers think that you either do not know your topic well or do not have your own ideas. Don't allow quotations to take over your paragraphs and shape your own words about the topic. In structuring your paragraphs, remember that your ideas and argument — your thesis — are what is most important to the readers and what justifies a quotation's being included at all.

Above all, taking an active stance when you quote means taking control of your own writing. You want to establish your own argument and guide your readers through it, allowing sources to contribute to but not dictate its direction. You are responsible for plotting and pacing your essay. Always keep in mind that your thesis is the skewer that runs through every paragraph, holding all of the ideas together. When you use quotations, then, you must organize them to enrich, substantiate, illustrate, and help support your central claim or thesis.

■ Explain the Quotations

When you quote an author to support or advance your argument, you must be sure that readers know exactly what they should learn from the quotation. Read the excerpt below from one student's early draft of an argument that focuses on the value of service learning in high schools as a means for creating change. The student reviews several relevant studies — but then simply drops in a quotation, expecting readers to know what they should pay attention to in the quotation.

> Other research emphasizes community service as an integral and integrated part of moral identity. In this understanding, community service activities are not isolated events but are woven into the context of students' everyday lives (Yates, 1995); the personal, the moral, and the civic become "inseparable" (Colby, Ehrlich, Beaumont, & Stephens, 2003, p. 15). In their study of minority high schoolers at an urban Catholic school who volunteered at a soup kitchen for the homeless as part of a class assignment, Youniss and Yates (1999) found that the students underwent significant identity changes, coming to perceive themselves as lifelong activists. The researchers' findings are worth quoting at length here because they depict the dramatic nature of the students' changed viewpoints. Youniss and Yates write:
>
> > Many students abandoned an initially negative view of homeless people and a disinterest in homelessness by gaining appreciation of the humanity of homeless people and by showing concern for homelessness in relation to poverty, job training, low-cost housing, prison reform, drug and alcohol rehabilitation, care for the mentally ill, quality urban education, and welfare policy.
> > Several students also altered perceptions of themselves from politically impotent teenagers to involved citizens who now and in the future could use their talent and power to correct social problems. They projected articulated pictures of themselves as adult citizens who could affect housing policies, education for minorities, and government programs within a clear framework of social justice. (p. 362)

The student's introduction to the quoted passage provided a rationale for quoting Youniss and Yates at length; but it did not help her readers see what was important about the research in relation to the student's own argument. Our student needed to frame the quotation for her readers. Instead of introducing the quotation by saying "Youniss and Yates write," she should have made explicit that the study supports the argument that community service can create change. A more appropriate frame for the quotation might have been a summary like this one:

Frames the quotation, explaining it in the context of the student's argument. One particular study underscores my argument that service can motivate change, particularly when that change begins within the students who are involved in service. Youniss and Yates (1999) write that over the course of their research, the students developed both an "appreciation of the humanity of homeless people" and a sense that they would someday be able to "use their talent and power to correct social problems" (p. 362).

In the following example, notice that the student writer uses Derrick Bell's text to say something about the ways the effects of desegregation have been muted by political manipulation.* The writer shapes what he wants readers to focus on, leaving nothing to chance.

> The effectiveness with which the meaning of *Brown v. Board of Education* has been manipulated, Derrick Bell argues, is also evidenced by the way in which such thinking has actually been embraced by minority groups. Bell claims that a black school board member's asking "But of what value is it to teach black children to read in all-black schools?" indicates this unthinking acceptance that whiteness is an essential ingredient to effective schooling for blacks. Bell continues:
>
> > The assumption that even the attaining of academic skills is worthless unless those skills are acquired in the presence of white students illustrates dramatically how a legal precedent, namely the Supreme Court's decision in *Brown v. Board of Education*, has been so constricted even by advocates that its goal — equal educational opportunity — is rendered inaccessible, even unwanted, unless it can be obtained through racial balancing of the school population. (p. 255)
>
> Bell's argument is extremely compelling, particularly when one considers the extent to which "racial balancing" has come to be defined in terms of large white majority populations and small nonwhite minority populations.

Notice how the student's last sentence helps readers understand what the quoted material suggests and why it's important by embedding and extending Bell's notion of racial balancing into his explanation.

In sum, you should always explain the information that you quote so that your readers can see how the quotation relates to your own argument ("Take your readers by the hand . . . "). As you read other people's writing, keep an eye open to the ways writers introduce and explain the sources they use to build their arguments.

*This quotation is from Derrick Bell's *Silent Covenants: Brown v. Board of Education and the Unfulfilled Hopes for Racial Reform* (NY: Oxford UP, 2005).

■ Attach Short Quotations to Your Own Sentences

The quotations we discussed above are **block quotations,** lengthy quotations, generally of more than five lines, that are set off from the text of a paper with indention. Make shorter quotations part of your own sentences so your readers can understand how the quotations connect to your argument and can follow along easily. How do you make a quotation part of your own sentences? There are two main methods:

- Integrate quotations within the grammar of your writing.
- Attach quotations with punctuation.

If possible, use both to make your integration of quotations more interesting and varied.

Integrate Quotations within the Grammar of a Sentence.   When you integrate a quotation into a sentence, the quotation must make grammatical sense and read as if it is part of the sentence:

> Fine, Weiss, and Powell (1998) expanded upon what others call "equal status contact theory" by using a "framework that draws on three traditionally independent literatures — those on community, difference, and democracy" (p. 37).

If you add words to the quotation, use square brackets around them to let readers know that the words are not original to the quotation:

> Smith and Wellner (2002) asserted that they "are not alone [in believing] that the facts have been incorrectly interpreted by Mancini" (p. 24).

If you omit any words in the middle of a quotation, use an **ellipsis,** three periods with spaces between them, to indicate the omission:

> Riquelme argues that "Eliot tries . . . to provide a definition by negations, which he also turns into positive terms that are meant to correct misconceptions" (156).

If you omit a sentence or more, make sure to put a period before the ellipsis points:

> Eagleton writes, "What Eliot was in fact assaulting was the whole ideology of middle-class liberalism. . . . Eliot's own solution is an extreme right-wing authoritarianism: men and women must sacrifice their petty 'personalities' and opinions to an impersonal order" (39).

Whatever you add (using square brackets) or omit (using ellipses), the sentence must read grammatically. And, of course, your additions and omissions must not distort the author's meaning.

Attach Quotations with Punctuation.   You also can attach a quotation to a sentence by using punctuation. For example, this passage attaches the run-in quotation with a colon:

> For these researchers, there needs to be recognition of differences in a way that will include and accept all students. Specifically, they ask: "Within multiracial settings,

when are young people invited to discuss, voice, critique, and re-view the very notions of race that feel so fixed, so hierarchical, so damaging, and so accepted in the broader culture?" (p. 132).

In conclusion, if you don't connect quotations to your argument, your readers may not understand why you've included them. You need to explain some significant point that each quotation reveals as you introduce or end it. This strategy helps readers know what to pay attention to in a quotation, particularly if the quotation is lengthy.

Steps to Integrating Quotations into Your Writing

1 **Take an active stance**. Your sources should contribute to your argument, not dictate its direction.

2 **Explain the quotations**. Explain what you quote so your readers understand how each quotation relates to your argument.

3 **Attach short quotations to your own sentences**. Integrate short quotations within the grammar of your own sentences, or attach them with appropriate punctuation.

A Practice Sequence: Integrating Quotations

1 Using several of the sources you are working with in developing your paper, try integrating quotations into your essay. Be sure you are controlling your sources. Carefully read the paragraphs where you've used quotations. Will your readers clearly understand why the quotations are there — the points the quotations support? Do the sentences with quotations read smoothly? Are they grammatically correct?

2 Working in a small group, agree on a substantial paragraph or passage (from this book or some other source) to write about. Each member should read the passage and take a position on the ideas, and then draft a page that quotes the passage using both strategies for integrating these quotations. Compare what you've written, examining similarities and differences in the use of quotations.

CITING AND DOCUMENTING SOURCES

You must provide a brief citation in the text of your paper for every quotation or idea taken from another writer, and you must list complete information at the end of your paper for the sources you use. This information is essential for readers who want to read the source to understand a quotation or idea in its original context. How you cite sources in the body of your paper and document them at the end of your paper varies from discipline to discipline, so it is important to ask your instructor what documentation style he or she prefers.

Even within academic disciplines, documentation styles can vary. Specific academic journals within disciplines will sometimes have their own set of style guidelines. The important thing is to adhere faithfully to your chosen (or assigned) style throughout your paper, observing all the niceties of form prescribed by the style. You may have noticed small differences in the citation styles in the examples throughout this chapter. That's because the examples are taken from the work of a variety of writers, both professionals and students, who had to conform to the documentation requirements of their publication or of their teachers.

For information on how to accurately cite and document sources, consult a writing handbook such as *The Everyday Writer*. Alternatively, the Web site for the University of Washington's Expository Writing Program provides links to online writing resources that can provide this information. You will find these links at <http://depts.washington.edu/engl/ewp/resources.php>.

■ ■ ■

Throughout this chapter we have emphasized two key points: that academic writing is researched — which means it is connected to a broader conversation — and that you should use sources strategically to develop your own thesis. The decisions you make about how to use the ideas of others matter: Will you paraphrase or summarize? Should you orchestrate a comparison of ideas in a synthesis? Should you use a direct quotation? Have you taken an active stance in using direct quotations? Have you analyzed the information in ways that clarify for readers why you are paraphrasing, summarizing, or quoting? Does the evidence you use support your thesis? Ultimately, sources should enhance and enrich the ideas you have developed through research, giving you the best chance of persuading your readers to listen to you, learn from you, and perhaps change their minds about an issue that is important to you.

PART FOUR

Writing and Revision
as Acts of Inquiry

11

Appealing to Your Readers

W ho you believe your readers are influences how you see a particular situation, define an issue, explain the ongoing conversation surrounding that issue, and formulate a question. You may need to read widely to understand how different writers have dealt with the issue you address. And you will need to anticipate how others might respond to your argument — whether they will be sympathetic or antagonistic — and to compose your essay so that readers will "listen" whether or not they agree with you. To achieve these goals, you will no doubt use reason in the form of evidence to sway readers. But you can also use other means of persuasion: That is, you can use your own character, by presenting yourself as someone who is knowledgeable, fair, and just; and you can appeal to your readers' emotions. Although you may believe that reason alone should provide the means for changing people's minds, people's emotions also color the way they see the world.

Your audience is more than your immediate reader, your instructor or a peer. Your audience encompasses those you cite in writing about a particular issue and those you anticipate responding to your argument. This is true no matter what you write about, from an interpretation of the novels of a particular author, or an analysis of the cultural work of horror films, to the ethics of treating boys and girls differently in schools, or the moral issues surrounding homelessness in America. In this chapter we discuss different ways of engaging your readers, centering on three kinds of appeals: **ethos**, appeals from character; **pathos**, appeals to emotion; and **logos**, appeals to reason. *Ethos, pathos,* and *logos* are terms derived from ancient Greek writers, but they are still of great value today when considering how to persuade your audience. Readers will judge your argument

---

Taken from Stuart Greene and April Lidinsky, *From Inquiry to Academic Writing: A Practical Guide*, pp. 167–200 (Chapter 8, "From Ethos to Logos: Appealing to Your Readers").

on whether or not you present an argument that is fair and just, one that creates a sense of goodwill. All three appeals rely on these qualities. You want your argument to convey that you are reasonable and value fairness, justice, and goodwill, that you trust that your readers are reasonable and value these qualities too; and that your argument makes reasonable use of evidence that appeals to your readers' sense of fairness, justice, and goodwill. Your task as a writer is to decide the proper balance of these different appeals in your argument, based on your thesis, the circumstances, and your audience.

CONNECTING WITH READERS: A SAMPLE ARGUMENT

To consider how an author connects with his audience, read the excerpt below from James W. Loewen's book *Lies My Teacher Told Me: Everything Your American History Textbook Got Wrong*. As you read the excerpt, note Loewen's main points, and select key examples that illustrate his argument. As a class, test the claims he makes — To what extent do you believe that what Loewen argues is true? This may entail recalling your own experiences in high school history classes or locating one or more of the books that Loewen mentions.

ABOUT THE READING

In addition to *Lies My Teacher Told Me* (1995), James Loewen, who holds a PhD in sociology, has written several other books, including *Lies Across America: What Our Historic Sites Get Wrong* (1999) and *Sundown Towns: A Hidden Dimension of American Racism* (2005). As the titles of these books suggest, Loewen is a writer who questions the assumptions about history that many people take for granted. This is especially true of the excerpt below, from a chapter in which Loewen challenges a common American belief — that everyone has an equal chance in what he calls the "land of opportunity" — by arguing that we live in a class system that privileges some people and raises barriers for others. History textbook writers, he points out, are guilty of complicity in this class system because they leave a great deal of history out of their textbooks.

JAMES W. LOEWEN

The Land of Opportunity

High school students have eyes, ears, and television sets (all too   *1*
many have their own TV sets), so they know a lot about relative privilege in America. They measure their family's social position against

that of other families, and their community's position against other communities. Middle-class students, especially, know little about how the American class structure works, however, and nothing at all about how it has changed over time. These students do not leave high school merely ignorant of the workings of the class structure; they come out as terrible sociologists. "Why are people poor?" I have asked first-year college students. Or, if their own class position is one of relative privilege, "Why is your family well off?" The answers I've received, to characterize them charitably, are half-formed and naïve. The students blame the poor for not being successful. They have no understanding of the ways that opportunity is not equal in America and no notion that social structure pushes people around, influencing the ideas they hold and the lives they fashion.

High school history textbooks can take some of the credit for this   *2*
state of affairs. Some textbooks cover certain high points of labor history, such as the 1894 Pullman strike near Chicago that President Cleveland broke with federal troops, or the 1911 Triangle Shirtwaist fire that killed 146 women in New York City, but the most recent event mentioned in most books is the Taft-Hartley Act of fifty years ago. No book mentions the Hormel meat-packers' strike in the mid-1980s or the air traffic controllers' strike broken by President Reagan. Nor do textbooks describe any continuing issues facing labor, such as the growth of multinational corporations and their exporting of jobs overseas. With such omissions, textbook authors can construe labor history as something that happened long ago, like slavery, and that, like slavery, was corrected long ago. It logically follows that unions appear anachronistic. The idea that they might be necessary in order for workers to have a voice in the workplace goes unstated.

Textbooks' treatments of events in labor history are never anchored in   *3*
any analysis of social class. This amounts to delivering the footnotes instead of the lecture! Six of the dozen high school American history textbooks I examined contain no index listing at all for "social class," "social stratification," "class structure," "income distribution," "inequality," or any conceivably related topic. Not one book lists "upper class," "working class," or "lower class." Two of the textbooks list "middle class," but only to assure students that America is a middle-class country. "Except for slaves, most of the colonists were members of the 'middling ranks,'" says *Land of Promise,* and nails home the point that we are a middle-class country by asking students to "Describe three 'middle-class' values that united free Americans of all classes." Several of the textbooks note the explosion of middle-class suburbs after World War II. Talking about the middle class is hardly equivalent to discussing social stratification, however; in fact, as Gregory Mantsios has pointed out, "such references appear to be acceptable precisely because they mute class differences."

Stressing how middle-class we all are is particularly problematic   *4*
today, because the proportion of households earning between 75 percent and 125 percent of the median income has fallen steadily

since 1967. The Reagan-Bush administrations accelerated this shrinkage of the middle class, and most families who left its ranks fell rather than rose. This is the kind of historical trend one would think history books would take as appropriate subject matter, but only four of the twelve books in my sample provide any analysis of social stratification in the United States. Even these fragmentary analyses are set mostly in colonial America. *Land of Promise* lives up to its reassuring title by heading its discussion of social class "Social Mobility." "One great difference between colonial and European society was that the colonists had more social mobility," echoes *The American Tradition.* "In contrast with contemporary Europe, eighteenth-century America was a shining land of equality and opportunity — with the notorious exception of slavery," chimes in *The American Pageant.* Although *The Challenge of Freedom* identifies three social classes — upper, middle, and lower — among whites in colonial society, compared to Europe "there was greater *social mobility.*"

Never mind that the most violent class conflicts in American history — Bacon's Rebellion and Shays's Rebellion — took place in and just after colonial times. Textbooks still say that colonial society was relatively classless and marked by upward mobility. And things have gotten rosier since. "By 1815," *The Challenge of Freedom* assures us, two classes had withered away and "America was a country of middle class people and of middle class goals." This book returns repeatedly, at intervals of every fifty years or so, to the theme of how open opportunity is in America. "In the years after 1945, *social mobility* — movement from one social class to another — became more widespread in America," *Challenge* concludes. "This meant that people had a better chance to move upward in society." The stress on upward mobility is striking. There is almost nothing in any of these textbooks about class inequalities or barriers of any kind to social mobility. "What conditions made it possible for poor white immigrants to become richer in the colonies?" *Land of Promise* asks. "What conditions made/make it difficult?" goes unasked. Textbook authors thus present an America in which, as preachers were fond of saying in the nineteenth century, men start from "humble origins" and attain "the most elevated positions."

Social class is probably the single most important variable in society. From womb to tomb, it correlates with almost all other social characteristics of people that we can measure. Affluent expectant mothers are more likely to get prenatal care, receive current medical advice, and enjoy general health, fitness, and nutrition. Many poor and working-class mothers-to-be first contact the medical profession in the last month, sometimes the last hours, of their pregnancies. Rich babies come out healthier and weighing more than poor babies. The infants go home to very different situations. Poor babies are more likely to have high levels of poisonous lead in their environments and their bodies. Rich babies get more time and verbal interaction with their parents and higher quality day care when not with their parents. When they enter kindergarten, and through the twelve years that follow, rich children benefit from suburban schools that spend two to three times as much money per student as schools in inner cities or impoverished rural areas. Poor children are taught in classes that are often 50 percent larger than the classes of affluent children. Differences such as these help account for the higher school-dropout rate among poor children.

Even when poor children are fortunate enough to attend the same 7 school as rich children, they encounter teachers who expect only children of affluent families to know the right answers. Social science research shows that teachers are often surprised and even distressed when poor children excel. Teachers and counselors believe they can predict who is "college material." Since many working-class children give off the wrong signals, even in first grade, they end up in the "general education" track in high school. "If you are the child of low-income parents, the chances are good that you will receive limited and often careless attention from adults in your high school," in the words of Theodore Sizer's best-selling study of American high schools, *Horace's Compromise.* "If you are the child of upper-middle-income parents, the chances are good that you will receive substantial and careful attention." Researcher Reba Page has provided vivid accounts of how high school American history courses use rote learning to turn off lower-class students. Thus schools have put into practice Woodrow Wilson's recommendation: "We want one class of persons to have a liberal education, and we want another class of persons, a very much larger class of necessity in every society, to forgo the privilege of a liberal education and fit themselves to perform specific difficult manual tasks."

As if this unequal home and school life were not enough, rich teenagers 8 then enroll in the Princeton Review or other coaching sessions for the Scholastic Aptitude Test. Even without coaching, affluent children are advantaged because their background is similar to that of the test-makers, so they are comfortable with the vocabulary and subtle subcultural assumptions of the test. To no one's surprise, social class correlates strongly with SAT scores.

All these are among the reasons why social class predicts the rate 9 of college attendance and the type of college chosen more effectively than does any other factor, including intellectual ability, however measured. After college, most affluent children get white-collar jobs, most working-class children get blue-collar jobs, and the class differences continue. As adults, rich people are more likely to have hired an attorney and to be a member of formal organizations that increase their civic power. Poor people are more likely to watch TV. Because affluent families can save some money while poor families must spend what they make, wealth differences are ten times larger than income differences. Therefore most poor and working-class families cannot accumulate the down payment required to buy a house, which in turn shuts them out from our most important tax shelter, the write-off of home mortgage interest. Working-class parents cannot afford to live in elite subdivisions or hire high-quality day care, so the process of educational inequality replicates itself in the next generation. Finally, affluent Americans also have longer life expectancies than lower- and working-class people, the largest single cause of which is better access to health care. Echoing the results of Helen Keller's study of blindness, research has determined that poor health is not distributed randomly about the social structure but is concentrated in the lower class. Social Security then becomes a huge transfer system, using monies contributed by all Americans to pay benefits disproportionately to longer-lived affluent Americans.

Ultimately, social class determines how people think about social   *10* class. When asked if poverty in America is the fault of the poor or the fault of the system, 57 percent of business leaders blamed the poor; just 9 percent blamed the system. Labor leaders showed sharply reversed choices: only 15 percent said the poor were at fault while 56 percent blamed the system. (Some replied "don't know" or chose a middle position.) The largest single difference between our two main political parties lies in how their members think about social class: 55 percent of Republicans blamed the poor for their poverty, while only 13 percent blamed the system for it; 68 percent of Democrats, on the other hand, blamed the system, while only 5 percent blamed the poor.

Few of these statements are news, I know, which is why I have not   *11* documented most of them, but the majority of high school students do not know or understand these ideas. Moreover, the processes have changed over time, for the class structure in America today is not the same as it was in 1890, let alone in colonial America. Yet in *Land of Promise,* for example, social class goes unmentioned after 1670.

For Analysis and Discussion

1. List what you think are Loewen's main points. What appeals does he seem to draw on most when he makes those points: appeals based on his own character (ethos), on the emotions of his reader (pathos), or on the reasonableness of his evidence (logos)? Are the appeals obvious or difficult to tease out? Does he combine them? Discuss your answers with your classmates.

2. Identify what you think is the main claim of Loewen's argument, and choose key examples to support your answer. Compare your chosen claim and examples to those chosen by your classmates. Do they differ significantly? Can you agree on Loewen's gist and his key examples?

3. As a class, test the claims Loewen makes by thinking about your own experiences in high school history classes. Do you remember finding out that

something you were taught from an American history textbook was not true? Did you discover on your own what you considered to be misrepresentations in or important omissions from your textbook? If so, did these misrepresentations or omissions tend to support or contradict the claims about history textbooks that Loewen makes?

APPEALING TO ETHOS

Although we like to believe that our decisions and beliefs are based on reason and logic, in fact often they are based on what amounts to character judgments. That is, if a person you trust makes a reasonable argument for one choice, and a person you distrust makes a reasonable argument for the opposite choice, you are more likely to be swayed by the argument of the person you trust. Similarly, the audience for your argument will be more disposed to agree with you if its members believe you are a fair, just person who is knowledgeable and has good judgment. Even the most well developed argument will fall short if you do not leave this kind of impression on your readers. Thus it is not surprising that ethos may be the most important component of your argument.

There are three strategies for evoking a sense of ethos: (1) Establish that you have good judgment; (2) convey to readers that you are knowledgeable; and (3) show that you understand the complexity of the issue. These strategies are interrelated: A writer who demonstrates good judgment is more often than not someone who is both knowledgeable about an issue and who acknowledges the complexity of it by weighing the strengths *and* weaknesses of different arguments. However, keep in mind that these characteristics do not exist apart from what readers think and believe.

■ Establish That You Have Good Judgment

Most readers of academic writing expect writers to demonstrate good judgment by identifying a problem that readers agree is worth addressing. In turn, good judgment gives writers credibility. Loewen crafts his introduction to capture the attention of educators as well as concerned citizens when he claims that students leave high school unaware of class structure and as a consequence "have no understanding of the ways that opportunity is not equal in America and no notion that social structure pushes people around, influencing the ideas they hold and the lives they fashion" (para. 1). Loewen does not blame students, or even instructors, for this lack of awareness. Instead, he writes, "textbooks can take some of the credit for this state of affairs" (para. 2) because, among other shortcomings, they leave out important events in "labor history" and relegate issues facing labor to the past. Whether or not an educator — or a general reader for that matter — will ultimately agree with Loewen's case is, at this point, up for grabs, but certainly the possibility that high schools in general, and history textbooks in particular, are failing students by leaving them vulnerable to class-based manipulation would be recognized as a problem by readers who believe America should be a society that offers equal opportunity for all. At this point, Loewen's readers are likely to agree that the problem of omission he identifies may be significant if its consequences are as serious as he believes them to be.

One could also argue that writers establish good judgment by conveying to readers that that they are fair-minded, just, and have the best interests of readers in mind. Loewen is particularly concerned that students understand the persistence of poverty and inequality in the United States and the historical circumstances of the poor, which they cannot do unless textbook writers take a more inclusive approach to addressing labor history, especially "the growth of multinational corporations and their exporting of jobs overseas" (para. 2). It's not fair to deny this important information to students, and it's not fair to the poor to leave them out of official histories of the United States. Loewen further demonstrates that he is fair and just when he calls attention in paragraph 6 to the inequality between rich and poor children in schools, a problem that persists despite our forebears' belief that class would not determine the fate of citizens of the United States.

■ Convey to Readers That You Are Knowledgeable

Being thoughtful about a subject goes hand in hand with being knowledgeable about the subject. Loewen demonstrates his knowledge of class issues and their absence from textbooks in a number of ways (not the least of which is his awareness that a problem exists — many people, including educators, may not be aware of this problem). In paragraph 3, Loewen makes a bold claim: "Textbooks' treatments of events in labor history are never anchored in any analysis of social class." As readers, we cannot help wondering: How does the author know this? How will he support this claim? Loewen anticipates these questions by demonstrating that he has studied the subject through a systematic examination of American history textbooks. He observes that six of the twelve textbooks he examined "contain no index listing at all for 'social class,' 'social stratification,' 'class structure,' 'income distribution,' 'inequality,' or any conceivably related topic; and that "not one book lists 'upper class,' 'working class,' or 'lower class.'" Loewen also demonstrates his grasp of class issues in American history, from — the "violent class conflicts" that "took place in and just after colonial times" (para. 5), which contradict textbook writers' assertions that class conflicts did not exist during this period, to the more recent conflicts in the 1980s and early 1990s (paras. 2 and 4). Moreover, Loewen backs up his own study of textbooks with references to a number of studies from the social sciences to illustrate that "social class is probably the single most important variable in society" (para. 6). Witness the statistics and findings he cites in paragraphs 6 through 10. The breadth of Loewen's historical knowledge and the range of his reading should convince readers that he is knowledgeable, and his trenchant analysis contributes to the authority he brings to the issue and to his credibility.

■ **Show That You Understand the Complexity of a Given Issue**

Recognizing the complexity of an issue helps readers see the extent to which authors know that any issue can be understood in a number of different ways. Academic readers value writing that displays inquisitiveness and curiosity. Loewen acknowledges that most of the history he recounts is not "news" (para. 11) to his educated readers, who by implication "know" and "understand" his references to historical events and trends. What may be news to his readers, he explains, is the extent to which class structure in the United States has changed over time. With the steady erosion of middle-class households since 1967, "class inequalities" and "barriers . . . to social mobility" (para. 5) are limiting more and more Americans' access to even the most fundamental of opportunities in a democratic society — health care and education.

Still, even though Loewen has introduced new thinking about the nature of class in the United States and has demonstrated a provocative play of mind by examining an overlooked body of data (high school history textbooks) that may influence the way class is perceived in America, there are still levels of complexity he hasn't addressed explicitly. Most important, perhaps, is the question of why history textbooks continue to ignore issues of class when there is so much research that indicates its importance in shaping the events history textbooks purport to explain.

Steps to Appealing to Ethos

1 **Establish that you have good judgment.** Identify an issue your readers will agree is worth addressing, and demonstrate that you are fair-minded and have the best interests of your readers in mind when you address it.

2 **Convey to readers that you are knowledgeable.** Support your claims with credible evidence that shows you have read widely, thought about, and understand the issue.

3 **Show that you understand the complexity of the issue.** Demonstrate that you understand the variety of viewpoints your readers may bring — or may not be able to bring — to the issue.

APPEALING TO PATHOS

An appeal to pathos recognizes that people are moved to action by their emotions as well as by reasonable arguments. In fact, pathos is a vital part of argument that can predispose readers one way or another. Do you want to arouse readers' sympathy? Anger? Passion? You can do that by knowing what readers value. Appeals to pathos are typically indirect. You can appeal to pathos by using examples or illustrations that you believe will arouse the appropriate emotions, and by presenting them using an appropriate tone.

To acknowledge that writers play on readers' emotions is not to endorse manipulative writing. Rather, it is to acknowledge that effective writers use all available means of persuasion to move readers to agree with them. After all, if your thoughtful reading and careful research have led you to believe that you must weigh in with a useful insight on an important issue, it stands to reason that you would want your argument to convince your readers to believe as strongly in what you assert as you do. For example, if you genuinely believe that the conditions some families are living in are abysmal and unfair, you want your readers to believe it too. And an effective way to persuade them to believe as you do, in addition to convincing them of the reasonableness of your argument and of your own good character and judgment, is to establish a kind of emotional common ground in your writing — the common ground of pathos.

■ Show That You Know What Your Readers Value

Let's consider some of the ways James Loewen signals that he knows what his readers value. In the first place, Loewen assumes that readers feel the same way he does: Educated people should know that the United States has a class structure despite the democratic principles that the nation was founded on. He also expects readers to identify with his unwillingness to accept the injustice that results from that class structure. He believes that women living in poverty should have access to appropriate health care, that children living in poverty should have a chance to attend college, and that certain classes of people should not be written off to "perform specific difficult manual tasks" (para. 7). Time and again, Loewen cites examples that reveal that the poor are discriminated against by the class structure in the United States not for lack of ability, lack of desire, lack of ambition, or lack of morality, but for no better reason than lack of money — and that such discrimination has been going on for a long time. He expects his readers also will find such discrimination an unacceptable affront to their values of fair play and democracy, and that they will experience the same sense of outrage that he does.

■ Use Illustrations and Examples That Appeal to Readers' Emotions

You can appeal to readers' emotions indirectly through the illustrations and examples you use to support your argument. In paragraph 2, Loewen contends that textbook writers share responsibility for high school students' not knowing about the continued relevance of class issues in American life.

Loewen's readers — parents, educators, historians — may very well be angered by the omissions he points out. Certainly he would expect them to be angry when they read about the effects of economic class on the health care expectant mothers and then their children receive (para. 6) and on their children's access to quality education (paras. 6–8). In citing the fact that social class "correlates strongly with SAT scores" (para. 8) and so "predicts the rate of collage attendance and the type of college chosen" (para. 9), Loewen forces his readers to acknowledge that the educational playing field is far from level. Finally, he calls attention to the fact that accumulated wealth accounts for deep class divisions in our society — that their inability to save prevents the poor from hiring legal counsel, purchasing a home, or taking advantage of tax shelters. The result, Loewen observes, is that "educational inequality replicates itself in the next generation" (para. 9). Together, these examples strengthen both Loewen's argument and what he hopes will be readers' outrage that history textbooks do not address class issues. Without that information, Americans cannot fully understand or act to change the existing class structure.

■ Consider How Your Tone May Affect Your Audience

The **tone** of your writing is your use of language that communicates your attitude toward yourself, your material, and your readers. Of course, your tone is important in everything you write, but it is particularly crucial when you are appealing to pathos. When you are appealing to your readers' emotions, it is tempting to use loaded, exaggerated, and even intemperate language to convey how you feel (and hope your readers will feel) about an issue. Consider these sentences: "The Republican Party has devised the most ignominious means of filling the pockets of corporations." "These wretched children suffer heartrending agonies that can barely be imagined, much less described." "The ethereal beauty of the Brandenburg concertos thrill one to the deepest core of one's being." All of these sentences express strong and probably sincere beliefs and emotions, but some readers might find them overwrought and coercive, and question the writer's reasonableness.

Some writers rely on irony or sarcasm to set the tone of their work. **Irony** is the use of language to say one thing while meaning quite another. **Sarcasm** is the use of heavy-handed irony to ridicule or attack someone or something. Although irony and sarcasm can make for vivid and entertaining writing, they also can backfire and end up alienating readers. The sentence "Liberals will be pleased to hear that the new budget will be making liberal use of their hard-earned dollars" may entertain some readers with its irony and wordplay, but others may assume that the writer's attitude toward liberals is likely to result in an unfairly slanted argument. And the sentence "In my opinion, there's no reason why Christians and Muslims shouldn't rejoice together over the common ground of their both being deluded about the existence of a God" may please some readers, but it risks alienating those who are uncomfortable with breezy comments about religious beliefs. Again, think of your readers and what they value, and weigh the benefits of a clever sentence against its potential to detract from your argument or offend your audience.

You often find colorful wording and irony in op-ed and opinion pieces, where a writer may not have the space to build a compelling argument using evidence and has to resort to shortcuts to readers' emotions. However, in academic writing, where the careful accumulation and presentation of evidence and telling examples are highly valued, the frequent use of loaded language, exaggeration, and sarcasm is looked on with distrust.

Consider Loewen's excerpt. Although his outrage comes through clearly, he never resorts to hectoring. For example, in paragraph 1, he writes that students are "ignorant of the workings of the class structure" and that their opinions are "half-formed and naïve." But he does not imply that students are ignoramuses or that their opinions are foolish. What they lack, he contends, is understanding. They need to be taught something about class structure that they are not now being taught. And paragraph 1 is about as close to name-calling as Loewen comes. Even textbook writers, who are the target of his anger, are not vilified. True, Loewen occasionally makes use of irony, for example in paragraph 5, where he points out inconsistencies and omissions in textbooks: "Never mind that the most violent class conflicts in American history — Bacon's Rebellion and Shays's Rebellion — took place in and just after colonial times. Textbooks still say that colonial society was relatively classless and marked by upward mobility. And things have gotten rosier since." But he doesn't resort to ridicule. Instead, he relies on examples and illustrations to connect with his readers' sense of values and appeal to their emotions.

Steps to Appealing to Pathos

1 **Show that you know what your readers value.** Start from your own values and imagine what assumptions and principles would appeal to your readers. What common ground can you imagine between your values and theirs? How will it need to be adjusted for different kinds of readers?

2 **Use illustrations and examples that appeal to readers' emotions.** Again, start from your own emotional position. What examples and illustrations resonate most with you? How can you present them to have the most emotional impact on your readers? How would you adjust them for different kinds of readers?

3 **Consider how your tone may affect your audience.** Be wary of using loaded, exaggerated, and intemperate language that may put off your readers; and be careful in your use of irony and sarcasm.

A Practice Sequence: Appealing to Ethos and Pathos

Discuss the language and strategies the writers use in the passages below to connect with their audience, in particular their appeals to both ethos and pathos. As you consider each excerpt, discuss who you think the implied audience is and whether you think the strategies the writers use to connect with their readers are effective or not.

1 Almost a half century after the U.S. Supreme Court concluded that Southern school segregation was unconstitutional and "inherently unequal," new statistics from the 1998–99 school year show that segregation continued to intensify throughout the 1990s, a period in which there were three major Supreme Court decisions authorizing a return to segregated neighborhood schools and limiting the reach and duration of desegregation orders. For African American students, this trend is particularly apparent in the South, where most blacks live and where the 2000 Census shows a continuing return from the North. From 1988 to 1998, most of the progress of the previous two decades in increasing integration in the region was lost. The South is still much more integrated than it was before the civil rights revolution, but it is moving backward at an accelerating rate.

—GARY ORFIELD, "Schools More Separate: Consequences of a Decade of Resegregation" (http://www.civilrightsproject.ucla.edu/research/deseg/ Schools_More_Separate.pdf)

2 No issue has been more saturated with dishonesty than the issue of racial quotas and preferences, which is now being examined by the Supreme Court of the United States. Many defenders of affirmative action are not even honest enough to admit that they are talking about quotas and preferences, even though everyone knows that that is what affirmative action amounts to in practice.

Despite all the gushing about the mystical benefits of "diversity" in higher education, a recent study by respected academic scholars found that "college diversity programs fail to raise standards" and that "a majority of faculty members and administrators recognize this when speaking anonymously."

This study by Stanley Rothman, Seymour Martin Lipset, and Neil Nevitte found that "of those who think that preferences have some impact on academic standards those believing it negative exceed those believing it positive by 15 to 1."

Poll after poll over the years has shown that most faculty members and most students are opposed to double standards in college admissions. Yet professors who will come out publicly and say what they say privately in these polls are as rare as hens' teeth.

Such two-faced talk is pervasive in academia and elsewhere. A few years ago, in Berkeley, there was a big fight over whether a faculty vote on affirmative action would be by secret ballot or open vote. Both sides knew that the result of a secret ballot would be the direct opposite of the result in a public vote at a faculty meeting.

—THOMAS SOWELL, "The Grand Fraud:
Affirmative Action for Blacks"
(http://www.capmag.com/article.asp?ID=2637)

3 When the judgment day comes for every high school student — that day when a final transcript is issued and sent to the finest institutions, with every sin of class selection written as with a burning chisel on stone — on that day a great cry will go up throughout the land, and there will be weeping, wailing, gnashing of teeth, and considerable grumbling against guidance counselors, and the cry of a certain senior might be, "WHY did no one tell me that Introduction to Social Poker wasn't a solid academic class?" At another, perhaps less wealthy school, a frustrated and under-nurtured sculptress will wonder, "Why can't I read, and why don't I care?" The reason for both of these oversights, as they may eventually discover, is that the idea of the elective course has been seriously mauled, mistreated, and abused under the current middle-class high school system. A significant amount of the blame for producing students who are stunted, both cognitively and morally, can be traced back to this pervasive fact. Elective courses, as shoddily planned and poorly funded as they may be, constitute the only formation that many students get in their own special types of intelligences. Following the model of Howard Gardner, these may be spatial, musical, or something else. A lack of stimulation to a student's own intelligence directly causes a lack of identification with the intelligence of others. Instead of becoming moderately interested in a subject by noticing the pleasure other people receive from it, the student will be bitter, jealous, and without empathy. These are the common ingredients in many types of tragedy, violent or benign. Schools must take responsibility for speaking in some way to each of the general types of intelligences. Failure to do so will result in students who lack skills, and also the inspiration to comfort, admire, emulate, and aid their fellow humans.

"All tasks that really call upon the power of attention are interesting for the same reason and to an almost equal degree," wrote Simone Weil in her *Reflections on Love and Faith*, her editor having defined attention as "a suspension of one's own self as a center of the world and making oneself available to the reality of another being." In Parker Palmer's *The Courage to Teach*, modern scientific theorist David Bohm describes "a holistic underlying implicate order whose information unfolds into the explicate order of particular fields." Rilke's euphemism for this "holistic . . . implicate order," which Palmer borrows, is "the grace of great things." Weil's term would be "God." However, both agree that eventual perception of this singular grace, or God, is accessible through education of a specific sort, and for both it is doubtless the most necessary experience of a lifetime. Realizing that this contention is raining down from different theorists, and keeping in mind that the most necessary experience of a lifetime should not be wholly irrelevant to the school system, educators should therefore reach the conclusion that this is a matter worth looking into. I assert that the most fruitful and practical results of their attention will be a wider range of electives coupled with a new acknowledgment and handling of them, one that treats each one seriously.

—ERIN MEYERS,
"The Educational Smorgasbord as Saving Grace"

APPEALING TO LOGOS: USING REASON AND EVIDENCE TO FIT THE SITUATION

To make an argument persuasive, you need to be in dialogue with your readers, using your own character (ethos) to demonstrate that you are a reasonable, credible, fair person and appealing to your readers' emotions (pathos), particularly their sense of right and wrong. Each type of appeal goes hand in hand with an appeal to logos, using converging pieces of evidence — statistics, facts, observations — to advance your claim. Remember that the type of evidence you use is determined by the issue, problem, situation, and readers' expectations. As an author, you should try to anticipate and address readers' beliefs and values. Ethos and pathos are concerned with the content of your argument; logos addresses both form and content.

An argument begins with one or more premises and ends with a conclusion. A **premise** is an assumption that you expect your readers to agree with, a statement that is either true or false — for example, "Alaska is cold in the winter" — that is offered in support of a claim. That claim is the **conclusion** you want your readers to draw from your premises. The conclusion is also a sentence that is either true or false. For instance, Loewen's major premise is that class is a key factor in Americans' access to health care, education, and wealth. Loewen also offers a second, more specific premise: that textbook writers provide little discussion of the ways class matters. Loewen crafts his argument to help readers draw the following conclusion: "We live in a class system that runs counter to the democratic principles that underlie the founding of the United States, and history textbooks must tell this story. Without this knowledge, citizens will be uninformed." Whether or not readers accept this as true depends on how Loewen moves from his initial premises to reach his conclusion — that is, whether or not we draw the same kinds of inferences, or reasoned judgments, that he does. He must do so in a way that meets readers' expectations of what constitutes relevant and persuasive evidence and guides them one step at a time toward his conclusion.

There are two main forms of argument: deductive and inductive. A **deductive argument** is an argument in which the premises support (or appear to support) the conclusion. If you join two premises to produce a conclusion that is taken to be true, you are stating a **syllogism.** This is the classic example of deductive reasoning through a syllogism:

1. All men are mortal. (First premise)
2. Socrates is a man. (Second premise)
3. Therefore, Socrates is mortal. (Conclusion)

In a deductive argument, it is impossible for both premises to be true and the conclusion to be false. That is, the truth of the premises means that the conclusion must also be true.

By contrast, an **inductive argument** relies on evidence and observation to reach a conclusion. Although readers may accept a writer's premises as true, it is possible for them to reject the writer's conclusion. Let's consider this for a moment in the context of Loewen's argument. Loewen introduces the premise that class matters, then offers the more specific premise that textbook writers leave class issues out of their narratives of American history, and finally draws the conclusion that citizens need to be informed of this body of knowledge in order to create change:

1. Although class is a key factor in Americans' access to health care, education, and wealth, students know very little about the social structure in the United States.
2. Textbook writers do not address the issue of class in their textbooks, an issue that people need to know about.
3. Therefore, if people had this knowledge, they would understand that poverty cannot be blamed on the poor.

Notice that Loewen's premises are not necessarily true. For example, readers could challenge the premise that "textbook writers do not address issues of class in their textbooks." After all, Loewen examined just twelve textbooks. What if he had examined a different set of textbooks? Would he have drawn the same conclusion? And even if Loewen's evidence convinces us that the two premises are true, we do not have to accept that the conclusion is true.

The conclusion in an inductive argument is never definitive. That is the nature of any argument that deals with human emotions and actions. Moreover, we have seen throughout history that people tend to disagree much more on the terms of an argument than on its form. Do we agree that Israel's leaders practice apartheid? (What do we mean by *apartheid* in this case?) Do we agree with the need to grant women reproductive rights? (When does life begin?) Do we agree that all people should be treated equally? (Would equality mean equal access to resources or to outcomes?)

Deductive arguments are conclusive. In a deductive argument, the premises are universal truths — laws of nature, if you will — and the conclusion must follow from those premises. That is, a^2 plus b^2 always equals c^2, and humans are always mortal. By contrast, an inductive argument is never conclusive. The premises may or may not be true; and even if they are true, the conclusion may be false. We might accept that class matters and that high school history textbooks don't address the issue of class structure in the United States; but we still would not know that students who have studied social stratification in America will necessarily understand the nature of poverty. It may be that social class is only one reason for poverty; or it may be that textbooks are only one source of information about social stratification in the United States, that textbook omissions are simply not as serious as Loewen claims. That the premises of an argument are true only establishes that the conclusion is probably true and, perhaps, only for some readers.

Inductive argument is the basis of academic writing; it is also the basis of any appeal to logos. The process of constructing an inductive argument involves three steps:

1. State the premises of your argument.

2. Use credible evidence to show readers that your argument has merit.

3. Demonstrate that the conclusion follows from the premises.

In following these three steps, you will want to determine the truth of your premises, help readers understand whether or not the inferences you draw are justified, and use word signals to help readers fully grasp the connections between your premises and conclusion.

■ State the Premises of Your Argument

Stating a premise establishes what you have found to be true and what you want to persuade readers to accept as truth as well. Let's return to Loewen, who asserts his premise at the very outset of the excerpt: "Middle-class students . . . know little about how the American class structure works . . . and nothing at all about how it has changed over time." Loewen elaborates on this initial premise a few sentences later, arguing that students "have no understanding of the ways that opportunity is not equal in America and no notion that the social structure pushes people around, influencing the ideas they hold and the lives they fashion." Implicit here is the point that class matters. Loewen makes this point explicit several paragraphs on, where he states that "social class is probably the single most important variable in society" (para. 6). He states his second, more specific premise in paragraph 2: "High school history textbooks can take some of the credit for this state of affairs." The burden of demonstrating that these premises are true is on Loewen. If readers find that either of the premises is not true, it will be difficult, if not impossible, for them to accept his conclusion that with more knowledge, people will understand that poverty is not the fault of the poor (para. 10).

▪ Use Credible Evidence

The validity of your argument depends on whether or not the inferences you draw are justified, and whether or not you can expect a reasonable person to draw the same conclusion from those premises. Loewen has to demonstrate throughout (1) that students do not have much, if any, knowledge about the class structure that exists in the United States and (2) that textbook writers are in large part to blame for this lack of knowledge. He also must help readers understand how this lack of knowledge contributes to (3) his conclusion that greater knowledge would lead Americans to understand that poor people are not responsible for poverty. He can help readers with the order in which he states his premises and by choosing the type and amount of evidence that will enable readers to draw the inferences that he does.

Interestingly, Loewen seems to assume that one group of readers — educators — will accept his first premise as true. He does not elaborate on what students know or do not know. Instead, he moves right to his second premise, which involves first acknowledging what high school history textbooks typically cover, then identifying what he believes are the important events that textbook writers exclude, and ultimately asserting that "treatments of events in labor history are never anchored in any analysis of social class" (para. 3). He supports this point with his own study of twelve textbooks (paras. 3–5) before returning to his premise that "social class is probably the single most important variable in society" (para. 6). What follows is a series of observations about the rich and references to researchers' findings on inequality (paras. 7–9). Finally, he asserts that "social class determines how people think about social class" (para. 10), implying that fuller knowledge would lead business leaders and conservative voters to think differently about the source of poverty. The question to explore is whether or not Loewen supports this conclusion.

▪ Demonstrate That the Conclusion Follows from the Premises

Authors signal their conclusion with words like *consequently, finally, in sum, in the end, subsequently, therefore, thus, ultimately,* and *as a result.* Here is how this looks in the structure of Loewen's argument:

1. Although class is a key factor in Americans' access to health care, education, and wealth, students know very little about the social structure in the United States.

2. Textbook writers do not address the issue of class in their textbooks, an issue that people need to know about.

3. Ultimately, if people had this knowledge, they would understand poverty cannot be blamed on the poor.

We've reprinted much of paragraph 9 of Loewen's excerpt below. Notice how Loewen pulls together what he has been discussing. He again underscores the importance of class and achievement ("All these are among the reasons."). And he points out that access to certain types of colleges puts people in a position to accumulate and sustain wealth. Of course, this is not true of the poor "because affluent families can save some money while poor families must spend what they make." This causal relationship ("Because") heightens readers' awareness of the class structure that exists in the United States.

> <u>All these are among the reasons</u> why social class predicts the rate of college attendance and the type of college chosen more effectively than does any other factor, including intellectual ability, however measured. After college, most affluent children get white-collar jobs, most working-class children get blue-collar jobs, and the class differences continue. As adults, rich people are more likely to have hired an attorney and to be a member of formal organizations that increase their civic power. Poor people are more likely to watch TV. <u>Because</u> affluent families can save some money while poor families must spend what they make, wealth differences are ten times larger than income differences. <u>Therefore</u> most poor and working-class families cannot accumulate the down payment required to buy a house, which in turn shuts them out from our most important tax shelter, the write-off of home mortgage interest. Working-class parents cannot afford to live in elite subdivisions or hire high-quality day care, so the process of educational inequality replicates itself in the next generation. <u>Finally</u>, affluent Americans also have longer life expectancies than lower- and working-class people, the largest single cause of which is better access to health care. . . .

Once Loewen establishes this causal relationship, he concludes ("Therefore," "Finally") with the argument that poverty persists from one generation to the next.

In paragraph 10, Loewen uses the transition word *ultimately* to make the point that social class matters, so much so that it limits the ways in which people see the world, that it even "determines how people think about social class." (We discuss how to write conclusions in Chapter 12.)

Steps to Appealing to Logos

1 **State the premises of your argument.** Establish what you have found to be true and what you want readers to accept as well.

2 **Use credible evidence.** Lead your readers from one premise to the next, making sure your evidence is sufficient and convincing and your inferences are logical and correct.

3 **Demonstrate that the conclusion follows from the premises.** In particular, use the right words to signal to your readers how the evidence and inferences lead to your conclusion.

RECOGNIZING LOGICAL FALLACIES

We turn now to **logical fallacies**, flaws in the chain of reasoning that lead to a conclusion that does not necessarily follow from the premises, or evidence. Logical fallacies are common in inductive arguments for two reasons: Inductive arguments rely on reasoning about probability, not certainty; and they derive from human beliefs and values, not facts or laws of nature.

Here we list fifteen logical fallacies. In examining them, think about how to guard against the sometimes-faulty logic behind statements you might hear from politicians, advertisers, and the like. That should help you examine the premises on which you base your own assumptions and the logic you use to help readers reach the same conclusions you do.

1. *Erroneous Appeal to Authority.* An authority is someone with expertise in a given subject. An *erroneous authority* is an author who claims to be an authority but is not, or someone an author cites as an authority who is not. In this type of fallacy, the claim might be true, but the fact that an unqualified person is making the claim means there is no reason for readers to accept the claim as true. Because the issue here is the legitimacy of authority, your concern should be to prove to yourself and your readers that you or the people you are citing have expertise in the subject. An awareness of this type of fallacy has become increasingly important as celebrities offer support for candidates running for office or act as spokespeople for curbing global warming or some other cause. The candidate may be the best person for the office, and there may be very good reasons to attack global warming; but we need to question the legitimacy of a nonexpert endorsement.

2. *Ad Hominem.* An ad hominem argument focuses on the person making a claim instead of on the claim itself. (*Ad hominem* is Latin for "to the person.") In most cases, an ad hominem argument does not have a bearing on the truth or the quality of a claim. Keep in mind that it is always important to address the claim or the reasoning behind it, rather than the person making the claim. "Of course Senator Wiley supports oil drilling in Alaska — he's in the pocket of the oil companies!" is an example of an ad hominem argument. Senator Wiley may have good reasons for supporting oil drilling in Alaska that have nothing to do with his alleged attachment to the oil industry. However, if an individual's character is relevant to the argument, then an ad hominem argument can be valid. If Senator Wiley has been found guilty of accepting bribes from an oil company, it makes sense to question both his credibility and his claims.

3. *Shifting the Issue.* This type of fallacy occurs when an author draws attention away from the issue instead of offering evidence that will enable people to draw their own conclusions about the soundness of an argument. For example:

> Affirmative action proponents accuse me of opposing equal opportunity in the workforce. I think my positions on military expenditures, education, and public health speak for themselves.

The author of this statement does not provide a chain of reasoning that would enable readers to judge his or her stance on the issue of affirmative action.

4. *Either/Or Fallacy.* At times, an author will take two extreme positions to force readers to make a choice between two seemingly contradictory positions. For example:

> Either you support the war in Iraq, or you are against it.

Although the author has set up an either/or condition, in reality one position does not exclude the other. Many people support the troops in Iraq even though they do not support the reasons for starting the war.

5. *Sweeping Generalizations.* When an author attempts to draw a conclusion without providing sufficient evidence to support the conclusion or examining possible counterarguments, he or she may be making sweeping generalizations. For example:

> Despite the women's movement in the 1960s and 1970s, women still do not receive equal pay for equal work. Obviously, any attempt to change the status quo for women is doomed to failure.

As is the case with many fallacies, the author's position may be reasonable, but we cannot accept the argument at face value. Reading critically entails testing assumptions like this one — that any attempt to create change is doomed to failure because women do not receive equal pay for equal work. We could ask, for example, whether inequities persist in the public sector. And we could point to other areas where the women's movement has had measurable success. Title IX, for example, has reduced the dropout rate among teenage girls; it has also increased the rate at which women earn college and graduate degrees.

6. *Bandwagon.* This is a fairly common mode of argument in advertising when, for example, a commercial attempts to persuade us to buy a certain product because it's popular.

> Because Harvard, Stanford, and Berkeley have all added a multicultural component to their graduation requirements, other institutions should do so as well.

The growing popularity of an idea is not sufficient reason to accept that it is true.

7. *Begging the Question.* This fallacy entails advancing a circular argument that asks readers to accept a premise that is also the conclusion readers are expected to draw:

> We could improve the undergraduate experience with coed dorms because both men and women benefit from living with members of the opposite gender.

Here readers are being asked to accept that the conclusion is true despite the fact that the premises — men benefit from living with women, and women benefit from living with men — are essentially the same as the conclusion.

Without evidence that a shift in dorm policy could improve on the undergraduate experience, we cannot accept the conclusion as true. Indeed, the conclusion does not necessarily follow from the premise.

8. *False Analogy.* Authors (and others) often try to persuade us that something is true by using a comparison. This approach is not in and of itself a problem, as long as the comparison is reasonable. For example:

> It is ridiculous to have a Gay and Lesbian Program and a Department of African American Culture. We don't have a Straight Studies Program or a Department of Caucasian Culture.

Here the author is urging readers to rethink the need for two academic departments by saying that the school doesn't have two other departments. That, of course, is not a reason for or against the new departments. What's needed is an analysis that compares the costs (economic and otherwise) of starting up and operating the new departments versus the contributions (economic and otherwise) of the new departments.

9. *Technical Jargon.* If you've ever had a salesperson try to persuade you to purchase a television or stereo with capabilities you absolutely *must* have — even if you don't understand a word the salesperson was saying about alternating currents and circuit splicers — then you're familiar with this type of fallacy. We found this passage in one of our student's papers:

> You should use this drug because it has been clinically proven that it inhibits the reuptake of serotonin and enhances the dopamine levels of the body's neurotransmitters.

The student's argument may very well be true, but he hasn't presented any substantive evidence to demonstrate that the premises are true and that the conclusion follows from the premises.

10. *Confusing Cause and Effect.* It is challenging to establish that one factor causes another. For example, how can we know for certain that economic class predicts, or is a factor in, academic achievement? How do we know that a new president's policies are the cause of a country's economic well-being? Authors often assume cause and effect when two factors are simply associated with each other:

> The current recession came right after President Bush was elected.

This fallacy states a fact; but it does not prove that the president's election caused the recession.

11. *Appeal to Fear.* One type of logical fallacy makes an appeal to readers' irrational fears and prejudices, preventing them from dealing squarely with a given issue and often confusing cause and effect:

> We should use whatever means possible to avoid further attack.

The reasoning here is something like this: "If we are soft on defense, we will never end the threat of terrorism." But we need to consider whether there is indeed a threat, and, if so, whether the presence of a threat should lead to action, and, if so, whether that action should include "whatever means possible." (Think of companies that sell alarm systems by pointing to people's vulnerability to harm and property damage.)

12. *Fallacy of Division.* A fallacy of division suggests that what is true of the whole must also be true of its parts:

> Conservatives have always voted against raising the minimum wage, against stem cell research, and for defense spending. Therefore, we can assume that conservative Senator Harrison will vote this way.

The author is urging readers to accept the premise without providing evidence of how the senator has actually voted on the three issues.

13. *Hasty Generalization.* This fallacy is committed when a person draws a conclusion about a group based on a sample that is too small to be representative. Consider this statement:

> Seventy-five percent of the seniors surveyed at the university study just 10 hours a week. We can conclude, then, that students at the university are not studying enough.

What you need to know is how many students were actually surveyed. Seventy-five percent may seem high, but not if the researcher surveyed just 400 of the 2,400 graduating seniors. This sample of students from a total population of 9,600 students at the university is too small to draw the conclusion that students in general are not studying enough.

14. *The Straw Man Argument.* A straw man fallacy makes a generalization about what a group believes without actually citing a specific writer or work:

> Democrats are more interested in running than in trying to win the war on terrorism.

Here the fallacy is that the author simply ignores a person's actual position and substitutes a distorted, exaggerated, or misrepresented version of that position. This kind of fallacy often goes hand in hand with assuming that what is true of the group is true of the individual, what we call the fallacy of division.

15. *Fallacy of the Middle Ground.* The fallacy of the middle ground assumes that the middle position between two extreme positions must be correct. Although the middle ground may be true, the author must justify this position with evidence.

> E. D. Hirsch argues that cultural literacy is the only sure way to increase test scores, and Jonathan Kozol believes schools will improve only if state legislators increase funding; but I would argue that school reform will occur if we change the curriculum *and* provide more funding.

This fallacy draws its power from the fact that a moderate or middle position is often the correct one. Again, however, the claim that the moderate or middle position is correct must be supported by legitimate reasoning.

ANALYZING THE APPEALS IN A TEXT

Now that you have studied the variety of appeals you can make to connect with your audience, we would like you to read a chapter from a study of education by Jean Anyon and analyze her strategies for appealing to her readers. The chapter is quite long and carefully argued, so we suggest you take detailed notes about her use of appeals to ethos, pathos, and logos as you read. You may want to refer to the Practice Sequence questions on p. 239 to help focus your reading. Ideally, you should work through the text with your classmates, in groups of three or four, appointing one student to record and share each group's analysis of Anyon's argument.

ABOUT THE READING

Jean Anyon teaches educational policy in the doctoral program in urban education at the City University of New York. Her articles on cities, race, social class, and schools have been reprinted in more than forty edited collections and translated into several languages. This chapter appears in her book *Radical Possibilities: Public Policy, Urban Education, and a New Social Movement* (2005).

JEAN ANYON

The Economic Is Political

It is widely acknowledged that one of the most important causes of poorly funded, staffed, and resourced schools is the poverty of the families and neighborhoods in which the schools are located. What is rarely acknowledged, however, is the proactive role of the federal government in maintaining this poverty and therefore poverty education. 1

All economies depend on government regulations in order to function. Capitalism would not be capitalism without constitutional and other federal provisions that make legal the private ownership of property, the right of business to charge more for products than the cost of producing them, or the right of corporations to keep those profits rather than sharing them with workers or employees. The 14th Amendment to the Constitution, passed in 1867, turns corporations into "persons" so they will be free from government "interference." Because economies are maintained by rules made by governments, economic institutions are inescapably political; they function according to determinative macroeconomic policies. 2

This chapter demonstrates that the poverty of U.S. families is considerably more widespread than commonly believed — and is catastrophic in low-income urban neighborhoods of color. I demonstrate that the 3 basic reason people are poor is that there are not enough jobs paying decent wages. In cities, the harsh economic realities of poverty shape the lives of parents of school children, and therefore the lives of their children as well. Neighborhood poverty also impacts the education students receive by contributing to low school funding levels, poorly paid teachers, and a lack of resources.

First, I provide an overview of national poverty as a backdrop to the situation in urban America. I then focus specifically on urban families of color. . . . 4

Income

Almost three-fourths (70%) of all American employees saw their wages fall between 1973 and 1995 (in constant dollars — that is, adjusted for inflation); even with the boom of the late 1990s, a majority of workers made less in 2000 than they had in 1973. New college graduates earned $1.10 less per hour in 1995 than their counterparts did in 1973. The earnings of the average American family did improve slightly over this period, but only through a dramatic increase in the number of hours worked and the share of families in which both parents worked (Lafer, 2002, p. 45; Mishel, Bernstein, and Boushey, 2003, p. 162). 5

Some of the largest long-term wage declines have been among entry-level workers (those with up to five years' work experience) with a high school education. Average wages for male entry-level high school graduates were 28% lower in 1997 than two decades earlier. The decline for comparable women was 18% (Economic Policy Institute, Feb. 17, 1999, p. 1). 6

Low wages are an important cause of poverty. Low-wage workers are those whose hourly wage is less than the earnings necessary to lift a family above the official poverty line — in 2004, $15,670 or less for a family of three, and $18,850 for a family of four. 7

The percentage of people who work full-time, year-round yet are poor is staggering. In 2000, at the height of a booming economy, almost a fifth of all men (19.5%), and almost a third of all women (33.1%) earned poverty-level wages working full-time, year-round. In the same year, over one in four Black men (26.3%), over one in three Black women (36.5%) and Hispanic men (37.6%), and almost half of Hispanic women (49.3%) earned poverty wages working full-time, year-round (Mishel, Bernstein, and Schmitt, 2001, pp. 137–139). 8

I analyzed figures provided by the Economic Policy Institute to calculate the overall percentage of people who work full-time, year-round, yet make *poverty-zone* wages. Poverty zone is defined here as wages up to 125% of the official poverty threshold needed to support a family of four at the poverty level (ibid., p. 133). The analysis demonstrates that in 1999, during the strong economy, almost half of people at work in the 9

U.S. (41.3%) earned poverty-zone wages — in 1999, $10.24/hour ($21,299/year) or less, working full-time, year-round (ibid., Table 2.10, p. 130). Two years later, in 2001, 38.4 earned poverty-zone wages working full-time, year-round (in 2001, 125% of the poverty line was a $10.88 hourly wage) (ibid., p. 134). These figures indicate that even in "good times" the U.S. pyramid of wages sits squarely on the shoulders of almost half of U.S. employees, who are the working poor.

In 2000, more than half (59.5%) of the working poor were women. Over   *10* 60% were White (60.4%). Thirty-five percent were Black or Latino (ibid., p. 353). Over 61.8% had a high school degree or less, while a quarter (24.2%) had some college, and 8% had a bachelor's degree (ibid., p. 353). This last figure indicates that *almost one in ten of the working poor is a college graduate.*

Seventy percent of the working poor had jobs in services or retail trade   *11* and 10% worked in manufacturing (ibid., p. 353). The vast majority (93.3%) were not in unions. More than half (57.7%) were under the age of 35 (ibid., p. 353). It is important to note that these workers are poor by official standards. As we will see below, a more realistic measure of poverty would literally double the amount of income under which people are defined as poor.

Moving up the income scale in the U.S. is more difficult than in other   *12* countries. As *Business Week* pointed out several years ago, economic mobility in the U.S. declined after the 1960s. Because most young people earn less than their parents, mobility here is second worst among similar countries recently studied — only Canada is worse (Dreier, Swanstrom, and Mollenkopf, 2001, pp. 18, 47). Low-wage workers in the U.S. are more likely to remain in the low-wage labor market longer than workers in Germany, France, Italy, the UK, Denmark, Finland, Sweden, and Canada (Mishel, Bernstein, and Schmitt, 2001, p. 12).

Relatively few U.S. individuals or families make high incomes. In   *13* 2000, only 7.8% of women and 16% of men earned at least three times the official poverty level (Mishel, Bernstein, and Boushey, 2003, p. 133). In 2001, only 19% of *families* earned more than $94,000, and only 4% made more than $164,000 (in 2001 dollars) (ibid., p. 56).

In the last two decades, income has skyrocketed at the tip of the distri-   *14* butional pyramid. The top one percent of tax filers, the 2.1 million people earning $700,000 a year or more, had after-tax income that jumped 31% in the last few years, while the after-tax income of the bottom 90% of tax filers rose only 3.4% (Mishel, Bernstein, and Schmitt, 2001, p. 83).

While employee pay has lagged, CEO pay has skyrocketed. And the   *15* ratio of CEO to worker pay has increased dramatically: In the 1960s and '70s, the ratio was between 26% and 37%. In the 1990s, it was between 102% and 310%. By 2001, the ratio had grown to 245% (Mishel, Bernstein, and Boushey, 2003, p. 215). In other words, in 2001, a CEO earned more in one workday (there are 260 in a year) than an average worker earned in 52 weeks (Economic Policy Institute, July 24, 2002, p. 1). In recent years, the average ratio of CEO pay to worker pay in all other advanced countries was considerably lower — 18.1 to 1 (Mishel, Bernstein, and Boushey, 2003, p. 216).

Jobs

What job opportunities are available for Americans? For two decades, numerous politicians, educators, and corporate spokespeople have been arguing that the U.S. must improve education because people need advanced skills in order to get a job. This is a myth, however. Most job openings in the next 10 years will not require either sophisticated skills or a college degree. Seventy-seven percent of new and projected jobs will be low-paying. Only a quarter of the new and projected jobs are expected to pay over $26,000 a year (Department of Labor, 2002, Chart 9; see also Economic Policy Institute, July 21, 2004). *16*

Most will require on-the-job training only, and will not require a college education; most will be in service and retail, where poverty-zone wages are the norm. Only 12.6% of new jobs will require a bachelor's degree. Of the 20 occupations expected to grow the fastest, only six require college — these six are in computer systems and information technology (Department of Labor, 2002, Chart 8), and there are relatively few of these jobs. *17*

The typical job of the future is not in information technology. Most job openings will be in food preparation and service and in fast-food restaurants, as telephone customer service representatives, and as cashiers (Department of Labor, 2002, Chart 9). In the next decade, about 5 million new jobs will be created for food workers, including waiters and waitresses. Another 4 million will be for cashiers and retail salespersons, and 3 million for clerks. Over 2 million will be for packagers, laborers, and truck drivers. Managerial and professional occupations will also need more workers, but their numbers pale compared with openings requiring less education. *18*

Indeed, a typical job of the future is retail sales at Wal-Mart. The average pay at Wal-Mart, which employs over a million people and is the largest private employer in the world, was $20,030 in 2000. According to *Business Week*, half of Wal-Mart's full-time employees are eligible for food stamps (households earning up to 130% of the official poverty line are eligible) (March 13, 2000, p. 78). *19*

A main determinant of whether one is poor or not is whether or not one has a decently paying job. The assertion that jobs are plentiful — if only workers were qualified to fill them — has been a central tenet of federal policy for 20 years. In 1982, the Reagan administration eliminated the Comprehensive Employment and Training Administration *20*

(CETA), which by 1978 had created almost 2 million full-time jobs, and substituted a major federal job training program (Job Partnership Training Act) (Lafer, 2002, pp. 1–2). Since then, and continuing today, job training has been the centerpiece of federal and state efforts to solve both the unemployment problem and the poverty problem. For almost all of this time, however, the federal government has not collected data on job availability (vacancies). If they had, and if they had consulted studies that had been carried out, they would have found that all the evidence demonstrates that at any given time there are far more unemployed people than there are job openings (ibid., p. 23; see also Pigeon and Wray, 1999, among others). The federal government has spent $85 billion on job training since the Reagan years, claiming all the while that there are jobs for those who want them (Lafer, 2002, p. 19).

In an exhaustive analysis, labor economist Gordon Lafer demon- _21_ strates that "over the period 1984 to 1996 — at the height of an alleged labor shortage — the number of people in need of work exceeded the total number of job openings by an average of five to one. In 1996, for example, the country would have needed 14.4 million jobs in order for all low-income people to work their way out of poverty. However, there were at most 2.4 million job openings available to meet this need; of these, only one million were in full-time, non-managerial positions" (ibid., 3, pp. 29–44). Thus, "there simply are not enough decently paying jobs for the number of people who need them — no matter how well trained they are" — and therefore job training programs cannot hope to address more than a small fraction of either the unemployment or poverty problems (ibid., 3, pp. 88–123; see also Jargowsky, 1998; and Eisenhower Foundation, 1998).

Lafer also demonstrates that throughout the 1984 to 1996 period, the _22_ total number of vacancies in jobs that paid above poverty wage was never more than one-seventh the number of people who needed those jobs, and "the gap between jobs needed and decently paying jobs available was never less than 16 million" (2002, pp. 34–35).

In the last 15 years or so, corporate pronouncements and federal eco- _23_ nomic policies (regarding expansion of visas for foreign workers, for example) have often been premised on the assumption that there has been a U.S. shortage of highly skilled computer technicians. And employers report that scientific and technical positions are often hard to fill (ibid., p. 54). Large corporations have argued that there are no skilled workers at home as a rationale for transferring computer-based operations to other countries. Although there are some shortages (nursing, for example), the evidence suggests that there is no actual shortage of programmers or systems analysts. "Rather, technology companies have hired lower-wage foreign programmers while thousands of more experienced (and more expensive) American programmers remained unemployed" (ibid., p. 54; see also Lardner, 1998).

Even in occupations such as nursing where there have been shortages,   *24*
most technical professions are quite small as a share of the overall workforce, and therefore the total number of such jobs going begging has
never been a significant source of job openings. For example, "the combined total of jobs for mathematicians, computer scientists, computer
programmers, numerical control tool programmers, science technicians,
electrical and electronic technicians, health technicians, and health
assessment and treating occupations amounted to only 4.1% of the total
workforce in 1984. After twenty years of unprecedented growth, this
share is projected to grow to only 6.4 by the year 2006" (Lafer, 2002, p. 54;
see also Galbraith, 1998; and Mishel, Bernstein, and Boushey, 2003).

Furthermore, as the technology has been adapted by business, "com-   *25*
puter work" has been highly differentiated, with technical knowledge
used by a relatively small group of well-paid specialists, and the vast
majority of daily computer operators carrying out tasks in relatively
low-wage occupations with few educational requirements (social workers, secretaries, credit card and computer call center operators, etc.)
(Lafer, 2002, p. 56; see also Frenkel, Korczynski, Shire, and Tam, 1999;
Galbraith, 1998; and Osterman, 2001).

To make the case for terminating the job-creation programs of CETA   *26*
in 1982, Ronald Reagan argued that "if you look at the want ads, you
see lots of available jobs" (Lafer, 2002, p. 44). As Lafer points out, however, "A look at the want ads in the newspapers shows that there are,
indeed jobs, but only for the number of people the ads specify; and this
illusion masks a deeper truth, which is that for large numbers of the
poor there are NO decently paying jobs, no matter how hard they work
or what training programs they enroll in" (ibid., p. 44).

A report in the *New York Times* in 1999 offered on-the-ground confir-   *27*
mation of the lack of jobs for workers who need them; Journalist Amy
Waldman reported that at the height of the "full economy" in 1999,
about 5,000 lined up for a job fair in the Bronx, New York. More than 40
employers were inside the Bronx County Building, trying to fill positions from sales clerk to registered nurse. Many of the people in line,
who had been waiting for over three hours, said they had been looking
for work, most often entry-level clerical positions, for months. Many of
the people in line were on public assistance and were trying to get off it.
"There is a huge pool of people with entry-level skills and not enough
jobs for them," said Lucy Mayo, an employment specialist. "Most of the
jobs that were available," she said, "offered low pay and no benefits. For
example, Barnes and Noble, which was scheduled to open a new bookstore at Bay Plaza in the Bronx, had 50–75 jobs to fill. The jobs pay
$7.25 an hour, are part-time with no benefits. Some of the large corpo-
rations there, however (Montefiore Medical Centers and the Correc-
tional Services Corporation), offered benefits after six months. One
man, aged 25, said he had left his last manufacturing job in Chatham,

NJ [a suburb of New York City], because the transportation was eating up half of his $7 hourly pay. With two children to support, he had been looking for work for six months. . . . There were 2,600 jobs created in the Bronx last year [1998], mostly in retail and construction. Still, 250,000 Bronx residents work outside the borough" (Waldman, Oct. 20, 1999).

Compounding the problem for entry-level workers, college-educated persons may be crowding them out. Research by Richard Murnane and Frank Levy shows that controlling for a person's mathematics or reading skill while a high school senior eliminates a substantial portion of the growth in the college-to-high school wage premium in a later period (for women essentially all, and for men about one-third). This suggests that it is basic high school–level skills that are increasingly in demand by employers, who are relying more and more on college completion as a screen to get the people who are more likely to have them (Murnane and Levy, 1996, p. 29; see also Pigeon and Wray, 1999).   28

That employers hire college-educated workers for jobs that require high school skills helps to explain why a more highly educated work-force does not necessarily earn higher wages. As entry-level employees obtain more education, employers merely ratchet up the requirements (see Galbraith, 1998; and Moss and Tilly, 2001).   29

Poverty

One consequence of a predominance of low-wage work and too few jobs in the U.S. is the numbers of poor people that approach the figures of 1959 before massive urban poverty became a national issue. Although the percentages are lower now, the numbers are still staggering: There were about as many people officially poor in 1993 (39.2 million) as in 1959 (39.4 million) — three years before Michael Harrington galvanized the nation's conscience, and ultimately a "war on poverty," by demon-strating that upwards of 40 million people were poor (Harrington, 1963, p. 9). (In 2003, almost 36 million — 35.8 million — were officially poor.)   30

Most poverty today is urban poverty. Demographic researcher Myron Orfield analyzed the distribution of poverty populations in the 25 largest metropolitan areas in the U.S. and found (confirmed by the 2000 Census) that about two-thirds of the U.S. poor today live in central cities and "urbanized," financially distressed suburbs.   31

As has been the case since the mid-1960s, most of the urban poor are Black or Latino. . . . The concentration of Black and Latino poor in low-income urban areas is due not only to a lack of jobs with decent pay (and insufficient income to support a move out if desired) but to the lack of federal and state implementation of antiracial discrimination laws, the lack of affordable housing outside of urban areas, and state-enabled local zoning exclusions based on social class (income).   32

The figures on poverty presented so far in this chapter are based on fed- 33
eral guidelines, and they underestimate the number of people who are
actually poor. The federal poverty formula in 1998 — during the height of
the '90s boom — determined that 13% of U.S. households (families and
unattached individuals) were poor. A single mother with two children was
officially poor if she earned $13,133 or less in that year. In 2003, a single
mother of two children was officially poor if she earned $15,260 or less.

Many social scientists have come to believe that these amounts are 34
too low, and that individuals and families with incomes up to 200% of
government thresholds are poor. The official formula for figuring
poverty — designed by federal employee Molly Orshansky in 1963 and
used in the war on poverty — utilized data collected in the 1950s. The
formula Orshansky devised was based on the price of a minimal food
budget (as determined by the Department of Agriculture). She multiplied the cost of food by three, to cover housing and health-care costs.
This figure, adjusted for family size, was the level below which families
and individuals were designated as poor.

Research in the 1950s showed that families spent about a third of 35
their budget on food. Since that time, however, the costs of housing and
health care have skyrocketed. Thus, most families today spend only
about a fifth of their income on food, and considerably more on housing
and health care (Bernstein, Brocht, and Spade-Aguilar, 2000, pp. 12–13;
see also Short, Iceland, and Garner, 1999; and recommendations by the
National Research Council, reported in Citro and Michael, 1995).

A recent national assessment of working families concluded that twice 36
the official poverty line is a more realistic measure of those who face critical and serious hardships in the U.S. This research documents that
working families with income up to 200% of the poverty line "experience
as many hardships" as families who are officially poor (Boushey,
Brocht, Gundersen, and Bernstein, 2001, p. 2).

A calculation of the individuals who earned less than 200% of the 37
poverty level in 2001 demonstrates a much larger percentage of poor
employees than is commonly acknowledged: 84.3% of Hispanic workers,
80% of Black workers, and 64.3% of White workers made wages at or
under 200% of the official poverty line (Mishel, Bernstein, and Schmitt,
2001, pp. 130–139). A calculation of *families* living with earnings up to
200% of the poverty line reveals that Black and Latino families face the
greatest financial hurdles. Over 50% of Black and Latino families earn
less than 200% of the poverty level, compared to only 20.3% of White
families, even though White families make up the majority (50.5%) of
families that fall below 200% of the poverty level (ibid., p. 12).

Families headed by a worker with less than a high school education 38
are the most likely to fall below 200% (68.6%), but over three-fourths of
families who fall below are headed by a worker with a high school education or more. An indication of the failure of higher education to
secure good wages is the fact that over a third (33.6%) are headed by a

worker with some college or a college degree (ibid., p. 13). And an indictment of the failure of full-time work to provide a decent living is the fact that a full half (50.0%) of families falling below 200% of the poverty line have a *full-time, year-round worker* (ibid., p. 15).

The statistics in this chapter relate in a fairly staid manner what is   *39* actually a potentially inflammatory political situation. A humane reckoning of poverty reveals that the vast majority of African Americans and Latinos who have jobs, and more than two-thirds of employed Whites, do not earn enough to live on. This outrages me, as the experience must anger those who live it. But the situation is not immutable. Economies are indeed political, regulated by officials elected and appointed who formulate legislation, legal decisions, and other policy. These officials, and their mandates, can be changed — but only if all of us who are incensed by the policies' indecency stand together.

In order for injustice to create an outrage that can ultimately be   *40* channeled into public demands, knowledge of the facts is necessary, and an appreciation of the consequences must be clear. I hope this chapter clarifies the situation regarding poverty. It is also extremely important . . . that people who are poor come to see their situation not as a result of their own failure but as a result of systemic causes. That is, if governments created enough jobs, and if businesses paid higher wages, workers would not be poor.

And knowledge is crucial to an accurate understanding of what   *41* plagues urban education. We must know where the problem lies in order to identify workable solutions. We can win the war against poverty and poor schools only if we know where the poverty originates. The next chapter describes one important source, federal policies that maintain low-wage work and unemployment in urban areas, and ways these can set up failure for the families and schools there.

BIBLIOGRAPHY

Bernstein, Jared, Brocht, Chauna, and Spade-Aguilar, Maggie. (2000). *How much is enough? Basic family budgets for working families.* Washington, DC: Economic Policy Institute.

Boushey, Heather, Brocht, Chauna, Gundersen, Betheny, and Bernstein, Jared. (2001). *Hardships in America: The real story of working families.* Washington, DC: Economic Policy Institute.

Citro, Constance, and Michael, Robert (Eds.). (1995). *Measuring poverty: A new approach.* Washington, DC: National Academy Press.

Department of Labor. (2002). *Occupation projections to 2010.* Washington, DC.

Economic Policy Institute. (1999, Feb. 17). *Entry-level workers face lower wages.* Washington, DC.

Economic Policy Institute. (2002, July 24). *Economic snapshots.* Washington, DC.

Economic Policy Institute. (2004, July 21). *Jobs in the future: No boom in the need for college graduates.* Washington, DC.

Eisenhower Foundation. (1998). *Background report.* Washington DC.

Frenkel, Stephen, Korczynski, Maretk, Shire, Karen, and Tam, May. (1999). *On the front line: Organization of work in the information economy.* Ithaca, NY: Cornell University Press.

Galbraith, James K. (1998). *Created unequal: The crisis in American pay.* Twentieth Century Fund Book. New York: Free Press, Simon and Schuster.

Harrington, Michael. (1963). *The other America: Poverty in the United States.* Baltimore, MD: Penguin.

Jargowsky, Paul. (1998). *Poverty and place: Ghettos, barrios, and the American city.* New York: Russell Sage.

Lafer, Gordon. (2002). *The job training charade.* Ithaca, NY: Cornell University Press.

Lardner, James. (1998, March 16). Too old to write code? *U.S. News & World Report.* Cited in Lafer, 2002 (p. 250).

Mishel, Lawrence, Bernstein, Jared, and Boushey, Heather. (2003). *The state of working America: 2002/2003.* Ithaca, NY: Cornell University Press.

Mishel, Lawrence, Bernstein, Jared, and Schmitt, John. (2001). *The state of working America: 2000/2001.* Ithaca, NY: Cornell University Press.

Moss, Philip, and Tilly, Chris. (2001). *Stories employers tell: Race, skill, and hiring in America.* New York: Russell Sage.

Murnane, Richard, and Levy, Frank. (1996). *Teaching the new basic skills: Principles for educating children to thrive in a changing economy.* New York: Free Press.

Orfield, Myron. (1997). *Metropolitics: A regional agenda for community and stability.* Washington, DC: Brookings Institute.

Osterman, Paul. (2001). *Working in America: A blueprint for the new labor market.* Cambridge, MA: MIT Press.

Pigeon, Marc-Andre, and Wray, Randall. (1999). Down and out in the United States: An inside look at the out of the labor force population. Public Policy Brief No. 54. Annandale-on-Hudson, NY: The Jerome Levy Economics Institute of Bard College.

Short, Kathleen, Iceland, John, and Garner, Thesia. (1999). *Experimental poverty measures.* Washington, DC: U.S. Census Bureau.

Waldman, Amy. (1999, Oct. 20). Long line in the Bronx, but for jobs, not the Yankees. *New York Times.*

A Practice Sequence: Analyzing the Appeals in a Text

1 Make a list of the major premises that inform Anyon's argument, and examine the evidence she uses to support them. To what extent do you find her evidence credible? Do you generally agree or disagree with the conclusions she draws? Be prepared to explain your responses to your class or peer group.

2 Note instances where Anyon appeals to ethos, pathos, and logos. How would you describe the ways she makes these three types of appeals? How does she present herself? What does she seem to assume? How does she help you understand the chain of reasoning by which she moves from premises to conclusion?

3 Working in groups of three or four, compose a letter to Anyon in which you take issue with her argument. This does not mean your group has to disagree with her entire argument, although of course you may. Rather, present your group's own contribution to

the conversation in which she is participating. You may want to ask her to further explain one or more of her points, or suggest what she might be leaving out, or add your own take or evidence to her argument. As a group, you will have to agree on your focus. In the letter, include a summary of Anyon's argument or the part of it on which your group is focusing. Pay close attention to your own strategies for appealing to her — how you present yourselves, how you appeal to her values and emotions, and how you present your reasons for your own premises and conclusion.

12

Drafting an Essay: Introductions, Supporting Paragraphs, Conclusions

In this chapter, we describe strategies for crafting introductions that set up your argument. We then describe the characteristics of well-formulated paragraphs that will help you build your argument. Finally, we provide you with some strategies for writing conclusions that reinforce what is new about your argument, what is at stake, and what readers should do with the knowledge you convey.

DRAFTING INTRODUCTIONS

The introduction is where you set up your argument. It's where you identify a widely held assumption, challenge that assumption, and state your thesis. Writers use a number of strategies to set up their arguments. In this section we look at five of them:

- Moving from a general topic to a specific thesis (inverted-triangle introduction)
- Introducing the topic with a story (narrative introduction)
- Beginning with a question (interrogative introduction)
- Capturing readers' attention with something unexpected (paradoxical introduction)
- Identifying a gap in knowledge (minding-the-gap introduction)

Remember that an introduction need not be limited to a single paragraph. It may take several paragraphs to effectively set up your argument.

Taken from Stuart Greene and April Lidinsky, *From Inquiry to Academic Writing: A Practical Guide*, pp. 201–26 (Chapter 9, "From Introductions to Conclusions: Drafting an Essay").

Keep in mind that you have to make these strategies your own. That is, we can suggest models, but you must make them work for your own argument. You must imagine your readers and what will engage them. What tone do you want to take? Playful? Serious? Formal? Urgent? The attitude you want to convey will depend on your purpose, your argument, and the needs of your audience.

■ The Inverted-Triangle Introduction

An **inverted-triangle introduction**, like an upside-down triangle, is broad at the top and pointed at the base. It begins with a general statement of the topic and then narrows its focus, ending with the point of the paragraph (and the triangle), the writer's thesis. We can see this strategy at work in the introduction from a student's essay below. The student writer (1) begins with a broad description of the problem she will address, (2) then focuses on a set of widely held but troublesome assumptions, and (3) finally, responding to what she sees as a pervasive problem, presents her thesis.

The student begins with a general set of assumptions about education that she believes people readily accept.

In today's world, many believe that education's sole purpose is to communicate information for students to store and draw on as necessary. By storing this information, students hope to perform well on tests. Good test scores assure good grades. Good grades eventually lead to acceptances into good colleges, which ultimately guarantee good jobs. Many teachers and students, convinced that education exists as a tool to secure good jobs, rely on the banking system. In her essay "Teaching to Transgress," bell hooks defines the banking system as an "approach to learning that is rooted in the notion that all students need to do is consume information fed to them by a professor and be able to memorize and store it" (185). Through the banking system, students focus solely on facts, missing the important themes and life lessons available in classes and school materials. The banking system misdirects the fundamental goals of education. Education's true purpose is to prepare students for the real world by allowing them access to pertinent life knowledge available in their studies. Education should then entice students to apply this pertinent life knowledge to daily life struggles through praxis. In addition to her definition of the banking system, hooks offers the idea of praxis from the work of Paulo Freire. When incorporated into education, praxis, or "action and reflection upon the world in order to change it" (185), offers an advantageous educational tool that enhances the true purpose of education and overcomes the banking system.

She then cites author bell hooks, to identify an approach that makes use of these assumptions — the "banking system" of education, a term hooks borrows from educator Paulo Freire.

The student then points to the banking system as the problem. This sets up her thesis about the "true purpose" of education.

The strategy of writing an introduction as an inverted triangle entails first identifying an idea, argument, or concept that people appear to accept as true; next, pointing out the problems with that idea, argument, or concept; and then, in a few sentences, setting out a thesis — how those problems can be resolved.

■ The Narrative Introduction

Opening with a short **narrative**, or story, is a strategy many writers use successfully to draw readers into a topic. A narrative introduction relates a sequence of events and can be especially effective if you think you need to coax indifferent or reluctant readers into taking an interest in the topic. Of course, a narrative introduction delays the declaration of your argument, so it's wise to choose a short story that clearly connects to your argument, and get to the thesis as quickly as possible (within a few paragraphs) before your readers start wondering "What's the point of this story?"

Notice how the student writer uses a narrative introduction to her argument in her essay titled "Throwing a Punch at Gender Roles: How Women's Boxing at Notre Dame Empowers Women."

The student's entire first paragraph is a narrative that takes us into the world of women's boxing and foreshadows her thesis.

Glancing at my watch, I ran into the gym, noting to myself that being late to the first day of boxing practice was not the right way to make a good first impression. I flew down the stairs into the basement, to the room the boxers have lovingly dubbed "The Pit." What greeted me when I got there was more than I could ever have imagined. Picture a room filled with boxing gloves of all sizes covering an entire wall, a mirror covering another, a boxing ring in a corner, and an awesome collection of framed newspaper and magazine articles chronicling the boxers whose pictures were hanging on every wall. Now picture that room with seventy-plus girls on the floor doing push-ups, sweat dripping down their faces. I was immediately struck by the discipline this sport would take from me, but I had no idea I would take so much more from it.

With her narrative as a backdrop, the student identifies a problem, using the transition word yet to mark her challenge to the conditions she observes in the university's women's boxing program.

The university offers the only nonmilitary-based college-level women's boxing program in America, and it also offers women the chance to push their physical limits in a regulated environment. Yet the program is plagued with disappointments. I have experienced for myself the stereotypes female boxers face and have dealt with the harsh reality that boxing is still widely recognized as only a men's sport. This paper will show that the women's boxing program at ND serves as a much-needed outlet for females to come face-to-face with aspects of themselves they would not typically get a chance to explore. It will

The writer then states her thesis (what her paper "will show"): Despite the problems of stereotyping, women's boxing offers women significant opportunities for growth.

also examine how viewing this sport as a positive opportunity for women at ND indicates that t'ere is growing hope that very soon more activities similar to women's boxing may be better received by society in general. I will accomplish these goals by analyzing scholarly journals, old <u>Observer</u> [the school newspaper] articles, and survey questions answered by the captains of the 2003 women's boxing team of ND.

The student writer uses a visually descriptive narrative to introduce us to the world of women's college boxing; then, in the second paragraph, she steers us toward the purpose of the paper and the methods she will use to develop her argument about what women's boxing offers to young women and to the changing world of sports.

■ The Interrogative Introduction

An **interrogative introduction** invites readers into the conversation of your essay by asking one or more questions, which the essay goes on to answer. You want to think of a question that will pique your readers' interest, enticing them to read on to discover how your insights shed light on the issue. Notice the question Daphne Spain, a professor of urban and environmental planning, uses to open her essay "Spatial Segregation and Gender Stratification in the Workplace."

Spain sets up her argument by asking a question and then tentatively answering it with a reference to a published study.

In the third sentence she states her thesis — that men and women have very little contact in the workplace.

Finally, she outlines the effects that this lack of contact has on women.

To what extent do women and men who work in different occupations also work in different space? Baran and Teegarden propose that occupational segregation in the insurance industry is "tantamount to spatial segregation by gender" since managers are overwhelmingly male and clerical staff are predominantly female. This essay examines the spatial conditions of women's work and men's work and proposes that working women and men come into daily contact with one another very infrequently. Further, women's jobs can be classified as "open floor," but men's jobs are more likely to be "closed door." That is, women work in a more public environment with less control of their space than men. This lack of spatial control both reflects and contributes to women's lower occupational status by limiting opportunities for the transfer of knowledge from men to women.

By the end of this introductory paragraph, Spain has explained some of the terms she will use in her essay (*open floor* and *closed door*) and has offered in her final sentence a clear statement of her thesis.

In "Harry Potter and the Technology of Magic," literature scholar Elizabeth Teare begins by contextualizing the Harry Potter publishing phenomenon. Then she raises a question about what is fueling this success story.

In her first four sentences, Teare describes something she is curious about and she hopes readers will be curious about — the growing popularity of the Harry Potter books.

The July/August 2001 issue of *Book* lists J. K. Rowling as one of the ten most influential people in publishing. She shares space on this list with John Grisham and Oprah Winfrey, along with less famous but equally powerful insiders in the book industry. What these industry leaders have in common is an almost magical power to make books succeed in the marketplace, and this magic, in addition to that performed with wands, Rowling's novels appear to practice. Opening weekend sales charted like those of a blockbuster movie (not to mention the blockbuster movie itself), the reconstruction of the venerable *New York Times* bestseller lists, the creation of a new nation's worth of web sites in the territory of cyberspace, and of course the legendary inspiration of tens of millions of child readers — the Harry Potter books have transformed both the technologies of reading and the way we

In the fifth sentence, Teare asks the question she will try to answer in the rest of the essay.

understand those technologies. What is it that makes these books — about a lonely boy whose first act on learning he is a wizard is to go shopping for a wand — not only an international phenomenon among children and parents and teachers but also a topic of compelling interest to literary, social, and cultural critics?

Finally, in the last sentence, Teare offers a partial answer to her question — her thesis.

I will argue that the stories the books tell, as well as the stories we're telling about them, enact both our fantasies and our fears of children's literature and publishing in the context of twenty-first-century commercial and technological culture.

In the final two sentences of the introduction, Teare raises her question about the root of this "international phenomenon" and then offers her thesis. By the end of the opening paragraph, then, the reader knows exactly what question is driving Teare's essay and the answer she proposes to explain throughout the essay.

■ The Paradoxical Introduction

A **paradoxical introduction** appeals to readers' curiosity by pointing out an aspect of the topic that runs counter to their expectations. Just as an interrogative introduction draws readers in by asking a question, a paradoxical introduction draws readers in by saying, in effect, "Here's something completely surprising and unlikely about this issue, but my essay will go on to show you how it is true." In this passage from "'Holding Back': Negotiating a Glass Ceiling on Women's Muscular

Strength," sociologist Shari L. Dworkin points to a paradox in our commonsense understanding of bodies as the product of biology, not culture.

In the first sentence, Dworkin quotes from a study to identify the thinking that she is going to challenge.

Current work in gender studies points to how "when examined closely, much of what we take for granted about gender and its causes and effects either does not hold up, or can be explained differently." These arguments become especially contentious when confronting nature/culture debates on gendered *bodies*.

Notice how Dworkin signals her own position (however) relative to commonly held assumptions.

After all, "common sense" frequently tells us that flesh and blood bodies are about biology. However, bodies are also shaped and constrained through cumulative social practices, structures of opportunity, wider cultural meanings, and more.

Dworkin ends by stating her thesis, noting a paradox that will surprise readers.

Paradoxically, then, when we think that we are "really seeing" naturally sexed bodies, perhaps we are seeing the effect of internalizing gender ideologies — carrying out social practices — and this constructs our vision of "sexed" bodies.

Dworkin's strategy in the first three sentences is to describe common practice, the understanding that bodies are biological. Then, in the sentences beginning "However" and "Paradoxically," she advances the surprising idea that our bodies — not just the clothes we wear, for example — carry cultural gender markers. Her essay then goes on to examine women's weight lifting, and the complex motives driving many women to create a body that is perceived as muscular but not masculine.

■ The Minding-the-Gap Introduction

This type of introduction takes its name from the British train system, the voice on the loudspeaker that intones "Mind the gap!" at every stop, to call riders' attention to the gap between the train car and the platform. In a **minding-the-gap introduction**, a writer calls readers' attention to a gap in the research on an issue, and then uses the rest of the essay to fill in the "gap." A minding-the-gap introduction says, in effect, "Wait a minute. There's something missing from this conversation, and my research and ideas will fill in this gap."

For example, in the introductory paragraphs to their book *Men's Lives*, Michael S. Kimmel and Michael A. Messner explain how the book is different from other books that discuss men's lives, and how it serves a different purpose.

The authors begin with an assumption and then challenge it. A transition word (but) signals the challenge.

This is a book about men. But, unlike other books about men, which line countless library shelves, this is a book about men as men. It is a book in which men's experiences are not taken for granted as we explore the "real" and significant accomplishments of men, but a book in which those experiences are treated as significant and important in themselves.

The authors follow with a question that provokes readers' interest and points to the gap they summarize in the last sentence.

But what does it mean to examine men "as men"? Most courses in a college curriculum are about men, aren't they? But these courses routinely deal with men only in their public roles, so we come to know and understand men as scientists, politicians, military figures, writers, and philosophers. Rarely, if ever, are men understood through the prism of gender.

Kimmel and Messner use these opening paragraphs to highlight both what they find problematic about the existing literature on men and to introduce readers to their own approach.

Strategies for Drafting Introductions

1 **Use an inverted triangle.** Begin with a broad situation, concept, or idea, and narrow the focus to your thesis.

2 **Begin with a narrative.** Capture readers' imagination and interest with a story that sets the stage for your argument.

3 **Ask a question that you will answer.** Provoke readers' interest with a question, and then use your thesis to answer the question.

4 **Present a paradox.** Begin with an assumption that readers accept as true and formulate a thesis that not only challenges that assumption but may very well seem paradoxical.

5 **Mind the gap.** Identify what readers know and then what they don't know (or what you believe they need to know).

A Practice Sequence: Drafting an Introduction

1 Write or rewrite your introduction (which, as you've seen, may involve more than one paragraph), using one of the strategies described above. Then share your introduction with one of your peers and ask the following questions:

- To what extent did the strategy compel you to want to read further?
- To what extent is my thesis clear?
- How effectively do I draw a distinction between what I believe others assume to be true and my own approach?
- Is there another way that I might have made my introduction more compelling?

After listening to the responses, try a second strategy and then ask your peer which introduction is more effective.

2 If you do not have your own introduction to work on, revise the introduction below from one of our students' essays, combining two of the strategies we describe above.

> News correspondent Pauline Frederick once commented, "When a man gets up to speak people listen then look. When a woman gets up, people look; then, if they like what they see, they listen." Ironically, the harsh reality of this statement is given life by the ongoing controversy over America's most recognizable and sometimes notorious toy, Barbie. Celebrating her 40th birthday this year, Barbie has become this nation's most beleaguered soldier (a woman no less) of idolatry who has been to the front lines and back more times than the average "Joe." This doll, a piece of plastic, a toy, incurs both criticism and praise spanning both ends of the ideological spectrum. Barbie's curvaceous and basically unrealistic body piques the ire of both liberals and conservatives, each contending that Barbie stands for the distinct view of the other. One hundred and eighty degrees south, others praise Barbie's (curves and all) ability to unlock youthful imagination and potential. M. G. Lord explains Barbie best: "To study Barbie, one sometimes has to hold seemingly contradictory ideas in one's head at the same time. . . . The doll functions like a Rorschach test: people project wildly dissimilar and often opposing meanings on it. . . . And her meaning, like her face, has not been static over time." In spite of the extreme polarity, a sole unconscious consensus manifests itself about Barbie. Barbie is "the icon" of womanhood and the twentieth century. She is the American dream. Barbie is "us." The question is always the same: What message does Barbie send? Barbie is a toy. She is the image of what we see.

DEVELOPING PARAGRAPHS

In your introduction, you set forth your thesis. Then, in subsequent paragraphs, you have to develop your argument. Remember our metaphor: If your thesis, or main claim, is the skewer that runs through each paragraph in your essay, then these paragraphs are the "meat" of your argument. The paragraphs that follow your introduction carry the burden of evidence in your argument. After all, a claim cannot stand on its own without supporting evidence. Generally speaking, each paragraph should include a topic sentence that brings the main idea of the paragraph into focus, be unified around the main idea of the topic sentence, and adequately develop the idea. At the same time, a paragraph does not stand on its own; as part of your overall argument, it can refer to what you've said earlier, gesture toward where you are heading, and connect to the larger conversation to which you are contributing.

We now ask you to read an excerpt from "Reinventing 'America': Call for a New National Identity," by Elizabeth Martínez, and answer some questions about how you think the author develops her argument, paragraph by paragraph. Then we discuss her work in the context of the three key elements of paragraphs: *topic sentences*, *unity*, and *adequate development*. As you read, pay attention to how, sentence by sentence, Martínez develops her paragraphs. We also ask that you consider how she makes her argument provocative, impassioned, and urgent for her audience.

┌─ ABOUT THE READING ────────────────────────────────

Elizabeth Martínez is a Chicana activist who since 1960 has worked in and documented different movements for change, including the civil rights, women's, and Chicano movements. She is the author of six books and numerous articles. Her best-known work is *500 Years of Chicano History in Pictures* (1991), which became the basis of a two-part video she scripted and codirected. Her latest book is *De Colores Means All of Us: Latina Views for a Multi-Colored Century* (1998). In "Reinventing 'America,'" Martínez argues that Americans' willingness to accept a "myth" as "the basis for [the] nation's self-defined identity" has brought the country to a crisis.

└──

ELIZABETH MARTÍNEZ

From Reinventing "America": Call for a New National Identity

For some fifteen years, starting in 1940, 85 percent of all U.S. elementary schools used the Dick and Jane series to teach children how to read. The series starred Dick, Jane, their white middle-class parents, their dog Spot and their life together in a home with a white picket fence.   1

"Look, Jane, look! See Spot run!" chirped the two kids. It was a house full of glorious family values, where Mom cooked while Daddy went to work in a suit and mowed the lawn on weekends. The Dick and Jane books also taught that you should do your job and help others. All this affirmed an equation of middle-class whiteness with virtue.   2

In the mid-1990s, museums, libraries and eighty Public Broadcasting Service (PBS) stations across the country had exhibits and programs commemorating the series. At one museum, an attendant commented, "When you hear someone crying, you know they are looking at the Dick   3 and Jane books." It seems nostalgia runs rampant among many Euro-Americans: a nostalgia for the days of unchallenged White Supremacy — both moral and material — when life was "simple."

We've seen that nostalgia before in the nation's history. But today it signifies a problem reaching a new intensity. It suggests a national identity crisis that promises to bring in its wake an unprecedented nervous breakdown for the dominant society's psyche. *4*

Nowhere is this more apparent than in California, which has long been on the cutting edge of the nation's present and future reality. Warning sirens have sounded repeatedly in the 1990s, such as the fierce battle over new history textbooks for public schools, Proposition 187's ugly denial of human rights to immigrants, the 1996 assault on affirmative action that culminated in Proposition 209, and the 1997 move to abolish bilingual education. Attempts to copycat these reactionary measures have been seen in other states. *5*

The attack on affirmative action isn't really about affirmative action. Essentially it is another tactic in today's war on the gains of the 1960s, a tactic rooted in Anglo resentment and fear. A major source of that fear: the fact that California will almost surely have a majority of people of color in 20 to 30 years at most, with the nation as a whole not far behind. *6*

Check out the February 3, 1992, issue of *Sports Illustrated* with its double-spread ad for *Time* magazine. The ad showed hundreds of newborn babies in their hospital cribs, all of them Black or brown except for a rare white face here and there. The headline says, "Hey, whitey! It's your turn at the back of the bus!" The ad then tells you, read *Time* magazine to keep up with today's hot issues. That manipulative image could have been published today; its implication of shifting power appears to be the recurrent nightmare of too many potential Anglo allies. *7*

Euro-American anxiety often focuses on the sense of a vanishing national identity. Behind the attacks on immigrants, affirmative action and multiculturalism, behind the demand for "English Only" laws and the rejection of bilingual education, lies the question: with all these new people, languages and cultures, what will it mean to be an American? If that question once seemed, to many people, to have an obvious, universally applicable answer, today new definitions must be found. But too often Americans, with supposed scholars in the lead, refuse to face that need and instead nurse a nostalgia for some bygone clarity. They remain trapped in denial. *8*

An array of such ostriches, heads in the sand, began flapping their feathers noisily with the publication of Allan Bloom's 1987 best-selling book, *The Closing of the American Mind*. Bloom bemoaned the decline of our "common values" as a society, meaning the decline of Euro-American cultural centricity (shall we just call it cultural imperialism?). Since then we have seen constant sniping at "diversity" goals across the land. The assault has often focused on how U.S. history is taught. And with reason, *9*

for this country's identity rests on a particular narrative about the historical origins of the United States as a nation.

The Great White Origin Myth

Every society has an origin narrative that explains that society to itself   *10*
and the world with a set of stories and symbols. The origin myth, as
scholar-activist Roxanne Dunbar Ortiz has termed it, defines how a society understands its place in the world and its history. The myth provides
the basis for a nation's self-defined identity. Most origin narratives can be
called myths because they usually present only the most flattering view of
a nation's history; they are not distinguished by honesty.

Ours begins with Columbus "discovering" a hemisphere where some 80   *11*
million people already lived but didn't really count (in what became the
United States, they were just buffalo-chasing "savages" with no grasp of
real estate values and therefore doomed to perish). It continues with the
brave Pilgrims, a revolution by independence-loving colonists against a
decadent English aristocracy and the birth of an energetic young republic
that promised democracy and equality (that is, to white male landowners).
In the 1840s, the new nation expanded its size by almost one-third, thanks
to a victory over that backward land of little brown people called Mexico.
Such has been the basic account of how the nation called the United
States of America came into being as presently configured.

The myth's omissions are grotesque. It ignores three major pillars of   *12*
our nationhood: genocide, enslavement and imperialist expansion (such
nasty words, who wants to hear them? — but that's the problem). The
massive extermination of indigenous peoples provided our land base;
the enslavement of African labor made our economic growth possible;
and the seizure of half of Mexico by war (or threat of renewed war)
extended this nation's boundaries north to the Pacific and south to the
Rio Grande. Such are the foundation stones of the United States, within
an economic system that made this country the first in world history to
be born capitalist. . . .

Racism as Linchpin of the U.S. National Identity

A crucial embellishment of the origin myth and key element of the   *13*
national identity has been the myth of the frontier, analyzed in Richard
Slotkin's *Gunfighter Nation*, the last volume of a fascinating trilogy. He
describes Theodore Roosevelt's belief that the West was won thanks to
American arms, "the means by which progress and nationality will be
achieved." That success, Roosevelt continued, "depends on the heroism
of men who impose on the course of events the latent virtues of their

'race.' " Roosevelt saw conflict on the frontier producing a series of virile "fighters and breeders" who would eventually generate a new leadership class. Militarism thus went hand in hand with the racialization of history's protagonists. . . .

The frontier myth embodied the nineteenth-century concept of Manifest Destiny, a doctrine that served to justify expansionist violence by means of intrinsic racial superiority. Manifest Destiny was Yankee conquest as the inevitable result of a confrontation between enterprise and progress (white) versus passivity and backwardness (Indian, Mexican). "Manifest" meant "God-given," and the whole doctrine is profoundly rooted in religious conviction going back to the earliest colonial times. In his short, powerful book *Manifest Destiny: American Expansion and the Empire of Right,* Professor Anders Stephanson tells how the Puritans reinvented the Jewish notion of chosenness and applied it to this hemisphere so that territorial expansion became God's will. . . .   *14*

Manifest Destiny Dies Hard

The concept of Manifest Destiny, with its assertion of racial superiority sustained by military power, has defined U.S. identity for 150 years. . . .   *15*

Today's origin myth and the resulting concept of national identity make for an intellectual prison where it is dangerous to ask big questions about this society's superiority. When otherwise decent people are trapped in such a powerful desire not to feel guilty, self-deception becomes unavoidable. To cease our present falsification of collective memory should, and could, open the doors of that prison. When together we cease equating whiteness with Americanness, a new day can dawn. As David Roediger, the social historian, has said, "[Whiteness] is the empty and therefore terrifying attempt to build an identity on what one isn't, and on whom one can hold back."   *16*

Redefining the U.S. origin narrative, and with it this country's national identity, could prove liberating for our collective psyche. It does not mean Euro-Americans should wallow individually in guilt. It does mean accepting collective responsibility to deal with the implications of our real origin. A few apologies, for example, might be a step in the right direction. In 1997, the idea was floated in Congress to apologize for slavery; it encountered opposition from all sides. But to reject the notion because corrective action, not an apology, is needed misses the point. Having defined itself as the all-time best country in the world, the United States fiercely denies the need to make a serious official apology for anything. . . . To press for any serious, official apology does imply a new origin narrative, a new self-image, an ideological sea-change.   *17*

Accepting the implications of a different narrative could also shed light on today's struggles. In the affirmative-action struggle, for example,   *18* opponents have said that that policy is no longer needed because racism ended with the Civil Rights Movement. But if we look at slavery as a fundamental pillar of this nation, going back centuries, it becomes obvious that racism could not have been ended by 30 years of mild reforms. If we see how the myth of the frontier idealized the white male adventurer as the central hero of national history, with the woman as sunbonneted helpmate, then we might better understand the dehumanized ways in which women have continued to be treated. A more truthful origin narrative could also help break down divisions among peoples of color by revealing common experiences and histories of cooperation.

For Analysis and Discussion

1. To what extent does the narrative Martínez begins with make you want to read further?
2. How does she connect this narrative to the rest of her argument?
3. How does she use repetition to create unity in her essay?
4. What assumptions does Martínez challenge?
5. How does she use questions to engage her readers?

■ Use Topic Sentences to Focus Your Paragraphs

The **topic sentence** states the main point of a paragraph. It should

- provide a partial answer to the question motivating the writer.
- act as an extension of the writer's thesis and the question motivating the writer's argument.
- serve as a guidepost, telling readers what the paragraph is about.
- help create unity and coherence both within the paragraph and within the essay.

Elizabeth Martínez begins by describing how elementary schools in the 1940s and 1950s used the Dick and Jane series not only to teach reading but also to foster a particular set of values — values that she believes do not serve all children enrolled in America's schools. In paragraph 4, she states her thesis, explaining that nostalgia in the United States has created "a national identity crisis that promises to bring in its wake an unprecedented nervous breakdown for the dominant society's psyche." This is a point that builds on an observation she makes in paragraph 3: "It seems nostalgia runs rampant among many Euro-Americans: a nostalgia for the days of unchallenged White Supremacy — both moral and material — when life was 'simple.'" Martínez often returns to this notion of nostalgia for a past that seems "simple" to explain what she sees as an impending crisis.

Consider the first sentence of paragraph 5 as a topic sentence. With Martínez's key points in mind, notice how she uses the sentence to make her thesis more specific. Notice too, how she ties in the crisis and break-down she alludes to in paragraph 4. Essentially, Martínez tells her readers that they can see these problems at play in California, an indicator of the "nation's present and future reality."

> *Nowhere is this more apparent than in California, which has long been on the cutting edge of the nation's present and future reality.* Warning sirens have sounded repeatedly in the 1990s, such as the fierce battle over new history textbooks for public schools, Proposition 187's ugly denial of human rights to immigrants, the 1996 assault on affirmative action that culminated in Proposition 209, and the 1997 move to abolish bilingual education. *Attempts to copycat these reactionary measures have been seen in other states.*

The final sentence of paragraph 5 sets up the remainder of the essay.

As readers, we expect each subsequent paragraph to respond in some way to the issue Martínez has raised. She meets that expectation by for-mulating a topic sentence that appears at the beginning of the paragraph. The topic sentence is what helps create unity and coherence in the essay.

■ Create Unity in Your Paragraphs

Each paragraph in an essay should focus on the subject suggested by the topic sentence. If a paragraph begins with one focus or major point of dis-cussion, it should not end with another. Several strategies can contribute to the unity of each paragraph:

Use details that follow logically from your topic sentence and maintain a single focus — a focus that is clearly an extension of your thesis. For example, in paragraph 5, Martínez's topic sentence ("Nowhere is this more apparent than in California, which has long been on the cutting edge of the nation's present and future reality") helps to create unity because it refers back to her thesis (*this* refers to the "national identity crisis" men-tioned in paragraph 4) and limits the focus of what she includes in the paragraph to "the fierce battle over new history textbooks" and recent pieces of legislation in California that follow directly from and support the claim of the topic sentence.

Repeat key words to guide your readers. A second strategy for creating unity is to repeat (or use synonyms for) key words within a given para-graph. You can see this at work in paragraph 12 (notice the words we've underscored), where Martínez explains that America's origin narrative omits significant details:

> The myth's omissions are grotesque. It ignores three major pillars of our nationhood: <u>genocide</u>, <u>enslavement</u> and <u>imperialist expansion</u> (such nasty words, who wants to hear them? — but that's the problem). The massive <u>extermination</u> of indigenous peoples provided our land base; the <u>enslavement</u> of African labor made our economic growth possible; and

the seizure of half of Mexico by war (or threat of renewed war) extended this nation's boundaries north to the Pacific and south to the Rio Grande. Such are the foundation stones of the United States, within an economic system that made this country the first in world history to be born capitalist. . . .

Specifically, Martínez tells us that the origin narrative ignores "three major pillars of our nationhood: genocide, enslavement and imperialist expansion." She then substitutes *extermination* for "genocide," repeats *enslavement,* and substitutes *seizure* for "imperialist expansionist." By connecting words in a paragraph, as Martínez does here, you help readers understand that the details you provide are all relevant to the point you want to make.

Use transition words to link ideas from different sentences.   A third strategy for creating unity within paragraphs is to establish a clear relationship among different ideas by using **transition words** or phrases. Transition words or phrases signal to your readers the direction your ideas are taking. Table 12.1 lists common transition words and phrases grouped by function — that is, for adding a new idea, presenting a contrasting idea, or drawing a conclusion about an idea.

Martínez uses transition words and phrases throughout the excerpt here. In several places, she uses the word *but* to make a contrast — to draw a distinction between an idea that many people accept as true and an alternative idea that she wants to pursue. Notice in paragraph 17 how she signals the importance of an official apology for slavery — and by implication genocide and the seizure of land from Mexico:

> . . . A few apologies, for example, might be a step in the right direction. In 1997, the idea was floated in Congress to apologize for slavery; it encountered opposition from all sides. But to reject the notion because corrective action, not an apology, is needed misses the point. Having defined itself as the all-time best country in the world, the United States fiercely denies the need to make a serious official apology for anything. . . . To press for any serious, official apology does imply a new origin narrative, a new self-image, an ideological sea-change.

TABLE 12.1   Common Transition Words and Phrases

Adding an Idea	Presenting a Contrasting Idea	Drawing a Logical Conclusion
also, and, further, moreover, in addition to, in support of, similarly	although, alternatively, as an alternative, but, by way of contrast, despite, even though, however, in contrast to, nevertheless, nonetheless, rather than, yet	as a result, because of, consequently, finally, in sum, in the end, subsequently, therefore, thus

Similarly, in the last paragraph, Martínez counters the argument that affirmative action is not necessary because racism no longer exists:

> . . . In the affirmative-action struggle, for example, opponents have said that that policy is no longer needed because racism ended with the Civil Rights Movement. But if we look at slavery as a fundamental pillar of this nation, going back centuries, it becomes obvious that racism could not have been ended by 30 years of mild reforms. . . .

There are a number of ways to rephrase what Martínez is saying in paragraph 18. We could substitute *however* for "but." Or, we could combine the two sentences into one to point to the relationship between the two competing ideas: *Although some people oppose affirmative action, believing that racism no longer exists, I would argue that racism remains a fundamental pillar of this nation.* Or we could pull together Martínez's different points to draw a logical conclusion using a transition word like *therefore*. Martínez observes that our country is in crisis as a result of increased immigration. *Therefore, we need to reassess our conceptions of national identity to account for the diversity that increased immigration has created.* We can substitute any of the transition words in Table 12.1 for drawing a logical conclusion.

The list of transition words and phrases in Table 12.1 is hardly exhaustive, but it gives you a sense of the ways to connect ideas so that readers understand how the ideas you write about are related. Are they similar ideas? Do they build on or support one another? Are you challenging accepted ideas? Or are you drawing a logical connection from a number of different ideas?

■ Use Critical Strategies to Develop Your Paragraphs

To develop a paragraph, you can use a range of strategies, depending on what you want to accomplish and what you believe your readers will need to be persuaded by what you argue. Among these strategies are using examples and illustrations; citing data (facts, statistics, evidence, details); analyzing texts; telling a story or anecdote; defining terms; making comparisons; and examining causes and evaluating consequences.

Use examples and illustrations.   Examples make abstract ideas concrete through illustration. Using examples is probably the most common way to develop a piece of writing. Of course, Martínez's essay is full of examples. In fact she begins with an example of a series of books — the Dick and Jane books — to show how a generation of school children were exposed to white middle-class values. She also uses examples in paragraph 5, where she lists several pieces of legislation (Propositions 187 and 209) to develop the claim in her topic sentence.

Cite data.   **Data** are factual pieces of information. They function in an essay as the bases of propositions. In the first few paragraphs of the excerpt, Martínez cites statistics ("85 percent of all U.S. elementary schools used the Dick and Jane series to teach children how to read") and facts ("In the mid-1990s, museums, libraries and eighty Public Broadcasting Service . . . stations across the country had exhibits and programs commemorating the series") to back up her claim about the popularity of the Dick and Jane series and the nostalgia the books evoke.

Analyze texts.   Analysis is the process of breaking something down into its elements to understand how they work together. When you analyze a text, you point out parts of the text that have particular significance to your argument and explain what they mean. By *texts,* we mean both verbal and visual texts. In paragraph 7, Martínez analyzes a visual text, an advertisement that appeared in *Sports Illustrated,* to reveal "its implication of shifting power" — a demographic power shift from Anglos to people of color.

Tell narratives or anecdotes.   Put simply, a narrative is an account of something that happened. More technically, a narrative relates a sequence of events that are connected in time; and an **anecdote** is a short narrative that recounts a particular incident. An anecdote, like an example, can bring an abstraction into focus. Consider Martínez's third paragraph, where the anecdote about the museum attendant brings her point about racially charged nostalgia among white Americans into memorable focus: The tears of the museum-goers indicate just how profound their nostalgia is. By contrast, a longer narrative, in setting out its sequence of events, often opens up possibilities for analysis. Why did these events occur? Why did they occur in this sequence? What might they lead to? What are the implications? What is missing? In paragraph 11, for example, Martínez relates several key events in the origin myth of America. Then, in the next paragraph, she explains what is omitted from the myth, or narrative, and builds her argument about the implications and consequences of those omissions.

Define terms.   A definition is an explanation of what something is and, by implication, what it is not. The simplest kind of definition is a synonym, but for the purpose of developing your argument, a one-word definition is rarely enough. When you define your terms, you are setting forth meanings that you want your readers to agree on, so that you can continue to build your argument on the foundation of that agreement. You may have to stipulate that your definition is part of a larger whole to develop your argument. For example: "Nostalgia is a bittersweet longing for things of the past; but for the purposes of my essay, I focus on white middle-class nostalgia, which combines a longing for a past that never existed with a hostile anxiety about the present."

In paragraph 10, Martínez defines the term *origin narrative* — a myth that explains "how a society understands its place in the world and its history . . . the basis for a nation's self-defined identity." The "Great White

Origin Myth" is an important concept in her developing argument about a national crisis of identity.

Make comparisons.   Technically, a **comparison** shows the similarities between two or more things, and a **contrast** shows the differences. In practice, however, it is very difficult, if not impossible, to develop a comparison that does not make use of contrast. Therefore, we use the term *comparison* to describe the strategy of comparing *and* contrasting. Doubtless you have written paragraphs or even whole essays that take as a starting point a version of this sentence: "X and Y are similar in some respects and different in others." This neutral formulation is seldom helpful when you are developing an argument. Usually, in making your comparison — in setting forth the points of similarity and difference — you have to take an evaluative or argumentative stance. Consider the comparison in this passage:

> Although there are similarities between the current nostalgias for Dick and Jane books and for rhythm and blues music of the same era — in both cases, the object of nostalgia can move people to tears — the nostalgias spring from emotional responses that are quite different and even contradictory. I will argue that the Dick and Jane books evoke a longing for a past that is colored by a fear of the present, a time when white middle-class values were dominant and unquestioned as they no longer are. By contrast, the nostalgia for R&B music may indicate a yearning for a past when multicultural musicians provided a sweaty release on the dance floor from those very same white-bread values of the time.

The writer does more than list similarities and differences; he offers an analysis of what they mean and is prepared to argue for his interpretation.

Certainly Elizabeth Martínez takes an evaluative stance when she compares versions of American history in paragraphs 11 and 12. In paragraph 11, she angrily relates the sanitized story of American history, setting up a contrast in paragraph 12 with the story that does not appear in history textbooks, a story of "genocide, enslavement and imperialist expansion." Her evaluative stance comes through clearly: She finds the first version repugnant and harmful, its omissions "grotesque."

Examine causes and evaluate consequences.   In any academic discipline, questions of cause and consequence are central. Whether you are analyzing the latest election results in a political science course, reading about the causes of the Vietnam War in a history course, or speculating about the long-term consequences of global warming in a science course, questions of why things happened, happen, or will happen are inescapable. Examining causes and consequences usually involves identifying a phenomenon and asking questions about it until you gather enough information to begin analyzing the relationships among its parts and deciding which are most significant. You can then begin to set forth your own analysis of what happened and why.

Of course, this kind of analysis is rarely straightforward, and any phenomenon worthy of academic study is bound to generate a variety of conversations about its causes and consequences. In your own thinking and research, avoid jumping to conclusions and continue to sift evidence until plausible connections present themselves. Be prepared to revise your thinking — perhaps several times — in light of new evidence.

In your writing, you also want to avoid oversimplifying. A claim like this — "The answer to curbing unemployment in the United States is to restrict immigration" — does not take into account corporate outsourcing of jobs overseas or the many other possible causes of unemployment. At the very least, you may need to explain the basis and specifics of your analysis, and qualify your claim: "Recent studies of patterns of immigration and unemployment in the United States suggest that unrestricted immigration is a major factor in the loss of blue-collar job opportunities in the Southwest." Certainly this sentence is less forceful and provocative than the other one, but it does suggest that you have done significant and focused research and respect the complexity of the issue.

Throughout her essay, Martínez analyzes causes and consequences. In paragraph 8, for example, she speculates that the *cause* of "attacks on immigrants, affirmative action and multiculturalism" is "Euro-American anxiety," "the sense of a vanishing national identity." In paragraph 13, she concludes that a *consequence* of Theodore Roosevelt's beliefs about race and war was a "militarism [that] went hand in hand with the racialization of history's protagonists." In paragraph 16, the topic sentence itself is a statement about causes and consequences: "Today's origin myth and the resulting concept of national identity make for an intellectual prison where it is dangerous to ask big questions about this society's superiority."

Having shown where and how Martínez uses critical strategies to develop her paragraphs, we must hasten to add that these critical strategies usually work in combination. Although you can easily develop an entire paragraph (or even an entire essay) using comparison, it is almost impossible to do so without relying on one or more of the other strategies. What if you need to tell an anecdote about the two authors you are comparing? What if you have to cite data about different rates of economic growth to clarify the main claim of your comparison? What if you are comparing different causes and consequences? Our point is that the strategies described here are methods for exploring your issue in writing. How you make use of them, individually or in combination, depends on which can help you best communicate your argument to your readers.

Steps to Developing Paragraphs

1 **Use topic sentences to focus your paragraphs.** Remember that a topic sentence partially answers the question motivating you to write; acts as an extension of your thesis; indicates to your readers what the paragraph is about; and helps create unity both within the paragraph and within the essay.

2 **Create unity in your paragraphs.** The details in your paragraph should follow logically from your topic sentence and maintain a single focus, one tied clearly to your thesis. Repetition and transition words also help create unity in paragraphs.

3 **Use critical strategies to develop your paragraphs.** Use examples and illustrations; cite data; analyze texts; tell stories or anecdotes; define terms; make comparisons; and examine causes and evaluate consequences.

A Practice Sequence: Working with Paragraphs

We would like you to work in pairs on paragraphing. The objective of this exercise is to gauge the effectiveness of your topic sentences and the degree to which your paragraphs are unified and fully developed.

Make a copy of your essay and cut it up into paragraphs. Shuffle the paragraphs to be sure they are no longer in the original order, and then exchange cut-up drafts with your partner. The challenge is to put your partner's essay back together again. When you both have finished, compare your reorderings with the original drafts. Were you able to reproduce the original organization exactly? If not, do the variations make sense? If one or the other of you had trouble putting the essay back together, talk about the adequacy of your topic sentences, ways to revise topic sentences in keeping with the details in a given paragraph, and strategies for making paragraphs more unified and coherent.

DRAFTING CONCLUSIONS

In writing a conclusion to your essay, you are making a final appeal to your audience. You want to convince readers that what you have written is a relevant, meaningful interpretation of a shared issue. You also want to remind them that your argument is reasonable. Rather than summarize all of the points you've made in the essay — assume your readers have carefully read what you've written — pull together the key components of your argument in the service of answering the question "So what?" Establish why your argument is important: What will happen if things stay the same? What will happen if things change? How effective your conclusion is depends on whether or not readers feel you have adequately addressed "So what?" — that you have made clear what is significant and of value.

In building on the specific details of your argument, you can also place what you have written in a broader context. What are the sociological implications of your argument? How far reaching are they? Are there political implications? Economic implications? Finally, explain again how your ideas contribute something new to the conversation by building on, extending, or even challenging what others have argued.

In her concluding paragraph, Elizabeth Martínez brings together her main points, puts her essay in a broader context, indicates what's new in her argument, and answers the question "So what?":

> Accepting the implications of a different narrative could also shed light on today's struggles. In the affirmative-action struggle, for example, opponents have said that that policy is no longer needed because racism ended with the Civil Rights Movement. But if we look at slavery as a fundamental pillar of this nation, going back centuries, it becomes obvious that racism could not have been ended by 30 years of mild reforms. If we see how the myth of the frontier idealized the white male adventurer as the central hero of national history, with the woman as sunbonneted helpmate, then we might better understand the dehumanized ways in which women have continued to be treated. A more truthful origin narrative could also help break down divisions among peoples of color by revealing common experiences and histories of cooperation.

Although Martínez refers back to important events and ideas she has discussed, she does not merely summarize. Instead, she suggests the implications of those important events and ideas in her first sentence (the topic sentence), which crystallizes the main point of her essay: Americans need a different origin narrative. Then she puts those implications in the broader context of contemporary racial and gender issues. She signals what's new in her argument with the word *if* (if we look at slavery in a new way, if we look at the frontier myth in a new way). Finally, her answers to "So what?" — important new insights into racial and gender issues — culminate in the last sentence, which also connects and extends the claim of her topic sentence, by asserting that a "more truthful origin narrative" could help heal divisions among peoples of color who have been misrepresented by the old origin myth. Clearly, she believes the implications of her argument matter: A new national identity has the potential to heal a country in crisis, a country on the verge of a "nervous breakdown" (para. 4).

Martínez also does something else in the last sentence of the concluding paragraph: She looks to the future, suggesting what the future implications of her argument could be. Looking to the future is one of five strategies for shaping a conclusion. The others we discuss are echoing the introduction, challenging the reader, posing questions, and concluding with a quotation. Each of these strategies appeals to readers in different ways; therefore, we suggest you try them all out in writing your own conclusions. Also, remember that some of these strategies can be combined. For example, you can write an introduction that challenges readers, poses a question, looks to the future, and ends with a quotation.

▪ Echo the Introduction

Echoing the introduction in your conclusion helps readers come full circle. It helps them see how you have developed your idea from beginning to end. In the example below, the student writer begins with a voice speaking from behind an Islamic veil, revealing the ways that Western culture misunderstands the symbolic value of wearing the veil. The writer repeats this visual image in her conclusion, quoting from the Koran: "Speak to them from behind a curtain."

Notice that the author begins with "a voice from behind the shrouds of an Islamic veil" and then echoes this quotation in her conclusion: "Speak to them from behind a curtain."

Introduction: A voice from behind the shrouds of an Islamic veil exclaims: "I often wonder whether people see me as a radical, fundamentalist Muslim terrorist packing an AK-47 assault rifle inside my jean jacket. Or maybe they see me as the poster girl for oppressed womanhood everywhere." In American culture where shameless public exposure, particularly of females, epitomizes ultimate freedom, the head-to-toe covering of a Muslim woman seems inherently oppressive. Driven by an autonomous national attitude, the inhabitants of the "land of the free" are quick to equate the veil with indisputable persecution. Yet Muslim women reveal the enslaving hijab as a symbolic display of the Islamic ideals — honor, modesty, and stability. Because of an unfair American assessment, the aura of hijab mystery cannot be removed until the customs and ethics of Muslim culture are genuinely explored. It is this form of enigmatic seclusion that forms the feminist controversy between Western liberals, who perceive the veil as an inhibiting factor against free will, and Islamic disciples, who conceptualize the veil as a sacred symbol of utmost morality.

Conclusion: By improperly judging an alien religion, the veil becomes a symbol of oppression and devastation, instead of a representation of pride and piety. Despite Western images, the hijab is a daily revitalization and reminder of the Islamic societal and religious ideals, thereby upholding the conduct and attitudes of the Muslim community. Americans share these ideals yet fail to recognize them in the context of a different culture. By sincerely exploring the custom of Islamic veiling, one will realize the vital role the hijab plays in shaping Muslim culture by sheltering women, and consequently society, from the perils that erupt from indecency. The principles implored in the Koran of modesty, honor, and stability construct a unifying and moral view of the Islamic Middle Eastern society when properly investigated. As it was transcribed from Allah, "Speak to them from behind a curtain. This is purer for your hearts and their hearts."

Notice how the conclusion echoes the introduction in its reference to a voice speaking from behind a curtain.

■ Challenge the Reader

By issuing a challenge to your readers, you create a sense of urgency, provoking them to act to change the status quo. In this example, the student writer explains the unacceptable consequences of preventing young women from educating themselves about AIDS and the spread of a disease that has already reached epidemic proportions.

Here the author cites a final piece of research to emphasize the extent of the problem.

Here she begins her explicit challenge to readers about what they have to do to protect themselves or their students from infection.

The changes in AIDS education that I am suggesting are necessary and relatively simple to make. Although the current curriculum in high school health classes is helpful and informative, it simply does not pertain to young women as much as it should. AIDS is killing women at an alarming rate, and many people do not realize this. According to Daniel DeNoon, AIDS is one of the six leading causes of death among women aged 18–45, and women "bear the brunt of the worldwide AIDS epidemic." For this reason, DeNoon argues, women are one of the most important new populations that are contracting HIV at a high rate. I challenge young women to be more well-informed about AIDS and their link to the disease; otherwise, many new cases may develop. As the epidemic continues to spread, women need to realize that they can stop the spread of the disease and protect themselves from infection and a number of related complications. It is the responsibility of health educators to present this to young women and inform them of the powerful choices that they can make.

■ Look to the Future

Looking to the future is particularly relevant when you are asking readers to take action. To move readers to action, you must establish the persistence of a problem and the consequences of letting a situation continue unchanged. In the concluding paragraph below, the student author points out a number of things that teachers need to do to involve parents in their children's education. She identifies a range of options before identifying what she believes is perhaps the most important action teachers can take.

The second through fifth sentences present an array of options.

First and foremost, teachers must recognize the ways in which some parents are positively contributing to their children's academic endeavors. Teachers must recognize nontraditional methods of participation as legitimate and work toward supporting parents in these tasks. For instance, teachers might send home suggestions for local after-school tutoring programs. Teachers must also try to make urban parents feel welcome and respected in their school. Teachers might call parents to ask their opinion about a certain difficulty their child is having, or invite them to talk about something of interest to them. One parent, for instance, spoke highly of the previous superintendent who had let him use his work as a film producer to help with a show for students during homeroom. If teachers can develop innovative ways to utilize parents' talents and interests rather than just inviting them to be passively involved in an already-in-place curriculum, more parents might respond. Perhaps, most importantly, if teachers want parents to be involved in their students' educations, they must make the parents feel as though their opinions and concerns have real weight. When parents such as those interviewed for this study voice concerns and questions over their child's progress, it is imperative that teachers acknowledge and answer them.

In the last two sentences, the writer looks to the future with her recommendations.

■ Pose Questions

Posing questions stimulates readers to think about the implications of your argument and to apply what you argue to other situations. This is the case in the paragraph below, in which the student writer focuses on immigration and then shifts readers' attention to racism and the possibility of hate crimes. It's useful to extrapolate from your argument, to raise questions that test whether what you write can be applied to different situations. These questions can help readers understand what is at issue.

The first question.

Other speculative questions follow from possible responses to the writer's first question.

Also, my research may apply to a broader spectrum of sociological topics. There has been recent discussion about the increasing trend of immigration. Much of this discussion has involved the distribution of resources to immigrants. Should immigrants have equal access to certain economic and educational resources in America? The decision is split. But, it will be interesting to see how this debate will play out. If immigrants are granted more resources, will certain Americans mobilize against the distribution of these resources? Will we see another rise in racist groups such as the Ku Klux Klan in order to prevent immigrants from obtaining more resources? My research can also be used to understand global conflict or war. In general, groups mobilize when their established resources are threatened by an external force. Moreover, groups use framing processes to justify their collective action to others.

■ Conclude with a Quotation

A quotation can add authority to your argument, indicating that others in positions of power and prestige support your stance. A quotation also can add poignancy to your argument, as it does in the excerpt below, in which the quotation amplifies the idea that people use Barbie to advance their own interests.

> The question still remains, what does Barbie mean? Is she the spokeswoman for the empowerment of women or rather is she performing the dirty work of conservative patriarchy? I do not think we will ever know the answer. Rather, Barbie is the undeniable "American Icon." She is a toy, and she is what we want her to be. A test performed by Albert M. Magro at Fairmont State College titled "Why Barbie Is Perceived as Beautiful" shows that Barbie is the epitome of what we as humans find beautiful. The test sought to find human preferences on evolutionary changes in the human body. Subjects were shown a series of photos comparing different human body parts, such as the size and shape of the eyes, and asked to decide which feature they preferred: the primitive or derived (more evolved traits). The test revealed that the subjects preferred the derived body traits. Ironically, it is these preferred evolutionary features that are utilized on the body of Barbie. Barbie is truly an extension of what we are and what we perceive.

The writer quotes an authority to amplify the idea that individually and collectively, we project significance on toys.

> Juel Best concludes his discourse on Barbie with these words: "Toys do not embody violence or sexism or occult meanings. People must assign toys their meanings." Barbie is whoever we make her out to be. Barbie grabs hold of our imaginations and lets us go wild.

Steps to Drafting Conclusions

1 **Pull together the main claims of your essay.** Don't simply repeat points you make in the paper. Instead, show readers how the points you make fit together.

2 **Answer the question "So What?"** Show your readers why your stand on the issue is significant.

3 **Place your argument in a larger context.** Discuss the specifics of your argument, but also indicate its broader implications.

4 **Show readers what is new.** As you synthesize the key points of your argument, explain how what you argue builds on, extends, or challenges the thinking of others.

5 **Decide on the best strategy for writing your conclusion.** Will you echo the introduction? Challenge the reader? Look to the future? Pose questions? Conclude with a quotation? Choose the best strategy or strategies to appeal to your readers.

A Practice Sequence: Drafting a Conclusion

1 Write your conclusion, using one of the strategies described in this section. Then share your conclusion with a classmate. Ask this person to address the following questions:

- Did I pull together the key points of the argument?
- Did I answer "So what?" adequately?
- Are the implications I want readers to draw from the essay clear?

After listening to the responses, try a second strategy, and then ask your classmate which conclusion is more effective.

2 If you do not have a conclusion of your own, analyze each example conclusion above to see how well each appears to (1) pull together the main claim of the essay, (2) answer "So what?" (3) place the argument in a larger context, and (4) show readers what is new.

13

Drafting an Essay: Well-Focused Sentences

When linguists describe languages, they categorize them according to the typical order of a sentence's key components. English is said to be an SVO language. The core of an English clause is made up of a Subject, Verb, and Object, most often in that order: *Cats eat mice; Matthew caught the ball; Elizabeth assumed the throne; Calculus teachers assign problem sets; I love you.*

We pick up the SVO pattern at an early age. When babies are learning to speak, they begin with one-word utterances — "ball," "Mama," "peekaboo," "hot," — but soon graduate to two-word and three-word strings. By the age of two, toddlers demonstrate an understanding of the SVO order: with remarkable consistency, they say "baby eat," "eat cereal," or "baby eat cereal," never mixing up the word order (never, for example, saying "cereal baby eat"). In English-speaking communities, we hear and produce hundreds of SVO sentences every day.

For writers, the SVO order has particular significance because it represents the norm. Without really thinking about it, readers develop an expectation that, as they approach a new sentence, they'll encounter first the subject, then the verb, and then an object. Of course, many English sentences are more complex than *Cats eat mice*, many are cast in other patterns (with, for example, an intransitive or linking verb), and some use alternative word order. Still, the SVO norm has a great deal of power in shaping readers' expectations and in determining how easily they process sentences.

In this chapter, I want to make a case for choosing subjects carefully, taking full advantage of the subject position. Because readers intuitively expect the first noun phrase in a clause to be the subject, they pay attention

---

Taken from Nora Bacon, *The Well-Crafted Sentence: A Writer's Guide to Style*, pp. 25–45 (Chapter 2, "Well-Focused Sentences: The Subject-Verb Pair").

to that noun phrase. A wise writer will direct the reader's attention to the key player, using the subject position to name the person or thing that the clause is really *about*. A sentence is well focused when the most important actor and action appear as the subject and verb.

POPULATED PROSE

We'll begin with some examples of well-focused sentences from Tim O'Brien's book *The Things They Carried*. In a chapter titled "On the Rainy River," the narrator describes a turning point in his life. In 1968, just out of college, he had to decide whether to comply with the military draft, virtually ensuring a tour in Vietnam, or flee to Canada. He spent a few days at a fishing lodge near the Canadian border, where his moral crisis was witnessed by the lodge's owner, Elroy Berdahl.

Note the subject of each clause:

> For ten or fifteen minutes Elroy held a course upstream, the river choppy and silver-gray, then he turned straight north and put the engine on full throttle. I felt the bow lift beneath me. I remember the wind in my ears, the sound of the old outboard Evinrude. For a time I didn't pay attention to anything, just feeling the cold spray against my face, but then it occurred to me that at some point we must've passed into Canadian waters, across that dotted line between two different worlds, and I remember a sudden tightness in my chest as I looked up and watched the far shore come at me. This wasn't a daydream. It was tangible and real. As we came in toward land, Elroy cut the engine, letting the boat fishtail lightly about twenty yards off shore. The old man didn't look at me or speak. Bending down, he opened up his tackle box and busied himself with a bobber and a piece of wire leader, humming to himself, his eyes down.

This paragraph is about two men. If you do a quick count, you'll find that twelve of the fifteen clauses have **human subjects**, nouns or pronouns referring to people. The narrator (*I*) appears as the subject of five clauses, Elroy Berdahl is the subject of five more, and *we*, referring to the pair of them, is the subject of two. By consistently placing the narrator and Elroy Berdahl in the subject position, O'Brien ensures that even as we're visualizing a fishing boat or a shoreline, the human beings have a presence. The consistent focus unifies the paragraph as a whole.

The same consistent focus appears in this passage where, in a striking move, O'Brien has the narrator address the reader directly:

> Twenty yards. I could've done it. I could've jumped and started swimming for my life. Inside me, in my chest, I felt a terrible squeezing

pressure. Even now, as I write this, I can still feel that tightness. And I want you to feel it — the wind coming off the river, the waves, the silence, the wooded frontier. You're at the bow of a boat on the Rainy River. You're twenty-one years old, you're scared, and there's a hard squeezing pressure in your chest.

Again, the subjects capture the essential relationship, the interaction between the narrator and the reader: until the final clause, every subject is *I* or *you*.

What would happen if the prose weren't so tightly focused? In the passage below, I've tried to retain as much of O'Brien's meaning as possible without using so many human subjects.

Twenty yards. It was do-able. It would have been possible to jump and start swimming for my life. Inside me, in my chest, there was a terrible squeezing pressure. Even now, as these words are being written, there is still that feeling of tightness. And it is important to me to share this feeling with you — the wind coming off the river, the waves, the silence, the wooded frontier. Imagine yourself at the bow of a boat on the Rainy River, twenty-one years old, scared, and there's a hard squeezing pressure in your chest.

To my ear, the altered passage is less effective — less cohesive, less vivid, with a slower pace. Words like *it* and *there* are just about meaning-free; as subjects, they have little power to focus a reader's attention or to steer a sentence in a clear direction. It's easy to understand O'Brien's preference for human subjects.

Exercise 13A

In the passages below, I've altered sentences from "On the Rainy River" by removing words referring to people from the subject position. Re-populate these passages to improve their focus. Ask who the passage is really about — who is doing something in the sentences — and whenever possible, use a noun or pronoun referring to that person as the subject.

Example
In the mornings it was sometimes our routine to go on long hikes into the woods, and at night there were usually Scrabble games or record-playing or reading in front of his big stone fireplace.

Restored to Original
In the mornings we sometimes went out on long hikes into the woods, and at night we played Scrabble or listened to records or sat reading in front of his big stone fireplace.

1. Even after two decades it is possible for me to close my eyes and return to that porch at the Tip Top Lodge. There is an image in my mind of the old guy staring at me. Elroy Berdahl: eighty-one years old, skinny and shrunken and mostly bald. His outfit was a flannel shirt and brown work pants. In one hand, if memory serves, was a green apple, a small paring knife in the other.

2. His fishing continued. His line was worked with the tips of his fingers, patiently, his eyes squinting out at his red and white bobber on the Rainy River. His eyes were flat and impassive. There was no speech. There was simply his presence, like the river and the late-summer sun.

Sentences with human subjects stand a good chance of having strong verbs. Compare, for example, the two versions of the example sentence in Exercise 13A:

> In the mornings it was sometimes our routine to go on long hikes into the woods, and at night there were usually Scrabble games or record-playing or reading in front of his big stone fireplace.

> In the mornings we sometimes went out on long hikes into the woods, and at night we played Scrabble or listened to records or sat reading in front of his big stone fireplace.

In the first sentence, the verbs are forms of *be*, the most colorless verb in our language. In the second sentence, the verbs are varied, and they name actions. This is a typical pattern in English prose: the writer who chooses a human subject has a wide range of verbs to choose from, and his or her sentences have life and energy.

You can see the contrast again in the passages in which the narrator contemplates a swim to the Canadian shore:

> Twenty yards. It was do-able. It would have been possible to jump and start swimming for my life. Inside me, in my chest, there was a terrible squeezing pressure. Even now, as these words are being written, there is still that feeling of tightness. And it is important to me to share this feeling with you — the wind coming off the river, the waves, the silence, the wooded frontier.

> Twenty yards. I could've done it. I could've jumped and started swimming for my life. Inside me, in my chest, I felt a terrible squeezing pressure. Even now, as I write this, I can still feel that tightness. And I want you to feel it — the wind coming off the river, the waves, the silence, the wooded frontier.

In the first version, five of the six verbs are forms of *be* (and the sixth, *are being written*, is in the passive voice, a topic discussed below). A subject like *it* or *there* can't be paired with very interesting verbs — *there* isn't capable of doing much. By contrast, people can do many things, so human subjects license a wide variety of verbs.

Exercise 13B

Observe the stylistic effects of choosing human subjects.

1. Return to Exercise 13A, underlining the subject-verb pairs in each passage before and after your revisions. When you shifted to human subjects, did your verbs shift as well? Do the revised passages rely less heavily on forms of *be*?

2. It often happens that the choice of a human subject makes a sentence more concise. Examine the passages in Exercise 13A, counting the words before and after revision. When you revised, were you able to capture the meaning in fewer words?

It's simple enough to populate the prose if you're writing about a person or group of people sharing an experience, but what happens when you're operating in the realm of ideas?

The paragraph below comes from "Say It Ain't So, Huck," Jane Smiley's 1996 article comparing *The Adventures of Huckleberry Finn* to *Uncle Tom's Cabin*. The paragraph illustrates a common pattern in academic writing: the main point — which is an idea, requiring abstract language — is spelled out at the beginning, and the writer continues by illustrating the point with specific examples. In the first few sentences, the writer uses (mostly) abstract nouns and relies heavily on *be* as the verb; in the examples, she uses (mostly) human or concrete nouns and verbs other than *be*.

> The power of *Uncle Tom's Cabin* is the power of brilliant analysis married to great wisdom of feeling. Stowe never forgets the logical end of any relationship in which one person is the subject and the other is the object. No matter how the two people feel, or what their intentions are, the logic of the relationship is inherently tragic and traps both parties until the false subject/object relationship is ended. Stowe's most oft-repeated and potent representation of this inexorable logic is the forcible separation of family members, especially of mothers from children. Eliza, faced with the sale of her child, Harry, escapes across the breaking ice of the Ohio River. Lucy, whose ten-month-old is sold behind her back, kills herself. Prue, who has been used for breeding, must listen to her last child cry itself to death

because her mistress won't let her save it; she falls into alcoholism and thievery and is finally whipped to death. Cassy, prefiguring a choice made by one of the characters in Toni Morrison's *Beloved*, kills her last child so that it won't grow up in slavery. All of these women have been promised something by their owners — love, education, the privilege and joy of raising their children — but, owing to slavery, all of these promises have been broken. . . .

If we isolate the subject-verb pairs in the opening sentences, where Smiley is explaining her point, we can easily see the reliance on abstract nouns and *be*:

power is
Stowe forgets
person is
other (person) is
people feel
intentions are
logic is . . . traps
relationship is ended
representation is

Five of the subjects (*power, intentions, logic, relationship, representation*) are abstractions, and six of the verbs are *is* or *are*.

By contrast, note the subject-verb pairs in Smiley's examples:

Eliza escapes
Lucy kills
ten-month-old is sold
Prue must listen
who has been used
mistress won't let
she falls . . . is whipped
Cassy kills
it won't grow up
women have been promised
promises have been broken

In these sentences, all of the clauses except the last have human subjects, and none has *be* as its main verb.

The passage below illustrates the same movement from stating an abstract point to supporting it with specific examples.

Stowe also <u>understands</u> that the real <u>root</u> of slavery <u>is</u> that <u>it</u> <u>is</u> profitable as well as customary. <u>Augustine</u> and his <u>brother</u> <u>live</u> with slavery because <u>it</u> <u>is</u> the system <u>they</u> <u>know</u> and because <u>they</u> <u>haven't</u> the imagination to live without it. <u>Simon Legree</u> <u>embraces</u> slavery because <u>he</u> <u>can make</u> money from it and because <u>it</u> <u>gives</u> him even more absolute power over his workers than <u>he</u> <u>could find</u> in the North or in England.

The first sentence explains Stowe's understanding about slavery. The sentence contains two clauses with abstract words as subjects (*root* and *it*, referring to slavery itself) and *is* as the verb. The subsequent sentences describe specific characters in the novel to show how Smiley has inferred Stowe's insight. Of the eight clauses in these sentences, six have human subjects:

<u>Augustine</u> . . . <u>brother</u> <u>live</u>
<u>they</u> <u>know</u>
<u>they</u> <u>haven't</u>
<u>Simon Legree</u> <u>embraces</u>
<u>he</u> <u>can make</u>
<u>he</u> <u>could find</u>

Harriet Beecher Stowe made the case against slavery come alive for a generation of readers by creating characters that touched their hearts. Her "brilliant analysis" of the institution reaches readers in the shape of men and women whose names we still recognize — Uncle Tom, Little Eva, Simon Legree — awakening our natural interest in human beings engaged in significant action. When Jane Smiley structures her paragraph by moving from analysis to specific examples, from "<u>power</u> <u>is</u>" to "<u>Eliza</u> <u>escapes</u>," she capitalizes on that same interest in human activity.

Exercise 13C

Choose one of the following as an opening sentence and write a short paragraph that develops the statement with specific examples. The opening sentence has an abstract subject. Use human subjects in most or all of the subsequent clauses.

1. The legacy of slavery still haunts America.
2. The local economy has experienced some unexpected reversals.
3. Communication is the key to employer-employee relationships.
4. Religious differences can cause friction in family life.

When the topic under discussion does not include any humans, the best subjects are concrete nouns — nouns naming something tangible, something a reader can visualize. Compare these sentences:

> In the last thirty years, there has been a decline in the quality of produce in freshness and flavor.

> In the last thirty years, a decline in the quality of produce in freshness and flavor has occurred.

> In the last thirty years, produce has declined in freshness and flavor.

Of the three sentences, the third is the leanest and strongest. Vegetables will never have much dramatic power, but a concrete subject is a step in the right direction, focusing the reader's attention on what the sentence is about.

ACTIVE VOICE AND PASSIVE VOICE

The distinction between active voice and passive voice is useful to know, especially if your writing handbook is one of the many that advises writers to prefer the active to the passive voice. I'd like to take a minute to explain these terms, and then I'll echo the conventional advice, with the caveat that the preference for the active voice is stronger on some occasions than others.

In an **active-voice** construction, the subject names the actor, performing the action described by the verb. In a **passive-voice** construction, the subject does not name the actor; instead, it names the person or thing that receives the action of the verb, the person or thing being acted upon. Compare the sentences below:

ACTIVE VOICE	PASSIVE VOICE
Jane Smiley admires *Uncle Tom's Cabin*.	*Uncle Tom's Cabin* is admired by Jane Smiley.
Stowe exposed the abuses of slavery to a wide audience.	The abuses of slavery were exposed to a wide audience by Stowe.
Early in the twentieth century, critics elevated *The Adventures of Huckleberry Finn* to the pantheon of great novels.	Early in the twentieth century, *The Adventures of Huckleberry Finn* was elevated to the pantheon of great novels by critics.
Our seminar will discuss both novels.	Both novels will be discussed by our seminar.

Because each of the sentences on the left has a transitive verb — which is to say, the verb has an object — these sentences can be transformed into the passive voice. The transformation moves the object into the subject position, and the verb is adjusted accordingly.

To forestall any confusion, let me point out immediately that voice is unrelated to tense. Whether a sentence is active or passive depends on whether the subject performs or receives the action, not on whether the action takes place in the past, present, or future. *The seminar discusses, the seminar discussed*, and *the seminar will discuss* are all active; *both novels are discussed, both novels were discussed*, and *both novels will be discussed* are all passive.

How do the passive-voice sentences on page 274 strike you? To my ear, the first three sound a bit odd. While the active-voice "Jane Smiley admires *Uncle Tom's Cabin*" sounds easy and natural, the passive-voice "*Uncle Tom's Cabin* is admired by Jane Smiley" sounds forced. Probably because ours is an SVO language, because the subject-verb-object order of the active voice is so very common, readers may pause or stumble over a passive-voice sentence. So, given a choice, most good writers on most occasions will place the actor in the subject position, generating an active-voice sentence.

Under some circumstances, however, the passive voice is more effective.

First, the passive voice is used when the actor is unimportant or unknown. Consider these sentences, for example:

> Early in the twentieth century, <u>critics</u> <u>elevated</u> *The Adventures of Huckleberry Finn* to the pantheon of great novels.

> Early in the twentieth century, *The Adventures of Huckleberry Finn* <u>was elevated</u> to the pantheon of great novels.

The actor in both sentences is *critics*: it is literary critics who have the power to elevate books to the pantheon of great novels. The active-voice construction *critics elevated* makes perfect sense. But perhaps your reader isn't likely to know much or care much about critics; perhaps he or she is more interested in *Huckleberry Finn*. In that case, it makes equally good sense to move the novel itself into the subject position. Similarly, when the actor is unknown, speakers and writers often choose the passive voice, so that we might say "My car was stolen" or "The lights were left on all night."

The passive voice may also be a good choice if you want to use the subject position to name a thing or idea carried over from an earlier sentence. In the cluster of passive-voice sentences on page 274, the last one is the least jarring.

> Both <u>novels</u> <u>will be discussed</u> by our seminar.

Because the previous sentences discuss *Uncle Tom's Cabin* and *The Adventures of Huckleberry Finn, novels* keeps the focus on the current topic, so it makes a fine subject. If you return to the Smiley passage on pages 271–72, you can see why the passive voice works so well in her final sentence: "All of these women have been promised something by their owners — love, education, the privilege and joy of raising their children — but, owing to slavery, all of these promises have been broken. . . ." *All of these women* refers to Eliza, Lucy, Prue, and Cassy, the characters who have just been discussed, so the paragraph coheres better for having *all of these women* in the subject position. In the second clause, *all of these promises* refers to the just-mentioned promises of love, education, and the privilege and joy of raising one's own children, so this phrase as subject lends coherence to the sentence.

Finally, the passive voice can emphasize the absence of agency and power in a person or thing that is acted upon. Smiley provides a good example in the sentence "Prue, who <u>has been used</u> for breeding, must listen to her last child cry itself to death because her mistress won't let her save it; <u>she</u> falls into alcoholism and thievery and <u>is</u> finally <u>whipped</u> to death."

In short, while writers usually prefer the active voice because of what we know about readers' expectations and their response as they process language, it is important to remember that the passive voice is available, too, as a stylistic option.

Exercise 13D

Rewrite the boldface clauses below to restore O'Brien's active-voice sentences. When you've rewritten each clause, underline the subject once and the verb twice to confirm that the subject performs the action.

> **Example**
> **I was never confronted about it by the old man.**
>
> **Restored to Active Voice**
> The old <u>man</u> never <u>confronted</u> me about it.

1. **Most graduate school deferments had been ended by the government.**
2. **Fight songs were played by a marching band.**
3. **Cartwheels were done along the banks of the Rainy River by a squad of cheerleaders.**
4. It seemed to me that when a nation goes to war it must have reasonable confidence in the justice and imperative of its cause. **Your mistakes can't be fixed.**
5. If you support a war, if you think it's worth the price, that's fine, but **your own precious fluids have to be put on the line.**

Exercise 13E

In the passage below, Jane Smiley opts to use the passive voice. Identify instances of the passive voice and underline the subject-verb pair to confirm that the subject names not the actor but a person or thing being acted upon. (I've underlined the first pair; there are four more.) Why might Smiley have chosen to cast these sentences in the passive voice?

> The <u>story</u>, familiar to most nineteenth-century Americans, . . . <u>may be sketched</u> briefly. A Kentucky slave, Tom, is sold to pay off a debt to a slave trader, who takes him to New Orleans. On the boat trip downriver, Tom is purchased by the wealthy Augustine St. Clare at the behest of his daughter, Eva. After Eva's death, and then St. Clare's, Tom is sold again, this time to Simon Legree, whose remote plantation is the site of every form of cruelty and degradation. The novel was immediately read and acclaimed by any number of excellent judges: Charles Dickens, George Eliot, Leo Tolstoy, George Sand — the whole roster of nineteenth-century liberals. . . .

VARIATION IN SENTENCE FOCUS

A general rule — even a fine, time-tested, oft-cited general rule like "prefer human or concrete subjects and active verbs" — is just a starting point. In the end, writing doesn't work by rules: it's a matter of judgment. And a writer's judgment will depend on his or her individual style and on what seems appropriate for the occasion — for the audience, purpose, and genre (memoir, editorial, short story, report).

To see how sentence focus varies, let's consider some model texts. Stories and memoirs describe people's experiences as they interact with one another, so you'd expect these texts to have a high frequency of human subjects and active verbs. By contrast, academic writing typically reports the findings of research, with the findings themselves — which may or may not have to do with human behavior — taking center stage. So you'd expect academic writing to have more abstract or non-human words as subjects and more verbs that can be paired with non-human subjects (*be*, passive-voice verbs). And sure enough, when I analyzed the model texts, these expectations were confirmed.

This table describes the subject-verb pairs in four texts.

	% OF CLAUSES WITH HUMAN SUBJECT	% OF CLAUSES WITH *I* AS SUBJECT	% OF CLAUSES WITH PASSIVE-VOICE VERB
Story Tim O'Brien, "On the Rainy River"	67	43	2
Memoir Henry Louis Gates Jr., "Sin Boldly"	77	23	4
Case study *(academic topic and genre,* *general audience)* Oliver Sacks, "Colorblind Painter"	47	2	30
Literary criticism *(academic topic and genre,* *general audience)* Jane Smiley, "Say It Ain't So, Huck"	54	3	14

The numbers demonstrate several points:

- Taken together, the four texts illustrate writers' strong preference for human subjects and active verbs.

- The preference for human subjects and active verbs is stronger in some genres than in others. (The patterns visible in this small sample have been observed in larger studies as well.)

- There is no law against using *I*! Teachers sometimes encourage young writers to avoid *I* to push them toward more worldly topics or more formal prose. But the choice to use *I* — like other choices writers make — depends on a number of factors including the writer's personal style, the topic, the audience, the purpose, and the genre.

Exercise 13F

Write two brief texts, just a few paragraphs each, about a past or present job.

First, write a narrative about yourself in relationship with a coworker, capturing a moment of interaction. Choose an incident that reveals the dynamics of the relationship; feel free to use dialogue.

Second, explain the purpose of your workplace, describing the product or service it provides and the processes that employees engage in to achieve the overriding purpose.

> When you've finished writing, identify the subject-verb pair in each clause. Are all of your sentences well focused? That is, do the subjects keep the reader's attention focused where it ought to be? Is the frequency of *I* or other human subjects about the same in the two texts, or does it differ? Is the frequency of active verbs, passive verbs, and *be* about the same, or does it differ? Might the similarities and/or differences be explained by the topics, by your rhetorical purposes, by your personal stylistic preferences?

SHARPENING THE FOCUS

In my experience, the concept of focus is useful at two points in the writing process. First, there's that moment early in a sentence's life, when it's not even a sentence yet but a thought waiting to be articulated. "Who is doing something?" I ask. "What is he or she doing?" When I can name the actor and action, when I can piece them together as the subject and verb of a clause, the sentence is on its way.

More frequently, I think about the subject-verb pair late in the writing process, when I read through a draft and find myself snagged by a clumsy, wordy, or confusing sentence. "Who is doing something? What is he or she doing?" These simple questions can be remarkably powerful in guiding a writer toward leaner, clearer sentences.

This section presents a series of exercises organized around five editing tips, all designed to keep the actor and action in focus:

- Double-check sentences that begin with an abstract subject.
- Double-check sentences with *there* in the subject position.
- In general, keep subject phrases short.
- When a sentence seems badly focused, see whether its subject is buried in an introductory phrase.
- When a sentence seems badly focused, see whether its verb is masquerading as a noun.

The tips overlap; for example, when an abstract word occupies the subject position (a problem you'll work on in Exercise 13G), it may have landed there because the sentence's natural subject is buried in an introductory phrase (see Exercise 13J). Please use the tips not to label faulty sentences but to guide your editing.

■ Double-Check Sentences with Abstract Subjects

When a sentence begins with an abstract subject, see whether you can streamline it by finding a human or concrete noun somewhere in the sentence and relocating that noun to the subject position.

ABSTRACT SUBJECT

The <u>phenomenon</u> of "boomerang children," young adults who return to live with their parents after graduating from college, is an occurrence faced by many families today.

<u>Disagreement</u> about financial matters such as the expectation of paying rent for the young adult's "own" room may be a point of difference between parents and children.

The first sentence links the abstract subject *phenomenon* to the equally abstract complement *occurrence*, so the heart of the sentence, "the phenomenon is an occurrence," says almost nothing. The second sentence similarly links two abstractions: "Disagreement may be a point of difference." To revise, find a human or concrete noun somewhere else in the sentence — find the actor — and move that noun to the front.

BETTER

"<u>Boomerang children</u>" are young adults who return to live with their parents after graduating from college; many families face this phenomenon today.

Many <u>families</u> face the phenomenon of "boomerang children," young adults who return to live with their parents after graduating from college.

<u>Parents and children</u> may disagree about financial matters such as rent for the young adult's "own" room.

<u>Parents</u> may expect payment for a room that the young adult considers his or her own room.

Sentences beginning *the next way, the second reason,* or *another aspect* are especially likely to appear as paragraph starters in academic papers. Yes, you have to make a transition — but you can do better than that!

ABSTRACT SUBJECT

A second <u>way</u> that families can address the ambiguities of their new situation is to establish ground rules.

Another <u>reason</u> that the U.S. invasion of Iraq was a mistake is that it caused the stature of the United States as a world leader to plummet.

BETTER

Second, <u>families</u> can address the ambiguities of their new situation by establishing ground rules.

Furthermore, when the <u>United States</u> invaded Iraq, its stature as a world leader plummeted.

Exercise 13G

In the sentences below, underline the abstract noun that occupies the subject position. Then circle the actor, the person who is *doing* something. Revise the sentence to place the actor in the subject position, once again underlining your subject.

> **Example**
> Compared with a generation ago, relationships between parents and children seem to be much better.
>
> **Suggested Revision**
> Parents and children get along better than they did a generation ago.

1. The incidence of moonlighting among schoolteachers is high.
2. The reason for Maybelle's desire to leave Minneapolis was her desire to avoid the harsh winter weather.
3. Similarities exist in the strategies Jackson and LeGuin use to portray the conflict between individual conscience and the influence of the social group.
4. The reason the characters in the stories are willing to victimize their neighbors is because they think their own comfort depends on somebody's sacrifice.
5. With the growing use of PowerPoint in academic and business settings, the advantages and disadvantages of the technology should be considered by speakers.

■ Double-Check Sentences with *There* in the Subject Position

In a sentence whose purpose is to assert that something exists, *there* may be just the right subject. Often, however, *there* just takes up space, delaying the appearance of a sentence's true subject. Since *there* is almost invariably followed by a form of *be*, it displaces not only the subject but the whole subject-verb pair.

THERE AS SUBJECT

There are some television news programs that tell only one side of the story.

BETTER

Some television news programs tell only one side of the story.

Exercise 13H

Revise the sentences below to eliminate *there* from the subject position. In the new sentence, underline the subject-verb pair.

Example
There are many young mothers who want to work.

Suggested Revision
Many young mothers want to work.

1. Consequently there are far too many children who are spending their days in underfunded daycare centers.
2. To comply with the new laws, there are too many extra expenses that a family daycare provider must contend with.
3. Outside, there was an ice cream truck ringing its bell, but the children were all indoors watching television.
4. In the story "The Ones Who Walk Away from Omelas," there is a single boy who is chosen to suffer in order for the rest of the town to prosper.
5. There are three points in the story where the author uses foreshadowing.

■ Keep Subject Phrases Short

Readers expect a subject-verb pair. If the subject is a lengthy phrase, the reader is held in suspense waiting for the verb, and the sentence feels awkward.

LONG SUBJECT PHRASE

Many hours of labor, several meetings, including an emergency meeting of the whole committee, and several revisions of the contract were the result of one hasty e-mail.

BETTER

One hasty e-mail resulted in many hours of labor, several meetings, including an emergency meeting of the whole committee, and several revisions of the contract.

As in the previous example, sometimes the best revision strategy is to see whether the sentence can be inverted.

Exercise 13I

In the sentences below, underline the long subject phrase. Then find a noun or noun phrase elsewhere in the sentence that would make a more concise subject. Rewrite the sentence, underlining the new subject.

Example
"Short-term temporary employment, or, in some cases, contract labor paid daily" describes the only promise the company will make.

Suggested Revision
The company will promise only "short-term temporary employment or, in some cases, contract labor paid daily."

1. Commitment to ethical behavior, respect for the rules of confidentiality, courtesy to coworkers and customers, and fully professional behavior on all occasions should be demonstrated by every employee.

2. Disorderly conduct, horseplay in the work area, fighting, threatening behavior, and profane or insulting remarks are strictly prohibited by company policy.

3. An unprecedented number of layoffs, a reduction of earnings, profits, and stock values, and a steadily worsening competitive position vis-à-vis the other high-tech companies in the area were among the factors being responded to by the CEO's decision to resign.

4. Accounting irregularities in both the purchasing office and the president's operating accounts were discovered by the auditors.

5. Planning your whole trip, from searching for the lowest airfare to finding an affordable rental car to locating a convenient hotel and even making restaurant reservations, can now be done using the Internet.

■ Uncover Subjects Buried in Introductory Phrases

The sentence below illustrates a trap into which many hapless subjects have fallen:

To the people of Minnesota, they develop a tolerance for freezing temperatures.

The writer has something to say about the people of Minnesota; the people are the sentence's natural subject. But because the sentence begins with *to*, the people of Minnesota appear as the object of a preposition, and the writer is forced to cast about for a substitute (*they*) to use as a subject.

An editor's task is simply to move the key noun phrase to the front of the sentence:

The <u>people</u> of Minnesota develop a tolerance for freezing temperatures.

Exercise 13J

In the sentences below, identify the key noun phrase and move it to the subject position. Underline the new subject.

> **Example**
> By having a large selection of organic vegetables, this appeals to the high-end buyer.
>
> **Suggested Revision**
> A large <u>selection</u> of organic vegetables appeals to the high-end buyer.

1. At the health food store, there are good bargains featured every weekend.
2. According to the store manager, he said he would be happy to stock more locally produced produce if he saw evidence of customer demand.
3. Because of the desk clerk at the hotel not knowing, it was unclear whether the rooms would be available both nights.
4. On San Francisco's beaches, it is beautiful but too cold for sunning or swimming.
5. After a visit to Chinatown, it made her nostalgic for her childhood in Shanghai.

■ Transform Nouns to Verbs

When a sentence seems badly focused, see whether its verb is masquerading as a noun.

An <u>emphasis</u> is placed on the development of research skills in our graduate program.

Emphasis makes a poor subject for reasons we've considered: as an abstraction, it can't do anything, so it leads to a passive-voice verb. But an alert editor will note that *emphasis* has a sister verb, *emphasize*, which names exactly the action that the writer wants to highlight:

Our graduate program <u>emphasizes</u> the development of research skills.

Exercise 13K

Each of the boldface nouns below has a sister verb. Refocus the sentence, pairing a well-chosen subject with the verb form of the word. Underline the subject-verb pair.

Example
As graduate students work on their dissertation projects, the **development** of sophisticated research skills is achieved.

Suggested Revision
As graduate students work on their dissertation projects, <u>they develop</u> sophisticated research skills.

1. The candidate's **decision** to drop out of the race occurred when she fell to sixth place in the polls.
2. There is a **tendency** in the main character to damage relationships with everyone she meets.
3. Every Saturday morning, the **distribution** of fresh, organic produce happens when local truck farmers bring organic produce to the farmer's market.
4. The **establishment** of a more equitable tax policy won't happen on the city council until council members have to answer to voters in district elections.
5. The **success** of the project will be achieved only if the **contribution** of every team member is a 100% effort.

These tips should help you produce tighter, more clearly focused sentences. But editing, like other aspects of writing, depends above all on your good judgment. If, as you work on your own prose, you follow these tips only to find that a sentence sounds worse, or that it suffers a loss of clarity, substance, or precision, then set the tip aside for another day.

14

Drafting an Essay:
Well-Balanced Sentences

In *Colored People: A Memoir*, Henry Louis Gates Jr. describes his first year of college in a chapter titled "Sin Boldly." The theme of bold sins is introduced in the chapter's first paragraph. Delivering his high school valedictory address, the young Gates rejected the "traditional prepared speech" he had practiced with his English teacher, instead writing a speech of his own about topics of the day:

> My speech was about Vietnam, abortion, and civil rights, about the sense of community our class shared, since so many of us had been together for twelve years, about the individual's rights and responsibilities in his or her community, and about the necessity to defy norms out of love.

Look carefully at that sentence. It's long — 49 words — but its structure is quite simple. The main clause begins with the subject-verb pair *speech was* and then describes the content of the speech in four prepositional phrases:

about Vietnam, abortion, and civil rights

about the sense of community our class shared, since so many of us had been together for twelve years

about the individual's rights and responsibilities in his or her community

about the necessity to defy norms out of love

Taken from Nora Bacon, *The Well-Crafted Sentence: A Writer's Guide to Style*, pp. 46–60 (Chapter 3, "Well-Balanced Sentences: Coordination and Parallel Structure").

The prepositional phrases are joined by a kind of glue you can buy for a penny at any sentence-structure shop: the coordinating conjunction *and*.

This chapter begins with some observations about Gates's work in "Sin Boldly" and goes on to examine other texts in which coordinating conjunctions join pairs or series, exploring the stylistic options that coordination makes available to writers.

COORDINATION

Let's take a moment to review the concept of coordination. English has seven coordinating conjunctions — *and, or, nor, but, for, yet, so* — which are used to join two or more independent clauses or smaller units within a clause. Almost always, the units joined by the coordinator will be similar in structure.

In the sentence about his valedictory speech, Gates has used coordinators not only to link a series of four prepositional phrases but also to connect some smaller units.

Vietnam, abortion, **and** civil rights,
The coordinator and *joins three noun phrases.*

the individual's rights **and** responsibilities
The coordinator and *joins two nouns.*

in his **or** her community
The coordinator or *joins two determiners. Since the phrase "his or her" is automatic for most writers and processed by readers as a single unit, it is of little stylistic interest.*

Coordinators can also link independent clauses.

Certainly Maura and I had been no strangers to controversy, **but** we usually took pains not to invite it.

We were apparently the first interracial couple in Mineral County, **and** there was hell to pay.

The Potomac Valley Hospital was called the meat factory because one of the doctors was reputed to be such a butcher, **so** we drove on past it and headed for my house.

Exercise 14A

The sentences below are by Henry Louis Gates Jr. ("Sin Boldly") and Louise Erdrich ("Shamengwa"). Circle every coordinating conjunction and identify the units being joined. Some sentences have more than one coordinator; identify them clearly using single and double underlining.

> #### Examples
> My one year at Potomac State College of West Virginia University, in Keyser, all of five miles away, was memorable for two reasons: because of <u>my English classes with Duke Anthony Whitmore</u> (and) <u>my first real love affair, with Maura Gibson</u>.
>
> It was he who showed me, by his example, <u>that ideas had a life of their own</u> (and) <u>that there were other professions as stimulating</u> (and) <u>as rewarding</u> as being a doctor.

1. Once we were at college, Maura and I started having long talks on the phone, first about nothing at all and then about everything.

2. In his own redneck way, 'Bama Gibson was a perfectly nice man, but he was not exactly mayoral material.

3. My grandfather was colored, my father was Negro, and I am black.

4. Geraldine, a dedicated, headstrong woman who six years back had borne a baby, dumped its father, and earned a degree in education, sometimes drove Shamengwa to fiddling contests.

5. He treated this instrument with the reverence we accord our drums, which are considered living beings and require from us food, water, shelter, and love.

6. I am a tribal judge, and things come to me through the grapevine of the court system or the tribal police.

7. I took my bedroll, a scrap of jerky, and a loaf of bannock, and sat myself down on the crackling lichen of the southern rock.

8. There were rivers flowing in and flowing out, secret currents, six kinds of weather working on its surface and a hidden terrain beneath.

9. Each wave washed in from somewhere unseen and washed out again to somewhere unknown.

10. He had taken the old man's fiddle because he needed money, but he hadn't thought much about where he would sell it or who would buy it.

Exercise 14B

Combine each group into a single sentence by creating a coordinate pair or series, joining the units with *and.*

Example

I made my way to Mr. Whitmore's table. I introduced myself tentatively. I stated my case, telling him my cousin Greg had said that he was a great teacher.

Suggested Revision

I made my way to Mr. Whitmore's table, introduced myself tentatively, and stated my case, telling him my cousin Greg had said that he was a great teacher.

1. I wrote to Harvard. I wrote to Yale. I wrote to Princeton.

2. Horse Lowe put his big red face into Maura's window. He beat on the windshield with his fist. He told me to get the hell off his property.

3. Geraldine was not surprised to see the lock of the cupboard smashed. She was not surprised to see the violin gone.

4. As the days passed, Corwin lay low. He picked up his job at the deep fryer.

5. He straightened out. He stayed sober. He used his best manners. When questioned, he was convincingly hopeful about his prospects. He was affable about his failures.

6. A surge of unfamiliar zeal filled him. He took up the instrument again. He threw back his hair. He began to play a swift, silent passage of music.

7. I remember my father playing chansons on his fiddle. He played reels. He played jigs.

8. He smiled. He shook his fine head. He spoke softly.

PARALLEL STRUCTURE

As a general rule, units in a series should have **parallel structure**; that is, they should be the same kind of grammatical unit, and they should fit into the same "slot" in the sentence. As I've noted, the series in Gates's sentence about his valedictory speech comprises four prepositional phrases, and any one of the phrases fits naturally after the subject and verb:

My speech was	about Vietnam, abortion, and civil rights
My speech was	about the sense of community our class shared, since so many of us had been together for twelve years
My speech was	about the individual's rights and responsibilities in his or her community
My speech was	about the necessity to defy norms out of love

In this sentence, the second prepositional phrase is longer and more complex than the others. Nevertheless, because all four units are prepositional phrases that fit naturally into the slot after *my speech was*, the series is parallel and the sentence is easy to read.

Sometimes the units in a well-crafted series match very closely:

My one year at Potomac State College of West Virginia University, in Keyser, all of five miles away, was memorable for two reasons: because of my English classes with Duke Anthony Whitmore **and** my first real love affair, with Maura Gibson.

Here, the noun phrases are about the same length, the nouns are signaled by the same determiner ("*my* English classes," "*my* first real love affair") and each noun is modified by a prepositional phrase beginning with *with* and ending with a person's name.

If a writer fails to use parallel structure in a series, the sentence will be awkward and potentially confusing. It's a good idea to check the parallelism in any series by applying two tests. First, are the units grammatically similar? Second, do they fit into the same slot in the sentence?

Somehow, for reasons having to do with nudity and sensuality, blacks were not allowed to walk along most beachfronts **or** attend resorts.

PARALLELISM TEST 1
Are the units grammatically similar?

| walk along most beachfronts | *verb phrase* |
| attend resorts | *verb phrase* |

PARALLELISM TEST 2
Do the units fit into the same slot in the sentence?

| blacks were not allowed to | walk along most beachfronts |
| blacks were not allowed to | attend resorts |

The sentence above passes both tests, so the most particular editor can be at peace. By contrast, note the faulty parallel structure in this sentence:

I was used to being stared at and somewhat used to being the only black person <u>on the beach</u>, **or** <u>in a restaurant</u>, **or** <u>a motel</u>.

PARALLELISM TEST 1
Are the units grammatically similar?

on the beach	*prepositional phrase*
in a restaurant	*prepositional phrase*
a motel	*noun phrase*

PARALLELISM TEST 2
Do the units fit into the same slot in the sentence?

the only black person	<u>on the beach</u>
the only black person	<u>in a restaurant</u>
the only black person	<u>a motel</u>

This sentence fails both tests, so it requires revision. The simplest revision is to restore the preposition that Gates used in his original sentence:

I was used to being stared at and somewhat used to being the only black person on the beach, or in a restaurant, or **at** a motel.

Exercise 14C

Each of these sentences contains a series in which the parallelism has gone awry. If you hear the problem immediately, revise the sentence. If you don't hear the problem right away, first identify the units in the series and test for parallel structure; then you'll be prepared to revise.

Example
He will probably be admitted to Officer Candidate School because he is young, strong, he can work hard, and has a good education.

The series is mixed, with two adjectives, then a clause, then a verb phrase.

Suggested Revisions
He will probably be admitted to Officer Candidate School because he is <u>young</u>, <u>strong</u>, <u>hardworking</u>, and <u>well educated</u>.
Four adjectives fit into the slot after "he is."

He will probably be admitted to Officer Candidate School because <u>he is young and strong</u>, <u>he can work hard</u>, and <u>he has a good education</u>.
Three clauses fit into the slot after "because."

1. He was always looking for money — scamming, betting, shooting pool, even now and then a job.

2. My mother out of grief became strict with my father, my older sister, and hard on me.

3. The U.S. government has, in a rush of publicity and embarrassing rhetoric, cobbled together an "international coalition against terror," mobilized its army, its air force, its navy and its media, and committing them to battle.

4. In fact, the problem for an invading army is that Afghanistan has no conventional coordinates or signposts to plot on a military map — no big cities, no highways, no industrial complexes, it doesn't have any water treatment plants.

5. Dropping more bombs on Afghanistan will only shuffle the rubble, scramble some old graves, and the dead will be disturbed.

6. During her first two years, Lucienne declared four majors: French, history, philosophy, and her favorite subject was still computer science.

7. The function of a university is to develop analytical skills of students and a place where they should learn to express themselves.

8. He argued for financial aid for the children of immigrants in order to ensure the equal right to study the liberal arts, an equal chance at higher-paying jobs, and to learn the communication skills that prepare young adults for full participation in a democracy.

CORRELATIVE CONJUNCTIONS

If you've heard a child describe his or her day ("We went to the playground and Jeremy fell off the high bar and there was blood all over his face and the teacher called his grandma . . ."), you get a sense of how heavily we depend on *and* (and, to a lesser extent, *but*) in our everyday speech. Naturally, then, all of us, from elementary school children to published authors, use coordination frequently when we write.

By contrast, coordinators' first cousins, the correlative conjunctions, are quite rare in spoken English, and you seldom see them in the work of young writers. It is experienced writers who use correlatives, exploiting their ability to join syntactic units and to manipulate emphasis.

Correlative conjunctions come in pairs:

both/and	not/but
either/or	not only/but (also)
neither/nor	

In living sentences, they sound like this:

> She shook her head as if she were **both** annoyed with me **and** exasperated with her father.

> The speck seemed to **both** advance **and** retreat.

> It was a canoe. But **either** the paddler was asleep in the bottom **or** the canoe was drifting.

The correlatives *not/but* and *not only/but (also)* give greater weight to the second unit in the pair. Consider the sentences below, from Arundhati Roy's "The Algebra of Infinite Justice."

> American people ought to know that it is **not** them **but** their government's policies that are so hated.

> Could it be that the stygian anger that led to the attacks has its taproot **not** in American freedom and democracy, **but** in the U.S. government's record of commitment and support to exactly the opposite things — to military and economic terrorism, insurgency, military dictatorship, religious bigotry, and unimaginable genocide (outside America)?

Roy's use of the correlative backgrounds the material following *not* while emphasizing the material following *but*.

Like other coordinators, correlatives call for parallel structure. The editor's task is to be sure that the two parts of the correlative conjunction are followed by similar grammatical units that fit into the same slot in the sentence:

> She shook her head as if she were **both** <u>annoyed with me</u> **and** <u>exasperated with her father.</u>

PARALLELISM TEST 1
Are the units grammatically similar?

annoyed with me	*adjective phrase*
exasperated with her father	*adjective phrase*

PARALLELISM TEST 2
Do the units fit into the same slot in the sentence?

She shook her head as if she were	<u>annoyed with me</u>
She shook her head as if she were	<u>exasperated with her father</u>

The sentence passes both tests. Now examine a sentence with faulty parallelism:

> I pretended to sleep, **not** <u>because I wanted to keep up the appearance of being sick</u> **but** <u>I could not bear to return to the way things had been.</u>

PARALLELISM TEST 1
Are the units grammatically similar?

because I wanted to keep up the appearance of being sick	*subordinate clause*
I could not bear to return to the way things had been	*independent clause*

PARALLELISM TEST 2
Do the units fit into the same slot in the sentence?

I pretended to sleep	because I wanted to keep up the appearance of being sick
I pretended to sleep	I could not bear to return to the way things had been

This sentence fails both tests, so it requires revision. In Erdrich's actual sentence, the subordinator *because* is repeated at the beginning of the second clause so that both clauses joined by *not/but* are subordinate:

> I pretended to sleep, **not** because I wanted to keep up the appearance of being sick **but** because I could not bear to return to the way things had been.

I sometimes like to experiment with the placement of correlative conjunctions, placing them early in the sentence to create some repetition or late in the sentence for maximum efficiency:

> The old woman knew enough **not** to trust her vision **but** to trust her touch.

> The old woman knew enough to trust **not** her vision **but** her touch.

> The purpose of dialogue is **not** to help participants reach agreement **but** to help them achieve mutual understanding.

> The purpose of dialogue is to help participants achieve **not** agreement **but** mutual understanding.

Exercise 14D

Join the following sentences, using the correlative conjunctions indicated.

> **Example**
> *both/and*
> When my father died he left the fiddle to my brother Edwin.
> He also left it to me.

> **Joined**
> When my father died he left the fiddle both to my brother Edwin and to me.

1. *both/and*
   Shamengwa loved the fiddle. Shamengwa's father loved the fiddle.
2. *both/and*
   His mother lost her capacity for joy. Ultimately, his father lost his capacity for joy.
3. *not/but*
   The narrator does not give Corwin a break because he believes he is innocent. He gives Corwin a break because he hopes he can be redeemed.
4. *either/or*
   He would learn to play the violin. Otherwise, he would do time.
5. *neither/nor*
   Billy Peace did not play fair in the race for the violin. His brother Edwin did not play fair in the race.
6. *both/and*
   Shamengwa can face the past without blinking. Billy Peace, who owned the violin before him, can face the past without blinking.
7. *both/and*
   The violin brings great heartache. It brings great joy.
8. *not only/but also*
   The violin brings great heartache. It brings great joy.
   The violin brings great joy. It brings great heartache.

VARIATION IN COORDINATE SERIES

▪ Length

The number of units in a series has a strong influence on its rhetorical effect. In general, a series with two or three units is unmarked — that is, the length of the series doesn't call attention to itself — so it simply suggests completeness.

> I wrote to Harvard, Yale, and Princeton.

A series with four units begins to feel long, and one with five or more conveys a sense of abundance, perhaps excess, perhaps exhaustion. This effect is even stronger when the writer omits the conjunction. In the sentence below, Gates describes his drives from Virginia to Delaware to meet Maura, stringing one prepositional phrase after another to create a long series and using no conjunction. By the end of the sentence, it's surprising to learn that he has any energy left:

I'd leave work on Friday at about four o'clock, then drive all the way to Delaware, through Washington and the Beltway, past Baltimore and Annapolis, over the Chesapeake Bridge, past Ocean City, arriving at Rehoboth before midnight, with as much energy as if I had just awakened.

In the following passage, Arundhati Roy places several long series in a row.

The September 11 attacks were a monstrous calling card from a world gone horribly wrong. The message may have been written by Bin Laden (who knows?) and delivered by his couriers, but it could well have been signed by the ghosts of the victims of America's old wars. The millions killed in Korea, Vietnam, and Cambodia; the 17,500 killed when Israel — backed by the U.S. — invaded Lebanon in 1982; the 200,000 Iraqis killed in Operation Desert Storm; the thousands of Palestinians who have died fighting Israel's occupation of the West Bank. And the millions who died, in Yugoslavia, Somalia, Haiti, Chile, Nicaragua, El Salvador, the Dominican Republic, Panama, at the hands of all the terrorists, dictators, and genocidists whom the American government supported, trained, bankrolled, and supplied with arms. And this is far from being a comprehensive list.

The power of the numbers Roy cites — millions, tens and hundreds of thousands, millions more — is heightened by the long series of military actions and the longer list of embattled countries. As readers, we perceive those lists as potentially continuing because of the number of units and, in the list of countries, the absence of a conjunction. Roy's closing assertion that the list could go on is already implicit in the structure of her sentences.

Exercise 14E

Choose a passage from a text you admire (which might be one of your own), and analyze the effect of a long coordinate series.

1. Spend some time with the passage: read it aloud and type it.
2. Make the structure of the series visible, identifying the units being joined and any coordinating conjunctions, as you did in Exercise 14A.
3. For each series, count the number of units. I've claimed that a series of three feels complete, a series of four feels longish, and a series of five or more suggests abundance or excess. Do these generalizations apply to the passage you've selected?
4. For each series, consider the writer's choice of a conjunction. Are the units joined by *and*? another coordinator? no conjunction at all? What is the effect of adding, deleting, or changing the conjunction?

5. Describe the role of the passage you've selected in the text as a whole. Is this an important moment in the development of the story or argument? Why? How does the use of coordinate series serve the writer's rhetorical purpose?

■ Repetition

One reason that coordinate series are so widely used is that they make sentences more concise: it is more efficient to write "I remember my father playing chansons, reels, and jigs on his fiddle" than to name the songs in three separate sentences. However, conciseness isn't the only virtue writers seek, and we sometimes opt to repeat a few words in a coordinate series. Compare these sentences:

> I wrote to Harvard, Yale, and Princeton.
>
> I wrote to Harvard, to Yale, and to Princeton.

One way to think about the difference in this pair is that they indicate different ways of defining the slot into which coordinate units fit. For example, in the first sentence, the slot begins after *to*, and it is filled with three nouns:

> I wrote to   Harvard
> Yale
> Princeton

In the second sentence, the slot begins after *wrote*, and it is filled with three prepositional phrases:

> I wrote   to Harvard
> to Yale
> to Princeton

Both versions of the sentence are perfectly correct, and both are concise and easy to read. In this case, Gates chose the first version, using the preposition *to* just once.

In the sentence below, Gates chose to repeat a preposition. Compare these sentences:

> My speech was about Vietnam, abortion, and civil rights, the sense of community our class shared, since so many of us had been together for twelve years, the individual's rights and responsibilities in his or her community, and the necessity to defy norms out of love.
>
> My speech was about Vietnam, abortion, and civil rights, about the sense of community our class shared, since so many of us had been

together for twelve years, about the individual's rights and responsibilities in his or her community, and about the necessity to defy norms out of love.

In the sentences above, the slots have been defined like this:

My speech was about   Vietnam, abortion, and civil rights
                       the sense of community our class shared . . .
                       the individual's rights and responsibilities . . .
                       the necessity to defy norms out of love.

My speech was   about Vietnam, abortion, and civil rights
                       about the sense of community our class
                       shared . . .
                       about the individual's rights and responsi-
                       bilities . . .
                       about the necessity to defy norms out of love.

Gates had a strong incentive to go with the second option, repeating the preposition *about* to make the four units match. The preposition functions like a bullet or a number, indicating that we're moving on to the next unit. It helps the reader piece the sentence together.

Finally, consider this pair:

Each wave washed in from somewhere unseen and out again to somewhere unknown.

Each wave washed in from somewhere unseen and washed out again to somewhere unknown.

Louise Erdrich wrote the second sentence, repeating the verb *washed*. It seems to me that the choice is easily explained on esthetic grounds. The repetition of *washed* makes the image more vivid, and it creates a rhythm in the sentence that captures the movement of the waves, washing in, washing out.

In short, a coordinate series creates the option of repeating words or phrases. Most writers strive for conciseness, so the default position may be to avoid repetition — but in the interest of clarity, emphasis, or beauty, repetition is sometimes a wise choice.

In "Shamengwa," Erdrich plays with repetition not just within sentences but from one sentence to the next. Shamengwa's story of finding his violin on the lake closes like this:

"That is how my fiddle came to me," Shamengwa said, raising his head to look steadily at me. He smiled, shook his fine head, and spoke softly. "And that is why no other fiddle will I play."

And, as the story of the violin's previous owner comes to a close, we again hear a repeated structure echoing over the lake:

> The uncles have returned to their houses, pastures, children, wives. I am alone on the shore. <u>As the night goes black, I sing for you.</u> <u>As the sun comes up, I call across the water.</u> White gulls answer. <u>As the time goes on, I begin to accept what I have done.</u> I begin to know the truth of things.

Exercise 14F

In "Sin Boldly," Gates presents a memorable scene in which he and his friends forcibly integrate the Swordfish nightclub. At the entrance of the four black men, Gates reports, everybody froze — and he breaks "everybody" into four sets of people.

> Everybody froze: the kids from Piedmont and Keyser who had grown up with us; the students from Potomac State; the rednecks and crackers from up the hollers, the ones who came to town once a week all dressed up in their Sears, Roebuck perma-pressed drawers, their Thom McAn semi-leather shoes, their ultimately *white* sox, and their hair slicked back and wet-looking. The kids of rednecks, who liked to drink gallons of 3.2 beer, threaten everybody within earshot, and puke all over themselves — they froze too, their worst nightmare staring them in the face.

A quick analysis of the passage shows that the four sets of people are presented in a coordinate series, with three groups in one sentence ("the kids from Piedmont and Keyser," "the students from Potomac State," "the rednecks and crackers from up the hollers") and the fourth group ("the kids of rednecks") in a separate sentence. Another coordinate series describes how the "rednecks and crackers" dressed, and another describes how their children liked to behave.

1. Rewrite the passage without using any series, instead breaking the passage into shorter sentences.
2. Consider the effect of the change. What is gained and what is lost?

15

Drafting an Essay: Special Effects

L inguists and educational researchers have studied how the mind processes written language. They have observed the order in which syntactic structures are acquired (which structures children master first,
which ones take longer) and the speed with which children and adults
comprehend sentences. The insights of these researchers can explain why
some texts strike us as reader-friendly while others require a hard slog.

Readers want sentences to be easy to process; they want subjects and
verbs to behave like subjects and verbs, sentences to be clear and complete, paragraphs to flow smoothly. These are reasonable expectations,
and we comply with them because we wish to be understood and, perhaps,
to give pleasure.

But occasionally, we don't give readers quite what they expect. Occasionally, we can communicate what we mean more powerfully or more
beautifully if we take readers by surprise. This chapter describes readers'
expectations primarily in order to recommend that you meet them —
stopping along the way to point out some examples of special effects
achieved by breaking with convention.

FOCUS ON THE SUBJECT

If you've read Chapter 13, you know all about focus. Writers create well-
focused sentences by placing actors — often, human actors — in the subject position of sentences. Well-focused sentences are easy for English
speakers to process because they follow the familiar SVO (subject-verb-

---

Taken from Nora Bacon, *The Well-Crafted Sentence: A Writer's Guide to Style*, pp. 120–36
(Chapter 8, "Special Effects: Expectations and Exceptions").

object) pattern, with the actor and action appearing right up front in the subject-verb positions. A well-focused sentence strikes readers as clear and easy to read precisely because it gives them what they expect, what they intuitively accept as the norm.

The sentences below are simple, straightforward examples of the subject-verb-object order:

> Elroy <u>fixed</u> breakfast for me.
>
> I <u>took</u> my suitcase out to the car.

Now, consider another option. In a passive voice construction, the actor is removed from the subject position:

ACTIVE VOICE	PASSIVE VOICE
Elroy fixed breakfast for me.	Breakfast was fixed for me by Elroy.
I took my suitcase out to the car.	My suitcase was taken out to the car by me.

Why might a writer use the passive voice? Writers sometimes make this choice for the sake of paragraph continuity; for example, imagine a paragraph about the three meals:

> <u>Breakfast was fixed for me by Elroy</u>. Lunch was Mary Lou's responsibility, and dinner was prepared by Jonathan.

And writers sometimes choose the passive voice in order to create that *by* phrase at the end, giving the actor even more stress than he or she would get in the subject position:

> My suitcase was taken out to the car <u>by me</u>! (Where in hell was the bellhop?)

A structure called *it*-cleft provides yet another option for manipulating emphasis.

ACTOR-ACTION WORD ORDER	*IT*-CLEFT
Elroy fixed breakfast for me.	It was Elroy who fixed breakfast for me.
I took my suitcase out to the car.	It was I who took my suitcase out to the car.

The *it*-cleft highlights the noun phrase immediately following the subject (*it*) and the verb (a form of *be*). The sentences above stress that *it was Elroy* and nobody else who fixed my breakfast; *it was I* and nobody else who carried the suitcase.

Placing a different noun phrase after the subject and verb shifts the stress:

ACTOR-ACTION WORD ORDER	*IT*-CLEFT
Elroy fixed breakfast for me.	It was breakfast that Elroy fixed for me.
I took my suitcase out to the car.	It was my suitcase that I took out to the car.

In this iteration, the first sentence tells us that *it was breakfast* and no other meal that Elroy fixed, the second that *it was my suitcase* and nothing else (or my suitcase and nobody else's) that I took to the car.

A similar effect can be achieved with the *what*-cleft.

ACTOR-ACTION WORD ORDER	*WHAT*-CLEFT
Elroy fixed breakfast for me.	What Elroy fixed for me was breakfast.
I took my suitcase out to the car.	What I took out to the car was my suitcase.

The *what*-cleft structure stresses a noun phrase — *breakfast, my suitcase* — by pushing it to the end of the sentence.

The clauses I've been playing with are taken from Tim O'Brien's story "On the Rainy River" where, in fact, he placed the actor in the subject position. If you read the surrounding sentences, you'll see that this is a sober, quiet moment in the story:

> I don't remember saying goodbye. The last night we had dinner together, and I went to bed early, and in the morning Elroy fixed breakfast for me . . .

> At some point later in the morning, it's possible that we shook hands — I just don't remember — but I do know that by the time I'd finished packing the old man had disappeared. Around noon, when I took my suitcase out to the car, I noticed that his old black pickup truck was no longer parked in front of the house. . . . I washed up the breakfast dishes, left his two hundred dollars on the kitchen counter, and drove south toward home.

At this point, O'Brien writes the lean, clear prose that most of us strive for on most occasions.

By contrast, let's look at some special occasions. Here is the first sentence of "On the Rainy River":

This is one story I've never told before.

O'Brien opens his story with a sentence that, like the *it*-cleft and *what*-cleft, violates our expectations for word order. If the sentence began with the actor as subject, it would read "I've never told this story before." To my mind, O'Brien's version is more effective because it stresses the story rather than the storyteller; it promises that this story to which I'm about to commit my time is something special. This effect is heightened in the sentences that follow:

This is one story I've never told before. Not to anyone. Not to my parents, not to my brother or sister, not even to my wife.

The story is a long-held secret — and he's telling it to me! "This is one story" . . . this is some story. I'm hooked.

Louise Erdrich's story "Shamengwa" also opens with an unconventional sentence. The word order is inverted, the verb appearing before the subject:

At the edge of our reservation settlement there <u>lived</u> an old <u>man</u> whose arm was twisted up winglike along his side, and who was for that reason named for a butterfly — Shamengwa.

If Erdrich had begun her sentence with the actor as subject, it would read:

An old <u>man</u> whose arm was twisted up winglike along his side, and who was for that reason named for a butterfly — Shamengwa — <u>lived</u> there at the edge of our reservation settlement.

That will never do. The noun phrase, modified as it is by two adjective clauses, is just too long to occupy the subject position; the reader has to wait too long to reach the verb. How about this one:

An old <u>man</u> <u>lived</u> there at the edge of our reservation settlement. His arm was twisted up winglike along his side, and he was for that reason named for a butterfly — Shamengwa.

Better, I think, but still not as effective as Erdrich's sentence for pulling the reader into the world of the story.

The point is this. The injunction to name the actor and action early in a sentence, in the subject-verb position, is a reliable guideline, and writers comply with it most of the time. "Except," as Dr. Seuss might say, "when they don't. Because, sometimes, they won't."

Exercise 15A

Practice the *it*-cleft and *what*-cleft constructions by revising these sentences. Use the unconventional word order to stress the phrase in boldface.

> **Example**
> *it*-cleft
> My mother lost a baby boy to diphtheria when I was but four years old, and **that loss** turned my mother to the Church.
>
> **Sample Response**
> My mother lost a baby boy to diphtheria when I was but four years old, and it was that loss that turned my mother to the Church.
>
> **Example**
> *what*-cleft
> **Diphtheria** took her youngest child from her.
>
> **Sample Response**
> What took her youngest child from her was diphtheria.

1. *it*-cleft

   About that time, I received a terrible kick from the cow.

2. *it*-cleft

   The cow's kick injured Shamengwa's arm.

3. *what*-cleft

   The cow's kick injured Shamengwa's arm.

4. *it*-cleft

   On the first hot afternoon in early May, I opened my window.

5. *it*-cleft

   I heard **the sound of Corwin's music**.

6. *what*-cleft

   I heard **the sound of Corwin's music**.

7. *it*-cleft

   The narrator finally learned the story of the violin's past.

8. *what*-cleft

   The date on the letter, 1897, stuck in my mind, woke me in the middle of the night.

COMPLETENESS AND EXPLICITNESS

Readers find sentences easy to read if they are complete and explicit, so that the syntactic structure of every phrase is immediately identifiable. For example, of the two sentences below, the second is easier to process:

> The stories you read in childhood shape your personality.

> The stories that you read in childhood shape your personality.

In this sentence, the relative pronoun *that* is optional; both sentences are perfectly correct, and you'll see sentences just like them everywhere in published prose. But readers grasp the second more easily, presumably because the presence of *that* signals the adjective clause, indicating how to piece the sentence together.

The same phenomenon can be observed when *that* introduces other structures, in this case a noun clause:

> I noticed his old black pickup truck was no longer parked in front of the house.

> I noticed that his old black pickup truck was no longer parked in front of the house.

In this pair, it's easier to see why the absence of *that* slows processing. As you read the first sentence, you would certainly understand *I noticed* as the subject and verb, and you might well interpret the next noun phrase, *his old black pickup truck*, as the object. But you'd be wrong: the object is the whole clause. (What did I notice? That the pickup truck was gone.) In the second sentence, the presence of *that* signals the beginning of a clause in the object position, so there's no risk of a misreading.

As I pointed out in Chapter 14, the presence of function words can be similarly helpful in lists. In her essay on the American response to the 9/11 terror attacks, Arundhati Roy quotes President Bush:

> "They hate our freedoms — our freedom of religion, our freedom of speech, our freedom to vote and assemble and disagree with each other."

> "They hate our freedoms — our freedom of religion, freedom of speech, freedom to vote and assemble and disagree with each other."

Later in the essay, Roy similarly repeats a function word in a list:

> In fact, the problem for an invading army is that Afghanistan has no conventional coordinates or signposts to plot on a military map — no big cities, no highways, no industrial complexes, no water treatment plants.

In fact, the problem for an invading army is that Afghanistan has no conventional coordinates or signposts to plot on a military map — no big cities, highways, industrial complexes, water treatment plants.

In either case, the second version is clear enough, but Bush's speech-writer chose to include the determiner *our* before every noun phrase, and Roy chose to include *no* four times. One effect of this repetition is to emphasize the meaning: these freedoms are *ours*, Afghanistan has *no* signs of advanced industrialism. Another effect is to promote easy processing. In short, to accommodate readers, writers usually make grammatical structures complete and explicit, using function words to signal syntactic relationships.

Because complete grammatical units are the norm, sentences that omit an expected word or phrase can be quite striking. Here, in three grammatically complete sentences, is the opening to "On the Rainy River":

> This is one story I've never told before. I haven't told it to anyone. I haven't told it to my parents, to my brother or sister, or even to my wife.

And here, again, is the opening as it appears in print:

> This is one story I've never told before. Not to anyone. Not to my parents, not to my brother or sister, not even to my wife.

O'Brien repeats the function word *not* — but he omits the grammatical core of the second and third sentences, writing just prepositional phrases punctuated with periods. He violates the expectation of explicitness and completeness, leaving it to the reader to find a grammatical home for the prepositional phrases by linking them to the first sentence.

O'Brien's second and third sentences are **fragments**, units punctuated as sentences but missing an independent clause. Fragments call attention to themselves; readers notice them, and reactions can range from puzzlement to admiration. To my ear, O'Brien's fragments make his prose sound like a speaking voice, especially in passages like these:

> In June of 1967, a month after graduating from Macalester College, I was drafted to fight a war I hated. I was twenty-one years old. <u>Young, yes, and politically naïve</u>, but even so the American war in Vietnam seemed to me wrong.

> In any case those were my convictions, and back in college I had taken a modest stand against the war. <u>Nothing radical, no hothead stuff, just ringing a few doorbells for Gene McCarthy, composing a few tedious, uninspired editorials for the campus newspaper.</u>

O'Brien also favors fragments in passages describing emotional turmoil, where the scraps of language recreate the turbulent current of the narrator's thoughts and feelings:

I remember a sound in my head. It wasn't thinking, just a silent howl. <u>A million things all at once</u> — I was too good for this war. <u>Too smart, too compassionate, too everything.</u> It couldn't happen. . . . <u>A mistake, maybe — a foul-up in the paperwork.</u>

Fragments appear in all genres of writing. They are infrequent in academic writing because its purposes are best served by explicitness and because, for better or worse, academic writers maintain a formal tone. Fragments are more frequent in fiction, where we value the artfulness of special effects.

Exercise 15B

In the paragraph below, Louise Erdrich describes the character Corwin Peace. Read the paragraph carefully, then work with it.

> Corwin was one of those I see again and again. A bad thing waiting for a worse thing to happen. A mistake, but one that we kept trying to salvage, because he was so young. Some thought he had no redeeming value whatsoever. A sociopath. A clever manipulator, who drugged himself dangerous each weekend. Others pitied him and blamed his behavior on his mother's drinking. F.A.E. F.A.S. A.D.D. He wore those initials after his name the way educated people append their degrees. Still others thought they saw something in him that could be saved — perhaps the most dangerous idea of all. . . . He was, unfortunately, good-looking, with the features of an Edward Curtis subject, though the crack and vodka were beginning to make him puffy.

1. Underline the fragments.
2. Rewrite the paragraph so that it contains only complete grammatical sentences, retaining the meaning as much as possible. What do you think? Are there places where your revisions improve the paragraph?

Exercise 15C

This passage is adapted from Tim O'Brien's "On the Rainy River." It continues the description of the narrator's reaction to receiving a draft notice.

> I was a *liberal*, for Christ sake: If they needed fresh bodies, why not draft some back-to-the-stone-age hawk? Why not draft some dumb jingo in his hard hat and Bomb Hanoi button, or one of LBJ's pretty daughters, or Westmoreland's whole

handsome family — nephews and nieces and baby grandson. There should be a law, I thought. If you support a war, if you think it's worth the price, that's fine, but you have to put your own precious fluids on the line. You have to head for the front and hook up with an infantry unit and help spill the blood. And you have to bring along your wife, or your kids, or your lover. There should be a law, I thought.

1. Rewrite the passage so that it has at least three fragments, using the material provided but cutting some units loose from their grammatical mooring in the sentences.
2. What do you think? Are there places where your revisions improve the passage?

SENTENCE VARIETY

Prose flows. It has a pace, a rhythm — and readers find it most pleasing when the rhythm is varied, with the pace speeding up or slowing down at appropriate points, the reader's voice sometimes rising, sometimes falling. Virginia Woolf said that when she wrote, she heard the rhythm first, and she filled in words to keep up with it.

The passage below appears about halfway through "On the Rainy River." These are not the kind of paragraphs that will echo in your mind for the rest of the afternoon; they don't come from a turning point in the story, they don't offer high drama. But they flow easily, as you'll hear if you read them aloud:

We spent six days together at the Tip Top Lodge. Just the two of us. Tourist season was over, and there were no boats on the river, and the wilderness seemed to withdraw into a great permanent stillness. Over those six days Elroy Berdahl and I took most of our meals together. In the mornings we sometimes went out on long hikes into the woods, and at night we played Scrabble or listened to records or sat reading in front of his big stone fireplace. At times I felt the awkwardness of an intruder, but Elroy accepted me into his quiet routine without fuss or ceremony. He took my presence for granted, the same way he might've sheltered a stray cat — no wasted sighs or pity — and there was never any talk about it. Just the opposite. What I remember more than anything is the man's willful, almost ferocious silence. In all that time together, all those hours, he never asked the obvious questions: Why was I there? Why alone? Why so preoccupied? If Elroy was curious about any of this, he was careful never to put it into words.

My hunch, though, is that he already knew. At least the basics. After all, it was 1968, and guys were burning draft cards, and Canada was just a boat ride away. Elroy Berdahl was no hick. His bedroom, I remember, was cluttered with books and newspapers. He killed me at the Scrabble board, barely concentrating, and on those occasions when speech was necessary he had a way of compressing large thoughts into small, cryptic packets of language. One evening, just at sunset, he pointed up at an owl circling over the violet-lighted forest to the west.

"Hey, O'Brien," he said. "There's Jesus."

Analyzing the paragraphs for sentence variety, you immediately notice the wide range of sentence lengths. The shortest sentences — "Why alone?" "There's Jesus" — contain just two words; the longest (beginning "In the mornings we sometimes went out") contains 33. There is no unbroken sequence of long sentences (more than 25 words), and the only extended sequence of short sentences (fewer than 15 words) is the one that ends the first paragraph.

We'll return to sentence length in a moment. But first, I'd like to point out two other kinds of variation. One way of classifying sentences is to note their functions. Sentences fall into four categories: declaratives (statements), interrogatives (questions), imperatives (commands), and exclamations. The previous passage, like most prose, relies primarily on declarative sentences. But the string of declaratives is interrupted by questions near the end of the first paragraph and by the quoted exclamation in the last.

Another way to classify sentences is to consider the complexity of their structure, observing the mix of independent clauses, dependent clauses, and modifiers. Here's how the first paragraph shakes out:

We spent six days together at the Tip Top Lodge.	*one independent clause*
Just the two of us.	*fragment*
Tourist season was over, and there were no boats on the river, and the wilderness seemed to withdraw into a great permanent stillness.	*three independent clauses joined by* and
Over those six days Elroy Berdahl and I took most of our meals together.	*one independent clause*
In the mornings we sometimes went out on long hikes into the woods, and at night we played Scrabble or listened to records or sat reading in front of his big stone fireplace.	*two independent clauses joined by* and; *the second clause contains a coordinate series*
At times I felt the awkwardness of an intruder, but Elroy accepted me into his quiet routine without fuss or ceremony.	*two independent clauses joined by* but

He took my presence for granted, the same way he might've sheltered a stray cat — no wasted sighs or pity — and there was never any talk about it.	*two independent clauses joined by* and; *the first clause contains an appositive and another noun phrase set off by dashes*
Just the opposite.	*fragment*
What I remember more than anything is the man's willful, almost ferocious silence.	*one independent clause;* what-*cleft*
In all that time together, all those hours, he never asked the obvious questions:	*one independent clause; introductory preposi- tional phrase contains an appositive*
Why was I there?	*one independent clause*
Why alone?	*fragment*
Why so preoccupied?	*fragment*
If Elroy was curious about any of this, he was careful never to put it into words.	*one dependent clause, one independent clause*

The second paragraph is equally varied in terms of the sentences' complexity.

It may well be that O'Brien, like Woolf, writes with his ear, producing sentences that vary in length, function, and complexity in response to an intuitive sense of what sounds right. Actually, I suspect that most of us write that way. We hear the music of language around us every day from birth — perhaps before birth — so that, as we write, we reach for words that will capture the right sound as well as the right meaning.

Exercise 15D

Analyze sentence variety in this passage from "Shamengwa."

> Shamengwa was a man of refinement, who prepared himself carefully to meet life every day. In the Ojibwa language that is spoken on our reservation, *owehzhee* is the way men get them- selves up — pluck stray hairs, brush each tooth, make a precise part in their hair, and, these days, press a sharp crease down the front of their blue jeans — in order to show that, although the government has tried in every way possible to destroy their manhood, they are undefeatable. *Owehzhee.* We still look good and we know it. The old man was never seen in disarray, and yet there was more to it.

He played the fiddle. How he played the fiddle! Although his arm was so twisted and disfigured that his shirts had to be carefully altered and pinned to accommodate the gnarled shape, he had agility in that arm, even strength. Ever since he was very young, Shamengwa had, with the aid of a white silk scarf, tied his elbow into a position that allowed the elegant hand and fingers at the end of the damaged arm full play across the fiddle's strings. With his other hand, he drew the bow.

1. How many words are in the shortest sentence?
2. How many words are in the longest sentence?
3. How many sentences are short, with fewer than 15 words?
4. How many are long, with more than 25 words?
5. Are there sequences of three or more very short sentences in a row?
6. Are there sequences of long sentences?
7. Where does Erdrich use something other than declarative sentences — questions, commands, exclamations, or fragments? (Think about the effect of these sentences, considering why she may have chosen to set them apart.)

Exercise 15E

If you'd like to examine sentence variety in an essay rather than a short story, work with this paragraph from Arundhati Roy's article "The Algebra of Infinite Justice."

For strategic, military and economic reasons, it is vital for the U.S. government to persuade its public that their commitment to freedom and democracy and the American Way of Life is under attack. In the current atmosphere of grief, outrage, and anger, it's an easy notion to peddle. However, if that were true, it's reasonable to wonder why the symbols of America's economic and military dominance — the World Trade Center and the Pentagon — were chosen as the targets of the attacks. Why not the Statue of Liberty? Could it be that the stygian anger that led to the attacks has its taproot not in American freedom and democracy, but in the U.S. government's record of commitment and support to exactly the opposite things — to military and economic terrorism, insurgency, military dictatorship, religious bigotry, and unimaginable genocide (outside America)? It must be hard for ordinary Americans, so recently bereaved, to look up at the world with their eyes full of tears and encounter

what might appear to them to be indifference. It isn't indifference. It's just augury. An absence of surprise. The tired wisdom
of knowing that what goes around eventually comes around.

1. How many words are in the shortest sentence?
2. How many words are in the longest sentence?
3. How many sentences are short, with fewer than 15 words?
4. How many are long, with more than 25 words?
5. Are there sequences of three or more very short sentences in
    a row?
6. Are there sequences of long sentences?
7. Where does Roy use something other than declarative sentences —
    questions, commands, exclamations, or fragments? (Think about
    the effect of these sentences, considering why she may have cho-
    sen to set them apart.)

Sentence length is always a topic of interest to writers, editors, and
teachers. Short sentences have much to recommend them: they are easy
for readers to process, and they are easy for writers to produce. For very
young or unskilled writers, short sentences seem a safe choice because
they don't present many opportunities for error. And some professional
writers, especially those who create technical documents, prefer short sentences, seeking an average sentence length of 15 to 20 words.

Long sentences have their virtues as well. For example, the use of
modifiers makes it possible for a writer to be specific and precise — and of
course, the more modification, the longer the sentence. And there is a relationship between sentence length and intellectual sophistication. Children
write short sentences; as they mature, the average sentence length in their
writing moves steadily upward. In some publications, especially academic
journals and high-prestige magazines like *Granta* and *The New Yorker*,
average sentence length climbs toward 25 words.

But in the end, we come back to the importance of variety. Even in a
genre where generally short-ish sentences and a low words-per-sentence
average are preferred, it's risky to write one short sentence after another
after another: the prose is likely to sound choppy and childlike. Even in a
genre where generally long-ish sentences and a high words-per-sentence
average are preferred, it's risky to write an unbroken sequence of long sentences or to let a sentence extend beyond, say, 60 words: the prose is likely
to strike readers as dense and difficult.

Let's have a look at some passages in which Louise Erdrich and Tim
O'Brien have taken the risk.

In the following passage, Erdrich renders a pivotal moment in
Shamengwa's story, relying heavily on very short sentences:

SENTENCE VARIETY**313**

The dream was simple. A voice. *Go to the lake and sit by the southern rock. Wait there. I will come to you.*

I decided to follow these instructions. I took my bedroll, a scrap of jerky, and a loaf of bannock, and sat myself down on the crackling lichen of the southern rock. That plate of stone jutted out into the water, which dropped off from its edges into a green-black depth. From that rock, I could see all that happened on the water. I put tobacco down for the spirits. All day I sat there waiting. Flies bit me. The wind boomed in my ears. Nothing happened. I curled up when the light left and I slept. Stayed on the next morning. The next day, too. It was the first time that I had ever slept out on the shores, and I began to understand why people said of the lake that there was no end to it, even though it was bounded by rocks.

Sentence length in this passage ranges from 2 words in the second sentence to 39 words in the last sentence. Still, the short sentences stand out because there are so many of them and because they are so very short. The passage has two series of short sentences, one describing the dream and the other describing the young Shamengwa's experience sitting beside the lake. Erdrich tells us how to read the first set of short sentences: they are a dream. And so we know how to read the second set as well. As I read about Shamengwa sitting on the southern rock, I imagine his frame of mind — dreamlike, surreal. Shamengwa is prepared — and by the rhythm of the prose, the reader is prepared — to accept a boat without an oarsman, floating across the lake with the gift of a violin.

Very short or very long sentences also indicate an altered consciousness in several passages of "On the Rainy River." The final crisis, the moment when the narrator's struggle with his conscience finally tears him apart, takes place as he sits in a boat on the river, the Canadian shore just twenty yards away:

My whole life seemed to spill out into the river, swirling away from me, everything I had ever been or ever wanted to be. I couldn't get my breath; I couldn't stay afloat; I couldn't tell which way to swim. A hallucination, I suppose, but as real as anything I would ever feel. . . . A squad of cheerleaders did cartwheels along the banks of the Rainy River; they had megaphones and pompoms and smooth brown thighs. The crowd swayed left and right. A marching band played fight songs. All my aunts and uncles were there, and Abraham Lincoln, and Saint George, and a nine-year-old girl named Linda who had died of a brain tumor back in fifth grade, and several members of the United States Senate, and a blind poet scribbling notes, and LBJ, and Huck Finn, and Abbie Hoffman, and all the dead soldiers back from the grave, and the many thousands who were later to die — villagers with terrible burns, little kids without arms or legs — yes, and the Joint Chiefs of Staff were there, and a couple of popes, and a first lieutenant named Jimmy Cross, and the last surviving veteran of the American Civil War, and Jane Fonda dressed up as Barbarella, and an old man sprawling beside a pigpen, and my grandfather, and Gary Cooper, and a kind-faced woman carrying an umbrella and a copy of Plato's *Republic*, and a million ferocious citizens waving flags of all shapes and colors — people in hard hats, people in head-bands — they were all whooping and chanting and urging me toward one shore or the other.

O'Brien follows this remarkable kaleidoscope of images with a return to the aluminum boat, rocking on the river. Elroy Berdahl "remained quiet. He kept fishing. . . . He made it real." The final paragraphs describing Berdahl's patient watchfulness and then the narrator's preparations to return home bring the reader back to earth with a conventional blend of sentences, varied in length but no longer extreme.

Very short sentences in sequence, or very long sentences, create special effects. Readers are surprised to see them. Brought up short, they read with special attention — and the writer has an opportunity to heighten the impact of words describing something frightening, something tumultuous, something magical.

Exercise 15F

In a paragraph of 100 to 200 words, describe a recent dream. Write two versions of your paragraph, keeping the content essentially the same, but experimenting with sentence variety:

1. Minimize sentence variety. Write every sentence in one or two clauses, and don't let the sentence length drop below 10 words or rise above 15. Try to make the prose sound dull, plodding, or singsong.

2. Maximize sentence variety. Experiment with different sentence types (questions, commands, exclamations) and with extreme sentence lengths — very short sentences and/or an ultra-long sentence like O'Brien's. Be as artful as you can, using the unconventional sentences to heighten the paragraph's effect.

16

Revision and Editing

A cademic writing is a collaborative enterprise. By reading and commenting on your drafts, your peers can support your work as a writer. And you can support the work of your peers by reading their drafts with a critical but constructive eye. As a critical reader of your peers' writing, you bring your knowledge, experiences, and interests to bear on what you read, and your responses to their texts can help other writers continue the conversations they have joined. The questions you raise may reveal what is missing from a writer's argument, motivating the writer to revise his or her work. It is easier to see problems in other people's writing than in our own because we have a critical distance from their work that we don't have from our own. At the same time, as you read other work critically, you will begin to internalize the questions that will help you revise your own arguments.

In this chapter, we set out the differences between revising and editing, discuss the peer editing process in terms of the composition pyramid, and then explain the writer's and reader's responsibilities through early drafts, later drafts, and final drafts, providing opportunities for you to practice peer response on three drafts of a student paper.

REVISING VERSUS EDITING

We make a distinction between revising and editing. By **revising**, we mean making changes to a paper to reflect new thinking or conceptualizing. If a reader finds that the real focus of your essay comes at the end of your draft, you need to revise the paper with this new focus in mind. Revising differs from **editing**, which involves minor changes to what will be the

---

Taken from Stuart Greene and April Lidinsky, *From Inquiry to Academic Writing: A Practical Guide*, pp. 227–30, 233–48 (Chapter 10, "From Revising to Editing: Working with Peer Groups").

final draft of a paper — replacing a word here and there, correcting misspellings, or substituting dashes for commas to create emphasis, for example. When you're reading a first or second draft, the niceties of style, spelling, and punctuation are not priorities. After all, if the writer had to change the focus of his or her argument, significant changes to words, phrases, and punctuation would be inevitable. Concentrating on editing errors early on, when the writer is still trying to develop an argument with evidence, organize information logically, and anticipate counterarguments, is inefficient and even counterproductive.

Here are some characteristics of revising and editing that can guide how you read your own writing and the comments you offer to other writers:

REVISING	EDITING
Treats writing as a work in progress	Treats writing as an almost-finished product
Focuses on new possibilities both within and beyond the text	Addresses obvious errors and deficiencies
Focuses on new questions or goals	Focuses on the text alone
Considers both purpose and readers' needs	Considers grammar, punctuation, spelling, and style
Encourages further discovery	Polishes up the essay

You should understand that writing is a process, and that revising is an integral part of that process. Your best writing will happen in the context of real readers' responding to your drafts. Look at the acknowledgments in any academic book, and you will see many people credited with having improved the book through their reading and discussion of drafts and ideas. All academic writers rely on conversations with others to strengthen their work.

THE PEER EDITING PROCESS

In sharing writing with others, you need to be clear about your responsibilities. You may find that you assume one role when you read a peer's early draft, trying to encourage and support the writer to find ways to strengthen his or her argument. Although you will need to be critical, asking probing questions, you also will need to be sure that your conversation is constructive, that you encourage your peer to continue writing. You play a very different role when the writer tells you, "This is it. It's finished."

We emphasize that the different stages of writing — early, later, and final — call for different work from both readers and writers because writers' needs vary with each successive draft. These stages correspond to what has been called the composition pyramid (Figure 16.1).* The

*We thank Susannah Brietz-Monta and Anthony Monta for this idea.

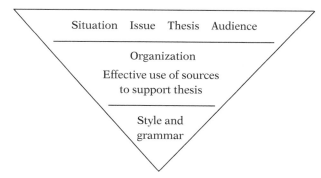

Figure 16.1   The Composition Pyramid

composition pyramid represents elements of writing that can help you decide what to pay attention to at different stages of writing.

The top of this inverted pyramid corresponds to the early stages of writing. At this point, members of the writing group should identify the situation the writer is responding to (for example, homelessness, inequality, or air pollution), the issue the writer has defined (for example, the economic versus the social costs of homelessness), the thesis or argument the writer advances, and the extent to which the writer addresses a given audience appropriately. The middle portion of the pyramid corresponds to a later stage of the writing process, the point at which members of the group should move on to discuss the extent to which the writer has organized the argument logically and used sources effectively to support the thesis. Has the writer integrated quotations smoothly into the paper? Is the evidence relevant, recent, and credible? Finally, the bottom of the pyramid corresponds to the final stages of drafting. As the writer's focus shifts to grammar and style, so should the group's. Questions to ask: Is this specific language appropriate to the intended audience? Has the writer presented the argument in ways that will compel readers — even those who disagree — to listen?

Steps in the Peer Editing Process

1 The writer distributes copies of the draft to each member of the writing group. (Ideally, the group should not exceed four students.)

2 The writer distributes a cover letter, setting an agenda for each member of the group.

3 The members read the cover letter.

4 The writer then reads the draft aloud, while members follow along, underlining passages and making notes to prepare themselves to discuss the draft.

5 Members ask questions that help the writer identify concepts that need further elaboration or clarification.

6 Discussion focuses on the strengths and weaknesses of the draft appropriate to the stage of writing and the writer's concerns. (Even in the early stage, readers and writer should sustain discussion for at least ten minutes before the next student takes a turn as writer.)

WORKING WITH EARLY DRAFTS

■ Consider the Writer's Responsibilities

When you present an early draft of your essay to your writing group, you want the group to focus on top-level pyramid concerns — situation, purpose, issue, thesis, and audience. You should explain this and any other concerns you have in a cover letter. Use the template in Figure 16.2 as a model for what needs explaining in the letter to your readers.

During the session it's important to be open to suggestions. Although you don't have to incorporate every suggestion your group makes when you revise your draft, be sure you at least understand the members' comments and concerns. If you don't understand what the members are saying about your draft, ask them to clarify or give you an example.

Finally, if you decide not to take someone's suggestion, have a good reason for doing so. It's fine to say no to a suggested change in the purpose or intended audience of your essay if that change means you won't be addressing the terms of the assignment or that you would no longer be interested in the issue.

FIGURE 16.2   The Writer's Cover Letter: Early Drafts

1. What is your question (or assignment)?
2. What is the issue motivating you to write?
3. How have published writers addressed the issue about which you are writing?
4. What is your working thesis?
5. Who is your audience, and what kind of response do you want from your readers?
6. What do you think is working best?
7. What specific aspect of the essay are you least satisfied with at this time?
8. What kind of feedback do you especially want today?

■ Consider the Reader's Responsibilities

Your task as a reader is to follow along as the early draft is read, paying special attention to the concerns the writer has explained in the cover letter and focusing on the top of the pyramid: situation, issue, thesis, and audience. Take notes directly on the draft copy, circling or underlining sections you find confusing or have questions about, so that you can refer to them specifically in the discussion.

When it's your turn to talk, have a conversation about your reactions to the draft — where the draft amused, confused, or persuaded you, for example. Don't just jump in and start telling the writer what he or she should be doing in the paper. Your role as a reader is to give the writer a live audience: Your responses can help the writer decide what parts of the paper are working and what parts need serious revision. There are times, however, when you should play the role of *deferring reader*, putting off certain comments. You don't want to overwhelm the writer with problems no matter how many questions the essay raises.

Offer both positive and negative remarks. Start by pointing out what is working well in the paper, so the writer knows where he or she is on the right track. This also leaves the writer more open to constructive criticism. But don't shy away from telling the writer what should be working better. It's your job as a reader to offer honest and specific responses to the draft, so the writer can develop it into an effective piece of writing. Figure 16.3 lists key questions you should ask as a reader of an early draft.

FIGURE 16.3   A Reader's Questions: Early Drafts

1. Are the questions and issues that motivate the writer clear?
2. Has the writer effectively related the conversation that published writers are engaged in?
3. What is at issue?
4. What is the writer's thesis?
5. Is the writer addressing the audience's concerns effectively?
6. What passages of the draft are most effective?
7. What passages of the draft are least effective?

■ Analyze an Early Draft

Keep these questions in mind as you read the following excerpt from a student's early draft. After reading a number of scholarly articles on the civil rights movement, Tasha Taylor decided to address what she sees as the difference between scholars' understanding of the movement and more popular treatments in textbooks and photographs. She also tries to tie in the larger question of historical memory to her analysis of southern blacks' struggle for equality — what people remember about the past and what they forget. In fact, she begins her essay with a quotation she believes summarizes what she wants to argue ("The struggle of man against power is the struggle of memory against forgetting").

As you read Taylor's essay, take detailed notes, and underline passages that concern you. Then write a paragraph or two explaining what she could do to strengthen the draft. Keep in mind that this is an early draft, so focus on the top level of the pyramid: the situation or assignment; the issue; the thesis; and the audience.

Taylor 1

Tasha Taylor
Professor Winters
English 111
October 23, 20--

Memory Through Photography

The struggle of man against power is the struggle of memory against forgetting.

–Milan Kundera

Ask the average American what the key components of the civil rights movement are, and most people will probably recall Martin Luther King, Jr. speaking of a dream in front of the Lincoln Memorial, Rosa Parks riding a bus, a few court decisions, and perhaps a photograph of Elizabeth Eckford cowering before an angry mob in front of Central High School in Little Rock. Few people are aware A. Philip Randolph planned the march on Washington. Few could describe Rosa Parks's connection to the civil rights movement (for example, the fact that she had been a member of the NAACP since 1943) before her legendary refusal to give up her seat in December 1955, which led to the Montgomery Bus Boycott. Few recognize the years of struggle that existed between the *Brown v. Board of Education* decision and the actual desegregation of schools. Few consider the fate of Elizabeth Eckford after the federal troops were sent to protect her and the other members of the Little Rock Nine had left Central High or the months of abuse (physical and emotional) that they endured in the name of integration. What most people know is limited to textbooks

1

Taylor 2

they read in school or the captions under photographs that describe
where a particular event occurred.

Why is it that textbooks exclusively feature the stories of larger
than life figures like Martin Luther King? Why is it that we remember
things the way we do? Historical events "have little meaning without
human interpretation, without our speaking about them within the
contexts of our lives and our culture, without giving them names and
meanings" (Kolker xix). Each person experiencing the exact same
event will carry a different memory from that event. Trying to decipher what memories reveal about each person is a fascinating yet
difficult endeavor, because each retelling of a memory and each additional memory alters existing ones.

The story that photographs and textbooks tell us does not even
begin to describe the depth of the movement or the thousands who
risked their lives and the lives of their families to make equality a
reality. Embracing this selective memory as a nation prevents understanding and acknowledgement of the harsh reality of other images
from the civil rights movement (demonstrators being plowed down by
fire hoses, beatings, and the charred bodies of bombing victims)
which are key aspects of understanding who we are as a society. The
question therefore is why. Why is it that textbook writers and
publishers have allowed so much of this history to be skewed and
forgotten? How can it be that barely 50 years after these events so
many have been forgotten or diluted?

For Analysis and Discussion

1. What is working well in Taylor's draft?
2. What is Taylor's thesis or argument?
3. To what extent does she connect her analysis of the civil rights movement and historical memory?
4. What parts of her analysis could Taylor explain further? (What do you still need to know?)
5. What would you suggest Taylor do next?

WORKING WITH LATER DRAFTS

■ Consider the Writer's Responsibilities

At a later stage, after you've had the opportunity to take readers' suggestions and do further research, you should be able to state your thesis more definitively than you did in your earlier draft. You also should be able to support your thesis with evidence, anticipating possible counterarguments. Ideally, your readers will still provide constructive criticism, offering their support, as in the first draft, but they will also question and challenge more than before.

Here, too, you want to help readers focus on your main concerns, which you should explain in a cover letter. You may still need to work on one or two top-level pyramid concerns; but your focus will likely be midlevel concerns — organization and the effective use of sources. Use the list of questions in Figure 16.4 to help you write your cover letter.

FIGURE 16.4   The Writer's Cover Letter: Later Drafts

1. What is your research question?
2. What is the issue motivating you to write?
3. What is your thesis?
4. How do you go about identifying a gap in readers' knowledge, modifying others' ideas, or trying to correct readers' misunderstandings?
5. To what extent do you distinguish your argument from the information you quote, summarize, or paraphrase from the sources you have read?
6. To what extent have you organized your ideas in ways that will help readers follow the logic of your argument?
7. To what extent have you anticipated potential counterarguments to your thesis?
8. What do you think is working best?
9. What specific aspect of the essay are you least satisfied with at this time?

■ Consider the Reader's Responsibilities

In a later draft, your focus as reader should be on midlevel concerns in the composition pyramid: places in the writer's text that are confusing, that require better transitions, or that could use sources more effectively. You can challenge writers at this stage of the composing process, perhaps playing the role of *naïve reader*, suggesting places in the draft where the writer has left something out or isn't clear. The naïve reader's comments tend to take the form of questions: "Do you mean to suggest that everyone who learns to write well succeeds in life? What kind of success are you talking about?"

Closely related to the naïve reader is the *devil's advocate reader*. This reader's comments also challenge the writer, often taking the form of a question like this: "But why couldn't this be attributed to the effects of socialization rather than heredity?" Figure 16.5 offers questions for reading later drafts.

FIGURE 16.5   A Reader's Questions: Later Drafts

1. To what extent is it clear what questions and issues motivate the writer?

2. What is the writer's thesis?

3. How effectively does the writer establish the conversation — identity a gap in people's knowledge, attempt to modify an existing argument, or try to correct some misunderstanding?

4. How effectively does the writer distinguish between his or her ideas and the ideas he or she summarizes, paraphrases, or quotes?

5. How well does the writer help you follow the logic of his or her argument?

6. To what extent are you persuaded by the writer's argument?

7. To what extent does the writer anticipate possible counterarguments?

8. To what extent does the writer make clear how he or she wants readers to respond?

9. What do you think is working best? Explain by pointing to specific passages in the writer's draft.

10. What specific aspect of the draft is least effective? Explain by pointing to a specific passage in the writer's draft.

■ Analyze a Later Draft

Now read the following excerpt from Taylor's second draft. You will see that she begins with her discussion of historical memory. She also has included an analysis of a book of photographs that Nobel Prize–winning author Toni Morrison compiled. Take notes as you read the draft and write a paragraph in which you describe what you see as some of the strengths of what Taylor has written and what she can do to make other elements stronger. In particular, focus on the middle level of the composition pyramid — on organization and the effective use of sources and evidence to support her thesis.

Taylor 1

Tasha Taylor
Professor Winters
English 111
November 14, 20--

Memory Through Photography

> The struggle of man against power is the struggle of memory
> against forgetting.
>
> –Milan Kundera

Memory is such an integral part of what it is to be human, yet is *1*
something so often taken for granted: people assume that their
memories are accurate to protect themselves from the harsh realities
of the atrocities committed by ordinary people. Even the pictures
used to represent the much-celebrated civil rights movement give us
a false sense of security and innocence. For example, the Ku Klux
Klan is most often depicted by covered faces and burning crosses; the
masks allow us to remove ourselves from responsibility. Few could
describe Rosa Parks's connection to the civil rights movement (for
example, the fact that she had been a member of the NAACP since
1943) before her legendary refusal to give up her seat in December
1955, which led to the Montgomery Bus Boycott. Few recognize the
years of struggle that existed between the *Brown v. Board of Education*
decision and the actual desegregation of schools. Few consider the
fate of Elizabeth Eckford after the federal troops were sent to protect
her and the other members of the Little Rock Nine had left Central
High or the months of abuse (physical and emotional) that they
endured in the name of integration. What most people know is limited to textbooks they read in school or the captions under photographs that describe where a particular event occurred.

It is important, therefore, to analyze what is remembered and even *2*
more importantly to recognize what it is forgotten: to question why it
is that it is forgotten, what that says about society today, how far it has
come and how much it has unwittingly fallen back into old patterns
such as prejudice and ignorance. The discrepancies in cultural memory
are due more to a society's desire to remember itself in the best light
and protect itself from the reality of its brutality and responsibility.
Such selective memory only temporarily heals the wounds of society;
lack of awareness does not cause healing. Although there have been

Taylor 2

many recent moves to increase awareness, they are tainted by unavoidable biases and therefore continue to perpetuate a distorted memory.

Images play a central role in the formation of cultural memory   3
because people can point to photographs and claim them as concrete
evidence: "Images entrance us because they provide a powerful illusion of owning reality. If we can photograph reality or paint or copy
it, we have exercised an important kind of power" (Kolker 3). A picture of black and white children sitting at a table together is used to
reinforce the cultural perception that the problems of racism are
over, that it has all been fixed.

In her book *Remember*, Toni Morrison strives to revitalize the   4
memory of school integration through photographs. The book is dedi-
cated to Denise McNair, Carole Robertson, Addie Mae Collins, and
Cynthia Wesley, the four girls killed in the 16th Street Baptist Church
bombing in 1963. Morrison writes, "Things are better now. Much,
much better. But remember why and please remember us" (Morrison
72). The pictures are of black and white children happily eating
together, solemnly saluting the flag together, and holding hands. The
photographs of the four murdered girls show them peacefully and
innocently smiling as if everything really is better now. In reality,
according to the Bureau of Alcohol, Tobacco and Firearms, between
1995 and 1997 there were 162 incidents of arson or bombing in
African American houses of worship (*ATF Online*). There are a few
images of people protesting integration, but they are also consistent
with the cultural memory (protesters are shown simply holding signs
and yelling, not beating and killing innocent children). Finally, the
captions are written in a child's voice. Yet it is not a child's voice at
all it is merely a top down view of children that serves to perpetuate
a distorted cultural memory.

The photographs used to suggest how things are much, much   5
better now are misleading. For example, the last photograph is of a
black girl and a white girl holding hands through a bus window,
which was transporting them to an integrated school. The caption
reads: "Anything can happen. Anything at all. See?" (71). It is a very
powerful image of how the evil of Jim Crow and segregation exist in a
distant past and the nation has come together and healed. However,
Morrison neglects to point out that the picture was taken in Boston,

Taylor 3

Massachusetts, not the deep south, the heart of racism. Children holding hands in Boston is much less significant than if they were in Birmingham where that action would be concrete evidence of how far we as a nation have come.

Morrison also glorifies of Martin Luther King, Jr. and Rosa Parks pointing to them as epitomizing the movement. Unfortunately, she perpetuates the story that one needs to be special or somehow larger than life to affect change. Paul Rogat Loeb writes in *Soul of a Citizen*:   6

> Once we enshrine our heroes, it becomes hard for mere mortals to measure up in our eyes . . . in our collective amnesia we lose the mechanisms through which grassroots social movements of the past successfully shifted public sentiment and challenged entrenched institutional power. Equally lost are the means by which their participants managed to keep on, sustaining their hope and eventually prevailing in circumstances at least as difficult as those we face today. (Loeb 38/36)

Placing a select few on pedestals and claiming them as next to divine heroes of the movement does society a disservice; people fail to realize that ordinary people can serve as agents of change.

Morrison's book ignores the thousand of ordinary people who risked their lives for the cause to bring about equality. The caption besides the picture of Rosa Parks in *Remember* reads "because if I ever feel helpless or lonely I just have to remember that all it takes is one person" (Morrison 62). Ironically, Morrison gives credit for the Montgomery Bus Boycott to one person, ignoring the months of planning and involved dozens of planners. Even the photograph presents Rosa Parks in a position of power. It is a low-angle shot up at Parks that makes her appear larger than life and authoritative. The photographs of Martin Luther King, Jr. also further the impression of power with a close up shot of his face as he stands above thousands of participants in the March on Washington. Although these photographs were selected to perpetuate the hero illusion, it is more inspiring to remember the ordinary people who took a stand and were able to accomplish extraordinary feats because of their dedication and persistence rather than glorify extraordinary people who were destined for greatness.   7

For Discussion and Analysis

1. What is Taylor's thesis or argument?
2. How well does she help you follow the logic of her argument with transitions?
3. How effectively does she distinguish between her ideas and the ideas she summarizes, paraphrases, or quotes?
4. To what extent are you persuaded by her argument?
5. What should Taylor do next?

WORKING WITH FINAL DRAFTS

■ Consider the Writer's Responsibilities

Your final draft should require editing, not revising. At this stage, readers should focus on errors in style and grammar in the text, not on the substance of your work. Here, too, indicate your main concerns in a cover letter (Figure 16.6).

FIGURE 16.6   The Writer's Cover Letter: Final Drafts

1. What is your unique perspective on your issue?
2. To what extent do the words and phrases you use reflect who you believe your readers are?
3. Does your style of citation reflect accepted conventions for academic writing?
4. What do you think is working best?
5. What specific aspect of the essay are you least satisfied with at this time?

■ Consider the Reader's Responsibilities

Once a writer's ideas are developed and in place, readers should turn their attention to the bottom level of the composition pyramid, to matters of style and grammar. At this stage, details are important: Is this the best word to use? Would this sentence be easier to follow if it was broken into two sentences? Which spelling is correct — *Freedman* or *Friedman*? Are citations handled consistently? Should this question mark precede or follow the quotation mark? The *grammatically correct reader* evaluates and makes judgments about the writer's work. This reader may simply indicate with a mark of some sort that there's a problem in a sentence or paragraph, or may even correct the writer's work. Figure 16.7 is a list of questions a reader should ask of a final draft.

FIGURE 16.7   A Reader's Questions: Final Drafts

1. How does the writer go about contributing a unique perspective on the issue?
2. To what extent does the writer use words and phrases that are appropriate for the intended audience?
3. To what extent does the style of citation reflect accepted conventions for academic writing?
4. What do you think is working best?
5. What specific aspect of the essay are you least satisfied with at this time?

■ Analyze a Near-Final Draft

Now read Taylor's near-final draft and write a paragraph detailing what she can do to strengthen it. Again, you will see that Taylor has made substantial changes. She compares Morrison's book of photographs to a Spike Lee documentary that she watched with her class. As you read the essay, focus on the bottom level of the composition pyramid: Does the writer use appropriate language? Does she adhere to appropriate conventions for using and citing sources?

Taylor 1

Tasha Taylor
Professor Winters
English 111
December 5, 20--

Memory Through Photography

Memory is such an integral part of what it is to be human, yet it is something so often taken for granted: people assume that their memories are accurate to protect themselves from the harsh realities of the atrocities committed by ordinary people. Even the pictures used to represent the much-celebrated civil rights movement give us a false sense of security and innocence. For example, the Ku Klux Klan is most often depicted by covered faces and burning crosses; the masks allow us to remove ourselves from responsibility. Few could describe Rosa Parks's connection to the civil rights movement before her legendary refusal to give up her seat in December 1955, which led to the Montgomery Bus Boycott (for example, the fact that she had been a member of the NAACP since 1943). Few recognize the

1

Taylor 2

years of struggle that existed between the 1954 *Brown v. Board of Education* decision and the actual desegregation of schools. Few consider the fate of Elizabeth Eckford after the federal troops sent to protect her and the other members of the Little Rock Nine had left Central High or the months of abuse (physical and emotional) that they endured in the name of integration. What most people know is limited to the textbooks they read in school or the captions under photographs that describe where a particular event occurred.

It is important, then, to analyze what is remembered, and even more important to recognize what is forgotten: to question why it is that it is forgotten, what that says about society today, how far it has come and how much it has unwittingly fallen back into old patterns of prejudice and ignorance. The discrepancies in cultural memory are due more to society's desire to remember itself in the best light and protect itself from the reality of its brutality and responsibility. Such selective memory only temporarily heals the wounds of society; lack of awareness does not cause healing. Although there have been many recent moves to increase awareness, they are tainted by unavoidable biases and therefore continue to perpetuate a distorted memory.

2

Images play a central role in the formation of cultural memory because people can point to photographs and claim them as concrete evidence: "Images entrance us because they provide a powerful illusion of owning reality. If we can photograph reality or paint or copy it, we have exercised an important kind of power" (Kolker 3). A picture of black and white children sitting at a table together is used to reinforce the cultural perception that the problems of racism are over, that they have all been fixed.

3

In her book *Remember*, Toni Morrison strives to revitalize the memory of school integration through photographs. The book is dedicated to Denise McNair, Carole Robertson, Addie Mae Collins, and Cynthia Wesley, the four girls killed in the 16th Street Baptist Church bombing in 1963. Morrison writes: "Things are better now. Much, much better. But remember why and please remember us" (72). The pictures are of black and white children happily eating together, solemnly saluting the flag together, and holding hands. The photographs of the four murdered girls show them peacefully and

4

Taylor 3

innocently smiling as if everything really is better now. In reality,
according to the Bureau of Alcohol, Tobacco, Firearms and
Explosives, between 1995 and 1997 there were 162 incidents of arson
or bombing in African American houses of worship (*ATF Online*).
There are a few images of people protesting integration, but they are
also consistent with the cultural memory (protesters are shown simply holding signs and yelling, not beating and killing innocent children). Finally, the captions are written in a child's voice. Yet it is not
a child's voice at all; it is merely a top-down view of children that
serves to perpetuate a distorted cultural memory.

The photographs used to suggest how things are much, much   5
better now are misleading. For example, the last photograph, taken
through a bus window, is of a black girl and a white girl holding
hands; the bus was transporting them to an integrated school. The
caption reads: "Anything can happen. Anything at all. See?" (71). It
is a very powerful image of how the evil of Jim Crow and segregation
exist in a distant past and the nation has come together and healed.
However, Morrison neglects to point out that the picture was taken
in Boston, not in the Deep South, the heart of racism. Children holding hands in Boston is much less significant than if they were in
Birmingham, where that action would be concrete evidence of how
far we as a nation have come.

Morrison also glorifies Martin Luther King Jr. and Rosa Parks,   6
pointing to them as epitomizing the movement. Unfortunately, she
perpetuates the story that one needs to be special or somehow larger
than life to effect change. Paul Rogat Loeb writes in *Soul of a Citizen*:

> Once we enshrine our heroes, it becomes hard for mere mortals
> to measure up in our eyes. . . . In our collective amnesia we lose
> the mechanisms through which grassroots social movements of
> the past successfully shifted public sentiment and challenged
> entrenched institutional power. Equally lost are the means by
> which their participants managed to keep on, sustaining their
> hope and eventually prevailing in circumstances at least as diffi-
> cult as those we face today. (38/36)

Placing a select few on pedestals and claiming them as next-to-
divine heroes of the movement does society a disservice; people
fail to realize that ordinary people can serve as agents of change.

Taylor 4

Morrison's book ignores the thousands of ordinary people who risked their lives for the cause to bring about equality. The caption beside the picture of Rosa Parks in *Remember* reads "Because if I ever feel helpless or lonely I just have to remember that all it takes is one person" (Morrison 62). Ironically, Morrison gives credit for the Montgomery Bus Boycott to one person, ignoring the months of planning that involved dozens of planners. Even the photograph presents Rosa Parks in a position of power. It is a low-angle shot up at Parks that makes her appear larger than life and authoritative. The photographs of Martin Luther King Jr. also further the impression of power with a close-up shot of his face as he stands above thousands of participants in the March on Washington. Although these photographs were selected to perpetuate the hero illusion, it is more inspiring to remember the ordinary people who took a stand and were able to accomplish extraordinary feats because of their dedication and persistence rather than to glorify extraordinary people who were destined for greatness.

7

In contrast, Spike Lee's 1998 documentary titled *4 Little Girls* is a stirring depiction of the lives and deaths of the girls who died in the 1963 16th Street Baptist Church bombing. In his film, Spike Lee looks behind what some would call "societal amnesia" to disclose the harsh realities of the civil rights movement. Lee interviews family members and friends of the murdered girls, revealing the pain and anger that they grapple with more than forty years after the tragedy. Lee not only includes images of the bombed church but also the charred and nearly unrecognizable bodies of the murdered girls. These disturbing images underscore the reality of their deaths without appearing sensationalist. The film does an exceptional job of reminding the viewer of the suffering and mindless hate that were prevalent during the civil rights movement.

8

However, the documentary is also biased. For instance, the girls were not little; they were fourteen, not really little girls. Lee chose to describe them as little to elicit emotion and sympathy for their tragic deaths. They were victims. They had not marched through the streets demanding equality; instead, Denise McNair, Carole Robertson, Addie Mae Collins, and Cynthia Wesley were simply attending Sunday school and were ruthlessly murdered. Victimizing Denise, Carole, Addie Mae, and Cynthia is not detrimental to the cultural memory in and of itself.

9

Taylor 5

The problem is that the victimization of the four girls is expanded to encompass the entire black community, undermining the power and achievement of the average black citizen. We need to remember the people who struggled to gain employment for blacks in the labor movement of the 1940s and 1950s that initiated the civil rights movement.

One can argue that despite the presence of misleading images in Spike Lee's film and Toni Morrison's book, at least some of the story is preserved. Still, it is easy to fall victim to the cliché: those who do not remember history are doomed to repeat it. Just because a portion of the story is remembered, it does not mean that society is immune to falling back into its old habits. This cultural amnesia not only perpetuates the injustices of the time but leaves open the possibility that these atrocities can occur again. If people believe the government can simply grant black equality, then they may believe that it can also take it away. In essence memory is about power: "The struggle of man against power is the struggle of memory against forgetting." Those who are remembered hold power over the forgotten. Their legacy is lost and so is their ability to inspire future generations through their memory.

10

Taylor 6

Works Cited

United States. Dept. of Justice. *ATF Online.* Bureau of Alcohol, Tobacco, Firearms and Explosives, 1 Dec. 2004. Web. 2 Dec. 2004.

Kolker, Robert. *Film, Form, and Culture.* New York: McGraw Hill, 1998. Print.

Kundera, Milan. *The Columbia World of Quotations.* New York: Columbia University Press, 1996. N. pag. *Bartleby.com.* Web. 2 Dec. 2004.

Loeb, Paul Rogat. *Soul of a Citizen.* New York: St. Martin's/Griffin, 1999. Print.

Morrison, Toni. *Remember.* Boston: Houghton Mifflin, 2004. Print.

For Analysis and Discussion

1. What would you say is Taylor's argument?
2. To what extent does she provide transitions to help you understand how her analysis supports her argument?
3. To what extent does she integrate quotations appropriately into the text of her argument?
4. To what extent does the style of citation reflect accepted conventions for academic writing?
5. If Taylor had more time to revise, what would you suggest she do?

PART FIVE

Readings: Methods and Objects of Inquiry

How Mali Lost Her Accent

Pacita Abad (1946–2004), an artist originally from the Philippines, created large and brightly colored mixed-media works that reflect both the country of her birth and her extensive experiences traveling around the world, including her experience as an immigrant in the United States. When she first came to this country, Abad found employment as a seamstress, a job that would profoundly impact her style as an artist. One of her best-known paintings, *How Mali Lost Her Accent* (1991) is an example of trapunto painting, a quilting technique Abad adapted by sewing and stuffing fabric on the canvas, thereby giving the two-dimensional painting a more sculptural quality. Images of Abad's artwork, including a reproduction of this painting in color, can be found on her Web site: http://www.pacitaabad.com/.

■ ■ ■

■ ADBUSTERS MEDIA FOUNDATION

Follow the Flock

Adbusters Media Foundation, founded in 1989 by Kalle Lasn and Bill Schmalz, supports a network of activists who call their audience's attention to the negative impact of consumerism on modern society. Based in Vancouver, British Columbia, Adbusters' philosophy is one of active participation rather than passive resistance. This participation is manifested through culture jamming, a form of protest in which mass media advertising is appropriated as a means of social critique. In this way, capitalism is subverted by its own language and symbols. In their spoof ads, Adbusters draws awareness to the political and economic power of large corporations, as well as to their unfair labor practices. The spoof ad *Follow the Flock*, among many others, can be found on the Adbusters Web site: https://www.adbusters.org/.

How to Tame a Wild Tongue

Gloria Anzaldúa (1942–2004), a sixth generation Tejana (a person of Hispanic origin born in Texas), was a poet, theorist, and activist. She was one of the first in her family to go to college and was about to finish her doctoral dissertation when she died unexpectedly from diabetes-related complications. Anzaldúa's writing, like her identity, is a mix of English and Spanish. Her work has won several awards, and she has been recognized particularly for promoting and reconceptualizing feminist and lesbian issues in literature and cultural studies. "How to Tame a Wild Tongue" is a chapter from her book *Borderlands/La Frontera: The New Mestiza* (1987), which is now a canonical work in Chicano studies.

■ ■ ■

"We're going to have to control your tongue," the dentist says, pulling out all the metal from my mouth. Silver bits plop and tinkle into the basin. My mouth is a motherlode.

The dentist is cleaning out my roots. I get a whiff of the stench when I gasp. "I can't cap that tooth yet, you're still draining," he says.

"We're going to have to do something about your tongue," I hear the anger rising in his voice. My tongue keeps pushing out the wads of cotton, pushing back the drills, the long thin needles. "I've never seen anything as strong or as stubborn," he says. And I think, how do you tame a wild tongue, train it to be quiet, how do you bridle and saddle it? How do you make it lie down?

> Who is to say that robbing a people of its language is less violent
> than war?
>
> — RAY GWYN SMITH[1]

I remember being caught speaking Spanish at recess — that was good for three licks on the knuckles with a sharp ruler. I remember being sent to the corner of the classroom for "talking back" to the Anglo teacher when all I was trying to do was tell her how to pronounce my name. "If you want to be American, speak 'American.' If you don't like it, go back to Mexico where you belong."

"I want you to speak English. *Pa' hallar buen trabajo tienes que saber hablar el inglés bien. Qué vale toda tu educación si todavía hablas inglés con un* 'accent,'" my mother would say, mortified that I spoke English like a Mexican. At Pan American University, I and all Chicano students were required to take two speech classes. Their purpose: to get rid of our accents.

Attacks on one's form of expression with the intent to censor are a violation of the First Amendment. *El Anglo con cara de inocente nos arrancó la lengua.* Wild tongues can't be tamed, they can only be cut out.

Overcoming the Tradition of Silence

Ahogadas, escupimos el oscuro.
Peleando con nuestra propia sombra
el silencio nos sepulta.

En boca cerrada no entran moscas. "Flies don't enter a closed mouth" is a saying I kept hearing when I was a child. *Ser habladora* was to be a gossip and a liar, to talk too much. *Muchachitas bien criadas,* well-bred girls don't answer back. *Es una falta de respeto* to talk back to one's mother or father. I remember one of the sins I'd recite to the priest in the confession box the few times I went to confession: talking back to my mother, *hablar pa' 'tras, repelar. Hocicona, repelona, chismosa,* having a big mouth, questioning, carrying tales are all signs of being *mal criada.* In my culture they are all words that are derogatory if applied to women — I've never heard them applied to men.

The first time I heard two women, a Puerto Rican and a Cuban, say the word *"nosotras,"* I was shocked. I had not known the word existed. Chicanas use *nosotros* whether we're male or female. We are robbed of our female being by the masculine plural. Language is a male discourse.

And our tongues have become
dry   the wilderness has
dried out our tongues   and
we have forgotten speech.
    — IRENA KLEPFISZ[2]

Even our own people, other Spanish speakers *nos quieren poner candados en la boca.* They would hold us back with their bag of *reglas de academia.*

Oyé Como Ladra: El Lenguaje de la Frontera

Quien tiene boca se equivoca.
    — MEXICAN SAYING

"Pocho, cultural traitor, you're speaking the oppressor's language by speaking English, you're ruining the Spanish language," I have been accused by various Latinos and Latinas. Chicano Spanish is considered by the purist and by most Latinos deficient, a mutilation of Spanish.

But Chicano Spanish is a border tongue which developed naturally. Change, *evolución, enriquecimiento de palabras nuevas por invención o adopción* have created variants of Chicano Spanish, *un nuevo lenguaje. Un lenguaje que corresponde a un modo de vivir.* Chicano Spanish is not incorrect, it is a living language.

For a people who are neither Spanish nor live in a country in which Spanish is the first language; for a people who live in a country in which English is the reigning tongue but who are not Anglo; for a people who cannot entirely identify with either standard (formal, Castillian) Spanish nor standard English, what recourse is left to them but to create their own language? A language which they can connect their identity to, one capable of communicating the realities and values true to themselves — a language with terms that are neither *español ni inglés*, but both. We speak a patois, a forked tongue, a variation of two languages.

Chicano Spanish sprang out of the Chicanos' need to identify ourselves as a distinct people. We needed a language with which we could communicate with ourselves, a secret language. For some of us, language is a homeland closer than the Southwest — for many Chicanos today live in the Midwest and the East. And because we are a complex, heterogeneous people, we speak many languages. Some of the languages we speak are

1. Standard English
2. Working-class and slang English
3. Standard Spanish
4. Standard Mexican Spanish
5. North Mexican Spanish dialect
6. Chicano Spanish (Texas, New Mexico, Arizona, and California have regional variations)
7. Tex-Mex
8. *Pachuco* (called *caló*)

My "home" tongues are the languages I speak with my sister and brothers, with my friends. They are the last five listed, with 6 and 7 being closest to my heart. From school, the media, and job situations, I've picked up standard and working-class English. From Mamagrande Locha and from reading Spanish and Mexican literature, I've picked up Standard Spanish and Standard Mexican Spanish. From *los recién llegados*, Mexican immigrants, and *braceros*, I learned the North Mexican dialect. With Mexicans I'll try to speak either Standard Mexican Spanish or the North Mexican dialect. From my parents and Chicanos living in the Valley, I picked up Chicano Texas Spanish, and I speak it with my mom, younger brother (who married a Mexican and who rarely mixes Spanish with English), aunts, and older relatives.

With Chicanas from *Nuevo México* or *Arizona* I will speak Chicano Spanish a little, but often they don't understand what I'm saying. With most California Chicanas I speak entirely in English (unless I forget). When I first moved to San Francisco, I'd rattle off something in Spanish, unintentionally embarrassing them. Often it is only with another Chicana *tejana* that I can talk freely.

Words distorted by English are known as anglicisms or *pochismos*. The *pocho* is an anglicized Mexican or American of Mexican origin who speaks Spanish with an accent characteristic of North Americans and who distorts and reconstructs the language according to the influence of English.[3] Tex-Mex, or Spanglish, comes most naturally to me. I may switch back and forth from English to Spanish in the same sentence or in the same word. With my sister and my brother Nune and with Chicano *tejano* contemporaries I speak in Tex-Mex.

From kids and people my own age I picked up *Pachuco*. *Pachuco* (the language of the zoot suiters) is a language of rebellion, both against Standard Spanish and Standard English. It is a secret language. Adults of the culture and outsiders cannot understand it. It is made up of slang words from both English and Spanish. *Ruca* means girl or woman, *vato* means guy or dude, *chale* means no, *simón* means yes, *churro* is sure, talk is *periquiar, pigionear* means petting, *que gacho* means how nerdy, *ponte águila* means watch out, death is called *la pelona*. Through lack of practice and not having others who can speak it, I've lost most of the *Pachuco* tongue.

Chicano Spanish

Chicanos, after 250 years of Spanish/Anglo colonization, have developed significant differences in the Spanish we speak. We collapse two adjacent vowels into a single syllable and sometimes shift the stress in certain words such as *maíz/maiz, cohete/cuete*. We leave out certain consonants when they appear between vowels: *lado/lao, mojado/mojao*. Chicanos from South Texas pronounce *f* as *j* as in *jue (fue)*. Chicanos use "archaisms," words that are no longer in the Spanish language, words that have been evolved out. We say *semos, truje, haiga, ansina*, and *naiden*. We retain the "archaic" *j*, as in *jalar*, that derives from an earlier *h* (the French *halar* or the Germanic *halon* which was lost to standard Spanish in the 16th century), but which is still found in several regional dialects such as the one spoken in South Texas. (Due to geography, Chicanos from the Valley of South Texas were cut off linguistically from other Spanish speakers. We tend to use words that the Spaniards brought over from Medieval Spain. The majority of the Spanish colonizers in Mexico and the Southwest came from Extremadura — Hernán Cortés was one of them — and Andalucía. Andalucians pronounce *ll* like a *y*, and their *d*'s tend to be absorbed by adjacent vowels: *tirado* becomes *tirao*. They brought *el lenguaje popular, dialectos y regionalismos*.[4])

Chicanos and other Spanish speakers also shift *ll* to *y* and *z* to *s*.[5] We leave out initial syllables, saying *tar* for *estar, toy* for *estoy, hora* for *ahora* (*cubanos* and *puertorriqueños* also leave out initial letters of some words). We also leave out the final syllable such as *pa* for *para*. The intervocalic *y*, the *ll* as in *tortilla, ella, botella*, gets replaced by *tortia* or *tortiya, ea, botea*. We add an additional syllable at the beginning of certain words: *atocar* for *tocar, agastar* for *gastar*. Sometimes we'll say *lavaste las vacijas*, other times *lavates* (substituting the *ates* verb endings for the *aste*).

We use anglicisms, words borrowed from English: *bola* from ball, *carpeta* from carpet, *máchina de lavar* (instead of *lavadora*) from washing machine. Tex-Mex argot, created by adding a Spanish sound at the beginning or end of an English word such as *cookiar* for cook, *watchar* for watch, *parkiar* for park, and *rapiar* for rape, is the result of the pressures on Spanish speakers to adapt to English.

We don't use the word *vosotros/as* or its accompanying verb form. We don't say *claro* (to mean yes), *imagínate*, or *me emociona*, unless we picked up Spanish from Latinas, out of a book, or in a classroom. Other Spanish-speaking groups are going through the same, or similar, development in their Spanish.

Linguistic Terrorism

> *Deslenguadas. Somos los del español deficiente.* We are your linguistic nightmare, your linguistic aberration, your linguistic *mestisaje*, the subject of your *burla*. Because we speak with tongues of fire we are culturally crucified. Racially, culturally, and linguistically *somos huérfanos* — we speak an orphan tongue.

Chicanas who grew up speaking Chicano Spanish have internalized the belief that we speak poor Spanish. It is illegitimate, a bastard language. And because we internalize how our language has been used against us by the dominant culture, we use our language differences against each other.

Chicana feminists often skirt around each other with suspicion and hesitation. For the longest time I couldn't figure it out. Then it dawned on me. To be close to another Chicana is like looking into the mirror. We are afraid of what we'll see there. *Pena*. Shame. Low estimation of self. In childhood we are told that our language is wrong. Repeated attacks on our native tongue diminish our sense of self. The attacks continue throughout our lives.

Chicanas feel uncomfortable talking in Spanish to Latinas, afraid of their censure. Their language was not outlawed in their countries. They had a whole lifetime of being immersed in their native tongue; generations, centuries in which Spanish was a first language, taught in school, heard on radio and TV, and read in the newspaper.

If a person, Chicana or Latina, has a low estimation of my native tongue, she also has a low estimation of me. Often with *mexicanas y latinas* we'll speak English as a neutral language. Even among Chicanas we tend to speak English at parties or conferences. Yet, at the same time, we're afraid the other will think we're *agringadas* because we don't speak Chicano Spanish. We oppress each other trying to out-Chicano each other, vying to be the "real" Chicanas, to speak like Chicanos. There is no one Chicano language just as there is no one Chicano experience. A monolingual Chicana whose first language is English or Spanish is just as much a Chicana as one who speaks several variants of Spanish. A Chicana from

Michigan or Chicago or Detroit is just as much a Chicana as one from the Southwest. Chicano Spanish is as diverse linguistically as it is regionally.

By the end of this century, Spanish speakers will comprise the biggest minority group in the U.S., a country where students in high schools and colleges are encouraged to take French classes because French is considered more "cultured." But for a language to remain alive it must be used.[6] By the end of this century English, and not Spanish, will be the mother tongue of most Chicanos and Latinos.

So, if you want to really hurt me, talk badly about my language. Ethnic identity is twin skin to linguistic identity — I am my language. Until I can take pride in my language, I cannot take pride in myself. Until I can accept as legitimate Chicano Texas Spanish, Tex-Mex, and all the other languages I speak, I cannot accept the legitimacy of myself. Until I am free to write bilingually and to switch codes without having always to translate, while I still have to speak English or Spanish when I would rather speak Spanglish, and as long as I have to accommodate the English speakers rather than having them accommodate me, my tongue will be illegitimate.

I will no longer be made to feel ashamed of existing. I will have my voice: Indian, Spanish, white. I will have my serpent's tongue — my woman's voice, my sexual voice, my poet's voice. I will overcome the tradition of silence.

> My fingers
> move sly against your palm
> Like women everywhere, we speak in code. . . .
> — MELANIE KAYE/KANTROWITZ[7]

"Vistas," Corridos, y Comida: My Native Tongue

In the 1960s, I read my first Chicano novel. It was *City of Night* by John Rechy, a gay Texan, son of a Scottish father and a Mexican mother. For days I walked around in stunned amazement that a Chicano could write and could get published. When I read *I Am Joaquín*[8] I was surprised to see a bilingual book by a Chicano in print. When I saw poetry written in Tex-Mex for the first time, a feeling of pure joy flashed through me. I felt like we really existed as a people. In 1971, when I started teaching High School English to Chicano students, I tried to supplement the required texts with works by Chicanos, only to be reprimanded and forbidden to do so by the principal. He claimed that I was supposed to teach "American" and English literature. At the risk of being fired, I swore my students to secrecy and slipped in Chicano short stories, poems, a play. In graduate school, while working toward a Ph.D., I had to "argue" with one advisor after the other, semester after semester, before I was allowed to make Chicano literature an area of focus.

Even before I read books by Chicanos or Mexicans, it was the Mexican movies I saw at the drive-in — the Thursday night special of $1.00 a carload — that gave me a sense of belonging. *"Vámonos a las vistas,"* my mother would call out and we'd all — grandmother, brothers, sister, and cousins — squeeze into the car. We'd wolf down cheese and bologna white bread sandwiches while watching Pedro Infante in melodramatic tearjerkers like *Nosotros los pobres*, the first "real" Mexican movie (that was not an imitation of European movies). I remember seeing *Cuando los hijos se van* and surmising that all Mexican movies played up the love a mother has for her children and what ungrateful sons and daughters suffer when they are not devoted to their mothers. I remember the singing-type "westerns" of Jorge Negrete and Miquel Aceves Mejía. When watching Mexican movies, I felt a sense of homecoming as well as alienation. People who were to amount to something didn't go to Mexican movies, or *bailes*, or tune their radios to *bolero, rancherita*, and *corrido* music.

The whole time I was growing up, there was *norteño* music sometimes called North Mexican border music, or Tex-Mex music, or Chicano music, or *cantina* (bar) music. I grew up listening to *conjuntos,* three- or four-piece bands made up of folk musicians playing guitar, *bajo sexto*, drums, and button accordion, which Chicanos had borrowed from the German immigrants who had come to Central Texas and Mexico to farm and build breweries. In the Rio Grande Valley, Steve Jordan and Little Joe Hernández were popular, and Flaco Jiménez was the accordion king. The rhythms of Tex-Mex music are those of the polka, also adapted from the Germans, who in turn had borrowed the polka from the Czechs and Bohemians.

I remember the hot, sultry evenings when *corridos* — songs of love and death on the Texas-Mexican borderlands — reverberated out of cheap amplifiers from the local *cantinas* and wafted in through my bedroom window.

Corridos first became widely used along the South Texas/Mexican border during the early conflict between Chicanos and Anglos. The *corridos* are usually about Mexican heroes who do valiant deeds against the Anglo oppressors. Pancho Villa's song, *"La cucaracha,"* is the most famous one. *Corridos* of John F. Kennedy and his death are still very popular in the Valley. Older Chicanos remember Lydia Mendoza, one of the great border *corrido* singers who was called *la Gloria de Tejas*. Her *"El tango negro,"* sung during the Great Depression, made her a singer of the people. The ever-present *corridos* narrated one hundred years of border history, bringing news of events as well as entertaining. These folk musicians and folk songs are our chief cultural mythmakers, and they made our hard lives seem bearable.

I grew up feeling ambivalent about our music. Country-western and rock-and-roll had more status. In the 50s and 60s, for the slightly educated and *agringado* Chicanos, there existed a sense of shame at being caught listening to our music. Yet I couldn't stop my feet from thumping to the music, could not stop humming the words, nor hide from myself the exhilaration I felt when I heard it.

There are more subtle ways that we internalize identification, especially in the forms of images and emotions. For me food and certain smells are tied to my identity, to my homeland. Woodsmoke curling up to an immense blue sky; woodsmoke perfuming my grandmother's clothes, her skin. The stench of cow manure and the yellow patches on the ground; the crack of a .22 rifle and the reek of cordite. Homemade white cheese sizzling in a pan, melting inside a folded *tortilla*. My sister Hilda's hot, spicy *menudo, chile colorado* making it deep red, pieces of *panza* and hominy floating on top. My brother Carito barbequing *fajitas* in the backyard. Even now and 3,000 miles away, I can see my mother spicing the ground beef, pork, and venison with *chile*. My mouth salivates at the thought of the hot steaming *tamales* I would be eating if I were home.

Si le Preguntas a Mi Mamá, "¿Qué Eres?"

"Identity is the essential core of who we are as individuals, the conscious experience of the self inside."

— GERSHEN KAUFMAN[9]

Nosotros los Chicanos straddle the borderlands. On one side of us, we are constantly exposed to the Spanish of the Mexicans, on the other side we hear the Anglos' incessant clamoring so that we forget our language. Among ourselves we don't say *nosotros los americanos, o nosotros los españoles, o nosotros los hispanos*. We say *nosotros los mexicanos* (by *mexicanos* we do not mean citizens of Mexico; we do not mean a national identity, but a racial one). We distinguish between *mexicanos del otro lado* and *mexicanos de este lado*. Deep in our hearts we believe that being Mexican has nothing to do with which country one lives in. Being Mexican is a state of soul — not one of mind, not one of citizenship. Neither eagle nor serpent, but both. And like the ocean, neither animal respects borders.

Dime con quien andas y te diré quien eres.
(Tell me who your friends are and I'll tell you who you are.)
— MEXICAN SAYING

Si le preguntas a mi mamá, "¿Qué eres?" te dirá, "*Soy mexicana*." My brothers and sister say the same. I sometimes will answer "*soy mexicana*" and at others will say "*soy Chicana*" o "*soy tejana*." But I identified as "*Raza*" before I ever identified as "*mexicana*" or "Chicana."

As a culture, we call ourselves Spanish when referring to ourselves as a linguistic group and when copping out. It is then that we forget our predominant Indian genes. We are 70–80 percent Indian.[10] We call ourselves

Hispanic[11] or Spanish-American or Latin American or Latin when linking ourselves to other Spanish-speaking peoples of the Western hemisphere and when copping out. We call ourselves Mexican-American[12] to signify we are neither Mexican nor American, but more the noun "American" than the adjective "Mexican" (and when copping out).

Chicanos and other people of color suffer economically for not acculturating. This voluntary (yet forced) alienation makes for psychological conflict, a kind of dual identity — we don't identify with the Anglo-American cultural values and we don't totally identify with the Mexican cultural values. We are a synergy of two cultures with various degrees of Mexicanness or Angloness. I have so internalized the borderland conflict that sometimes I feel like one cancels out the other and we are zero, nothing, no one. *A veces no soy nada ni nadie. Pero hasta cuando no lo soy, lo soy.*

When not copping out, when we know we are more than nothing, we call ourselves Mexican, referring to race and ancestry; *mestizo* when affirming both our Indian and Spanish (but we hardly ever own our Black ancestry); Chicano when referring to a politically aware people born and/or raised in the U.S.; *Raza* when referring to Chicanos; *tejanos* when we are Chicanos from Texas.

Chicanos did not know we were a people until 1965 when Ceasar Chavez and the farmworkers united and *I Am Joaquín* was published and *la Raza Unida* party was formed in Texas. With that recognition, we became a distinct people. Something momentous happened to the Chicano soul — we became aware of our reality and acquired a name and a language (Chicano Spanish) that reflected that reality. Now that we had a name, some of the fragmented pieces began to fall together — who we were, what we were, how we had evolved. We began to get glimpses of what we might eventually become.

Yet the struggle of identities continues, the struggle of borders is our reality still. One day the inner struggle will cease and a true integration take place. In the meantime, *tenémos que hacer la lucha. ¿Quién está protegiendo los ranchos de mi gente? ¿Quién está tratando de cerrar la fisura entre la india y el blanco en nuestra sangre? El Chicano, si, el Chicano que anda como un ladrón en su propia casa.*

Los Chicanos, how patient we seem, how very patient. There is the quiet of the Indian about us.[13] We know how to survive. When other races have given up their tongue, we've kept ours. We know what it is to live under the hammer blow of the dominant *norteamericano* culture. But more than we count the blows, we count the days the weeks the years the centuries the eons until the white laws and commerce and customs will rot in the deserts they've created, lie bleached. *Humildes* yet proud, *quietos* yet wild, *nosotros los mexicanos-Chicanos* will walk by the crumbling ashes as we go about our business. Stubborn, persevering, impenetrable as stone, yet possessing a malleability that renders us unbreakable, we, the *mestizas* and *mestizos*, will remain.

NOTES

1. Ray Gwyn Smith, *Moorland Is Cold Country*, unpublished book.

2. Irena Klepfisz, *"Di rayze aheym*/The Journey Home," in *The Tribe of Dina: A Jewish Women's Anthology*, Melanie Kaye/Kantrowitz and Irena Klepfisz, eds. (Montpelier, VT: Sinister Wisdom Books, 1986), 49.

3. R. C. Ortega, *Dialectología Del Barrio*, trans. Hortencia S. Alwan (Los Angeles, CA: R. C. Ortega Publisher & Bookseller, 1977), 132.

4. Eduardo Hernandéz-Chávez, Andrew D. Cohen, and Anthony F. Beltramo, *El Lenguaje de los Chicanos: Regional and Social Characteristics of Language Used by Mexican Americans* (Arlington, VA: Center for Applied Linguistics, 1975), 39.

5. Hernandéz-Chávez, xvii.

6. Irena Klepfisz, "Secular Jewish Identity: Yidishkayt in America," in *The Tribe of Dina*, Kaye/Kantrowitz and Klepfisz, eds., 43.

7. Melanie Kaye/Kantrowitz, "Sign," in *We Speak in Code: Poems and Other Writings* (Pittsburgh, PA: Motheroot Publications, Inc., 1980), 85.

8. Rodolfo Gonzales, *I Am Joaquín/Yo Soy Joaquín* (New York, NY: Bantam Books, 1972). It was first published in 1967.

9. Gershen Kaufman, *Shame: The Power of Caring* (Cambridge, MA: Schenkman Books, Inc., 1980), 68.

10. John R. Chávez, *The Lost Land: The Chicago Images of the Southwest* (Albuquerque, NM: University of New Mexico Press, 1984), 88–90.

11. "Hispanic" is derived from *Hispanis* (*España*, a name given to the Iberian Peninsula in ancient times when it was a part of the Roman Empire) and is a term designated by the U.S. government to make it easier to handle us on paper.

12. The Treaty of Guadalupe Hidalgo created the Mexican-American in 1848.

13. Anglos, in order to alleviate their guilt for dispossessing the Chicano, stressed the Spanish part of us and perpetrated the myth of the Spanish Southwest. We have accepted the fiction that we are Hispanic, that is Spanish, in order to accommodate ourselves to the dominant culture and its abhorrence of Indians. Chávez, 88–91.

■ JAMES BALDWIN ─────────────────────────────────

If Black English Isn't a Language, Then Tell Me, What Is?

James Baldwin (1924–1987) was an American writer who explored how race and sexuality shape one's identity. Baldwin's writing was considered controversial because some of his characters were homosexual and were in interracial relationships. His first novel, *Go Tell It on the Mountain* (1953), recounts his childhood in Harlem, where he became a preacher at the age of fourteen. Disenchanted with the racism he witnessed in the United States, Baldwin spent much of his adult life in France and Turkey, returning briefly to participate in the civil rights movement. The essay

"If Black English Isn't a Language, Then Tell Me, What Is?" was originally published in the *New York Times* in 1979 and was later reprinted in a collection of Baldwin's essays called *The Price of the Ticket* (1985).

■ ■ ■

The argument concerning the use, or the status, or the reality, of black English is rooted in American history and has absolutely nothing to do with the question the argument supposes itself to be posing. The argument has nothing to do with language itself but with the role of language. Language, incontestably, reveals the speaker. Language, also, far more dubiously, is meant to define the other — and, in this case, the other is refusing to be defined by a language that has never been able to recognize him.

People evolve a language in order to describe and thus control their circumstances or in order not to be submerged by a situation that they cannot articulate. (And if they cannot articulate it, they are submerged.) A Frenchman living in Paris speaks a subtly and crucially different language from that of the man living in Marseilles; neither sounds very much like a man living in Quebec; and they would all have great difficulty in apprehending what the man from Guadeloupe, or Martinique, is saying, to say nothing of the man from Senegal — although the "common" language of all these areas is French. But each has paid, and is paying, a different price for this "common" language, in which, as it turns out, they are not saying, and cannot be saying, the same things: They each have very different realities to articulate, or control.

What joins all languages, and all men, is the necessity to confront life, in order, not inconceivably, to outwit death: The price for this is the acceptance, and achievement, of one's temporal identity. So that, for example, though it is not taught in the schools (and this has the potential of becoming a political issue) the south of France still clings to its ancient and musical Provençal, which resists being described as a "dialect." And much of the tension in the Basque countries, and in Wales, is due to the Basque and Welsh determination not to allow their languages to be destroyed. This determination also feeds the flames in Ireland for among the many indignities the Irish have been forced to undergo at English hands is the English contempt for their language.

It goes without saying, then, that language is also a political instrument, means, and proof of power. It is the most vivid and crucial key to identity: It reveals the private identity, and connects one with, or divorces one from, the larger, public, or communal identity. There have been, and are, times and places, when to speak a certain language could be dangerous, even fatal. Or, one may speak the same language, but in such a way that one's antecedents are revealed, or (one hopes) hidden. This is true in France, and is absolutely true in England: The range (and reign) of accents on that damp little island make England coherent for the English and totally incomprehensible for everyone else. To open your mouth in England is (if I may use black English) to "put your business in the street." You have confessed your parents, your youth, your school, your salary, your self-esteem, and, alas, your future.

Now, I do not know what white Americans would sound like if there had never been any black people in the United States, but they would not sound the way they sound. *Jazz*, for example, is a very specific sexual term, as in *jazz me, baby*, but white people purified it into the Jazz Age. *Sock it to me*, which means, roughly, the same thing, has been adopted by Nathaniel Hawthorne's descendants with no qualms or hesitations at all, along with *let it all hang out* and *right on! Beat to his socks*, which was once the black's most total and despairing image of poverty, was transformed into a thing called the Beat Generation, which phenomenon was, largely, composed of *uptight*, middle-class white people, imitating poverty, trying to *get down*, to *get with it*, doing their *thing*, doing their despairing best to be *funky*, which we, the blacks, never dreamed of doing — we were funky, baby, like *funk* was going out of style.

Now, no one can eat his cake, and have it, too, and it is late in the day to attempt to penalize black people for having created a language that permits the nation its only glimpse of reality, a language without which the nation would be even more *whipped* than it is.

I say that the present skirmish is rooted in American history, and it is. Black English is the creation of the black diaspora. Blacks came to the United States chained to each other, but from different tribes. Neither could speak the other's language. If two black people, at that bitter hour of the world's history, had been able to speak to each other, the institution of chattel slavery could never have lasted as long as it did. Subsequently, the slave was given, under the eye, and the gun, of his master, Congo Square, and the Bible — or, in other words, and under those conditions, the slave began the formation of the black church, and it is within this unprecedented tabernacle that black English began to be formed. This was not, merely, as in the European example, the adoption of a foreign tongue, but an alchemy that transformed ancient elements into a new language: *A language comes into existence by means of brutal necessity, and the rules of the language are dictated by what the language must convey.*

There was a moment, in time, and in this place, when my brother, or my mother, or my father, or my sister, had to convey to me, for example, the danger in which I was standing from the white man standing just behind me, and to convey this with a speed and in a language, that the white man could not possibly understand, and that, indeed, he cannot understand, until today. He cannot afford to understand it. This understanding would reveal to him too much about himself and smash that mirror before which he has been frozen for so long.

Now, if this passion, this skill, this (to quote Toni Morrison) "sheer intelligence," this incredible music, the mighty achievement of having brought a people utterly unknown to, or despised by "history" — to have brought this people to their present, troubled, troubling, and unassailable and unanswerable place — if this absolutely unprecedented journey does not indicate that black English is a language, I am curious to know what definition of languages is to be trusted.

A people at the center of the western world, and in the midst of so hostile a population, has not endured and transcended by means of what is patronizingly called a "dialect." We, the blacks, are in trouble, certainly, but we are not inarticulate because we are not compelled to defend a morality that we know to be a lie.

The brutal truth is that the bulk of the white people in America never had any interest in educating black people, except as this could serve white purposes. It is not the black child's language that is despised. It is his experience. A child cannot be taught by anyone who despises him, and a child cannot afford to be fooled. A child cannot be taught by anyone whose demand, essentially, is that the child repudiate his experience, and all that gives him sustenance, and enter a limbo in which he will no longer be black, and in which he knows that he can never become white. Black people have lost too many black children that way.

And, after all, finally, in a country with standards so untrustworthy, a country that makes heroes of so many criminal mediocrities, a country unable to face why so many of the nonwhite are in prison, or on the needle, or standing, futureless, in the streets — it may very well be that both the child, and his elder, have concluded that they have nothing whatever to learn from the people of a country that has managed to learn so little.

■ **JOHN BERGER**

Ways of Seeing

John Berger (b. 1926) is a British artist, art critic, and writer whose work has been very influential in visual studies. He is particularly interested in how technology and ideology affect perception. This selection, the first chapter from his book *Ways of Seeing*, accompanied a British Broadcasting Corporation television series in 1972. Three of the seven chapters of the book are visual arguments about images of women in art and advertising. Berger's political leanings are evident in his work and his actions. For example, in *Ways of Seeing*, Berger draws heavily from Walter Benjamin's Marxist essay "The Work of Art in the Age of Mechanical Reproduction." Further, in 1972, Berger donated half of the money he received for winning the prestigious Booker Prize for his novel *G.* to the Black Panther Party, which also supported a Marxist ideology.

■ ■ ■

Seeing comes before words. The child looks and recognizes before it can speak.

But there is also another sense in which seeing comes before words. It is seeing which establishes our place in the surrounding world; we explain that world with words, but words can never undo the fact that we are surrounded by it. The relation between what we see and what we know is never settled. Each evening we *see* the sun set. We *know* that the earth is turning away from it. Yet the knowledge, the explanation, never quite fits the sight. The Surrealist painter Magritte commented on this always-present gap between words and seeing in a painting called *The Key of Dreams*.

The way we see things is affected by what we know or what we believe. In the Middle Ages when men believed in the physical existence of Hell the sight of fire must have meant something different from what it means today. Nevertheless their idea of Hell owed a lot to the sight of fire consuming and the ashes remaining — as well as to their experience of the pain of burns.

When in love, the sight of the beloved has a completeness which no words and no embrace can match: a completeness which only the act of making love can temporarily accommodate.

Yet this seeing which comes before words, and can never be quite covered by them, is not a question of mechanically reacting to stimuli. (It can

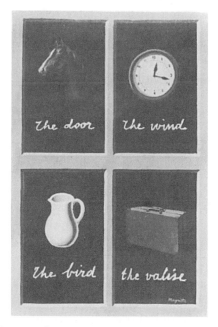

The Key of Dreams by Magritte [1898–1967]

only be thought of in this way if one isolates the small part of the process which concerns the eye's retina.) We only see what we look at. To look is an act of choice. As a result of this act, what we see is brought within our reach — though not necessarily within arm's reach. To touch something is to situate oneself in relation to it. (Close your eyes, move round the room and notice how the faculty of touch is like a static, limited form of sight.) We never look at just one thing; we are always looking at the relation between things and ourselves. Our vision is continually active, continually moving, continually holding things in a circle around itself, constituting what is present to us as we are.

Soon after we can see, we are aware that we can also be seen. The eye of the other combines with our own eye to make it fully credible that we are part of the visible world.

If we accept that we can see that hill over there, we propose that from that hill we can be seen. The reciprocal nature of vision is more fundamental than that of spoken dialogue. And often dialogue is an attempt to verbalize this — an attempt to explain how, either metaphorically or literally, "you see things," and an attempt to discover how "he sees things."

In the sense in which we use the word in this book, all images are manmade [see p. 355]. An image is a sight which has been recreated or reproduced. It is an appearance, or a set of appearances, which has been detached from the place and time in which it first made its appearance and preserved — for a few moments or a few centuries. Every image embodies a way of seeing. Even a photograph. For photographs are not, as is often assumed, a mechanical record. Every time we look at a photograph, we are aware, however slightly, of the photographer selecting that sight from an infinity of other possible sights. This is true even in the most casual family snapshot. The photographer's way of seeing is reflected in his choice of subject. The painter's way of seeing is reconstituted by the marks he makes on the canvas or paper. Yet, although every image embodies a way of seeing, our perception or appreciation of an image depends also upon our own way of seeing. (It may be, for example, that Sheila is one figure among twenty; but for our own reasons she is the one we have eyes for.)

Images were first made to conjure up the appearance of something that was absent. Gradually it became evident that an image could outlast what it represented; it then showed how something or somebody had once looked — and thus by implication how the subject had once been seen by other people. Later still the specific vision of the image-maker was also recognized as part of the record. An image became a record of how X had seen Y. This was the result of an increasing consciousness of individuality, accompanying an increasing awareness of history. It would be rash to try to date this last development precisely. But certainly in Europe such consciousness has existed since the beginning of the Renaissance.

No other kind of relic or text from the past can offer such a direct testimony about the world which surrounded other people at other times. In

this respect images are more precise and richer than literature. To say this is not to deny the expressive or imaginative quality of art, treating it as mere documentary evidence; the more imaginative the work, the more profoundly it allows us to share the artist's experience of the visible.

Yet when an image is presented as a work of art, the way people look at it is affected by a whole series of learnt assumptions about art. Assumptions concerning:

Beauty
Truth
Genius
Civilization
Form
Status
Taste, etc.

Many of these assumptions no longer accord with the world as it is. (The world-as-it-is is more than pure objective fact, it includes consciousness.) Out of true with the present, these assumptions obscure the past. They mystify rather than clarify. The past is never there waiting to be discovered, to be recognized for exactly what it is. History always constitutes the relation between a present and its past. Consequently fear of the present leads to mystification of the past. The past is not for living in; it is a well of conclusions from which we draw in order to act. Cultural mystification of the past entails a double loss. Works of art are made unnecessarily remote. And the past offers us fewer conclusions to complete in action.

When we "see" a landscape, we situate ourselves in it. If we "saw" the art of the past, we would situate ourselves in history. When we are prevented from seeing it, we are being deprived of the history which belongs to us. Who benefits from this deprivation? In the end, the art of the past is being mystified because a privileged minority is striving to invent a history which can retrospectively justify the role of the ruling classes, and such a justification can no longer make sense in modern terms. And so, inevitably, it mystifies.

Let us consider a typical example of such mystification. A two-volume study was recently published on Frans Hals.[1] It is the authoritative work to date on this painter. As a book of specialized art history it is no better and no worse than the average.

The last two great paintings by Frans Hals [p. 357] portray the Governors and the Governesses of an Alms House for old paupers in the Dutch seventeenth-century city of Haarlem. They were officially commissioned portraits. Hals, an old man of over eighty, was destitute. Most of his life he had been in debt. During the winter of 1664, the year he began painting these pictures, he obtained three loads of peat on public charity, otherwise he would have frozen to death. Those who now sat for him were administrators of such public charity.

The author records these facts and then explicitly says that it would be incorrect to read into the paintings any criticism of the sitters. There is no evidence, he says, that Hals painted them in a spirit of bitterness. The author considers them, however, remarkable works of art and explains why. Here he writes of the Regentesses:

> Each woman speaks to us of the human condition with equal importance. Each woman stands out with equal clarity against the *enormous* dark surface, yet they are linked by a firm rhythmical arrangement and the subdued diagonal pattern formed by their heads and hands. Subtle modulations of the *deep*, glowing blacks contribute to the *harmonious fusion* of the whole and form an *unforgettable contrast* with the *powerful* whites and vivid flesh tones where the detached strokes reach *a peak of breadth and strength*. [Berger's italics]

The compositional unity of a painting contributes fundamentally to the power of its image. It is reasonable to consider a painting's composition. But here the composition is written about as though it were in itself the emotional charge of the painting. Terms like *harmonious fusion, unforgettable contrast*, reaching *a peak of breadth and strength* transfer the emotion provoked by the image from the plane of lived experience, to that of disinterested "art appreciation." All conflict disappears. One is left with the unchanging "human condition," and the painting considered as a marvellously made object.

Very little is known about Hals or the Regents who commissioned him. It is not possible to produce circumstantial evidence to establish what their relations were. But there is the evidence of the paintings themselves: the evidence of a group of men and a group of women as seen by another man, the painter. Study this evidence and judge for yourself.

Regents of the Old Men's Alms House by Hals [1580–1666]

Regentesses of the Old Men's Alms House by Hals [1580–1666]

The art historian fears such direct judgement:

> As in so many other pictures by Hals, the penetrating characterizations almost seduce us into believing that we know the personality traits and even the habits of the men and women portrayed.

What is this "seduction" he writes of? It is nothing less than the paintings working upon us. They work upon us because we accept the way Hals saw his sitters. We do not accept this innocently. We accept it in so far as it corresponds to our own observation of people, gestures, faces, institutions. This is possible because we still live in a society of comparable social relations and moral values. And it is precisely this which gives the paintings

their psychological and social urgency. It is this — not the painter's skill as a "seducer" — which convinces us that we *can* know the people portrayed.
    The author continues:

> In the case of some critics the seduction has been a total success. It has, for example, been asserted that the Regent in the tipped slouch hat, which hardly covers any of his long, lank hair, and whose curiously set eyes do not focus, was shown in a drunken state. [below]

This, he suggests, is a libel. He argues that it was a fashion at that time to wear hats on the side of the head. He cites medical opinion to prove that

the Regent's expression could well be the result of a facial paralysis. He insists that the painting would have been unacceptable to the Regents if one of them had been portrayed drunk. One might go on discussing each of these points for pages. (Men in seventeenth-century Holland wore their hats on the side of their heads in order to be thought of as adventurous and pleasure-loving. Heavy drinking was an approved practice. Etcetera.) But such a discussion would take us even farther away from the only confrontation which matters and which the author is determined to evade.

In this confrontation the Regents and Regentesses stare at Hals, a destitute old painter who has lost his reputation and lives off public charity; he examines them through the eyes of a pauper who must nevertheless try to be objective; i.e., must try to surmount the way he sees as a pauper. This is the drama of these paintings. A drama of an "unforgettable contrast."

Mystification has little to do with the vocabulary used. Mystification is the process of explaining away what might otherwise be evident. Hals was the first portraitist to paint the new characters and expressions created by capitalism. He did in pictorial terms what Balzac did two centuries later in literature. Yet the author of the authoritative work on these paintings sums up the artist's achievement by referring to

> Hals's unwavering commitment to his personal vision, which enriches our consciousness of our fellow men and heightens our awe for the ever-increasing power of the mighty impulses that enabled him to give us a close view of life's vital forces.

That is mystification.

In order to avoid mystifying the past (which can equally well suffer pseudo-Marxist mystification) let us now examine the particular relation which now exists, so far as pictorial images are concerned, between the present and the past. If we can see the present clearly enough, we shall ask the right questions of the past.

Today we see the art of the past as nobody saw it before. We actually perceive it in a different way.

This difference can be illustrated in terms of what was thought of as perspective. The convention of perspective, which is unique to European art and which was first established in the early Renaissance, centers everything on the eye of the beholder. It is like a beam from a lighthouse — only

instead of light travelling outwards, appearances travel in. The conventions called those appearances *reality*. Perspective makes the single eye the center of the visible world. Everything converges on to the eye as to the vanishing point of infinity. The visible world is arranged for the spectator as the universe was once thought to be arranged for God.

According to the convention of perspective there is no visual reciprocity. There is no need for God to situate himself in relation to others: he is himself the situation. The inherent contradiction in perspective was that it structured all images of reality to address a single spectator who, unlike God, could only be in one place at a time.

After the invention of the camera this contradiction gradually became apparent.

> I'm an eye. A mechanical eye. I, the machine, show you a world the way only I can see it. I free myself for today and forever from human immobility. I'm in constant movement. I approach and pull away from objects. I creep under them. I move alongside a running horse's mouth. I fall and rise with the falling and rising bodies. This is I, the machine, maneuvring in the chaotic movements, recording one movement after another in the most complex combinations.
>
> Freed from the boundaries of time and space, I coordinate any and all points of the universe, wherever I want them to be. My way leads towards the creation of a fresh perception of the world. Thus I explain in a new way the world unknown to you.[2]

The camera isolated momentary appearances and in so doing destroyed the idea that images were timeless. Or, to put it another way, the camera showed that the notion of time passing was inseparable from the experience of the visual (except in paintings). What you saw depended upon where you were when. What you saw was relative to your position in time and space. It was no longer possible to imagine everything converging on the human eye as on the vanishing point of infinity.

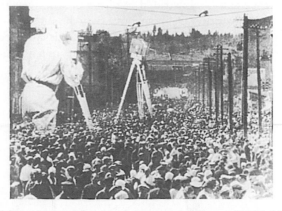

Still from *Man with a Movie Camera* by Vertov [1895–1954]

This is not to say that before the invention of the camera men believed that everyone could see everything. But perspective organized the visual field as though that were indeed the ideal. Every drawing or painting that used perspective proposed to the spectator that he was the unique center of the world. The camera — and more particularly the movie camera — demonstrated that there was no center.

The invention of the camera changed the way men saw. The visible came to mean something different to them. This was immediately reflected in painting.

For the Impressionists the visible no longer presented itself to man in order to be seen. On the contrary, the visible, in continual flux, became fugitive. For the Cubists the visible was no longer what confronted the single eye, but the totality of possible views taken from points all round the object (or person) being depicted [below].

The invention of the camera also changed the way in which men saw paintings painted long before the camera was invented. Originally paintings were an integral part of the building for which they were designed. Sometimes in an early Renaissance church or chapel one has the feeling that the images on the wall are records of the building's interior life, that together they make up the building's memory — so much are they part of the particularity of the building [p. 362].

The uniqueness of every painting was once part of the uniqueness of the place where it resided. Sometimes the painting was transportable. But it could never be seen in two places at the same time. When the camera reproduces a painting, it destroys the uniqueness of its image. As a result its meaning changes. Or, more exactly, its meaning multiplies and fragments into many meanings.

Still Life with Wicker Chair by Picasso [1881–1973]

Church of St. Francis at Assisi

This is vividly illustrated by what happens when a painting is shown on a television screen. The painting enters each viewer's house. There it is surrounded by his wallpaper, his furniture, his mementos. It enters the atmosphere of his family. It becomes their talking point. It lends its meaning to their meaning. At the same time it enters a million other houses and, in each of them, is seen in a different context. Because of the camera, the painting now travels to the spectator rather than the spectator to the painting. In its travels, its meaning is diversified.

One might argue that all reproductions more or less distort, and that therefore the original painting is still in a sense unique. Here [below] is a reproduction of the *Virgin of the Rocks* by Leonardo da Vinci.

Having seen this reproduction, one can go to the National Gallery to look at the original and there discover what the reproduction lacks. Alternatively one can forget about the quality of the reproduction and simply be reminded, when one sees the original, that it is a famous painting of which somewhere one has already seen a reproduction. But in either case the uniqueness of the original now lies in it being *the original of a reproduction*. It is no longer what its image shows that strikes one as unique; its first meaning is no longer to be found in what it says, but in what it is.

This new status of the original work is the perfectly rational consequence of the new means of reproduction. But it is at this point that a process of mystification again enters. The meaning of the original work no longer lies in what it uniquely says but in what it uniquely is. How is its unique existence evaluated and defined in our present culture? It is defined as an object whose value depends upon its rarity. This market is affirmed and gauged by the price it fetches on the market. But because it is nevertheless "a work of art" — and art is thought to be greater than commerce — its market price is said to be a reflection of its spiritual value. Yet the spiritual value of an object, as distinct from a message or an example, can only be explained in terms of magic or religion. And since in

Virgin of the Rocks by Leonardo da Vinci [1452–1519]. *Reproduced by courtesy of the Trustees, The National Gallery, London*

modern society neither of these is a living force, the art object, the "work of art," is enveloped in an atmosphere of entirely bogus religiosity. Works of art are discussed and presented as though they were holy relics: relics which are first and foremost evidence of their own survival. The past in which they originated is studied in order to prove their survival genuine. They are declared art when their line of descent can be certified.

Before the *Virgin of the Rocks* the visitor to the National Gallery would be encouraged by nearly everything he might have heard and read about the painting to feel something like this: "I am in front of it. I can see it. This painting by Leonardo is unlike any other in the world. The National Gallery has the real one. If I look at this painting hard enough, I should somehow be able to feel its authenticity. The *Virgin of the Rocks* by Leonardo da Vinci: it is authentic and therefore it is beautiful."

To dismiss such feelings as naive would be quite wrong. They accord perfectly with the sophisticated culture of art experts for whom the National Gallery catalogue is written. The entry on the *Virgin of the Rocks* is one of the longest entries. It consists of fourteen closely printed pages.

National Gallery

Virgin of the Rocks **by Leonardo da Vinci**
[1452–1519]. *Louvre Museum*

They do not deal with the meaning of the image. They deal with who commissioned the painting, legal squabbles, who owned it, its likely date, the families of its owners. Behind this information lie years of research. The aim of the research is to prove beyond any shadow of doubt that the painting is a genuine Leonardo. The secondary aim is to prove that an almost identical painting in the Louvre is a replica of the National Gallery version.

French art historians try to prove the opposite [see p. 364].

The National Gallery sells more reproductions of Leonardo's cartoon of *The Virgin and Child with St. Anne and St. John the Baptist* [below] than any other picture in their collection. A few years ago it was known only to scholars. It became famous because an American wanted to buy it for two and a half million pounds.

Now it hangs in a room by itself. The room is like a chapel. The drawing is behind bullet-proof perspex. It has acquired a new kind of impressiveness. Not because of what it shows — not because of the meaning of its image. It has become impressive, mysterious, because of its market value.

The bogus religiosity which now surrounds original works of art, and which is ultimately dependent upon their market value, has become the substitute for what paintings lost when the camera made them reproducible. Its function is nostalgic. It is the final empty claim for the continuing values of an oligarchic, undemocratic culture. If the image is no longer unique and exclusive, the art object, the thing, must be made mysteriously so.

The Virgin and Child with St. Anne and St. John the Baptist by Leonardo da Vinci [1452–1519]. *Reproduced by courtesy of the Trustees, The National Gallery, London*

The majority of the population do not visit art museums. The following table shows how closely an interest in art is related to privileged education.

National Proportion of Art Museum Visitors According to Level of Education: Percentage of Each Educational Category Who Visit Art Museums

	GREECE	POLAND	FRANCE	HOLLAND
With no educational qualification	0.02	0.12	0.15	—
Only primary education	0.30	1.50	0.45	0.50
Only secondary education	10.5	10.4	10	20
Further and higher education	11.5	11.7	12.5	17.3

SOURCE: Pierre Bourdieu and Alain Darbel, *L'Amour de l'art*, Editions de Minuit, Paris 1969, Appendix 5, table 4

The majority take it as axiomatic that the museums are full of holy relics which refer to a mystery which excludes them: the mystery of unaccountable wealth. Or, to put this another way, they believe that original masterpieces belong to the preserve (both materially and spiritually) of the rich. Another table indicates what the idea of an art gallery suggests to each social class.

Of the Places Listed Below Which Does a Museum Remind You of Most?

	MANUAL WORKERS	SKILLED AND WHITE COLLAR WORKERS	PROFESSIONAL AND UPPER MANAGERIAL
	%	%	%
Church	66	45	30.5
Library	9	34	28
Lecture hall	—	4	4.5
Department store or entrance hall in public building	—	7	2
Church and library	9	2	4.5
Church and lecture hall	4	2	—
Library and lecture hall	—	—	2
None of these	4	2	19.5
No reply	8	4	9
	100 (n = 53)	100 (n = 98)	100 (n = 99)

SOURCE: as above, Appendix 4, table 8

In the age of pictorial reproduction the meaning of paintings is no longer attached to them; their meaning becomes transmittable: that is to say it becomes information of a sort, and, like all information, it is either put to use or ignored; information carries no special authority within itself. When a painting is put to use, its meaning is either modified or totally changed. One should be quite clear about what this involves. It is not a question of reproduction failing to reproduce certain aspects of an image faithfully; it is a question of reproduction making it possible, even inevitable, that an image will be used for many different purposes and that the reproduced image, unlike an original work, can lend itself to them all. Let us examine some of the ways in which the reproduced image lends itself to such usage.

Venus and Mars by Botticelli [1445–1510]. *Reproduced by courtesy of the Trustees, The National Gallery, London*

Reproduction isolates a detail of a painting from the whole. The detail is transformed. An allegorical figure becomes a portrait of a girl [see bottom, p. 367].

When a painting is reproduced by a film camera it inevitably becomes material for the film-maker's argument.

A film which reproduces images of a painting leads the spectator, through the painting, to the film-maker's own conclusions. The painting lends authority to the film-maker. This is because a film unfolds in time and a painting does not. In a film the way one image follows another, their succession, constructs an argument which becomes irreversible. In a painting all its elements are there to be seen simultaneously. The spectator may need time to examine each element of the painting but whenever he reaches a conclusion, the simultaneity of the whole painting is there to reverse or qualify his conclusion. The painting maintains its own authority [below]. Paintings are often reproduced with words around them [see top, p. 369].

Procession to Calvary by Breughel [1525–1569]

This is a landscape of a cornfield with birds flying out of it. Look at it for a moment [below]. Then turn the page [p. 370].

It is hard to define exactly how the words have changed the image but undoubtedly they have. The image now illustrates the sentence.

In this essay each image reproduced has become part of an argument which has little or nothing to do with the painting's original independent meaning. The words have quoted the paintings to confirm their own verbal authority. . . .

Reproduced paintings, like all information, have to hold their own against all the other information being continually transmitted [see bottom, p. 370].

Wheatfield with Crows by Van Gogh [1853–1890]

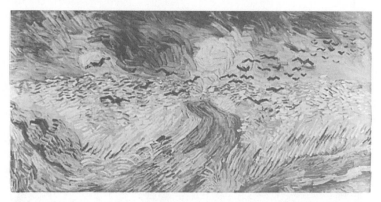

This is the last picture that Van Gogh painted before he killed himself.

Consequently a reproduction, as well as making its own references to the image of its original, becomes itself the reference point for other images. The meaning of an image is changed according to what one sees immediately beside it or what comes immediately after it. Such authority as it retains, is distributed over the whole context in which it appears [see p. 371].

Because works of art are reproducible, they can, theoretically, be used by anybody. Yet mostly — in art books, magazines, films, or within gilt frames in living-rooms — reproductions are still used to bolster the illusion that nothing has changed, that art, with its unique undiminished authority, justifies most other forms of authority, that art makes inequality seem noble and hierarchies seem thrilling. For example, the whole concept of the National Cultural Heritage exploits the authority of art to glorify the present social system and its priorities.

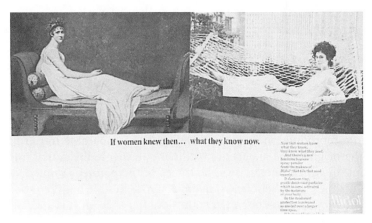

If women knew then... what they know now.

The means of reproduction are used politically and commercially to disguise or deny what their existence makes possible. But sometimes individuals use them differently [p. 372].

Adults and children sometimes have boards in their bedrooms or living-rooms on which they pin pieces of paper: letters, snapshots, reproductions of paintings, newspaper cuttings, original drawings, postcards. On each board all the images belong to the same language and all are more or less equal within it, because they have been chosen in a highly personal way to match and express the experience of the room's inhabitant. Logically, these boards should replace museums.

What are we saying by that? Let us first be sure about what we are not saying.

We are not saying that there is nothing left to experience before original works of art except a sense of awe because they have survived. The way original works of art are usually approached — through museum catalogues, guides, hired cassettes, etc. — is not the only way they might be approached. When the art of the past ceases to be viewed nostalgically, the works will cease to be holy relics — although they will never re-become what they were before the age of reproduction. We are not saying original works of art are now useless.

Original paintings are silent and still in a sense that information never is. Even a reproduction hung on a wall is not comparable in this respect for in the original the silence and stillness permeate the actual material, the paint, in which one follows the traces of the painter's immediate gestures. This has the effect of closing the distance in time between the painting of the picture and one's own act of looking at it. In this special sense all paintings are contemporary. Hence the immediacy of their testimony. Their historical moment is literally there before our eyes. Cézanne made a similar observation from the painter's point of view. "A minute in the world's life passes! To paint it in its reality, and forget everything for that! To become that minute, to be the sensitive plate . . . give the image of what we see, forgetting everything that has appeared before our time. . . ." What we make of that painted moment when it is before our eyes depends upon what we expect of art, and that in turn depends today upon how we have already experienced the meaning of paintings through reproductions.

Nor are we saying that all art can be understood spontaneously. We are not claiming that to cut out a magazine reproduction of an archaic Greek head, because it is reminiscent of some personal experience, and to pin it to a board beside other disparate images, is to come to terms with the full meaning of that head.

The idea of innocence faces two ways. By refusing to enter a conspiracy, one remains innocent of that conspiracy. But to remain innocent may also be to remain ignorant. The issue is not between innocence and knowledge (or between the natural and the cultural) but between a total approach to art which attempts to relate it to every aspect of experience and the esoteric approach of a few specialized experts who are the clerks of the nostalgia of a ruling class in decline. (In decline, not before the proletariat, but before the new power of the corporation and the state.) The

Woman Pouring Milk by Vermeer [1632–1675]

real question is: to whom does the meaning of the art of the past properly belong? to those who can apply it to their own lives, or to a cultural hierarchy of relic specialists?

The visual arts have always existed within a certain preserve; originally this preserve was magical or sacred. But it was also physical: it was the place, the cave, the building, in which, or for which, the work was made. The experience of art, which at first was the experience of ritual, was set apart from the rest of life — precisely in order to be able to exercise power over it. Later the preserve of art became a social one. It entered the culture of the ruling class, whilst physically it was set apart and isolated in their palaces and houses. During all this history the authority of art was inseparable from the particular authority of the preserve.

What the modern means of reproduction have done is to destroy the authority of art and to remove it — or, rather, to remove its images which they reproduce — from any preserve. For the first time ever, images of art have become ephemeral, ubiquitous, insubstantial, available, valueless, free. They surround us in the same way as a language surrounds us. They have entered the mainstream of life over which they no longer, in themselves, have power.

Yet very few people are aware of what has happened because the means of reproduction are used nearly all the time to promote the illusion that nothing has changed except that the masses, thanks to reproductions, can now begin to appreciate art as the cultured minority once did. Under-standably, the masses remain uninterested and sceptical.

If the new language of images were used differently, it would, through its use, confer a new kind of power. Within it we could begin to define our experiences more precisely in areas where words are inadequate. (Seeing comes before words.) Not only personal experience, but also the essential historical experience of our relation to the past: that is to say the experi-ence of seeking to give meaning to our lives, of trying to understand the history of which we can become the active agents.

The art of the past no longer exists as it once did. Its authority is lost. In its place there is a language of images. What matters now is who uses that language for what purpose. This touches upon questions of copyright for reproduction, the ownership of art presses and publishers, the total policy of public art galleries and museums. As usually presented, these are narrow professional matters. One of the aims of this essay has been to show that what is really at stake is much larger. A people or a class which is cut off from its own past is far less free to choose and to act as a people or class than one that has been able to situate itself in history. This is why — and this is the only reason why — the entire art of the past has now be-come a political issue.

Many of the ideas in the preceding essay have been taken from another, written over forty years ago by the German critic and philosopher Walter Benjamin.

His essay was entitled The Work of Art in the Age of Mechanical Repro-duction. *This essay is available in English in a collection called* Illumina-tions *(Cape, London, 1970).*

NOTES

1. Seymour Slive, *Frans Hals* (Phaidon, London).
2. This quotation is from an article written in 1923 by Dziga Vertov, the revolutionary Soviet film director.

Hybrid Academic Discourses: What, Why, How

Patricia Bizzell (b. 1948) is a professor of English at the College of the Holy Cross in Worcester, Massachusetts, where she started the Writing across the Curriculum Program in 1978. She has also served as the president of the Rhetoric Society of America. An influential scholar in the field of composition studies, Bizzell has authored and edited numerous articles and books on writing. Because she views writing as a means of teaching self-awareness and inspiring political motivation, Bizzell considers her work in rhetoric and composition to be in the service of social justice and equality. Her article "Hybrid Academic Discourses: What, Why, How" was originally published in the journal *Composition Studies* in the fall of 1999. She has written and edited several books on hybrid or alternative discourses.

Almost twenty years ago, David Bartholomae and I and other scholars defined a pedagogical position that argued for using first-year composition to initiate students into the academic discourse community. Wherever students are in their language-using practices when they come to college, we said, what they must learn to do is to write within traditional academic discourse. In a 1985 essay, Bartholomae called this learning process "inventing the university," and we usually talked as if it were fundamentally a one-way street. Students, it seemed, had to leave behind their home discourses and conform totally to the academic.

It is important to remember that this pedagogical position was defined against work that labeled struggling academic writers as linguistically and cognitively deficient. For example, in 1983, Thomas J. Farrell published an essay in which he claimed that Black English actually produced cognitive deficiency, causing its speakers to perform poorly on I.Q. tests. As can be seen by reviewing my 1982 essay "Cognition, Convention, and Certainty," those of us taking the opposing view advanced the notion of "academic discourse community" to provide an alternative explanation for some students' struggles. They most definitely were not linguistically or cognitively deficient, we argued, but simply unfamiliar with what Mina Shaughnessy called the "ways of winning arguments in academia" ("Some Needed" 319). Shaughnessy's ground-breaking 1977 book, *Errors and Expectations*, had helped us see these writers not as "remedial" cases, but as what she called "basic writers" who needed instruction in the basics of Standard English and academic discourse conventions. Her work went a long way toward showing us how such instruction might proceed.

This position, advocating the teaching of academic discourse, has in turn been attacked, supplemented, and modified by later scholarship. For example, Min-Zhan Lu's powerful 1987 essay on her own struggles with the different discourses of her schooling in Maoist China, her parents' Western education, and her graduate work in English at the University of Pittsburgh show that our early arguments on the possibility of teaching academic discourse were too sanguine about the conflicts such teaching might generate for students coming from home discourse communities at great remove from the academic. Joseph Harris won the Braddock Award for his 1989 essay critiquing the fundamental idea of "community" that underlay our work, exposing the unfair pressures of conformity it places on students and the ways it disguises internal disagreements. I have been strongly affected by these challenges and, as the introduction to my 1992 book *Academic Discourse and Critical Consciousness* explains, have modified my views on teaching academic discourse. I would no longer want to defend a pedagogical position that sees its inculcation as a one-way street.

From my experience through these years of debate over teaching academic discourse, I would now say that two points hold constant for me. One is that first-year college students are surely linguistically and cognitively competent, not to mention deserving of respect as human beings! The other is that it is my job as an English teacher to help them develop their language-using abilities so that they can succeed in college and in whatever work in the world they choose to do. I can say further that I still believe that there is such a thing as academic discourse, and I can even still say that I think it should be taught to students who are unfamiliar with it. But I now think defining "academic discourse" is a more complex task than I earlier realized, which concomitantly complicates the pedagogical strategies needed to teach it.

More specifically, while I still believe that a sort of traditional academic discourse can be defined, I contend that it no longer holds the field alone. To be sure, it still has many adherents, and students will encounter its hidebound proponents in more than one college class. But in many, many academic disciplines today, traditional academic discourse must share the field with new forms of discourse that are clearly doing serious intellectual work and are received and evaluated as such, even as they violate many of the conventions of traditional academic discourse. If I am going to do my job of preparing students for success in college, then, I cannot ignore these new forms of academic discourse, what I am calling "hybrid" academic discourses, in my teaching.

Moreover, it now seems to me that students are not ignoring these new forms either. Whereas once upon a time, I might have understood a nontraditional academic paper as simply the product of someone who did not know how to do traditional academic discourse, now, increasingly, I believe I am seeing work by students who are deliberately experimenting with new forms. If this is true, of course, I still need to know how to evaluate this new work and how to help students do it better, as well as to prepare them for those situations in which only traditional academic discourse will do. But as I noted above, the advent of hybrid forms of academic discourse complicates the demands placed on my teaching.

What I propose to do here is to explore the nature of these hybrid discourses, and then to offer some suggestions for how to teach them. I will begin by outlining the characteristics of traditional academic discourse, both because I believe it still needs to be taught and because it provides the "baseline" discourse against which the experiments of hybrid forms can be understood. Next I will try to analyze some examples of the new hybrid discourses, to help show what I mean by *hybrid* and to provide suggestions for hybrid rhetorical strategies that may be helpful to share with students. Finally, I will offer some tentative suggestions on teaching intended mainly to stimulate dialogue on these pedagogical issues.

Traditional Academic Discourse

I initially grasped academic discourse as the discourse of a community — hence the phrase, academic discourse community. *Community*, of course, is a word that invokes the presence of people. I believe it resonated for me precisely because the people around me — my students, graduate professors, fellow teaching assistants, among others — and their written and oral interactions first prompted me to study language in use in the academy. I was acutely conscious of how people were affected by the ways they used language, especially how individual students felt when their ways of using language were praised or disapproved. Thus it appeared to me, first and foremost, that what mattered most was who had access to what discourse. This led me to conceptualize "discourse community" as a group of people who share language-using practices. I considered that these practices are conventionalized, that is, there are certain customary ways of doing things. The way one employs these language-using conventions (with familiarity, grace, or tentative bravado, for example) establishes one's place within the community: people of higher status use language (within the shared conventions) differently than do people of lower status. Following these language-using conventions shapes participants' way of looking at the world — their world view — including notions of what's real, normal, natural, good, and true. The people in the group use the shared language to work together on some shared project in the world — something they are trying to do together.

In short: in a discourse community, shared conventions of language use affect social status, world view, and work. These elements are so powerful that the discourse could be said to take on a life of its own, independent of individual participants; it could be said, even, to "create" the participants that suit its conventions by allowing individuals no other options if they wish to be counted as participants. Thus, unlike a neighborhood in which people encounter one another face to face, a discourse community casts its discursive net over boundaries of geographic location, cultural background, socio-economic status, and even time — the dead may participate in discourse communities if their ideas and their texts survive. There are many discourse "communities" — perhaps the term should go into quotation marks to clarify that we are not talking about human neighborhoods but rather fields of communication. Actual humans are usually acquainted with more than one discourse, without being essentially defined by any — which helps give rise to hybrid discursive forms in which the language-using practices of more than one discourse are blended, sometimes not smoothly.

The characteristics of the traditional discourse of the academic community may be summarized as follows. First, it employs a form of language called a "grapholect." A grapholect, as the name suggests, is meant to be written and read, not spoken. It typically uses the most formal and ultra-correct form of its participants' native language, treating as "errors" usages that would be unproblematic in casual conversation, which is why even students who have been fluent writers in less demanding situations in high school may struggle with it. The grapholect is too elaborate to be spoken. Audiences often have trouble listening to it when people give lectures in classes or read papers at conferences that are written in the grapholect.

Also, traditional academic genres shape whole pieces of writing, determining what the parts are and what the structure is. My first-year students often come provided with the five-paragraph essay as a sort of proto-academic genre, a baby version, consisting of an introductory paragraph, supposedly including a thesis statement, three paragraphs presenting three supporting points or examples, and a concluding paragraph, which restates the thesis. This format usually cracks under the strain of more advanced college-level academic work, which is why I've seen papers with five paragraphs, each paragraph a couple of pages long! Academic genres as used by all but the rankest beginners are more complex, and often discipline-specific: students use genres such as the lab report, the reflective journal, the critical essay, the research paper, and so on, and these have their counterparts for practicing scholars in the various academic fields.

Finally, and perhaps most important, the traditional academic discourse community enforces a typical world view, such that the persona speaking through academic writing projects the following characteristics. First, the persona is objective, evidently trying to prevent any emotions or prejudices from influencing the ideas in the writing (hence the traditional ban on the first person, the "I," in academic discourse). Also, the persona is skeptical, responding with doubt and questions to any claim that something is true or good or beautiful (my husband has a quintessentially academic colleague whose license plate reads, "DOUBT"). Not surprisingly, the persona is argumentative, favoring debate, believing that if we are going to find out whether something is true or good or beautiful, the only way we will do that is by arguing for opposing views of it, to see who wins (this method goes back to ancient Greece — some scholars would say to the Sophists; it can be seen in Plato's dialogues; and it is also embodied in our adversarial legal system). In this view, only debate can produce knowledge, which is not immediately available to experience or revealed from transcendent sources. Additionally, the persona is extremely precise, exacting, rigorous — if debate is going to generate knowledge, all participants must use language carefully (hence the ultra-correctness of the grapholect), demonstrate their knowledge of earlier scholarly work, argue logically and fairly, use sound evidence, and so on.

It might also be said that this persona is male, and white, and economically privileged. It might be said that the characteristics I have just outlined are most congenial to those actual humans who are white men of the upper social classes, that is, that these characteristics are most in accord with the personality traits that they are already socialized to develop. Certainly, for example, women are not encouraged to take aggressive postures, attacking the ideas of others and so on. Traditional academic discourse seemed to be quite a white male preserve until very recently, as can be readily verified by reading any scholarship written, say, before 1970, and looking at the range of references, kinds of jokes, cultural allusions made, etc. James Sosnoski has gone so far as to characterize this traditional discourse as a "mindless man-driven theory machine," arguing that its preferred agonistic stance, which in his analysis comes to sacrifice really useful scholarship to merely winning an argument, is linked to traditional male socialization.

Hybrid Academic Discourses

As I said earlier, the traditional academic discourse that I have just described is certainly not dead. It still has many proponents. But it is sharing the field with new forms of discourse, and I believe that this is happening at least in part because the academic population is becoming more diverse. More people who are not white males of the upper social classes are gaining access to post-secondary education and to positions as post-secondary teachers and scholars. With the diverse population, slowly but surely, come diverse discourses from people's various home communities. Previously non-academic discourses are blending with traditional academic discourses to form the new hybrids. These new discourses are still "academic," in that they are doing the intellectual work of the academy — rigorous, reflective scholarship. We find these discourses appearing in articles in top-rank academic journals and in books from prestigious academic presses. But they have combined elements of traditional academic discourse with elements of other ways of using language that are more comfortable for the new academics — after all, in how many communities is it considered appropriate to critically question everything one's interlocutor says, picking apart the other person's statements and even her or his grammar and word choice, while keeping one's own emotions and investments in the topic carefully hidden?

Perhaps these new discourses are gaining ground, too, because they enable new kinds of intellectual work. I want to emphasize that I see these hybrid forms not simply as more comfortable or more congenial but as allowing their practitioners to do intellectual work in ways they could not if confined to traditional academic discourse. That is why these discourse forms are pervading so many academic disciplines today — new discourse forms that are openly subjective, incorporating an author's emotions and prejudices, forms that seek to find common ground among opposing positions rather than setting them against one another head to head, forms that deviate form the traditional grapholect by using language that is more informal, that includes words from other languages, that employs cultural references from the wide variety of world cultures rather than only the canonical Western tradition, and so on. These hybrid discourses enable scholarship to take account of new variables, to explore new methods, and to communicate findings in new venues, including broader reading publics than the academic.

Let me mention a few examples of the kinds of discourse I am talking about, taken from the field of composition studies (but examples could be found in literary studies, history, anthropology, or many other fields): a book on struggling college writers that was much acclaimed in the popular press as well as in scholarly venues, *Lives on the Boundary*, by Mike Rose, an Italian American of working-class background; Helen Fox's book *Listening to the World*, on teaching traditional American academic writing to foreign students in U.S. universities; and two academic-prize-winning accounts of how the authors, coming from home discourse communities at great remove from the academic, succeeded in the academy and came to use composition scholarship to understand their own struggles, namely African American Keith Gilyard's *Voices of the Self* and Puerto Rican American Victor Villanueva, Jr.'s *Bootstraps: From an American Academic of Color*. None of these authors is a white male from the upper social classes — probably not a coincidence. Reflecting the relatively recent advent into the academy of people from more diverse communities. Rose's book was published in 1989 and all the others in the early 1990s (Gilyard's in 1991, Villanueva's in 1993, and Fox's in 1994).

Each of these writers has his or her own distinctive hybrid discourse, yet I believe that their new forms of academic discourse have some traits in common, which I derive from my analysis of Villanueva's *Bootstraps* ("Rhetorics"). Hence what I am going to do here is to try to summarize some of these hybrid discourse traits, using my analysis of Villanueva and some additional guidance from Fox's work.

First, the grapholect issue. Clearly, none of these books is written in the traditional academic grapholect. I do not think, however, that the dialects typically found in hybrid academic discourses can be helpfully conceptualized as forms taken directly from other discourse communities. True, there has been some debate in composition studies about "students' right to their own language," as it was phrased by Richard Lloyd-Jones and colleagues in a 1974 resolution at the Conference on College Composition and Communication. This way of thinking poses a conflict between traditional academic discourse and the home community discourses of students whose home communities are socio-economically and politically marginalized, far from the privileged position of the upper-class white male paradigm. This conflict can be dramatized, for example, as a conflict between Black English and the traditional academic gratholect: some say Black English cannot be used for intellectual work; Geneva Smitherman, for one, shows that it can be by writing scholarly work in Black English. But increasingly, I think we will see hybrid forms such as exemplified in Villanueva's writing. *Bootstraps* is written in neither traditional academic discourse nor what some of my students call "newyorican English," but in a hybrid form that borrows from both and is greater than the sum of its parts, accomplishing intellectual work that could not be done in either of the parent discourses alone.

Along with using a hybrid form of English in his writing, Villanueva also exemplifies another common trait of hybrid discourses, namely his willingness to use a variant range of cultural references. Although he shows himself to be fully conversant with the traditional published scholarship in the field of composition studies, he also does not hesitate to use Puerto Rican American cultural references to make his points. For example, he illustrates his difficulties in adjusting to a move to California when he was a teen-ager by describing his shock upon learning that local school custom requires him to shave off his mustache:

> *Que portorro* doesn't have a mustache? His is respectable, nearly trimmed always, never did wear a *chibo*, the little strip of hair from the bottom lip to the chin; never did let the mustache turn into a *chinchow*, the Charlie-Chan like droop below the lipline. He wore his mustache like his father had, like his uncle Diego, like the respectable men of the block, like Zorro. But this is not TV California; it's his new world, and he'll comply. (37)

Villanueva apparently assumes that most of his readers will recognize the reference to Zorro (whom he has already discussed, ironically, as one of the few Latino images available to him in the popular media when he was a child). But he provides some minimal interpretation here for those of his readers who are unfamiliar with the culture of facial hair in the Puerto Rican American community — probably more guidance than traditional academic writers would be likely to give when alluding, for instance, to Midwestern white Fourth of July picnic customs. I suspect, however (not being initiated into the culture of facial hair myself), that he does not give enough information for the uninformed to fully understand the reference. This does not worry him. Note, too, that he does not bother to translate all the Spanish words he uses. Such cultural mixing or hybridization would be anathema in traditional academic discourse, at least without lengthy footnotes.

Now some larger generic issues. Once again, these are illustrated from *Bootstraps* but can be found in variant forms in other hybrid discourses. For one thing, personal experience, which is absolutely taboo in traditional academic discourse, may be used in hybrid forms to add persuasive force to a point by invoking an emotional response from the reader. In Villanueva this strategy is used, for example, to convince us that change is needed by invoking our sympathy for the writer's suffering under the current educational system, in which he was advised that he was not college material and that he should consider a manual vocation. Personal experience may also be used in a less emotionally charged way, as a source of illustrative examples, as when Villanueva uses vignette portraits of his childhood friends to illustrate John Ogbu's distinction between "immigrant" and "caste-like" minorities. These personal examples present shades of meaning more clearly than an abstract description of traits could do.

Another violation of academic tradition, in this case the agonistic stance in argument, can be found in a strategy I call "offhand refutation." This is not a rigorous frontal assault on an opposed scholarly position but a casual critical remark. This non-confrontational strategy still leaves the reader in no doubt as to Villanueva's position. One example occurs in his discussion of the work of Carl Bereiter and other proponents of deficit theories of African American children's school difficulties. Having described several of these theories, when Villanueva is ready to begin his argument against them, he says, "Round and 'round she goes. Since the question is always 'what's wrong with them,' the answer gets repeated too: bad language equals insufficient cognitive development" (11). He does not say, "What Bereiter ignores is . . ." or any of the other combative lead-ins that we might expect. Thus, perhaps, he wins a better hearing from readers who might be disposed to believe Bereiter. He does not antagonize them even before presenting the points that he hopes will change their minds.

In the paragraph that follows this offhand remark, however, Villanueva, while maintaining a relatively informal and non-aggressive style, nevertheless cites a number of scholarly sources to support his position against the deficit theorists. Thus, as in traditional academic discourse, he pays his respects to existing scholarship by acknowledging its conclusions and alluding to them with proper documentation. He blends traditional and non-traditional discursive approaches.

When the conclusions of established scholarship are believed to be tainted by prejudice, however, such respect may be unwarranted. Then, instead of committing oneself to a lengthy process of refutation, one might employ a strategy I call "appropriative history": a creative retelling of traditional history in which the writer's agenda for needed new research is highlighted, as when Villanueva traces a genealogy from the Greek Sophists to American Latino rhetoric. This is a common strategy in women's studies — no more "The pioneers crossed the plains with their wives and children. . . ." I don't think this strategy is intended to substitute for the work of re-writing scholarly history; but it is meant as an intellectual prod, to alert readers that new research is needed.

Of course, humor is absolutely forbidden in traditional academic discourse save for the very occasional and very dry donnish witticism.

Villanueva, on the other hand, makes frequent use of wry humor, as, for example, when he tells us how he succeeded in graduate school by employing what he calls "Professorial Discourse Analysis." The term itself seems to mock disciplinary jargon. "Professorial Discourse Analysis" is what Villanueva did when he went to the library and read a professor's published work before attempting to write for that professor; he then imitated the professor's style as closely as he could in his own work. Villanueva reports on the success of this practice: along with the As and Bs he got comments such as "I never saw this before" and "too novel" (71).

As with several of the other strategies I've discussed, such as the uses of personal experience, this free use of humor seems designed to court the audience, to woo readers' attention, and to persuade them that the author is a likable person, that is, to enhance the author's ethos. Using humor to get a hearing is a time-honored strategy of people addressing others who have social power over them and who may be negatively disposed toward them; here Villanueva adapts it to an academic form.

I want to emphasize that Villanueva's book is not a personal memoir. It is a scholarly work, published with a prestigious press in the field of composition studies, in which he shows wide familiarity with previous scholarship and in which he makes a serious argument about American education. But it is not written in traditional academic discourse, and, I have attempted to show, it is therefore the more effective.

I can add to this list of generalizable traits of hybrid academic discourses by looking at how Helen Fox describes characteristics that can be found in the writing of students who have been schooled in other academic traditions before coming to the United States. English is a second language for these students, although it may be close to second nature from early childhood study; and it may be a form of English other than American — Indian or African inflected, for example. I will summarize some of the textual features she finds, as follows.

One is a stylistic preference for indirection — deliberately not coming to the point quickly, stating a thesis at the outset clearly, or proceeding to the conclusion linearly. Indirection may be evidenced in an extended metaphor or narrative that might seem "off the point" to a traditional American academic; or in heavy use of abstraction and generalization; or in sentences that seem too long and elaborately entangled for traditional American academic readers. Her students have told Fox that they intend to show respect for the reader's powers of inference by using indirection, as well as to tantalize the reader into reading on. In a May 1998 workshop I attended conducted by Fox, she gave the example of Paulo Freire, whose work has been widely read and respected in composition studies, as a heavy user of this strategy of indirection — a comment I found very helpful in understanding the difficulties I always have with reading his work.

Fox also notes that her students are governed by assumptions of a group-oriented culture, in which people are highly attuned to each other's unexpressed thoughts and feelings and in which collective views are assumed to exist and to be valued. Thus the posture of the traditional academic arguer may seem arrogant. For these students, something like Villanueva's strategy of off-hand refutation would be preferable because it avoids direct confrontation. However, as Fox points out, the traditional academic reader has to be schooled to understand that such a way of presenting points is fully rigorous and representative of neither fuzzy thinking nor a desire to disguise fuzzy thinking.

Another group-oriented attitude, related to this reluctance to attack and completely discredit scholars with whom one disagrees, can be found in foreign students' views on what constitutes "original" work. Fox uses a friend's play on the word "original" to get at these writers' attitudes toward scholarship that has already been done. Whereas the traditional American academic views "original" work as work that corrects or supersedes what has already been done, these writers view "original" as going back to the origins, that is, relying heavily on the most highly respected work that has already been done. These writers might quote lengthy passages from this work, sometimes without attribution since the "original" work, a source of wisdom, is assumed to be community property.

I want to emphasize that the traits Fox finds enter these students' writing from other academic discourses in which they have participated. These traits describe writing that does serious intellectual work — just not in the way favored by traditional American academic discourse.

Let me now quickly review the traits of hybrid academic discourses that have been sketched here.

- Writing in a variant form of English, not the standard grapholect.
- Using a non-traditional range of cultural references, including words and concepts from cultures other than upper-class male European, and sometime not providing exhaustive explanations of these.
- Using personal experience to evoke the reader's emotional response and sympathy.
- Using personal experience as a source of detailed, nuanced illustrations.
- Employing "off-hand refutation," in which an opponent is not attacked head-on, but more casually, indirectly, or gently questioned.
- Employing "appropriative history," or writing oneself into the story.
- Using humor — especially ironic, wry humor, which is hard to see at first.
- Coming at one's main points indirectly, meandering, holding off the main point.
- Assuming that all readers know and share the writer's emotions and cultural assumptions, rather than claiming and valuing an individual and individualistic viewpoint.
- Showing respect for important earlier work by reproducing it, rather than seeking to be "creative" by superseding earlier work.

This is by no means a complete list. It is meant merely to illustrate the possibilities for successfully varying traditional academic discourse. These traits are all drawn from successful, published academic discourse that nevertheless takes hybrid forms.

A teacher can learn more about the diversities of hybrid discourses not only by alertly reading the increasing number of examples to be found in published scholarship in the field, but also by performing a thought experiment: she should give herself the task of writing about something valuable she has learned about teaching writing, discussing at least one piece of published scholarship that helped her learn it (the traditional academic argumentative move), and also bringing in at least one instance of personal experience — instantiation, illustration, whatever — that helped her learn it (the hybrid move). This is a kind of writing that academics have traditionally performed in private reading journals, from which ideas for publishable work may come, but it is an interesting experiment to try to produce such writing with the idea in mind that other scholars might read it.

Teaching Hybrid Academic Discourses

The thought experiment I have just described is also a useful exercise for the teacher who wants to expand her repertoire of academic discourse teaching strategies to include the new hybrid discourses. It exemplifies the kind of teaching I think will work best, namely to give students opportunities to experiment. I do not recommend taking into class a taxonomy of hybrid discourses, such as I have just sketched, and requiring your students to produce texts that conform to it. That can hardly be done even with long-established, traditional, and exhaustively analyzed academic genres. So it certainly can't be done with these sorts of academic discourses that are hybrid, experimental, and in the process of emerging. Rather, it seems to me that what we have to do is to create conditions in which students are encouraged to experiment with their own forms of hybrid discourse.

Course conditions that will encourage experimentation, I believe, must focus on what the students are reading as well as what they are writing. A key feature of hybrid academic discourses is that these discourses attend to reading, to previously published scholarship — as I noted above in reference to Villanueva, these discourses are not memoirs, not purely personal essays. So, the course must have "outside reading," that is, something other than the writing of the students in the course.

This outside reading should focus on a cultural crux of our day, the sort of vexed problem that professional academic scholarship grapples with, such as gender role definition, the limits and possibilities of political protest, the immigrant experience and what it means to be or to become an "American," and more. Whatever crux is chosen should be carefully derived from local conditions, in what the teacher's own students might be interested. Although students might be asked to choose their own area of study, a difficulty in pursuing that route is that gathering, copying, and distributing the reading material would take a lot of time. It might be better for the teacher to do some research before the class begins, analogous to that which Paulo Freire recommends to his literacy educators when they are identifying generative words, to find a good crux to explore and to collect, if not all, at least a substantial amount of reading material before the class begins, to which the students can add.

I suggest that this "outside reading" be a collection of materials from what Mary Louise Pratt would call a "contact zone." Pratt works in comparative literature, and she's interested in texts produced in a time and place where different cultures and possibly also different languages are coming into contact with each other in uneasy ways, where there is something at issue, where some groups have more power than others. A "contact zone" is her name for such a historical moment and the texts it generates (for more on the application of this concept to composition, see my essay "Contact Zones and English Studies"). Bruce Herzberg and I have published a composition textbook called *Negotiating Difference* in which we have compiled several collections of the kinds of materials I am talking about, for "contact zones" such as the antebellum debate over the uses of the Declaration of Independence in arguments about slavery, or the controversy during and after World War II about the American internment of the Nikkei, Japanese Americans. Be it noted that these contact zones, like the ones Pratt discusses, have historical roots and develop over time — such richness is a valuable asset, whatever collection of materials is used.

It is crucially important, in my view, that such a collection of materials not be conceived as a traditional "case study," which usually devolves into "pro" and "con" sides. Contact zones are typically much more complex than that, as Pratt's research and my own suggest, and students are helped to appreciate the necessary complexity and ambiguity of serious argumentative positions if they see a crux addressed in a variety of ways. For example, in the *Negotiating Difference* collection on antebellum debate about "woman's sphere," a range of positions is taken both by the men and women who want to restrict women's activities and by the men and women who want to enlarge them. Some who argue for restriction adduce female inferiority, while others hotly denying this, still urge women to subordinate themselves in the interests of domestic and civil order. Some who argue for enlargement base their case on special spiritual powers presumed to inhere in women, which society is presumed to need, while others insist that restrictions are absurd for women because they are exactly the same in their mental and spiritual powers as men. Race comes into these arguments in complicated ways as well: Louisa McCord argues that all white women, like all African Americans of both sexes, are inferior to white men; Elizabeth Cady Stanton argues that the oppression of white, married women is similar to, and equally reprehensible as, the oppression of black slaves. These are the kinds of complexities that will stimulate students to experiment, as they may well feel that the charged material cannot be adequately addressed in traditional academic forms.

Let me also note that what Pratt and I both mean by "texts" are not only all sorts of written texts (letters, sermons, histories, poems, captivity narratives, etc.) but also any human artifact that can be "read" or interpreted — all sorts of visual representations, from drawings to computer screens, craft objects, music, films, posters, etc. Again, I think it's a good idea that whatever collection of materials is used be generically diverse, to provide students with a lot of examples of discursive strategies to adapt.

What should students do with these readings? That is, what should they be writing about? I suggest that they both analyze and imitate the materials. Reading comprehension questions to be addressed in class journals and/or discussed in class would not be amiss for materials of the level of challenge that I am recommending. While one does not want to talk down to students, it is also damaging to assume they understand when they do not: the object should be to create a classroom environment in which questions can be asked without embarrassment. Imitation exercises, too, are excellent facilitators of analysis, helping students really to see how a text works.

Students should also be writing papers in which they connect the materials with their own experience. They must cite these texts and engage them rigorously; but they must also talk about their own experience in ways that feel right to them. For example, texts on the Japanese internment raise issues of citizenship in poignant ways, which students can relate to their own experiences and notions of what it means to be a citizen, what rights and responsibilities are entailed, whether or not they were born in the U.S. It will not be easy for students to control such hybrid experiments, and their texts will probably need a fair amount of revising; but the students will probably be able to go far beyond the usual stale, rush-to-closure "this is my opinion." In attempting to inter-weave rigorous responses to their reading and their own reflections, it could be said that they are devising a new version of the essay genre for the academic setting. If, at the same time, students are asked to write some more traditional academic papers — which I think would be a good idea — they might also be able to make these papers more essayistic, more charged with their own particular blends of discourses. They might research in greater depth some aspect of the crux or contact zone under study. For example, I have asked students to write papers in which they do research and argue, in traditional academic fashion, for the inclusion of some author or selection of material into the unit we are studying.

Incidentally, since we are talking about developing experimental discourses, for which no sure models can be provided and in which every writer will have to find something of his or her own path, within the constraints of the available discourses that may be hybridized, I think it's a good idea to build in a lot of class attention to process and revising. With materials clustered around a particular crux, too, students will find that similar issues come up for them in consecutive papers, and I like to encourage students to cannibalize earlier papers for parts to use in later papers and generally to think of themselves as intellectuals whose ideas on the issues under discussion are developing. Class discussion and collaborative projects, too, contribute powerfully to this process.

In all this, the goal is to help students develop a range of experimental discourses. I don't think we should encourage them to think that each one has a unique, "authentic-voice" sort of hybrid discourse that he or she must discover. Rather, I am encouraging a sort of craft-person attitude toward writing, in which various tools are developed and students learn to deploy them with greater facility. bell hooks, for one, has written eloquently about the need to allow students to develop this sort of range and above all, not to essentialize their supposedly appropriate discourses based on race, gender, or other variables. She says this about her college creative writing class:

> Whenever I read a poem written in the particular dialect of southern black speech, the teacher and fellow students would praise me for using my "true," authentic voice, and encouraged me to develop this "voice," to write more of these poems. From the onset this troubled me. Such comments seemed to mask racial biases about what my authentic voice would or should be. . . .
> I had come to understand black poets as being capable of speaking in many voices, that the Dunbar of a poem written in dialect was no more or less authentic than the Dunbar writing a sonnet. Yet it was listening to black musicians like Duke Ellington, Louis Armstrong, and later John Coltrane that impressed upon [my] consciousness a sense of versatility — they played all kinds of music, had multiple voices. So it was with poetry. (11)

If it can be so with academic discourses as well, I believe students will be well served. That is why, while not forgetting that students will need to know how to "write a sonnet" — how to employ the conventions of traditional academic discourse — I am encouraging more attention to the development of hybrid discourses.

WORKS CITED

Bartholomae, David. "Inventing the University." In *When a Writer Can't Write: Studies in Writer's Block and Other Composing Process Problems*. Ed. Mike Rose. New York: Guilford, 1985.

Bizzell, Patricia. "Cognition, Convention, and Certainty: What We Need to Know about Writing." *PRE/TEXT* 3 (1982): 213–43.

———. "Contact Zones and English Studies." *College English* 56 (1994): 163–69.

———. Introduction. *Academic Discourse and Critical Consciousness*. By Patricia Bizzell. Pittsburgh: U of Pittsburgh P, 1992.

———. "Rhetorics of Color." Conference on College Composition and Communication Convention. Grand Hyatt, Washington, DC. 24 Mar. 1995.

Bizzell, Patricia, and Bruce Herzberg. *Negotiating Difference*. Boston: Bedford Books of St. Martin's, 1996.

Farrell, Thomas J. "I.Q. and Standard English." *College Composition and Communication* 34 (1983): 470–84.

Fox, Helen. *Listening to the World: Cultural Issues in Academic Writing*. Urbana: NCTE, 1994.

Freire, Paulo. *Pedagogy of the Oppressed*. Trans. Myra Ramos. New York: Seabury, 1970.

Gilyard, Keith. *Voices of the Self: A Study of Language Competence.* Detroit: Wayne State UP, 1991.

Harris, Joseph. "The Idea of Community in the Study of Writing." *College Composition and Communication* 40 (1989): 11–22.

hooks, bell. *Talking Back: Thinking Feminist, Thinking Black.* Boston: South End Press, 1989.

Lloyd-Jones, Richard, et al. "Students' Right to Their Own Language." Spec. issue of *College Composition and Communication* 25 (1974): 1–33.

Lu, Min-Zhan. "From Silence to Words: Writing as Struggle." *College English* 49 (1987): 437–48.

Pratt, Mary Louise. "Arts of the Contact Zone." *Profession 91* (1991): 33–40.

Rose, Mike. *Lives on the Boundary: The Struggle and Achievements of America's Underprepared.* New York: Free Press, 1989.

Shaughnessy, Mina. *Errors and Expectations: A Guide for the Teacher of Basic Writing.* New York: Oxford UP, 1977.

———. "Some Needed Research on Writing." *College Composition and Communication* 28 (1977): 317–320.

Smitherman, Geneva. *Talkin' and Testifyin'.* Boston: Houghton Mifflin, 1977.

Sosnoski, James J. "A Mindless, Man-driven Theory Machine: Intellectuality, Sexuality, and the Institution of Criticism." *Feminism and Institutions: Dialogues on Feminist Theory.* Ed. Linda Kauffman. Oxford: Basil Blackwell, 1989. Rpt. In *Feminisms.* Ed. Robyn R. Warhol and Diane Price Herndl. New Brunswick, NJ: Rutgers UP, 1991.

Villanueva, Victor, Jr. *Bootstraps: From an American Academic of Color.* Urbana: NCTE, 1993.

■ THE BLACK PANTHER PARTY

Ten Point Plan

The Black Panther Party was a civil rights organization started in 1966 in Oakland, California, by Huey P. Newton and Bobby Seale. Driven by the assassination of Malcolm X, the Black Panther Party was committed to overturning racism and social oppression in order to create a global socialist community. The organization's founding principles were called the Ten Point Plan (or Platform). The Black Panther Party was controversial because of its militant ideology and reputation for violence, particularly toward the police. This militaristic stance put the Black Panther Party in sharp contrast to Martin Luther King Jr.'s Southern Christian Leadership Conference. The Black Panther Party eventually disbanded in the early 1970s while Newton was on trial for killing a police officer.

1. **WE WANT FREEDOM. WE WANT POWER TO DETERMINE THE DESTINY OF OUR BLACK AND OPPRESSED COMMUNITIES.** We believe that Black and oppressed people will not be free until we are able to determine our destinies in our own communities ourselves, by fully controlling all the institutions which exist in our communities.

2. **WE WANT FULL EMPLOYMENT FOR OUR PEOPLE.** We believe that the federal government is responsible and obligated to give every person employment or a guaranteed income. We believe that if the American businessmen will not give full employment, then the technology and means of production should be taken from the businessmen and placed in the community so that the people of the community can organize and employ all of its people and give a high standard of living.

3. **WE WANT AN END TO THE ROBBERY BY THE CAPITALISTS OF OUR BLACK AND OPPRESSED COMMUNITIES.** We believe that this racist government has robbed us and now we are demanding the overdue debt of forty acres and two mules. Forty acres and two mules were promised 100 years ago as restitution for slave labor and mass murder of Black people. We will accept the payment in currency which will be distributed to our many communities. The American racist has taken part in the slaughter of our fifty million Black people. Therefore, we feel this is a modest demand that we make.

4. **WE WANT DECENT HOUSING, FIT FOR THE SHELTER OF HUMAN BEINGS.** We believe that if the landlords will not give decent housing to our Black and oppressed communities, then housing and the land should be made into cooperatives so that the people in our communities, with government aid, can build and make decent housing for the people.

5. **WE WANT DECENT EDUCATION FOR OUR PEOPLE THAT EXPOSES THE TRUE NATURE OF THIS DECADENT AMERICAN SOCIETY. WE WANT EDUCATION THAT TEACHES US OUR TRUE HISTORY AND OUR ROLE IN THE PRESENT-DAY SOCIETY.** We believe in an educational system that will give to our people a knowledge of the self. If you do not have knowledge of yourself and your position in the society and in the world, then you will have little chance to know anything else.

6. **WE WANT COMPLETELY FREE HEALTH CARE FOR All BLACK AND OPPRESSED PEOPLE.** We believe that the government must provide, free of charge, for the people, health facilities which will not only treat our illnesses, most of which have come about as a result of our oppression, but which will also develop preventive medical programs to guarantee our future survival. We believe that mass health education and research programs must be developed to give all Black and oppressed people access to advanced scientific and medical information, so we may provide ourselves with proper medical attention and care.

7. **WE WANT AN IMMEDIATE END TO POLICE BRUTALITY AND MURDER OF BLACK PEOPLE, OTHER PEOPLE OF COLOR, ALL OPPRESSED PEOPLE INSIDE THE UNITED STATES.** We believe

that the racist and fascist government of the United States uses its domestic enforcement agencies to carry out its program of oppression against black people, other people of color and poor people inside the United States. We believe it is our right, therefore, to defend ourselves against such armed forces and that all Black and oppressed people should be armed for self defense of our homes and communities against these fascist police forces.

8. **WE WANT AN IMMEDIATE END TO ALL WARS OF AGGRESSION.** We believe that the various conflicts which exist around the world stem directly from the aggressive desire of the United States' ruling circle and government to force its domination upon the oppressed people of the world. We believe that if the United States government or its lackeys do not cease these aggressive wars it is the right of the people to defend themselves by any means necessary against their aggressors.

9. **WE WANT FREEDOM FOR ALL BLACK AND OPPRESSED PEOPLE NOW HELD IN U.S. FEDERAL, STATE, COUNTY, CITY AND MILITARY PRISONS AND JAILS. WE WANT TRIALS BY A JURY OF PEERS FOR All PERSONS CHARGED WITH SO-CALLED CRIMES UNDER THE LAWS OF THIS COUNTRY.** We believe that the many Black and poor oppressed people now held in United States prisons and jails have not received fair and impartial trials under a racist and fascist judicial system and should be free from incarceration. We believe in the ultimate elimination of all wretched, inhuman penal institutions, because the masses of men and women imprisoned inside the United States or by the United States military are the victims of oppressive conditions which are the real cause of their imprisonment. We believe that when persons are brought to trial they must be guaranteed, by the United States, juries of their peers, attorneys of their choice and freedom from imprisonment while awaiting trial.

10. **WE WANT LAND, BREAD, HOUSING, EDUCATION, CLOTHING, JUSTICE, PEACE AND PEOPLE'S COMMUNITY CONTROL OF MODERN TECHNOLOGY.** When, in the course of human events, it becomes necessary for one people to dissolve the political bonds which have connected them with another, and to assume, among the powers of the earth, the separate and equal station to which the laws of nature and nature's God entitle them, a decent respect to the opinions of mankind requires that they should declare the causes which impel them to the separation.

We hold these truths to be self-evident, that all men are created equal; that they are endowed by their Creator with certain unalienable rights; that among these are life, liberty, and the pursuit of happiness. That to secure these rights, governments are instituted among men, deriving their just powers from the consent of the governed; that, whenever any form of government becomes destructive of these ends, it is the right of the people to alter or to abolish it, and to institute a new government, laying its foundation on such principles, and organizing its powers in such form as to them shall seem most likely to effect their safety and happiness. Prudence, indeed, will dictate that governments long established should not be changed for light and transient causes; and, accordingly, all experience hath shown that mankind are most disposed to suffer, while evils are sufferable, than to right themselves by abolishing the forms to which they are accustomed. But, when a long train of abuses and usurpation, pursuing invariably the same object, evinces a design to reduce them under absolute despotism, it is their right, it is their duty, to throw off such government, and to provide new guards for their future security.

■ **BLUE SCHOLARS**

The Ave.

The Blue Scholars are composed of MC Geologic, also known as Prometheus Brown or George Quibuyen, and DJ Sabzi, also known as Alexei Saba Mohajerjasbi. The two met while they were members of a student organization called S.H.O.W. (the Student Hip-Hop Organization of Washington) at the University of Washington and joined together to form the hip hop group the Blue Scholars in 2002. Many of the Blue Scholars' songs revolve around life in and the politics of the Pacific Northwest, Seattle in particular. The song "The Ave." — which is on their first album, a self-titled release from 2004 — was written in a studio apartment in the University District.

I be a patient man, waiting for the rain to come down
My feet touch the ground but my head's in the clouds
I be Prometheus Brown stealing the fire outta heaven
The setting is several city blocks, off the 71 stop
I walk around the district, distracted by
the decadent madness of all the undergrads and addicts
club rats and heads, space cadets and pragmatics
one of a few places they coexist on the planet
whatever happened to the avenue before the summer of 2002
Lounging with crew on 42nd
My how time flies when we're waiting for the chariot
Eating vegan sandwiches with cannibis subtracting our sobriety
Pondering society and self
He's eyeing me like I aint gonna bring it to his health

He don't want it, cause certainly he knows he's just another
Sucka without his fraternity brothas to back him up
Campus Park Way up to 41st 42nd
43rd 45th / and past 47th
to the edge of the bubble, delinquent we laugh
saying "Fuck class - get your education on the Ave."
Campus Park Way up to 41st 42nd
43rd 45th / and past 47th
to the edge of the bubble, delinquent we laugh
saying "Fuck class - get your education on the Ave."
I be a patient man waiting and checking for the sound
of potential break records up at 2nd time around, in fact
we made this track from a sample we jacked
from some vinyl that we dug out of the crates
on the ave, the rats escaped the lab / infestations and all
there be cracks in the sidewalk, made from the fall
a natty dreadlock strumming on his broken guitar
singing Babylon fall outside of the bookstore
where I purchased the journal in which the verses I recite
reside, I write vividly to capture the vibe I'm like
hey kid walk straight, master your high
if you listen you can hear the eye of the city cry
but the sound is often drowned by hollering scholars
intoxicated or jaded like the coffeeshop philosophers
the so-called artists, the poets and the profits
scenery is changing but nobody can stop it
Campus Park Way up to 41st 42nd
43rd 45th / and past 47th
to the edge of the bubble, delinquent we laugh
saying "Fuck class - get your education on the Ave."
Campus Park Way up to 41st 42nd
43rd 45th / and past 47th
to the edge of the bubble, delinquent we laugh
saying "Fuck class - get your education on the Ave."

■ JIM BORGMAN

A New Ghetto

Jim Borgman (b. 1954), born and raised in Cincinnati, Ohio, has been an
editorial cartoonist for the *Cincinnati Enquirer* since 1977. Claiming to be
neither a liberal nor a conservative, Borgman has won many prestigious
awards throughout his career, including the Pulitzer Prize in 1991 and the
National Cartoonists Society's Reuben Award for Outstanding Cartoonist
of the Year in 1993. Borgman is also the cocreator of the popular comic

strip *Zits* and has published many book collections of his work. The cartoon *A New Ghetto* (1997) responds to the controversial decision of the
school board of Oakland, California, in December 1996, recognizing Ebonics as a dialect that should be used to help students learn Standard English.

■   JUSTICE WILLIAM J. BRENNAN JR.

Majority Opinion of the U.S. Supreme Court in *Texas v. Johnson* (1989)

In *Texas v. Johnson* (1989), the U.S. Supreme Court considered whether
the First Amendment granting freedom of speech also protects nonspeech
acts or nonverbal communication, such as flag burning. The case centered
on the actions of Gregory Johnson during the 1984 Republican National
Convention. Johnson, a member of the Revolutionary Communist Youth
Brigade, burned an American flag to protest the Reagan administration
and was consequently sentenced to a year in jail and fined $2,000. In a
five-to-four decision, the Supreme Court found in favor of Johnson,
thereby overturning laws in forty-eight states that considered flag burning
to be illegal. As a result of *Texas v. Johnson*, numerous proposals have been
introduced in Congress to amend the Constitution to prohibit flag burning, most recently in 2006.

After publicly burning an American flag as a means of political protest, Gregory Lee Johnson was convicted of desecrating a flag in violation of Texas law. This case presents the question whether his conviction is consistent with the First Amendment. We hold that it is not.

While the Republican National Convention was taking place in Dallas in 1984, respondent Johnson participated in a political demonstration dubbed the "Republican War Chest Tour." . . .

The demonstration ended in front of Dallas City Hall, where Johnson unfurled the American flag, doused it with kerosene, and set it on fire. While the flag burned, the protestors chanted: "America, the red, white, and blue, we spit on you." After the demonstrators dispersed, a witness to the flag burning collected the flag's remains and buried them in his backyard. No one was physically injured or threatened with injury, though several witnesses testified that they had been seriously offended by the flag burning.

Of the approximately 100 demonstrators, Johnson alone was charged with a crime. The only criminal offense with which he was charged was the desecration of a venerated object in violation of Texas Penal Code Ann. Sec. 42.09 (a)(3) (1989) ["Desecration of a Venerated Object"]. After a trial, he was convicted, sentenced to one year in prison, and fined $2,000. The Court of Appeals for the Fifth District of Texas at Dallas affirmed Johnson's conviction, but the Texas Court of Criminal Appeals reversed, holding that the State could not, consistent with the First Amendment, punish Johnson for burning the flag in these circumstances. . . .

State Asserted Two Interests

To justify Johnson's conviction for engaging in symbolic speech, the State asserted two interests: preserving the flag as a symbol of national unity and preventing breaches of the peace. The Court of Criminal Appeals held that neither interest supported his conviction.

Acknowledging that this Court had not yet decided whether the Government may criminally sanction flag desecration in order to preserve the flag's symbolic value, the Texas court nevertheless concluded that our decision in *West Virginia Board of Education v. Barnette*, 319 U.S. 624 (1943), suggested that furthering this interest by curtailing speech was impermissible.

The First Amendment literally forbids the abridgment only of "speech," but we have long recognized that its protection does not end at the spoken or written word. . . .

Especially pertinent to this case are our decisions recognizing the communicative nature of conduct relating to flags. Attaching a peace sign to the flag, *Spence v. Washington*, 1974; saluting the flag, *Barnette*, and displaying a red flag, *Stromberg v. California* (1931), we have held, all may find shelter under the First Amendment. . . . That we have had little difficulty identifying an expressive element in conduct relating to flags should not be surprising. The very purpose of a national flag is to serve as a symbol of our country; it is, one might say, "the one visible manifestation of two hundred years of nationhood." . . .

Pregnant with expressive content, the flag as readily signifies this Nation as does the combination of letters found in "America."

The Government generally has a freer hand in restricting expressive conduct than it has in restricting the written or spoken word. . . . It may not, however, proscribe particular conduct because it has expressive elements. . . . It is, in short, not simply the verbal or nonverbal nature of the expression, but the governmental interest at stake, that helps to determine whether a restriction on that expression is valid.

The State offers two separate interests to justify this conviction: preventing breaches of the peace and preserving the flag as a symbol of nationhood and national unity. We hold that the first interest is not implicated on this record and that the second is related to the suppression of expression. . . .

We thus conclude that the State's interest in maintaining order is not implicated on these facts. The State need not worry that our holding will disable it from preserving the peace. We do not suggest that the First Amendment forbids a state to prevent "imminent lawless action." And, in fact, Texas already has a statute specifically prohibiting breaches of the peace, Texas Penal Code Ann. Sec. 42.01 (1989), which tends to confirm that Texas need not punish this flag desecration in order to keep the peace.

If there is a bedrock principle underlying the First Amendment, it is that the Government may not prohibit the expression of an idea simply because society finds the idea itself offensive or disagreeable. . . .

We have not recognized an exception to this principle even where our flag has been involved. In *Street v. New York*, 394 U.S. 576 (1969), we held that a state may not criminally punish a person for uttering words critical of the flag. . . .

Nor may the Government, we have held, compel conduct that would evince respect for the flag. . . .

We never before have held that the Government may ensure that a symbol be used to express only one view of that symbol or its referents. . . . To conclude that the Government may permit designated symbols to be used to communicate only a limited set of messages would be to enter territory having no discernible or defensible boundaries.

Which Symbols Warrant Unique Status?

Could the Government, on this theory, prohibit the burning of state flags? Of copies of the Presidential seal? Of the Constitution? In evaluating these choices under the First Amendment, how would we decide which symbols were sufficiently special to warrant this unique status? To do so, we would be forced to consult our own political preferences, and impose them on the citizenry, in the very way that the First Amendment forbids us to do.

There is, moreover, no indication — either in the text of the Constitution or in our cases interpreting it — that a separate juridical category exists for the American flag alone. Indeed, we would not be surprised to learn that the persons who framed our Constitution and wrote the Amendment that we now construe were not known for their reverence for the Union Jack.

The First Amendment does not guarantee that other concepts virtually sacred to our Nation as a whole — such as the principle that discrimination on the basis of race is odious and destructive — will go unquestioned in the marketplace of ideas. We decline, therefore, to create for the flag an exception to the joust of principles protected by the First Amendment.

We are fortified in today's conclusion by our conviction that forbidding criminal punishment for conduct such as Johnson's will not endanger the special role played by our flag or the feelings it inspires. . . .

A Reaffirmation of Principles

We are tempted to say, in fact, that the flag's deservedly cherished place in our community will be strengthened, not weakened, by our holding today. Our decision is a reaffirmation of the principles of freedom and inclusiveness that the flag best reflects, and of the conviction that our toleration of criticism such as Johnson's is a sign and source of our strength.

The way to preserve the flag's special role is not to punish those who feel differently about these matters. It is to persuade them that they are wrong. . . .

We can imagine no more appropriate response to burning a flag than waving one's own, no better way to counter a flag burner's message than by saluting the flag that burns, no surer means of preserving the dignity even of the flag that burned than by — as one witness here did — according its remains a respectful burial. We do not consecrate the flag by punishing its desecration, for in doing so we dilute the freedom that this cherished emblem represents.

■ **CHIEF JUSTICE WILLIAM H. REHNQUIST**

Dissenting Opinion in *Texas v. Johnson* (1989)

In holding this Texas statute unconstitutional, the Court ignores Justice Holmes's familiar aphorism that "a page of history is worth a volume of logic." For more than 200 years, the American flag has occupied a unique position as the symbol of our nation, a uniqueness that justifies a governmental prohibition against flag burning in the way respondent Johnson did here.

At the time of the American Revolution, the flag served to unify the Thirteen Colonies at home while obtaining recognition of national sovereignty abroad. Ralph Waldo Emerson's "Concord Hymn" describes the first skirmishes of the Revolutionary War in these lines:

> By the rude bridge that arched the flood,
> Their flag to April's breeze unfurled,
> Here once the embattled farmers stood,
> And fired the shot heard round the world.

In the First and Second World Wars, thousands of our countrymen died on foreign soil fighting for the American cause. At Iwo Jima in the Second World War, United States Marines fought hand to hand against thousands of Japanese. By the time the marines reached the top of Mount Suribachi, they raised a piece of pipe upright and from one end fluttered a flag. That ascent had cost nearly 6,000 American lives. . . .

The flag symbolizes the nation in peace as well as in war. It signifies our national presence on battleships, airplanes, military installations, and public buildings from the United States Capitol to the thousands of county courthouses and city halls throughout the country. . . .

No other American symbol has been as universally honored as the flag. In 1931, Congress declared "The Star Spangled Banner" to be our national anthem. In 1949 Congress declared June 14th to be Flag Day. In 1987, John Philip Sousa's "The Stars and Stripes Forever" was designated as the national march. Congress has also established "The Pledge of Allegiance to the Flag" and the manner of its deliverance. . . . All of the states now have statutes prohibiting the burning of the flag. . . .

The result of the Texas statute is obviously to deny one in Johnson's frame of mind one of many means of "symbolic speech." Far from being a case of "one picture being worth a thousand words," flag burning is the equivalent of an inarticulate grunt or roar that, it seems fair to say, is most likely to be indulged in not to express any particular idea, but to antagonize others. . . .

The Texas statute deprived Johnson of only one rather inarticulate symbolic form of protest — a form of protest that was profoundly offensive to many — and left him with a full panoply of other symbols and every conceivable form of verbal expression to express his deep disapproval of national policy. . . .

But the Court today will have none of this. The uniquely deep awe and respect for our flag felt by virtually all of us are bundled off under the rubric of "designated symbols," that the First Amendment prohibits the Government from "establishing." But the Government has not "established" this feeling; 200 years of history have done that. The Government is simply recognizing as a fact the profound regard for the American flag created by that history when it enacts statutes prohibiting the disrespectful public burning of the flag.

The Court concludes its opinion with a regrettably patronizing civics lecture, presumably addressed to the Members of both Houses of Congress, the members of the 48 state legislatures that enacted prohibitions against flag burning, and the troops fighting under that flag in Vietnam who objected to its being burned: "The way to preserve the flag's special role is not to punish those who feel differently about these matters. It is to persuade them that they are wrong."

The Court's role as the final expositor of the Constitution is well established, but its role as a platonic guardian admonishing those responsible to public opinion as if they were truant school children has no similar place in our system of government. . . .

Even if flag burning could be considered just another species of symbolic speech under the logical application of the rules that the Court has developed in its interpretation of the First Amendment in other contexts, this case has an intangible dimension that makes those rules inapplicable.

A country's flag is a symbol of more than "nationhood and national unity." It also signifies the ideas that characterize the society that has chosen that emblem, as well as the special history that has animated the growth and power of those ideas. . . .

So it is with the American flag. It is more than a proud symbol of the courage, the determination and the gifts of nature that transformed 13 fledgling colonies into a world power. It is a symbol of freedom, of equal opportunity, of religious tolerance and of good will for other peoples who share our aspirations. . . .

The value of the flag as a symbol cannot be measured. Even so, I have no doubt that the interest in preserving that value for the future is both significant and legitimate. . . . The creation of a Federal right to post bulletin boards and graffiti on the Washington Monument might enlarge the market for free expression, but at a cost I would not pay.

Similarly, in my considered judgment, sanctioning the public desecration of the flag will tarnish its value — both for those who cherish the ideas for which it waves and for those who desire to don the robes of martyrdom by burning it. That tarnish is not justified by the trivial burden on free expression occasioned by requiring that an available, alternative mode of expression — including uttering words critical of the flag — be employed.

The ideas of liberty and equality have been an irresistible force in motivating leaders like Patrick Henry, Susan B. Anthony, and Abraham Lincoln, schoolteachers like Nathan Hale and Booker T. Washington, the Philippine Scouts who fought at Bataan, and the soldiers who scaled the bluff at Omaha Beach. If those ideas are worth fighting for — and our history demonstrates that they are — it cannot be true that the flag that uniquely symbolizes their power is not itself worthy of protection from unnecessary desecration.

Standard English

Chris Britt (b. 1959), a nationally syndicated editorial cartoonist for Illinois's *State Journal-Register*, is a recipient of the National Press Association's Editorial Cartoonist of the Year Award. He has been the staff cartoonist for several major newspapers, including the *Seattle Times*. Known for his unapologetically caustic cartoons, Britt said of his profession in the *Illinois Times* in 2005: "Cartooning is not meant to soothe the psyche. It just stakes out a position, and that's it." His position is usually on the liberal side, although his cartoons are equally critical of Democratic politicians. Like Jim Borgman's editorial cartoon of the same year, Britt's cartoon *Standard English* (1997) expresses his position on Ebonics after the Oakland School Board decision.

■ ■ ■

131 Course Syllabus

Cathryn Cabral (b. 1978) was born on the Big Island of Hawai'i. She received her bachelor's and master's degrees in English from the University of Hawai'i at Mānoa and is currently a doctoral candidate in the English Department at the University of Washington. She has taught several sections of English 131, from which this syllabus was taken, and served as an assistant director for English 109/110. Her research interests in rhetoric and composition include language rights and alternative discourses, particularly Hawai'i Creole English and African American English.

■ ■ ■

English 131: Introductory Composition

Who I Stay: Cathryn Michiko Noelani Cabral   **Can Email:** cathrync@u.washington.edu

Wen You Can See Me: T/TH 10:30a–11:30p   **Wea I Stay:** Padelford A11B

Wen We Going Meet: MTWTH 9:30a–10:20a   **And Wea:** SMI 313

Wat We Going Do Hea:

Welcom to da class, introductory composition. In dis class we going learn and practice da skills needed fo' succeed in college writing, and try figga out wat dat success means. Ova da quatta, we going make niele an' tink about how we going read 'uku hard stuffs by da kine akamai folks, how dey wen construct dese texts — how dey wen say what dey wen say (wen like make big we call 'um da rhetorical conventions or strategies writers use) — an' how we going write fo' dis audience of akamai (an' maybe da fake akamai; no be scared) people.

We going be writing 'uku plenny stuffs. Some going be handwritten an' manini, like reading responses or summaries. Some going be short papahs (1–2 pages). You also going get two long papahs (5–7-pages) dat going be da kine argument you like make. Expect fo' write every day, fo' real kine. We going practice developing argument, applying da stuffs we wen read, using good kine evidence, an' writing fo' all kine peoples an' purposes. Dis going be good stuff. Bumbye you going turn in one portfolio wit all your stuffs in 'um but wit only a small, manini, selection dat going be graded. Das going be sweet!

Now we going get to our explicit (like plain or exact) goals fo' da course (dis going be wat you going have to do, but also wat I going have to get you ready fo' do, so talk back if you no tink we doing dis stuff, kay?):

- we going make da kine complex, analytic (like wea you investigate sumting, da kine analyze, yea?), persuasive argument dat going matter to uddah academics (das right, you one academic too) an' going make some difference in wat we tink, how we tink, li'dat.
- we going read, analyze an' synthesize (jus' mean we going bring 'uku plenny tings/ideas together so dey talk to each uddah, work togeddah or contradict each uddah) da kine complex texts purposefully (not jus' cuz you wen read 'um) fo' make an' support your own writing (da readings gotta do sumting), an' explore all kine method fo' researching one subject.
- we going show dat we aware of da strategies (da "how dey an' we say wat dey an' we say" stuff) writers use fo' different writing situations (wat you like your writing fo' do).
- we going develop da kine flexible strategies fo' revising, editing, an' proofreading our writing (dey all different tings, yea; dats why dey stay listed separately).

So wat we going look at as we do dese tings going be language, power, an' identity. Ho' big stuffs! We going look at da different kine language **we** use, an' **wen** we use 'um; who get fo' decide wat count as one "appropriate" language; an' wat going happen to da people dat no speak or write in da "appropriate" way. We going explore da multiple kine language, vernacular an' dialect we speak, sometime we going even see dem written, an' talk story about da consequences (da good an' bad stuffs) speaking/writing dis kine language in certain places bring.

Wat You Going Need Fo' Class

- *Situating Inquiry: An Introduction to Reading, Researching, and Writing at UW*
- *They Say, I Say*, Graff an' Birkenstein
- One notebook for in-class writing
- One working UW email account dat you going check often

Wat We Going Read

- Gloria Anzaldúa, "How to Tame a Wild Tongue"
- Patricia Bizzell, "Hybrid Academic Discourses: What, Why, How"
- Frank Delima (video)
- bell hooks, "Language: Teaching Worlds/Teaching Words"
- Lisa Kanae, *Sista Tongue* (excerpt)
- Mary Louise Pratt, "Arts of the Contact Zone"
- Lee Tonouchi, "Da State of Pidgin Address"

Making Da Grade

No Make Any Kine (Preparation): 10%

Eh, you gotta come class ready fo' talk an' intahact. I no like come in every-day an' hear myself talk. I know wat I tink. I like you guys run da discussion, ask an' answer da questions, an' make da class be useful fo' wat you like discuss an' learn. Dis mean you wen read da reading, write da writing, brought your books an' your supplies (no be asking everytime if I get one pen), an' have some tauts fo' share. Preparation also mean dat you come to class **on time**. We not going wait for you get hea fo' start tings, an' if you miss sumting, ho' going be hard fo' you get into 'em. So come on time. You come late all da time an' I going tink your preparation not so good, eh?

Make Sure I Know You In Da Class (Participation): 20%

I was shy kine kid in skoo. I know stay hard fo' speak up in class wen you no like make shame. But you gotta try make one effort. Discussion an' da group work stay big part of dis class. We going read hard stuff, but we going try tackle 'um togeddah. You going have to share your ideas, wea you had trouble, wat you tink, an' you going have to listen to wat everyone else tink fo' dis work out. I like you all fo' talk in discussion, but dat don't mean you jus' say any kine. Gotta be on topic. But, good participation also mean you doing da readings, taking notes, asking questions an' trying fo' answer 'um, working in your groups, an' dat your written stuff stay tautful, you wen put some effort in 'um an' neva jus' write 'um on da bus dat morning, kay? Fo' your papah fo' count, gotta be turned in at da start of class wen due. I no take da kine late work 'cuz back me up an' I no can read 'um good. So I no grade or make notes on late stuff.

I also like talk to you individually, so dey going be two mandatory (you gotta show up or going count against you) conferences wit me during da quatta. Only going be 15–20 minutes, so no sweat 'um good. I going tell you wat fo' bring to da conference wen come up.

No worries. Stay easy fo' get good participation in dis class. Jus' make sure I know you part of da class an' making one effort. I know like see you at da end an' wondah who you stay.

Da Big Kahuna (Portfolio): 70%

Dis da big one. Seventy percent (no joke) of your grade going be base on a portfolio you put togeddah at da end of da quatta. Going include all da major writing you wen do dis quatta, but I only going grade wat you tell me fo' grade. How you like dat one?

So hea how going work: you not going throw anyting away, an' you not going lose anyting. (Dis fo' real, now. You lose sumting an' you going have to rewrite da buggah.) Ova da quatta you going complete two assignment series dat end wit one long papah each. To get to dis papah, you going write 'uku plenny short stuff (da kine summary, definition, interview, li'dat). Two weeks before da portfolio due, you going choose 4–6 of dese short papahs, an' one of da two long papahs fo' revise an' den have me grade. I going check dat you wen complete everyting, but I not going grade wat you no like. Ho', you get da chance fo' tell me wat you like graded an' wat you no like graded? Wat kine dat? Nah, nah, dis one good ting. You no like one papah, you no need get one grade on 'um!

You going get plenny time fo' revise your papahs an' make sure dey meet da goals I wen tell you about on da first page. Da last ting you going write fo' me is one lettah dat tell me how da papahs in da portfolio meet dese goals. Rememba dat I suppose to make sure we meeting da goals too. If you no feel like we doing enuff or wat we doing stay kapakahi, lemme know an' we go make da kine adjustments.

Talk Story (but no be emailing me da kine homework)

No be one stranjah, yeah? I get da office hours set aside jus' for' you! I no going be doing anyting but waiting fo' you fo' come in an' talk story. Dis is not jus' fo' if you have one problem or fall behind. Dat's cool too, but you no like wait fo' one sumo-size problem fo' come see me. Any kine question, concern, one epiphany you having, I like hear 'um all. You get one good idea, come talk. You no like wat we doing an' get one suggestion, come talk. It's your kuleana fo' come in, but no be scared. I stay easy-going.

Da best way fo' reach me is email, but I not on all da time, eh? I going try hard fo' answer you in 24 hours, but weekend might take longer. So no leave 'um fo' da last minute. I know we in da tech age, but I going be pakiki head an' say I not going accept homework or papahs ova email. I serious, now. You gotta make da arrangements if you going miss class. If you get one serious ting, like one documented illness or wat, we can try work 'um out. Jus' keep in touch, yeah? You go MIA fo' weeks den going be more hard fo' make da accommodations.

How We Going Act

I going leave dis space open fo' us establish our own rules fo' how we going act in class. We going read an' discuss da kine controversial, passionate, maybe offensive, maybe our response offend someone, stuff, an' we no like make dis one violent class atmosphere. I like everyone be able to say wat dey tink without tinking someone going attack 'um or dey going be called stupid or wat. We need fo' determine wat going make us all feel safe fo' say wat need fo' say. I no like da racist, sexist, homophobic language, but we got fo' determine wat dat mean.

I Like Hear You, Not One Moke You Pretending Fo' Be (Plagiarism)

I one mellow tita, but dea's one ting that make me huhu more dan anyting else. Da kine plagiarism pisses me off. I know wat uddahs tink. I can go read wat uddahs tink. I want fo' hear wat you tink. You go make like someone else's idea yours an' I going make like you no care about dis class, your tauts or your learning.

But dey could be times wea you no know you stay plagiarizing. So plagiarism mean you present someone else's words or tauts fo' your own. Dis include:

- not citing wea you got da idea
- not citing wen you wen paraphrase (neva use da text word-fo'-word, but wen take da idea an' rephrase little bit) da material
- not citing da kine word-for'-word quote (even if it's jus' a phrase dat someone else wen coin)
- using someone else's papah fo' your own
- using a papah you wen write fo' anuddah class fo' my class

It can be hard fo' know if you plagiarizing or not, an' I say if you wondah if you are, jus' cite da buggah, but if you get one question, please come fo' see me. I going help you know if you need cite da info or not.

It's policy fo' any student who plagiarize fo' be reported to da College of Arts an' Sciences fo' one review. Dis is one policy I going be hard-ass about. I no like intentional (da kine wea you know you trying fo' make me da ass) plagiarism. Once you get da review, dea's little I can do fo' step in an' help you. Come talk to me, no plagiarize, an' we going work 'um out.

Going Help You Out

UW get da kine lots of assistance fo' you. You jus' gotta seek 'um out. If you need accommodations fo' anyting (large print texts, li'dat), I can work wit UW Disabled Student Services (da DSS) fo' get you wat you need. No worry about asking, yeah? I going take da suggestions fo' meet da needs you have. You can reach da DSS at dso@u.washington.edu, or if you like call you can at (206) 543–6450/V, (206) 543–6452/TTY.

No Be Shame

More dan DSS, UW also get plenny writing assistance dat you can use fo' free.

Da English Department Writing Center

You gotta make one appointment, but dey devote 50 minutes to helping you wit your writing. Dey **not** one editing/proofreading center. Come in fo' brainstorm an assignment, figga out wat I asking in an assignment, work out ideas fo' one papah, any 'uku plenny oddah tings, but no be taking your papah dea an' asking, "eh, can proofread dis?" Dey stay highly trained an' akamai people. Dey want fo' help, so make use of 'um, eh?

You can all fo' one appointment (685–2876); stop by fo' make one appointment (dey not going take you if you no have one appointment) in (B12 Padelford Hall); or make one appointment online (http://depts.washing .edu/wcenter/)

Da CLUE Writing Center

Like da English Department Writing Center, CLUE is not one editing/ proofreading service. Dey will do everyting the uddah place will, but dey stay open late night. You got full day of classes or work, an' can't make da uddah hours, CLUE get your back. Dey open from 7pm to 12am in 242 Mary Gates Hall, an' day take drop-ins (dat means you no need one appointment an' can jus' show up!).

Get One Beef Wit Me

I stay open to feedback, da critiques about wat we doing li'dat, but if you get one issue you no feel comfortable talking to me about, dese your superheroes. I hope you can talk wit me first, but if you no can, call, email, or stop an' see dese folks on da Expository Writing staff in Padelford A-11:

Anis Bawarshi, Director   543–2190   bawarshi@u.washington.edu

■ CHICAGO WOMEN'S CLUB ─────────────────────────

Pledge for Children

Women's Clubs are volunteer organizations that developed in the late nineteenth and early twentieth centuries with an agenda for promoting issues of social justice, primarily in regard to education. Their membership was generally white and middle class. In the spring of 1917, the American Speech Committee of the Chicago Women's Club surveyed local schools to determine how the English language was being taught to children. In the March 1918 issue of *English Journal*, chairperson Katharine Knowles Robbins explained that the purpose of the research was "to find out what was the attitude of different sections of the Chicago public with regard to the standard of speech in daily life" (163). They determined that "the influence of the school and companions is equal to and perhaps greater than that of the home, for our observation is that the lovely voice and speech of little children are often spoiled in the first few years in school" (165). According to Robbins, the *Pledge for Children* provided a means for "good" speech habits to be practiced at home.

■ ■ ■

I love the United States of America. I love my country's flag. I love my country's language. I promise:

1. That I will not dishonor my country's speech by leaving off the last syllables of words.
2. That I will say a good American "yes" and "no" in place of an Indian grunt "um-hum" and "nup-um" or a foreign "ya" or "yeh" and "nope."
3. That I will do my best to improve American speech by avoiding loud, rough tones, by enunciating clearly, and speaking pleasantly, clearly, and sincerely.
4. That I will learn to articulate correctly as many words as possible during the year.

■ STANLEY E. FISH

How to Recognize a Poem When You See One

Stanley E. Fish (b. 1938) is the Davidson-Kahn Distinguished University Professor of Humanities and Law at Florida International University and Dean Emeritus of the College of Liberal Arts and Sciences at the University of Illinois at Chicago. An expert on the poet John Milton, Fish is also known for his theory of interpretative communities. He discusses this theory in his essay "How to Recognize a Poem When You See One," which is a selection from his book *Is There a Text in This Class?* (1980). Fish, who has also become known for his views on the politics of higher education, often writes as a columnist for the *New York Times*.

■ ■ ■

Last time I sketched out an argument by which meanings are the property neither of fixed and stable texts nor of free and independent readers but of interpretive communities that are responsible both for the shape of a reader's activities and for the texts those activities produce. In this lecture I propose to extend that argument so as to account not only for the meanings a poem might be said to have but for the fact of its being recognized as a poem in the first place. And once again I would like to begin with an anecdote.

In the summer of 1971 I was teaching two courses under the joint auspices of the Linguistic Institute of America and the English Department of the State University of New York at Buffalo. I taught these courses in the morning and in the same room. At 9:30 I would meet a group of students who were interested in the relationship between linguistics and literary criticism. Our nominal subject was stylistics but our concerns were finally theoretical and extended to the presuppositions and assumptions which underlie both linguistic and literary practice. At 11:00 these students were replaced by another group whose concerns were exclusively literary and were in fact confined to English religious poetry of the seventeenth century. These students had been learning how to identify Christian symbols and how to recognize typological patterns and how to move from the observation of these symbols and patterns to the specification of a poetic intention that was usually didactic or homiletic. On the day I am thinking about, the only connection between the two classes was an assignment given to the first which was still on the blackboard at the beginning of the second. It read:

Jacobs-Rosenbaum
Levin
Thorne
Hayes
Ohman (?)

I am sure that many of you will already have recognized the names on this list, but for the sake of the record, allow me to identify them. Roderick Jacobs and Peter Rosenbaum are two linguists who have coauthored a number of textbooks and coedited a number of anthologies. Samuel Levin is a linguist who was one of the first to apply the operations of transformational grammar to literary texts. J. P. Thorne is a linguist at Edinburgh who, like Levin, was attempting to extend the rules of transformational grammar to the notorious irregularities of poetic language. Curtis Hayes is a linguistic who was then using transformational grammar in order to establish an objective basis for his intuitive impression that the language of Gibbon's *Rise and Fall of the Roman Empire* is more complex than the language of Hemingway's novels. And Richard Ohmann is the literary critic who, more than any other, was responsible for introducing the vocabulary of transformational grammar to the literary community. Ohmann's name was spelled as you see it here because I could not remember whether it contained one or two n's. In other words, the question mark in parenthesis signified nothing more than a faulty memory and a desire on my part to appear scrupulous. The fact that the names appeared in a list that was arranged vertically, and that Levin, Thorne, and Hayes formed a column that was more or less centered in relation to the paired names of Jacobs and Rosenbaum, was similarly accidental and was evidence only of a certain compulsiveness if, indeed, it was evidence of anything at all.

In the time between the two classes I made only one change. I drew a frame around the assignment and wrote on the top of that frame "p. 43." When the members of the second class filed in I told them that what they saw on the blackboard was a religious poem of the kind they had been studying and I asked them to interpret it. Immediately they began to perform in a manner that, for reasons which will become clear, was more or less predictable. The first student to speak pointed out that the poem was probably a hieroglyph, although he was not sure whether it was in the shape of a cross or an altar. This question was set aside as the other students, following his lead, began to concentrate on individual words, interrupting each other with suggestions that came so quickly that they seemed spontaneous. The first line of the poem (the very order of events assumed the already constituted status of the object) received the most attention: Jacobs was explicated as a reference to Jacob's ladder, traditionally allegorized as a figure for the Christian ascent to heaven. In this poem, however, or so my students told me, the means of ascent is not a ladder but a tree, a rose tree or rosenbaum. This was seen to be an obvious reference to the Virgin Mary who was often characterized as a rose without thorns, itself an emblem of the immaculate conception. At this point the poem appeared to the students to be operating in the familiar manner of an iconographic riddle. It at once posed the question, "How is it that a man can climb to heaven by means of a rose tree?" and directed the reader to the inevitable answer: by the fruit of that tree, the fruit of Mary's womb, Jesus. Once this interpretation was established it received support from, and conferred significance on, the word "thorne," which could only be an allusion to the crown of thorns, a symbol of the trial suffered by Jesus and of the price he paid to save us all. It was only a short step (really no step at all) from this insight to the recognition of Levin as a double reference, first to the tribe of Levi, of whose priestly function Christ was the fulfillment, and second to the unleavened bread carried by the children of Israel on their exodus from Egypt, the place of sin, and in response to the call of Moses, perhaps the most familiar of the old testament types of Christ. The final word of the poem was given at least three complementary readings: it could be "omen," especially since so much of the poem is concerned with foreshadowing and prophecy; it could be Oh Man, since it is man's story as it intersects with the divine plan that is the poem's subject; and it could, of course, be simply "amen," the proper conclusion to a poem celebrating the love and mercy shown by a God who gave his only begotten son so that we may live.

In addition to specifying significances for the words of the poem and relating those significances to one another, the students began to discern larger structural patterns. It was noted that of the six names in the poem three — Jacobs, Rosenbaum, and Levin — are Hebrew, two — Thorne and Hayes — are Christian, and one — Ohman — is ambiguous, the ambiguity being marked in the poem itself (as the phrase goes) by the question mark in parenthesis. This division was seen as a reflection of the basic distinction between the old dispensation and the new, the law of sin and the law of love. That distinction, however, is blurred and finally dissolved by the typological perspective which invests the old testament events and heroes with new testament meanings. The structure of the poem, my students concluded, is therefore a double one, establishing and undermining its basic pattern (Hebrew vs. Christian) at the same time. In this context there is finally no pressure to resolve the ambiguity of Ohman since the two possible readings — the name is Hebrew, the name is Christian — are both authorized by the reconciling presence in the poem of Jesus Christ. Finally, I must report that one student took to counting letters and found, to no one's surprise, that the most prominent letters in the poem were S, O, N.

Some of you will have noticed that I have not yet said anything about Hayes. This is because of all the words in the poem it proved the most recalcitrant to interpretation, a fact not without consequence, but one which I will set aside for the moment since I am less interested in the details of the exercise than in the ability of my students to perform it. What is the source of that ability? How is it that they were able to do what they did? What is it that they did? These questions are important because they bear directly on a question often asked in literary theory, What are the distinguishing features of literary language? Or, to put the matter more colloquially, How do you recognize a poem when you see one? The commonsense answer, to which many literary critics and linguists are committed, is that the act of recognition is triggered by the observable presence of distinguishing features. That is, you know a poem when you see one because its language displays the characteristics that you know to be proper to poems. This, however, is a model that quite obviously does not fit the present example. My students did not proceed from the noting of distinguishing features to the recognition that they were confronted by a poem; rather, it was the act of recognition that came first — they knew in advance that they were dealing with a poem — and the distinguishing features then followed.

In other words, acts of recognition, rather than being triggered by formal characteristics, are their source. It is not that the presence of poetic qualities compels a certain kind of attention but that the paying of a certain kind of attention results in the emergence of poetic qualities. As soon as my students were aware that it was poetry they were seeing, they began to look with poetry-seeing eyes, that is, with eyes that saw everything in relation to the properties they knew poems to possess. They knew, for example (because they were told by their teachers), that poems are (or are supposed to be) more densely and intricately organized than ordinary communications; and that knowledge translated itself into a willingness — one might even say a determination — to see connections between one word and another and between every word and the poem's central insight. Moreover, the assumption that there *is* a central insight is itself poetry-specific, and presided over its own realization. Having assumed that the collection of words before them was unified by an informing purpose (because unifying purposes are what poems have), my students proceeded to find one and to formulate it. It was in the light of that purpose (now assumed) that significances for the individual words began to suggest themselves, significances which then fleshed out the assumption that had generated them in the first place. Thus the meanings of the words and the interpretation in which those words were seen to be embedded emerged together, as a consequence of the operations my students began to perform once they were told that this was a poem.

It was almost as if they were following a recipe — if it's a poem do this, if it's a poem, see it that way — and indeed definitions of poetry *are* recipes, for by directing readers as to what to look for in a poem, they instruct them in ways of looking that will produce what they expect to see. If your definition of poetry tells you that the language of poetry is complex, you will scrutinize the language of something identified as a poem in such a way as to bring out the complexity you know to be "there." You will, for example, be on the look-out for latent ambiguities; you will attend to the presence of alliterative and consonantal patterns (there will always be some), and you will try to make something of them (you will always succeed); you will search for meanings that subvert, or exist in a tension with the meanings that first present themselves; and if these operations fail to produce the anticipated complexity, you will even propose a significance for the words that are *not* there, because, as everyone knows, everything about a poem, including its omissions, is significant. Nor, as you do these things, will you have any sense of performing in a willful manner, for you will only be doing what you learned to do in the course of becoming a skilled reader of poetry. Skilled reading is usually thought to be a matter of discerning what is there, but if the example of my students can be generalized, it is a matter of knowing how to *produce* what can thereafter be said to be there. Interpretation is not the art of construing but the art of constructing. Interpreters do not decode poems; they make them.

To many, this will be a distressing conclusion, and there are a number of arguments that could be mounted in order to forestall it. One might point out that the circumstances of my students' performance were special. After all, they had been concerned exclusively with religious poetry for some weeks, and therefore would be uniquely vulnerable to the deception I had practiced on them and uniquely equipped to impose religious themes and patterns on words innocent of either. I must report, however, that I have duplicated this experiment any number of times at nine or ten universities in three countries, and the results are always the same, even when the participants know from the beginning that what they are looking at was originally an assignment. Of course this very fact could itself be turned into an objection: doesn't the reproducibility of the exercise prove that there is something about these words that leads everyone to perform in the same way? Isn't it just a happy accident that names like Thorne and Jacobs have counterparts or near counterparts in biblical names and symbols? And wouldn't my students have been unable to do what they did if the assignment I gave to the first class had been made up of different names? The answer to all of these questions is no. Given a firm belief that they were confronted by a religious poem, my students would have been able to turn any list of names into the kind of poem we have before us now, because they would have read the names within the assumption that they were informed with Christian significances. (This is nothing more than a literary analogue to Augustine's rule of faith.) You can test this assertion by replacing Jacobs-Rosenbaum, Levin, Thorne, Hayes, and Ohman with names drawn from the faculty of Kenyon College — Temple, Jordan, Seymour, Daniels, Star, Church. I will not exhaust my time or your patience by performing a full-dress analysis, which would involve, of course, the relation between those who saw the River Jordan and those who saw *more* by seeing the Star of Bethlehem, thus fulfilling the prophecy by which the temple of Jerusalem was replaced by the inner temple or church built up in the heart of every Christian. Suffice it to say that it could easily be done (you can take the poem home and do it yourself) and that the shape of its doing would be constrained not by the names but by the interpretive assumptions that gave them a significance even before they were seen. This would be true even if there were no names on the list, if the paper or blackboard were blank; the blankness would present no problem to the interpreter, who would immediately see in it the void out of which God created the earth, or the abyss into which unregenerate sinners fall, or, in the best of all possible poems, both.

Even so, one might reply, all you've done is demonstrate how an interpretation, if it is prosecuted with sufficient vigor, can impose itself on material which has its own proper shape. Basically, at the ground level, in the first place, when all is said and done, "Jacobs-Rosenbaum Levin Thorne Hayes Ohman(?)" is an assignment; it is only a trick that allows you to transform it into a poem, and when the effects of the trick have worn off, it will return to its natural form and be seen as an assignment once again. This is a powerful argument because it seems at once to give interpretation its due (as an act of the will) and to maintain the independence of that on which interpretation works. It allows us, in short, to preserve our commonsense intuition that interpretation must be interpretation of *something*. Unfortunately, the argument will not hold because the assignment we all see is no less the product of interpretation than the poem into which it was turned. That is, it requires just as much work, and work of the same kind, to see this as an assignment as it does to see it as a poem. If this seems counterintuitive, it is only because the work required to see it as an assignment is work we have already done, in the course of acquiring the huge amount of background knowledge that enables you and me to function in the academic world. In order to know what an assignment is, that is, in order to know what to do with something identified as an assignment, you must first know what a class is (know that it isn't an economic grouping) and know that classes meet at specified times for so many weeks, and that one's performance in a class is largely a matter of performing between classes.

Think for a moment of how you would explain this last to someone who did not already know it. "Well," you might say, "a class is a group situation in which a number of people are instructed by an informed person in a particular subject." (Of course the notion of "subject" will itself require explication.) "An assignment is something you do when you're not in class." "Oh, I see," your interlocutor might respond, "an assignment is something you do to take your mind off what you've been doing in class." "No, an assignment is a part of a class." "But how can that be if you only do it when the class is not meeting?" Now it would be possible, finally, to answer that question, but only by enlarging the horizons of your explanation to include the very concept of a university, what it is one might be doing there, why one might be doing it instead of doing a thousand other things, and so on. For most of us these matters do not require explanation, and indeed, it is hard for us to imagine someone for whom they do, but that is because our tacit knowledge of what it means to move around in academic life was acquired so gradually and so long ago that it doesn't seem like knowledge at all (and therefore something someone else might *not* know) but a part of the world. You might think that when you're on campus (a phrase that itself requires volumes) that you are simply walking around on the two legs God gave you; but your walking is informed by an internalized awareness of institutional goals and practices, of norms of behavior, of lists of do's and don't's, of invisible lines and the dangers of crossing them; and, as a result, you see everything as *already* organized in relation to those same goals and practices. It would never occur to you, for example, to wonder if the people pouring out of that building are fleeing from a fire; you *know* that they are exiting from a class (what could be more obvious?) and you know that because your perception of their action occurs within a knowledge of what people in a university could possibly be doing and the reasons they could have for doing it (going to the next class, going back to the dorm, meeting someone in the student union). It is within the same knowledge that an assignment becomes intelligible so that it appears to you immediately as an obligation, as a set of directions, as something with parts, some of which may be more significant than others. That is, it is a proper question to ask of an assignment whether some of its parts might be omitted or slighted, whereas readers of poetry know that no part of a poem can be slighted (the rule is "everything counts") and they do not rest until every part has been given a significance.

In a way this amounts to no more than saying what everyone already knows: poems and assignments are different, but my point is that the differences are a result of the different interpretive operations we perform and not of something inherent in one or the other. An assignment no more compels its own recognition than does a poem; rather, as in the case of a poem, the shape of an assignment emerges when someone looks at something identified as one with assignment-seeing eyes, that is, with eyes which are capable of seeing the words as already embedded within the instructional structure that makes it possible for assignments to have a sense. The ability to see, and therefore to make, an assignment is no less a learned ability than the ability to see, and therefore to make, a poem. Both are constructed artifacts, the products and not the producers of interpretation, and while the differences between them are real, they are interpretive and do not have their source in some bedrock level of objectivity.

Of course one might want to argue that there is a bedrock level at which these names constitute neither an assignment nor a poem but are merely a list. But that argument too falls because a list is no more a natural object — one that wears its meaning on its face and can be recognized by anyone — than an assignment or a poem. In order to see a list, one must already be equipped with the concepts of seriality, hierarchy, subordination, and so on, and while these are by no mean esoteric concepts and seem available to almost everyone, they are nonetheless learned, and if there were someone who had not learned them, he or she would not be able to see a list. The next recourse is to descend still lower (in the direction of atoms) and to claim objectivity for letters, paper, graphite, black marks on white spaces, and so on; but these entities too have palpability and shape only because of the assumption of some or other system of intelligibility, and they are therefore just as available to a deconstructive dissolution as are poems, assignments, and lists.

The conclusion, therefore, is that all objects are made and not found, and that they are made by the interpretive strategies we set in motion. This does not, however, commit me to subjectivity because the means by which they are made are social and conventional. That is, the "you" who does the interpretative work that puts poems and assignments and lists into the world is a communal you and not an isolated individual. No one of us wakes up in the morning and (in French fashion) reinvents poetry or thinks up a new educational system or decides to reject seriality in favor of some other, wholly original, form of organization. We do not do these things because we could not do them, because the mental operations we can perform are limited by the institutions in which we are *already* embedded. These institutions precede us, and it is only by inhabiting them, or being inhabited by them, that we have access to the public and conventional senses they make. Thus while it is true to say that we create poetry (and assignments and lists), we create it through interpretive strategies that are finally not our own but have their source in a publicly available system of intelligibility. Insofar as the system (in this case a literary system) constrains us, it also fashions us, furnishing us with categories of understanding, with which we in turn fashion us, furnishing us with categories of understanding, with which we in turn fashion the entities to which we can then point. In short, to the list of made or constructed objects we must add ourselves, for we no less than the poems and assignments we see are the products of social and cultural patterns of thought.

To put the matter in this way is to see that the opposition between objectivity and subjectivity is a false one because neither exists in the pure form that would give the opposition its point. This is precisely illustrated by my anecdote in which we do *not* have free-standing readers in a relationship of perceptual adequacy or inadequacy to an equally free-standing text. Rather, we have readers whose consciousness are constituted by a set of conventional notions which when put into operation constitute in turn a conventional, and conventionally seen, object. My students could do what they did, and do it in unison, because as members of a literary community they knew what a poem was (their knowledge was public), and that knowledge led them to look in such a way as to populate the landscape with what they knew to be poems.

Of course poems are not the only objects that are constituted in unison by shared ways of seeing. Every object or event that becomes available within an institutional setting can be so characterized. I am thinking, for example, of something that happened in my classroom just the other day. While I was in the course of vigorously making a point, one of my students, William Newlin by name, was just as vigorously waving his hand. When I asked the other members of the class what it was that Mr. Newlin was doing, they all answered that he was seeking permission to speak. I then asked them how they knew that. The immediate reply was that it was obvious; what else could he be thought to be doing? The meaning of his gesture, in other words, was right there on its surface, available for reading by anyone who had the eyes to see. That meaning, however, would not have been available to someone without any knowledge of what was involved in being a student. Such a person might have thought that Mr. Newlin was pointing to the fluorescent lights hanging from the ceiling, or calling our attention to some object that was about to fall ("the sky is falling," "the sky is falling"). And if the someone in question were a child of elementary or middle-school age, Mr. Newlin might well have been seen as seeking permission not to speak but to go to the bathroom, an interpretation or reading that would never occur to a student at Johns Hopkins or any other institution of "higher learning" (and how would we explain to the uninitiated the meaning of *that* phrase).

The point is the one I have made so many times before: it is neither the case that the significance of Mr. Newlin's gesture is imprinted on its surface where it need only be read off, or that the construction put on the gesture by everyone in the room was individual and idiosyncratic. Rather, the source of our interpretive unanimity was a structure of interests and understood goals, a structure whose categories so filled our individual consciousnesses that they were rendered as one, immediately investing phenomena with the significance they *must* have, given the already-in-place assumptions about what someone could possibly be intending (by word or gesture) in a classroom. By seeing Mr. Newlin's raised hand with a single shaping eye, we were demonstrating what Harvey Sacks has characterized as "the fine power of a culture. It does not, so to speak, merely fill brains in roughly the same way, it fills them so that they are alike in fine detail."[1] The occasion of Sacks's observation was the ability of his hearers to understand a sequence of two sentences — "The baby cried. The mommy picked it up." — exactly as he did (assuming, for example that "the 'mommy' who picks up the 'baby' is the mommy of that baby"), despite the fact that alternative ways of understanding were demonstrably possible. That is, the mommy of the second sentence could well have been the mommy of some other baby, and it need not even have been a baby that this "floating" mommy was picking up. One is tempted to say that in the absence of a specific context we are authorized to take the words literally, which is what Sacks's hearers do; but as Sacks observes, it is within the assumption of a context — one so deeply assumed that we are unaware of it — that the words acquire what seems to be their literal meaning. There is nothing *in the words* that tells Sacks and his hearers how to relate the mommy and the baby of this story, just as there is nothing *in the form* of Mr. Newlin's gesture that tells his fellow students how to determine its significance. In both cases the determination (of relation and significance) is the work of categories of organization — the family, being a student — that are from the very first giving shape and value to what is heard and seen.

Indeed, these categories are the very shape of seeing itself, in that we are not to imagine a perceptual ground more basic than the one they afford. That is, we are not to imagine a moment when my students "simply see" a physical configuration of atoms and *then* assign that configuration a significance, according to the situation they happen to be in. To be in the situation (this or any other) is to "see" with the eyes of its interests, its goals, its understood practices, values, and norms, and so to be conferring significance *by* seeing, not after it. The categories of my students' vision are the categories by which they understand themselves to be functioning as students (what Sacks might term "doing studenting"), and objects will appear to them in forms related to that way of functioning rather than in some objective or preinterpretive form. (This is true even when an object is seen as not related, since nonrelation is not a pure but a differential category — the specification of something by enumerating what it is not; in short, nonrelation is merely one form of relation, and its perception is always situation-specific.)

Of course, if someone who was not functioning as a student was to walk into my classroom, he might very well see Mr. Newlin's raised hand (and "raised hand" is already an interpretation-laden description) in some other way, as evidence of a disease, as the salute of a political follower, as a muscle-improving exercise, as an attempt to kill flies; but he would always see it in *some* way, and never as purely physical data waiting for his interpretation. And, moreover, the way of seeing, whatever it was, would never be individual or idiosyncratic, since its source would always be the institutional structure of which the "see-er" was an extending agent. This is what Sacks means when he says that a culture fills brains "so that they are alike in fine detail"; it fills them so that no one's interpretive acts are exclusively his own but fall to him by virtue of his position in some socially organized environment and are therefore always shared and public. It follows, then, that the fear of solipsism, of the imposition by the unconstrained self of its own prejudices, is unfounded because the self does not exist apart from the communal or conventional categories of thought that enable its operations (of thinking, seeing, reading). Once one realizes that the conceptions that fill consciousness, including any conception of its own status, are culturally derived, the very notion of an unconstrained self, of a consciousness wholly and dangerously free, becomes incomprehensible.

But without the notion of the unconstrained self, the arguments of Hirsch, Abrams, and the other proponents of objective interpretation are deprived of their urgency. They are afraid that in the absence of the controls afforded by a normative system of meanings, the self will simply substitute its own meanings for the meanings (usually identified with the intentions of the author) that texts bring with them, the meanings that texts *"have"*; however, if the self is conceived of not as an independent entity but as a social construct whose operations are delimited by the systems of intelligibility that inform it, then the meanings it confers on texts are not its own but have their source in the interpretive community (or communities) of which it is a function. Moreover, these meanings will be neither subjective nor objective, at least in the terms assumed by those who argue within the traditional framework: they will not be objective because they will always have been the product of a point of view rather than having been simply "read off"; and they will not be subjective because that point of view will always be social or institutional. Or by the same reasoning one could say that they are *both* subjective and objective: they are subjective because they inhere in a particular point of view and are therefore not universal; and they are objective because the point of view that delivers them is public and conventional rather than individual or unique.

To put the matter in either way is to see how unhelpful the terms "subjective" and "objective" finally are. Rather than facilitating inquiry, they close it down, by deciding in advance what shape inquiry can possibly take. Specifically, they assume, without being aware that it is an assumption and therefore open to challenge, the very distinction I have been putting into question, the distinction between interpreters and the objects they interpret. That distinction in turn assumes that interpreters and their objects are two different kinds of *a*contextual entities, and within these twin assumptions the issue can only be one of control: will texts be allowed to constrain their own interpretation or will irresponsible interpreters be allowed to obscure and overwhelm texts. In the spectacle that ensues, the spectacle of Anglo-American critical controversy, texts and selves fight it out in the persons of their respective champions, Abrams, Hirsch, Reichert, Graff on the one hand, Holland, Bleich, Slatoff, and (in some characterizations of him) Barthes on the other. But if selves are constituted by the ways of thinking and seeing that inhere in social organizations, and if these constituted selves in turn constitute texts according to these same ways, then there can be no adversary relationship between text and self because they are the necessarily related products of the same cognitive possibilities. A text cannot be overwhelmed by an irresponsible reader and one need not worry about protecting the purity of a text from a reader's idiosyncracies. It is only the distinction between subject and object that gives rise to these urgencies, and once the distinction is blurred they simply fall away. One can respond with a cheerful yes to the question "Do readers make meanings?" and commit oneself to very little because it would be equally true to say that meanings, in the form of culturally derived interpretive categories, make readers.

Indeed, many things look rather different once the subject–object dichotomy is eliminated as the assumed framework within which critical discussion occurs. Problems disappear, not because they have been solved but because they are shown never to have been problems in the first place. Abrams, for example, wonders how, in the absence of a normative system of stable meanings, two people could ever agree on the interpretation of a work or even of a sentence; but the difficulty is only a difficulty if the two (or more) people are thought of as isolated individuals whose agreement must be compelled by something external to them. (There is something of the police state in Abrams's vision, complete with posted rules and boundaries, watchdogs to enforce them, procedures for identifying their violators as criminals.) But if the understandings of the people in question are informed by the same notions of what counts as a fact, of what is central, peripheral, and worthy of being noticed — in short, by the same interpretive principles — then agreement between them will be assured, and its source will not be a text that enforces its own perception but a way of perceiving that results in the emergence to those who share it (or those whom it shares) of the same text. That text might be a poem, as it was in the case of those who first "saw" "Jacobs-Rosenbaum Levin Hayes Thorne Ohman(?)," or a hand, as it is every day in a thousand classrooms; but whatever it is, the shape and meaning it appears immediately to have will be the "ongoing accomplishment"[2] of those who agree to produce it.

NOTES

1. "On the Analysability of Stories by Children," in *Ethnomethodology*, ed. Roy Turner (Baltimore: Penguin, 1974), p. 218.

2. A phrase used by the ethnomethodologists to characterize the interpretive activities that create and maintain the features of everyday life. See, for example, Don H. Zimmerman, "Fact as a Practical Accomplishment," in *Ethnomethodology*, pp. 128–143.

Panopticism

Michel Foucault (1926–1984), a French philosopher and theorist, was a chair at the Collège de France and also a professor at the University of California, Berkeley. Foucault is considered one of the most important scholars of the twentieth century because of the influence his work has had in shaping lines of inquiry in academic disciplines throughout the university. Foucault is best known for his critique of social institutions, such as the prison system and psychiatry, and his analysis of the relationship among language, knowledge, and power. "Panopticism" is a selection from his book *Discipline and Punish: The Birth of the Prison* (1977), which explores how power in contemporary society is exerted through disciplinarity and surveillance.

■ ■ ■

The following, according to an order published at the end of the seventeenth century, were the measures to be taken when the plague appeared in a town.[1]

First, a strict spatial partitioning: the closing of the town and its outlying districts, a prohibition to leave the town on pain of death, the killing of all stray animals; the division of the town into distinct quarters, each governed by an intendant. Each street is placed under the authority of a syndic, who keeps it under surveillance; if he leaves the street, he will be condemned to death. On the appointed day, everyone is ordered to stay indoors: it is forbidden to leave on pain of death. The syndic himself comes to lock the door of each house from the outside; he takes the key with him and hands it over to the intendant of the quarter; the intendant keeps it until the end of the quarantine. Each family will have made its own provisions; but, for bread and wine, small wooden canals are set up between the street and the interior of the houses, thus allowing each person to receive his ration without communicating with the suppliers and other residents; meat, fish, and herbs will be hoisted up into the houses with pulleys and baskets. If it is absolutely necessary to leave the house, it will be done in turn, avoiding any meeting. Only the intendants, syndics, and guards will move about the streets and also, between the infected houses, from one corpse to another, the "crows," who can be left to die: these are "people of little substance who carry the sick, bury the dead, clean, and do many vile and abject offices." It is a segmented, immobile, frozen space. Each individual is fixed in his place. And, if he moves, he does so at the risk of his life, contagion, or punishment.

Inspection functions ceaselessly. The gaze is alert everywhere: "A considerable body of militia, commanded by good officers and men of substance," guards at the gates, at the town hall, and in every quarter to ensure the prompt obedience of the people and the most absolute authority of the magistrates, "as also to observe all disorder, theft and extortion." At each of the town gates there will be an observation post; at the end of each street sentinels. Every day, the intendant visits the quarter in his charge, inquires whether the syndics have carried out their tasks, whether the inhabitants have anything to complain of; they "observe their actions." Every day, too, the syndic goes into the street for which he is responsible; stops before each house: gets all the inhabitants to appear at the windows (those who live overlooking the courtyard will be allocated a window looking onto the street at which no one but they may show themselves); he calls each of them by name; informs himself as to the state of each and every one of them — "in which respect the inhabitants will be compelled to speak the truth under pain of death"; if someone does not appear at the window, the syndic must ask why: "In this way he will find out easily enough whether dead or sick are being concealed." Everyone locked up in his cage, everyone at his window, answering to his name and showing himself when asked — it is the great review of the living and the dead.

This surveillance is based on a system of permanent registration: reports from the syndics to the intendants, from the intendants to the magistrates or mayor. At the beginning of the "lock up," the role of each of the inhabitants present in the town is laid down, one by one; this document bears "the name, age, sex of everyone, notwithstanding his condition": a copy is sent to the intendant of the quarter, another to the office of the town hall, another to enable the syndic to make his daily roll call. Everything that may be observed during the course of the visits — deaths, illnesses, complaints, irregularities — is noted down and transmitted to the intendants and magistrates. The magistrates have complete control over medical treatment; they have appointed a physician in charge; no other practitioner may treat, no apothecary prepare medicine, no confessor visit a sick person without having received from him a written note "to prevent anyone from concealing and dealing with those sick of the contagion, unknown to the magistrates." The registration of the pathological must be constantly centralized. The relation of each individual to his disease and to his death passes through the representatives of power, the registration they make of it, the decisions they take on it.

Five or six days after the beginning of the quarantine, the process of purifying the houses one by one is begun. All the inhabitants are made to leave; in each room "the furniture and goods" are raised from the ground or suspended from the air; perfume is poured around the room; after carefully sealing the windows, doors, and even the keyholes with wax, the perfume is set alight. Finally, the entire house is closed while the perfume is consumed; those who have carried out the work are searched, as they were on entry, "in the presence of the residents of the house, to see that they did not have something on their persons as they left that they did not have on entering." Four hours later, the residents are allowed to reenter their homes.

This enclosed, segmented space, observed at every point, in which the individuals are inserted in a fixed place, in which the slightest movements are supervised, in which all events are recorded, in which an uninterrupted work of writing links the center and periphery, in which power is exercised without division, according to a continuous hierarchical figure, in which each individual is constantly located, examined, and distributed among the living beings, the sick, and the dead — all this constitutes a compact model of the disciplinary mechanism. The plague is met by order; its function is to sort out every possible confusion: that of the disease, which is transmitted when bodies are mixed together; that of the evil, which is increased when fear and death overcome prohibitions. It lays down for each individual his place, his body, his disease, and his death, his well-being, by means of an omnipresent and omniscient power that subdivides itself in a regular, uninterrupted way even to the ultimate determination of the individual, of what characterizes him, of what belongs to him, of what happens to him. Against the plague, which is a mixture, discipline brings into play its power, which is one of analysis. A whole literary fiction of the festival grew up around the plague: suspended laws, lifted prohibitions, the frenzy of passing time, bodies mingling together without respect, individuals unmasked, abandoning their statutory identity and the figure under which they had been recognized, allowing a quite different truth to appear. But there was also a political dream of the plague, which was exactly its reverse: not the collective festival, but strict divisions; not laws transgressed, but the penetration of regulation into even the smallest details of everyday life through the mediation of the complete hierarchy that assured the capillary functioning of power; not masks that were put on and taken off, but the assignment to each individual of his "true" name, his "true" place, his "true" body, his "true" disease. The plague as a form, at once real and imaginary, of disorder had as its medical and political correlative discipline. Behind the disciplinary mechanisms can be read the haunting memory of "contagions," of the plague, of rebellions, crimes, vagabondage, desertions, people who appear and disappear, live and die in disorder.

If it is true that the leper gave rise to rituals of exclusion, which to a certain extent provided the model for and general form of the great Confinement, then the plague gave rise to disciplinary projects. Rather than the massive, binary division between one set of people and another, it called for multiple separations, individualizing distributions, an organization in depth of surveillance and control, an intensification and a ramification of power. The leper was caught up in a practice of rejection, of exile-enclosure; he was left to his doom in a mass among which it was useless to differentiate; those sick of the plague were caught up in a meticulous tactical partitioning in which individual differentiations were the constricting effects of a power that multiplied, articulated, and subdivided itself; the great confinement on the one hand; the correct training on the other. The leper and his separation; the plague and its segmentations. The first is marked; the second analyzed and distributed. The exile of the leper and the arrest of the plague do not bring with them the same political dream. The first is that of a pure community, the second that of a disciplined society. Two ways of exercising power over men, of controlling their relations, of separating out their dangerous mixtures. The plague-stricken town, traversed throughout with hierarchy, surveillance, observation, writing; the town immobilized by the functioning of an extensive power that bears in a distinct way over all individual bodies — this is the utopia of the perfectly governed city. The plague (envisaged as a possibility at least) is the trial in the course of which one may define ideally the exercise of disciplinary power. In order to make rights and laws function according to pure theory, the jurists place themselves in imagination in the state of nature; in order to see perfect disciplines functioning, rulers dreamed of the state of plague. Underlying disciplinary projects the image of the plague stands for all forms of confusion and disorder; just as the image of the leper, cut off from all human contact, underlies projects of exclusion.

They are different projects, then, but not incompatible ones. We see them coming slowly together, and it is the peculiarity of the nineteenth century that it applied to the space of exclusion of which the leper was the symbolic inhabitant (beggars, vagabonds, madmen, and the disorderly formed the real population) the technique of power proper to disciplinary partitioning. Treat "lepers" as "plague victims," project the subtle segmentations of discipline onto the confused space of internment, combine it with the methods of analytical distribution proper to power, individualize the excluded, but use procedures of individualization to mark exclusion — this is what was operated regularly by disciplinary power from the beginning of the nineteenth century in the psychiatric asylum, the penitentiary, the reformatory, the approved school, and to some extent, the hospital. Generally speaking, all the authorities exercising individual control function according to a double mode; that of binary division and branding (mad/sane; dangerous/harmless; normal/abnormal); and that of coercive assignment, of differential distribution (who he is; where he must be; how he is to be characterized; how he is to be recognized; how a constant surveillance is to be exercised over him in an individual way, etc.). On the one hand, the lepers are treated as plague victims; the tactics of individualizing disciplines are imposed on the excluded; and, on the other hand, the universality of disciplinary controls makes it possible to brand the "leper" and to bring into play against him the dualistic mechanisms of exclusion. The constant division between the normal and the abnormal, to which every individual is subjected, brings us back to our own time, by applying the binary branding and exile of the leper to quite different objects; the existence of a whole set of techniques and institutions for measuring, supervising, and correcting the abnormal brings into play the disciplinary mechanisms to which the fear of the plague gave rise. All the mechanisms of power which, even today, are disposed around the abnormal individual, to brand him and to alter him, are composed of those two forms from which they distantly derive.

Bentham's *Panopticon* is the architectural figure of this composition. We know the principle on which it was based: at the periphery, an annular building; at the center, a tower; this tower is pierced with wide windows that open onto the inner side of the ring; the peripheric building is divided into cells, each of which extends the whole width of the building; they have two windows, one on the inside, corresponding to the windows of the tower; the other, on the outside, allows the light to cross the cell from one end to the other. All that is needed, then, is to place a supervisor in a central tower and to shut up in each cell a madman, a patient, a condemned man, a worker, or a schoolboy. By the effect of backlighting, one can observe from the tower, standing out precisely against the light, the small captive shadows in the cells of the periphery. They are like so many cages, so many small theaters, in which each actor is alone, perfectly individualized and constantly visible. The panoptic mechanism arranges spatial unities that make it possible to see constantly and to recognize immediately. In short, it reverses the principle of the dungeon; or rather of its three functions — to enclose, to deprive of light, and to hide — it preserves only the first and eliminates the other two. Full lighting and the eye of a supervisor capture better than darkness, which is ultimately protected. Visibility is a trap.

To begin with, this made it possible — as a negative effect — to avoid those compact, swarming, howling masses that were to be found in places of confinement, those painted by Goya or described by Howard. Each individual, in his place, is securely confined to a cell from which he is seen from the front by the supervisor; but the side walls prevent him from coming into contact with his companions. He is seen, but he does not see; he is the object of information, never a subject in communication. The arrangement of his room, opposite the central tower, imposes on him an axial visibility; but the divisions of the ring, those separated cells, imply a lateral invisibility. And this invisibility is a guarantee of order. If the inmates are convicts, there is no danger of a plot, an attempt at collective escape, the planning of new crimes for the future, bad reciprocal influences; if they are patients, there is no danger of contagion; if they are madmen, there is no risk of their committing violence upon one another; if they are schoolchildren, there is no copying, no noise, no chatter, no waste of time; if they are workers, there are no disorders, no theft, no coalitions, none of those distractions that slow down the rate of work, make it less perfect, or cause accidents. The crowd, a compact mass, a locus of multiple exchanges, individualities merging together, a collective effect, is abolished and replaced by a collection of separated individualities. From the point of view of the guardian, it is replaced by a multiplicity that can be numbered and supervised; from the point of view of the inmates, by a sequestered and observed solitude (Bentham 60–64).

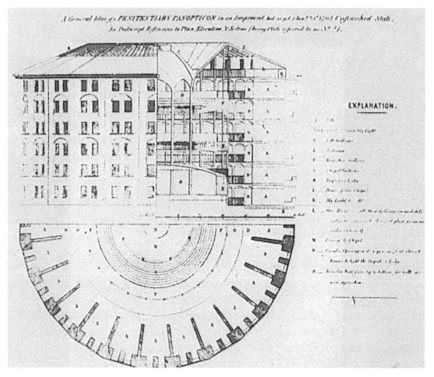

Plan of the Panopticon by J. Bentham (The Works of Jeremy Bentham, *ed.*
Bowring, vol. IV, 1843, 172–73)

Hence the major effect of the Panopticon: to induce in the inmate a
state of conscious and permanent visibility that assures the automatic
functioning of power. So to arrange things that the surveillance is permanent in its effects even if it is discontinuous in its action; that the perfection of power should tend to render its actual exercise unnecessary; that
this architectural apparatus should be a machine for creating and sustaining a power relation independent of the person who exercises it; in short,
that the inmates should be caught up in a power situation of which they
are themselves the bearers. To achieve this, it is at once too much and too
little that the prisoner should be constantly observed by an inspector: too
little, for what matters is that he knows himself to be observed; too much,
because he has no need in fact of being so. In view of this, Bentham laid
down the principle that power should be visible and unverifiable. Visible:
the inmate will constantly have before his eyes the tall outline of the central tower from which he is spied upon. Unverifiable: the inmate must
never know whether he is being looked at at any one moment; but he must
be sure that he may always be so. In order to make the presence or absence
of the inspector unverifiable, so that the prisoners, in their cells, cannot
even see a shadow, Bentham envisaged not only venetian blinds on the

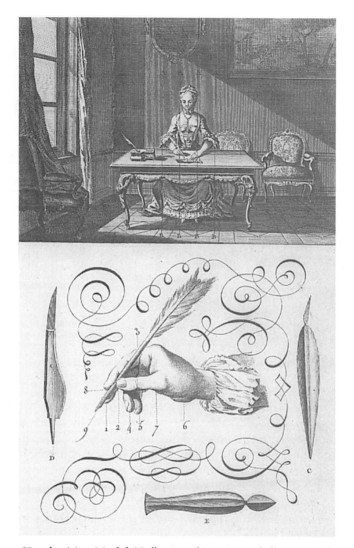

Handwriting Model *(Collections historiques de l'I.N.R.D.P.)*

windows of the central observation hall, but, on the inside, partitions that intersected the hall at right angles and, in order to pass from one quarter to the other, not doors but zigzag openings; for the slightest noise, a gleam of light, a brightness in a half-opened door would betray the presence of the guardian.[2] The Panopticon is a machine for dissociating the see/being seen dyad: in the peripheric ring, one is totally seen, without ever seeing; in the central tower, one sees everything without ever being seen.[3]

It is an important mechanism, for it automatizes and disindividualizes power. Power has its principle not so much in a person as in a certain concerted distribution of bodies, surfaces, lights, gazes; in an arrangement

Interior of the Penitentiary at Stateville, United States, Twentieth Century

whose internal mechanisms produce the relation in which individuals are caught up. The ceremonies, the rituals, the marks by which the sovereign's surplus power was manifested are useless. There is a machinery that assures dissymmetry, disequilibrium, difference. Consequently, it does not matter who exercises power. Any individual, taken almost at random, can operate the machine: in the absence of the director, his family, his friends, his visitors, even his servants (Bentham 45). Similarly, it does not matter what motive animates him: the curiosity of the indiscreet, the malice of a child, the thirst for knowledge of a philosopher who wishes to visit this museum of human nature, or the perversity of those who take pleasure in spying and punishing. The more numerous those anonymous and temporary observers are, the greater the risk for the inmate of being surprised and the greater his anxious awareness of being observed. The Panopticon is a marvelous machine which, whatever use one may wish to put it to, produces homogeneous effects of power.

A real subjection is born mechanically from a fictitious relation. So it is not necessary to use force to constrain the convict to good behavior, the madman to calm, the worker to work, the schoolboy to application, the patient to the observation of the regulations. Bentham was surprised that panoptic institutions could be so light: there were no more bars, no more chains, no more heavy locks; all that was needed was that the separations should be clear and the openings well arranged. The heaviness of the old

Lecture on the Evils of Alcoholism in the Auditorium of Fresnes Prison

"houses of security," with their fortresslike architecture, could be replaced by the simple, economic geometry of a "house of certainty." The efficiency of power, its constraining force have, in a sense, passed over to the other side — to the side of its surface of application. He who is subjected to a field of visibility, and who knows it, assumes responsibility for the constraints of power; he makes them play spontaneously upon himself; he inscribes in himself the power relation in which he simultaneously plays both roles; he becomes the principle of his own subjection. By this very fact, the external power may throw off its physical weight; it tends to the noncorporal; and, the more it approaches this limit, the more constant, profound, and permanent are its effects: it is a perpetual victory that avoids any physical confrontation and which is always decided in advance.

Bentham does not say whether he was inspired, in his project, by Le Vaux's menagerie at Versailles: the first menagerie in which the different elements are not, as they traditionally were, distributed in a park (Loisel 104–7). At the center was an octagonal pavilion which, on the first floor, consisted of only a single room, the king's *salon*; on every side large windows looked out onto seven cages (the eighth side was reserved for the entrance), containing different species of animals. By Bentham's time, this menagerie had disappeared. But one finds in the program of the Panopticon a similar concern with individualizing observation, with characterization and classification, with the analytical arrangement of space. The Panopticon is a royal menagerie; the animal is replaced by man, individual distribution by specific grouping, and the king by the machinery of a furtive power. With this exception, the Panopticon also does the work of a naturalist. It makes it possible to draw up differences: among patients, to observe the symptoms of each individual, without the proximity of beds, the circulation of miasmas, the effects of contagion confusing the clinical tables; among schoolchildren, it makes it possible to observe performances (without there being any imitation or copying), to map aptitudes, to assess characters, to draw up rigorous classifications, and in relation to normal development, to distinguish "laziness and stubbornness" from "incurable imbecility"; among workers, it makes it possible to note the aptitudes of each worker, compare the time he takes to perform a task, and if they are paid by the day, to calculate their wages (Bentham 60–64).

So much for the question of observation. But the Panopticon was also a laboratory; it could be used as a machine to carry out experiments, to alter behavior, to train or correct individuals. To experiment with medicines and monitor their effects. To try out different punishments on prisoners, according to their crimes and character, and to seek the most effective ones. To teach different techniques simultaneously to the workers, to decide which is the best. To try out pedagogical experiments — and in particular to take up once again the well-debated problem of secluded education, by using orphans. One would see what would happen when, in their sixteenth or eighteenth year, they were presented with other boys or girls; one could verify whether, as Helvetius thought, anyone could learn anything; one would follow "the genealogy of every observable idea"; one could bring up different children according to different systems of thought, making certain children believe that two and two do not make four or that the moon is a cheese, then put them together when they are twenty or twenty-five years old; one would then have discussions that would be worth a great deal more than the sermons or lectures on which so much money is spent; one would have at least an opportunity of making discoveries in the domain of metaphysics. The Panopticon is a privileged place for experiments on men, and for analyzing with complete certainty the transformations that may be obtained from them. The Panopticon may even provide an apparatus for supervising its own mechanisms. In this central tower, the director may spy on all the employees that he has under his orders: nurses, doctors, foremen, teachers, warders; he will be able to judge them continuously, alter their behavior, impose upon them the methods he thinks best; and it will even be possible to observe the director himself. An inspector arriving unexpectedly at the center of the Panopticon will be able to judge at a glance, without anything being concealed from him, how the entire establishment is functioning. And, in any case, enclosed as he is in the middle of this architectural mechanism, is not the director's own fate entirely bound up with it? The incompetent physician who has allowed contagion to spread, the incompetent prison governor or workshop manager will be the first victims of an epidemic or a revolt. "'By every tie I could devise,' said the master of the Panopticon, 'my own fate had been bound up by me with theirs'" (Bentham 177). The Panopticon functions as a kind of laboratory of power. Thanks to its mechanisms of observation, it gains in efficiency and in the ability to penetrate into men's behavior; knowledge follows the advances of power, discovering new objects of knowledge over all the surfaces on which power is exercised.

The plague-stricken town, the panoptic establishment — the differences are important. They mark, at a distance of a century and a half, the transformations of the disciplinary program. In the first case, there is an exceptional situation: against an extraordinary evil, power is mobilized; it makes itself everywhere present and visible; it invents new mechanisms; it separates, it immobilizes, it partitions; it constructs for a time what is both a counter-city and the perfect society; it imposes an ideal functioning, but one that is reduced, in the final analysis, like the evil that it combats, to a simple dualism of life and death: that which moves brings death, and one kills that which moves. The Panopticon, on the other hand, must be understood as a generalizable model of functioning; a way of defining power relations in terms of the everyday life of men. No doubt Bentham presents it as a particular institution, closed in upon itself. Utopias, perfectly closed in upon themselves, are common enough. As opposed to the ruined prisons, littered with mechanisms of torture, to be seen in Piranese's engravings, the Panopticon presents a cruel, ingenious cage. The fact that it should have given rise, even in our own time, to so many variations, projected or realized, is evidence of the imaginary intensity that it has possessed for almost two hundred years. But the Panopticon must not be understood as a dream building: it is the diagram of a mechanism of power reduced to its ideal form; its functioning, abstracted from any obstacle, resistance, or friction, must be represented as a pure architectural and optical system: it is in fact a figure of political technology that may and must be detached from any specific use.

It is polyvalent in its applications; it serves to reform prisoners, but also to treat patients, to instruct schoolchildren, to confine the insane, to supervise workers, to put beggars and idlers to work. It is a type of location of bodies in space, of distribution of individuals in relation to one another, of hierarchical organization, of disposition of centers and channels of power, of definition of the instruments and modes of intervention of power, which can be implemented in hospitals, workshops, schools, prisons. Whenever one is dealing with a multiplicity of individuals on whom a task or a particular form of behavior must be imposed, the panoptic schema may be used. It is — necessary modifications apart — applicable "to all establishments whatsoever, in which, within a space not too large to be covered or commanded by buildings, a number of persons are meant to be kept under inspection" (Bentham 40; although Bentham takes the penitentiary house as his prime example, it is because it has many different functions to fulfill — safe custody, confinement, solitude, forced labor, and instruction).

In each of its applications, it makes it possible to perfect the exercise of power. It does this in several ways: because it can reduce the number of those who exercise it, while increasing the number of those on whom it is exercised. Because it is possible to intervene at any moment and because the constant pressure acts even before the offenses, mistakes, or crimes have been committed. Because, in these conditions, its strength is that it never intervenes, it is exercised spontaneously and without noise, it constitutes a mechanism whose effects follow from one another. Because, without any physical instrument other than architecture and geometry, it acts directly on individuals; it gives "power of mind over mind." The panoptic schema makes any apparatus of power more intense: it assures its economy (in material, in personnel, in time); it assures its efficacity by its preventative character, its continuous functioning and its automatic mechanisms. It is a way of obtaining from power "in hitherto unexampled quantity," "a great and new instrument of government . . . ; its great excellence consists in the great strength it is capable of giving to *any* institution it may be thought proper to apply it to" (Bentham 66).

It's a case of "it's easy once you've thought of it" in the political sphere. It can in fact be integrated into any function (education, medical treatment, production, punishment); it can increase the effect of this function, by being linked closely with it; it can constitute a mixed mechanism in which relations of power (and of knowledge) may be precisely adjusted, in the smallest detail, to the processes that are to be supervised; it can establish a direct proportion between "surplus power" and "surplus production." In short, it arranges things in such a way that the exercise of power is not added on from the outside, like a rigid, heavy constraint, to the functions it invests, but is so subtly present in them as to increase their efficiency by itself increasing its own points of contact. The panoptic mechanism is not simply a hinge, a point of exchange between a mechanism of power and a function; it is a way of making power relations function in a function, and of making a function function through these power relations. Bentham's preface to *Panopticon* opens with a list of the benefits to be obtained from his "inspection-house": "*Morals reformed — health preserved — industry invigorated — instruction diffused — public burthens lightened —* Economy seated, as it were, upon a rock — the gordian knot of the Poor-Laws not cut, but untied — all by a simple idea in architecture!" (Bentham 39).

Furthermore, the arrangement of this machine is such that its enclosed nature does not preclude a permanent presence from the outside: we have seen that anyone may come and exercise in the central tower the functions of surveillance, and that, this being the case, he can gain a clear idea of the way in which the surveillance is practiced. In fact, any panoptic institution, even if it is as rigorously closed as a penitentiary, may without difficulty be subjected to such irregular and constant inspections: and not only by the appointed inspectors, but also by the public; any member of society will have the right to come and see with his own eyes how the schools, hospitals, factories, prisons function. There is no risk, therefore, that the increase of power created by the panoptic machine may degenerate into tyranny; the disciplinary mechanism will be democratically controlled, since it will be constantly accessible "to the great tribunal committee of the world."[4] This Panopticon, subtly arranged so that an observer may observe, at a glance, so many different individuals, also enables everyone to come and observe any of the observers. The seeing machine was once a sort of dark room into which individuals spied; it has become a transparent building in which the exercise of power may be supervised by society as a whole.

The panoptic schema, without disappearing as such or losing any of its properties, was destined to spread throughout the social body; its vocation was to become a generalized function. The plague-stricken town provided an exceptional disciplinary model: perfect, but absolutely violent; to the disease that brought death, power opposed its perpetual threat of death; life inside it was reduced to its simplest expression; it was, against the power of death, the meticulous exercise of the right of the sword. The Panopticon, on the other hand, has a role of amplification; although it arranges power, although it is intended to make it more economic and more effective, it does so not for power itself, nor for the immediate salvation of a threatened society: its aim is to strengthen the social forces — to increase production, to develop the economy, spread education, raise the level of public morality; to increase and multiply.

How is power to be strengthened in such a way that, far from impeding progress, far from weighing upon it with its rules and regulations, it actually facilitates such progress? What intensificator of power will be able at the same time to be a multiplicator of production? How will power, by increasing its forces, be able to increase those of society instead of confiscating them or impeding them? The Panopticon's solution to this problem is that the productive increase of power can be assured only if, on the one hand, it can be exercised continuously in the very foundations of society, in the subtlest possible way, and if, on the other hand, it functions outside these sudden, violent, discontinuous forms that are bound up with the exercise of sovereignty. The body of the king, with its strange material and physical presence, with the force that he himself deploys or transmits to some few others, is at the opposite extreme of this new physics of power represented by panopticism; the domain of panopticism is, on the contrary, that whole lower region, that region of irregular bodies, with their details, their multiple movements, their heterogeneous forces, their spatial relations; what are required are mechanisms that analyze distributions, gaps, series, combinations, and which use instruments that render visible, record, differentiate, and compare: a physics of a relational and multiple power, which has its maximum intensity not in the person of the king, but in the bodies that can be individualized by these relations. At the theoretical level, Bentham defines another way of analyzing the social body and the power relations that traverse it; in terms of practice, he defines a procedure of subordination of bodies and forces that must increase the utility of power while practicing the economy of the prince. Panopticism is the general principle of a new "political anatomy" whose object and end are not the relations of sovereignty but the relations of discipline.

The celebrated, transparent, circular cage, with its high tower, powerful and knowing, may have been for Bentham a project of a perfect disciplinary institution; but he also set out to show how one may "unlock" the disciplines and get them to function in a diffused, multiple, polyvalent way throughout the whole social body. These disciplines, which the classical age had elaborated in specific, relatively enclosed places — barracks, schools, workshops — and whose total implementation had been imagined only at the limited and temporary scale of a plague-stricken town, Bentham dreamed of transforming into a network of mechanisms that would be everywhere and always alert, running through society without interruption in space or in time. The panoptic arrangement provides the formula for this generalization. It programs, at the level of an elementary and easily transferable mechanism, the basic functioning of a society penetrated through and through with disciplinary mechanisms.

There are two images, then, of discipline. At one extreme, the discipline-blockade, the enclosed institution, established on the edges of society, turned inwards towards negative functions: arresting evil, breaking communications, suspending time. At the other extreme, with panopticism, is the discipline-mechanism: a functional mechanism that must improve the exercise of power by making it lighter, more rapid, more effective, a design of subtle coercion for a society to come. The movement from one project to the other, from a schema of exceptional discipline to one of a generalized surveillance, rests on a historical transformation: the gradual extension of the mechanisms of discipline throughout the seventeenth and eighteenth centuries, their spread throughout the whole social body, the formation of what might be called in general the disciplinary society.

A whole disciplinary generalization — the Benthamite physics of power represents an acknowledgment of this — had operated throughout the classical age. The spread of disciplinary institutions, whose network was beginning to cover an ever larger surface and occupying above all a less and less marginal position, testifies to this: what was an islet, a privileged place, a circumstantial measure, or a singular model, became a general formula; the regulations characteristic of the Protestant and pious armies of William of Orange or of Gustavus Adolphus were transformed into regulations for all the armies of Europe; the model colleges of the Jesuits, or the schools of Batencour or Demia, following the example set by Sturm, provided the outlines for the general forms of educational discipline; the ordering of the naval and military hospitals provided the model for the entire reorganization of hospitals in the eighteenth century.

But this extension of the disciplinary institutions was no doubt only the most visible aspect of various, more profound processes.

1. *The functional inversion of the disciplines.* At first, they were expected to neutralize dangers, to fix useless or disturbed populations, to avoid the inconveniences of over-large assemblies; now they were being asked to play a positive role, for they were becoming able to do so, to increase the possible utility of individuals. Military discipline is no longer a mere means of preventing looting, desertion, or failure to obey orders among the troops; it has become a basic technique to enable the army to exist, not as an assembled crowd, but as a unity that derives from this very unity an increase in its forces; discipline increases the skill of each individual, coordinates these skills, accelerates movements, increases fire power, broadens the fronts of attack without reducing their vigor, increases the capacity for resistance, etc. The discipline of the workshop, while remaining a way of enforcing respect for the regulations and authorities, of preventing thefts or losses, tends to increase aptitudes, speeds, output, and therefore profits; it still exerts a moral influence over behavior, but more and more it treats actions in terms of their results, introduces bodies into a machinery, forces into an economy. When, in the seventeenth century, the provincial schools or the Christian elementary schools were founded, the justifications given for them were above all negative: those poor who were unable to bring up their children left them "in ignorance of their obligations: given the difficulties they have in earning a living, and themselves having been badly brought up, they are unable to communicate a sound upbringing that they themselves never had"; this involves three major inconveniences: ignorance of God, idleness (with its consequent drunkenness, impurity, larceny, brigandage), and the formation of those gangs of beggars, always ready to stir up public disorder and "virtually to exhaust the funds of the Hôtel-Dieu" (Demia 60–61). Now, at the beginning of the Revolution, the end laid down for primary education was to be, among

other things, to "fortify," to "develop the body," to prepare the child "for a future in some mechanical work," to give him "an observant eye, a sure hand and prompt habits" (Talleyrand's Report to the Constituent Assembly, 10 September 1791, quoted by Léon 106). The disciplines function increasingly as techniques for making useful individuals. Hence their emergence from a marginal position on the confines of society, and detachment from the forms of exclusion or expiation, confinement, or retreat. Hence the slow loosening of their kinship with religious regularities and enclosures. Hence also their rooting in the most important, most central, and most productive sectors of society. They become attached to some of the great essential functions: factory production, the transmission of knowledge, the diffusion of aptitudes and skills, the war-machine. Hence, too, the double tendency one sees developing throughout the eighteenth century to increase the number of disciplinary institutions and to discipline the existing apparatuses.

2. *The swarming of disciplinary mechanisms.* While, on the one hand, the disciplinary establishments increase, their mechanisms have a certain tendency to become "deinstitutionalized," to emerge from the closed fortresses in which they once functioned and to circulate in a "free" state; the massive, compact disciplines are broken down into flexible methods of control, which may be transferred and adapted. Sometimes the closed apparatuses add to their internal and specific function a role of external surveillance, developing around themselves a whole margin of lateral controls. Thus the Christian School must not simply train docile children; it must also make it possible to supervise the parents, to gain information as to their way of life, their resources, their piety, their morals. The school tends to constitute minute social observatories that penetrate even to the adults and exercise regular supervision over them: the bad behavior of the child, or his absence, is a legitimate pretext, according to Demia, for one to go and question the neighbors, especially if there is any reason to believe that the family will not tell the truth; one can then go and question the parents themselves, to find out whether they know their catechism and the prayers, whether they are determined to root out the vices of their children, how many beds there are in the house and what the sleeping arrangements are; the visit may end with the giving of alms, the present of a religious picture, or the provision of additional beds (Demia 39–40). Similarly, the hospital is increasingly conceived of as a base for the medical observation of the population outside; after the burning down of the Hôtel-Dieu in 1772, there were several demands that the large buildings, so heavy and so disordered, should be replaced by a series of smaller hospitals; their function would be to take in the sick of the quarter, but also to gather information, to be alert to any endemic or epidemic phenomena, to open dispensaries, to give advice to the inhabitants, and to keep the authorities informed of the sanitary state of the region.[5]

One also sees the spread of disciplinary procedures, not in the form of enclosed institutions, but as centers of observation disseminated throughout society. Religious groups and charity organizations had long played this role of "disciplining" the population. From the Counter-Reformation to the philanthropy of the July monarchy, initiatives of this type continued to increase; their aims were religious (conversion and moralization), economic (aid and encouragement to work), or political (the struggle against discontent or agitation). One has only to cite by way of example the regulations for the charity associations in the Paris parishes. The territory to be covered was divided into quarters and cantons and the members of the associations divided themselves up along the same lines. These members had to visit their respective areas regularly. "They will strive to eradicate places of ill-repute, tobacco shops, life-classes, gaming house, public scandals, blasphemy, impiety, and any other disorders that may come to their knowledge." They will also have to make individual visits to the poor; and the information to be obtained is laid down in regulations: the stability of the lodging, knowledge of prayers, attendance at the sacraments, knowledge of a trade, morality (and "whether they have not fallen into poverty through their own fault"); lastly, "one must learn by skillful questioning in what way they behave at home. Whether there is peace between them and their neighbors, whether they are careful to bring up their children in the fear of God . . . , whether they do not have their older children of different sexes sleeping together and with them, whether they do not allow licentiousness and cajolery in their families, especially in their older daughters. If one has any doubts as to whether they are married, one must ask to see their marriage certificate."[6]

3. *The state-control of the mechanisms of the discipline.* In England, it was private religious groups that carried out, for a long time, the functions of social discipline (cf. Radzinovitz 203–14); in France, although a part of this role remained in the hands of parish guilds or charity associations, another — and no doubt the most important part — was very soon taken over by the police apparatus.

The organization of a centralized police had long been regarded, even by contemporaries, as the most direct expression of royal absolutism; the sovereign had wished to have "his own magistrate to whom he might directly entrust his orders, his commissions, intentions, and who was entrusted with the execution of orders and orders under the King's private seal" (a note by Duval, first secretary at the police magistrature, quoted in Funck-Brentano I). In effect, in taking over a number of preexisting functions — the search for criminals, urban surveillance, economic and political supervision — the police magistratures and the magistrature-general that presided over them in Paris transposed them into a single, strict, administrative machine: "All the radiations of force and information that spread from the circumference culminate in the magistrate-general. . . . It is he who operates all the wheels that together produce order and harmony. The effects of his administration cannot be better compared than to the movement of the celestial bodies" (Des Essarts 344, 528).

But, although the police as an institution were certainly organized in the form of a state apparatus, and although this was certainly linked directly to the center of political sovereignty, the type of power that it exercises, the mechanisms it operates, and the elements to which it applies them are specific. It is an apparatus that must be coextensive with the entire social body and not only by the extreme limits that it embraces, but by the minuteness of the details it is concerned with. Police power must bear "over everything": it is not, however, the totality of the state nor of the kingdom as visible and invisible body of the monarch; it is the dust of events, actions, behavior, opinions — "everything that happens";[7] the police are concerned with "those things of every moment," those "unimportant things," of which Catherine II spoke in her Great Instruction (Supplement to the *Instruction for the Drawing Up of a New Code*, 1769, article 535). With the police, one is in the indefinite world of a supervision that seeks ideally to reach the most elementary particle, the most passing phenomenon of the social body: "The ministry of the magistrates and police officers is of the greatest importance; the objects that it embraces are in a sense definite, one may perceive them only by a sufficiently detailed examination" (Delamare, unnumbered preface): the infinitely small of political power.

And, in order to be exercised, this power had to be given the instrument of permanent, exhaustive, omnipresent surveillance, capable of making all visible, as long as it could itself remain invisible. It had to be like a faceless gaze that transformed the whole social body into a field of perception: thousands of eyes posted everywhere, mobile attentions ever on the alert, a long, hierarchized network which, according to Le Maire, comprised for Paris the forty-eight *commissaires*, the twenty *inspecteurs*, then the "observers," who were paid regularly, the *"basses mouches,"* or secret agents, who were paid by the day, then the informers, paid according to the job done, and finally the prostitutes. And this unceasing observation had to be accumulated in a series of reports and registers; throughout the eighteenth century, an immense police text increasingly covered society by means of a complex documentary organization (on the police registers in the eighteenth century, cf. Chassaigne). And, unlike the methods of judicial or administrative writing, what was registered in this way were forms of behavior, attitudes, possibilities, suspicions — a permanent account of individuals' behavior.

Now, it should be noted that, although this police supervision was entirely "in the hands of the king," it did not function in a single direction. It was in fact a double-entry system: it had to correspond, by manipulating the machinery of justice, to the immediate wishes of the king, but it was also capable of responding to solicitations from below; the celebrated *lettres de cachet*, or orders under the king's private seal, which were long the symbol of arbitrary royal rule and which brought detention into disrepute on political grounds, were in fact demanded by families, masters, local notables, neighbors, parish priests; and their function was to punish by confinement a whole infrapenality, that of disorder, agitation, disobedience, bad conduct; those things that Ledoux wanted to exclude from his architecturally perfect city and which he called "offenses of nonsurveillance." In short, the eighteenth-century police added a disciplinary function to its role as the auxiliary of justice in the pursuit of criminals and as an instrument for the political supervision of plots, opposition movements, or revolts. It was a complex function since it linked the absolute power of the monarch to the lowest levels of power disseminated in society; since, between these different, enclosed institutions of discipline (workshops, armies, schools), it extended an intermediary network, acting where they could not intervene, disciplining the nondisciplinary spaces; but it filled in the gaps, linked them together, guaranteed with its armed force an interstitial discipline and a metadiscipline. "By means of a wise police, the sovereign accustoms the people to order and obedience" (Vattel 162).

The organization of the police apparatus in the eighteenth century sanctioned a generalization of the disciplines that became coextensive with the state itself. Although it was linked in the most explicit way with everything in the royal power that exceeded the exercise of regular justice, it is understandable why the police offered such slight resistance to the rearrangement of the judicial power; and why it has not ceased to impose its prerogatives upon it, with ever-increasing weight, right up to the present day; this is no doubt because it is the secular arm of the judiciary; but it is also because, to a far greater degree than the judicial institution, it is identified, by reason of its extent and mechanisms, with a society of the disciplinary type. Yet it would be wrong to believe that the disciplinary functions were confiscated and absorbed once and for all by a state apparatus.

"Discipline" may be identified neither with an institution nor with an apparatus; it is a type of power, a modality for its exercise, comprising a whole set of instruments, techniques, procedures, levels of application, targets; it is a "physics" or an "anatomy" of power, a technology. And it may be taken over either by "specialized" institutions (the penitentiaries or "houses of correction" of the nineteenth century), or by institutions that use it as an essential instrument for a particular end (schools, hospitals), or by preexisting authorities that find in it a means of reinforcing or reorganizing their internal mechanisms of power (one day we should show how intrafamilial relations, essentially in the parents-children cell, have become "disciplined," absorbing since the classical age external schemata, first educational and military, then medical, psychiatric, psychological, which have made the family the privileged locus of emergence for the disciplinary question of the normal and the abnormal), or by apparatuses that have made discipline their principle of internal functioning (the disciplinarization of the administrative apparatus from the Napoleonic period), or finally by state apparatuses whose major, if not exclusive, function is to assure that discipline reigns over society as a whole (the police).

On the whole, therefore, one can speak of the formation of a disciplinary society in this movement that stretches from the enclosed disciplines, a sort of social "quarantine," to an indefinitely generalizable mechanism of "panopticism." Not because the disciplinary modality of power has replaced all the others; but because it has infiltrated the others, sometimes undermining them, but serving as an intermediary between them, linking them together, extending them, and above all making it possible to bring the effects of power to the most minute and distant elements. It assures an infinitesimal distribution of the power relations.

A few years after Bentham, Julius gave this society its birth certificate (Julius 384–86). Speaking of the panoptic principle, he said that there was much more there than architectural ingenuity: it was an event in the "history of the human mind." In appearance, it is merely the solution of a technical problem; but, through it, a whole type of society emerges. Antiquity had been a civilization of spectacle. "To render accessible to a multitude of men the inspection of a small number of objects": this was the problem to which the architecture of temples, theaters, and circuses responded. With spectacle, there was a predominance of public life, the intensity of festivals, sensual proximity. In these rituals in which blood flowed, society found new vigor and formed for a moment a single great body. The modern age poses the opposite problem: "To procure for a small number, or even for a single individual, the instantaneous view of a great multitude." In a society in which the principal elements are no longer the community and public life, but, on the one hand, private individuals and, on the other, the state, relations can be regulated only in a form that is the exact reverse of the spectacle: "It was to the modern age, to the ever-growing influence of the state, to its ever more profound intervention in all the details and all the relations of social life, that was reserved the task of increasing and perfecting its guarantees, by using and directing towards that great aim the building and distribution of buildings intended to observe a great multitude of men at the same time."

Julius saw as a fulfilled historical process that which Bentham had described as a technical program. Our society is one not of spectacle, but of surveillance; under the surface of images, one invests bodies in depth; behind the great abstraction of exchange, there continues the meticulous, concrete training of useful forces; the circuits of communication are the supports of an accumulation and a centralization of knowledge; the play of signs defines the anchorages of power; it is not that the beautiful totality of the individual is amputated, repressed, altered by our social order, it is rather that the individual is carefully fabricated in it, according to a whole technique of forces and bodies. We are much less Greeks than we believe. We are neither in the amphitheater, nor on the stage, but in the panoptic machine, invested by its effects of power, which we bring to ourselves since we are part of its mechanism. The importance, in historical mythology, of the Napoleonic character probably derives from the fact that it is at the point of junction of the monarchical, ritual exercise of sovereignty and the hierarchical, permanent exercise of indefinite discipline. He is the individual who looms over everything with a single gaze which no detail, however minute, can escape: "You may consider that no part of the Empire is without surveillance, no crime, no offense, no contravention that remains unpunished, and that the eye of the genius who can enlighten all embraces the whole of this vast machine, without, however, the slightest detail escaping his attention" (Treilhard 14). At the moment of its full blossoming, the disciplinary society still assumes with the Emperor the old aspect of the power of spectacle. As a monarch who is at one and the same time a usurper of the ancient throne and the organizer of the new state, he combined into a single symbolic, ultimate figure the whole of the long process by which the pomp of sovereignty, the necessarily spectacular manifestations of power, were extinguished one by one in the daily exercise of surveillance, in a panopticism in which the vigilance of intersecting gazes was soon to render useless both the eagle and the sun.

The formation of the disciplinary society is connected with a number of broad historical processes — economic, juridico-political, and lastly, scientific — of which it forms part.

1. Generally speaking, it might be said that the disciplines are techniques for assuring the ordering of human multiplicities. It is true that there is nothing exceptional or even characteristic in this: every system of power is presented with the same problem. But the peculiarity of the disciplines is that they try to define in relation to the multiplicities a tactics of power that fulfills three criteria: firstly, to obtain the exercise of power at the lowest possible cost (economically, by the low expenditure it involves; politically, by its discretion, its low exteriorization, its relative invisibility, the little resistance it arouses); secondly, to bring the effects of this social power to their maximum intensity and to extend them as far as possible, without either failure or interval; thirdly, to link this "economic" growth of power with the output of the apparatuses (educational, military, industrial, or medical) within which it is exercised; in short, to increase both the docility and the utility of all the elements of the system. This triple objective of the disciplines corresponds to a well-known historical conjuncture. One aspect of this conjuncture was the large demographic thrust of the eighteenth century; an increase in the floating population (one of the primary objects of discipline is to fix; it is an antinomadic technique); a change of quantitative scale in the groups to be supervised or manipulated (from the beginning of the seventeenth century to the eve of the French Revolution, the school population had been increasing rapidly, as had no doubt the hospital population; by the end of the eighteenth century, the peacetime army exceeded 200,000 men). The other aspect of the conjuncture was the growth in the apparatus of production, which was becoming more and more extended and complex; it was also becoming more costly and its profitability had to be increased. The development of the disciplinary methods corresponded to these two processes, or rather, no doubt, to the new need to adjust their correlation. Neither the residual forms of

feudal power nor the structures of the administrative monarchy, nor the local mechanisms of supervision, nor the unstable, tangled mass they all formed together could carry out this role: they were hindered from doing so by the irregular and inadequate extension of their network, by their often conflicting functioning, but above all by the "costly" nature of the power that was exercised in them. It was costly in several senses: because directly it cost a great deal to the Treasury; because the system of corrupt offices and farmed-out taxes weighed indirectly, but very heavily, on the population; because the resistance it encountered forced it into a cycle of perpetual reinforcement; because it proceeded essentially by levying (levying on money or products by royal, seigniorial, ecclesiastical taxation; levying on men or time by *corvées* of press-ganging, by locking up or banishing vagabonds). The development of the disciplines marks the appearance of elementary techniques belonging to a quite different economy: mechanisms of power which, instead of proceeding by deduction, are integrated into the productive efficiency of the apparatuses from within, into the growth of this efficiency and into the use of what it produces. For the old principle of "levying-violence," which governed the economy of power, the disciplines substitute the principle of "mildness-production-profit." These are the techniques that make it possible to adjust the multiplicity of men and the multiplication of the apparatuses of production (and this means not only "production" in the strict sense, but also the production of knowledge and skills in the school, the production of health in the hospitals, the production of destructive force in the army).

In this task of adjustment, discipline had to solve a number of problems for which the old economy of power was not sufficiently equipped. It could reduce the inefficiency of mass phenomena: reduce what, in a multiplicity, makes it much less manageable than a unity; reduce what is opposed to the use of each of its elements and of their sum; reduce everything that may counter the advantages of number. That is why discipline fixes; it arrests or regulates movements; it clears up confusion; it dissipates compact groupings of individuals wandering about the country in unpredictable ways; it establishes calculated distributions. It must also master all the forces that are formed from the very constitution of an organized multiplicity; it must neutralize the effects of counterpower that spring from them and which form a resistance to the power that wishes to dominate it: agitations, revolts, spontaneous organizations, coalitions — anything that may establish horizontal conjunctions. Hence the fact that the disciplines use procedures of partitioning and verticality, that they introduce, between the different elements at the same level, as solid separations as possible, that they define compact hierarchical networks, in short, that they oppose to the intrinsic, adverse force of multiplicity the technique of the continuous, individualizing pyramid. They must also increase the particular utility of each element of the multiplicity, but by means that are the most rapid and the least costly, that is to say, by using the multiplicity itself as an instrument of this growth. Hence, in order to extract from bodies the maximum time and force, the use of those overall methods known as timetables, collective training, exercises, total and detailed surveillance. Furthermore, the disciplines must increase the effect of utility proper to the multiplicities, so that each is made more useful than the simple sum of its elements: it is in order to increase the utilizable effects of the multiple that the disciplines define tactics of distribution, reciprocal adjustment of bodies, gestures, and rhythms, differentiation of capacities, reciprocal co-ordination in relation to apparatuses or tasks. Lastly, the disciplines have to bring into play the power relations, not above but inside the very texture of the multiplicity, as discreetly as possible, as well articulated on the other functions of these multiplicities and also in the least expensive way possible: to this correspond anonymous instruments of power, coextensive with the multiplicity that they regiment, such as hierarchical surveillance, continuous registration, perpetual assessment, and classification. In short, to substitute for a power that is manifested through the brilliance of those who exercise it, a power that insidiously objectifies those on whom it is applied; to form a body of knowledge about these individuals, rather than to deploy the ostentatious signs of sovereignty. In a word, the disciplines are the ensemble of minute technical inventions that made it possible to increase the useful size of multiplicities by decreasing the inconveniences of the power which, in order to make them useful, must control them. A multiplicity, whether in a workshop or a nation, an army or a school, reaches the threshold of a discipline when the relation of the one to the other becomes favorable.

If the economic take-off of the West began with the techniques that made possible the accumulation of capital, it might perhaps be said that the methods for administering the accumulation of men made possible a political take-off in relation to the traditional, ritual, costly, violent forms of power, which soon fell into disuse and were superseded by a subtle, calculated technology of subjection. In fact, the two processes — the accumulation of men and the accumulation of capital — cannot be separated; it would not have been possible to solve the problem of the accumulation of men without the growth of an apparatus of production capable of both sustaining them and using them; conversely, the techniques that made the cumulative multiplicity of men useful accelerated the accumulation of capital. At a less general level, the technological mutations of the apparatus of production, the division of labor and the elaboration of the disciplinary techniques sustained an ensemble of very close relations (cf. Marx, *Capital*, vol. I, chapter XIII and the very interesting analysis in Guerry and Deleule). Each makes the other possible and necessary; each provides a model for the other. The disciplinary pyramid constituted the small cell of power within which the separation, coordination, and supervision of tasks was imposed and made efficient; and analytical partitioning of time, gestures, and bodily forces constituted an operational schema that could easily be transferred from the groups to be subjected to the mechanisms of production; the massive projection of military methods onto industrial organization was an example of this modeling of the division of labor following the model laid down by the schemata of power. But, on the other hand, the technical analysis of the process of production, its "mechanical" breaking-down, were projected onto the labor force whose task it was to implement it: the constitution of those disciplinary machines in which the individual forces that they bring together are composed into a whole and therefore increased is the effect of this projection. Let us say that discipline is the unitary technique by which the body is reduced as a "political" force at the least cost and maximized as a useful force. The growth of a capitalist economy gave rise to the specific modality of disciplinary power, whose general formulas, techniques of submitting forces and bodies, in short, "political anatomy," could be operated in the most diverse political regimes, apparatuses, or institutions.

2. The panoptic modality of power — at the elementary, technical, merely physical level at which it is situated — is not under the immediate dependence or a direct extension of the great juridico-political structures of a society; it is nonetheless not absolutely independent. Historically, the process by which the bourgeoisie became in the course of the eighteenth century the politically dominant class was masked by the establishment of an explicit, coded, and formally egalitarian juridical framework, made possible by the organization of a parliamentary, representative regime. But the development and generalization of disciplinary mechanisms constituted the other, dark side of these processes. The general juridical form that guaranteed a system of rights that were egalitarian in principle was supported by these tiny, everyday, physical mechanisms, by all those systems of micropower that are essentially nonegalitarian and asymmetrical that we call the disciplines. And although, in a formal way, the representative regime makes it possible, directly or indirectly, with or without relays, for the will of all to form the fundamental authority of sovereignty, the disciplines provide, at the base, a guarantee of the submission of forces and bodies. The real, corporal disciplines constituted the foundation of the formal, juridical liberties. The contract may have been regarded as the ideal foundation of law and political power; panopticism constituted the technique, universally widespread, of coercion. It continued to work in depth on the juridical structures of society, in order to make the effective mechanisms of power function in opposition to the formal framework that it had acquired. The "Enlightenment," which discovered the liberties, also invented the disciplines.

In appearance, the disciplines constitute nothing more than an infra-law. They seem to extend the general forms defined by law to the infinitesimal level of individual lives; or they appear as methods of training that enable individuals to become integrated into these general demands. They seem to constitute the same type of law on a different scale, thereby making it more meticulous and more indulgent. The disciplines should be regarded as a sort of counterlaw. They have the precise role of introducing insuperable asymmetries and excluding reciprocities. First, because discipline creates between individuals a "private" link, which is a relation of constraints entirely different from contractual obligation; the acceptance of a discipline may be underwritten by contract; the way in which it is imposed, the mechanisms it brings into play, the nonreversible subordination of one group of people by another, the "surplus" power that is always fixed on the same side, the inequality of position of the different "partners" in relation to the common regulation, all these distinguish the disciplinary link from the contractual link, and make it possible to distort the contractual link systematically from the moment it has as its content a mechanism of discipline. We know, for example, how many real procedures undermine the legal fiction of the work contract: workshop discipline is not the least important. Moreover, whereas the juridical systems define juridical subjects according to universal norms, the disciplines characterize, classify, specialize; they distribute along a scale, around a norm, hierarchize individuals in relation to one another and, if necessary, disqualify and invalidate. In any case, in the space and during the time in which they exercise their control and bring into play the asymmetries of their power, they effect a suspension of the law that is never total, but is never annulled either. Regular and institutional as it may be, the discipline, in its mechanism, is a "counterlaw." And, although the universal juridicism of modern society seems to fix limits on the exercise of power, its universally widespread panopticism enables it to operate, on the underside of the law, a machinery that is both immense and minute, which supports, reinforces, multiplies the asymmetry of power and undermines the limits that are traced around the law. The minute disciplines, the panopticisms of every day may well be below the level of emergence of the great apparatuses and the great political struggles. But, in the genealogy of modern society, they have been, with the class domination that traverses it, the political counterpart of the juridical norms according to which power was redistributed. Hence, no doubt, the importance that has been given for so long to the small techniques of discipline, to those apparently insignificant tricks that it has invented, and even to those "sciences" that give it a respectable face; hence the fear of abandoning them if one cannot find any substitute; hence the affirmation that they are at the very foundation of society, and an element in its equilibrium, whereas they are a series of mechanisms for unbalancing power relations definitively and everywhere; hence the persistence in regarding them as the humble, but concrete form of every morality, whereas they are a set of physico-political techniques.

To return to the problem of legal punishments, the prison with all the corrective technology at its disposal is to be resituated at the point where the codified power to punish turns into a disciplinary power to observe; at the point where the universal punishments of the law are applied selectively to certain individuals and always the same ones; at the point where the redefinition of the juridical subject by the penalty becomes a useful training of the criminal; at the point where the law is inverted and passes outside itself, and where the counterlaw becomes the effective and institutionalized content of the juridical forms. What generalizes the power to punish, then, is not the universal consciousness of the law in each juridical subject; it is the regular extension, the infinitely minute web of panoptic techniques.

3. Taken one by one, most of these techniques have a long history behind them. But what was new, in the eighteenth century, was that, by being combined and generalized, they attained a level at which the formation of knowledge and the increase of power regularly reinforce one another in a circular process. At this point, the disciplines crossed the "technological" threshold. First the hospital, then the school, then, later, the workshop were not simply "reordered" by the disciplines; they became, thanks to them, apparatuses such that any mechanism of objectification could be used in them as an instrument of subjection, and any growth of power could give rise in them to possible branches of knowledge; it was this link, proper to the technological systems, that made possible within the disciplinary element the formation of clinical medicine, psychiatry, child psychology, educational psychology, the rationalization of labor. It is a double process, then: an epistemological "thaw" through a refinement of power relations; a multiplication of the effects of power through the formation and accumulation of new forms of knowledge.

The extension of the disciplinary methods is inscribed in a broad historical process: the development at about the same time of many other technologies — agronomical, industrial, economic. But it must be recognized that, compared with the mining industries, the emerging chemical industries or methods of national accountancy, compared with the blast furnaces or the steam engine, panopticism has received little attention. It is regarded as not much more than a bizarre little utopia, a perverse dream — rather as though Bentham had been the Fourier of a police society, and the Phalanstery had taken on the form of the Panopticon. And yet this represented the abstract formula of a very real technology, that of individuals. There were many reasons why it received little praise; the most obvious is that the discourses to which it gave rise rarely acquired, except in the academic classifications, the status of sciences; but the real reason is no doubt that the power that it operates and which it augments is a direct, physical power that men exercise upon one another. An inglorious culmination had an origin that could be only grudgingly acknowledged. But it would be unjust to compare the disciplinary techniques with such inventions as the steam engine or Amici's microscope. They are much less; and yet, in a way, they are much more. If a historical equivalent or at least a point of comparison had to be found for them, it would be rather in the "inquisitorial" technique.

The eighteenth century invented the techniques of discipline and the examination, rather as the Middle Ages invented the judicial investigation.

But it did so by quite different means. The investigation procedure, an old fiscal and administrative technique, had developed above all with the reorganization of the Church and the increase of the princely states in the twelfth and thirteenth centuries. At this time it permeated to a very large degree the jurisprudence first of the ecclesiastical courts, then of the lay courts. The investigation as an authoritarian search for a truth observed or attested was thus opposed to the old procedures of the oath, the ordeal, the judicial duel, the judgment of God, or even of the transaction between private individuals. The investigation was the sovereign power arrogating to itself the right to establish the truth by a number of regulated techniques. Now, although the investigation has since then been an integral part of Western justice (even up to our own day), one must not forget either its political origin, its link with the birth of the states and of monarchical sovereignty, or its later extension and its role in the formation of knowledge. In fact, the investigation has been the no doubt crude, but fundamental, element in the constitution of the empirical sciences; it has been the juridico-political matrix of this experimental knowledge, which, as we know, was very rapidly released at the end of the Middle Ages. It is perhaps true to say that, in Greece, mathematics were born from techniques of measurement; the sciences of nature, in any case, were born, to some extent, at the end of the Middle Ages, from the practices of investigation. The great empirical knowledge that covered the things of the world and transcribed them into the ordering of an indefinite discourse that observes, describes, and establishes the "facts" (at a time when the Western world was beginning the economic and political conquest of this same world) had its operating model no doubt in the Inquisition — that immense invention that our recent mildness has placed in the dark recesses of our memory. But what this politico-juridical, administrative, and criminal, religious and lay, investigation was to the sciences of nature, disciplinary analysis has been to the sciences of man. These sciences, which have so delighted our "humanity" for over a century, have their technical matrix in the petty, malicious minutiae of the disciplines and their investigations. These investigations are perhaps to psychology, psychiatry, pedagogy, criminology, and so many other strange sciences, what the terrible power of investigation was to the calm knowledge of the animals, the plants, or the earth. Another power, another knowledge. On the threshold of the classical age, Bacon, lawyer and statesman, tried to develop a methodology of investigation for the empirical sciences. What Great Observer will produce the methodology of examination for the human sciences? Unless, of course, such a thing is not possible. For, although it is true that, in becoming a technique for the empirical sciences, the investigation has detached itself from the inquisitorial procedure, in which it was historically rooted, the examination has remained extremely close to the disciplinary power that shaped it. It has always been and still is an intrinsic element of the disciplines. Of course it seems to have undergone a speculative purification by integrating itself with such sciences as psychology and psychiatry. And, in effect, its appearance in the form of tests, interviews, interrogations, and consultations is apparently in order to rectify the mechanisms of discipline: educational psychology is supposed to correct the rigors of the school, just as the medical or psychiatric interview is supposed to rectify the effects of the discipline of work. But we must not be misled; these techniques merely refer individuals from one disciplinary authority to another, and they reproduce, in a concentrated or formalized form, the schema of power-knowledge proper to each discipline (on this subject, cf. Tort). The great investigation that gave rise to the sciences of nature has become detached from its politico-juridical model; the examination, on the other hand, is still caught up in disciplinary technology.

In the Middle Ages, the procedure of investigation gradually superseded the old accusatory justice, by a process initiated from above; the disciplinary technique, on the other hand, insidiously and as if from below, has invaded a penal justice that is still, in principle, inquisitorial. All the great movements of extension that characterize modern penality — the problematization of the criminal behind his crime, the concern with a punishment that is a correction, a therapy, a normalization, the division of the act of judgment between various authorities that are supposed to measure, assess, diagnose, cure, transform individuals — all this betrays the penetration of the disciplinary examination into the judicial inquisition.

What is now imposed on penal justice as its point of application, its "useful" object, will no longer be the body of the guilty man set up against the body of the king; nor will it be the juridical subject of an ideal contract; it will be the disciplinary individual. The extreme point of penal justice under the Ancien Régime was the infinite segmentation of the body of the regicide: a manifestation of the strongest power over the body of the greatest criminal, whose total destruction made the crime explode into its truth. The ideal point of penality today would be an indefinite discipline: an interrogation without end, an investigation that would be extended without limit to a meticulous and ever more analytical observation, a judgment that would at the same time be the constitution of a file that was never closed, the calculated leniency of a penalty that would be interlaced with the ruthless curiosity of an examination, a procedure that would be at the same time the permanent measure of a gap in relation to an inaccessible norm and the asymptotic movement that strives to meet in infinity. The public execution was the logical culmination of a procedure governed by the Inquisition. The practice of placing individuals under "observation" is a natural extension of a justice imbued with disciplinary methods and examination procedures. Is it surprising that the cellular prison, with its regular chronologies, forced labor, its authorities of surveillance and registration, its experts in normality, who continue and multiply the functions of the judge, should have become the modern instrument of penalty? Is it surprising that prisons resemble factories, schools, barracks, hospitals, which all resemble prisons?

NOTES

1. Archives militaires de Vincennes, A 1,516 91 sc. Pièce. This regulation is broadly similar to a whole series of others that date from the same period and earlier.

2. In the *Postscript to the Panopticon*, 1791, Bentham adds dark inspection galleries painted in black around the inspector's lodge, each making it possible to observe two stories of cells.

3. In his first version of the *Panopticon*, Bentham had also imagined an acoustic surveillance, operated by means of pipes leading from the cells to the central tower. In the *Postscript* he abandoned the idea, perhaps because he could not introduce into it the principle of dissymmetry and prevent the prisoners from hearing the inspector as well as the inspector hearing them. Julius tried to develop a system of dissymmetrical listening (Julius 18).

4. Imagining this continuous flow of visitors entering the central tower by an underground passage and then observing the circular landscape of the Panopticon, was Bentham aware of the Panoramas that Barker was constructing at exactly the same period (the first seems to have dated from 1787) and in which the visitors, occupying the central place, saw unfolding around them a landscape, a city, or a battle. The visitors occupied exactly the place of the sovereign gaze.

5. In the second half of the eighteenth century, it was often suggested that the army should be used for the surveillance and general partitioning of the population. The army, as yet to undergo discipline in the seventeenth century, was regarded as a force capable of instilling it. Cf., for example, Servan, *Le Soldat citoyen*, 1780.

6. Arsenal, MS. 2565. Under this number, one also finds regulations for charity associations of the seventeenth and eighteenth centuries.

7. Le Maire in a memorandum written at the request of Sartine, in answer to sixteen questions posed by Joseph II on the Parisian police. This memorandum was published by Gazier in 1879.

BIBLIOGRAPHY

Archives militaires de Vincennes, A 1,516 91 sc.
Bentham, J., *Works*, ed. Bowring, IV, 1843.
Chassaigne, M., *La Lieutenance générale de police*, 1906.
Delamare, N., *Traité de police*, 1705.
Demia, C., *Règlement pour les écoles de la ville de Lyon*, 1716.
Des Essarts, T. N., *Dictionnaire universel de police*, 1787.
Funck-Brentano, F., *Catalogue des manuscrits de la bibliothèque de l'Arsenal*, IX.
Guerry, F., and Deleule, D., *Le Corps productif*, 1973.
Julius, N. H., *Leçons sur les prisons*, I, 1831 (Fr. trans.).
Léon, A., *La Révolution française et l'éducation technique*, 1968.
Loisel, G., *Histoire des ménageries*, II, 1912.
Marx, Karl, *Capital*, vol. I, ed. 1970.
Radzinovitz, L., *The English Criminal Law*, II, 1956.
Servan, J., *Le Soldat citoyen*, 1780.
Tort, Michel, *Q.I.*, 1974.
Treilhard, J. B., *Motifs du code d'instruction criminelle*, 1808.
Vattel, E. de, *Le Droit des gens*, 1768.

The "Banking" Concept of Education

Paulo Freire (1921–1997) was a Brazilian educator who was awarded the UNESCO Prize for Peace Education in 1986. Freire is best known for promoting a way of teaching called critical pedagogy, which stresses that students should question power relations in society, particularly those that serve as a means of oppression. As a result of this questioning of authority, those who are oppressed become liberated. Although critical pedagogy is now widely applied, Freire originally practiced this approach with Brazilian peasants, encouraging them to become politically active against those in power. Because of this, Freire was exiled from Brazil after a military coup in 1964, at which point he traveled and taught in Europe and the United States. Upon his return to Brazil sixteen years later, Freire was appointed to the position of minister of education of São Paulo. "The 'Banking' Concept of Education" is a selection from Freire's best-known book, *Pedagogy of the Oppressed* (1970).

■ ■ ■

A careful analysis of the teacher-student relationship at any level inside or outside the school, reveals its fundamentally *narrative* character. This relationship involves a narrating subject (the teacher) and patient, listening objects (the students). The contents, whether values or empirical dimensions of reality, tend in the process of being narrated to become lifeless and petrified. Education is suffering from narration sickness.

The teacher talks about reality as if it were motionless, static, compartmentalized, and predictable. Or else he expounds on a topic completely alien to the existential experience of the students. His task is to "fill" the students with the contents of his narration — contents which are detached from reality, disconnected from the totality that engendered them and could give them significance. Words are emptied of their concreteness and become a hollow, alienated, and alienating verbosity.

The outstanding characteristic of this narrative education, then, is the sonority of words, not their transforming power. "Four times four is sixteen; the capital of Pará is Belém." The student records, memorizes, and repeats these phrases without perceiving what four times four really means, or realizing the true significance of "capital" in the affirmation "the capital of Pará is Belém," that is, what Belém means for Pará and what Pará means for Brazil.

Narration (with the teacher as narrator) leads the students to memorize mechanically the narrated content. Worse yet, it turns them into "containers," into "receptacles" to be "filled" by the teacher. The more completely she fills the receptacles, the better a teacher she is. The more meekly the receptacles permit themselves to be filled, the better students they are.

Education thus becomes an act of depositing, in which the students are the depositories and the teacher is the depositor. Instead of communicating, the teacher issues communiqués and makes deposits which the students patiently receive, memorize, and repeat. This is the "banking" concept of education, in which the scope of action allowed to the students extends only as far as receiving, filing, and storing the deposits. They do, it is true, have the opportunity to become collectors or catalogers of the things they store. But in the last analysis, it is the people themselves who are filed away through the lack of creativity, transformation, and knowledge in this (at best) misguided system. For apart from inquiry, apart from the praxis, individuals cannot be truly human. Knowledge emerges only through invention and reinvention, through the restless, impatient, continuing, hopeful inquiry, human beings pursue in the world, with the world, and with each other.

In the banking concept of education, knowledge is a gift bestowed by those who consider themselves knowledgeable upon those whom they consider to know nothing. Projecting an absolute ignorance onto others, a characteristic of the ideology of oppression, negates education and knowledge as processes of inquiry. The teacher presents himself to his students as their necessary opposite; by considering their ignorance absolute, he justifies his own existence. The students, alienated like the slave in the Hegelian dialectic, accept their ignorance as justifying the teacher's existence — but, unlike the slave, they never discover that they educate the teacher.

The raison d'être of libertarian education, on the other hand, lies in its drive towards reconciliation. Education must begin with the solution of the teacher-student contradiction, by reconciling the poles of the contradiction so that both are simultaneously teachers *and* students.

This solution is not (nor can it be) found in the banking concept. On the contrary, banking education maintains and even stimulates the contradiction through the following attitudes and practices, which mirror oppressive society as a whole:

a. the teacher teaches and the students are taught;
b. the teacher knows everything and the students know nothing;
c. the teacher thinks and the students are thought about;
d. the teacher talks and the students listen — meekly;
e. the teacher disciplines and the students are disciplined;
f. the teacher chooses and enforces his choice, and the students comply;
g. the teacher acts and the students have the illusion of acting through the action of the teacher;
h. the teacher chooses the program content, and the students (who were not consulted) adapt to it;

i. the teacher confuses the authority of knowledge with his or her own professional authority, which she and he sets in opposition to the freedom of the students;

j. the teacher is the Subject of the learning process, while the pupils are mere objects.

It is not surprising that the banking concept of education regards men as adaptable, manageable beings. The more students work at storing the deposits entrusted to them, the less they develop the critical consciousness which would result from their intervention in the world as transformers of that world. The more completely they accept the passive role imposed on them, the more they tend simply to adapt to the world as it is and to the fragmented view of reality deposited in them.

The capability of banking education to minimize or annul the students' creative power and to stimulate their credulity serves the interests of the oppressors, who care neither to have the world revealed nor to see it transformed. The oppressors use their "humanitarianism" to preserve a profitable situation. Thus they react almost instinctively against any experiment in education which stimulates the critical faculties and is not content with a partial view of reality but always seeks out the ties which link one point to another and one problem to another.

Indeed, the interests of the oppressors lie in "changing the consciousness of the oppressed, not the situation which oppresses them"[1] for the more the oppressed can be led to adapt to that situation, the more easily they can be dominated. To achieve this end, the oppressors use the banking concept of education in conjunction with a paternalistic social action apparatus, within which the oppressed receive the euphemistic title of "welfare recipients." They are treated as individual cases, as marginal persons who deviate from the general configuration of a "good, organized, and just" society. The oppressed are regarded as the pathology of the healthy society, which must therefore adjust these "incompetent and lazy" folk to its own patterns by changing their mentality. These marginals need to be "integrated," "incorporated" into the healthy society that they have "forsaken."

The truth is, however, that the oppressed are not "marginals," are not people living "outside" society. They have always been "inside" — inside the structure which made them "beings for others." The solution is not to "integrate" them into the structure of oppression, but to transform that structure so that they can become "beings for themselves." Such transformation, of course, would undermine the oppressors' purposes; hence their utilization of the banking concept of education to avoid the threat of student *conscientização*.

The banking approach to adult education, for example, will never propose to students that they critically consider reality. It will deal instead with such vital questions as whether Roger gave green grass to the goat, and insist upon the importance of learning that on the contrary, Roger gave green grass to the rabbit. The "humanism" of the banking approach masks the effort to turn women and men into automatons — the very negation of their ontological vocation to be more fully human.

Those who use the banking approach, knowingly or unknowingly (for there are innumerable well-intentioned bank-clerk teachers who do not realize that they are serving only to dehumanize), fail to perceive that the deposits themselves contain contradictions about reality. But, sooner or later, these contradictions may lead formerly passive students to turn against their domestication and the attempt to domesticate reality. They may discover through existential experience that their present way of life is irreconcilable with their vocation to become fully human. They may perceive through their relations with reality that reality is really a *process*, undergoing constant transformation. If men and women are searchers and their ontological vocation is humanization, sooner or later they may perceive the contradiction in which banking education seeks to maintain them, and then engage themselves in the struggle for their liberation.

But the humanist, revolutionary educator cannot wait for this possibility to materialize. From the outset, her efforts must coincide with those of the students to engage in critical thinking and the quest for mutual humanization. His efforts must be imbued with a profound trust in people and their creative power. To achieve this, they must be partners of the students in their relations with them.

The banking concept does not admit to such partnership — and necessarily so. To resolve the teacher-student contradiction, to exchange the role of depositor, prescriber, domesticator, for the role of student among students would be to undermine the power of oppression and serve the cause of liberation.

Implicit in the banking concept is the assumption of a dichotomy between human beings and the world: a person is merely *in* the world, not *with* the world or with others; the individual is spectator, not re-creator. In this view, the person is not a conscious being (*corpo consciente*); he or she is rather the possessor of *a* consciousness: an empty "mind" passively open to the reception of deposits of reality from the world outside. For example, my desk, my books, my coffee cup, all the objects before me — as bits of the world which surrounds me — would be "inside" me, exactly as I am inside my study right now. This view makes no distinction between being accessible to consciousness and entering consciousness. The distinction, however, is essential: The objects which surround me are simply accessible to my consciousness, not located within it. I am aware of them, but they are not inside me.

It follows logically from the banking notion of consciousness that the educator's role is to regulate the way the world "enters into" the students. The teacher's task is to organize a process which already occurs spontaneously, to "fill" the students by making deposits of information which he or she considers to constitute true knowledge.[2] And since people "receive" the world as passive entities, education should make them more passive still, and adapt them to the world. The educated individual is the adapted person, because she or he is a better "fit" for the world. Translated into practice, this concept is well suited to the purposes of the oppressors, whose tranquility rests on how well people fit the world the oppressors have created, and how little they question it.

The more completely the majority adapt to the purposes which the dominant minority prescribe for them (thereby depriving them of the right to their own purposes), the more easily the minority can continue to prescribe. The theory and practice of banking education serve this end quite efficiently. Verbalistic lessons, reading requirements,[3] the methods for evaluating "knowledge," the distance between the teacher and the taught, the criteria for promotion: everything in this ready-to-wear approach serves to obviate thinking.

The bank-clerk educator does not realize that there is no true security in his hypertrophied role, that one must seek to live *with* others in solidarity. One cannot impose oneself, nor even merely, coexist with one's students. Solidarity requires true communication, and the concept by which such an educator is guided fears and proscribes communication.

Yet only through communication can human life hold meaning. The teacher's thinking is authenticated only by the authenticity of the students' thinking. The teacher cannot think for her students, nor can she impose her thought on them. Authentic thinking, thinking that is concerned about *reality*, does not take place in ivory-tower isolation, but only in communication. If it is true that thought has meaning only when generated by action upon the world, the subordination of students to teachers becomes impossible.

Because banking education begins with a false understanding of men and women as objects, it cannot promote the development of what Fromm calls "biophily," but instead produces its opposite: "necrophily."

> While life is characterized by growth in a structured, functional manner, the necrophilous person loves all that does not grow, all that is mechanical. The necrophilous person is driven by the desire to transform the organic into the inorganic, to approach life mechanically, as if all living persons were things. . . . Memory, rather than experience; having, rather than being, is what counts. The necrophilous person can relate to an object — a flower or a person — only if he possesses it; hence a threat to his possession is a threat to himself; if he loses possession he loses contact with the world. . . . He loves control, and in the act of controlling he kills life.[4]

Oppression — overwhelming control — is necrophilic; it is nourished by love of death, not life. The banking concept of education, which serves the interests of oppression, is also necrophilic. Based on a mechanistic, static, naturalistic, spatialized view of consciousness, it transforms students into receiving objects. It attempts to control thinking and action, leads women and men to adjust to the world, and inhibits their creative power.

When their efforts to act responsibly are frustrated, when they find themselves unable to use their faculties, people suffer. "This suffering due to impotence is rooted in the very fact that the human equilibrium has been disturbed."[5] But the inability to act which causes people's anguish also causes them to reject their impotence, by attempting

> . . . to restore [their] capacity to act. But can [they], and how? One way is to submit to and identify with a person or group having power. By this symbolic participation in another person's life, [men have] the illusion of acting, when in reality [they] only submit to and become a part of those who act.[6]

Populist manifestations perhaps best exemplify this type of behavior by the oppressed, who, by identifying with charismatic leaders, come to feel that they themselves are active and effective. The rebellion they express as they emerge in the historical process is motivated by that desire to act effectively. The dominant elites consider the remedy to be more domination and repression, carried out in the name of freedom, order, and social peace (that is, the peace of the elites). Thus they can condemn — logically, from their point of view — "the violence of a strike by workers and [can] call upon the state in the same breath to use violence in putting down the strike."[7]

Education as the exercise of domination stimulates the credulity of students, with the ideological intent (often not perceived by educators) of indoctrinating them to adapt to the world of oppression. This accusation is not made in the naive hope that the dominant elites will thereby simply abandon the practice. Its objective is to call the attention of true humanists to the fact that they cannot use banking educational methods in the pursuit of liberation, for they would only negate that very pursuit. Nor may a revolutionary society inherit these methods from an oppressor society. The revolutionary society which practices banking education is either misguided or mistrusting of people. In either event, it is threatened by the specter of reaction.

Unfortunately, those who espouse the cause of liberation are themselves surrounded and influenced by the climate which generates the banking concept, and often do not perceive its true significance or its dehumanizing power. Paradoxically, then, they utilize this same instrument of alienation in what they consider an effort to liberate. Indeed, some "revolutionaries" brand as "innocents," "dreamers," or even "reactionaries" those who would challenge this educational practice. But one does not liberate people by alienating them. Authentic liberation — the process of humanization — is not another deposit to be made in men. Liberation is a praxis: the action and reflection of men and women upon their world in order to transform it. Those truly committed to the cause of liberation can accept neither the mechanistic concept of consciousness as an empty vessel to be filled, nor the use of banking methods of domination (propaganda, slogans — deposits) in the name of liberation.

Those truly committed to liberation must reject the banking concept in its entirety, adopting instead a concept of women and men as conscious beings, and consciousness as consciousness intent upon the world. They must abandon the educational goal of deposit-making and replace it with the posing of the problems of human beings in their relations with the world. "Problem-posing" education, responding to the essence of consciousness — *intentionality* — rejects communiqués and embodies communications. It epitomizes the special characteristic of consciousness: being *conscious of*, not only as intent on objects but as turned in upon itself in a Jasperian "split" — consciousness as consciousness *of* consciousness.

Liberating education consists in acts of cognition, not transferrals of information. It is a learning situation in which the cognizable object (far from being the end of the cognitive act) intermediates the cognitive actors — teacher on the one hand and students on the other. Accordingly, the practice of problem-posing education entails at the outset that the teacher-student contradiction be resolved. Dialogical relations — indispensable to the capacity of cognitive actors to cooperate in perceiving the same cognizable object — are otherwise impossible.

Indeed, problem-posing education, which breaks with the vertical patterns characteristic of banking education, can fulfil its function as the practice of freedom only if it can overcome the above contradiction. Through dialogue, the teacher-of-the-students and the students-of-the-teacher cease to exist and a new term emerges: teacher-student with students-teachers. The teacher is no longer merely the-one-who-teaches, but one who is himself taught in dialogue with the students, who in turn while being taught also teach. They become jointly responsible for a process in which all grow. In this process, arguments based on "authority" are no longer valid; in order to function, authority must be *on the side of* freedom, not *against* it. Here, no one teaches another, nor is anyone self-taught. People teach each other, mediated by the world, by the cognizable objects which in banking education are "owned" by the teacher.

The banking concept (with its tendency to dichotomize everything) distinguishes two stages in the action of the educator. During the first, he cognizes a cognizable object while he prepares his lessons in his study or his laboratory; during the second, he expounds to his students about that object. The students are not called upon to know, but to memorize the contents narrated by the teacher. Nor do the students practice any act of cognition, since the object towards which that act should be directed is the property of the teacher rather than a medium evoking the critical reflection of both teacher and students. Hence in the name of the "preservation of culture and knowledge" we have a system which achieves neither true knowledge nor true culture.

The problem-posing method does not dichotomize the activity of the teacher-student: she is not "cognitive" at one point and "narrative" at another. She is always "cognitive," whether preparing a project or engaging in dialogue with the students. He does not regard cognizable objects as his private property but as the object of reflection by himself and the students. In this way, the problem-posing educator constantly re-forms his reflections in the reflection of the students. The students — longer docile listeners — are now critical coinvestigators in dialogue with the teacher. The teacher presents the material to the students for their consideration, and reconsiders her earlier considerations as the students express their own. The role of the problem-posing educator is to create, together with the students, the conditions under which knowledge at the level of the *doxa* is superseded by true knowledge, at the level of the *logos*.

Whereas banking education anesthetizes and inhibits creative power, problem-posing education involves a constant unveiling of reality. The former attempts to maintain the *submersion* of consciousness; the latter strives for the *emergence* of consciousness and *critical intervention* in reality.

Students, as they are increasingly posed with problems relating to themselves in the world and with the world, will feel increasingly challenged and obliged to respond to that challenge. Because they apprehend the challenge as interrelated to other problems within a total context, not as a theoretical question, the resulting comprehension tends to be increasingly critical and thus constantly less alienated. Their response to the challenge evokes new challenges, followed by new understandings; and gradually the students come to regard themselves as committed.

Education as the practice of freedom — as opposed to education as the practice of domination — denies that man is abstract, isolated, independent, and unattached to the world; it also denies that the world exists as a reality apart from people. Authentic reflection considers neither abstract man nor the world without people, but people in their relations with the world. In these relations consciousness and world are simultaneous: Consciousness neither precedes the world nor follows it.

> La conscience et le monde sont donnés d'un même coup: extérieur par essence à la conscience, le monde est, par essence relatif à elle.[8]

In one of our culture circles in Chile, the group was discussing (based on a codification) the anthropological concept of culture. In the midst of the discussion, a peasant who by banking standards was completely ignorant said: "Now I see that without man there is no world." When the educator responded: "Let's say, for the sake of argument, that all the men on earth were to die, but that the earth itself remained, together with trees, birds, animals, rivers, seas, the stars. . . . wouldn't all this be a world?" "Oh no," the peasant replied emphatically. "There would be no one to say: 'This is a world.'"

The peasant wished to express the idea that there would be lacking the consciousness of the world which necessarily implies the world of consciousness. *I* cannot exist without a *non-I*. In turn, the *not-I* depends on that existence. The world which brings consciousness into existence becomes the world *of* that consciousness. Hence, the previously cited affirmation of Sartre: "*La conscience et le mond sont donnés d'un même coup.*"

As women and men, simultaneously reflecting on themselves and on the world, increase the scope of their perception, they begin to direct their observations towards previously inconspicuous phenomena:

> In perception properly so-called, as an explicit awareness [*Gewahren*], I am turned towards the object, to the paper, for instance. I apprehend it as being this here and now. The apprehension is a singling out, every object having a background in experience. Around and about the paper lie books, pencils, inkwell, and so forth, and these in a certain sense are also "perceived," perceptually there, in the "field of intuition"; but whilst I was turned towards the paper there was no turning in their direction, nor any apprehending of them, not even in a secondary sense. They appeared and yet were not singled out, were not posited on their own account. Every perception of a thing has such a zone of background intuitions or background awareness, if "intuiting" already includes the state of being turned towards, and this also is a "conscious experience," or more briefly a "consciousness of" all indeed that in point of fact lies in the co-perceived objective background.[9]

That which had existed objectively but had not been perceived in its deeper implications (if indeed it was perceived at all) begins to "stand out," assuming the character of a problem and therefore of challenge. Thus, men and women begin to single out elements from their "background awareness" and to reflect upon them. These elements are now objects of their consideration, and, as such, objects of their action and cognition.

In problem-posing education, people develop their power to perceive critically *the way they exist* in the world *with which* and *in which* they find themselves; they come to see the world not as a static reality, but as a reality in process, in transformation. Although the dialectical relations of women and men with the world exist independently of how these relations are perceived (or whether or not they are perceived at all), it is also true that the form of action they adopt is to a large extent a function of how they perceive themselves in the world. Hence, the teacher-student and the students-teachers reflect simultaneously on themselves and the world without dichotomizing this reflection from action, and thus establish an authentic form of thought and action.

Once again, the two educational concepts and practices under analysis come into conflict. Banking education (for obvious reasons) attempts, by mythicizing reality, to conceal certain facts which explain the way human beings exist in the world; problem-posing education sets itself the task of demythologizing. Banking education resists dialogue; problem-posing education regards dialogue as indispensable to the act of cognition which unveils reality. Banking education treats students as objects of assistance; problem-posing education makes them critical thinkers. Banking education inhibits creativity and domesticates (although it cannot completely destroy) the *intentionality* of consciousness by isolating consciousness from the world, thereby denying people their ontological and historical vocation of becoming more fully human. Problem-posing education bases itself on creativity and stimulates true reflection and action upon reality; thereby responding to the vocation of persons as beings who are authentic only when engaged in inquiry and creative transformation. In sum: Banking theory and practice, as immobilizing and fixating forces, fail to acknowledge men and women as historical beings; problem-posing theory and practice take the people's historicity as their starting point.

Problem-posing education affirms men and women as beings in the process of *becoming* — as unfinished, uncompleted beings in and with a likewise unfinished reality. Indeed, in contrast to other animals who are unfinished, but not historical, people know themselves to be unfinished; they are aware of their incompletion. In this incompletion and this awareness lie the very roots of education as an exclusively human manifestation. The unfinished character of human beings and the transformational character of reality necessitate that education be an ongoing activity.

Education is thus constantly remade in the praxis. In order to *be*, it must *become*. Its "duration" (in the Bergsonian meaning of the word) is found in the interplay of the opposites *permanence* and *change*. The banking method emphasizes permanence and becomes reactionary; problem-posing education — which accepts neither a "well-behaved" present nor a predetermined fixture — roots itself in the dynamic present and becomes revolutionary.

Problem-posing education is revolutionary futurity. Hence it is prophetic (and, as such, hopeful). Hence, it corresponds to the historical nature of humankind. Hence, it affirms women and men as beings who transcend themselves, who move forward and look ahead, for whom immobility represents a fatal threat, for whom looking at the past must only be a means of understanding more clearly what and who they are so that they can more wisely build the future. Hence, it identifies with the movement which engages people as beings aware of their incompletion — an historical movement which has its point of departure, its Subjects and its objective.

The point of departure of the movement lies in the people themselves. But since people do not exist apart from the world, apart from reality, the movement must begin with the human-world relationship. Accordingly, the point of departure must always be with men and women in the "here and now," which constitutes the situation within which they are submerged, from which they emerge, and in which they intervene. Only by starting from this situation — which determines their perception of it — can they begin to move. To do this authentically they must perceive their state not as fated and unalterable, but merely as limiting — and therefore challenging.

Whereas the banking method directly or indirectly reinforces men's fatalistic perception of their situation, the problem-posing method presents this very situation to them as a problem. As the situation becomes the object of their cognition, the naive or magical perception which produced their fatalism gives way to perception which is able to perceive itself even as it perceives reality, and can thus be critically objective about that reality.

A deepened consciousness of their situation leads people to apprehend that situation as a historical reality susceptible of transformation. Resignation gives way to the drive for transformation and inquiry, over which men feel themselves to be in control. If people, as historical beings necessarily engaged with other people in a movement of inquiry, did not control that movement, it would be (and is) a violation of their humanity. Any situation in which some individuals prevent others from engaging in the process of inquiry is one of violence. The means used are not important; to alienate human beings from their own decision-making is to change them into objects.

This movement of inquiry must be directed towards humanization — the people's historical vocation. The pursuit of full humanity, however, cannot be carried out in isolation or individualism, but only in fellowship and solidarity; therefore it cannot unfold in the antagonistic relations between oppressors and oppressed. No one can be authentically human while he prevents others from being so. Attempting *to be more* human, individualistically, leads to *having more*, egotistically, a form of dehumanization. Not that it is not fundamental *to have* in order *to be* human. Precisely because it *is* necessary, some men's *having* must not be allowed to constitute an obstacle to others, *having*, must not consolidate the power of the former to crush the latter.

Problem-posing education, as a humanist and liberating praxis, posits as fundamental that the people subjected to domination must fight for their emancipation. To that end, it enables teachers and students to become Subjects of the educational process by overcoming authoritarianism and an alienating intellectualism; it also enables people to overcome their false perception of reality. The world — no longer something to be described with deceptive words — becomes the object of that transforming action by men and women which results in their humanization.

Problem-posing education does not and cannot serve the interests of the oppressor. No oppressive order could permit the oppressed to begin to question: Why? While only a revolutionary society can carry out this education in systematic terms, the revolutionary leaders need not take full power before they can employ the method. In the revolutionary process, the leaders cannot utilize the banking method as an interim measure, justified on grounds of expediency, with the intention of *later* behaving in a genuinely revolutionary fashion. They must be revolutionary — that is to say dialogical — from the outset.

NOTES

1. Simone de Beauvoir, *La pensée de droite, aujourd'hui* (Paris); ST, *El pensamiento político de la derecha* (Buenos Aires, 1963), p. 34.

2. This concept corresponds to what Sartre calls the "digestive" or "nutritive" concept of education, in which knowledge is "fed" by the teacher to the students to "fill them out." See Jean-Paul Sartre, "Une idée fondamentale de la phénoménologie de Husserl: L'intentionalité," *Situations* I (Paris, 1947).

3. For example, some professors specify in their reading lists that a book should be read from pages 10 to 15 — and do this to "help" their students!

4. Eric Fromm, *The Heart of Man* (New York, 1966), p. 41.

5. Ibid., p. 31.

6. Ibid.

7. Reinhold Niebuhr, *Moral Man and Immoral Society* (New York, 1960), p. 130.

8. Sartre, op. cit., p. 32. [The passage is obscure but could be read as "Consciousness and the world are given simultaneously: The outside world as it enters consciousness is relative to our ways of perceiving it." — Editor's note]

9. Edmund Husserl, *Ideas — General Introduction to Pure Phenomenology* (London, 1969), pp. 105–06.

■ **CLIFFORD GEERTZ** ─────────────────────────

Thick Description: Toward an Interpretive Theory of Culture

Clifford Geertz (1926–2006) was a cultural anthropologist whose theories of cultural interpretation are still highly influential, both in anthropology and in other social sciences. In addition to teaching at UC Berkeley, University of Chicago, and Oxford University, Geertz performed field research in Java, Morocco, and Bali. It was through this field research that he came to believe that anthropology could not make universal claims regarding cultures; rather, cultures must be considered as texts, and as such they always demand an act of interpretation. Interpretative anthropology, therefore, cannot seek universal principles of culture, but instead must search for the meaning and context of cultural behavior. This topic is explored in detail in "Thick Description," a selection from Geertz's collection of essays *The Interpretation of Cultures* (1973), which is considered to be one of the most influential social science texts of the last century.

■ ■ ■

I

In her book, *Philosophy in a New Key*, Susanne Langer remarks that certain ideas burst upon the intellectual landscape with a tremendous force. They resolve so many fundamental problems at once that they seem also to promise that they will resolve all fundamental problems, clarify all obscure issues. Everyone snaps them up as the open sesame of some new positive science, the conceptual center-point around which a comprehensive system of analysis can be built. The sudden vogue of such a *grande idée*, crowding out almost everything else for a while, is due, she says, "to the fact that all sensitive and active minds turn at once to exploiting it. We try it in every connection, for every purpose, experiment with possible stretches of its strict meaning, with generalizations and derivatives."

After we have become familiar with the new idea, however, after it has become part of our general stock of theoretical concepts, our expectations are brought more into balance with its actual uses, and its excessive popularity is ended. A few zealots persist in the old key-to-the-universe view of it; but less driven thinkers settle down after a while to the problems the idea has really generated. They try to apply it and extend it where it applies and where it is capable of extension; and they desist where it does not apply or cannot be extended. It becomes, if it was, in truth, a seminal idea in the first place, a permanent and enduring part of our intellectual armory. But it no longer has the grandiose, all-promising scope, the infinite versatility of apparent application, it once had. The second law of thermodynamics, or the principle of natural selection, or the notion of unconscious motivation, or the organization of the means of production does not explain everything, not even everything human, but it still explains something; and our attention shifts to isolating just what that something is, to disentangling ourselves from a lot of pseudoscience to which, in the first flush of its celebrity, it has also given rise.

Whether or not this is, in fact, the way all centrally important scientific concepts develop, I don't know. But certainly this pattern fits the concept of culture, around which the whole discipline of anthropology arose, and whose domination that discipline has been increasingly concerned to limit, specify, focus, and contain. It is to this cutting of the culture concept down to size, therefore actually insuring its continued importance rather than undermining it, that the essays below are all, in their several ways and from their several directions, dedicated. They all argue, sometimes explicitly, more often merely through the particular analysis they develop, for a narrowed, specialized, and, so I imagine, theoretically more powerful concept of culture to replace E. B. Tylor's famous "most complex whole," which, its originative power not denied, seems to me to have reached the point where it obscures a good deal more than it reveals.

The conceptual morass into which the Tylorean kind of *pot-au-feu* theorizing about culture can lead, is evident in what is still one of the better general introductions to anthropology, Clyde Kluckhohn's *Mirror for Man*. In some twenty-seven pages of his chapter on the concept, Kluckhohn managed to define culture in turn as: (1) "the total way of life of a people"; (2) "the social legacy the individual acquires from his group"; (3) "a way of thinking, feeling, and believing"; (4) "an abstraction from behavior"; (5) a theory on the part of the anthropologist about the way in which a group of people in fact behave; (6) a "storehouse of pooled learning"; (7) "a set of standardized orientations to recurrent problems"; (8) "learned behavior"; (9) a mechanism for the normative regulation of behavior; (10) "a set of techniques for adjusting both to the external environment and to other men"; (11) "a precipitate of history"; and turning, perhaps in desperation, to similes, as a map, as a sieve, and as a matrix. In the face of this sort of theoretical diffusion, even a somewhat constricted and not entirely standard concept of culture, which is at least internally coherent and, more important, which has a definable argument to make is (as, to be fair, Kluckhohn himself keenly realized) an improvement. Eclecticism is self-defeating not because there is only one direction in which it is useful to move, but because there are so many: it is necessary to choose.

The concept of culture I espouse, and whose utility the essays below attempt to demonstrate, is essentially a semiotic one. Believing, with Max Weber, that man is an animal suspended in webs of significance he himself has spun, I take culture to be those webs, and the analysis of it to be therefore not an experimental science in search of law but an interpretive one in search of meaning. It is explication I am after, construing social expressions on their surface enigmatical. But this pronouncement, a doctrine in a clause, demands itself some explication.

II

Operationalism as a methodological dogma never made much sense so far as the social sciences are concerned, and except for a few rather too well-swept corners — Skinnerian behaviorism, intelligence testing, and so on — it is largely dead now. But it had, for all that, an important point to make, which, however we may feel about trying to define charisma or alienation in terms of operations, retains a certain force: if you want to understand what a science is, you should look in the first instance not at its theories or its findings, and certainly not at what its apologists say about it; you should look at what the practitioners of it do.

In anthropology, or anyway social anthropology, what the practitioners do is ethnography. And it is in understanding what ethnography is, or more exactly *what doing ethnography is*, that a start can be made toward grasping what anthropological analysis amounts to as a form of knowledge. This, it must immediately be said, is not a matter of methods. From one point of view, that of the textbook, doing ethnography is establishing rapport, selecting informants, transcribing texts, taking genealogies, mapping fields, keeping a diary, and so on. But it is not these things, techniques and received procedures, that define the enterprise. What defines it is the kind of intellectual effort it is: an elaborate venture in, to borrow a notion from Gilbert Ryle, "thick description."

Ryle's discussion of "thick description" appears in two recent essays of his (now reprinted in the second volume of his *Collected Papers*) addressed to the general question of what, as he puts it, *"Le Penseur"* is doing: "Thinking and Reflecting" and "The Thinking of Thoughts." Consider, he says, two boys rapidly contracting the eyelids of their right eyes. In one, this is an involuntary twitch; in the other, a conspiratorial signal to a friend. The two movements are, as movements, identical; from an I-am-a-camera, "phenomenalistic" observation of them alone, one could not tell which was twitch and which was wink, or indeed whether both or either was twitch or wink. Yet the difference, however unphotographable, between a twitch and a wink is vast; as anyone unfortunate enough to have had the first taken for the second knows. The winker is communicating, and indeed communicating in a quite precise and special way: (1) deliberately, (2) to someone in particular, (3) to impart a particular message, (4) according to a socially established code, and (5) without cognizance of the rest of the company. As Ryle points out, the winker has not done two things, contracted his eyelids and winked, while the twitcher has done only one, contracted his eyelids. Contracting your eyelids on purpose when there exists a public code in which so doing counts as a conspiratorial signal *is* winking. That's all there is to it: a speck of behavior, a fleck of culture, and — *voilà!* — a gesture.

That, however, is just the beginning. Suppose, he continues, there is a third boy, who, "to give malicious amusement to his cronies," parodies the first boy's wink, as amateurish, clumsy, obvious, and so on. He, of course, does this in the same way the second boy winked and the first twitched: by contracting his right eyelids. Only this boy is neither winking nor twitching, he is parodying someone else's, as he takes it, laughable, attempt at winking. Here, too, a socially established code exists (he will "wink" laboriously, overobviously, perhaps adding a grimace — the usual artifices of the clown); and so also does a message. Only now it is not conspiracy but ridicule that is in the air. If the others think he is actually winking, his whole project misfires as completely, though with somewhat different results, as if they think he is twitching. One can go further: uncertain of his mimicking abilities, the would-be satirist may practice at home before the mirror, in which case he is not twitching, winking, or parodying, but rehearsing; though so far as what a camera, a radical behaviorist, or a believer in protocol sentences would record he is just rapidly contracting his right eyelids like all the others. Complexities are possible, if not practically without end, at least logically so. The original winker might, for example, actually have been fake-winking, say, to mislead outsiders into imagining there was a conspiracy afoot when there in fact was not, in which case our descriptions of what the parodist is parodying and the rehearser rehearsing of course shift accordingly. But the point is that between what Ryle calls the "thin description" of what the rehearser (parodist, winker, twitcher . . .) is doing ("rapidly contracting his right eyelids") and the "thick description" of what he is doing ("practicing a burlesque of a friend faking a wink to deceive an innocent into thinking a conspiracy is in motion") lies the object of ethnography: a stratified hierarchy of meaningful structures in terms of which twitches, winks, fake-winks, parodies, rehearsals of parodies are produced, perceived, and interpreted, and without which they would not (not even the zero-form twitches, which, *as a cultural category*, are as much nonwinks as winks are nontwitches) in fact exist, no matter what anyone did or didn't do with his eyelids.

Like so many of the little stories Oxford philosophers like to make up for themselves, all this winking, fake-winking, burlesque-fake-winking, rehearsed-burlesque-fake-winking, may seem a bit artificial. In way of adding a more empirical note, let me give, deliberately unpreceded by any prior explanatory comment at all, a not untypical excerpt from my own field journal to demonstrate that, however evened off for didactic purposes, Ryle's example presents an image only too exact of the sort of piled-up structures of inference and implication through which an ethnographer is continually trying to pick his way:

> The French [the informant said] had only just arrived. They set up twenty or so small forts between here, the town, and the Marmusha area up in the middle of the mountains, placing them on promontories so they could survey the countryside. But for all this they couldn't guarantee safety, especially at night, so although the *mezrag*, trade-pact, system was supposed to be legally abolished it in fact continued as before.
>
> One night, when Cohen (who speaks fluent Berber), was up there, at Marmusha, two other Jews who were traders to a neighboring tribe came by to purchase some goods from him. Some Berbers, from yet another neighboring tribe, tried to break into Cohen's place, but he fired his rifle in the air. (Traditionally, Jews were not allowed to carry weapons; but at this period things were so unsettled many did so anyway.) This attracted the attention of the French and the marauders fled.
>
> The next night, however, they came back, one of them disguised as a woman who knocked on the door with some sort of a story. Cohen was suspicious and didn't want to let "her" in, but the other Jews said, "oh, it's all right, it's only a woman," So they opened the door and the whole lot came pouring in. They killed the two visiting Jews, but Cohen managed to barricade himself in an adjoining room. He heard the robbers planning to burn him alive in the shop after they removed his goods, and so he opened the door and, laying about him wildly with a club, managed to escape through a window.
>
> He went up to the fort, then, to have his wounds dressed, and complained to the local commandant, one Captain Dumari, saying he wanted his *'ar* — i.e., four or five times the value of the merchandise stolen from him. The robbers were from a tribe which had not yet submitted to French authority and were in open rebellion against it, and he wanted authorization to go with his *mezrag*-holder, the Marmusha tribal *sheikh*, to collect the indemnity, that, under traditional rules, he had coming to him. Captain Dumari couldn't officially give him permission to do this, because of the French prohibition of the *mezrag* relationship, but he gave him verbal authorization, saying, "If you get killed, it's your problem."
>
> So the *sheikh*, the Jew, and a small company of armed Marmushans went off ten or fifteen kilometers up into the rebellious area, where there were of course no French, and, sneaking up, captured the thief-tribe's shepherd and stole its herds. The other tribe soon came riding out on horses after them, armed with rifles and ready to attack. But when they saw who the "sheep thieves" were, they thought better of it and said, "all right, we'll talk." They couldn't really deny what had happened — that some of their men had robbed

Cohen and killed the two visitors — and they weren't prepared to start the serious feud with the Marmusha a scuffle with the invading party would bring on. So the two groups talked, and talked, and talked, there on the plain amid the thousands of sheep, and decided finally on five-hundred-sheep damages. The two armed Berber groups then lined up on their horses at opposite ends of the plain, with the sheep herded between them, and Cohen, in his black gown, pillbox hat, and flapping slippers, went out alone among the sheep, picking out, one by one and at his own good speed, the best ones for his payment.

So Cohen got his sheep and drove them back to Marmusha. The French, up in their fort, heard them coming from some distance ("Ba, ba, ba" said Cohen, happily, recalling the image) and said, "What the hell is that?" And Cohen said, "That is my '*ar*." The French couldn't believe he had actually done what he said he had done, and accused him of being a spy for the rebellious Berbers, put him in prison, and took his sheep. In the town, his family, not having heard from him in so long a time, thought he was dead. But after a while the French released him and he came back home, but without his sheep. He then went to the Colonel in the town, the Frenchman in charge of the whole region, to complain. But the Colonel said, "I can't do anything about the matter. It's not my problem."

Quoted raw, a note in a bottle, this passage conveys, as any similar one similarly presented would do, a fair sense of how much goes into ethnographic description of even the most elemental sort — how extraordinarily "thick" it is. In finished anthropological writings, including those collected here, this fact — that what we call our data are really our own constructions of other people's constructions of what they and their compatriots are up to — is obscured because most of what we need to comprehend a particular event, ritual, custom, idea, or whatever is insinuated as background information before the thing itself is directly examined. (Even to reveal that this little drama took place in the highlands of central Morocco in 1912 — and was recounted there in 1968 — is to determine much of our understanding of it.) There is nothing particularly wrong with this, and it is in any case inevitable. But it does lead to a view of anthropological research as rather more of an observational and rather less of an interpretive activity than it really is. Right down at the factual base, the hard rock, insofar as there is any, of the whole enterprise, we are already explicating: and worse, explicating explications. Winks upon winks upon winks.

Analysis, then, is sorting out the structures of signification — what Ryle called established codes, a somewhat misleading expression, for it makes the enterprise sound too much like that of the cipher clerk when it is much more like that of the literary critic — and determining their social ground and import. Here, in our text, such sorting would begin with distinguishing the three unlike frames of interpretation ingredient in the situation, Jewish, Berber, and French, and would then move on to show how (and why) at that time, in that place, their copresence produced a situation in which systematic misunderstanding reduced traditional form to social farce. What tripped Cohen up, and with him the whole, ancient pattern of social and economic relationships within which he functioned, was a confusion of tongues.

I shall come back to this too-compacted aphorism later, as well as to the details of the text itself. The point for now is only that ethnography is thick description. What the ethnographer is in fact faced with — except when (as, of course, he must do) he is pursuing the more automatized routines of data collection — is a multiplicity of complex conceptual structures, many of them superimposed upon or knotted into one another, which are at once strange, irregular, and inexplicit, and which he must contrive somehow first to grasp and then to render. And this is true at the most down-to-earth, jungle field work levels of his activity: interviewing informants, observing rituals, eliciting kin terms, tracing property lines, censusing households . . . writing his journal. Doing ethnography is like trying to read (in the sense of "construct a reading of") a manuscript — foreign, faded, full of ellipses, incoherencies, suspicious emendations, and tendentious commentaries, but written not in conventionalized graphs of sound but in transient examples of shaped behavior.

III

Culture, this acted document, thus is public, like a burlesqued wink or a mock sheep raid. Though ideational, it does not exist in someone's head; though unphysical, it is not an occult entity. The interminable, because unterminable, debate within anthropology as to whether culture is "subjective" or "objective," together with the mutual exchange of intellectual insults ("idealist!" — "materialist!"; "mentalist!" — "behaviorist!"; "impressionist!" — "positivist!") which accompanies it, is wholly misconceived. Once human behavior is seen as (most of the time; there *are* true twitches) symbolic action — action which, like phonation in speech, pigment in painting, line in writing, or sonance in music, signifies — the question as to whether culture is patterned conduct or a frame of mind, or even the two somehow mixed together, loses sense. The thing to ask about a burlesqued wink or a mock sheep raid is not what their ontological status is. It is the same as that of rocks on the one hand and dreams on the other — they are things of this world. The thing to ask is what their import is: what it is, ridicule or challenge, irony or anger, snobbery or pride, that, in their occurrence and through their agency, is getting said.

This may seem like an obvious truth, but there are a number of ways to obscure it. One is to imagine that culture is a self-contained "superorganic" reality with forces and purposes of its own; that is, to reify it. Another is to claim that it consists in the brute pattern of behavioral events we observe in fact to occur in some identifiable community or other; that is, to reduce it. But though both these confusions still exist, and doubtless will be always with us, the main source of theoretical muddlement in contemporary anthropology is a view which developed in reaction to them and is right now very widely held — namely, that, to quote Ward Goodenough, perhaps its leading proponent, "culture [is located] in the minds and hearts of men."

Variously called ethnoscience, componential analysis, or cognitive anthropology (a terminological wavering which reflects a deeper uncertainty), this school of thought holds that culture is composed of psychological structures by means of which individuals or groups of individuals guide their behavior. "A society's culture," to quote Goodenough again, this time in a passage which has become the *locus classicus* of the whole movement, "consists of whatever it is one has to know or believe in order to operate in a manner acceptable to its members." And from this view of what culture is follows a view, equally assured, of what describing it is — the writing out of systematic rules, an ethnographic algorithm, which, if followed, would make it possible so to operate, to pass (physical appearance aside) for a native. In such a way, extreme subjectivism is married to extreme formalism, with the expected result: an explosion of debate as to whether particular analyses (which come in the form of taxonomies, paradigms, tables, trees, and other ingenuities) reflect what the natives "really" think or are merely clever simulations, logically equivalent but substantively different, of what they think.

As, on first glance, this approach may look close enough to the one being developed here to be mistaken for it, it is useful to be explicit as to what divides them. If, leaving our winks and sheep behind for the moment, we take, say, a Beethoven quartet as an, admittedly rather special but, for these purposes, nicely illustrative, sample of culture, no one would, I think, identify it with its score, with the skills and knowledge needed to play it, with the understanding of it possessed by its performers or auditors, nor, to take care, *en passant*, of the reductionists and reifiers, with a particular performance of it or with some mysterious entity transcending material existence. The "no one" is perhaps too strong here, for there are always incorrigibles. But that a Beethoven quartet is a temporally developed tonal structure, a coherent sequence of modeled sound — in a word, music — and not anybody's knowledge of or belief about anything, including how to play it, is a proposition to which most people are, upon reflection, likely to assent.

To play the violin it is necessary to possess certain habits, skills, knowledge, and talents, to be in the mood to play, and (as the old joke goes) to have a violin. But violin playing is neither the habits, skills, knowledge, and so on, nor the mood, nor (the notion believers in "material culture" apparently embrace) the violin. To make a trade pact in Morocco, you have to do certain things in certain ways (among others, cut, while chanting Quranic Arabic, the throat of a lamb before the assembled, undeformed, adult male members of your tribe) and to be possessed of certain psychological characteristics (among others, a desire for distant things).

But a trade pact is neither the throat cutting nor the desire, though it is real enough, as seven kinsmen of our Marmusha sheikh discovered when, on an earlier occasion, they were executed by him following the theft of one mangy, essentially valueless sheepskin from Cohen.

Culture is public because meaning is. You can't wink (or burlesque one) without knowing what counts as winking or how, physically, to contract your eyelids, and you can't conduct a sheep raid (or mimic one) without knowing what it is to steal a sheep and how practically to go about it. But to draw from such truths the conclusion that knowing how to wink is winking and knowing how to steal a sheep is sheep raiding is to betray as deep a confusion as, taking thin descriptions for thick, to identify winking with eyelid contractions or sheep raiding with chasing woolly animals out of pastures. The cognitivist fallacy — that culture consists (to quote another spokesman for the movement, Stephen Tyler) of "mental phenomena which can [he means "should"] be analyzed by formal methods similar to those of mathematics and logic" — is as destructive of an effective use of the concept as are the behaviorist and idealist fallacies to which it is a misdrawn correction. Perhaps, as its errors are more sophisticated and its distortions subtler, it is even more so.

The generalized attack on privacy theories of meaning is, since early Husserl and late Wittgenstein, so much a part of modern thought that it need not be developed once more here. What is necessary is to see to it that the news of it reaches anthropology; and in particular that it is made clear that to say that culture consists of socially established structures of meaning in terms of which people do such things as signal conspiracies and join them or perceive insults and answer them, is no more to say that it is a psychological phenomenon, a characteristic of someone's mind, personality, cognitive structure, or whatever, than to say that Tantrism, genetics, the progressive form of the verb, the classification of wines, the Common Law, or the notion of "a conditional curse" (as Westermarck defined the concept of 'ar in terms of which Cohen pressed his claim to damages) is. What, in a place like Morocco, most prevents those of us who grew up winking other winks or attending other sheep from grasping what people are up to is not ignorance as to how cognition works (though, especially as, one assumes, it works the same among them as it does among us, it would greatly help to have less of that too) as a lack of familiarity with the imaginative universe within which their acts are signs. As Wittgenstein has been invoked, he may as well be quoted:

> We . . . say of some people that they are transparent to us. It is, however, important as regards this observation that one human being can be a complete enigma to another. We learn this when we come into a strange country with entirely strange traditions; and, what is more, even given a mastery of the country's language. We do not *understand* the people. (And not because of not knowing what they are saying to themselves.) We cannot find our feet with them.

IV

Finding our feet, an unnerving business which never more than distantly succeeds, is what ethnographic research consists of as a personal experience; trying to formulate the basis on which one imagines, always excessively, one has found them is what anthropological writing consists of as a scientific endeavor. We are not, or at least I am not, seeking either to become natives (a compromised word in any case) or to mimic them. Only romantics or spies would seem to find point in that. We are seeking, in the widened sense of the term in which it encompasses very much more than talk, to converse with them, a matter a great deal more difficult, and not only with strangers, than is commonly recognized. "If speaking *for* someone else seems to be a mysterious process," Stanley Cavell has remarked, "that may be because speaking *to* someone does not seem mysterious enough."

Looked at in this way, the aim of anthropology is the enlargement of the universe of human discourse. That is not, of course, its only aim — instruction, amusement, practical counsel, moral advance, and the discovery of natural order in human behavior are others; nor is anthropology the only discipline which pursues it. But it is an aim to which a semiotic concept of culture is peculiarly well adapted. As interworked systems of construable signs (what, ignoring provincial usages, I would call symbols), culture is not a power, something to which social events, behaviors, institutions, or processes can be causally attributed; it is a context, something within which they can be intelligibly — that is, thickly — described.

The famous anthropological absorption with the (to us) exotic — Berber horsemen, Jewish peddlers, French Legionnaires — is, thus, essentially a device for displacing the dulling sense of familiarity with which the mysteriousness of our own ability to relate perceptively to one another is concealed from us. Looking at the ordinary in places where it takes unaccustomed forms brings out not, as has so often been claimed, the arbitrariness of human behavior (there is nothing especially arbitrary about taking sheep theft for insolence in Morocco), but the degree to which its meaning varies according to the pattern of life by which it is informed. Understanding a people's culture exposes their normalness without reducing their particularity. (The more I manage to follow what the Moroccans are up to, the more logical, and the more singular, they seem.) It renders them accessible: setting them in the frame of their own banalities, it dissolves their opacity.

It is this maneuver, usually too casually referred to as "seeing things from the actor's point of view," too bookishly as "the *verstehen* approach," or too technically as "emic analysis," that so often leads to the notion that anthropology is a variety of either long-distance mind reading or cannibalisle fantasizing, and which, for someone anxious to navigate past the wrecks of a dozen sunken philosophies, must therefore be executed with a great deal of care. Nothing is more necessary to comprehending what anthropological interpretation is, and the degree to which it *is* interpretation, than an exact understanding of what it means — and what it does not mean — to say that our formulations of other peoples' symbol systems must be actor-oriented.[1]

What it means is that descriptions of Berber, Jewish, or French culture must be cast in terms of the constructions we imagine Berbers, Jews, or Frenchmen to place upon what they live through, the formulae they use to define what happens to them. What it does not mean is that such descriptions are themselves Berber, Jewish, or French — that is, part of the reality they are ostensibly describing; they are anthropological — that is, part of a developing system of scientific analysis. They must be cast in terms of the interpretations to which persons of a particular denomination subject their experience, because that is what they profess to be descriptions of; they are anthropological because it is, in fact, anthropologists who profess them. Normally, it is not necessary to point out quite so laboriously that the object of study is one thing and the study of it another. It is clear enough that the physical world is not physics and *A Skeleton Key to Finnegan's Wake* not *Finnegan's Wake*. But, as, in the study of culture, analysis penetrates into the very body of the object — that is, *we begin with our own interpretations of what our informants are up to, or think they are up to, and then systematize those* — the line between (Moroccan) culture as a natural fact and (Moroccan) culture as a theoretical entity tends to get blurred. All the more so, as the latter is presented in the form of an actor's-eye description of (Moroccan) conceptions of everything from violence, honor, divinity, and justice, to tribe, property, patronage, and chiefship.

In short, anthropological writings are themselves interpretations, and second and third order ones to boot. (By definition, only a "native" makes first order ones: it's *his* culture.)[2] They are, thus, fictions; fictions, in the sense that they are "something made," "something fashioned" — the original meaning of *fictiō* — not that they are false, unfactual, or merely "as if" thought experiments. To construct actor-oriented descriptions of the involvements of a Berber chieftain, a Jewish merchant, and a French soldier with one another in 1912 Morocco is clearly an imaginative act, not all that different from constructing similar descriptions of, say, the involvements with one another of a provincial French doctor, his silly,

---

[1]Not only other peoples': anthropology *can* be trained on the culture of which it is itself a part, and it increasingly is; a fact of profound importance, but which, as it raises a few tricky and rather special second order problems, I shall put to the side for the moment.

[2]The order problem is, again, complex. Anthropological works based on other anthropological works (Lévi-Strauss', for example) may, of course, be fourth order or higher, and informants frequently, even habitually, make second order interpretations — what have come to be known as "native models." In literate cultures, where "native" interpretation can proceed to higher levels — in connection with the Maghreb, one has only to think of Ibn Khaldun; with the United States, Margaret Mead — these matters become intricate indeed.

adulterous wife, and her feckless lover in nineteenth century France. In the latter case, the actors are represented as not having existed and the events as not having happened, while in the former they are represented as actual, or as having been so. This is a difference of no mean importance; indeed, precisely the one Madame Bovary had difficulty grasping. But the importance does not lie in the fact that her story was created while Cohen's was only noted. The conditions of their creation, and the point of it (to say nothing of the manner and the quality) differ. But the one is as much a *fictiō* — "a making" — as the other.

Anthropologists have not always been as aware as they might be of this fact: that although culture exists in the trading post, the hill fort, or the sheep run, anthropology exists in the book, the article, the lecture, the museum display, or, sometimes nowadays, the film. To become aware of it is to realize that the line between mode of representation and substantive content is as undrawable in cultural analysis as it is in painting; and that fact in turn seems to threaten the objective status of anthropological knowledge by suggesting that its source is not social reality but scholarly artifice.

It does threaten it, but the threat is hollow. The claim to attention of an ethnographic account does not rest on its author's ability to capture primitive facts in faraway places and carry them home like a mask or a carving, but on the degree to which he is able to clarify what goes on in such places, to reduce the puzzlement — what manner of men are these? — to which unfamiliar acts emerging out of unknown backgrounds naturally give rise. This raises some serious problems of verification, all right — or, if "verification" is too strong a word for so soft a science (I, myself, would prefer "appraisal"), of how you can tell a better account from a worse one. But that is precisely the virtue of it. If ethnography is thick description and ethnographers those who are doing the describing, then the determining question for any given example of it, whether a field journal squib or a Malinowski-sized monograph, is whether it sorts winks from twitches and real winks from mimicked ones. It is not against a body of uninterpreted data, radically thinned descriptions, that we must measure the cogency of our explications, but against the power of the scientific imagination to bring us into touch with the lives of strangers. It is not worth it, as Thoreau said, to go round the world to count the cats in Zanzibar.

V

Now, this proposition, that it is not in our interest to bleach human behavior of the very properties that interest us before we begin to examine it, has sometimes been escalated into a larger claim: namely, that as it is only those properties that interest us, we need not attend, save cursorily, to behavior at all. Culture is most effectively treated, the argument goes, purely as a symbolic system (the catch phrase is, "in its own terms"), by isolating its elements, specifying the internal relationships among those elements, and then characterizing the whole system in some general way — according to the core symbols around which it is organized, the underlying structures of which it is a surface expression, or the ideological principles upon which it is based. Though a distinct improvement over "learned behavior" and "mental phenomena" notions of what culture is, and the source of some of the most powerful theoretical ideas in contemporary anthropology, this hermetical approach to things seems to me to run the danger (and increasingly to have been overtaken by it) of locking cultural analysis away from its proper object, the informal logic of actual life. There is little profit in extricating a concept from the defects of psychologism only to plunge it immediately into those of schematicism.

Behavior must be attended to, and with some exactness, because it is through the flow of behavior — or, more precisely, social action — that cultural forms find articulation. They find it as well, of course, in various sorts of artifacts, and various states of consciousness; but these draw their meaning from the role they play (Wittgenstein would say their "use") in an ongoing pattern of life, not from any intrinsic relationships they bear to one another. It is what Cohen, the sheikh, and "Captain Dumari" were doing when they tripped over one another's purposes — pursuing trade, defending honor, establishing dominance — that created our pastoral drama, and that is what the drama is, therefore, "about." Whatever, or wherever, symbol systems "in their own terms" may be, we gain empirical access to them by inspecting events, not by arranging abstracted entities into unified patterns.

A further implication of this is that coherence cannot be the major test of validity for a cultural description. Cultural systems must have a minimal degree of coherence, else we would not call them systems; and, by observation, they normally have a great deal more. But there is nothing so coherent as a paranoid's delusion or a swindler's story. The force of our interpretations cannot rest, as they are now so often made to do, on the tightness with which they hold together, or the assurance with which they are argued. Nothing has done more, I think, to discredit cultural analysis than the construction of impeccable depictions of formal order in whose actual existence nobody can quite believe.

If anthropological interpretation is constructing a reading of what happens, then to divorce it from what happens — from what, in this time or that place, specific people say, what they do, what is done to them, from the whole vast business of the world — is to divorce it from its applications and render it vacant. A good interpretation of anything — a poem, a person, a history, a ritual, an institution, a society — takes us into the heart of that of which it is the interpretation. When it does not do that, but leads us instead somewhere else — into an admiration of its own elegance, of its author's cleverness, or of the beauties of Euclidean order — it may have its intrinsic charms; but it is something else than what the task at hand — figuring out what all that rigamarole with the sheep is about — calls for.

The rigamarole with the sheep — the sham theft of them, the repara-tive transfer of them, the political confiscation of them — is (or was) essentially a social discourse, even if, as I suggested earlier, one conducted in multiple tongues and as much in action as in words.

Claiming his *'ar*, Cohen invoked the trade pact; recognizing the claim, the sheikh challenged the offenders' tribe; accepting responsibility, the offenders' tribe paid the indemnity; anxious to make clear to sheikhs and peddlers alike who was now in charge here, the French showed the impe-rial hand. As in any discourse, code does not determine conduct, and what was actually said need not have been. Cohen might not have, given its ille-gitimacy in Protectorate eyes, chosen to press his claim. The sheikh might, for similar reasons, have rejected it. The offenders' tribe, still resisting French authority, might have decided to regard the raid as "real" and fight rather than negotiate. The French, were they more *habile* and less *dur* (as, under Mareschal Lyautey's seigniorial tutelage, they later in fact became), might have permitted Cohen to keep his sheep, winking — as we say — at the continuance of the trade pattern and its limitation to their authority. And there are other possibilities: the Marmushans might have regarded the French action as too great an insult to bear and gone into dissidence themselves; the French might have attempted not just to clamp down on Cohen but to bring the sheikh himself more closely to heel; and Cohen might have concluded that between renegade Berbers and Beau Geste sol-diers, driving trade in the Atlas highlands was no longer worth the candle and retired to the better-governed confines of the town. This, indeed, is more or less what happened, somewhat further along, as the Protectorate moved toward genuine sovereignty. But the point here is not to describe what did or did not take place in Morocco. (From this simple incident one can widen out into enormous complexities of social experience.) It is to demonstrate what a piece of anthropological interpretation consists in: tracing the curve of a social discourse; fixing it into an inspectable form.

The ethnographer "inscribes" social discourse; *he writes it down*. In so doing, he turns it from a passing event, which exists only in its own moment of occurrence, into an account, which exists in its inscriptions and can be reconsulted. The sheikh is long dead, killed in the process of being, as the French called it, "pacified"; "Captain Dumari," his pacifier, lives, retired to his souvenirs, in the south of France; and Cohen went last year, part refugee, part pilgrim, part dying patriarch, "home" to Israel. But what they, in my extended sense, "said" to one another on an Atlas plateau sixty years ago is — very far from perfectly — preserved for study. "What," Paul Ricoeur, from whom this whole idea of the inscription of action is borrowed and somewhat twisted, asks, "what does writing fix?"

> Not the event of speaking, but the "said" of speaking, where we understand by the "said" of speaking that intentional exteriorization constitutive of the aim of discourse thanks to which the *sagen* — the saying — wants to become *Aus-sage* — the enunciation, the enunciated. In short, what we write is the *noema* ["thought," "content," "gist"] of the speaking. It is the meaning of the speech event, not the event as event.

This is not itself so very "said" — if Oxford philosophers run to little stories, phenomenological ones run to large sentences; but it brings us anyway to a more precise answer to our generative question, "What does the ethnographer do?" — he writes.[3] This, too, may seem a less than startling discovery, and to someone familiar with the current "literature," an implausible one. But as the standard answer to our question has been, "He observes, he records, he analyzes" — a kind of *veni, vidi, vici* conception of the matter — it may have more deep-going consequences than are at first apparent, not the least of which is that distinguishing these three phases of knowledge-seeking may not, as a matter of fact, normally be possible; and, indeed, as autonomous "operations" they may not in fact exist.

The situation is even more delicate, because, as already noted, what we inscribe (or try to) is not raw social discourse, to which, because, save very marginally or very specially, we are not actors, we do not have direct access, but only that small part of it which our informants can lead us into understanding.[4] This is not as fatal as it sounds, for, in fact, not all Cretans are liars, and it is not necessary to know everything in order to understand something. But it does make the view of anthropological analysis as the conceptual manipulation of discovered facts, a logical reconstruction of a mere reality, seem rather lame. To set forth symmetrical crystals of significance, purified of the material complexity in which they were located, and then attribute their existence to autogenous principles or order, universal properties of the human mind, or vast, a priori *weltanschauungen*, is to pretend a science that does not exist and imagine a reality that cannot be found. Cultural analysis is (or should be) guessing at meanings, assessing the guesses, and drawing explanatory conclusions from the better guesses, not discovering the Continent of Meaning and mapping out its bodiless landscape.

VI

So, there are three characteristics of ethnographic description: it is interpretive; what it is interpretive of is the flow of social discourse; and the interpreting involved consists in trying to rescue the "said" of such discourse from its perishing occasions and fix it in perusable terms. The *kula*

---

[3]Or, again, more exactly, "inscribes." Most ethnography is in fact to be found in books and articles, rather than in films, records, museum displays, or whatever; but even in them there are, of course, photographs, drawings, diagrams, tables, and so on. Self-consciousness about modes of representation (not to speak of experiments with them) has been very lacking in anthropology.

[4]So far as it has reinforced the anthropologist's impulse to engage himself with his informants as persons rather than as objects, the notion of "participant observation" has been a valuable one. But, to the degree it has led the anthropologist to block from his view the very special, culturally bracketed nature of his own role and to imagine himself something more than an interested (in both senses of that word) sojourner, it has been our most powerful source of bad faith.

is gone or altered; but, for better or worse, *The Argonauts of the Western Pacific* remains. But there is, in addition, a fourth characteristic of such description, at least as I practice it: it is microscopic.

This is not to say that there are no large-scale anthropological interpretations of whole societies, civilizations, world events, and so on. Indeed, it is such extension of our analyses to wider contexts that, along with their theoretical implications, recommends them to general attention and justifies our constructing them. No one really cares anymore, not even Cohen (well . . . maybe, Cohen), about those sheep as such. History may have its unobtrusive turning points, "great noises in a little room"; but this little go-round was surely not one of them.

It is merely to say that the anthropologist characteristically approaches such broader interpretations and more abstract analyses from the direction of exceedingly extended acquaintances with extremely small matters. He confronts the same grand realities that others — historians, economists, political scientists, sociologists — confront in more fateful settings: Power, Change, Faith, Oppression, Work, Passion, Authority, Beauty, Violence, Love, Prestige; but he confronts them in contexts obscure enough — places like Marmusha and lives like Cohen's — to take the capital letters off them. These all-too-human constancies, "those big words that make us all afraid," take a homely form in such homely contexts. But that is exactly the advantage. There are enough profundities in the world already.

Yet, the problem of how to get from a collection of ethnographic miniatures on the order of our sheep story — an assortment of remarks and anecdotes — to wall-sized culturescapes of the nation, the epoch, the continent, or the civilization is not so easily passed over with vague allusions to the virtues of concreteness and the down-to-earth mind. For a science born in Indian tribes, Pacific islands, and African lineages and subsequently seized with grander ambitions, this has come to be a major methodological problem, and for the most part a badly handled one. The models that anthropologists have themselves worked out to justify their moving from local truths to general visions have been, in fact, as responsible for undermining the effort as anything their critics — sociologists obsessed with sample sizes, psychologists with measures, or economists with aggregates — have been able to devise against them.

Of these, the two main ones have been: the Jonesville-is-the-USA "microcosmic" model; and the Easter-Island-is-a-testing-case "natural experiment" model. Either heaven in a grain of sand, or the farther shores of possibility.

The Jonesville-is-America writ small (or America-is-Jonesville writ large) fallacy is so obviously one that, the only thing that needs explanation is how people have managed to believe it and expected others to believe it. The notion that one can find the essence of national societies, civilizations, great religions, or whatever summed up and simplified in so-called "typical" small towns and villages is palpable nonsense. What one finds in small towns and villages is (alas) small-town or village life. If localized, microscopic studies were really dependent for their greater relevance upon such a premise — that they captured the great world in the little — they wouldn't have any relevance.

But, of course, they are not. The locus of study is not the object of study. Anthropologists don't study villages (tribes, towns, neighborhoods . . .); they study *in* villages. You can study different things in different places, and some things — for example, what colonial domination does to established frames of moral expectation — you can best study in confined localities. But that doesn't make the place what it is you are studying. In the remoter provinces of Morocco and Indonesia I have wrestled with the same questions other social scientists have wrestled with in more central locations — for example, how comes it that men's most importunate claims to humanity are cast in the accents of group pride? — and with about the same conclusiveness. One can add a dimension — one much needed in the present climate of size-up-and-solve social science; but that is all. There is a certain value, if you are going to run on about the exploitation of the masses in having seen a Javanese sharecropper turning earth in a tropical downpour or a Moroccan tailor embroidering kaftans by the light of a twenty-watt bulb. But the notion that this gives you the thing entire (and elevates you to some moral vantage ground from which you can look down upon the ethically less privileged) is an idea which only someone too long in the bush could possibly entertain.

The "natural laboratory" notion has been equally pernicious, not only because the analogy is false — what kind of a laboratory is it where *none* of the parameters are manipulable? — but because it leads to a notion that the data derived from ethnographic studies are purer, or more fundamental, or more solid, or less conditioned (the most favored word is "elementary") than those derived from other sorts of social inquiry. The great natural variation of cultural forms is, of course, not only anthropology's great (and wasting) resource, but the ground of its deepest theoretical dilemma: how is such variation to be squared with the biological unity of the human species? But it is not, even metaphorically, experimental variation, because the context in which it occurs varies along with it, and it is not possible (though there are those who try) to isolate the y's from x's to write a proper function.

The famous studies purporting to show that the Oedipus complex was backwards in the Trobriands, sex roles were upside down in Tchambuli, and the Pueblo Indians lacked aggression (it is characteristic that they were all negative — "but not in the South"), are, whatever their empirical validity may or may not be, not "scientifically tested and approved" hypotheses. They are interpretations, or misinterpretations, like any others, arrived at in the same way as any others, and as inherently inconclusive as any others, and the attempt to invest them with the authority of physical experimentation is but methodological sleight of hand. Ethnographic findings are not privileged, just particular: another country heard from. To regard them as anything more (*or anything less*) than that distorts both them and their implications, which are far profounder than mere primitivity, for social theory.

Another country heard from: the reason that protracted descriptions of distant sheep raids (and a really good ethnographer would have gone into what kind of sheep they were) have general relevance is that they present the sociological mind with bodied stuff on which to feed. The important thing about the anthropologist's findings is their complex specificness, their circumstantiality. It is with the kind of material produced by long-term, mainly (though not exclusively) qualitative, highly participative, and almost obsessively fine-comb field study in confined contexts that the mega-concepts with which contemporary social science is afflicted — legitimacy, modernization, integration, conflict, charisma, structure, . . . meaning — can be given the sort of sensible actuality that makes it possible to think not only realistically and concretely *about* them, but, what is more important, creatively and imaginatively *with* them.

The methodological problem which the microscopic nature of ethnography presents is both real and critical. But it is not to be resolved by regarding a remote locality as the world in a teacup or as the sociological equivalent of a cloud chamber. It is to be resolved — or, anyway, decently kept at bay — by realizing that social actions are comments on more than themselves; that where an interpretation comes from does not determine where it can be impelled to go. Small facts speak to large issues, winks to epistemology, or sheep raids to revolution, because they are made to.

VII

Which brings us, finally, to theory. The besetting sin of interpretive approaches to anything — literature, dreams, symptoms, culture — is that they tend to resist, or to be permitted to resist, conceptual articulation and thus to escape systematic modes of assessment. You either grasp an interpretation or you do not, see the point of it or you do not, accept it or you do not. Imprisoned in the immediacy of its own detail, it is presented as self-validating, or, worse, as validated by the supposedly developed sensitivities of the person who presents it; any attempt to cast what it says in terms other than its own is regarded as a travesty — as, the anthropologist's severest term of moral abuse, ethnocentric.

For a field of study which, however timidly (though I, myself, am not timid about the matter at all), asserts itself to be a science, this just will not do. There is no reason why the conceptual structure of a cultural interpretation should be any less formulable, and thus less susceptible to explicit canons of appraisal, than that of, say, a biological observation or a physical experiment — no reason except that the terms in which such formulations can be cast are, if not wholly nonexistent, very nearly so. We are reduced to insinuating theories because we lack the power to state them.

At the same time, it must be admitted that there are a number of characteristics of cultural interpretation which make the theoretical development of it more than usually difficult. The first is the need for theory to stay rather closer to the ground than tends to be the case in sciences more able to give themselves over to imaginative abstraction. Only short flights of ratiocination tend to be effective in anthropology; longer ones tend to drift off into logical dreams, academic bemusements with formal symmetry. The whole point of a semiotic approach to culture is, as I have said, to aid us in gaining access to the conceptual world in which our subjects live so that we can, in some extended sense of the term, converse with them. The tension between the pull of this need to penetrate an unfamiliar universe of symbolic action and the requirements of technical advance in the theory of culture, between the need to grasp and the need to analyze, is, as a result, both necessarily great and essentially irremovable. Indeed, the further theoretical development goes, the deeper the tension gets. This is the first condition for cultural theory: it is not its own master. As it is unseverable from the immediacies thick description presents, its freedom to shape itself in terms of its internal logic is rather limited. What generality it contrives to achieve grows out of the delicacy of its distinctions, not the sweep of its abstractions.

And from this follows a peculiarity in the way, as a simple matter of empirical fact, our knowledge of culture ... cultures ... a culture ... grows: in spurts. Rather than following a rising curve of cumulative findings, cultural analysis breaks up into a disconnected yet coherent sequence of bolder and bolder sorties. Studies do build on other studies, not in the sense that they take up where the others leave off, but in the sense that, better informed and better conceptualized, they plunge more deeply into the same things. Every serious cultural analysis starts from a sheer beginning and ends where it manages to get before exhausting its intellectual impulse. Previously discovered facts are mobilized, previously developed concepts used, previously formulated hypotheses tried out; but the movement is not from already proven theorems to newly proven ones, it is from an awkward fumbling for the most elementary understanding to a supported claim that one has achieved that and surpassed it. A study is an advance if it is more incisive — whatever that may mean — than those that preceded it; but it less stands on their shoulders than, challenged and challenging, runs by their side.

It is for this reason, among others, that the essay, whether of thirty pages or three hundred, has seemed the natural genre in which to present cultural interpretations and the theories sustaining them, and why, if one looks for systematic treatises in the field, one is so soon disappointed, the more so if one finds any. Even inventory articles are rare here, and anyway of hardly more than bibliographical interest. The major theoretical contributions not only lie in specific studies — that is true in almost any field — but they are very difficult to abstract from such studies and integrate into anything one might call "culture theory" as such. Theoretical formulations hover so low over the interpretations they govern that they don't make much sense or hold much interest apart from them. This is so, not because they are not general (if they are not general, they are not theoretical), but because, stated independently of their applications, they seem either commonplace or vacant. One can, and this in fact is how the field progresses conceptually, take a line of theoretical attack developed in connection with one exercise in ethnographic interpretation and employ it in another, pushing it forward to greater precision and broader relevance; but one cannot write a "General Theory of Cultural Interpretation." Or, rather, one can, but there appears to be little profit in it, because the essential task of theory building here is not to codify abstract regularities but to make thick description possible, not to generalize across cases but to generalize within them.

To generalize within cases is usually called, at least in medicine and depth psychology, clinical inference. Rather than beginning with a set of observations and attempting to subsume them under a governing law, such inference begins with a set of (presumptive) signifiers and attempts to place them within an intelligible frame. Measures are matched to theoretical predictions, but symptoms (even when they are measured) are scanned for theoretical peculiarities — that is, they are diagnosed. In the study of culture the signifiers are not symptoms or clusters of symptoms, but symbolic acts or clusters of symbolic acts, and the aim is not therapy but the analysis of social discourse. But the way in which theory is used — to ferret out the unapparent import of things — is the same.

Thus we are lead to the second condition of cultural theory: it is not, at least in the strict meaning of the term, predictive. The diagnostician doesn't predict measles; he decides that someone has them, or at the very most *anticipates* that someone is rather likely shortly to get them. But this limitation, which is real enough, has commonly been both misunderstood and exaggerated, because it has been taken to mean that cultural interpretation is merely post facto: that, like the peasant in the old story, we first shoot the holes in the fence and then paint the bull's-eyes around them. It is hardly to be denied that there is a good deal of that sort of thing around, some of it in prominent places. It is to be denied, however, that it is the inevitable outcome of a clinical approach to the use of theory.

It is true that in the clinical style of theoretical formulation, conceptualization is directed toward the task of generating interpretations of matters already in hand, not toward projecting outcomes of experimental manipulations or deducing future states of a determined system. But that does not mean that theory has only to fit (or, more carefully, to generate cogent interpretations of) realities past; it has also to survive — intellectually survive — realities to come. Although we formulate our interpretation of an outburst of winking or an instance of sheep-raiding after its occurrence, sometimes long after, the theoretical framework in terms of which such an interpretation is made must be capable of continuing to yield defensible interpretations as new social phenomena swim into view. Although one starts any effort at thick description, beyond the obvious and superficial, from a state of general bewilderment as to what the devil is going on — trying to find one's feet — one does not start (or ought not) intellectually empty-handed. Theoretical ideas are not created wholly anew in each study; as I have said, they are adopted from other, related studies, and, refined in the process, applied to new interpretive problems. If they cease being useful with respect to such problems, they tend to stop being used and are more or less abandoned. If they continue being useful, throwing up new understandings, they are further elaborated and go on being used.[5]

Such a view of how theory functions in an interpretive science suggests that the distinction, relative in any case, that appears in the experimental or observational sciences between "description" and "explanation" appears here as one, even more relative, between "inscription" ("thick description") and "specification" ("diagnosis") — between setting down the meaning particular social actions have for the actors whose actions they are, and stating, as explicitly as we can manage, what the knowledge thus attained demonstrates about the society in which it is found and, beyond that, about social life as such. Our double task is to uncover the conceptual structures that inform our subjects' acts, the "said" of social discourse, and to construct a system of analysis in whose terms what is generic to those structures, what belongs to them because they are what they are, will stand out against the other determinants of human behavior. In ethnography, the office of theory is to provide a vocabulary in which what symbolic action has to say about itself — that is, about the role of culture in human life — can be expressed.

Aside from a couple of orienting pieces concerned with more foundational matters, it is in such a manner that theory operates in the essays collected here. A repertoire of very general, made-in-the-academy concepts and systems of concepts — "integration," "rationalization," "symbol," "ideology," "ethos," "revolution," "identity," "metaphor," "structure," "ritual," "world view," "actor," "function," "sacred," and, of course, "culture" itself — is woven into the body of thick-description ethnography in the hope of rendering mere occurrences scientifically eloquent.[6] The aim is

---

[5]Admittedly, this is something of an idealization. Because theories are seldom if ever decisively disproved in clinical use but merely grow increasingly awkward, unproductive, strained, or vacuous, they often persist long after all but a handful of people (though *they* are often most passionate) have lost much interest in them. Indeed, so far as anthropology is concerned, it is almost more of a problem to get exhausted ideas out of the literature than it is to get productive ones in, and so a great deal more of theoretical discussion than one would prefer is critical rather than constructive, and whole careers have been devoted to hastening the demise of moribund notions. As the field advances one would hope that this sort of intellectual weed control would become a less prominent part of our activities. But, for the moment, it remains true that old theories tend less to die than to go into second editions.

[6]The overwhelming bulk of the following chapters concern Indonesia rather than Morocco, for I have just begun to face up to the demands of my North African material which, for the most part, was gathered more recently. Field work in Indonesia was carried out in 1952–1954, 1957–1958, and 1971; in Morocco in 1964, 1965–1966, 1968–1969, and 1972.

to draw large conclusions from small, but very densely textured facts; to support broad assertions about the role of culture in the construction of collective life by engaging them exactly with complex specifics.

Thus it is not only interpretation that goes all the way down to the most immediate observational level: the theory upon which such interpretation conceptually depends does so also. My interest in Cohen's story, like Ryle's in winks, grew out of some very general notions indeed. The "confusion of tongues" model — the view that social conflict is not something that happens when, out of weakness, indefiniteness, obsolescence, or neglect, cultural forms cease to operate, but rather something which happens when, like burlesqued winks, such forms are pressed by unusual situations or unusual intentions to operate in unusual ways — is not an idea I got from Cohen's story. It is one, instructed by colleagues, students, and predecessors, I brought to it.

Our innocent-looking "note in a bottle" is more than a portrayal of the frames of meaning of Jewish peddlers, Berber warriors, and French proconsuls, or even of their mutual interference. It is an argument that to rework the pattern of social relationships is to rearrange the coordinates of the experienced world. Society's forms are culture's substance.

VIII

There is an Indian story — at least I heard it as an Indian story — about an Englishman who, having been told that the world rested on a platform which rested on the back of an elephant which rested in turn on the back of a turtle, asked (perhaps he was an ethnographer; it is the way they behave), what did the turtle rest on? Another turtle. And that turtle? "Ah, Sahib, after that it is turtles all the way down."

Such, indeed, is the condition of things. I do not know how long it would be profitable to meditate on the encounter of Cohen, the sheikh, and "Dumari" (the period has perhaps already been exceeded); but I do know that however long I did so I would not get anywhere near to the bottom of it. Nor have I ever gotten anywhere near to the bottom of anything I have ever written about, either in the essays below or elsewhere. Cultural analysis is intrinsically incomplete. And, worse than that, the more deeply it goes the less complete it is. It is a strange science whose most telling assertions are its most tremulously based, in which to get somewhere with the matter at hand is to intensify the suspicion, both your own and that of others, that you are not quite getting it right. But that, along with plaguing subtle people with obtuse questions, is what being an ethnographer is like.

There are a number of ways to escape this — turning culture into folklore and collecting it, turning it into traits and counting it, turning it into institutions and classifying it, turning it into structures and toying with it. But they *are* escapes. The fact is that to commit oneself to a semiotic concept of culture and an interpretive approach to the study of it is to commit oneself to a view of ethnographic assertion as, to borrow W. B. Gallie's by now famous phrase, "essentially contestable." Anthropology, or at least interpretive anthropology, is a science whose progress is marked less by a perfection of consensus than by a refinement of debate. What gets better is the precision with which we vex each other.

This is very difficult to see when one's attention is being monopolized by a single party to the argument. Monologues are of little value here, because there are no conclusions to be reported; there is merely a discussion to be sustained. Insofar as the essays here collected have any importance, it is less in what they say than what they are witness to: an enormous increase in interest, not only in anthropology, but in social studies generally, in the role of symbolic forms in human life. Meaning, that elusive and ill-defined pseudoentity we were once more than content to leave philosophers and literary critics to fumble with, has now come back into the heart of our discipline. Even Marxists are quoting Cassirer; even positivists, Kenneth Burke.

My own position in the midst of all this has been to try to resist subjectivism on the one hand and cabbalism on the other, to try to keep the analysis of symbolic forms as closely tied as I could to concrete social events and occasions, the public world of common life, and to organize it in such a way that the connections between theoretical formulations and descriptive interpretations were unobscured by appeals to dark sciences. I have never been impressed by the argument that, as complete objectivity is impossible in these matters (as, of course, it is), one might as well let one's sentiments run loose. As Robert Solow has remarked, that is like saying that as a perfectly aseptic environment is impossible, one might as well conduct surgery in a sewer. Nor, on the other hand, have I been impressed with claims that structural linguistics, computer engineering, or some other advanced form of thought is going to enable us to understand men without knowing them. Nothing will discredit a semiotic approach to culture more quickly than allowing it to drift into a combination of intuitionism and alchemy, no matter how elegantly the intuitions are expressed or how modern the alchemy is made to look.

The danger that cultural analysis, in search of all-too-deep-lying turtles, will lose touch with the hard surfaces of life — with the political, economic, stratificatory realities within which men are everywhere contained — and with the biological and physical necessities on which those surfaces rest, is an ever-present one. The only defense against it, and against, thus, turning cultural analysis into a kind of sociological aestheticism, is to train such analysis on such realities and such necessities in the first place. It is thus that I have written about nationalism, about violence, about identity, about human nature, about legitimacy, about revolution, about ethnicity, about urbanization, about status, about death, about time, and most of all about particular attempts by particular peoples to place these things in some sort of comprehensible, meaningful frame.

To look at the symbolic dimensions of social action — art, religion, ideology, science, law, morality, common sense — is not to turn away from the existential dilemmas of life for some empyrean realm of de-emotionalized forms; it is to plunge into the midst of them. The essential vocation of interpretive anthropology is not to answer our deepest questions, but to make available to us answers that others, guarding other sheep in other valleys, have given, and thus to include them in the consultable record of what man has said.

■ JESSE GORDON

What Is America?

Jesse Gordon is a writer and filmmaker living in New York City. His op-art piece *What Is America?* was published in the *New York Times* on July 3, 2000. In a letter to the editor, a reader responded to these photographs by stating, "Those who were born here provided much of the tired cynicism. Those who immigrated provided much of the energetic optimism and joy. This is more proof that America does not just have an immigrant past; it has an immigrant future."

■ ■ ■

"freedom"
Yen, Vietnam

"money"
Frankie, Queens

"imperialism"
Aaron, New York City

"diversity"
Karine, New York City

"religious freedom"
Dhananjay, India

"plastics"
Ian, Canada

"possibility"
Raymond, St. Kitts

"choice"
Melissa, New York City

"ignorance"
Devo, Kansas City

"my adopted country"
Sister Mary, England

"needs healing"
Elijah, South Carolina

"hope"
Pat, Staten Island

"open-minded"
Isaac, Brooklyn

"jazz"
Valerie, Connecticut

"ketchup"
Constantino, Greece

"original ideas"
Charles, New York City

"business"
Adaib, Yemen

"consumerism"
Silvia, Barcelona

"fun"
Nobuhisa, Japan

"lost opportunities"
Dan, Seattle

"excess"
Katherine, Boston

"*sundar* (beautiful)"
Sharada, India

"everything"
Larry, Puerto Rico

"ahhhh!"
Jadah and Joziah,
New York City

Life in Hell

Matt Groening (b. 1954) grew up in Portland, Oregon, and attended the Evergreen State College in Olympia, Washington, where he served as a writer and cartoonist for the school paper. Upon graduation, Groening moved to Los Angeles to pursue a career as a writer. The comic *Life in Hell*, which began in 1977 as a way for Groening to document his experiences in Los Angeles for his friends and family, caught the attention of publishers and is now nationally syndicated. Because of the popularity of *Life in Hell*, Groening was asked to create a comic for television. In response, he created *The Simpsons*, one of the longest running and most successful television shows in history. There are often references to *Life in Hell* in *The Simpsons*.

Bitch

Beverly Gross (b. 1938) is an English professor and a public intellectual at Queens College of the City University of New York, having taught previously at Northwestern University and Vassar College. In the 1960s and 1970s, Gross worked as a literary editor for several journals and magazines, including the *Chicago Review* and *The Nation*. Her writing has also appeared in a number of literary journals. The essay "Bitch" was first published in *Salmagundi*, a humanities- and social sciences–based quarterly magazine, in 1994. Although Gross isn't explicit about redefining and reappropriating the word *bitch* from its historically derogatory usages, this essay can be viewed as part of the larger movement to reclaim sexist and racist language.

■ ■ ■

We were discussing Mary McCarthy's *The Group* in a course called Women Writers and Literary Tradition. McCarthy's biographer Carol Gelderman, I told the class, had been intrigued by how often critics called Mary McCarthy a bitch. I read a few citations. "Her novels are crammed with cerebration and bitchiness" (John Aldridge). "Her approach to writing [is] reflective of the modern American bitch" (Paul Schlueter). Why McCarthy? a student asked. Her unrelenting standards, I ventured, her tough-minded critical estimates — there was no self-censoring, appeasing Angel in the House of Mary McCarthy's brain. Her combativeness (her marital battles with Edmund Wilson became the stuff of academic legend). Maybe there were other factors. But the discussion opened up to the more inclusive issue of the word *bitch* itself. What effect does that appellation have on women? What effect might it have had on McCarthy? No one ever called Edmund Wilson a bitch. Do we excuse, even pay respect when a man is critical, combative, assertive? What is the male equivalent of the word bitch, I asked the class.

"Boss," said Sabrina Sims.

This was an evening class at a branch of the City University of New York. Most of the students are older adults trying to fit a college education into otherwise busy lives. Most of them have full-time jobs during the day. Sabrina Sims works on Wall Street, is a single mother raising a ten-year-old daughter, is black, and had to take an Incomplete in the course because she underwent a kidney transplant in December.

Her answer gave us all a good laugh. I haven't been able to get it out of my mind. I've been thinking about *bitch*, watching how it is used by writers and in conversation, and have explored its lexical history. "A name of reproach for a woman" is how Doctor Johnson's Dictionary dealt with the word in the eighteenth century, as though anticipating the great adaptability of this particular execration, a class of words that tends toward early obsolescence. Not *bitch*, however, which has been around for a millennium, outlasting a succession of definitions. Its longevity is perhaps attributable to its satisfying misogyny. Its meaning matters less than its power to denounce and subjugate. Francis Grose in *A Classical Dictionary of the Vulgar Tongue* (1785) considered *bitch* "the most offensive appellation that can be given to an English woman, even more provoking than that of whore." He offered as evidence "a low London woman's reply on being called a bitch" in the late-eighteenth century: "I may be a whore but can't be a bitch!" The meaning of *bitch* has changed over the centuries but it remains the word that comes immediately to the tongue, still "the most offensive appellation" the English language provides to hurl at a woman.

The *Oxford English Dictionary* records two main meanings for the noun *bitch* up through the nineteenth century.

1. The female of the dog
2. Applied opprobriously to a woman; strictly a lewd or sensual woman. Not now in decent use.

It was not until the twentieth century that *bitch* acquired its opprobrious application in realms irrespective of sensuality. The Supplement to the *OED* (1972) adds:

2a: "In mod. use, esp. a malicious or treacherous woman."

Every current desk dictionary supplies some such meaning:

A spiteful, ill-tempered woman [*World Book Dictionary*]
A malicious, unpleasant, selfish woman, esp. one who stops at nothing to reach her goal. [*Random House Dictionary*]

But malice and treachery only begin to tell the story. The informal questionnaire that I administered to my students and a number of acquaintances elicited ample demonstration of the slippery adaptability of bitch as it might be used these days:

a conceited person, a snob
a self-absorbed woman
a complainer
a competitive woman
a woman who is annoying, pushy, possibly underhanded (in short, a man in a woman's body)
someone rich, thin, and free!

"A word used by men who are threatened by women" was one astute response. Threat lurks everywhere: for women the threat is in being called a bitch. "Someone whiny, threatening, crabby, pestering" is what one woman offered as her definition. "Everything I try hard not to be," she added, "though it seeps through." I offer as a preliminary conclusion that *bitch* means to men whatever they find threatening in a woman and it means to women whatever they particularly dislike about themselves. In either case the word functions as a misogynistic club. I will add that the woman who defined *bitch* as everything she tries hard not to be when asked to free associate about the word came up immediately with "mother." That woman happens to be my sister. We share the same mother, who was often whiny and crabby, though I would never have applied the word *bitch* to her, but then again, I don't consider whiny, crabby and pestering to be prominent among my own numerous flaws.

Dictionaries of slang are informative sources, in touch as they are with nascent language and the emotive coloration of words, especially words of abuse. A relatively restrained definition is offered by the only female lexicographer I consulted for whom *bitch* is "a nasty woman" or "a difficult task" (Anita Pearl, *Dictionary of Popular Slang*). The delineations of *bitch* by the male lexicographers abound with such cascading hostility that the compilers sometimes seem to be reveling in their task. For example, Howard Wentworth and Stuart Berg Flexner in *Dictionary of American Slang*:

> A woman, usu., but not necessarily, a mean, selfish, malicious, deceiving, cruel, or promiscuous woman.

Eugene E. Landy's *The Underground Dictionary* (1971) offers:

> 1. Female who is mean, selfish, cruel, malicious, deceiving, a.k.a. cunt.
> 2. Female. See Female.

I looked up the entry for *Female* (Landy, by the way, provides no parallel entry for *Male*):

> beaver, bird, bitch, broad, bush, cat, chick, crack, cunt, douche, fish, fox, frail, garbage can, heffer, pussy, quail, ruca, scag, snatch, stallion, slave, sweet meat, tail, trick, tuna. See GIRLFRIEND; WIFE.

Richard A. Spear's *Slang and Euphemism* comments on the derivative adjective:

> bitchy 1. pertaining to a mood wherein one complains incessantly about anything. Although this applies to men or women, it is usually associated with women, especially when they are menstruating. Cf. DOG DAYS

Robert L. Chapman's definition in *Thesaurus of American Slang* starts off like a feminist analysis:

> 1 n. A woman one dislikes or disapproves of.

Followed, however, by a sobering string of synonyms: "broad, cunt, witch."

And then this most interesting note:

> Female equivalents of the contemptuous terms for men, listed in this book under *asshole*, are relatively rare. Contempt for females, in

slang, stresses their putative sexual promiscuity and weakness rather than their moral vileness and general odiousness. Some terms under *asshole*, though, are increasingly used of women.

"See ball-buster." Chapman suggests under his second definition for *bitch* ("anything arduous or very disagreeable"). I looked up "ball-buster":

n. Someone who saps or destroys masculinity.
ball-whacker
bitch
nut-cruncher.

Some*thing* has become some*one*. The ball-buster is not a disagreeable thing but a disagreeable (disagreeing?) person. A female person. "A woman one dislikes or disapproves of." For someone so sensitive to the nuances of hostility and verbal put-down, Chapman certainly takes a circuitous route to get to the underlying idea that no other dictionary even touches: *Bitch* means ball-buster.

What one learns from the dictionaries: there is no classifiable thing as a bitch, only a label produced by the act of name-calling. The person named is almost always a female. The name-calling refers to alleged faults of ill-temper, selfishness, malice, cruelty, spite, all of them faults in the realm of interpersonal relating — women's faults: It is hard to think of a put-down word encompassing these faults in a man. *Bastard* and even *son of a bitch* have bigger fish to fry. And an asshole is an asshole in and of himself. A bitch is a woman who makes the name-caller feel uncomfortable. Presumably that name-caller is a man whose ideas about how a woman should behave toward him are being violated.

"Women," wrote Virginia Woolf, "have served all these centuries as looking-glasses possessing the magic and delicious power of reflecting the figure of man at twice its natural size." The woman who withholds that mirror is a bitch. Bitchiness is the perversion of womanly sweetness, compliance, pleasantness, ego-building. (Male ego-building, of course, though that is a virtual tautology; women have egos but who builds them?) If a woman is not building ego she is busting balls.

Ball-buster? The word is a nice synecdoche (like asshole) with great powers of revelation. A ball-buster, one gathers, is a demanding bitch who insists on overexertion from a man to satisfy her sexual or material voraciousness. "The bitch is probably his wife." But balls also bust when a disagreeable woman undermines a guy's ego and "saps or destroys masculinity." The bitch could be his wife, but also his boss, Gloria Steinem, the woman at the post office, the woman who spurns his advances. The familiar Freudian delineation of the male-female nexus depicts male sexuality as requiring the admiration, submission, and subordination of the female. The ultimate threat of (and to) the back-talking woman is male impotence.

Bitch, the curse and concept, exists to insure male potency and female submissiveness. Men have deployed it to defend their power by attacking and neutralizing the upstart. *Bitch* is admonitory, like *whore*, like *dyke*. Borrowing something from both words, *bitch* is one of those verbal missiles with the power of shackling women's actions and impulses.

The metamorphosis of *bitch* from the context of sexuality (a carnal woman, a promiscuous woman) to temperament (an angry woman, a malicious woman) to power (a domineering woman, a competitive woman) is a touchstone to the changing position of women through this century. As women have become more liberated, individually and collectively, the word has taken on connotations of aggressive, hostile, selfish. In the old days a bitch was a harlot; nowadays she is likely to be a woman who won't put out. Female sensuality, even carnality, even infidelity, have been supplanted as what men primarily fear and despise in women. Judging by the contemporary colorations of the word *bitch*, what men primarily fear and despise in women is power.

Some anecdotes:

1. Barbara Bush's name-calling of Geraldine Ferraro during the 1984 presidential election: "I can't say it but it rhymes with 'rich.'"

How ladylike of the future First Lady to avoid uttering the unmentionable. The slur did its dirty work, particularly among those voters disturbed by the sudden elevation of a woman to such unprecedented political heights. In what possible sense did Barbara Bush mean that Geraldine Ferraro is a bitch? A loose woman? Hardly. A nasty woman? Not likely. A pushy woman? Almost certainly. The unspoken syllable was offered as a response to Ferraro's lofty ambitions, potential power, possibly her widespread support among feminists. Imagine a woman seeking to be vice president instead of vice husband.

The ascription of bitchery seems to have nothing to do with Ferraro's bearing and behavior. Certainly not the Ferraro who wrote about the event in her autobiography:

> Barbara Bush realized what a gaffe she had made. . . .
>
> "I just want to apologize to you for what I said," she told me over the phone while I was in the middle of another debate rehearsal. "I certainly didn't mean anything by it."
>
> "Don't worry about it," I said to her. "We all say things at times we don't mean. It's all right."
>
> "Oh," she said breathlessly. "You're such a lady."
>
> All I could think of when I hung up was: Thank God for my convent school training.

2. Lady Ashley at the end of *The Sun Also Rises*: "It makes one feel rather good, deciding not to be a bitch." The context here is something like this: A bitch is a woman who ruins young heroic bullfighters. A woman who is propelled by her sexual drive, desires, and vanity. The fascination of Brett Ashley is that she lives and loves like a man: Her sexuality is unrepressed and she doesn't care much for monogamy. (Literary critics until the 1960s commonly called her a nymphomaniac.) She turns her male

admirers into women — Mike becomes a self-destructive alcoholic, Robert a moony romantic, Pedro a sacrificial virgin, and Jake a frustrated eunuch. At her entrance in the novel she is surrounded by an entourage of twittering fairies. Lady Ashley is a bitch not because she is nasty, bossy, or ill-tempered (she has lovely manners and a terrific personality). And perhaps not even because of her freewheeling, strident sexuality. She is a bitch because she overturns the male/female nexus. What could be a more threatening infraction in a Hemingway novel?

2a. Speaking of Hemingway: After his falling out with Gertrude Stein who had made unflattering comments about his writing in *The Autobiography of Alice B. Toklas*, Hemingway dropped her off a copy of his newly published *Death in the Afternoon* with the handwritten inscription, "A bitch is a bitch is a bitch."

[Q.] Why was Gertrude Stein a bitch?

[A.] For no longer admiring Hemingway. A bitch is a woman who criticizes.

3. "Ladies and gentlemen. I don't believe Mrs. Helmsley is charged in the indictment with being a tough bitch" is how her defense lawyer Gerald A. Feffer addressed the jury in Leona Helmsley's trial for tax fraud and extortion. He acknowledged that she was "sometimes rude and abrasive," and that she "may have overcompensated for being a woman in a hard-edged men's business world." Recognizing the difficulty of defending what the New York *Post* called "the woman that everyone loves to hate," his tactic was to preempt the prosecution by getting there first with "tough bitch." He lost.

4. *Esquire* awarded a Dubious Achievement of 1990 to Victor Kiam, owner of the New England Patriots football team, for saying "he could never have called Boston *Herald* reporter Lisa Olson 'a classic bitch' because he doesn't use the word *classic*." Some background on what had been one of that year's most discussed controversies: Olson aroused the ire of the Patriots for showing up in their locker room with the male reporters after a game. Members of the Patriots, as *Esquire* states, surrounded her, "thrusting their genitals in her face and daring her to touch them."

Why is Lisa Olson a bitch? For invading the male domain of sports reportage and the male territory of the locker room? For telling the world, instead of swallowing her degradation, pain, and anger? The club owner's use of "bitch" seems meant to conjure up the lurking idea of castrating female. Seen in that light the Patriots' act of "thrusting their genitals in her face" transforms an act of loutishness into a position of innocent vulnerability.

5. Bumper sticker observed on back of pickup truck:

Impeach Jane Fonda, American Traitor Bitch

The bumper sticker seemed relatively new and fresh. I observed it a full two decades after Jane Fonda's journey to North Vietnam which is the event that surely inspired this call to impeachment (from what? aerobics class?). *Bitch* here is an expletive. It originates in and sustains anger.

Calling Jane Fonda a "traitor" sounds a bit dated in the 1990s, but adding "bitch" gives the accusation timelessness and does the job of rekindling old indignation.

6. Claude Brown's account in *Manchild in the Promised Land* of how he learned about women from a street-smart older friend:

> Johnny was always telling us about bitches. To Johnny, every chick was a bitch. Even mothers were bitches. Of course there were some nice bitches, but they were still bitches. And a man had to be a dog in order to handle a bitch.
>
> Johnny said once, "If a bitch ever tells you she's only got a penny to buy the baby some milk, take it. You take it, 'cause she's gon git some more. Bitches can always git some money." He really knew about bitches. Cats would say, "I saw your sister today, and she is a fine bitch." Nobody was offended by it. That's just the way things were. It was easy to see all women as bitches.

Bitch in black male street parlance seems closer to its original meaning of a female breeder — not a nasty woman and not a powerful woman, but the biological bearer of litters. The word is likely to be used in courting as well as in anger by males seeking the sexual favor or a female, and a black female addressed as bitch by an admirer is expected to feel not insulted but honored by the attention. (*Bitch* signifies something different when black women use it competitively about other black women.) But even as an endearment, from male to female, there is no mistaking the lurking contempt.

A *Dictionary of Afro-American Slang* compiled by Clarence Major (under the imprint of the leftist International Publishers) provides only that *bitch* in black parlance is "a mean, flaunting homosexual," entirely omitting any reference to its rampant use in black street language as the substitute word for woman. A puzzling omission. Perhaps the word is so taken for granted that its primary meaning is not even recognized as black vernacular.

Bitch, mama, motherfucker — how frequently motherhood figures in street language. Mothers are the object of insults when playing the dozens. The ubiquitous motherfucker simultaneously strikes out at one's immediate foe as well as the sanctity of motherhood. Mama, which Clarence Major defines as "a pretty black girl," is an endearment that a man might address to a sexy contemporary. "Hey mama" is tinged with a certain sweetness. "Hey bitch" has more of an edge, more likely to be addressed to a woman the man no longer needs to sweet-talk. It is hard to think of white males coming on by evoking motherhood or of white women going for it. A white male addressing a woman as bitch is not likely to be expecting a sexual reward. She will be a bitch behind her back and after the relationship is over or didn't happen.

The widespread use of *bitch* by black men talking to black women, its currency in courting, and its routine acceptance by women are suggestive of some powerful alienation in male-female relations and in black self-identity. Although there may be the possibility of ironic inversion, as in calling a loved one nigger, a black man calling a loved one bitch is expressing contempt for the object of his desire with the gratuitous fillip of associative contempt for the woman who gave him life. Bitch, like motherfucker, bespeaks something threatening to the male sense of himself, a furious counter to emasculation in a world where, as the young Claude Brown figured out, mothers have all the power. It is not hard to see that the problem of black men is much more with white racism than it is with black women. Whatever the cause, however, the language sure doesn't benefit the women. Here is still one more saddening instance of the victim finding someone even more hapless to take things out on. (Does this process explain why Clarence Major's only reference for *bitch* is to the "mean, flaunting homosexual"?)

7. "Do you enjoy playing that role of castrating bitch" is a question put to Madonna by an interviewer for the *Advocate*. Madonna's answer: "I enjoy expressing myself. . . ."

A response to another question about the public's reaction to her movie *Truth or Dare*: "They already think I'm a cunt bitch, they already think I'm Attila the Hun. They already compare me to Adolf Hitler and Saddam Hussein."

Bitch has lost its power to muzzle Madonna. Unlike other female celebrities who have cringed from accusations of bitchiness (Joan Rivers, Imelda Marcos, Margaret Thatcher, Nancy Reagan), Madonna has made her fortune by exploiting criticism. Her career has skyrocketed with the media's charges of obscenity and sacrilege; she seems to embrace the *bitch* label with the same eager opportunism.

"I enjoy expressing myself" is not merely the explanation for why Madonna gets called bitch; "I enjoy expressing myself" is the key to defusing the power of *bitch* to fetter and subdue. Madonna has appropriated the word and turned the intended insult to her advantage. This act of appropriation, I predict, will embolden others with what consequences and effects it is impossible to foresee.

■ SUHEIR HAMMAD ━━━━━━━━━━━━━━━━━━━━━━━━━━━━━━━━

First Writing Since

Born to Palestinian parents in Jordan, Suheir Hammad (b. 1973) grew up mostly in Brooklyn, New York, moving there when she was five years old. Hammad is a political activist and slam poet who has won numerous awards, including a Tony for her participation in *Def Poetry Jam on Broadway* in 2003. Her poems, which are often meditations on her identity as a Palestinian American, have been published in a variety of journals and anthologies. In 1996, Hammad also published a book of her poetry, *Born Palestinian, Born Black*, and a memoir, *Drops of This Story*.

1. there have been no words.
i have not written one word.
no poetry in the ashes south of canal street.
no prose in the refrigerated trucks driving debris and dna.
not one word.

today is a week, and seven is of heavens, gods, science.
evident out my kitchen window is an abstract reality.
sky where once was steel.
smoke where once was flesh.

fire in the city air and i feared for my sister's life in a way never
before. and then, and now, i fear for the rest of us.

first, please god, let it be a mistake, the pilot's heart failed,
the plane's engine died.
then please god, let it be a nightmare, wake me now.
please god, after the second plane, please, don't let it be anyone
who looks like my brothers.

i do not know how bad a life has to break in order to kill.
i have never been so hungry that i willed hunger
i have never been so angry as to want to control a gun over a pen.
not really.
even as a woman, as a palestinian, as a broken human being.
never this broken.

more than ever, i believe there is no difference.
the most privileged nation, most americans do not know
the difference between indians, afghanis, syrians, muslims, sikhs, hindus.
more than ever, there is no difference.

2. thank you korea for kimchi and bibim bob, and corn tea and the
genteel smiles of the wait staff at wonjo — smiles never revealing
the heat of the food or how tired they must be working long midtown
shifts. thank you korea, for the belly craving that brought me into
the city late the night before and diverted my daily train ride into
the world trade center.

there are plenty of thank yous in ny right now.
thank you for my lazy procrastinating late ass.
thank you to the germs that had me call in sick.
thank you, my attitude, you had me fired the week before.
thank you for the train that never came,
the rude nyer who stole my cab going downtown.
thank you for the sense my mama gave me to run.
thank you for my legs, my eyes, my life.

3. the dead are called lost and their families hold up shaky
printouts in front of us through screens smoked up.

we are looking for iris, mother of three. please call with any
information. we are searching for priti, last seen on the 103rd
floor. she was talking to her husband on the phone and the line
went. please help us find george, also known as adel. his family is
waiting for him with his favorite meal. i am looking for my son, who
was delivering coffee. i am looking for my sister girl,
she started her job on monday.

i am looking for peace. i am looking for mercy. i am looking for
evidence of compassion. any evidence of life. i am looking for life.

4. ricardo on the radio said in his accent thick as yuca, "i will
feel so much better when the first bombs drop over there. and my
friends feel the same way."

on my block, a woman was crying in a car parked and stranded in hurt.
i offered comfort, extended a hand she did not see before she said,
"we're gonna burn them so bad, i swear, so bad." my hand went to my
head and my head went to the numbers within it of the dead iraqi
children, the dead in nicaragua. the dead in rwanda who had to vie
with fake sport wrestling for america's attention.

yet when people sent emails saying, this was bound to happen, lets
not forget u.s. transgressions, for half a second i felt resentful.
hold up with that, cause i live here, these are my friends and fam,
and it could have been me in those buildings, and we're not bad
people, do not support america's bullying.
can i just have a half second to feel bad?

if i can find through this exhaust people who were left behind to
mourn and to resist mass murder, i might be alright.

thank you to the woman who saw me brinking my cool and blinking back
tears. she opened her arms before she asked "do you want a hug?" a
big white woman, and her embrace was the kind only people with the
warmth of flesh can offer. i wasn't about to say no to any comfort.
"my brother's in the navy," i said. "and we're arabs".
"wow, you got double trouble." word.

5. one more person ask me if i knew the hijackers.
one more motherfucker ask me what navy my brother is in.
one more person assume no arabs or muslims were killed.
one more person assume they know me, or that i represent a people.
or that a people represent an evil.
or that evil is as simple as a flag and words on a page.

we did not vilify all white men when mcveigh bombed oklahoma.
america did not give out his family's addresses or where he went to
church. or blame the bible or pat robertson.

and when the networks air footage of palestinians dancing in the street, there is no apology that hungry children are bribed with sweets that turn their teeth brown. that correspondents edit images. that archives are there to facilitate lazy and inaccurate journalism.

and when we talk about holy books and hooded men and death, why do we never mention the kkk?

if there are any people on earth who understand
how new york is feeling right now,
they are in the west bank and the gaza strip.

6. today it is ten days. last night bush waged war on a man once openly funded by the cia. i do not know who is responsible. read too many books, know too many people to believe what i am told. i don't give a fuck about bin laden. his vision of the world does not include me or those i love. and petitions have been going around for years trying to get the u.s. sponsored taliban out of power. shit is complicated, and i don't know what to think.

but i know for sure who will pay.

in the world, it will be women, mostly colored and poor. women will have to bury children, and support themselves through grief. "either you are with us, or with the terrorists" meaning keep your people under control and your resistance censored. meaning we got the loot and the nukes.

in america, it will be those amongst us who refuse blanket attacks on the shivering. those of us who work toward social justice, in support of civil liberties, in opposition to hateful foreign policies.

i have never felt less american and more new yorker — particularly brooklyn, than these past days. the stars and stripes on all these cars and apartment windows represent the dead as citizens first not family members, not lovers.

i feel like my skin is real thin, and that my eyes are only going to get darker. the future holds little light.

my baby brother is a man now, and on alert, and praying five times a day that the orders he will take in a few days time are righteous and will not weigh his soul down from the afterlife he deserves.

both my brothers — my heart stops when i try to pray — not a beat to disturb my fear. one a rock god, the other a sergeant, and both palestinian, practicing muslim, gentle men. both born in brooklyn and their faces are of the archetypal arab man, all eyelashes and nose and beautiful color and stubborn hair.

what will their lives be like now?

over there is over here.

7. all day, across the river, the smell of burning rubber and limbs
floats through. the sirens have stopped now.
the advertisers are back on the air.
the rescue workers are traumatized.
the skyline is brought back to human size.
no longer taunting the gods with its height.

i have not cried at all while writing this. i cried when i saw those
buildings collapse on themselves like a broken heart. i have never
owned pain that needs to spread like that. and i cry daily that my
brothers return to our mother safe and whole.

there is no poetry in this. there are causes and effects. there are
symbols and ideologies. mad conspiracy here, and information we will
never know. there is death here, and there are promises of more.

there is life here. anyone reading this is breathing, maybe hurting,
but breathing for sure. and if there is any light to come, it will
shine from the eyes of those who look for peace and justice after the
rubble and rhetoric are cleared and the phoenix has risen.

affirm life.
affirm life.
we got to carry each other now.
you are either with life, or against it.
affirm life.

■ LANGSTON HUGHES

Theme for English B

Langston Hughes (1902–1967) was one of the most popular and influential writers of the Harlem Renaissance. Although he is arguably best
known for his poems, Hughes was also a prolific writer of novels, short
stories, plays, and essays, as well as two autobiographies: *The Big Sea* and
I Wonder as I Wander. He won numerous awards throughout his lifetime
for his literary achievements. In his poems, the style of which was heavily
influenced by the emerging musical genre of jazz, Hughes recorded the
experience of African Americans in the early twentieth century. Through
his poetry, he sought to dispel racial stereotypes and celebrate working-
class African Americans. *Weary Blues* (1926) was his first collection of
poetry. The poem "Theme for English B" was published in the collection
Montage of a Dream Deferred (1951).

■ ■ ■

The instructor said,

> *Go home and write*
> *a page tonight.*
> *And let that page come out of you —*
> *Then, it will be true.*

I wonder if it's that simple?
I am twenty-two, colored, born in Winston-Salem.
I went to school there, then Durham, then here
to this college on the hill above Harlem.
I am the only colored student in my class.
The steps from the hill lead down into Harlem,
through a park, then I cross St. Nicholas,
Eighth Avenue, Seventh, and I come to the Y,
the Harlem Branch Y, where I take the elevator
up to my room, sit down, and write this page:

It's not easy to know what is true for you or me
at twenty-two, my age. But I guess I'm what
I feel and see and hear, Harlem, I hear you:
hear you, hear me — we two — you, me, talk on this page.
(I hear New York too.) Me — who?
Well, I like to eat, sleep, drink, and be in love.
I like to work, read, learn, and understand life.
I like a pipe for a Christmas present,
or records — Bessie, obop, or Bach.
I guess being colored doesn't make me *not* like
the same things other folks like who are other races.
So will my page be colored that I write?
Being me, it will not be white.
But it will be
a part of you, instructor.
You are white —
yet a part of me, as I am a part of you.
That's American.
Sometimes perhaps you don't want to be a part of me.
Nor do I often want to be a part of you.
But we are, that's true!
As I learn from you,
I guess you learn from me —
although you're older — and white —
and somewhat more free.

This is my page for English B.

■ MARTIN LUTHER KING JR.

Letter from Birmingham Jail

Martin Luther King Jr. (1929–1968) was a Baptist minister from Atlanta, Georgia, who was instrumental in the success of the civil rights movement. In 1955, King led the Montgomery Bus Boycott after the arrest of Rosa Parks. In 1957, he helped organize the Southern Christian Leadership Conference, a civil rights organization that promoted nonviolent means of protest. Even though King believed in nonviolence, he was arrested several times for his efforts to desegregate the South. King wrote "Letter from Birmingham Jail" during an eight-day prison sentence for protesting. This open letter responded to a statement by eight Alabama clergymen called "A Call for Unity," which claimed that legal action, rather than civil disobedience, was the way to overcome segregation and other social injustices. The letter was first published in *The Christian Century* on June 12, 1963. Because of his "I Have a Dream" speech, which he delivered at the March on Washington in 1963, King is regarded as one of the best American orators. King was awarded the Nobel Peace Prize in 1964. He was assassinated on April 4, 1968, in Memphis, Tennessee.

■ ■ ■

April 16, 1963

My Dear Fellow Clergymen:

While confined here in the Birmingham city jail, I came across your recent statement calling my present activities "unwise and untimely." Seldom do I pause to answer criticism of my work and ideas. If I sought to answer all the criticisms that cross my desk, my secretaries would have little time for anything other than such correspondence in the course of the day, and I would have no time for constructive work. But since I feel that you are men of genuine good will and that your criticisms are sincerely set forth, I want to try to answer your statement in what I hope will be patient and reasonable terms.

I think I should indicate why I am here in Birmingham, since you have been influenced by the view which argues against "outsiders coming in." I have the honor of serving as president of the Southern Christian Leadership Conference, an organization operating in every southern state, with headquarters in Atlanta, Georgia. We have some eighty-five affiliated organizations across the South, and one of them is the Alabama Christian Movement for Human Rights. Frequently we share staff, educational, and financial resources with our affiliates. Several months ago the affiliate here in Birmingham asked us to be on call to engage in a nonviolent direct-action program if such were deemed necessary. We readily consented, and when the hour came we lived up to our promise. So I, along with several members of my staff, am here because I was invited here. I am here because I have organizational ties here.

But more basically, I am in Birmingham because injustice is here. Just as the prophets of the eighth century B.C. left their villages and carried their "thus saith the Lord" far beyond the boundaries of their home towns, and just as the Apostle Paul left his village of Tarsus and carried the gospel of Jesus Christ to the far corners of the Greco-Roman world, so am I compelled to carry the gospel of freedom beyond my own home town. Like Paul, I must constantly respond to the Macedonian call for aid.

Moreover, I am cognizant of the interrelatedness of all communities and states. I cannot sit idly by in Atlanta and not be concerned about what happens in Birmingham. Injustice anywhere is a threat to justice everywhere. We are caught in an inescapable network of mutuality, tied in a single garment of destiny. Whatever affects one directly, affects all indirectly. Never again can we afford to live with the narrow, provincial "outside agitator" idea. Anyone who lives inside the United States can never be considered an outsider anywhere within its bounds.

You deplore the demonstrations taking place in Birmingham. But your statement, I am sorry to say, fails to express a similar concern for the conditions that brought about the demonstrations. I am sure that none of you would want to rest content with the superficial kind of social analysis that deals merely with effects and does not grapple with underlying causes. It is unfortunate that demonstrations are taking place in Birmingham, but it is even more unfortunate that the city's white power structure left the Negro community with no alternative.

In any nonviolent campaign there are four basic steps: collection of the facts to determine whether injustices exist; negotiation; self-purification; and direct action. We have gone through all these steps in Birmingham. There can be no gainsaying the fact that racial injustice engulfs this community. Birmingham is probably the most thoroughly segregated city in the United States. Its ugly record of brutality is widely known. Negroes have experienced grossly unjust treatment in the courts. There have been more unsolved bombings of Negro homes and churches in Birmingham than in any other city in the nation. These are the hard, brutal facts of the case. On the basis of these conditions, Negro leaders sought to negotiate with the city fathers. But the latter consistently refused to engage in good-faith negotiation.

Then, last September, came the opportunity to talk with leaders of Birmingham's economic community. In the course of the negotiations, certain promises were made by the merchants — for example, to remove the stores' humiliating racial signs. On the basis of these promises, the Reverend Fred Shuttlesworth and the leaders of the Alabama Christian Movement for Human Rights agreed to a moratorium on all demonstrations. As the weeks and months went by, we realized that we were the victims of a broken promise. A few signs, briefly removed, returned; the others remained.

As in so many past experiences, our hopes had been blasted, and the shadow of deep disappointment settled upon us. We had no alternative except to prepare for direct action, whereby we would present our very bodies as a means of laying our case before the conscience of the local and the national community. Mindful of the difficulties involved, we decided to undertake a process of self-purification. We began a series of workshops on nonviolence, and we repeatedly asked ourselves: "Are you able to accept blows without retaliating?" "Are you able to endure the ordeal of jail?" We decided to schedule our direct-action program for the Easter season, realizing that except for Christmas, this is the main shopping period of the year. Knowing that a strong economic withdrawal program would be the by-product of direct action, we felt that this would be the best time to bring pressure to bear on the merchants for the needed change.

Then it occurred to us that Birmingham's mayoral election was coming up in March, and we speedily decided to postpone action until after election day. When we discovered that the Commissioner of Public Safety, Eugene "Bull" Connor, had piled up enough votes to be in the run-off, we decided again to postpone action until the day after the run-off so that the demonstrations could not be used to cloud the issues. Like many others, we wanted to see Mr. Connor defeated, and to this end we endured postponement after postponement. Having aided in this community need, we felt that our direct-action program could be delayed no longer.

You may well ask, "Why direct action? Why sit-ins, marches, and so forth? Isn't negotiation a better path?" You are quite right in calling for negotiation. Indeed, this is the very purpose of direct action. Nonviolent direct action seeks to create such a crisis and foster such a tension that a community which has constantly refused to negotiate is forced to confront the issue. It seeks so to dramatize the issue that it can no longer be ignored. My citing the creation of tension as part of the work of the nonviolent-resister may sound rather shocking. But I must confess that I am not afraid of the word "tension." I have earnestly opposed violent tension, but there is a type of constructive, nonviolent tension which is necessary for growth. Just as Socrates felt that it was necessary to create a tension in the mind so that individuals could rise from the bondage of myths and half-truths to the unfettered realm of creative analysis and objective appraisal, so must we see the need for nonviolent gadflies to create the kind of tension in society that will help men rise from the dark depths of prejudice and racism to the majestic heights of understanding and brotherhood.

The purpose of our direct-action program is to create a situation so crisis-packed that it will inevitably open the door to negotiation. I therefore concur with you in your call for negotiation. Too long has our beloved Southland been bogged down in a tragic effort to live in monologue rather than dialogue.

One of the basic points in your statement is that the action that I and my associates have taken in Birmingham is untimely. Some have asked: "Why didn't you give the new city administration time to act?" The only answer that I can give to this query is that the new Birmingham administration must be prodded about as much as the outgoing one, before it will act. We are sadly mistaken if we feel that the election of Albert Boutwell as mayor will bring the millennium to Birmingham. While Mr. Boutwell is a much more gentle person than Mr. Connor, they are both segregation-ists, dedicated to maintenance of the status quo. I have hoped that Mr. Boutwell will be reasonable enough to see the futility of massive resistance to desegregation. But he will not see this without pressure from devotees of civil rights. My friends, I must say to you that we have not made a single gain in civil rights without determined legal and nonviolent pressure. Lamentably, it is an historical fact that privileged groups seldom give up their privileges voluntarily. Individuals may see the moral light and volun-tarily give up their unjust posture, but, as Reinhold Niebuhr has reminded us, groups tend to be more immoral than individuals.

We know through painful experience that freedom is never voluntarily given by the oppressor; it must be demanded by the oppressed. Frankly, I have yet to engage in a direct-action campaign that was "well timed" in the view of those who have not suffered unduly from the disease of segrega-tion. For years now I have heard the word "Wait!" It rings in the ear of every Negro with piercing familiarity. This "Wait" has almost always meant "Never." We must come to see, with one of our distinguished jurists, that "justice too long delayed is justice denied."

We have waited for more than 340 years for our constitutional and God-given rights. The nations of Asia and Africa are moving with jet-like speed toward gaining political independence, but we still creep at horse-and-buggy pace toward gaining a cup of coffee at a lunch counter. Perhaps it is easy for those who have never felt the stinging darts of segregation to say, "Wait." But when you have seen vicious mobs lynch your mothers and fathers at will and drown your sisters and brothers at whim; when you have seen hate-filled policemen curse, kick, and even kill your black broth-ers and sisters; when you see the vast majority of your twenty million Negro brothers smothering in an airtight cage of poverty in the midst of an affluent society; when you suddenly find your tongue twisted and your speech stammering as you seek to explain to your six-year-old daughter why she can't go to the public amusement park that has just been adver-tised on television, and see tears welling up in her eyes when she is told that Funtown is closed to colored children, and see ominous clouds of inferiority beginning to form in her little mental sky, and see her beginning to distort her personality by developing an unconscious bitterness toward white people; when you have to concoct an answer for a five-year-old son who is asking, "Daddy, why do white people treat colored people so mean?"; when you take a cross-country drive and find it necessary to sleep night after night in the uncomfortable corners of your automobile because no motel will accept you; when you are humiliated day in and day out by nagging signs reading "white" and "colored"; when your first name becomes "nigger," your middle name becomes "boy" (however old you are) and your last name becomes "John," and your wife and mother are never given the respected title "Mrs."; when you are harried by day and haunted by night by the fact that you are a Negro, living constantly at tiptoe stance, never quite knowing what to expect next, and are plagued with inner fears and outer resentments; when you are forever fighting a degenerating sense of "nobodiness" — then you will understand why we find it difficult to wait. There comes a time when the cup of endurance runs over, and men are no longer willing to be plunged into the abyss of despair. I hope, sirs, you can understand our legitimate and unavoidable impatience.

You express a great deal of anxiety over our willingness to break laws. This is certainly a legitimate concern. Since we so diligently urge people to obey the Supreme Court's decision of 1954 outlawing segregation in the public schools, at first glance it may seem rather paradoxical for us consciously to break laws. One may well ask: "How can you advocate breaking some laws and obeying others?" The answer lies in the fact that there are two types of laws: just and unjust. I would be the first to advocate obeying just laws. One has not only a legal but a moral responsibility to obey just laws. Conversely, one has a moral responsibility to disobey unjust laws. I would agree with St. Augustine that "an unjust law is no law at all."

Now, what is the difference between the two? How does one determine whether a law is just or unjust? A just law is a man-made code that squares with the moral law or the law of God. An unjust law is a code that is out of harmony with the moral law. To put it in the terms of St. Thomas Aquinas: An unjust law is a human law that is not rooted in eternal law and natural law. Any law that uplifts human personality is just. Any law that degrades human personality is unjust. All segregation statutes are unjust because segregation distorts the soul and damages the personality. It gives the segregator a false sense of superiority and the segregated a false sense of inferiority. Segregation, to use the terminology of the Jewish philosopher Martin Buber, substitutes an "I-it" relationship for an "I-thou" relationship and ends up relegating persons to the status of things. Hence segregation is not only politically, economically, and sociologically unsound, it is morally wrong and sinful. Paul Tillich has said that sin is separation. Is not segregation an existential expression of man's tragic separation, his awful estrangement, his terrible sinfulness? Thus it is that I can urge men to obey the 1954 decision of the Supreme Court, for it is morally right; and I can urge them to disobey segregation ordinances, for they are morally wrong.

Let us consider a more concrete example of just and unjust laws. An unjust law is a code that a numerical or power majority group compels a minority group to obey but does not make binding on itself. This is *difference* made legal. By the same token, a just law is a code that a majority compels a minority to follow and that it is willing to follow itself. This is *sameness* made legal.

Let me give another explanation. A law is unjust if it is inflicted on a minority that, as a result of being denied the right to vote, had no part in enacting or devising the law. Who can say that the legislature of Alabama which set up that state's segregation laws was democratically elected? Throughout Alabama all sorts of devious methods are used to prevent Negroes from becoming registered voters, and there are some counties in which, even though Negroes constitute a majority of the population, not a single Negro is registered. Can any law enacted under such circumstances be considered democratically structured?

Sometimes a law is just on its face and unjust in its application. For instance, I have been arrested on a charge of parading without a permit. Now, there is nothing wrong in having an ordinance which requires a permit for a parade. But such an ordinance becomes unjust when it is used to maintain segregation and to deny citizens the First Amendment privilege of peaceful assembly and protest.

I hope you are able to see the distinction I am trying to point out. In no sense do I advocate evading or defying the law, as would the rabid segregationist. That would lead to anarchy. One who breaks an unjust law must do so openly, lovingly, and with a willingness to accept the penalty. I submit that an individual who breaks a law that conscience tells him is unjust, and who willingly accepts the penalty of imprisonment in order to arouse the conscience of the community over its injustice, is in reality expressing the highest respect for law.

Of course, there is nothing new about this kind of civil disobedience. It was evidenced sublimely in the refusal of Shadrach, Meshach, and Abednego to obey the laws of Nebuchadnezzar, on the ground that a higher moral law was at stake. It was practiced superbly by the early Christians, who were willing to face hungry lions and the excruciating pain of chopping blocks rather than submit to certain unjust laws of the Roman Empire. To a degree, academic freedom is a reality today because Socrates practiced civil disobedience. In our own nation, the Boston Tea Party represented a massive act of civil disobedience.

We should never forget that everything Adolf Hitler did in Germany was "legal" and everything the Hungarian freedom fighters did in Hungary was "illegal." It was "illegal" to aid and comfort a Jew in Hitler's Germany. Even so, I am sure that, had I lived in Germany at the time, I would have aided and comforted my Jewish brothers. If today I lived in a Communist country where certain principles dear to the Christian faith are suppressed, I would openly advocate disobeying that country's antireligious laws.

I must make two honest confessions to you, my Christian and Jewish brothers. First, I must confess that over the past few years I have been gravely disappointed with the white moderate. I have almost reached the regrettable conclusion that the Negro's great stumbling block in his stride toward freedom is not the White Citizen's Counciler or the Ku Klux Klanner, but the white moderate, who is more devoted to "order" than to justice; who prefers a negative peace which is the absence of tension to a positive peace which is the presence of justice; who constantly says, "I agree with you in the goal you seek, but I cannot agree with your methods of direct action"; who paternalistically believes he can set the timetable for another man's freedom; who lives by a mythical concept of time and who constantly advises the Negro to wait for a "more convenient season." Shallow understanding from people of good will is more frustrating than absolute misunderstanding from people of ill will. Lukewarm acceptance is much more bewildering than outright rejection.

I had hoped that the white moderate would understand that law and order exist for the purpose of establishing justice and that when they fail in this purpose they become the dangerously structured dams that block the flow of social progress. I had hoped that the white moderate would understand that the present tension in the South is a necessary phase of the transition from an obnoxious negative peace, in which the Negro passively accepted his unjust plight, to a substantive and positive peace, in which all men will respect the dignity and worth of human personality. Actually, we who engage in nonviolent direct action are not the creators of tension. We merely bring to the surface the hidden tension that is already alive. We bring it out in the open, where it can be seen and dealt with. Like a boil that can never be cured so long as it is covered up but must be opened with all its ugliness to the natural medicines of air and light, injustice must be exposed, with all the tension its exposure creates, to the light of human conscience and the air of national opinion, before it can be cured.

In your statement you assert that our actions, even though peaceful, must be condemned because they precipitate violence. But is this a logical assertion? Isn't this like condemning a robbed man because his possession of money precipitated the evil act of robbery? Isn't this like condemning Socrates because his unswerving commitment to truth and his philosophical inquiries precipitated the act by the misguided populace in which they made him drink hemlock? Isn't this like condemning Jesus because his unique God-consciousness and never-ceasing devotion to God's will precipitated the evil act of crucifixion? We must come to see that, as the federal courts have consistently affirmed, it is wrong to urge an individual to cease his efforts to gain his basic constitutional rights because the quest may precipitate violence. Society must protect the robbed and punish the robber.

I had also hoped that the white moderate would reject the myth concerning time in relation to the struggle for freedom. I have just received a letter from a white brother in Texas. He writes: "All Christians know that the colored people will receive equal rights eventually, but it is possible that you are in too great a religious hurry. It has taken Christianity almost two thousand years to accomplish what it has. The teachings of Christ take time to come to earth." Such an attitude stems from a tragic misconception of time, from the strangely irrational notion that there is something in the very flow of time that will inevitably cure all ills. Actually, time itself is neutral; it can be used either destructively or constructively. More and more I feel that the people of ill will have used time much more effectively than have the people of good will. We will have to repent in this generation not merely for the hateful words and actions of the bad people, but for the appalling silence of the good people. Human progress never rolls in on wheels of inevitability; it comes through the tireless efforts of men willing to be co-workers with God, and without this hard work, time itself becomes an ally of the forces of social stagnation. We must use time creatively, in the knowledge that the time is always ripe to do right. Now is

the time to make real the promise of democracy and transform our pend-
ing national elegy into a creative psalm of brotherhood. Now is the time to
lift our national policy from the quicksand of racial injustice to the solid
rock of human dignity.

You speak of our activity in Birmingham as extreme. At first I was
rather disappointed that fellow clergymen would see my nonviolent efforts
as those of an extremist. I began thinking about the fact that I stand in the
middle of two opposing forces in the Negro community. One is a force of
complacency, made up in part of Negroes who, as a result of long years of
oppression, are so drained of self-respect and a sense of "somebodiness"
that they have adjusted to segregation; and in part of a few middle-class
Negroes who, because of a degree of academic and economic security and
because in some ways they profit by segregation, have become insensitive
to the problems of the masses. The other force is one of bitterness and
hatred, and it comes perilously close to advocating violence. It is expressed
in the various black nationalist groups that are springing up across the
nation, the largest and best-known being Elijah Muhammad's Muslim
movement. Nourished by the Negro's frustration over the continued existence of racial discrimination, this movement is made up of people who
have lost faith in America, who have absolutely repudiated Christianity,
and who have concluded that the white man is an incorrigible "devil."

I have tried to stand between these two forces, saying that we need
emulate neither the "do-nothingism" of the complacent nor the hatred and
despair of the black nationalist. For there is the more excellent way of love
and nonviolent protest. I am grateful to God that, through the influence of
the Negro church, the way of nonviolence became an integral part of our
struggle.

If this philosophy had not emerged, by now many streets of the South
would, I am convinced, be flowing with blood. And I am further convinced
that if our white brothers dismiss as "rabble-rousers" and "outside agitators" those of us who employ nonviolent direct action, and if they refuse to
support our nonviolent efforts, millions of Negroes will, out of frustration
and despair, seek solace and security in black nationalist ideologies — a
development that would inevitably lead to a frightening racial nightmare.

Oppressed people cannot remain oppressed forever. The yearning for
freedom eventually manifests itself, and that is what has happened to the
American Negro. Something within has reminded him of his birthright of
freedom, and something without has reminded him that it can be gained.
Consciously or unconsciously, he has been caught up by the *Zeitgeist*, and
with his black brothers of Africa and his brown and yellow brothers of
Asia, South America, and the Caribbean, the United States Negro is moving
with a sense of great urgency toward the promised land of racial justice. If
one recognizes this vital urge that has engulfed the Negro community, one
should readily understand why public demonstrations are taking place.
The Negro has many pent-up resentments and latent frustrations, and he
must release them. So let him march; let him make prayer pilgrimages to

the city hall; let him go on freedom rides — and try to understand why he must do so. If his repressed emotions are not released in nonviolent ways, they will seek expression through violence; this is not a threat but a fact of history. So I have not said to my people, "Get rid of your discontent." Rather, I have tried to say that this normal and healthy discontent can be channeled into the creative outlet of nonviolent direct action. And now this approach is being termed extremist.

But though I was initially disappointed at being categorized as an extremist, as I continued to think about the matter I gradually gained a measure of satisfaction from the label. Was not Jesus an extremist for love: "Love your enemies, bless them that curse you, do good to them that hate you, and pray for them which despitefully use you, and persecute you." Was not Amos an extremist for justice: "Let justice roll down like waters and righteousness like an ever-flowing stream." Was not Paul an extremist for the Christian gospel: "I bear in my body the marks of the Lord Jesus." Was not Martin Luther an extremist: "Here I stand; I cannot do otherwise, so help me God." And John Bunyan: "I will stay in jail to the end of my days before I make a butchery of my conscience." And Abraham Lincoln: "This nation cannot survive half slave and half free." And Thomas Jefferson: "We hold these truths to be self-evident, that all men are created equal. . . ." So the question is not whether we will be extremists, but what kind of extremists we will be. Will we be extremists for hate or for love? Will we be extremists for the preservation of injustice or for the extension of justice? In that dramatic scene on Calvary's hill three men were crucified. We must never forget that all three were crucified for the same crime — the crime of extremism. Two were extremists for immorality, and thus fell below their environment. The other, Jesus Christ, was an extremist for love, truth, and goodness, and thereby rose above his environment. Perhaps the South, the nation, and the world are in dire need of creative extremists.

I had hoped that the white moderate would see this need. Perhaps I was too optimistic; perhaps I expected too much. I suppose I should have realized that few members of the oppressor race can understand the deep groans and passionate yearnings of the oppressed race, and still fewer have the vision to see that injustice must be rooted out by strong, persistent, and determined action. I am thankful, however, that some of our white brothers in the South have grasped the meaning of this social revolution and committed themselves to it. They are still all too few in quantity, but they are big in quality. Some — such as Ralph McGill, Lillian Smith, Harry Golden, James McBridge Dabbs, Ann Braden, and Sarah Patton Boyle — have written about our struggle in eloquent and prophetic terms. Others have marched with us down nameless streets of the South. They have languished in filthy, roach-infested jails, suffering the abuse and brutality of policemen who view them as "dirty nigger-lovers." Unlike so many of their moderate brothers and sisters, they have recognized the urgency of the moment and sensed the need for powerful "action" antidotes to combat the disease of segregation.

Let me take note of my other major disappointment. I have been so greatly disappointed with the white church and its leadership. Of course, there are some notable exceptions. I am not unmindful of the fact that each of you has taken some significant stands on this issue. I commend you, Reverend Stallings, for your Christian stand on this past Sunday, in welcoming Negroes to your worship service on a nonsegregated basis. I commend the Catholic leaders of this state for integrating Spring Hill College several years ago.

But despite these notable exceptions, I must honestly reiterate that I have been disappointed with the church. I do not say this as one of those negative critics who can always find something wrong with the church. I say this as a minister of the gospel, who loves the church; who was nurtured in its bosom; who has been sustained by its spiritual blessings and who will remain true to it as long as the cord of life shall lengthen.

When I was suddenly catapulted into the leadership of the bus protest in Montgomery, Alabama, a few years ago, I felt we would be supported by the white church. I felt that the white ministers, priests, and rabbis of the South would be among our strongest allies. Instead, some have been outright opponents, refusing to understand the freedom movement and misrepresenting its leaders; all too many others have been more cautious than courageous and have remained silent behind the anesthetizing security of stained-glass windows.

In spite of my shattered dreams, I came to Birmingham with the hope that the white religious leadership of this community would see the justice of our cause and, with deep moral concern, would serve as the channel through which our just grievances could reach the power structure. I had hoped that each of you would understand. But again I have been disappointed. . . .

There was a time when the church was very powerful — in the time when the early Christians rejoiced at being deemed worthy to suffer for what they believed. In those days the church was not merely a thermometer that recorded the ideas and principles of popular opinion; it was a thermostat that transformed the mores of society. Whenever the early Christians entered a town, the people in power became disturbed and immediately sought to convict the Christians for being "disturbers of the peace" and "outside agitators." But the Christians pressed on, in the conviction that they were "a colony of heaven," called to obey God rather than man. Small in number, they were big in commitment. They were too God-intoxicated to be "astronomically intimidated." By their effort and example they brought an end to such ancient evils as infanticide and gladiatorial contests.

Things are different now. So often the contemporary church is a weak, ineffectual voice with an uncertain sound. So often it is an archdefender of the status quo. Far from being disturbed by the presence of the church, the power structure of the average community is consoled by the church's silent — and often even vocal — sanction of things as they are.

But the judgment of God is upon the church as never before. If today's church does not recapture the sacrificial spirit of the early church, it will lose its authenticity, forfeit the loyalty of millions, and be dismissed as an irrelevant social club with no meaning for the twentieth century. Every day I meet young people whose disappointment with the church has turned into outright disgust.

Perhaps I have once again been too optimistic. Is organized religion too inextricably bound to the status quo to save our nation and the world? Perhaps I must turn my faith to the inner spiritual church, the church within the church, as the true *ekklesia* and the hope of the world. But again I am thankful to God that some noble souls from the ranks of organized religion have broken loose from the paralyzing chains of conformity and joined us as active partners in the struggle for freedom. They have left their secure congregations and walked the streets of Albany, Georgia, with us. They have gone down the highways of the South on tortuous rides for freedom. Yes, they have gone to jail with us. Some have been dismissed from their churches, have lost the support of their bishops and fellow ministers. But they have acted in the faith that right defeated is stronger than evil triumphant. Their witness has been the spiritual salt that has preserved the true meaning of the gospel in these troubled times. They have carved a tunnel of hope through the dark mountain of disappointment.

I hope the church as a whole will meet the challenge of this decisive hour. But even if the church does not come to the aid of justice, I have no despair about the future. I have no fear about the outcome of our struggle in Birmingham, even if our motives are at present misunderstood. We will reach the goal of freedom in Birmingham and all over the nation, because the goal of America is freedom. Abused and scorned though we may be, our destiny is tied up with America's destiny. Before the pilgrims landed at Plymouth, we were here. Before the pen of Jefferson etched the majestic words of the Declaration of Independence across the pages of history, we were here. For more than two centuries our forebears labored in this country without wages: they made cotton king; they built the homes of their masters while suffering gross injustice and shameful humiliation — and yet out of a bottomless vitality they continued to thrive and develop. If the inexpressible cruelties of slavery could not stop us, the opposition we now face will surely fail. We will win our freedom because the sacred heritage of our nation and the eternal will of God are embodied in our echoing demands.

Before closing I feel impelled to mention one other point in your statement that has troubled me profoundly. You warmly commended the Birmingham police force for keeping "order" and "preventing violence." I doubt that you would have so warmly commended the police force if you had seen its dogs sinking their teeth into unarmed, nonviolent Negroes. I doubt that you would so quickly commend the policemen if you were to observe their ugly and inhumane treatment of Negroes here in the city jail; if you were to watch them push and curse old Negro women and young

Negro girls; if you were to see them slap and kick old Negro men and young boys; if you were to observe them, as they did on two occasions, refuse to give us food because we wanted to sing our grace together. I cannot join you in your praise of the Birmingham police department.

It is true that the police have exercised a degree of discipline in handling the demonstrators. In this sense they have conducted themselves rather "nonviolently" in public. But for what purpose? To preserve the evil system of segregation. Over the past few years I have consistently preached that nonviolence demands that the means we use must be as pure as the ends we seek. I have tried to make clear that it is wrong to use immoral means to attain moral ends. But now I must affirm that it is just as wrong, or perhaps even more so, to use moral means to preserve immoral ends. Perhaps Mr. Connor and his policemen have been rather nonviolent in public, as was Chief Pritchett in Albany, Georgia, but they have used the moral means of nonviolence to maintain the immoral end of racial injustice. As T. S. Eliot has said. "The last temptation is the greatest treason: To do the right deed for the wrong reason."

I wish you had commended the Negro sit-inners and demonstrators of Birmingham for their sublime courage, their willingness to suffer, and their amazing discipline in the midst of great provocation. One day the South will recognize its real heroes. They will be the James Merediths, with the noble sense of purpose that enables them to face jeering and hostile mobs, and with the agonizing loneliness that characterizes the life of the pioneer. They will be old, oppressed, battered Negro women, symbolized in a seventy-two-year-old woman in Montgomery, Alabama, who rose up with a sense of dignity and with her people decided not to ride segregated buses, and who responded with ungrammatical profundity to one who inquired about her weariness: "My feets is tired, but my soul is at rest." They will be the young high school and college students, the young ministers of the gospel and a host of their elders, courageously and nonviolently sitting in at lunch counters and willingly going to jail for conscience' sake. One day the South will know that when these disinherited children of God sat down at lunch counters, they were in reality standing up for what is best in the American dream and for the most sacred values in our Judaeo-Christian heritage, thereby bringing our nation back to those great wells of democracy which were dug deep by the founding fathers in their formulation of the Constitution and the Declaration of Independence.

Never before have I written so long a letter. I'm afraid it is much too long to take your precious time. I can assure you that it would have been much shorter if I had been writing from a comfortable desk, but what else can one do when he is alone in a narrow jail cell, other than write long letters, think long thoughts, and pray long prayers?

If I have said anything in this letter that overstates the truth and indicates an unreasonable impatience, I beg you to forgive me. If I have said anything that understates the truth and indicates my having a patience that allows me to settle for anything less than brotherhood, I beg God to forgive me.

I hope this letter finds you strong in the faith. I also hope that circumstances will soon make it possible for me to meet each of you, not as an integrationist or a civil rights leader but as a fellow clergyman and a Christian brother. Let us all hope that the dark clouds of racial prejudice will soon pass away and the deep fog of misunderstanding will be lifted from our fear-drenched communities, and in some not too distant tomorrow the radiant stars of love and brotherhood will shine over our great nation with all their scintillating beauty.

Yours for the cause of
Peace and Brotherhood,
Martin Luther King Jr.

■   JONATHAN LETHEM ─────────────────────────────

The Ecstasy of Influence: A Plagiarism

Jonathan Lethem (b. 1964) is a writer of fiction and nonfiction who grew up in New York City. His novel *Motherless Brooklyn*, one of his best-known works, won several awards, including a National Book Critic's Circle Award. In 2005, Lethem received a MacArthur Fellowship. Lethem is interested in both the literary and the music worlds; he interviewed Bob Dylan for *Rolling Stone* in 2006 and was the keynote speaker at the Experience Music Project Pop Conference in 2007. The essay "The Ecstasy of Influence: A Plagiarism," published in the February 2007 issue of *Harper's*, explores the paradoxical assumptions about copyright laws and intellectual property in visual, musical, and literary works of art. Inspired by his research for this essay, Lethem created the Promiscuous Materials Project, a collection of stories and song lyrics that writers and musicians can take and adapt for their own purposes: http://www.jonathanlethem.com/promiscuous_materials.html.

■ ■ ■

All mankind is of one author, and is one volume; when one man dies, one chapter is not torn out of the book, but translated into a better language; and every chapter must be so translated. . . .

— JOHN DONNE

Love and Theft

Consider this tale: a cultivated man of middle age looks back on the story of an *amour fou*, one beginning when, traveling abroad, he takes a room as a lodger. The moment he sees the daughter of the house, he is lost. She is a preteen, whose charms instantly enslave him. Heedless of her age, he becomes intimate with her. In the end she dies, and the narrator — marked by her forever — remains alone. The name of the girl supplies the title of the story: *Lolita*.

The author of the story I've described, Heinz von Lichberg, published his tale of Lolita in 1916, forty years before Vladimir Nabokov's novel. Lichberg later became a prominent journalist in the Nazi era, and his youthful works faded from view. Did Nabokov, who remained in Berlin until 1937, adopt Lichberg's tale consciously? Or did the earlier tale exist for Nabokov as a hidden, unacknowledged memory? The history of literature is not without examples of this phenomenon, called cryptomnesia. Another hypothesis is that Nabokov, knowing Lichberg's tale perfectly well, had set himself to that art of quotation that Thomas Mann, himself a master of it, called "higher cribbing." Literature has always been a crucible in which familiar themes are continually recast. Little of what we admire in Nabokov's *Lolita* is to be found in its predecessor; the former is in no way deducible from the latter. Still: did Nabokov consciously borrow and quote?

"When you live outside the law, you have to eliminate dishonesty." The line comes from Don Siegel's 1958 film noir, *The Lineup*, written by Stirling Silliphant. The film still haunts revival houses, likely thanks to Eli Wallach's blazing portrayal of a sociopathic hit man and to Siegel's long, sturdy auteurist career. Yet what were those words worth — to Siegel, or Silliphant, or their audience — in 1958? And again: what was the line worth when Bob Dylan heard it (presumably in some Greenwich Village repertory cinema), cleaned it up a little, and inserted it into "Absolutely Sweet Marie"? What are they worth now, to the culture at large?

Appropriation has always played a key role in Dylan's music. The songwriter has grabbed not only from a panoply of vintage Hollywood films but from Shakespeare and F. Scott Fitzgerald and Junichi Saga's *Confessions of a Yakuza*. He also nabbed the title of Eric Lott's study of minstrelsy for his 2001 album *Love and Theft*. One imagines Dylan liked the general resonance of the title, in which emotional misdemeanors stalk the sweetness of love, as they do so often in Dylan's songs. Lott's title is, of course, itself a riff on Leslie Fiedler's *Love and Death in the American Novel*, which famously identifies the literary motif of the interdependence of a white man and a dark man, like Huck and Jim or Ishmael and Queequeg — a series of nested references to Dylan's own appropriating, minstrel-boy self. Dylan's art offers a paradox: while it famously urges us not to look back, it also encodes a knowledge of past sources that might otherwise have little home in contemporary culture, like the Civil War poetry of the Confederate bard Henry Timrod, resuscitated in lyrics on Dylan's newest record, *Modern Times*. Dylan's originality and his appropriations are as one.

The same might be said of *all* art. I realized this forcefully when one day I went looking for the John Donne passage quoted above. I know the lines, I confess, not from a college course but from the movie version of *84, Charing Cross Road* with Anthony Hopkins and Anne Bancroft. I checked out *84, Charing Cross Road* from the library in the hope of finding the Donne passage, but it wasn't in the book. It's alluded to in the play that was adapted from the book, but it isn't reprinted. So I rented the movie again, and there was the passage, read in voice-over by Anthony Hopkins but without attribution. Unfortunately, the line was also abridged so that, when I finally turned to the Web, I found myself searching for the line "all mankind is of one volume" instead of "all mankind is of one author, and is one volume."

My Internet search was initially no more successful than my library search. I had thought that summoning books from the vasty deep was a matter of a few keystrokes, but when I visited the website of the Yale library, I found that most of its books don't yet exist as computer text. As a last-ditch effort I searched the seemingly more obscure phrase "every chapter must be so translated." The passage I wanted finally came to me, as it turns out, not as part of a scholarly library collection but simply because someone who loves Donne had posted it on his homepage. The lines I sought were from Meditation 17 in *Devotions upon Emergent Occasions*, which happens to be the most famous thing Donne ever wrote, containing as it does the line "never send to know for whom the bell tolls; it tolls for thee." My search had led me from a movie to a book to a play to a website and back to a book. Then again, those words may be as famous as they are only because Hemingway lifted them for his book title.

Literature has been in a plundered, fragmentary state for a long time. When I was thirteen I purchased an anthology of Beat writing. Immediately, and to my very great excitement, I discovered one William S. Burroughs, author of something called *Naked Lunch*, excerpted there in all its coruscating brilliance. Burroughs was then as radical a literary man as the world had to offer. Nothing, in all my experience of literature since, has ever had as strong an effect on my sense of the sheer possibilities of writing. Later, attempting to understand this impact, I discovered that Burroughs had incorporated snippets of other writers' texts into his work, an action I knew my teachers would have called plagiarism. Some of these borrowings had been lifted from American science fiction of the Forties and Fifties, adding a secondary shock of recognition for me. By then I knew that this "cut-up method," as Burroughs called it, was central to whatever he thought he was doing, and that he quite literally believed it to be akin to magic. When he wrote about his process, the hairs on my neck stood up, so palpable was the excitement. Burroughs was interrogating the universe with scissors and a paste pot, and the least imitative of authors was no plagiarist at all.

Contamination Anxiety

In 1941, on his front porch, Muddy Waters recorded a song for the folk-lorist Alan Lomax. After singing the song, which he told Lomax was entitled "Country Blues," Waters described how he came to write it. "I made it on about the eighth of October '38," Waters said. "I was fixin' a puncture on a car. I had been mistreated by a girl. I just felt blue, and the song fell into my mind and it come to me just like that and I started singing." Then Lomax, who knew of the Robert Johnson recording called "Walkin' Blues," asked Waters if there were any other songs that used the same tune. "There's been some blues played like that," Waters replied. "This song comes from the cotton field and a boy once put a record out — Robert Johnson. He put it out as named 'Walkin' Blues.' I heard the tune before I heard it on the record. I learned it from Son House." In nearly one breath, Waters offers five accounts: his own active authorship: he "made it" on a specific date. Then the "passive" explanation: "it come to me just like that." After Lomax raises the question of influence, Waters, without shame, misgivings, or trepidation, says that he heard a version by Johnson, but that his mentor, Son House, taught it to him. In the middle of that complex genealogy, Waters declares that "this song comes from the cotton field."

Blues and jazz musicians have long been enabled by a kind of "open source" culture, in which pre-existing melodic fragments and larger musical frameworks are freely reworked. Technology has only multiplied the possibilities; musicians have gained the power to *duplicate* sounds literally rather than simply approximate them through allusion. In Seventies Jamaica, King Tubby and Lee "Scratch" Perry deconstructed recorded music, using astonishingly primitive pre-digital hardware, creating what they called "versions." The recombinant nature of their means of production quickly spread to DJs in New York and London. Today an endless, gloriously impure, and fundamentally social process generates countless hours of music.

Visual, sound, and text collage — which for many centuries were relatively fugitive traditions (a cento here, a folk pastiche there) — became explosively central to a series of movements in the twentieth century: futurism, cubism, Dada, musique concrète, situationism, pop art, and appropriationism. In fact, collage, the common denominator in that list, might be called *the* art form of the twentieth century, never mind the twenty-first. But forget, for the moment, chronologies, schools, or even centuries. As examples accumulate — Igor Stravinsky's music and Daniel Johnston's, Francis Bacon's paintings and Henry Darger's, the novels of the Oulipo group and of Hannah Crafts (the author who pillaged Dickens's *Bleak House* to write *The Bondwoman's Narrative*), as well as cherished texts that become troubling to their admirers after the discovery of their "plagiarized" elements, like Richard Condon's novels or Martin Luther King Jr.'s sermons — it becomes apparent that appropriation, mimicry, quotation, allusion, and sublimated collaboration consist of a kind of sine qua non of the creative act, cutting across all forms and genres in the realm of cultural production.

In a courtroom scene from *The Simpsons* that has since entered into the television canon, an argument over the ownership of the animated characters Itchy and Scratchy rapidly escalates into an existential debate on the very nature of cartoons. "Animation is built on plagiarism!" declares the show's hot-tempered cartoon-producer-within-a-cartoon, Roger

Meyers Jr. "You take away our right to steal ideas, where are they going to come from?" If nostalgic cartoonists had never borrowed from *Fritz the Cat*, there would be no *Ren & Stimpy Show*; without the Rankin/Bass and Charlie Brown Christmas specials, there would be no *South Park*; and without *The Flintstones* — more or less *The Honeymooners* in cartoon loincloths — The Simpsons would cease to exist. If those don't strike you as essential losses, then consider the remarkable series of "plagiarisms" that links Ovid's "Pyramus and Thisbe" with Shakespeare's *Romeo and Juliet* and Leonard Bernstein's *West Side Story*, or Shakespeare's description of Cleopatra, copied nearly verbatim from Plutarch's life of Mark Antony and also later nicked by T. S. Eliot for *The Waste Land*. If these are examples of plagiarism, then we want more plagiarism.

Most artists are brought to their vocation when their own nascent gifts are awakened by the work of a master. That is to say, most artists are converted to art by art itself. Finding one's voice isn't just an emptying and purifying oneself of the words of others but an adopting and embracing of filiations, communities, and discourses. Inspiration could be called inhaling the memory of an act never experienced. Invention, it must be humbly admitted, does not consist in creating out of void but out of chaos. Any artist knows these truths, no matter how deeply he or she submerges that knowing.

What happens when an allusion goes unrecognized? A closer look at *The Waste Land* may help make this point. The body of Eliot's poem is a vertiginous mélange of quotation, allusion, and "original" writing. When Eliot alludes to Edmund Spenser's "Prothalamion" with the line "Sweet Thames, run softly, till I end my song," what of readers to whom the poem, never one of Spenser's most popular, is unfamiliar? (Indeed, the Spenser is now known largely because of Eliot's use of it.) Two responses are possible: grant the line to Eliot, or later discover the source and understand the line as plagiarism. Eliot evidenced no small anxiety about these matters; the notes he so carefully added to *The Waste Land* can be read as a symptom of modernism's contamination anxiety. Taken from this angle, what exactly is postmodernism, except modernism without the anxiety?

Surrounded by Signs

The surrealists believed that objects in the world possess a certain but unspecifiable intensity that had been dulled by everyday use and utility. They meant to reanimate this dormant intensity, to bring their minds once again into close contact with the matter that made up their world. André Breton's maxim "Beautiful as the chance encounter of a sewing machine and an umbrella on an operating table" is an expression of the belief that simply placing objects in an unexpected context reinvigorates their mysterious qualities.

This "crisis" the surrealists identified was being simultaneously diagnosed by others. Martin Heidegger held that the essence of modernity was found in a certain technological orientation he called "enframing." This tendency encourages us to see the objects in our world only in terms of how they can serve us or be used by us. The task he identified was to find ways to resituate ourselves vis-à-vis these "objects," so that we may see them as "things" pulled into relief against the ground of their functionality. Heidegger believed that art had the great potential to reveal the "thing-ness" of objects.

The surrealists understood that photography and cinema could carry out this reanimating process automatically; the process of framing objects in a lens was often enough to create the charge they sought. Describing the effect, Walter Benjamin drew a comparison between the photographic apparatus and Freud's psychoanalytic methods. Just as Freud's theories "isolated and made analyzable things which had heretofore floated along unnoticed in the broad stream of perception," the photographic apparatus focuses on "hidden details of familiar objects," revealing "entirely new structural formations of the subject."

It's worth noting, then, that early in the history of photography a series of judicial decisions could well have changed the course of that art: courts were asked whether the photographer, amateur or professional, required permission before he could capture and print an image. Was the photographer *stealing* from the person or building whose photograph he shot, pirating something of private and certifiable value? Those early decisions went in favor of the pirates. Just as Walt Disney could take inspiration from Buster Keaton's *Steamboat Bill, Jr.*, the Brothers Grimm, or the existence of real mice, the photographer should be free to capture an image without compensating the source. The world that meets our eye through the lens of a camera was judged to be, with minor exceptions, a sort of public commons, where a cat may look at a king.

Novelists may glance at the stuff of the world too, but we sometimes get called to task for it. For those whose ganglia were formed pre-TV, the mimetic deployment of pop-culture icons seems at best an annoying tic and at worst a dangerous vapidity that compromises fiction's seriousness by dating it out of the Platonic Always, where it ought to reside. In a graduate workshop I briefly passed through, a certain gray eminence tried to convince us that a literary story should always eschew "any feature which serves to date it" because "serious fiction must be Timeless." When we protested that, in his own well-known work, characters moved about electrically lit rooms, drove cars, and spoke not Anglo-Saxon but postwar English — and further, that fiction he'd himself ratified as great, such as Dickens, was liberally strewn with innately topical, commercial, and time-bound references — he impatiently amended his proscription to those explicit references that would date a story in the "frivolous Now." When pressed, he said of course he meant the "trendy mass-popular-media" reference. Here, transgenerational discourse broke down.

I was born in 1964; I grew up watching Captain Kangaroo, moon landings, zillions of TV ads, the Banana Splits, *M*A*S*H*, and *The Mary Tyler*

Moore Show. I was born with words in my mouth — "Band-Aid," "Q-tip," "Xerox" — object-names as fixed and eternal in my logosphere as "taxi-cab" and "toothbrush." The world is a home littered with pop-culture products and their emblems. I also came of age swamped by parodies that stood for originals yet mysterious to me — I knew Monkees before Beatles, Belmondo before Bogart, and "remember" the movie *Summer of '42* from a *Mad* magazine satire, though I've still never seen the film itself. I'm not alone in having been born backward into an incoherent realm of texts, products, and images, the commercial and cultural environment with which we've both supplemented and blotted out our natural world. I can no more claim it as "mine" than the sidewalks and forests of the world, yet I do dwell in it, and for me to stand a chance as either artist or citizen, I'd probably better be permitted to name it.

Consider Walker Percy's *The Moviegoer*:

> Other people, so I have read, treasure memorable moments in their lives: the time one climbed the Parthenon at sunrise, the summer night one met a lonely girl in Central Park and achieved with her a sweet and natural relation-ship, as they say in books. I too once met a girl in Central Park, but it is not much to remember. What I remember is the time John Wayne killed three men with a carbine as he was falling to the dusty street in *Stagecoach*, and the time the kitten found Orson Welles in the doorway in *The Third Man*.

Today, when we can eat Tex-Mex with chopsticks while listening to reggae and watching a YouTube rebroadcast of the Berlin Wall's fall — i.e., when damn near *everything* presents itself as familiar — it's not a surprise that some of today's most ambitious art is going about trying to *make the familiar strange*. In so doing, in reimagining what human life might truly be like over there across the chasms of illusion, mediation, demographics, marketing, imago, and appearance, artists are paradoxically trying to restore what's taken for "real" to three whole dimensions, to reconstruct a univocally round world out of disparate streams of flat sights.

Whatever charge of tastelessness or trademark violation may be attached to the artistic appropriation of the media environment in which we swim, the alternative — to flinch, or tiptoe away into some ivory tower of irrelevance — is far worse. We're surrounded by signs; our imperative is to ignore none of them.

Usemonopoly

The idea that culture can be property — *intellectual* property — is used to justify everything from attempts to force the Girl Scouts to pay royalties for singing songs around campfires to the infringement suit brought by the estate of Margaret Mitchell against the publishers of Alice Randall's *The Wind Done Gone*. Corporations like Celera Genomics have filed for patents for human genes, while the Recording Industry Association of

America has sued music downloaders for copyright infringement, reaching out-of-court settlements for thousands of dollars with defendants as young as twelve. ASCAP bleeds fees from shop owners who play background music in their stores; students and scholars are shamed from placing texts facedown on photocopy machines. At the same time, copyright is revered by most established writers and artists as a birthright and bulwark, the source of nurture for their infinitely fragile practices in a rapacious world. Plagiarism and piracy, after all, are the monsters we working artists are taught to dread, as they roam the woods surrounding our tiny preserves of regard and remuneration.

A time is marked not so much by ideas that are argued about as by ideas that are taken for granted. The character of an era hangs upon what needs no defense. In this regard, few of us question the contemporary construction of copyright. It is taken as a law, both in the sense of a universally recognizable moral absolute, like the law against murder, and as naturally inherent in our world, like the law of gravity. In fact, it is neither. Rather, copyright is an ongoing social negotiation, tenuously forged, endlessly revised, and imperfect in its every incarnation.

Thomas Jefferson, for one, considered copyright a necessary evil: he favored providing just enough incentive to create, nothing more, and thereafter allowing ideas to flow freely, as nature intended. His conception of copyright was enshrined in the Constitution, which gives Congress the authority to "promote the Progress of Science and useful Arts, by securing for limited Times to Authors and Inventors the exclusive Right to their respective Writings and Discoveries." This was a balancing act between creators and society as a whole; second comers might do a much better job than the originator with the original idea.

But Jefferson's vision has not fared well, has in fact been steadily eroded by those who view the culture as a market in which everything of value should be owned by someone or other. The distinctive feature of modern American copyright law is its almost limitless bloating — its expansion in both scope and duration. With no registration requirement, every creative act in a tangible medium is now subject to copyright protection: your email to your child or your child's finger painting, both are automatically protected. The first Congress to grant copyright gave authors an initial term of fourteen years, which could be renewed for another fourteen if the author still lived. The current term is the life of the author plus seventy years. It's only a slight exaggeration to say that each time Mickey Mouse is about to fall into the public domain, the mouse's copyright term is extended.

Even as the law becomes more restrictive, technology is exposing those restrictions as bizarre and arbitrary. When old laws fixed on reproduction as the compensable (or actionable) unit, it wasn't because there was anything fundamentally invasive of an author's rights in the making of a copy. Rather it was because copies were once easy to find and count, so they made a useful benchmark for deciding when an owner's rights had been invaded. In the contemporary world, though, the act of "copying" is in no meaningful sense equivalent to an infringement — we make a copy every time we accept an emailed text, or send or forward one — and is impossible anymore to regulate or even describe.

At the movies, my entertainment is sometimes lately preceded by a dire trailer, produced by the lobbying group called the Motion Picture Association of America, in which the purchasing of a bootleg copy of a Hollywood film is compared to the theft of a car or a handbag — and, as the bullying supertitles remind us, "You wouldn't steal a handbag!" This conflation forms an incitement to quit thinking. If I were to tell you that pirating DVDs or downloading music is in no way different from loaning a friend a book, my own arguments would be as ethically bankrupt as the MPAA's. The truth lies somewhere in the vast gray area between these two overstated positions. For a car or a handbag, once stolen, no longer is available to its owner, while the appropriation of an article of "intellectual property" leaves the original untouched. As Jefferson wrote, "He who receives an idea from me, receives instruction himself without lessening mine; as he who lights his taper at mine, receives light without darkening me."

Yet industries of cultural capital, who profit not from creating but from distributing, see the sale of culture as a zero-sum game. The piano-roll publishers fear the record companies, who fear the cassette-tape manufacturers, who fear the online vendors, who fear whoever else is next in line to profit most quickly from the intangible and infinitely reproducible fruits of an artist's labor. It has been the same in every industry and with every technological innovation. Jack Valenti, speaking for the MPAA: "I say to you that the VCR is to the American film producer and the American public as the Boston Strangler is to the woman home alone."

Thinking clearly sometimes requires unbraiding our language. The word "copyright" may eventually seem as dubious in its embedded purposes as "family values," "globalization," and, sure, "intellectual property." Copyright is a "right" in no absolute sense; it is a government-granted monopoly on the use of creative results. So let's try calling it that — not a right but a *monopoly on use*, a "usemonopoly" — and then consider how the rapacious expansion of monopoly rights has always been counter to the public interest, no matter if it is Andrew Carnegie controlling the price of steel or Walt Disney managing the fate of his mouse. Whether the monopolizing beneficiary is a living artist or some artist's heirs or some corporation's shareholders, the loser is the community, including living artists who might make splendid use of a healthy public domain.

The Beauty of Second Use

A few years ago someone brought me a strange gift, purchased at MoMA's downtown design store: a copy of my own first novel, *Gun, With Occasional Music*, expertly cut into the contours of a pistol. The object was the work of Robert The, an artist whose specialty is the reincarnation of everyday materials. I regard my first book as an old friend, one who never fails to remind me of the spirit with which I entered into this game of art and commerce — that to be allowed to insert the materials of my imagination onto the shelves of bookstores and into the minds of readers (if only a handful) was a wild privilege. I was paid $6,000 for three years of writing, but at the time I'd have happily published the results for nothing. Now my old friend had come home in a new form, one I was unlikely to have imagined for it myself. The gun-book wasn't readable, exactly, but I couldn't take offense at that. The fertile spirit of stray connection this appropriated object conveyed back to me — the strange beauty of its second use — was a reward for being a published writer I could never have fathomed in advance. And the world makes room for both my novel and Robert The's gun-book. There's no need to choose between the two.

In the first life of creative property, if the creator is lucky, the content is sold. After the commercial life has ended, our tradition supports a second life as well. A newspaper is delivered to a doorstep, and the next day wraps fish or builds an archive. Most books fall out of print after one year, yet even within that period they can be sold in used bookstores and stored in libraries, quoted in reviews, parodied in magazines, described in conversations, and plundered for costumes for kids to wear on Halloween. The demarcation between various possible uses is beautifully graded and hard to define, the more so as artifacts distill into and repercuss through the realm of culture into which they've been entered, the more so as they engage the receptive minds for whom they were presumably intended.

Active reading is an impertinent raid on the literary preserve. Readers are like nomads, poaching their way across fields they do not own — artists are no more able to control the imaginations of their audiences than the culture industry is able to control second uses of its artifacts. In the children's classic *The Velveteen Rabbit*, the old Skin Horse offers the Rabbit a lecture on the practice of textual poaching. The value of a new toy lies not it its material qualities (not "having things that buzz inside you and a stick-out handle"), the Skin Horse explains, but rather in how the toy is used. "Real isn't how you are made. . . . It's a thing that happens to you. When a child loves you for a long, long time, not just to play with, but REALLY loves you, then you become Real." The Rabbit is fearful, recognizing that consumer goods don't become "real" without being actively reworked: "Does it hurt?" Reassuring him, the Skin Horse says: "It doesn't happen all at once. . . . You become. It takes a long time. . . . Generally, by the time you are Real, most of your hair has been loved off, and your eyes drop out and you get loose in the joints and very shabby." Seen from the perspective of the toymaker, the Velveteen Rabbit's loose joints and missing eyes represent vandalism, signs of misuse and rough treatment; for others, these are marks of its loving use.

Artists and their surrogates who fall into the trap of seeking recompense for every possible second use end up attacking their own best audience members for the crime of exalting and enshrining their work. The Recording Industry Association of America prosecuting their own record-buying public makes as little sense as the novelists who bristle at autographing used copies of their books for collectors. And artists, or their heirs, who fall into the trap of attacking the collagists and satirists and digital samplers of their work are attacking the next generation of creators for the crime of being influenced, for the crime of responding with the same mixture of intoxication, resentment, lust, and glee that characterizes all artistic successors. By doing so they make the world smaller, betraying what seems to me the primary motivation for participating in the world of culture in the first place: to make the world larger.

Source Hypocrisy, or, Disnial

The Walt Disney Company has drawn an astonishing catalogue from the work of others: *Snow White and the Seven Dwarfs, Fantasia, Pinocchio, Dumbo, Bambi, Song of the South, Cinderella, Alice in Wonderland, Robin Hood, Peter Pan, Lady and the Tramp, Mulan, Sleeping Beauty, The Sword in the Stone, The Jungle Book*, and, alas, *Treasure Planet*, a legacy of cultural sampling that Shakespeare, or De La Soul, could get behind. Yet Disney's protectorate of lobbyists has policed the resulting cache of cultural materials as vigilantly as if it were Fort Knox — threatening legal action, for instance, against the artist Dennis Oppenheim for the use of Disney characters in a sculpture, and prohibiting the scholar Holly Crawford from using any Disney-related images — including artwork by Lichtenstein, Warhol, Oldenburg, and others — in her monograph *Attached to the Mouse: Disney and Contemporary Art*.

This peculiar and specific act — the enclosure of commonwealth culture for the benefit of a sole or corporate owner — is close kin to what could be called *imperial plagiarism*, the free use of Third World or "primitive" artworks and styles by more privileged (and better-paid) artists. Think of Picasso's Les Demoiselles d'Avignon, or some of the albums of Paul Simon or David Byrne: even without violating copyright, those creators have sometimes come in for a certain skepticism when the extent of their outsourcing became evident. And, as when Led Zeppelin found themselves sued for back royalties by the bluesman Willie Dixon, the act can occasionally be an expensive one. *To live outside the law, you must be honest*: perhaps it was this, in part, that spurred David Byrne and Brian Eno to recently launch a "remix" website, where anyone can download easily disassembled versions of two songs from *My Life in the Bush of Ghosts*, an album reliant on vernacular speech sampled from a host of sources. Perhaps it also explains why Bob Dylan has never refused a request for a sample.

Kenneth Koch once said, "I'm a writer who likes to be influenced." It was a charming confession, and a rare one. For so many artists, the act of creativity is intended as a Napoleonic imposition of one's uniqueness upon the universe — *après moi le déluge* of copycats! And for every James Joyce or Woody Guthrie or Martin Luther King Jr., or Walt Disney, who gathered a constellation of voices in his work, there may seem to be some corporation or literary estate eager to stopper the bottle: cultural debts flow in, but they don't flow out. We might call this tendency "source hypocrisy." Or we could name it after the most pernicious source hypocrites of all time: Disnial.

You Can't Steal a Gift

My reader may, understandably, be on the verge of crying, "Communist!" A large, diverse society cannot survive without property; a large, diverse, and modern society cannot flourish without some form of intellectual property. But it takes little reflection to grasp that there is ample value that the term "property" doesn't capture. And works of art exist simultaneously in two economies, a market economy and a *gift economy*.

The cardinal difference between gift and commodity exchange is that a gift establishes a feeling-bond between two people, whereas the sale of a commodity leaves no necessary connection. I go into a hardware store, pay the man for a hacksaw blade, and walk out. I may never see him again. The disconnectedness is, in fact, a virtue of the commodity mode. We don't want to be bothered, and if the clerk always wants to chat about the family, I'll shop elsewhere. I just want a hacksaw blade. But a gift makes a connection. There are many examples, the candy or cigarette offered to a stranger who shares a seat on the plane, the few words that indicate goodwill between passengers on the late-night bus. These tokens establish the simplest bonds of social life, but the model they offer may be extended to the most complicated of unions — marriage, parenthood, mentorship. If a value is placed on these (often essentially unequal) exchanges, they degenerate into something else.

Yet one of the more difficult things to comprehend is that the gift economies — like those that sustain open-source software — coexist so naturally with the market. It is precisely this doubleness in art practices that we must identify, ratify, and enshrine in our lives as participants in culture, either as "producers" or "consumers." Art that matters to us — which moves the heart, or revives the soul, or delights the senses, or offers courage for living, however we choose to describe the experience — is received as a gift is received. Even if we've paid a fee at the door of the museum or concert hall, when we are touched by a work of art something comes to us that has nothing to do with the price. The daily commerce of our lives proceeds at its own constant level, but a gift conveys an uncommodifiable surplus of inspiration.

The way we treat a thing can change its nature, though. Religions often prohibit the sale of sacred objects, the implication being that their sanctity is lost if they are bought and sold. We consider it unacceptable to sell sex, babies, body organs, legal rights, and votes. The idea that something should never be commodified is generally known as *inalienability* or *unalienability* — a concept most famously expressed by Thomas Jefferson in the phrase "endowed by their Creator with certain unalienable Rights . . ." A work of art seems to be a hardier breed; it can be sold in the market and still emerge a work of art. But if it is true that in the essential commerce of art a gift is carried by the work from the artist to his audience, if I am right to say that where there is no gift there is no art, then it may be possible to destroy a work of art by converting it into a pure commodity. I don't maintain that art can't be bought and sold, but that the gift portion of the work places a constraint upon our merchandising. This is the reason why even a really beautiful, ingenious, powerful ad (of which there are a lot) can never be any kind of real art: an ad has no status as gift; i.e., it's never really *for* the person it's directed at.

The power of a gift economy remains difficult for the empiricists of our market culture to understand. In our times, the rhetoric of the market presumes that everything should be and can be appropriately bought, sold, and owned — a tide of alienation lapping daily at the dwindling redoubt of the unalienable. In free-market theory, an intervention to halt propertization is considered "paternalistic," because it inhibits the free action of the citizen, now reposited as a "potential entrepreneur." Of course, in the real world, we know that child-rearing, family life, education, socialization, sexuality, political life, and many other basic human activities require insulation from market forces. In fact, paying for many of these things can ruin them. We may be willing to peek at *Who Wants to Marry a Multi-millionaire* or an eBay auction of the ova of fashion models, but only to reassure ourselves that some things are still beneath our standards of dignity.

What's remarkable about gift economies is that they can flourish in the most unlikely places — in run-down neighborhoods, on the Internet, in scientific communities, and among members of Alcoholics Anonymous. A classic example is commercial blood systems, which generally produce blood supplies of lower safety, purity, and potency than volunteer systems. A gift economy may be superior when it comes to maintaining a group's commitment to certain extra-market values.

The Commons

Another way of understanding the presence of gift economies — which dwell like ghosts in the commercial machine — is in the sense of a *public commons*. A commons, of course, is anything like the streets over which we drive, the skies through which we pilot airplanes, or the public parks or beaches on which we dally. A commons belongs to everyone and no one, and its use is controlled only by common consent. A commons describes resources like the body of ancient music drawn on by composers and folk musicians alike, rather than the commodities, like "Happy Birthday to You," for which ASCAP, 114 years after it was written, continues to collect a fee. Einstein's theory of relativity is a commons. Writings in the public domain are a commons. Gossip about celebrities is a commons. The silence in a movie theater is a transitory commons, impossibly fragile, treasured by those who crave it, and constructed as a mutual gift by those who compose it.

The world of art and culture is a vast commons, one that is salted through with zones of utter commerce yet remains gloriously immune to any overall commodification. The closest resemblance is to the commons of a *language*: altered by every contributor, expanded by even the most passive user. That a language is a commons doesn't mean that the community owns it; rather it belongs *between* people, possessed by no one, not even by society as a whole.

Nearly any commons, though, can be encroached upon, partitioned, enclosed. The American commons include tangible assets such as public forests and minerals, intangible wealth such as copyrights and patents, critical infrastructures such as the Internet and government research, and cultural resources such as the broadcast airwaves and public spaces. They include resources we've paid for as taxpayers and inherited from previous generations. They're not just an inventory of marketable assets; they're social institutions and cultural traditions that define us as Americans and enliven us as human beings. Some invasions of the commons are sanctioned because we can no longer muster a spirited commitment to the public sector. The abuse goes unnoticed because the theft of the commons is seen in glimpses, not in panorama. We may occasionally see a former wetland paved; we may hear about the breakthrough cancer drug that tax dollars helped develop, the rights to which pharmaceutical companies acquired for a song. The larger movement goes too much unremarked. The notion of a *commons of cultural materials* goes more or less unnamed.

Honoring the commons is not a matter of moral exhortation. It is a practical necessity. We in Western society are going through a period of intensifying belief in private ownership, to the detriment of the public good. We have to remain constantly vigilant to prevent raids by those who would selfishly exploit our common heritage for their private gain. Such raids on our natural resources are not examples of enterprise and initiative. They are attempts to take from all the people just for the benefit of a few.

Undiscovered Public Knowledge

Artists and intellectuals despondent over the prospects for originality can take heart from a phenomenon identified about twenty years ago by Don Swanson, a library scientist at the University of Chicago. He called it "undiscovered public knowledge." Swanson showed that standing problems in medical research may be significantly addressed, perhaps even solved, simply by systematically surveying the scientific literature. Left to its own devices, research tends to become more specialized and abstracted from the real-world problems that motivated it and to which it remains relevant. This suggests that such a problem may be tackled effectively not by commissioning more research but by assuming that most or all of the solution can already be found in various scientific journals, waiting to be assembled by someone willing to read across specialties. Swanson himself did this in the case of Raynaud's syndrome, a disease that causes the fingers of young women to become numb. His finding is especially striking — perhaps even scandalous — because it happened in the ever-expanding biomedical sciences.

Undiscovered public knowledge emboldens us to question the extreme claims to originality made in press releases and publishers' notices: Is an intellectual or creative offering truly novel, or have we just forgotten a worthy precursor? Does solving certain scientific problems really require massive additional funding, or could a computerized search engine, creatively deployed, do the same job more quickly and cheaply? Lastly, does our appetite for creative vitality require the violence and exasperation of another avant-garde, with its wearisome killing-the-father imperatives, or might we be better off ratifying the *ecstasy of influence* — and deepening our willingness to understand the commonality and timelessness of the methods and motifs available to artists?

Give All

A few years ago, the Film Society of Lincoln Center announced a retrospective of the works of Dariush Mehrjui, then a fresh enthusiasm of mine. Mehrjui is one of Iran's finest filmmakers, and the only one whose subject was personal relationships among the upper-middle-class intelligentsia. Needless to say, opportunities to view his films were — and remain — rare indeed. I headed uptown for one, an adaptation of J. D. Salinger's *Franny and Zooey*, titled *Pari*, only to discover at the door of the Walter Reade Theater that the screening had been canceled: its announcement had brought threat of a lawsuit down on the Film Society. True, these were Salinger's rights under the law. Yet why would he care that some obscure Iranian filmmaker had paid him homage with a meditation on his heroine? Would it have damaged his book or robbed him of some crucial remuneration had the screening been permitted? The fertile spirit of stray connection — one stretching across what is presently seen as the direst of international breaches — had in this case been snuffed out. The cold, undead hand of one of my childhood literary heroes had reached out from its New Hampshire redoubt to arrest my present-day curiosity.

A few assertions, then:

Any text that has infiltrated the common mind to the extent of *Gone With the Wind* or *Lolita* or *Ulysses* inexorably joins the language of culture.

A map-turned-to-landscape, it has moved to a place beyond enclosure or control. The authors and their heirs should consider the subsequent parodies, refractions, quotations, and revisions an honor, or at least the price of a rare success.

A corporation that has imposed an inescapable notion — Mickey Mouse, Band-Aid — on the cultural language should pay a similar price.

The primary objective of copyright is not to reward the labor of authors but "to promote the Progress of Science and useful Arts." To this end, copyright assures authors the right to their original expression, but encourages others to build freely upon the ideas and information conveyed by a work. This result is neither unfair nor unfortunate.

Contemporary copyright, trademark, and patent law is presently corrupted. The case for perpetual copyright is a denial of the essential gift-aspect of the creative act. Arguments in its favor are as un-American as those for the repeal of the estate tax.

Art is sourced. Apprentices graze in the field of culture.

Digital sampling is an art method like any other, neutral in itself.

Despite hand-wringing at each technological turn — radio, the Internet — the future will be much like the past. Artists will sell some things but also give some things away. Change may be troubling for those who crave less ambiguity, but the life of an artist has never been filled with certainty.

The dream of a perfect systematic remuneration is nonsense. I pay rent with the price my words bring when published in glossy magazines and at the same moment offer them for almost nothing to impoverished literary quarterlies, or speak them for free into the air in a radio interview. So what are they worth? What would they be worth if some future Dylan worked them into a song? Should I care to make such a thing impossible?

Any text is woven entirely with citations, references, echoes, cultural languages, which cut across it through and through in a vast stereophony. The citations that go to make up a text are anonymous, untraceable, and yet *already read*; they are quotations without inverted commas. The kernel, the soul — let us go further and say the substance, the bulk, the actual and valuable material of all human utterances — is plagiarism. For substantially all ideas are secondhand, consciously and unconsciously drawn from a million outside sources, and daily used by the garnerer with a pride and satisfaction born of the superstition that he originated them; whereas there is not a rag of originality about them anywhere except the little discoloration they get from his mental and moral caliber and his temperament, and which is revealed in characteristics of phrasing. Old and new make the warp and woof of every moment. There is no thread that is not a twist of these two strands. By necessity, by proclivity, and by delight, we all quote. Neurological study has lately shown that memory, imagination, and consciousness itself is stitched, quilted, pastiched. If we cut-and-paste our selves, might we not forgive it of our artworks?

Artists and writers — and our advocates, our guilds and agents — too often subscribe to implicit claims of originality that do injury to these truths. And we too often, as hucksters and bean counters in the tiny enterprises of our selves, act to spite the gift portion of our privileged roles. People live differently who treat a portion of their wealth as a gift. If we devalue and obscure the gift-economy function of our art practices, we turn our works into nothing more than advertisements for themselves. We may console ourselves that our lust for subsidiary rights in virtual perpetuity is some heroic counter to rapacious corporate interests. But the truth is that with artists pulling on one side and corporations pulling on the other, the loser is the collective public imagination from which we were nourished in the first place, and whose existence as the ultimate repository of our offerings makes the work worth doing in the first place.

As a novelist, I'm a cork on the ocean of story, a leaf on a windy day. Pretty soon I'll be blown away. For the moment I'm grateful to be making a living, and so must ask that for a limited time (in the Thomas Jefferson sense) you please respect my small, treasured usemonopolies. Don't pirate my editions; do plunder my visions. The name of the game is Give All. You, reader, are welcome to my stories. They were never mine in the first place, but I gave them to you. If you have the inclination to pick them up, take them with my blessing.

Key: I Is Another

This key to the preceding essay names the source of every line I stole, warped, and cobbled together as I "wrote" (except, alas, those sources I forgot along the way). Nearly every sentence I culled I also revised, at least slightly — for necessities of space, in order to produce a more consistent tone, or simply because I felt like it.

Title

The phrase "the ecstasy of influence," which embeds a rebuking play on Harold Bloom's "anxiety of influence," is lifted from spoken remarks by Professor Richard Dienst of Rutgers.

Love and Theft

". . . a cultivated man of middle age . . ." to ". . . hidden, unacknowledged memory?" These lines, with some adjustments for tone, belong to the anonymous editor or assistant who wrote the dust-flap copy of Michael Maar's *The Two Lolitas*. Of course, in my own experience, dust-flap copy is often a collaboration between author and editor. Perhaps this was also true for Maar.

"The history of literature . . ." to ". . . borrow and quote?" comes from Maar's book itself.

"Appropriation has always . . ." to ". . . Ishmael and Queequeg . . ." This paragraph makes a hash of remarks from an interview with Eric Lott conducted by David McNair and Jayson Whitehead, and incorporates both interviewers' and interviewee's observations. (The text-interview form can be seen as a commonly accepted form of multivocal writing. Most interviewers prime their subjects with remarks of their own — leading the witness, so to speak — and gently refine their subjects' statements in the final printed transcript.)

"I realized this . . ." to ". . . for a long time." The anecdote is cribbed, with an elision to avoid appropriating a dead grandmother, from Jonathan Rosen's *The Talmud and the Internet*. I've never seen *84, Charing Cross Road*, nor searched the Web for a Donne quote. For me it was through Rosen to Donne, Hemingway, website, et al.

"When I was thirteen . . ." to ". . . no plagiarist at all." This is from William Gibson's "God's Little Toys," in *Wired* magazine. My own first encounter with William Burroughs, also at age thirteen, was less epiphanic. Having grown up with a painter father who, during family visits to galleries or museums, approvingly noted collage and appropriation techniques in the visual arts (Picasso, Claes Oldenburg, Stuart Davis), I was gratified, but not surprised, to learn that literature could encompass the same methods.

Contamination Anxiety

"In 1941, on his front porch . . ." to ". . . 'this song comes from the cotton field.'" Siva Vaidhyanathan, *Copyrights and Copywrongs*.

". . . enabled by a kind . . . freely reworked." Kembrew McLeod, *Freedom of Expression*. In *Owning Culture*, McLeod notes that, as he was writing, he

> happened to be listening to a lot of old country music, and in my casual listening I noticed that *six* country songs shared *exactly* the same vocal melody, including Hank Thompson's "Wild Side of Life," the Carter Family's "I'm Thinking Tonight of My Blue Eyes," Roy Acuff's "Great Speckled Bird," Kitty Wells's "It Wasn't God Who Made Honky Tonk Angels," Reno & Smiley's "I'm Using My Bible for a Roadmap," and Townes Van Zandt's "Heavenly Houseboat Blues." . . . In his extensively researched book, *Country: The Twisted Roots of Rock 'n' Roll*, Nick Tosches documents that the melody these songs share is both "ancient and British." There were no recorded lawsuits stemming from these appropriations. . . .

". . . musicians have gained . . . through allusion." Joanna Demers, *Steal This Music*.

"In Seventies Jamaica . . ." to ". . . hours of music." Gibson.

"Visual, sound, and text collage . . ." to ". . . realm of cultural production." This plunders, rewrites, and amplifies paragraphs from McLeod's *Owning Culture*, except for the line about collage being the art form of the twentieth and twenty-first centuries, which I heard filmmaker Craig Baldwin say, in defense of sampling, in the trailer for a forthcoming documentary, *Copyright Criminals*.

"In a courtroom scene . . ." to ". . . would cease to exist." Dave Itzkoff, *New York Times*.

". . . the remarkable series of 'plagiarisms' . . ." to ". . . we want more plagiarism." Richard Posner, combined from The Becker-Posner Blog and *The Atlantic Monthly*.

"Most artists are brought . . ." to ". . . by art itself." These words, and many more to follow, come from Lewis Hyde's *The Gift*. Above any other book I've here plagiarized, I commend *The Gift* to your attention.

"Finding one's voice . . . filiations, communities, and discourses." Semanticist George L. Dillon, quoted in Rebecca Moore Howard's "The New Abolitionism Comes to Plagiarism."

"Inspiration could be . . . act never experienced." Ned Rorem, found on several "great quotations" sites on the Internet.

"Invention, it must be humbly admitted . . . out of chaos." Mary Shelley, from her introduction to *Frankenstein*.

"What happens . . ." to ". . . contamination anxiety." Kevin J. H. Dettmar, from "The Illusion of Modernist Allusion and the Politics of Postmodern Plagiarism."

Surrounded by Signs

"The surrealists believed . . ." to the Walter Benjamin quote. Christian Keathley's *Cinephilia and History, or the Wind in the Trees*, a book that treats fannish fetishism as the secret at the heart of film scholarship. Keathley notes, for instance, Joseph Cornell's surrealist-influenced 1936 film *Rose Hobart*, which simply records "the way in which Cornell himself watched the 1931 Hollywood potboiler *East of Borneo*, fascinated and distracted as he was by its B-grade star" — the star, of course, being Rose Hobart herself. This, I suppose, makes Cornell a sort of father to computer-enabled fan-creator reworkings of Hollywood product, like the version of George Lucas's *The Phantom Menace* from which the noxious Jar Jar Binks character was purged; both incorporate a viewer's subjective preferences into a revision of a filmmaker's work.

". . . early in the history of photography" to ". . . without compensating the source." From *Free Culture*, by Lawrence Lessig, the greatest of public advocates for copyright reform, and the best source if you want to get radicalized in a hurry.

"For those whose ganglia . . ." to ". . . discourse broke down." From David Foster Wallace's essay "E Unibus Pluram," reprinted in *A Supposedly*

Fun Thing I'll Never Do Again. I have no idea who Wallace's "gray eminence" is or was. I inserted the example of Dickens into the paragraph; he
strikes me as overlooked in the lineage of authors of "brand-name" fiction.

"I was born . . . *Mary Tyler Moore Show*." These are the reminiscences
of Mark Hosler from Negativland, a collaging musical collective that was
sued by U2's record label for their appropriation of "I Still Haven't Found
What I'm Looking For." Although I had to adjust the birth date, Hosler's
cultural menu fits me like a glove.

"The world is a home . . . pop-culture products . . ." McLeod.

"Today, when we can eat . . ." to ". . . flat sights." Wallace.

"We're surrounded by signs, ignore none of them." This phrase, which
I unfortunately rendered somewhat leaden with the word "imperative,"
comes from Steve Erickson's novel *Our Ecstatic Days*.

Usemonopoly

". . . everything from attempts . . ." to "defendants as young as twelve."
Robert Boynton, *The New York Times Magazine*, "The Tyranny of Copyright?"

"A time is marked . . ." to ". . . what needs no defense." Lessig, this
time from *The Future of Ideas*.

"Thomas Jefferson, for one . . ." to "'. . . respective Writings and Discoveries.'" Boynton.

". . . second comers might do a much better job than the originator . . ." I found this phrase in Lessig, who is quoting Vaidhyanathan, who
himself is characterizing a judgment written by Learned Hand.

"But Jefferson's vision . . . owned by someone or other." Boynton.

"The distinctive feature . . ." to ". . . term is extended." Lessig, again
from *The Future of Ideas*.

"When old laws . . ." to ". . . had been invaded." Jessica Litman, *Digital
Copyright*.

"'I say to you . . . woman home alone.'" I found the Valenti quote in
McLeod. Now fill in the blank: Jack Valenti is to the public domain as
_____ is to _____.

The Beauty of Second Use

"In the first . . ." to ". . . builds an archive." Lessig.

"Most books . . . one year . . ." Lessig.

"Active reading is . . ." to ". . . do not own . . ." This is a mashup of
Henry Jenkins, from his *Textual Poachers: Television Fans and Participatory
Culture*, and Michel de Certeau, whom Jenkins quotes.

"In the children's classic . . ." to ". . . its loving use." Jenkins. (Incidentally, have the holders of the copyright to *The Velveteen Rabbit* had a close
look at *Toy Story*? There could be a lawsuit there.)

Source Hypocrisy, or, Disnial

"The Walt Disney Company . . . alas, *Treasure Planet* . . ." Lessig.

"Imperial Plagiarism" is the title of an essay by Marilyn Randall.

". . . spurred David Byrne . . . *My Life in the Bush of Ghosts* . . ." Chris Dahlen, *Pitchfork* — though in truth by the time I'd finished, his words were so utterly dissolved within my own that had I been an ordinary cutting-and-pasting journalist it never would have occurred to me to give Dahlen a citation. The effort of preserving another's distinctive phrases as I worked on this essay was sometimes beyond my capacities; this form of plagiarism was oddly hard work.

"Kenneth Koch . . ." to ". . . *déluge* of copycats!" Emily Nussbaum, *The New York Times Book Review*.

You Can't Steal a Gift

"You can't steal a gift." Dizzy Gillespie, defending another player who'd been accused of poaching Charlie Parker's style: "You can't steal a gift. Bird gave the world his music, and if you can hear it you can have it."

"A large, diverse society . . . intellectual property." Lessig.

"And works of art . . . " to ". . . marriage, parenthood, mentorship." Hyde.

"Yet one . . . so naturally with the market." David Bollier, *Silent Theft*.

"Art that matters . . ." to ". . . bought and sold." Hyde.

"We consider it unacceptable . . ." to "'. . . certain unalienable Rights . . .'" Bollier, paraphrasing Margaret Jane Radin's *Contested Commodities*.

"A work of art . . ." to ". . . constraint upon our merchandising." Hyde.

"This is the reason . . . person it's directed at." Wallace.

"The power of a gift . . ." to ". . . certain extra-market values." Bollier, and also the sociologist Warren O. Hagstrom, whom Bollier is paraphrasing.

The Commons

"Einstein's theory . . ." to ". . . public domain are a commons." Lessig.

"That a language is a commons . . . society as a whole." Michael Newton, in the *London Review of Books*, reviewing a book called *Echolalias: On the Forgetting of Language* by Daniel Heller-Roazen. The paraphrases of book reviewers are another covert form of collaborative culture; as an avid reader of reviews, I know much about books I've never read. To quote Yann Martel on how he came to be accused of imperial plagiarism in his Booker-winning novel *Life of Pi*,

> Ten or so years ago, I read a review by John Updike in the *New York Times Review of Books* [sic]. It was of a novel by a Brazilian writer, Moacyr Scliar. I forget the title, and John Updike did worse: he clearly thought the book as

> a whole was forgettable. His review — one of those that makes you suspicious by being mostly descriptive . . . oozed indifference. But one thing about it struck me: the premise. . . . Oh, the wondrous things I could do with this premise.

Unfortunately, no one was ever able to locate the Updike review in question.

"The American commons . . ." to ". . . for a song." Bollier.

"Honoring the commons . . ." to ". . . practical necessity." Bollier.

"We in Western . . . public good." John Sulston, Nobel Prize–winner and co-mapper of the human genome.

"We have to remain . . ." to ". . . benefit of a few." Harry S Truman, at the opening of the Everglades National Park. Although it may seem the height of presumption to rip off a president — I found claiming Truman's stolid advocacy as my own embarrassing in the extreme — I didn't rewrite him at all. As the poet Marianne Moore said, "If a thing had been said in the *best* way, how can you say it better?" Moore confessed her penchant for incorporating lines from others' work, explaining, "I have not yet been able to outgrow this hybrid method of composition."

Undiscovered Public Knowledge

". . . intellectuals despondent . . ." to ". . . quickly and cheaply?" Steve Fuller, *The Intellectual*. There's something of Borges in Fuller's insight here; the notion of a storehouse of knowledge waiting passively to be assembled by future users is suggestive of both "The Library of Babel" and "Kafka and his Precursors."

Give All

". . . one of Iran's finest . . ." to ". . . meditation on his heroine?" Amy Taubin, *Village Voice*, although it was me who was disappointed at the door of the Walter Reade Theater.

"The primary objective . . ." to ". . . unfair nor unfortunate." Sandra Day O'Connor, 1991.

". . . the future will be much like the past" to ". . . give some things away." Open-source film archivist Rick Prelinger, quoted in McLeod.

"Change may be troubling . . . with certainty." McLeod.

". . . woven entirely . . ." to ". . . without inverted commas." Roland Barthes.

"The kernel, the soul . . ." to ". . . characteristics of phrasing." Mark Twain, from a consoling letter to Helen Keller, who had suffered distressing accusations of plagiarism (!). In fact, her work included unconsciously memorized phrases; under Keller's particular circumstances, her writing could be understood as a kind of allegory of the "constructed" nature of artistic perception. I found the Twain quote in the aforementioned *Copyrights and Copywrongs*, by Siva Vaidhyanathan.

"Old and new . . ." to ". . . we all quote." Ralph Waldo Emerson. These guys all sound alike!

"People live differently . . . wealth as a gift." Hyde.

". . . I'm a cork . . ." to ". . . blown away." This is adapted from The Beach Boys song " 'Til I Die," written by Brian Wilson. My own first adventure with song-lyric permissions came when I tried to have a character in my second novel quote the lyrics "There's a world where I can go and/Tell my secrets to/In my room/In my room." After learning the likely expense, at my editor's suggestion I replaced those with "You take the high road/I'll take the low road/I'll be in Scotland before you," a lyric in the public domain. This capitulation always bugged me, and in the subsequent British publication of the same book I restored the Brian Wilson lyric, without permission. *Ocean of Story* is the title of a collection of Christina Stead's short fiction.

Saul Bellow, writing to a friend who'd taken offense at Bellow's fictional use of certain personal facts, said: "The name of the game is Give All. You are welcome to all my facts. You know them, I give them to you. If you have the strength to pick them up, take them with my blessing." I couldn't bring myself to retain Bellow's "strength," which seemed presumptuous in my new context, though it is surely the more elegant phrase. On the other hand, I was pleased to invite the suggestion that the gifts in question may actually be light and easily lifted.

Key to the Key

The notion of a collage text is, of course, not original to me. Walter Benjamin's incomplete *Arcades Project* seemingly would have featured extensive interlaced quotations. Other precedents include Graham Rawle's novel *Diary of an Amateur Photographer*, its text harvested from photography magazines, and Eduardo Paolozzi's collage-novel *Kex*, cobbled from crime novels and newspaper clippings. Closer to home, my efforts owe a great deal to the recent essays of David Shields, in which diverse quotes are made to closely intertwine and reverberate, and to conversations with editor Sean Howe and archivist Pamela Jackson. Last year David Edelstein, in *New York* magazine, satirized the Kaavya Viswanathan plagiarism case by creating an almost completely plagiarized column denouncing her actions. Edelstein intended to demonstrate, through ironic example, how bricolage such as his own was ipso facto facile and unworthy. Although Viswanathan's version of "creative copying" was a pitiable one, I differ with Edelstein's conclusions.

The phrase *Je est un autre*, with its deliberately awkward syntax, belongs to Arthur Rimbaud. It has been translated both as "I is another" and "I is someone else," as in this excerpt from Rimbaud's letters:

For *I* is someone else. If brass wakes up a trumpet, it is not its fault. To me this is obvious: I witness the unfolding of my own thought: I watch it, I listen to it: I make a stroke of the bow: the symphony begins to stir in the depths, or springs on to the stage.

If the old fools had not discovered only the *false* significance of the Ego, we should not now be having to sweep away those millions of skeletons which, since time immemorial, have been piling up the fruits of their one-eyed intellects, and claiming to be, themselves, the authors!

■ JAMES W. LOEWEN ━━━━━━━━━━━━━━━━━━━━━━━━━

Handicapped by History: The Process of Hero-Making

James W. Loewen (b. 1942) is currently a sociology professor at the Catholic University of America, although he spent most of his career at the University of Vermont. In 1980, he was involved in a First Amendment case when his history textbook *Mississippi: Conflict and Change* was considered too controversial for the public school system because of its heavy focus on race relations. After this case, Loewen analyzed the content of twelve history textbooks and published his results in the book *Lies My Teacher Told Me: Everything Your American History Textbook Got Wrong* (1995), which won the American Book Award that year. "Handicapped by History: The Process of Hero-Making" is the book's introduction.

■ ■ ■

What passes for identity in America is a series of myths about one's heroic ancestors.

— JAMES BALDWIN[1]

One is astonished in the study of history at the recurrence of the idea that evil must be forgotten, distorted, skimmed over. We must not remember that Daniel Webster got drunk but only remember that he was a splendid constitutional lawyer. We must forget that George Washington was a slave owner . . . and simply remember the things we regard as creditable and inspiring. The difficulty, of course, with this philosophy is that history loses its value as an incentive and example; it paints perfect men and noble nations, but it does not tell the truth.

— W. E. B. DU BOIS[2]

By idolizing those whom we honor, we do a disservice both to them and to ourselves. . . . We fail to recognize that we could go and do likewise.

— CHARLES V. WILLIE[3]

This chapter is about heroification, a degenerative process (much like calcification) that makes people over into heroes. Through this process, our educational media turn flesh-and-blood individuals into pious, perfect creatures without conflicts, pain, credibility, or human interest.

Many American history textbooks are studded with biographical vignettes of the very famous (*Land of Promise* devotes a box to each president) and the famous (*The Challenge of Freedom* provides "Did You Know?" boxes about Elizabeth Blackwell, the first woman to graduate from medical school in the United States, and Lorraine Hansberry, author of *A Raisin in the Sun*, among many others). In themselves, vignettes are not a bad idea. They instruct by human example. They show diverse ways that people can make a difference. They allow textbooks to give space to characters such as Blackwell and Hansberry, who relieve what would otherwise be a monolithic parade of white male political leaders. Biographical vignettes also provoke reflection as to our purpose in teaching history: Is Chester A. Arthur more deserving of space than, say, Frank Lloyd Wright? Who influences us more today — Wright, who invented the carport and transformed domestic architectural spaces, or Arthur, who, um, signed the first Civil Service Act? Whose rise to prominence provides more drama — Blackwell's or George Bush's (the latter born with a silver Senate seat in his mouth)?[4] The choices are debatable, but surely textbooks should include *some* people based not only on what they achieved but also on the distance they traversed to achieve it.

We could go on to third- and fourth-guess the list of heroes in textbook pantheons. My concern here, however, is not who gets chosen, but rather what happens to the heroes when they are introduced into our history textbooks and our classrooms. Two twentieth-century Americans provide case studies of heroification: Woodrow Wilson and Helen Keller. Wilson was unarguably an important president, and he receives extensive textbook coverage. Keller, on the other hand, was a "little person" who pushed through no legislation, changed the course of no scientific discipline, declared no war. Only one of the twelve history textbooks I surveyed includes her photograph. But teachers love to talk about Keller and often show audiovisual materials or recommend biographies that present her life as exemplary. All this attention ensures that students retain something about both of these historical figures, but they may be no better off for it. Heroification so distorts the lives of Keller and Wilson (and many others) that we cannot think straight about them.

Teachers have held up Helen Keller, the blind and deaf girl who overcame her physical handicaps, as an inspiration to generations of schoolchildren. Every fifth-grader knows the scene in which Anne Sullivan spells *water* into young Helen's hand at the pump. At least a dozen movies and filmstrips have been made on Keller's life. Each yields its version of the same cliché. A McGraw-Hill educational film concludes: "The gift of Helen Keller and Anne Sullivan to the world is to constantly remind us of the wonder of the world around us and how much we owe those who taught us what it means, for there is no person that is unworthy or incapable of being helped, and the greatest service any person can make is to help another reach true potential."[5]

To draw such a bland maxim from the life of Helen Keller, historians and filmmakers have disregarded her actual biography and left out the lessons she specifically asked us to learn from it. Keller, who struggled so valiantly to learn to speak, has been made mute by history. The result is that we really don't know much about her.

Over the past ten years, I have asked dozens of college students who Helen Keller was and what she did. They all know that she was a blind and deaf girl. Most of them know that she was befriended by a teacher, Anne Sullivan, and learned to read and write and even to speak. Some students can recall rather minute details of Keller's early life: that she lived in Alabama, that she was unruly and without manners before Sullivan came along, and so forth. A few know that Keller graduated from college. But about what happened next, about the whole of her adult life, they are ignorant. A few students venture that Keller became a "public figure" or a "humanitarian," perhaps on behalf of the blind or deaf. "She wrote, didn't she?" or "she spoke" — conjectures without content. Keller, who was born in 1880, graduated from Radcliffe in 1904 and died in 1968. To ignore the sixty-four years of her adult life or to encapsulate them with the single word *humanitarian* is to lie by omission.

The truth is that Helen Keller was a radical socialist. She joined the Socialist party of Massachusetts in 1909. She had become a social radical even before she graduated from Radcliffe, and *not*, she emphasized, because of any teachings available there. After the Russian Revolution, she sang the praises of the new communist nation: "In the East a new star is risen! With pain and anguish the old order has given birth to the new, and behold in the East a man-child is born! Onward, comrades, all together! Onward to the campfires of Russia! Onward to the coming dawn!"[6] Keller hung a red flag over the desk in her study. Gradually she moved to the left of the Socialist party and became a Wobbly, a member of the Industrial Workers of the World (IWW), the syndicalist union persecuted by Woodrow Wilson.

Keller's commitment to socialism stemmed from her experience as a disabled person and from her sympathy for others with handicaps. She began by working to simplify the alphabet for the blind, but soon came to realize that to deal solely with blindness was to treat symptom, not cause. Through research she learned that blindness was not distributed randomly throughout the population but was concentrated in the lower class. Men who were poor might be blinded in industrial accidents or by inadequate medical care; poor women who became prostitutes faced the additional danger of syphilitic blindness. Thus Keller learned how the social class system controls people's opportunities in life, sometimes determining even whether they can see. Keller's research was not just book-learning: "I have visited sweatshops, factories, crowded slums. If I could not see it, I could smell it."[7]

At the time Keller became a socialist, she was one of the most famous women on the planet. She soon became the most notorious. Her conversion to socialism caused a new storm of publicity — this time outraged. Newspapers that had extolled her courage and intelligence now emphasized her handicap. Columnists charged that she had no independent sensory input and was in thrall to those who fed her information. Typical was the editor of the Brooklyn *Eagle*, who wrote that Keller's "mistakes spring out of the manifest limitations of her development."

Keller recalled having met this editor: "At that time the compliments he paid me were so generous that I blush to remember them. But now that I have come out for socialism he reminds me and the public that I am blind and deaf and especially liable to error. I must have shrunk in intelligence during the years since I met him." She went on, "Oh, ridiculous Brooklyn *Eagle!* Socially blind and deaf, it defends an intolerable system, a system that is the cause of much of the physical blindness and deafness which we are trying to prevent."[8]

Keller, who devoted much of her later life to raising funds for the American Foundation for the Blind, never wavered in her belief that our society needed radical change. Having herself fought so hard to speak, she helped found the American Civil Liberties Union to fight for the free speech of others. She sent $100 to the NAACP with a letter of support that appeared in its magazine *The Crisis* — a radical act for a white person from Alabama in the 1920s. She supported Eugene V. Debs, the Socialist candidate, in each of his campaigns for the presidency. She composed essays on the women's movement, on politics, on economics. Near the end of her life, she wrote to Elizabeth Gurley Flynn, leader of the American Communist party, who was then languishing in jail, a victim of the McCarthy era: "Loving birthday greetings, dear Elizabeth Flynn! May the sense of serving mankind bring strength and peace into your brave heart!"[9]

One may not agree with Helen Keller's positions. Her praise of the USSR now seems naïve, embarrassing, to some even treasonous. But she *was* a radical — a fact few Americans know, because our schooling and our mass media left it out.[10]

What we did not learn about Woodrow Wilson is even more remarkable. When I ask my college students to tell me what they recall about President Wilson, they respond with enthusiasm. They say that Wilson led our country reluctantly into World War I and after the war led the struggle nationally and internationally to establish the League of Nations. They associate Wilson with progressive causes like women's suffrage. A handful of students recall the Wilson administration's Palmer Raids against left-wing unions. But my students seldom know or speak about two antidemocratic policies that Wilson carried out: his racial segregation of the federal government and his military interventions in foreign countries.

Under Wilson, the United States intervened in Latin America more often than at any other time in our history. We landed troops in Mexico in 1914, Haiti in 1915, the Dominican Republic in 1916, Mexico again in

1916 (and nine more times before the end of Wilson's presidency), Cuba in 1917, and Panama in 1918. Throughout his administration Wilson maintained forces in Nicaragua, using them to determine Nicaragua's president and to force passage of a treaty preferential to the United States.

In 1917 Woodrow Wilson took on a major power when he started sending secret monetary aid to the "White" side of the Russian civil war. In the summer of 1918 he authorized a naval blockade of the Soviet Union and sent expeditionary forces to Murmansk, Archangel, and Vladivostok to help overthrow the Russian Revolution. With the blessing of Britain and France, and in a joint command with Japanese soldiers, American forces penetrated westward from Vladivostok to Lake Baikal, supporting Czech and White Russian forces that had declared an anticommunist government headquartered at Omsk. After briefly maintaining front lines as far west as the Volga, the White Russian forces disintegrated by the end of 1919, and our troops finally left Vladivostok on April 1, 1920.[11]

Few Americans who were not alive at the time know anything about our "unknown war with Russia," to quote the title of Robert Maddox's book on this fiasco. Not one of the twelve American history textbooks in my sample even mentions it. Russian history textbooks, on the other hand, give the episode considerable coverage. According to Maddox: "The immediate effect of the intervention was to prolong a bloody civil war, thereby costing thousands of additional lives and wreaking enormous destruction on an already battered society. And there were longer-range implications. Bolshevik leaders had clear proof . . . that the Western powers meant to destroy the Soviet government if given the chance."[12]

This aggression fueled the suspicions that motivated the Soviets during the Cold War, and until its breakup the Soviet Union continued to claim damages for the invasion.

Wilson's invasions of Latin America are better known than his Russian adventure. Textbooks do cover some of them, and it is fascinating to watch textbook authors attempt to justify these episodes. Any accurate portrayal of the invasions could not possibly show Wilson or the United States in a favorable light. With hindsight we know that Wilson's interventions in Cuba, the Dominican Republic, Haiti, and Nicaragua set the stage for the dictators Batista, Trujillo, the Duvaliers, and the Somozas, whose legacies still reverberate.[13] Even in the 1910s, most of the invasions were unpopular in this country and provoked a torrent of criticism abroad. By the mid-1920s, Wilson's successors reversed his policies in Latin America. The authors of history textbooks know this, for a chapter or two after Wilson they laud our "Good Neighbor Policy," the renunciation of force in Latin America by Presidents Coolidge and Hoover, which was extended by Franklin D. Roosevelt.

Textbooks might (but don't) call Wilson's Latin American actions a "Bad Neighbor Policy" by comparison. Instead, faced with unpleasantries, textbooks wriggle to get the hero off the hook, as in this example from *The Challenge of Freedom*: "President Wilson wanted the United States to build friendships with the countries of Latin America. However, he found this difficult. . . ." Some textbooks blame the invasions on the countries invaded: "Necessity was the mother of armed Caribbean intervention," states *The American Pageant*. *Land of Promise* is vague as to who caused the invasions but seems certain they were not Wilson's doing: "He soon discovered that because of forces he could not control, his ideas of morality and idealism had to give way to practical action." *Promise* goes on to assert Wilson's innocence: "Thus, though he believed it morally undesirable to send Marines into the Caribbean, he saw no way to avoid it." This passage is sheer invention. Unlike his secretary of the navy, who later complained that what Wilson "forced [me] to do in Haiti was a bitter pill for me," no documentary evidence suggests that Wilson suffered any such qualms about dispatching troops to the Caribbean.[14]

All twelve of the textbooks I surveyed mention Wilson's 1914 invasion of Mexico, but they posit that the interventions were not Wilson's fault. "President Wilson was urged to send military forces into Mexico to protect American investments and to restore law and order," according to *Triumph of the American Nation*, whose authors emphasize that the president at first chose *not* to intervene. But "as the months passed, even President Wilson began to lose patience." Walter Karp has shown that this version contradicts the facts — the invasion was Wilson's idea from the start, and it outraged Congress as well as the American people.[15] According to Karp, Wilson's intervention was so outrageous that leaders of both sides of Mexico's ongoing civil war demanded that the U.S. forces leave; the pressure of public opinion in the United States and around the world finally influenced Wilson to recall the troops.

Textbook authors commonly use another device when describing our Mexican adventures: they identify Wilson as ordering our forces to withdraw, but nobody is specified as having ordered them in! Imparting information in a passive voice helps to insulate historical figures from their own unheroic or unethical deeds.

Some books go beyond omitting the actor and leave out the act itself. Half of the twelve textbooks do not even mention Wilson's takeover of Haiti. After U.S. marines invaded the country in 1915, they forced the Haitian legislature to select our preferred candidate as president. When Haiti refused to declare war on Germany after the United States did, we dissolved the Haitian legislature. Then the United States supervised a pseudo-referendum to approve a new Haitian constitution, less democratic than the constitution it replaced; the referendum passed by a hilarious 98,225 to 768. As Piero Gleijesus has noted, "It is not that Wilson failed in his earnest efforts to bring democracy to these little countries. He never tried. He intervened to impose hegemony, not democracy."[16] The United States also attacked Haiti's proud tradition of individual ownership of small tracts of land, which dated back to the Haitian Revolution, in favor of the establishment of large plantations. American troops forced peasants in shackles to work on road construction crews. In 1919 Haitian citizens rose up and resisted U.S. occupation troops in a guerrilla war that cost more than 3,000 lives, most of them Haitian. Students who read *Triumph of the American Nation* learn this about Wilson's intervention in Haiti: "Neither the treaty nor the continued presence of American troops restored order completely. During the next four or five years, nearly 2,000 Haitians were killed in riots and other outbreaks of violence." This passive construction veils the circumstances about which George Barnett, a U.S. marine general, complained to his commander in Haiti: "Practically indiscriminate killing of natives has gone on for some time." Barnett termed this violent episode "the most startling thing of its kind that has ever taken place in the Marine Corps."[17]

During the first two decades of this century, the United States effectively made colonies of Nicaragua, Cuba, the Dominican Republic, Haiti, and several other countries. Wilson's reaction to the Russian Revolution solidified the alignment of the United States with Europe's colonial powers. His was the first administration to be obsessed with the specter of communism, abroad and at home. Wilson was blunt about it. In Billings, Montana, stumping the West to seek support for the League of Nations, he warned, "There are apostles of Lenin in our own midst. I can not imagine what it means to be an apostle of Lenin. It means to be an apostle of the night, of chaos, of disorder."[18] Even after the White Russian alternative collapsed. Wilson refused to extend diplomatic recognition to the Soviet Union. He participated in barring Russia from the peace negotiations after World War I and helped oust Béla Kun, the communist leader who had risen to power in Hungary. Wilson's sentiment for self-determination and democracy never had a chance against his three bedrock "ism"s: colonialism, racism, and anticommunism. A young Ho Chi Minh appealed to Woodrow Wilson at Versailles for self-determination for Vietnam, but Ho had all three strikes against him. Wilson refused to listen, and France retained control of Indochina.[19] It seems that Wilson regarded self-determination as all right for, say, Belgium, but not for the likes of Latin America or Southeast Asia.

At home, Wilson's racial policies disgraced the office he held. His Republican predecessors had routinely appointed blacks to important offices, including those of port collector for New Orleans and the District of Columbia and register of the treasury. Presidents sometimes appointed African Americans as postmasters, particularly in southern towns with large black populations. African Americans took part in the Republican Party's national conventions and enjoyed some access to the White House. Woodrow Wilson, for whom many African Americans voted in 1912, changed all that. A southerner, Wilson had been president of Princeton, the only major northern university that refused to admit blacks. He was an outspoken white supremacist — his wife was even worse — and told "darky" stories in cabinet meetings. His administration submitted a legislative program intended to curtail the civil rights of African Americans, but Congress would not pass it. Unfazed, Wilson used his power as chief executive to segregate the federal government. He appointed southern whites to offices traditionally reserved for blacks. Wilson personally vetoed a clause on racial equality in the Covenant of the League of Nations. The one occasion on which Wilson met with African American leaders in the White House ended in a fiasco as the president virtually threw the visitors out of his office. Wilson's legacy was extensive: he effectively closed the Democratic Party to African Americans for another two decades, and parts of the federal government remained segregated into the 1950s and beyond.[20] In 1916 the Colored Advisory Committee of the Republican National Committee issued a statement on Wilson that, though partisan, was accurate: "No sooner had the Democratic Administration come into power than Mr. Wilson and his advisors entered upon a policy to eliminate all colored citizens from representation in the Federal Government."[21]

Of the twelve history textbooks I reviewed, only four accurately describe Wilson's racial policies. *Land of Promise* does the best job:

> Woodrow Wilson's administration was openly hostile to black people. Wilson was an outspoken white supremacist who believed that black people were inferior. During his campaign for the presidency, Wilson promised to press for civil rights. But once in office he forgot his promises. Instead, Wilson ordered that white and black workers in federal government jobs be segregated from one another. This was the first time such segregation had existed since Reconstruction! When black federal employees in Southern cities protested the order, Wilson had the protesters fired. In November, 1914, a black delegation asked the President to reverse his policies. Wilson was rude and hostile and refused their demands.

Unfortunately, except for one other textbook, *The United States — A History of the Republic, Promise* stands alone. Most of the textbooks that treat Wilson's racism give it only a sentence or two. Five of the books never even mention this "black mark" on Wilson's presidency. One that does, *The American Way*, does something even more astonishing: it invents a happy ending! "Those in favor of segregation finally lost support in the administration. Their policies gradually were ended." This is simply not true.

Omitting or absolving Wilson's racism goes beyond concealing a character blemish. It is overtly racist. No black person could ever consider Woodrow Wilson a hero. Textbooks that present him as a hero are written from a white perspective. The coverup denies all students the chance to learn something important about the interrelationship between the leader and the led. White Americans engaged in a new burst of racial violence during and immediately after Wilson's presidency. The tone set by the administration was one cause. Another was the release of America's first epic motion picture.[22]

The filmmaker David W. Griffith quoted Wilson's two-volume history of the United States, now notorious for its racist view of Reconstruction, in his infamous masterpiece *The Clansman*, a paean to the Ku Klux Klan for its role in putting down "black-dominated" Republican state governments during reconstruction. Griffith based the movie on a book by

Wilson's former classmate, Thomas Dixon, whose obsession with race was "unrivaled until *Mein Kampf*." At a private White House showing, Wilson saw the movie, now retitled *Birth of a Nation*, and returned Griffith's compliment: "It is like writing history with lightning, and my only regret is that it is all so true." Griffith would go on to use this quotation in successfully defending his film against NAACP charges that it was racially inflammatory.[23]

This landmark of American cinema was not only the best technical production of its time but also probably the most racist major movie of all time. Dixon intended "to revolutionize northern sentiment by a presentation of history that would transform every man in my audience into a good Democrat! . . . And make no mistake about it — we are doing just that."[24] Dixon did not overstate by much. Spurred by *Birth of a Nation*, William Simmons of Georgia reestablished the Ku Klux Klan. The racism seeping down from the White House encouraged this Klan, distinguishing it from its Reconstruction predecessor, which President Grant had succeeded in virtually eliminating in one state (South Carolina) and discouraging nationally for a time. The new KKK quickly became a national phenomenon. It grew to dominate the Democratic Party in many southern states, as well as in Indiana, Oklahoma, and Oregon. During Wilson's second term, a wave of antiblack race riots swept the country. Whites lynched blacks as far north as Duluth.[25]

If Americans had learned from the Wilson era the connection between racist presidential leadership and like-minded public response, they might not have put up with a reprise on a far smaller scale during the Reagan-Bush years.[26] To accomplish such education, however, textbooks would have to make plain the relationship between cause and effect, between hero and followers. Instead, they reflexively ascribe noble intentions to the hero and invoke "the people" to excuse questionable actions and policies. According to *Triumph of the American Nation*: "As President, Wilson seemed to agree with most white Americans that segregation was in the best interests of black as well as white Americans."

Wilson was not only antiblack; he was also far and away our most nativist president, repeatedly questioning the loyalty of those he called "hyphenated Americans." "Any man who carries a hyphen about with him," said Wilson, "carries a dagger that he is ready to plunge into the vitals of this Republic whenever he gets ready."[27] The American people responded to Wilson's lead with a wave of repression of white ethnic groups; again, most textbooks blame the people, not Wilson. *The American Tradition* admits that "President Wilson set up" the Creel Committee on Public Information, which saturated the United States with propaganda linking Germans to barbarism. But *Tradition* hastens to shield Wilson from the ensuring domestic fallout: "Although President Wilson had been careful in his war message to sate that most Americans of German descent were 'true and loyal citizens,' the anti-German propaganda often caused them suffering."

Wilson displayed little regard for the rights of anyone whose opinions differed from his own. But textbooks take pains to insulate him from wrongdoing. "Congress," not Wilson, is credited with having passed the Espionage Act of June 1917 and the Sedition Act of the following year, probably the most serious attacks on the civil liberties of Americans since the short-lived Alien and Sedition Acts of 1798. In fact, Wilson tried to strengthen the Espionage Act with a provision giving broad censorship powers directly to the president. Moreover, with Wilson's approval, his postmaster general used his new censorship powers to suppress all mail that was socialist, anti-British, pro-Irish, or that in any other way might, in his view, have threatened the war effort. Robert Goldstein served ten years in prison for producing *The Spirit of 76*, a film about the Revolutionary War that depicted the British, who were now our allies, unfavorably.[28] Textbook authors suggest that wartime pressures excuse Wilson's suppression of civil liberties, but in 1920, when World War I was long over, Wilson vetoed a bill that would have abolished the Espionage and Sedition acts.[29] Textbook authors blame the anticommunist and anti-labor union witch hunts of Wilson's second term on his illness and on an attorney general run amok. No evidence supports this view. Indeed, Attorney General Palmer asked Wilson in his last days as president to pardon Eugene V. Debs, who was serving time for a speech attributing World War I to economic interests and denouncing the Espionage Act as undemocratic.[30] The president replied, "Never!" and Debs languished in prison until Warren Harding pardoned him.[31] *The American Way* adopts perhaps the most innovative approach to absolving Wilson of wrongdoing: *Way* simply moves the "red scare" to the 1920s, after Wilson had left office!

Because heroification prevents textbooks from showing Wilson's shortcomings, textbooks are hard pressed to explain the results of the 1920 election. James Cox, the Democratic candidate who was Wilson's would-be successor, was crushed by the nonentity Warren G. Harding, who never even campaigned. In the biggest landslide in the history of American presidential politics, Harding got almost 64 percent of the major-party votes. The people were "tired," textbooks suggest, and just wanted a "return to normalcy." The possibility that the electorate knew what it was doing in rejecting Wilson never occurs to our authors.[32] It occurred to Helen Keller, however. She called Wilson "the greatest individual disappointment the world has ever known!"

It isn't only high school history courses that heroify Wilson. Textbooks such as *Land of Promise*, which discusses Wilson's racism, have to battle uphill, for they struggle against the archetypal Woodrow Wilson commemorated in so many history museums, public television documentaries, and historical novels.

For some years now, Michael Frisch has been conducting an experiment in social archetypes at the State University of New York at Buffalo. He asks his first-year college students for "the first ten names that you think of" in American history before the Civil War. When Frisch found that his students listed the same political and military figures year after year, replicating the privileged positions afforded them in high school text-books, he added the proviso, "excluding presidents, generals, statesmen, etc." Frisch still gets a stable list, but one less predictable on the basis of history textbooks. Seven years out of eight, Betsy Ross had led the list. (Paul Revere usually comes in second.)

What is interesting about this choice is that Betsy Ross never did anything. Frisch notes that she played "no role whatsoever in the actual creation of any actual first flag." Ross came to prominence around 1876, when some of her descendants, seeking to create a tourist attraction in Philadelphia, largely invented the myth of the first flag. With justice, high school textbooks universally ignore Betsy Ross; not one of my twelve books lists her in its index. So how and why does her story get transmit-ted? Frisch offers a hilarious explanation: If George Washington is the Father of Our Country, then Betsy Ross is our Blessed Virgin Mary! Frisch describes the pageants reenacted (or did we only imagine them?) in our elementary school years: "Washington [the god] calls on the humble seam-stress Betsy Ross in her tiny home and asks her if she will make the nation's flag, to his design. And Betsy promptly brings forth — from her lap! — the nation itself, and the promise of freedom and natural rights for all mankind."[33]

I think Frisch is onto something, but maybe he is merely on some-thing. Whether or not one buys his explanation, Betsy Ross's ranking among students surely proves the power of the social archetype. In the case of Woodrow Wilson, textbooks actually participate in creating the social archetype. Wilson is portrayed as "good," "idealist," "for self-determination, not colonial intervention," "foiled by an isolationist Sen-ate," and "ahead of his time." We name institutions after him, from the Woodrow Wilson Center at the Smithsonian Institution to Woodrow Wil-son Junior High School in Decatur, Illinois, where I misspent my adoles-cence. If a fifth face were to be chiseled into Mount Rushmore, many Americans would propose that it should be Wilson's.[34] Against such arche-typal goodness, even the unusually forthright treatment of Wilson's racism in *Land of Promise* cannot but fail to stick in students' minds.

Curators of history museums know that their visitors bring archetypes in with them. Some curators consciously design exhibits to confront these archetypes when they are inaccurate. Textbook authors, teachers, and moviemakers would better fulfill their educational mission if they also taught against inaccurate archetypes. Surely Woodrow Wilson does not need their flattering omissions, after all. His progressive legislative accom-plishments in just his first two years, including tariff reform, an income tax, the Federal Reserve Act, and the Workingmen's Compensation Act, are almost unparalleled. Wilson's speeches on behalf of self-determination stirred the world, even if his actions did not live up to his words.

Why do textbooks promote wartless stereotypes? The authors' omis-sions and errors can hardly be accidental. The producers of the filmstrips, movies, and other educational materials on Helen Keller surely know she was a socialist; no one can read Keller's writings without becoming aware of her political and social philosophy. At least one textbook author, Thomas Bailey, senior author of *The American Pageant*, clearly knew of the 1918 U.S. invasion of Russia, for he wrote in a different venue in 1973, "American troops shot it out with Russian armed forces on Russian soil in two theatres from 1918 to 1920."[35] Probably several other authors knew of it, too. Wilson's racism is also well known to professional historians. Why don't they let the public in on these matters?

Heroification itself supplies a first answer. Socialism is repugnant to most Americans. So are racism and colonialism. Michael Kammen suggests that authors selectively omit blemishes in order to make certain historical figures sympathetic to as many people as possible.[36] The textbook critic Norma Gabler has testified that textbooks should "present our nation's patriots in a way that would honor and respect them"; in her eyes, admitting Keller's socialism and Wilson's racism would hardly do that.[37] In the early 1920s the American Legion said that authors of textbooks "are at fault in placing before immature pupils the blunders, foibles and frailties of prominent heroes and patriots of our Nation."[38] The Legion would hardly be able to fault today's history textbooks on this count.

Perhaps we can go further. I began with Helen Killer because omitting the last sixty-four years of her life exemplifies the sort of culture-serving distortion that will be discussed later in this book. We teach Keller as an ideal, not a real person, to inspire our young people to emulate her. Keller becomes a mythic figure, the "woman who overcame" — but for *what?* There is no content! Just look what *she* accomplished, we're exhorted — yet we haven't a clue as to what that really was.

Keller did not want to be frozen in childhood. She herself stressed that the meaning of her life lay in what she did once she overcame her disability. In 1929, when she was nearing fifty, she wrote a second volume of autobiography, entitled *Midstream*, that described her social philosophy in some detail. Keller wrote about visiting mill towns, mining towns, and packing towns where workers were on strike. She intended that we learn of these experiences and of the conclusions to which they led her. Consistent with our American ideology of individualism, the truncated version of Helen Keller's story sanitizes a hero, leaving only the virtues of self-help and hard work. Keller herself, while scarcely opposing hard work, explicitly rejected this ideology.

> I had once believed that we were all masters of our fate — that we could mould our lives into any form we pleased. . . . I had overcome deafness and blindness sufficiently to be happy, and I supposed that anyone could come out victorious if he threw himself valiantly into life's struggle. But as I went more and more about the country I learned that I had spoken with assurance on a subject I knew little about. I forgot that I owed my success partly to the advantages of my birth and environment. . . . Now, however, I learned that the power to rise in the world is not within the reach of everyone.[39]

Textbooks don't want to touch this idea. "There are three great taboos in textbook publishing," an editor at one of the biggest houses told me, "sex, religion, and social class." While I had been able to guess the first two, the third floored me. Sociologists know the importance of social class, after all. Reviewing American history textbooks convinced me that this editor was right, however. The notion that opportunity might be unequal in America, that not everyone has "the power to rise in the world," is anathema to textbook authors, and to many teachers as well. Educators would much rather present Keller as a bland source of encouragement and inspiration to our young — if she can do it, you can do it! So they leave out her adult life and make her entire existence over into a vague "up by the bootstraps" operation. In the process, they make this passionate fighter for the poor into something she never was in life: boring.

Woodrow Wilson gets similarly whitewashed. Although some history textbooks disclose more than others about the seamy underside of Wilson's presidency, all twelve books reviewed share a common tone: respectful, patriotic, even adulatory. Ironically, Wilson was widely despised in the 1920s, and it was only after World War II that he came to be viewed kindly by policymakers and historians. Our postwar bipartisan foreign policy, one of far-reaching interventions sheathed in humanitarian explanations, was "shaped decisively by the ideology and the international program developed by the Wilson Administration," according to N. Gordon Levin, Jr.[40] Textbook authors are thus motivated to underplay or excuse Wilson's foreign interventions, many of which were counterproductive blunders, as well as other unsatisfactory aspects of his administration.

A host of other reasons — pressure from the "ruling class," pressure from textbook adoption committees, the wish to avoid ambiguities, a desire to shield children from harm or conflict, the perceived need to control children and avoid classroom disharmony, pressure to provide answers — may help explain why textbooks omit troublesome facts. A certain etiquette coerces us all into speaking in respectful tones about the past, especially when we're passing on Our Heritage to our young. Could it be that we don't *want* to think badly of Woodrow Wilson? We seem to feel that a person like Helen Keller can be an inspiration only so long as she remains uncontroversial, one-dimensional. We don't want complicated icons. "People do not like to think. If one thinks, one must reach conclusions," Helen Keller pointed out. "Conclusions are not always pleasant."[41] Most of us automatically shy away from conflict, and understandably so. We particularly seek to avoid conflict in the classroom. One reason is habit: we are so accustomed to blandness that the textbook or teacher who brought real intellectual controversy into the classroom would strike us as a violation of polite rhetoric, of classroom norms. We are supposed to speak well of the deceased, after all. Probably we are supposed to maintain the same attitude of awe, reverence, and respect when we read about our national heroes as when we visit our National Cathedral and view the final resting places of Helen Keller and Woodrow Wilson, as close physically in death as they were distant ideologically in life.

Whatever the causes, the results of heroification are potentially crippling to students. Helen Keller is not the only person this approach treats like a child. Denying students the humanness of Keller, Wilson, and others keeps students in intellectual immaturity. It perpetuates what might be called a Disney version of history: The Hall of Presidents at Disneyland similarly presents our leaders as heroic statesmen, not imperfect human beings.[42] Our children end up without realistic role models to inspire them. Students also develop no understanding of causality in history. Our nation's thirteen separate forays into Nicaragua, for instance, are surely worth knowing about as we attempt to understand why that country embraced a communist government in the 1980s. Textbooks should show history as contingent, affected by the power of ideas and individuals. Instead, they present history as a "done deal."

Do textbooks, filmstrips, and American history courses achieve the results they seek with regard to our heroes? Surely textbook authors want us to think well of the historical figures they treat with such sympathy. And, on a superficial level at least, we do. Almost no recent high school graduates have anything "bad" to say about either Keller or Wilson. But are these two considered heroes? I have asked hundreds of (mostly white) college students on the first day of class to tell me who their heroes in American history are. As a rule, they do not pick Helen Keller, Woodrow Wilson, Christopher Columbus, Miles Standish or anyone else in Plymouth, John Smith or anyone else in Virginia, Abraham Lincoln, or indeed anyone else in American history whom the textbooks implore them to choose.[43] Our post-Watergate students view all such "establishment" heroes cynically. They're bor-r-ring.

Some students choose "none" — that is, they say they have no heroes in American history. Other students display the characteristically American sympathy for the underdog by choosing African Americans: Martin Luther King, Jr., Malcolm X, perhaps Rosa Parks, Harriet Tubman, or Frederick Douglass. Or they choose men and women from other countries: Gandhi, Mother Teresa, Nelson Mandela, or (now fading fast) Mikhail Gorbachev or Boris Yeltsin.

In one sense that is a healthy development. Surely we want students to be skeptical. Probably we want them to challenge being told whom to believe it. But replying "none" is too glib, too nihilistic, for my taste. It is, however, an understandable response to heroification. For when textbook authors leave out the warts, the problems, the unfortunate character traits, and the mistaken ideas, they reduce heroes from dramatic men and women to melodramatic stick figures. Their inner struggles disappear and they become goody-goody, not merely good.

Students poke fun at the goody-goodiest of them all by passing on Helen Keller jokes. In so doing, schoolchildren are not poking cruel fun at a disabled person, they are deflating a pretentious symbol that is too good to be real. Nonetheless, our loss of Helen Keller as anything but a source of jokes is distressing. Knowing the reality of her quite amazing life might empower not only deaf or blind students, but any schoolgirl, and perhaps boys as well. For like other peoples around the world, we Americans need heroes. Statements such as "If Martin Luther King were alive, he'd . . ." suggest one function of historical figures in our contemporary society. Most of us tend to think well of ourselves when we have acted as we imagine our heroes might have done. Who our heroes are and whether they are presented in a way that makes them lifelike, hence usable as role models, could have a significant bearing on our conduct in the world.

We now turn to our first hero, Christopher Columbus. "Care should be taken to vindicate great names from pernicious erudition," wrote Washington Irving, defending heroification.[44] Irving's three-volume biography of Columbus, published in 1828, still influences what high school teachers and textbooks say about the Great Navigator. Therefore it will come as no surprise that heroification has stolen from us the important facets of his life, leaving only melodramatic minutiae.

NOTES

1. James Baldwin, "A Talk to Teachers," *Saturday Review*, December 21, 1963, reprinted in Rick Simonson and Scott Walker, eds., *Multicultural Literacy* (St. Paul, Minn.: Graywolf Press, 1988), 9.

2. W. E. B. Du Bois, *Black Reconstruction* (Cleveland: World Meridian, 1964 [1935]), 722.

3. Charles V. Willie, quoted in David J. Garrow, *Bearing the Cross* (New York: William Morrow, 1986), 625.

4. The phrase refers, of course, to his *father's* wealth and Senate seat.

5. *Helen Keller* (New York: McGraw-Hill Films, 1969).

6. Helen Keller, "Onward, Comrades," address at the Rand School of Social Science, New York, December 31, 1920, reprinted in Philip S. Foner, ed., *Helen Keller: Her Socialist Years* (New York: International Publishers, 1967), 107.

7. Quoted in Jonathan Kozol, *The Night Is Dark and I Am Far from Home* (New York: Simon & Schuster, 1990 [1975]), 101.

8. Foner, ed., *Helen Keller: Her Socialist Years*, 26.

9. Joseph P. Lash, *Helen and Teacher* (New York: Delacorte, 1980), 454; Dennis Wepman, *Helen Keller* (New York: Chelsea House, 1987), 69; Foner, ed., *Helen Keller: Her Socialist Years*, 17–18. The United States did not allow Flynn to receive the letter.

10. Jonathan Kozol brought this suppression to my attention in an address at the University of Wyoming in 1975.

Nazi leaders knew her radicalism: in 1933 they burned Keller's books because of their socialist content and banned her from their libraries. We overlook her socialist content, thus learning no more than the German public about her ideas. See Irving Wallace, David Wallechinsky, and Amy Wallace, *Significa* (New York: Dutton, 1983), 1–2.

11. N. Gordon Levin, Jr., *Woodrow Wilson and World Politics: America's Response to War and Revolution* (New York: Oxford University Press, 1968), 67. Everett M. Dirksen, "Use of U.S. Armed Forces in Foreign Countries," *Congressional Record*, June 23, 1969, 16840–43.

12. Robert J. Maddox, *The Unknown War with Russia* (San Rafael, Calif.: Presidio Press, 1977), 137.

13. Hans Schmidt, *The United States Occupation of Haiti, 1915–1934* (New Brunswick, N.J.: Rutgers University Press, 1971), 86.

14. Ibid., 66, 74.

15. Walter Karp, *The Politics of War* (New York: Harper and Row, 1979), 158–67.

16. Piero Gleijesus, "The Other Americas," *Washington Post Book World*, December 27, 1992, 5.

17. "Reports Unlawful Killing of Haitians by Our Marines," *New York Times*, October 14, 1920, 1ff. Also see Schmidt, *The United States Occupation of Haiti*.

18. *Addresses of President Wilson*. 66th Congress, Senate Document 120 (Washington, D.C.: Government Printing Office, 1919), 133.

19. Jean Lacouture, *Ho Chi Minh* (New York: Random House, 1968), 24, 265.

20. Rayford W. Logan, *The Betrayal of the Negro* (New York: Collier, 1965 [1954]), 360–70; Nancy J. Weiss, "Wilson Draws the Color Line," in Arthur Mann, ed., *The Progressive Era* (Hinsdale, Ill.: Dryden, 1975), 144; Harvey Wasserman, *American Born and Reborn* (New York: Macmillan, 1983), 131; Kathleen Wolgemuth, "Woodrow Wilson and Federal Segregation," *Journal of Negro History* 44 (1959): 158–73; and Morton Sosna, "The South in the Saddle," *Wisconsin Magazine of History* 54 (Fall 1970): 30–49.

21. Colored Advisory Committee of the Republican National Committee, "Address to the Colored Voters," October 6, 1916, reprinted in Herbert Aptheker, ed., *A Documentary History of the Negro People in the United States, 1910–1932* (Secaucus, N.J.: Citadel, 1973), 140.

22. Wyn C. Wade, *The Fiery Cross* (New York: Simon & Schuster, 1987), 115–51.

23. Ibid., 135–37.

24. Ibid., 138.

25. Lerone Bennett, Jr., *Before the Mayflower* (Baltimore: Penguin, 1966 [1962]), 292–94. Bennett counts twenty-six major race riots in 1919 alone, including riots in Omaha; Knoxville; Longview, Texas; Chicago; Phillips County, Arkansas; and Washington, D.C. Also see Herbert Shapiro. *White Violence and Black Response* (Amherst: University of Massachusetts Press, 1988), 123–54.

26. See Studs Terkel, "Interview," *Modern Maturity* 36, no. 2 (April 1993): 76.

27. *Addresses of President Wilson*, 108–09.

28. William Bruce Wheeler and Susan D. Becker, *Discovering the American Past*, vol. 2 (Boston: Houghton Mifflin, 1990), 127.

29. Ronald Schaffer, *Americans in the Great War* (New York: Oxford University Press, 1991), quoted in Garry Wills, "The Presbyterian Nietzsche," *New York Review of Books*, January 16, 1992, 6.

30. Karp, *The Politics of War*, 326–28; Charles D. Ameringer, *U.S. Foreign Intelligence* (Lexington, Mass.: D.C. Heath, 1990), 109. Ironically, after the war Wilson agreed with Debs on the power of economic interests: "Is there any man here . . . who does not know that the seed of war in the modern world is industrial and commercial rivalry?" (Speech in Saint Louis, September 5, 1919; *Addresses of President Wilson*, 41.)

31. Ameringer, *U.S. Foreign Intelligence*, 109.

32. Ibid. Ameringer points out that Wilson's attacks on civil liberties had become a political liability and Attorney General Palmer a pathetic joke by the fall of 1920.

33. Michael H. Frisch, *A Shared Authority* (Albany: State University of New York Press, 1990), 39–47.

34. In Arthur M. Schlesinger's 1962 poll of seventy-five "leading historians," Wilson came in fourth, ahead of Thomas Jefferson (Kenneth S. Davis, "Not So Common Man," *New York Review of Books*, December 4, 1986, 29). Eight hundred and forty-six professors of American history rated Wilson sixth, after FDR and the four gentlemen already on Mount Rushmore (Robert K. Murray and Tim Blessing, "The Presidential Performance Study," *Journal of American History* 70 [December 1983]: 535–55). See also George Hornby, ed., *Great Americana Scrap Book* (New York: Crown, 1985), 121.

35. Thomas A. Bailey, *Probing America's Past*, vol. 2 (Lexington, Mass.: D.C. Heath, 1973), 575.

36. Michael Kammen, *Mystic Chords of Memory* (New York: Alfred A. Knopf, 1991), 701.

37. Quoted in Marjory Kline, "Social Influences in Textbook Publishing," in *Educational Forum* 48, no. 2 (1984): 230.

38. Bessie Pierce, *Public Opinion and the Teaching of History in the United States* (New York: Alfred A. Knopf, 1926), 332.

39. Helen Keller, *Midstream: My Later Life* (New York: Greenwood, 1968 [1929]), 156.

40. Levin, *Woodrow Wilson and World Politics*, 1. Since Wilson's was the only Democratic administration in the first third of the twentieth century, it was natural that many of Franklin Roosevelt's statesmen, including FDR himself, had received their foreign policy experience under Wilson.

41. Quoted in Kozol, *The Night Is Dark and I Am Far from Home*, 101.

42. Kammen, *Mystic Chords of Memory*, 639.

43. See also Arthur Levine, *When Dreams and Heroes Died* (San Francisco: Jossey-Bass, 1980), and Frisch, *A Shared Authority*.

44. Quoted in Claudia Bushman, "America Discovers Columbus" (Costa Mesa, Calif.: American Studies Association Annual Meeting, 1992), 9.

■ RONALD MACAULAY

Extremely Interesting, Very Interesting, or Only Quite Interesting? Adverbs and Social Class[1]

Ronald Macaulay is a professor emeritus of linguistics at Pitzer College. He is the author of *Language, Social Class, and Education: A Glasgow Study*; *Locating Dialect in Discourse: The Language of Honest Men and Bonnie Lasses in Ayr*; and *Standards and Variation in Urban Speech*. In "Extremely Interesting, Very Interesting, or Only Quite Interesting? Adverbs and Social Class," Macaulay revisits the work of sociologist and linguist Basil Bernstein, who researched and reported on the connection between language use and social class in the 1960s and 1970s. Macaulay conducted his own research in order to verify the validity of Bernstein's findings. "Adverbs and Social Class," published in 2002 in the *Journal of Sociolinguistics*, is a good example of the genre of the research article, in which researchers situate and explore research questions and then present and analyze findings. Research articles are generally divided into individual sections that discuss the researcher's questions, methods, data, analysis, and conclusions.

■ ■ ■

I am glad you like adverbs — I adore them; they are the only qualifications I really much respect . . .

— HENRY JAMES, letter to a young admirer, 1902

Introduction

Social class figured prominently in early sociolinguistic investigations (Macaulay and Trevelyan 1973; Trudgill 1974) but became less central as the focus moved to ethnicity, networking (Milroy 1980) and gender (Coates 1986). There continue to be studies of social class differences (e.g., Foulkes and Docherty 1999) usually with particular attention to the role of social class differences in language change. There have, however, been fewer studies of stable social class differences. Macaulay (1991) examined a range of features in a small sample of speakers in the town of Ayr in the west of Scotland. Many of the clearest social class differences were in pronunciation and morphology, similar to those found in other sociolinguistic studies, but there were also differences in syntax, lexical choice, and discourse features. Some of the latter differences resembled those examined by Basil Bernstein in his early attempts to characterize social class differences in language (Bernstein 1962).

As a young man working with boys' clubs in the east end of London and later teaching adolescents at a day college, Bernstein was struck by the difference between the boys' verbal skills and their performance skills (Bernstein 1971: 2–5). He later demonstrated this by comparing the results of two polarized groups on tests of verbal and non-verbal intelligence. He was able to show that the verbal scores of the working-class boys were depressed in comparison with their non-verbal scores, while there was no difference for the middle-class subjects (Bernstein 1960). Bernstein had some intuitions about the actual linguistic differences that he set out in a paper not based on his own research (Bernstein 1959). Among the characteristics of what he was then calling a *public language* (used by, among others, "the unskilled and semi-skilled strata") was "rigid and limited use of adjectives and adverbs" (1971: 42).[2] Bernstein later investigated this notion empirically in a study based on discussion groups with two middle-class groups of five boys and two working-class groups of five boys and one of four (Bernstein 1962). A sample of 1,800 words was taken from each session but this number was reduced by the omission of certain forms and the contribution of two working-class boys who contributed fewer than 90 words each. The total number of words analyzed was 7,892.

Bernstein identified a category of "uncommon adverbs" by excluding adverbs of degree and place, *just*, and *really*, in addition to a number of items that would not normally be considered adverbs (e.g., *not*, *how*). Bernstein does not give the actual frequencies but only the results of the statistical analysis: "[a] greater proportion of the adverbs of the middle class are uncommon and the difference is significant beyond the 0.001 level of confidence" (1971: 101). This difference in adverb use has similarities to one found in the Ayr study, and I later examined a corpus of conversations recorded in Glasgow (Stuart-Smith 1999) where the same social class difference in the frequency with which the speakers used adverbs emerged. This paper reports the results from the two studies and explores possible explanations for this consistent difference.

The Sample

In 1978 and 1979 I conducted interviews in Ayr as part of a proposed (but never completed) comparative study of urban speech in Scotland. From these interviews I chose twelve speakers, six middle-class and six lower-class, for detailed analysis (Macaulay 1991). The sample was clearly polarized in social class terms on grounds of occupation, education, and residence. The tapes were transcribed in their entirety and searched for phonological, morphological, syntactic, lexical, and discourse features (Macaulay 1991). The size of the corpus is 120,669 words (lower-class speakers 69,711; middle-class speakers 50,898).

The second set of recordings was collected for an investigation of language variation and change in Glasgow, Scotland (Stuart-Smith 1999). The study is one of several (Foulkes and Docherty 1999) carried out to discover what changes, if any, had occurred in British urban speech since the earlier studies of the 1970s (e.g., Macaulay and Trevelyan 1973; Trudgill 1974). In the summer of 1997, 33 Glaswegians were recorded in same-sex dyadic conversations of approximately 35 minutes long. The speakers were drawn from two areas of the city, representing broadly urban working-class and suburban middle-class areas.

The sample consists of two age groups: adolescents (13–14) and adults (40+), with equal numbers of males and females.[3] For each session one speaker was selected and asked to choose someone they would feel comfortable talking to in the presence of a tape-recorder for about half an hour. The participants were free to talk about anything they wished. The resulting tapes provide material for an examination of age, social class, and gender differences in this particular form of discourse, and are free from any addressee effect (Bell 1984) that might be caused by an academic interviewer. Although there are more adult speakers in the Glasgow study the total amount of speech recorded from the adults is less than in the Ayr study, 84,616 words (working-class speakers 50,307; middle-class speakers 34,309). The main reason is that the Ayr interviews lasted longer than half an hour.

In the Glasgow sample, unlike the Ayr sample, there were also adolescents aged 13–14. They produced considerably less speech overall than the adults, 43,046 words (working-class adolescents 21,093; middle-class adolescents 21,953) and there were social class and gender differences in the amount of talk recorded. The working-class boys produced less speech than the others and the working-class girls the most, so the adolescent corpus is unbalanced in gender terms but there is enough speech from all four categories to justify quantitative analysis.

Bernstein emphasized that the kinds of differences he found between working-class and middle-class speakers were not absolute but relative: "[t]he difference on individual measures was always one of relative frequency" (1971: 13). The key measure used in the present paper is the frequency of use per one thousand words. The Ayr and Glasgow samples were transcribed in their entirety, both as dialogues and with the contribution of each speaker separated. The contributions of individual speakers were analyzed by means of the WordCruncher concordance program. The resulting lists were then manually searched for items that might vary in their distribution. Among these were derived adverbs in -*ly*.

The Data

1. Adverbs in -ly

Adults. Table 1 gives the frequency of adverbs in -*ly* for the Ayr sample, from Macaulay (1995: 44), and for the Glasgow adult sample. It can be seen that while there are minor differences, the general pattern is remarkably similar in both, with the middle-class speakers using derived adverbs in -*ly* more than twice as frequently as the working-class speakers. This similarity was reassuring because I had worried that the social class differences in the use of derivative adverbs found in the Ayr study might be an artifact of the interview situation (Macaulay 1995). The figures in Table 1 cannot be directly compared with Bernstein's findings because they include *really* and degree adverbs, and Bernstein reports only the proportion of "uncommon adverbs" rather than frequencies, but the pattern is presumably similar.

Figure 1 shows that for the Glasgow adults the individual frequencies reflect the general pattern with two outliers, one middle-class woman with a frequency of 6.5 and one working-class woman with a frequency of 12.2. Figure 1 also shows that it is the middle-class men who are the most frequent users of these adverbs.

TABLE 1   Relative frequency of derivative adverbs in -*ly* in Ayr and Glasgow

| | AYR | | | | GLASGOW | | | |
| | LOWER-CLASS | | MIDDLE-CLASS | | WORKING-CLASS | | MIDDLE-CLASS | |
	#	FREQ.	#	FREQ.	#	FREQ.	#	FREQ.
Manner	28	0.40	82	1.61	11	0.22	32	0.93
Time/Freq.	41	0.58	70	1.38	19	0.38	33	0.96
Degree	47	0.67	121	2.38	35	0.69	42	1.22
Sentence	76	1.08	174	3.42	92	1.82	197	5.74
really	55	0.79	106	2.08	93	1.85	104	3.03
Totals	247	3.52	553	10.87	250	4.97	408	11.89

Freq. = per 1,000 words

At this point it may be helpful to point out that while the differences in adverb use are not salient and are not indexical of social class membership in Silverstein's (1996) sense, there are many obvious differences in pronunciation and morphology that distinguish the two groups. The differences between the two groups in Ayr are summarized in Macaulay (1991: 257). The differences in pronunciation in Glasgow are presented in Stuart-Smith (1999). Nobody from Ayr or Glasgow would have the slightest difficulty in assigning any of the speakers to one social class or the other on the

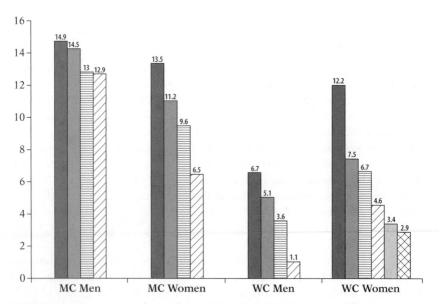

FIGURE 1   Frequency of use of adverbs in -*ly* by 18 Glasgow adults (freq. = per 1,000 words)

basis of a short extract from the tapes. The two groups are clearly polarized within the local speech community.

Macaulay (1995) also examined the use of adjectives by the two groups of speakers in Ayr and found that the middle-class speakers used adjectives with a frequency of 22.41 per thousand in contrast to the lower-class speakers with a frequency of 11.74. The figures for the Glasgow sample show the middle-class speakers with a frequency of 34.16 and the working-class speakers with a frequency of 24.74. Once again, the pattern is repeated, though the distance between the groups is less in Glasgow.

Adolescents. What about the adolescents in Glasgow? The overall frequency of derivative adverbs in -*ly* for the Glasgow adolescents is given in Table 2. Although the overall frequency of use is lower than in the adult sessions the pattern of social class differences is similar and the difference is still substantial. The individual figures are shown in Figure 2. Here the outliers are two middle-class boys who use very few adverbs in -*ly* and one working-class boy who uses these adverbs with a frequency of 8.2. It is the other two middle-class boys that use these adverbs most frequently, like the middle-class men.

Given the overall higher frequency with which these adverbs are used in the middle-class sessions, it is not surprising that the variety of adverbs is greater. In the middle-class adult conversations there are 74 different adverbs in -*ly* used; in the working-class conversations, 37 different adverbs are used. Of the total, 22 adverbs are used by both groups, the most frequent being *really* (MC 3.03/WC 1.85) and *actually* (MC 2.8/WC 0.74). In the case of the adolescents, the middle-class speakers use 32 different adverbs in -*ly*, and the working-class 21, with 15 used by both. As with the adults, the most frequent are *really* (MC 3.14/WC 0.85) and *actually* (MC 0.73/WC 0.57). However, the list of adverbs unique to either social class group does not suggest that the source of the difference lies in education. It is unlikely that educational differences account for the failure of working-class speakers to use adverbs such as *badly, clearly, fairly, happily,* etc. or

TABLE 2   Frequency of adverbs in -*ly* in Glasgow adolescent conversations, by gender and social class

	N	FREQ.
Middle-class girls	84	8.1
Middle-class boys	101	8.8
Working-class girls	50	3.7
Working-class boys	29	3.9
MC adolescents	185	8.4
WC adolescents	79	3.9

Freq. = per 1,000 words

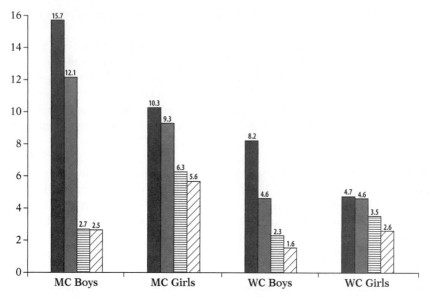

FIGURE 2   Frequency of use of adverbs in -*ly* by 16 Glasgow adolescents (freq. = per 1,000 words)

their use of such adverbs as *automatically, basically, entirely,* and *literally* that do not occur in the middle-class conversations. Nor is there any indication that the working-class speakers are using uninflected forms (suffixless adjectives, zero forms) instead of inflected adverbs. These forms are more common in American English (Opdahl 2000) and they have also been found to occur fairly frequently in northern British English (Tagliamonte and Ito 2001). In both the Ayr and the Glasgow recordings uninflected forms were too rare to affect the results.

As regards the use of adjectives, the social class difference found among the adults is repeated in the adolescent conversations. The middle-class adolescents use adjectives with a frequency of 29.79 per thousand words and for the working-class adolescents the frequency is 21.86. The social class differences that were found in the Ayr interviews have thus been repeated in the Glasgow conversations, among both adults and adolescents.

2. Other adverbs

It is not only derived adverbs that show this marked social class difference. In the Ayr interviews the middle-class speakers used *very* with a frequency of 3.03 per thousand words compared with a frequency of only 0.82 in the lower-class interviews. A similar pattern is found in the Glasgow conversations (see Figure 3). It can be seen from Figure 3 that *very* is almost categorically a middle-class word. Eleven (61%) of the 18 working-class speakers do not use it even once in their conversations. The Glasgow adolescents have two additional intensifiers that are not found in the adult sessions, *pure* and *dead*. The frequencies are shown in Figure 4.

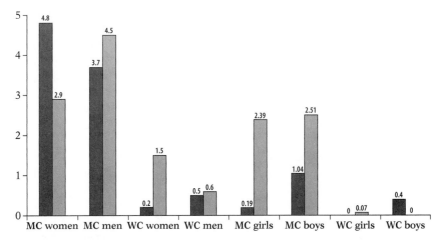

FIGURE 3 Frequency of use of *very* and *quite* by Glasgow adults and adolescents (freq. = per 1,000 words)

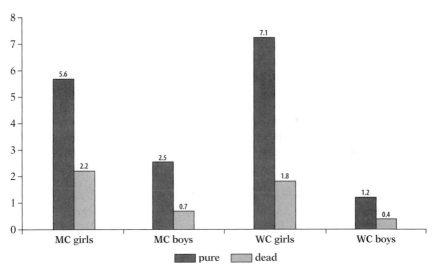

FIGURE 4 Frequence of use of *pure* and *dead* by Glasgow adolescents (freq. = per 1,000 words)

Examples of the use of *pure* and *dead* can be seen in 1:

1. a. this is **pure** embarrassing
   b. this is **dead** embarrassing
   c. it's **pure** funny but
   d. I'd look **dead** funny without a fringe wouldn't I?
   e. and I was like **really** close to Chi
   f. I was standing **pure** close to him
   g. she used to be **dead** fat
   h. she's **dead** skinny now

Examples 1e and 1f show that *pure* is most likely an alternative to *really* but many of the examples of *dead* are like those in 1g and 1h modifying an adjective and could be an alternative to *very*. It can be seen from Figure 4 that while both boys and girls use these forms, girls use them three times as frequently. The overall social class difference for the two intensifiers is very slight (MC 5.4/WC 6.4).

Another adverb whose use varies socially is *quite*. In the Ayr interviews, the middle-class speakers also used *quite* more frequently (2.49 per 1,000 words) compared with the lower-class speakers (1.00 per 1,000 words). A similar pattern can be seen in the Glasgow conversations, as shown in Figure 3, which shows that *quite* is predominantly a middle-class item in both age-groups.

The use of *quite* can either be emphatic (what Quirk, Greenbaum, Leech, and Svartvik 1985: 590 call "maximizers"), as in the examples in 2, or a hedge (what Quirk et al. 1985: 577–578 call "downtoners"), as in the examples in 3. All the examples in 2 and 3 are from middle-class conversations:

2. a. but I think clothes-wise were *quite* different
   b. and I was *quite* proud because I was still thirty nine
   c. I do it *quite* quickly
      I can do it in about fifteen seconds
   d. San Francisco's actually *quite* chilly so —
   e. it's *quite quite quite quite* different

3. a. it is actually *quite* nice
   b. I mean Alison's still *quite* sort of young
   c. the actual wee beach is — is *quite* nice because it's sort of rough sand
   d. it's *quite* pleasant it's — it's sand-dunish and em
   e. but it's — it's er *quite* interesting to find how different people do speak

Deciding between these two functions is sometimes difficult so any figures reflect an interpretative decision. The middle-class speakers appear to use *quite* more frequently in its emphatic function (67%) than in its hedging function (33%). For the working-class speakers the difference is less: 56 percent emphatic, 44 percent hedging. However, the middle-class speakers use *quite* with an overall frequency of 3.64 per thousand words compared with the working-class frequency of 1.19. The frequency with which the middle-class speakers use *quite* in its emphatic function is 2.42 per thousand words compared with the working-class frequency of 0.66. In the hedging function the frequencies are: middle-class 1.2, working-class 0.52. The middle-class thus use *quite* twice as often as the working-class speakers in a hedging function and almost four times as often in the emphatic function.

The final adverb to be examined is *just*. In the Ayr interviews the difference in the frequencies of *just* was minimal (MC 5.01/WC 4.84). The frequencies for the Glasgow speakers are shown in Figure 5. It can be seen that the social class differences are slight. This is the only example of a

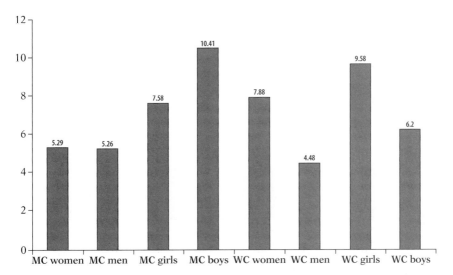

FIGURE 5 Frequency of use of *just* by Glasgow adults and adolescents (freq. = per 1,000 words)

very common adverb that the working-class adults use more frequently (6.72 per 1,000 words) than the middle-class adults (5.28). There are, however, also social class differences in the use of *just*. While the working-class adults use *just* slightly more frequently (6.18 per 1,000 words) than the middle-class adults (5.22 per 1,000 words), they do not use *just* in exactly the same way.

In Ayr, following the analysis presented in Lee (1987), I separated the uses of *just* into four categories. The first is with reference to time, usually the immediate past, as in examples la and lb. The second use is as an intensifier with the general sense of "exactly," as in examples 2a and 2b. The third use is in the sense of "only," as in examples 3a and 3b. Finally, there is the sense of "simply," as shown in examples 4a and 4b:

4. (the *a* examples are middle-class, *b* examples working-class)
   1a. I've *just* realized something (speaker 10R)
   1b. that's it *just* opened up again (13R)
   2a. yes that's *just* what I was thinking (12L)
   2b. well *just* as it turns round the bend (15L)
   3a. but it's *just* a baby (12L)
   3b. it was *just* the two of us (14L)
   4a. I'll *just* take everything out of the dining room (10R)
   4b. I'll *just* go alang (13R)

The examples in 4 show that both groups use *just* in all four senses but they do not use them equally frequently as shown in Figure 6. The working-class adults use *just* more often in the "simply" sense, while the middle-

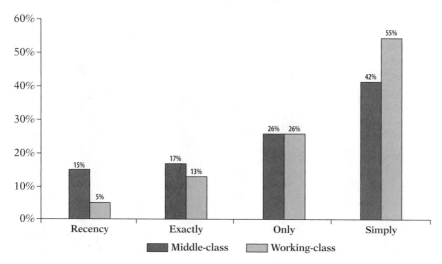

FIGURE 6 Social class differences in the use of *just* in four senses by Glasgow adults (% of group usage)

class adults make more frequent use of the "recency" and "exactly" senses than do the working-class speakers. The latter middle-class use is most distinctive when employed emphatically with adjectives and verbs as in 5:

5. a. It's *just* awful. I mean that's my lot plus another three — it's *just* horrendous you know absolute madness (10R)
   b. and I mean she was *just* impeccable (16R)
   c. and it *just* poured (16L)
   d. oh it's *just* out of this world (12R)

There is nothing remarkable about this emphatic use but it does not occur in the working-class sessions. The middle-class speakers also use *just* with hedges, as in 6:

6. (Hedges in bold)
   a. Truro's really *just* a **sort of** market town (10L)
   b. to stop and *just* **sort of** pitch their camp there for the day (16R)
   c. it's really *just* a **sort of** buffer (10R)
   d. it **kind of** had been programmed to really **sort of** *just* keep you in order (12R)

There are not many examples of these uses in the middle-class conversations but there is none in the working-class conversations.

In the adolescent conversations there are only minor social class differences, with the middle-class adolescents using *just* with a frequency of 8.88 per thousand words and the working-class adolescents with a frequency of 8.30 per thousand words. The pattern and frequencies are remarkably similar to those in the adult conversations, showing that unlike *very* and *quite*, the adolescents are using the word in much the same way as the adults. There are even examples of the emphatic evaluative use (examples 7a and 7b) and of the use of *just* with hedges (examples 7c and 7d) that occur only in the conversations between middle-class adolescents:

7. (Hedges in bold)
   a. she's *just* dead annoying (5L)
   b. and I mean that's *just* stupid (5R)
   c. she's *just* **sort of** standing in for Mister Weir (3L)
   d. and eventually they *just* **sort of** ran out (4R)

As with the adults, there are few examples but they occur only in the middle-class conversations.

Discussion

Since the Ayr interviews and the Glasgow conversations were recorded under very different circumstances, their similarity is striking and raises questions as to why this situation should arise. However, as Bernstein pointed out, the difficulty is "the problem of inferring from micro counts of specific linguistic choices to macro characteristics of the speech as a whole" (1971: 13). The remainder of this paper will be devoted to examining possible explanations for the social class difference in the use of inflected and other adverbs. It may be helpful to take as a starting-point three examples of empirical investigation.

Bernstein (1971[1962]) included adverb use in a list of features that he identified as characteristic of what he was then calling a *restricted code* rather than a *public language*:

> The restriction on the use of adjectives, uncommon adjectives, uncommon adverbs, the relative simplicity of the verbal form and the low proportion of subordinations supports the thesis that the working-class subjects do not explicate intent verbally and inasmuch as this is so the speech is relatively non-individuated. (Bernstein 1971: 109)

It is not immediately obvious what "explicate intent verbally" or "non-individuated" mean or what role adverbs might play in either. Bernstein (1971) went on to explain the different character of an *elaborated code*:

> Individuated speech presupposes a history of a particular role relationship if it is to be prepared and delivered appropriately. Inasmuch as difference is part of the expectation, there is less reliance or dependency on the listener; or rather this dependency is reduced by the explication of meaning. (Bernstein 1971: 113)

In other words, "uncommon adverbs" help to make utterances more explicit. Labov, on the other hand, includes adverbs such as *really* as signals of intensity:

"Intensity" is defined here as the emotional expression of social orientation toward the linguistic proposition: the commitment of the self to the proposition. (Labov 1984: 43–44)

Powell (1992), in a historical examination of the development of interpersonal and metalinguistic senses of stance adverbs, observes that certain adverbs can "act preemptively to inform and to persuade a hearer of the nature and importance of the speaker's evaluation" (1992: 76). She regards as interpersonal use "any use which the OED defines as emphatic, emphatic use being preeminently expressive in function" (1992: 83).

What evidence is there in the transcripts to support the hypothesis that the middle-class speakers use adverbs in -ly: (1) to be more explicit; (2) to express intensity; or (3) to signal the speaker's evaluation? The Oxford English Dictionary gives as its definition for the word *explicit* in relation to knowledge: "[d]eveloped in detail; hence, clear, definite." In the Glasgow middle-class conversations there are examples of derived adverbs that might come under this heading, as in the examples in 8:

8. a. they're *slightly* different but they're *exactly* the same color (10R)
   b. and it's *immediately* at the roadside (16L)
   c. it just goes downhill *slowly* (16L)
   d. a wee bit ambiguous here and there but *generally* okay (11L)

In the examples in 8 the speakers appear to be trying to make the point clearly. There are, however, similar examples in the working-class sessions, as shown in 9:

9. a. you would just go along until you get to *roughly* the first street (15L)
   b. there's *really* nothing to see in it but it's *really* quiet (18L)
   c. two *completely* different people (13R)
   d. he's aboot — he's *nearly* as tall as — taller than John must be aboot six two — six four or something (14R)

There are not many examples in either set of conversations and if this is what Bernstein meant by explicitness, then it does not appear to explain the social class difference in the frequency of derived adverbs. I will return to the significance of details later.

As regards intensity, the examples in 10 are taken from the middle-class interviews in Ayr (Macaulay 1991: 125):

10. a. I found it *extraordinarily* boring (1M)
    b. I got *absolutely* sick of doing nothing (1M)
    c. but this zombie of a mother — *completely* apathetic (WG)
    d. a *terribly* crippled bent old woman (DN)

These examples support Labov's view of these adverbs as expressing intensity. There are 25 clear examples in the Ayr middle-class interviews but only three in the working-class interviews. Similar examples can be found in the Glasgow middle-class conversations:

11. a. and she was apparently *absolutely* horrendous (10L)
    b. who's got *absolutely* no sense of golfing etiquette (11L)
    c. whereas the lady describing it thought it was *absolutely* perfect (11L)
    d. you're either running around going d — *absolutely* scatty chasing your tail or (10R)

However, there are similar examples in the working-class sessions, though fewer, and most of the examples come from one man (18L):

12. a. I was there it was — oh it was *absolutely* brilliant (18L)
    b. oh I mean it's amazing it's *absolutely* fantastic (18L)
    c. it seemed to me to be a *perfectly* good place (18L)
    d. everything's all just draining doon like that you know just *completely totally* unwinding (13R)

So, there is some support for the view that the use of derived adverbs to express intensity contributes to the difference in frequency between the two social classes.

What about Powell's notion that adverbs are used to express the speaker's evaluation? The most obvious examples are evidentials, as in examples 13a and 13b but more important are examples such as the hedge in 13c and the intensifier in 13d where the personal attitude is clearly stated:

13. a. but *funnily* enough I gave out (10L)
    b. *interestingly* enough that one of these programs on the telly (16R)
    c. I thought *technically* it was brilliant but — but it was boring (12L)
    d. San Francisco's *actually* quite chilly . . . it's — it's *amazingly* chilly (16L)

The examples in 13 are from the middle-class sessions. There are a few in the working-class conversations as well:

14. a. *funnily* enough we got that one (13R)
    b. but hmm *unfortunately* my trade went (18L)
    c. urban decay I mean you can get right into that *politically* (18R)
    d. but as I say I *normally* drink whisky (13R)

However, there are few examples in either set of conversations, so the explanation for the difference in frequency is unlikely to lie here. However, some of the adverbs used by the middle-class Glasgow adults suggest an attitude of confidence in making categorical judgments that is less apparent in the working-class conversations: *amazingly, awfully, badly, drastically, enormously, overly, properly,* and *terribly.* Even the other adverbs can have this effect when combined with adjectives as in the examples in 2, the kind of effect Louw (1993) describes as "semantic prosody."

15. L10: mmhm her mother had me in stitches one day
         when I bumped into them in town
         and I think I'd had a *particularly* bad day with Kim
         and she was telling me all about her Fiona

and what she was like at Kim's age
who — and she was *apparently absolutely* horrendous

In 15 the adverbs emphasize the categorical judgments expressed by the adjectives.

As was shown earlier the Glasgow middle-class adults use adjectives with a frequency of 34.16 per thousand words and the working-class adults with a frequency of 24.74. However, the difference is greater when evaluative adjectives (Hunston and Sinclair 2000) are compared. The middle-class adults use evaluative adjectives with a frequency of 12.88 per thousand words and the working-class adults with a frequency of 8.67. Moreover, there is a difference in the kind of evaluative adjectives used. In the working-class conversations 52 percent of the adjectives are simple words of approval or disapproval (e.g., *good*, *bad*, *nice*); in the middle-class conversations only 36 percent of the evaluative adjectives are of this kind. The middle-class adults use adjectives such as *horrendous, horrible, hellish, chauvinistic, unattractive, messy, impressive, interesting, tremendous, fantastic, substantial*, and *impeccable*, but none of these or similar adjectives is used by the working-class adults.

Of the three possible explanations examined so far, the use of derived adverbs to show intensity seems to be the most plausible though it may be difficult to separate this from evaluation. Moreover, it is not only derived adverbs that show this difference. The difference in the use of *very* is hardly one that can be explained in terms of register or education. It would also appear to be unrelated to explicitness. It is obviously used to express intensity and emphasis so that it can be used in the expression of evaluation, as in 16 where its use reflects the speaker's assessment:

16. (Middle-class man)
    16L: there's a *very* steep descent to it from the road
          it's a *very* gradual descent to the bay
          and it is actually a *very* nice walk

Biber and Finegan in their cluster analysis of styles of stance found that the cluster that corresponds to "involved, intense conversational style" (1989: 110) was characterized by "frequent use of emphatics, hedges, and other general evidential markers" (1989: 111). Since the London-Lund Corpus of Spoken English (Svartvik and Quirk 1980) consists mainly of middle-class speakers and is the basis for Biber and Finegan's findings it is not surprising that this description would also fit the middle-class conversations in Glasgow. The middle-class Glasgow adults in general use more hedges than the working-class adults. For example, the middle-class speakers use *sort of* with a frequency of 1.84 instances per thousand words. The frequency for the working-class speakers is only 0.54 but even this is misleading because one of the working-class women uses *sort of* with a frequency of 2.3 per thousand words; the rest of the working-class speakers use *sort of* with a frequency of only 0.23. There is essentially no difference in the use of *kind of/kinda* (MC 0.49 vs. WC 0.45). The middle-class Glasgow adults are also more likely to use *you know* in hedges (see Macaulay 2002). The middle-class Glasgow adults sometimes use derived adverbs along with hedges, as in the examples in 17:

17. (Adverbs in italics, hedges in bold)
    a. Truro's *really just* **a sort of** market town (10L)
    b. although the carpet was much thinner it was **sort of** *badly* fitted (10R)
    c. and they were trying to **sort of** *actually* extend the ladies' rights (11L)
    d. it **kind of** had been programmed to *really* **sort of** *just* keep you in order (12L)

Biber and Finegan suggest that the certainty and emphatic forms in their conversational sample:

> seem to reflect a sense of heightened emphatic excitement about the inter-action, while the hedges seem to reflect a lack of concern with precise details, indicating that the focus is on involved interaction rather than precise seman-tic expression. (Biber and Finegan 1989: 110)

Biber and Finegan were interested in different styles employed in different genres, including written materials as well as spoken, so their emphasis is not on variation within conversational styles and cannot be expected to draw distinctions of this kind. Nevertheless, their conclusions are consis-tent with the middle-class Glasgow conversations. The question then be-comes: what is it that characterizes the working-class speakers? One clue may lie in the phrase "a lack of concern with precise details" (Biber and Finegan 1989: 110) with reference to hedges in the London-Lund Corpus materials. It was apparent in the Ayr interviews that the working-class speakers were concerned about details. The most extreme example of this was Andrew Sinclair (Macaulay 1985, 1991: 249–254):

18. I mean as one of thirteen of a family — eh
    and I'm one of the oldest ones
    well there were four — two boys and two girls older than me

Here Sinclair takes care to make it clear just where he came in the birth order. He also gave many details of work in the coal mines.

The Glasgow working-class speakers also include many details:

19. (Conversation #13, working-class women)
    R13: and eh that's what happened there
         everybody was aw watching their bottles going doon you know
         doon and doon and doon
         the next thing oor table —
         it was like a half bottle of vodka and a half bottle of whisky and

six cans of Pils and th — there was near enough another carry-oot was getting ordered

L13:   do you know you know that's what I would have ha — had with me
I wouldn't have had the vodka
I'd have had like that my Pils maybe

R13:   aye

L13:   but I thought "Oh to hell
I'm going — I'm going to drink vodka tonight for a change"

R13:   aye but see that last one?
the *Times* were gieing a can of Pils oot free in the Coop at the time
can you mind o that?

L13:   oh right

R13:   so everybody was aw on Pils
everybody that came in aw had aw these Pils
they must have all been buying the *Times*
and g — giving — giving aw these Pi — cans of Pils

L13:   you were get — you were getting — you —

R13:   cause their tables were full of them
Everybody
you could guarantee there was aboot six at each table aw drinking Pils
and aw these cans were up
and a big black bag at the — the bottom of the hall aw the cans were getting put into
cause that's what I was on an aw
and then as I say we ended up going on to Haddows and getting mair

This is a narrative about a night's drinking but nothing much happens in the story. Yet the details are important: the vodka, the whisky, the cans of Pils (beer). The evaluation comes in the line "there was near enough another carry-oot was getting ordered." This means that despite the amount of drink on the table they were thinking of getting more from the off-licence (liquor store), and in the end they did: "we ended up going on to Haddows and getting mair." It was clearly a night of prodigious drinking and the way it is communicated is through the details. There are no summarizing adjectives or adverbs.

In the Ayr interviews, the lower-class speakers made use of several syntactic constructions that have a highlighting or intensifying effect (Macaulay 1991: 118–123). The five different constructions: demonstrative focusing; clefting; noun phrase preposing; left dislocation; and right dislocation are illustrated in 20:

20. (Ayr, lower-class speakers)
    a. *Demonstrative focusing*
        i. that's us going for another game (WL)
        ii. and that was you shut in the house for a week (EL)

b. *Clefting*
 i. it's a queer man and wife that doesnae have an argument (EL)
 ii. it's them that's running it now (MR)
c. *Noun phrase preposing*
 i. an auld auld man he was you ken (WR)
 ii. and one of them he had been out with once or twice (AS)
d. *Left dislocation*
 i. Mr Patterson he was a gentleman (WL)
 ii. but my own family they've had a lot of leeway (EL)
e. *Right dislocation*
 i. she was a very quiet woman my mother (WR)
 ii. in fact he offered me a job Mr. Cunningham (WL)

The lower-class speakers in Ayr used these constructions with a frequency of 2.91 per thousand words, in comparison to a frequency of 0.58 in the middle-class interviews. A similar difference was found in the Glasgow adult conversations, with the working-class speakers using these constructions with a frequency of 2.4 per thousand words and the middle-class speakers 0.23. The actual figures are shown in Figure 7. It can be seen that with the exception of demonstrative focusing, the middle-class speakers in both Ayr and Glasgow (columns 1 and 3) make some use of these constructions but very slight in comparison with the working-class speakers. This is the reverse of the situation with adverbs.

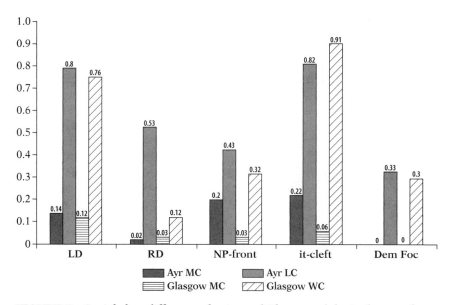

FIGURE 7 Social class differences by Ayr and Glasgow adults in the use of highlighting constructions (left dislocation, right dislocation, NP-fronting, it-clefting, demonstrative focusing) (freq. = per 1,000 words)

Conclusion

The examination of the Ayr interviews and the Glasgow conversations reveals a difference in discourse style between the two social classes. The middle-class speakers appear to adopt two complementary strategies. One is to use adverbs (and adjectives) to make emphatic statements, making quite clear their opinions and their attitudes. The other is to soften their statements with hedges of various kinds. Both of these strategies are consistent with Biber and Finegan's conclusions from the London-Lund Corpus about an "involved, intense conversational style" (1989: 110). The working-class speakers, on the other hand, seem to avoid these strategies and instead depend upon an accumulation of details and several movement rules to focus attention on certain constituents. Neither of these styles fits the kind of distinction between an elaborated code and a restricted code that Bernstein sought to draw from his investigation. Indeed, it could be argued that the working-class speakers are more explicit than the middle-class speakers.

In the earlier paper (Macaulay 1995: 51–53), I argued that the working-class use of quoted dialogue allowed the hearer more freedom to interpret the situation than did the use of evaluative adverbs and adjectives, which impose the speaker's interpretation on the listener. In the same way, the greater emphasis on details in the Glasgow working-class conversations provides the hearer with the information necessary to understand the situation. In contrast, the Glasgow middle-class speakers seem anxious to make sure that there is no doubt about their attitude or opinion ("very user-friendly really" L12; "it's actually quite nice for swimming" L16) and to do so they often employ adverbs.

Given the different ways in which the data for the two studies were collected, the results cannot simply be the effect of the methodology. The consistency of the social class differences is remarkable since there is nothing that stands out in the choice of topics that might affect the use of adverbs (or adjectives). Nor can the patterns of use be the result of interviewer bias, since there were no interviewers in the Glasgow sessions. One way of validating results is by testing again and again, by the same or different methods, in similar or different settings, with similar or different samples (Campbell and Fiske 1959). Since quantitative studies of discourse variation are not yet common it would be unwise to place too much significance on the results of two small-scale studies, but the fact that the social class differences show up so strongly in two quite different kinds of sample is some validation for the claim that something fundamental in the speech style used by the two social class groups in western Scotland governs their use of adverbs.

NOTES

1. In the years in which I have been presenting papers on this topic I have received comments from a wide variety of scholars, including anonymous

reviewers and the editors of this journal. To all of them I express my gratitude and my apologies for perhaps not benefiting as much as I should have done from their help.

2. All page references are to the collected versions in Bernstein 1971.

3. For technical reasons three sessions were recorded with working-class women; one speaker was recorded twice with different interlocutors. As a result the number of participants in each social class/age/gender category is not totally consistent but since the results are presented in terms of frequencies, the difference in absolute numbers need not materially affect any conclusions.

REFERENCES

Bell, Allan. 1984. Language style as audience design. *Language in Society* 13: 145–204.
Bernstein, Basil. 1959. A public language: Some sociological implications of a linguistic form. *British Journal of Sociology* 10: 311–326 (reprinted in Bernstein 1971: 41–60).
Bernstein, Basil. 1960. Language and social class. *British Journal of Sociology* 11: 271–276 (reprinted in Bernstein 1971: 61–67).
Bernstein, Basil. 1962. Social class, linguistic codes, and grammatical elements. *Language and Speech* 5: 31–46 (reprinted in Bernstein 1971: 95–117).
Bernstein, Basil. 1971. *Theoretical studies towards a sociology of language (Class, Codes and Control*, Volume 1). London: Routledge and Kegan Paul.
Biber, Douglas and Edward Finegan. 1989. Styles of stance in English: Lexical and grammatical marking of evidentiality and affect. *Text* 9: 93–124.
Campbell, Donald T. and Donald W. Fiske. 1959. Convergent and discriminant validation by the multitrait-multimethod matrix. *Psychological Bulletin* 56: 81–105.
Coates, Jennifer. 1986. *Women, Men and Language*. London: Longman.
Foulkes, Paul and Gerry Docherty (eds.). 1999. *Urban Voices: Variation and Change in British Accents*. London: Arnold.
Hunston, Susan and John Sinclair. 1990. A local grammar of evaluation. In Susan Hunston and Geoff Thompson (eds.) *Evaluation in Text: Authorial Stance and the Construction of Discourse*. Oxford: Oxford University Press. 75–101.
Labov, William. 1984. Intensity. In Deborah Schiffrin (ed.) *Meaning, Form, and Use in Context: Linguistic Applications*. Washington, D.C.: Georgetown University Press. 43–70.
Lee, David. 1987. The semantics of *just*. *Journal of Pragmatics* 11: 377–398.
Louw, Bill. 1993. Irony in the text or insincerity in the writer? The diagnostic potential of semantic prosodies. In Mona Baker, Gill Francis, and Elena Tognini-Bognelli (eds.) *Text and Technology: In Honour of John Sinclair*. Amsterdam: John Benjamins. 157–176.
Macaulay, Ronald K. S. 1985. The narrative skills of a Scottish coal miner. In Manfred Görlach (ed.) *Focus on: Scotland*. Amsterdam: John Benjamins. 101–124.
Macaulay, Ronald K. S. 1991. *Locating Dialect in Discourse: The Language of Honest Men and Bonnie Lasses in Ayr*. New York: Oxford University Press.
Macaulay, Ronald K. S. 1995. The adverbs of authority. *English World-Wide* 16: 37–60 (reprinted in Macaulay 1997).
Macaulay, Ronald K. S. 1997. *Standards and Variation in Urban Speech: Examples from Lowland Scots*. Amsterdam: John Benjamins.
Macaulay, Ronald K. S. 2000. Women talk about people, men talk about things. Paper given at IGALA 1, Stanford University, May 5, 2000.
Macaulay, Ronald K. S. 2002. You know, it depends. To appear in *Journal of Pragmatics*.
Macaulay, Ronald K. S. and Gavin D. Trevelyan. 1973. *Language, Education and Employment in Glasgow*. (Final report to the Social Science Research Council.) Edinburgh: The Scottish Council for Research in Education.
Milroy, Lesley. 1980. *Language and Social Networks*. Oxford: Blackwell.

Opdahl, Lise. 2000. *LY or Zero Suffix?: A Study in Variation of Dual-form Adverbs in Present-day English* (two volumes). Frankfurt: Peter Lang.

Powell, Mava Jo. 1992. The systematic development of correlated interpersonal and metalinguistic uses in stance adverbs. *Cognitive Linguistics* 3: 75–110.

Quirk, Randolph, Sidney Greenbaum, Geoffrey Leech, and Jan Svartvik. 1985. *A Comprehensive Grammar of the English Language.* London: Longman.

Silverstein, Michael. 1996. Monoglot "standard" in America: Standardization and metaphors of linguistic hegemony. In Donald Brenneis and Ronald K. S. Macaulay (eds.) *The Matrix of Language.* Boulder, Colorado: Westview Press. 284–306.

Stuart-Smith, Jane. 1999. Glasgow. In Paul Foulkes and Gerry Docherty (eds.) *Urban Voices: Variation and Change in British Accents.* London: Arnold. 203–222.

Svartvik, Jan and Randolph Quirk (eds.). 1980. *A Corpus of English Conversation.* Lund: C. W. K. Gleerup.

Tagliamonte, Sali and Rika Ito. 2001. Think *really different*: Continuity and specialization in the English adverb. Unpublished manuscript.

Trudgill, Peter. 1974. *The Social Differentiation of English in Norwich.* Cambridge: Cambridge University Press.

■ EMILY MARTIN ───────────────────────────

The Egg and the Sperm: How Science Has Constructed a Romance Based on Stereotypical Male-Female Roles

Emily Martin (b. 1944) is a professor of anthropology at New York University. Her work focuses on the intersection of medicine and culture, particularly disease and reproduction, as she examines the impact of cultural ideology on medical discourse. She is also particularly interested in issues of feminism — that is, how the language used to describe biological processes such as menstruation and pregnancy reinforces cultural stereotypes about gender. Martin explores this issue in the article "The Egg and the Sperm: How Science Has Constructed a Romance Based on Stereotypical Male-Female Roles," which was originally published in *Signs: Journal of Women in Culture and Society* (1991). This research was later presented in her book *The Woman in the Body: A Cultural Analysis of Reproduction* (1992).

■ ■ ■

> The theory of the human body is always a part of a world-picture. . . . The theory of the human body is always a part of a *fantasy.*
> — JAMES HILLMAN, *The Myth of Analysis*[1]

As an anthropologist, I am intrigued by the possibility that culture shapes how biological scientists describe what they discover about the natural world. If this were so, we would be learning about more than the natural world in high school biology class; we would be learning about cultural beliefs and practices as if they were part of nature. In the course of my research I realized that the picture of egg and sperm drawn in popular as well as scientific accounts of reproductive biology relies on stereotypes central to our cultural definitions of male and female. The stereotypes imply not only that female biological processes are less worthy than their male counterparts but also that women are less worthy than men. Part of my goal in writing this article is to shine a bright light on the gender stereotypes hidden within the scientific language of biology. Exposed in such a light, I hope they will lose much of their power to harm us.

Egg and Sperm: A Scientific Fairy Tale

At a fundamental level, all major scientific textbooks depict male and female reproductive organs as systems for the production of valuable substances, such as eggs and sperm.[2] In the case of women, the monthly cycle is described as being designed to produce eggs and prepare a suitable place for them to be fertilized and grown — all to the end of making babies. But the enthusiasm ends there. By extolling the female cycle as a productive enterprise, menstruation must necessarily be viewed as a failure. Medical texts describe menstruation as the "debris" of the uterine lining, the result of necrosis, or death of tissue. The descriptions imply that a system has gone awry, making products of no use, not to specification, unsalable, wasted, scrap. An illustration in a widely used medical text shows menstruation as a chaotic disintegration of form, complementing the many texts that describe it as "ceasing," "dying," "losing," "denuding," "expelling."[3]

Male reproductive physiology is evaluated quite differently. One of the texts that sees menstruation as failed production employs a sort of breathless prose when it describes the maturation of sperm: "The mechanisms which guide the remarkable cellular transformation from spermatid to mature sperm remain uncertain. . . . Perhaps the most amazing characteristic of spermatogenesis is its sheer magnitude: The normal human male may manufacture several hundred million sperm per day."[4] In the classic text *Medical Physiology*, edited by Vernon Mountcastle, the male/female, productive/destructive comparison is more explicit: "Whereas the female *sheds* only a single gamete each month, the seminiferous tubules *produce* hundreds of millions of sperm each day" (emphasis mine).[5] The female author of another text marvels at the length of the microscopic seminiferous tubules, which, if uncoiled and placed end to end, "would span almost one-third of a mile!" She writes, "In an adult male these structures produce millions of sperm cells each day." Later she asks, "How is this feat accomplished?"[6] None of these texts expresses such intense enthusiasm for any female processes. It is surely no accident that the "remarkable" process of making sperm involves precisely what, in the medical view, menstruation does not: production of something deemed valuable.[7]

One could argue that menstruation and spermatogenesis are not analogous processes and, therefore, should not be expected to elicit the same
kind of response. The proper female analogy to spermatogenesis, biologically, is ovulation. Yet ovulation does not merit enthusiasm in these texts
either. Textbook descriptions stress that all of the ovarian follicles containing ova are already present at birth. Far from being *produced*, as sperm
are, they merely sit on the shelf, slowly degenerating and aging like over-
stocked inventory: "At birth, normal human ovaries contain an estimated
one million follicles [each], and no new ones appear after birth. Thus, in
marked contrast to the male, the newborn female already has all the germ
cells she will ever have. Only a few, perhaps 400, are destined to reach full
maturity during her active productive life. All the others degenerate at
some point in their development so that few, if any, remain by the time she
reaches menopause at approximately 50 years of age."[8] Note the "marked
contrast" that this description sets up between male and female: the male,
who continuously produces fresh germ cells, and the female, who has
stockpiled germ cells by birth and is faced with their degeneration.

Nor are the female organs spared such vivid descriptions. One scientist writes in a newspaper article that a woman's ovaries become old and
worn out from ripening eggs every month, even though the woman herself
is still relatively young: "When you look through a laparoscope . . . at an
ovary that has been through hundreds of cycles, even in a superbly healthy
American female, you see a scarred, battered organ."[9]

To avoid the negative connotations that some people associate with
the female reproductive system, scientists could begin to describe male
and female processes as homologous. They might credit females with
"producing" mature ova one at a time, as they're needed each month, and
describe males as having to face problems of degenerating germ cells. This
degeneration would occur throughout life among spermatogonia, the
undifferentiated germ cells in the testes that are the long-lived, dormant
precursors of sperm.

But the texts have an almost dogged insistence on casting female processes in a negative light. The texts celebrate sperm production because it
is continuous from puberty to senescence, while they portray egg production as inferior because it is finished at birth. This makes the female seem
unproductive, but some texts will also insist that it is she who is wasteful.[10]
In a section heading for *Molecular Biology of the Cell*, a best-selling text, we
are told that "Oogenesis is wasteful." The text goes on to emphasize that of
the seven million oogonia, or egg germ cells, in the female embryo, most
degenerate in the ovary. Of those that do go on to become oocytes, or
eggs, many also degenerate, so that at birth only two million eggs remain
in the ovaries. Degeneration continues throughout a woman's life: By puberty 300,000 eggs remain, and only a few are present by menopause. "During the forty or so years of a woman's reproductive life, only 400 to 500
eggs will have been released," the authors write. "All the rest will have

degenerated. It is still a mystery why so many eggs are formed only to die in the ovaries."[11]

The real mystery is why the male's vast production of sperm is not seen as wasteful.[12] Assuming that a man "produces" 100 million (10^8) sperm per day (a conservative estimate) during an average reproductive life of sixty years, he would produce well over two trillion sperm in his lifetime. Assuming that a woman "ripens" one egg per lunar month, or thirteen per year, over the course of her forty-year reproductive life, she would total five hundred eggs in her lifetime. But the word "waste" implies an excess, too much produced. Assuming two or three offspring, for every baby a woman produces, she wastes only around two hundred eggs. For every baby a man produces, he wastes more than one trillion (10^{12}) sperm.

How is it that positive images are denied to the bodies of women? A look at language — in this case, scientific language — provides the first clue. Take the egg and the sperm.[13] It is remarkable how "femininely" the egg behaves and how "masculinely" the sperm.[14] The egg is seen as large and passive.[15] It does not *move* or *journey*, but passively "is transported," "is swept,"[16] or even "drifts"[17] along the fallopian tube. In utter contrast, sperm are small, "streamlined,"[18] and invariably active. They "deliver" their genes to the egg, "activate the developmental program of the egg,"[19] and have a "velocity" that is often remarked upon.[20] Their tails are "strong" and efficiently powered.[21] Together with the forces of ejaculation, they can "propel the semen into the deepest recesses of the vagina."[22] For this they need "energy," "fuel,"[23] so that with a "whiplashlike motion and strong lurches"[24] they can "burrow through the egg coat"[25] and "penetrate" it.[26]

At its extreme, the age-old relationship of the egg and the sperm takes on a royal or religious patina. The egg coat, its protective barrier, is sometimes called its "vestments," a term usually reserved for sacred, religious dress. The egg is said to have a "corona,"[27] a crown, and to be accompanied by "attendant cells."[28] It is holy, set apart and above, the queen to the sperm's king. The egg is also passive, which means it must depend on sperm for rescue. Gerald Schatten and Helen Schatten liken the egg's role to that of Sleeping Beauty: "a dormant bride awaiting her mate's magic kiss, which instills the spirit that brings her to life."[29] Sperm, by contrast, have a "mission,"[30] which is to "move through the female genital tract in quest of the ovum."[31] One popular account has it that the sperm carry out a "perilous journey" into the "warm darkness," where some fall away "exhausted." "Survivors" "assault" the egg, the successful candidates "surrounding the prize."[32] Part of the urgency of this journey, in more scientific terms, is that "once released from the supportive environment of the ovary, an egg will die within hours unless rescued by a sperm."[33] The wording stresses the fragility and dependency of the egg, even though the same text acknowledges elsewhere that sperm also live for only a few hours.[34]

In 1948, in a book remarkable for its early insights into these matters, Ruth Herschberger argued that female reproductive organs are seen as biologically interdependent, while male organs are viewed as autonomous, operating independently and in isolation:

> At present the functional is stressed only in connection with women: It is in them that ovaries, tubes, uterus, and vagina have endless interdependence. In the male, reproduction would seem to involve "organs" only.
>
> Yet the sperm, just as much as the egg, is dependent on a great many related processes. There are secretions which mitigate the urine in the urethra before ejaculation, to protect the sperm. There is the reflex shutting off of the bladder connection, the provision of prostatic secretions, and various types of muscular propulsion. The sperm is no more independent of its milieu than the egg, and yet from a wish that it were, biologists have lent their support to the notion that the human female, beginning with the egg, is congenitally more dependent than the male.[35]

Bringing out another aspect of the sperm's autonomy, an article in the journal *Cell* has the sperm making an "existential decision" to penetrate the egg: "Sperm are cells with a limited behavioral repertoire, one that is directed toward fertilizing eggs. To execute the decision to abandon the haploid state, sperm swim to an egg and there acquire the ability to effect membrane fusion."[36] Is this a corporate manager's version of the sperm's activities — "executing decisions" while fraught with dismay over difficult options that bring with them very high risk?

There is another way that sperm, despite their small size, can be made to loom in importance over the egg. In a collection of scientific papers, an electron micrograph of an enormous egg and tiny sperm is titled "A Portrait of the Sperm."[37] This is a little like showing a photo of a dog and calling it a picture of the fleas. Granted, microscopic sperm are harder to photograph than eggs, which are just large enough to see with the naked eye. But surely the use of the term *portrait*, a word associated with the powerful and wealthy, is significant. Eggs have only micrographs or pictures, not portraits.

One depiction of sperm as weak and timid, instead of strong and powerful — the only such representation in Western civilization, so far as I know — occurs in Woody Allen's movie *Everything You Always Wanted to Know About Sex* *But Were Afraid to Ask*. Allen, playing the part of an apprehensive sperm inside a man's testicles, is scared of the man's approaching orgasm. He is reluctant to launch himself into the darkness, afraid of contraceptive devices, afraid of winding up on the ceiling if the man masturbates.

The more common picture — egg as damsel in distress, shielded only by her sacred garments; sperm as heroic warrior to the rescue — cannot be proved to be dictated by the biology of these events. While the "facts" of biology may not *always* be constructed in cultural terms, I would argue that in this case they are. The degree of metaphorical content in these descriptions, the extent to which differences between egg and sperm are emphasized, and the parallels between cultural stereotypes of male and female behavior and the character of egg and sperm all point to this conclusion.

New Research, Old Imagery

As new understandings of egg and sperm emerge, textbook gender imagery is being revised. But the new research, far from escaping the stereotypical representations of egg and sperm, simply replicates elements of textbook gender imagery in a different form. The persistence of this imagery calls to mind what Ludwik Fleck termed "the self-contained" nature of scientific thought. As he described it, "the interaction between what is already known, what remains to be learned, and those who are to apprehend it, go to ensure harmony within the system. But at the same time they also preserve the harmony of illusions, which is quite secure within the confines of a given thought style."[38] We need to understand the way in which the cultural content in scientific descriptions changes as biological discoveries unfold, and whether that cultural content is solidly entrenched or easily changed.

In all of the texts quoted above, sperm are described as penetrating the egg, and specific substances on a sperm's head are described as binding to the egg. Recently, this description of events was rewritten in a biophysics lab at Johns Hopkins University — transforming the egg from the passive to the active party.[39]

Prior to this research, it was thought that the zona, the inner vestments of the egg, formed an impenetrable barrier. Sperm overcame the barrier by mechanically burrowing through, thrashing their tails and slowly working their way along. Later research showed that the sperm released digestive enzymes that chemically broke down the zona; thus, scientists presumed that the sperm used mechanical *and* chemical means to get through to the egg.

In this recent investigation, the researchers began to ask questions about the mechanical force of the sperm's tail. (The lab's goal was to develop a contraceptive that worked topically on sperm.) They discovered, to their great surprise, that the forward thrust of sperm is extremely weak, which contradicts the assumption that sperm are forceful penetrators.[40] Rather than thrusting forward, the sperm's head was now seen to move mostly back and forth. The sideways motion of the sperm's tail makes the head move sideways with a force that is ten times stronger than its forward movement. So even if the overall force of the sperm were strong enough to mechanically break the zona, most of its force would be directed sideways rather than forward. In fact, its strongest tendency, by tenfold, is to escape by attempting to pry itself off the egg. Sperm, then, must be exceptionally efficient at *escaping* from any cell surface they contact. And the surface of the egg must be designed to trap the sperm and prevent their escape. Otherwise, few if any sperm would reach the egg.

The researchers at Johns Hopkins concluded that the sperm and egg stick together because of adhesive molecules on the surfaces of each. The egg traps the sperm and adheres to it so tightly that the sperm's head is forced to lie flat against the surface of the zona, a little bit, they told me, "like Br'er Rabbit getting more and more stuck to tar baby the more he wriggles." The trapped sperm continues to wiggle ineffectually side to side. The mechanical force of its tail is so weak that a sperm cannot break even one chemical bond. This is where the digestive enzymes released by the sperm come in. If they start to soften the zona just at the tip of the sperm and the sides remain stuck, then the weak, flailing sperm can get oriented in the right direction and make it through the zona — provided that its bonds to the zona dissolve as it moves in.

Although this new version of the saga of the egg and the sperm broke through cultural expectations, the researchers who made the discovery continued to write papers and abstracts as if the sperm were the active party who attacks, binds, penetrates, and enters the egg. The only difference was that sperm were now seen as performing these actions weakly.[41] Not until August 1987, more than three years after the findings described above, did these researchers reconceptualize the process to give the egg a more active role. They began to describe the zona as an aggressive sperm catcher, covered with adhesive molecules that can capture a sperm with a single bond and clasp it to the zona's surface.[42] In the words of their published account: "The innermost vestment, the *zona pellucide*, is a glycoprotein shell, which captures and tethers the sperm before they penetrate it . . . The sperm is captured at the initial contact between the sperm tip and the *zona*. . . . Since the thrust [of the sperm] is much smaller than the force needed to break a single affinity bond, the first bond made upon the tip-first meeting of the sperm and *zona* can result in the capture of the sperm."[43]

Experiments in another lab reveal similar patterns of data interpretation. Gerald Schatten and Helen Schatten set out to show that, contrary to conventional wisdom, the "egg is not merely a large, yolk-filled sphere into which the sperm burrows to endow new life. Rather, recent research suggests the almost heretical view that sperm and egg are mutually active partners."[44] This sounds like a departure from the stereotypical textbook view, but further reading reveals Schatten and Schatten's conformity to the aggressive-sperm metaphor. They describe how "the sperm and egg first touch when, from the tip of the sperm's triangular head, a long, thin filament shoots out and harpoons the egg." Then we learn that "remarkably, the harpoon is not so much fired as assembled at great speed, molecule by molecule, from a pool of protein stored in a specialized region called the acrosome. The filament may grow as much as twenty times longer than the sperm head itself before its tip reaches the egg and sticks."[45] Why not call this "making a bridge" or "throwing out a line" rather than firing a harpoon? Harpoons pierce prey and injure or kill them, while this filament only sticks. And why not focus, as the Hopkins lab did, on the stickiness of the egg, rather than the stickiness of the sperm?[46] Later in the article, the Schattens replicate the common view of the sperm's perilous journey into the warm darkness of the vagina, this time for the purpose of explaining its journey into the egg itself: "[The sperm] still has an arduous journey ahead. It must penetrate farther into the egg's huge sphere of cytoplasm and somehow locate the nucleus, so that the two cells' chromosomes can fuse. The sperm dives down into the cytoplasm, its tail beating. But it is soon interrupted by the sudden and swift migration of the egg nucleus, which rushes toward the sperm with a velocity triple that of the movement of chromosomes during cell division, crossing the entire egg in about a minute."[47]

Like Schatten and Schatten and the biophysicists at Johns Hopkins, another researcher has recently made discoveries that seem to point to a more interactive view of the relationship of egg and sperm. This work, which Paul Wassarman conducted on the sperm and eggs of mice, focuses on identifying the specific molecules in the egg coat (the zona pellucida) that are involved in egg-sperm interaction. At first glance, his descriptions seem to fit the model of an egalitarian relationship. Male and female gametes "recognize one another," and "interactions . . . take place between sperm and egg."[48] But the article in *Scientific American* in which those descriptions appear begins with a vignette that presages the dominant motif of their presentation: "It has been more than a century since Hermann Fol, a Swiss zoologist, peered into his microscope and became the first person to see a sperm penetrate an egg, fertilize it, and form the first cell of a new embryo."[49] This portrayal of the sperm as the active party — the one that *penetrates* and *fertilizes* the egg and *produces* the embryo — is not cited as an example of an earlier, now outmoded view. In fact, the author reiterates the point later in the article: "Many sperm can bind to and penetrate the zona pellucida, or outer coat, of an unfertilized mouse egg, but only one sperm will eventually fuse with the thin plasma membrane surrounding the egg proper (*inner sphere*), fertilizing the egg and giving rise to a new embryo."[50]

The imagery of sperm as aggressor is particularly startling in this case: The main discovery being reported is isolation of a particular molecule *on the egg coat* that plays an important role in fertilization! Wassarman's choice of language sustains the picture. He calls the molecule that has been isolated, ZP3, a "sperm receptor." By allocating the passive, waiting role to the egg, Wassarman can continue to describe the sperm as the actor, the one that makes it all happen: "The basic process begins when many sperm first attach loosely and then bind tenaciously to receptors on the surface of the egg's thick outer coat, the zona pellucida. Each sperm, which has a large number of egg-binding proteins on its surface, binds to many sperm receptors on the egg. More specifically, a site on each of the egg-binding proteins fits a complementary site on a sperm receptor, much as a key fits a lock."[51] With the sperm designated as the "key" and the egg the "lock," it is obvious which one acts and which one is acted upon. Could this imagery not be reversed, letting the sperm (the lock) wait until the egg produces the key? Or could we speak of two halves of a locket matching, and regard the matching itself as the action that initiates the fertilization?

It is as if Wassarman were determined to make the egg the receiving partner. Usually in biological research, the *protein* member of the pair of binding molecules is called the receptor, and physically it has a pocket in it rather like a lock. As the diagrams that illustrate Wassarman's article show, the molecules on the sperm are proteins and have "pockets." The small, mobile molecules that fit into these pockets are called ligands. As shown in the diagrams, ZP3 on the egg is a polymer of "keys"; many small knobs stick out. Typically, molecules on the sperm would be called receptors and molecules on the egg would be called ligands. But Wassarman chose to name ZP3 on the egg the receptor and to create a new term, "the egg-binding protein," for the molecule on the sperm that otherwise would have been called the receptor.[52]

Wassarman does credit the egg coat with having more functions than those of a sperm receptor. While he notes that "the zona pellucida has at times been viewed by investigators as a nuisance, a barrier to sperm and hence an impediment to fertilization," his new research reveals that the egg coat "serves as a sophisticated biological security system that screens incoming sperm, selects only those compatible with fertilization and development, prepares sperm for fusion with the egg and later protects the resulting embryo from polyspermy [a lethal condition caused by fusion of more than one sperm with a single egg]."[53] Although this description gives the egg an active role, that role is drawn in stereotypically feminine terms. The egg *selects* an appropriate mate, *prepares* him for fusion, and then *protects* the resulting offspring from harm. This is courtship and mating behavior as seen through the eyes of a sociobiologist: woman as the hard-to-get prize, who, following union with the chosen one, becomes woman as servant and mother.

And Wassarman does not quit there. In a review article for *Science*, he outlines the "chronology of fertilization."[54] Near the end of the article are two subject headings. One is "Sperm Penetration," in which Wassarman describes how the chemical dissolving of the zona pellucida combines with the "substantial propulsive force generated by sperm." The next heading is "Sperm-Egg Fusion." This section details what happens inside the zona after a sperm "penetrates" it. Sperm "can make contact with, adhere to, and fuse with (that is, fertilize) an egg."[55] Wassarman's word choice, again, is astonishingly skewed in favor of the sperm's activity, for in the next breath he says that sperm *lose* all motility upon fusion with the egg's surface. In mouse and sea urchin eggs, the sperm enters at the *egg's* volition, according to Wassarman's description: "Once fused with egg plasma membrane [the surface of the egg], how does a sperm enter the egg? The surface of both mouse and sea urchin eggs is covered with thousands of plasma membrane-bound projections, called microvilli [tiny "hairs"]. Evidence in sea urchins suggests that, after membrane fusion, a group of elongated microvilli cluster tightly around and interdigitate over the sperm head. As these microvilli are resorbed, the sperm is drawn into the egg. Therefore, sperm motility, which ceases at the time of fusion in both sea urchins and mice, is not required for sperm entry."[56] The section called "Sperm Penetration" more logically would be followed by a section called "The Egg Envelops," rather than "Sperm-Egg Fusion." This would give a parallel — and more accurate — sense that both the egg and the sperm initiate action.

Another way that Wassarman makes less of the egg's activity is by describing components of the egg but referring to the sperm as a whole entity. Deborah Gordon has described such an approach as "atomism" ("the part is independent of and primordial to the whole") and identified it as one of the "tenacious assumptions" of Western science and medicine.[57] Wassarman employs atomism to his advantage. When he refers to processes going on within sperm, he consistently returns to descriptions that remind us from whence these activities came: They are part of sperm that penetrate an egg or generate propulsive force. When he refers to processes going on within eggs, he stops there. As a result, any active role he grants them appears to be assigned to the parts of the egg, and not to the egg itself. In the quote above, it is the microvilli that actively cluster around the sperm. In another example, "the driving force for engulfment of a fused sperm comes from a region of cytoplasm just beneath an egg's plasma membrane."[58]

Social Implications: Thinking Beyond

All three of these revisionist accounts of egg and sperm cannot seem to escape the hierarchical imagery of older accounts. Even though each new account gives the egg a larger and more active role, taken together they bring into play another cultural stereotype: woman as a dangerous and aggressive threat. In the Johns Hopkins lab's revised model, the egg ends up as the female aggressor who "captures and tethers" the sperm with her sticky zona, rather like a spider lying in wait in her web.[59] The Schatten lab has the egg's nucleus "interrupt" the sperm's dive with a "sudden and swift" rush by which she "clasps the sperm and guides its nucleus to the center."[60] Wassarman's description of the surface of the egg "covered with thousands of plasma membrane-bound projections, called microvilli" that reach out and clasp the sperm adds to the spiderlike imagery.[61]

These images grant the egg an active role but at the cost of appearing disturbingly aggressive. Images of woman as dangerous and aggressive, the femme fatale who victimizes men, are widespread in Western literature and culture.[62] More specific is the connection of spider imagery with the idea of an engulfing, devouring mother.[63] New data did not lead scientists to eliminate gender stereotypes in their descriptions of egg and sperm. Instead, scientists simply began to describe egg and sperm in different, but no less damaging, terms.

Can we envision a less stereotypical view? Biology itself provides another model that could be applied to the egg and the sperm. The cybernetic

model — with its feedback loops, flexible adaptation to change, coordination of the parts within a whole, evolution over time, and changing response to the environment — is common in genetics, endocrinology, and
ecology and has a growing influence in medicine in general.[64] This model
has the potential to shift our imagery from the negative, in which the
female reproductive system is castigated both for not producing eggs after
birth and for producing (and thus wasting) too many eggs overall, to
something more positive. The female reproductive system could be seen
as responding to the environment (pregnancy or menopause), adjusting
to monthly changes (menstruation), and flexibly changing from reproduc-
tivity after puberty to nonreproductivity later in life. The sperm and egg's
interaction could also be described in cybernetic terms. J. F. Hartman's
research in reproductive biology demonstrated fifteen years ago that if an
egg is killed by being pricked with a needle, live sperm cannot get through
the zona.[65] Clearly, this evidence shows that the egg and sperm *do* interact
on more mutual terms, making biology's refusal to portray them that way
all the more disturbing.

We would do well to be aware, however, that cybernetic imagery is
hardly neutral. In the past, cybernetic models have played an important
part in the imposition of social control. These models inherently provide
a way of thinking about a "field" of interacting components. Once the
field can be seen, it can become the object of new forms of knowledge,
which in turn can allow new forms of social control to be exerted over
the components of the field. During the 1950s, for example, medicine
began to recognize the psychosocial *environment* of the patient: the patient's family and its psychodynamics. Professions such as social work
began to focus on this new environment, and the resulting knowledge
became one way to further control the patient. Patients began to be seen
not as isolated, individual bodies, but as psychosocial entities located in an
"ecological" system: Management of "the patient's psychology was a new
entrée to patient control."[66]

The models that biologists use to describe their data can have important social effects. During the nineteenth century, the social and natural
sciences strongly influenced each other: The social ideas of Malthus about
how to avoid the natural increase of the poor inspired Darwin's *Origin of
Species*.[67] Once the *Origin* stood as a description of the natural world, complete with competition and market struggles, it could be reimported into
social science as social Darwinism, in order to justify the social order of
the time. What we are seeing now is similar: the importation of cultural
ideas about passive females and heroic males into the "personalities" of
gametes. This amounts to the "implanting of social imagery on representations of nature so as to lay a firm basis for reimporting exactly that same
imagery as natural explanations of social phenomena."[68]

Further research would show us exactly what social effects are being
wrought from the biological imagery of egg and sperm. At the very least,
the imagery keeps alive some of the hoariest old stereotypes about weak

damsels in distress and their strong male rescuers. That these stereotypes are now being written in at the level of the *cell* constitutes a powerful move to make them seem so natural as to be beyond alteration.

The stereotypical imagery might also encourage people to imagine that what results from the interaction of egg and sperm — a fertilized egg — is the result of deliberate "human" action at the cellular level. Whatever the intentions of the human couple, in this microscopic "culture" a cellular "bride" (or femme fatale) and a cellular "groom" (her victim) make a cellular baby. Rosalind Petchesky points out that through visual representations such as sonograms, we are given *"images* of younger and younger, and tinier and tinier, fetuses being 'saved.'" This leads to "the point of visibility being 'pushed back' *indefinitely*."[69] Endowing egg and sperm with intentional action, a key aspect of personhood in our culture, lays the foundation for the point of viability being pushed back to the moment of fertilization. This will likely lead to greater acceptance of technological developments and new forms of scrutiny and manipulation, for the benefit of these inner "persons": court-ordered restrictions on a pregnant woman's activities in order to protect her fetus, fetal surgery, amniocentesis, and rescinding of abortion rights, to name but a few examples.[70]

Even if we succeed in substituting more egalitarian, interactive metaphors to describe the activities of egg and sperm, and manage to avoid the pitfalls of cybernetic models, we would still be guilty of endowing cellular entities with personhood. More crucial, then, than what *kinds* of personalities we bestow on cells is the very fact that we are doing it at all. This process could ultimately have the most disturbing social consequences.

One clear feminist challenge is to wake up sleeping metaphors in science, particularly those involved in descriptions of the egg and the sperm. Although the literary convention is to call such metaphors "dead," they are not so much dead as sleeping, hidden within the scientific context of texts — and all the more powerful for it.[71] Waking up such metaphors, by becoming aware of when we are projecting cultural imagery onto what we study, will improve our ability to investigate and understand nature. Waking up such metaphors, by becoming aware of their implications, will rob them of their power to naturalize our social conventions about gender.

NOTES

Portions of this article were presented as the 1987 Becker Lecture, Cornell University. I am grateful for the many suggestions and ideas I received on this occasion. For especially pertinent help with my arguments and data I thank Richard Cone, Kevin Whaley, Sharon Stephens, Barbara Duden, Susanne Kuechler, Lorna Rhodes, and Scott Gilbert. The article was strengthened and clarified by the comments of the anonymous *Signs* reviewers as well as the superb editorial skills of Amy Gage.

1. James Hillman, *The Myth of Analysis* (Evanston, Ill.: Northwestern University Press, 1972), 220.

2. The textbooks I consulted are the main ones used in classes for undergraduate premedical students or medical students (or those held on reserve in the library for these classes) during the past few years at Johns Hopkins University. These texts are widely used at other universities in the country as well.

3. Arthur C. Guyton, *Physiology of the Human Body*, 6th ed. (Philadelphia: Saunders College Publishing, 1984), 624.

4. Arthur J. Vander, James H. Sherman, and Dorothy S. Luciano, *Human Physiology: The Mechanism of Body Function*, 3d ed. (New York: McGraw-Hill, 1980), 483–84.

5. Vernon B. Mountcastle, *Medical Physiology*, 14th ed. (London: Mosby, 1980), 2:1624.

6. Eldra Pearl Solomon, *Human Anatomy and Physiology* (New York: CBS College Publishing, 1983), 678.

7. For elaboration, see Emily Martin, *The Woman in the Body: A Cultural Analysis of Reproduction* (Boston: Beacon, 1987), 27–53.

8. Vander, Sherman, and Luciano, 568.

9. Melvin Konner, "Childbearing and Age," *New York Times Magazine* (December 27, 1987), 22–23, esp. 22.

10. I have found but one exception to the opinion that the female is wasteful: "Smallpox being the nasty disease it is, one might expect nature to have designed antibody molecules with combining sites that specifically recognize the epitopes on smallpox virus. Nature differs from technology, however: It thinks nothing of wastefulness. (For example, rather than improving the chance that a spermatozoon will meet an egg cell, nature finds it easier to produce millions of spermatozoa.)" (Niels Kaj Jerne, "The Immune System," *Scientific American* 229, no. 1 [July 1973]: 53). Thanks to a *Signs* reviewer for bringing this reference to my attention.

11. Bruce Alberts et al., *Molecular Biology of the Cell* (New York: Garland, 1983), 795.

12. In her essay "Have Only Men Evolved?" (in *Discovering Reality: Feminist Perspectives on Epistemology, Metaphysics, Methodology, and Philosophy of Science*, ed. Sandra Harding and Merrill B. Hintikka [Dordrecht: Reidel, 1983], 45–69, esp. 60–61), Ruth Hubbard points out that sociobiologists have said the female invests more energy than the male in the production of her large gametes, claiming that this explains why the female provides parental care. Hubbard questions whether it "really takes more 'energy' to generate the one or relatively few eggs than the large excess of sperms required to achieve fertilization." For further critique of how the greater size of eggs is interpreted in sociobiology, see Donna Haraway, "Investment Strategies for the Evolving Portfolio of Primate Females," in *Body/Politics*, ed. Mary Jacobus, Evelyn Fox Keller, and Sally Shuttleworth (New York: Routledge, 1990), 155–56.

13. The sources I used for this article provide compelling information on interactions among sperm. Lack of space prevents me from taking up this theme here, but the elements include competition, hierarchy, and sacrifice. For a newspaper report, see Malcolm W. Browne, "Some Thoughts on Self Sacrifice," *New York Times* (July 5, 1988), C6. For a literary rendition, see John Barth, "Night-Sea Journey," in his *Lost in the Funhouse* (Garden City, NY: Doubleday, 1968), 3–13.

14. See Carol Delaney, "The Meaning of Paternity and the Virgin Birth Debate," *Man* 21, no. 3 (September 1986): 494–513. She discusses the differ-

ence between this scientific view that women contribute genetic material to the fetus and the claim of long-standing Western folk theories that the origin and identity of the fetus comes from the male, as in the metaphor of planting a seed in soil.

15. For a suggested direct link between human behavior and purportedly passive eggs and active sperm, see Erik H. Erikson, "Inner and Outer Space: Reflections on Womanhood," *Daedalus* 93, no. 2 (Spring 1964): 582–606, esp. 591.

16. Guyton (n. 3 above), 619; and Mountcastle (n. 5 above), 1609.

17. Jonathan Miller and David Pelham, *The Facts of Life* (New York: Viking Penguin, 1984), 5.

18. Alberts et al., 796.

19. Ibid., 796.

20. See, e.g., William F. Ganong, *Review of Medical Physiology*, 7th ed. (Los Altos, Calif. Lange Medical Publications, 1975), 322.

21. Alberts et al. (n. 11 above), 796.

22. Guyton, 615.

23. Solomon (n. 6 above), 683.

24. Vander, Sherman, and Luciano (n. 4 above), 4th ed. (1985), 580.

25. Alberts et al., 796.

26. All biology texts quoted above use the word *penetrate*.

27. Solomon, 700.

28. A. Beldecos et al., "The Importance of Feminist Critique for Contemporary Cell Biology," *Hypatia* 3, no. 1 (Spring 1988): 61–76.

29. Gerald Schatten and Helen Schatten, "The Energetic Egg," *Medical World News* 23 (January 23, 1984): 51–53, esp. 51.

30. Alberts et al., 796.

31. Guyton (n. 3 above), 613.

32. Miller and Pelham (n. 17 above), 7.

33. Alberts et al. (n. 11 above), 804.

34. Ibid., 801.

35. Ruth Herschberger, *Adam's Rib* (New York: Pelligrini & Cudaby, 1948), esp. 84. I am indebted to Ruth Hubbard for telling me about Herschberger's work, although at a point when this paper was already in draft form.

36. Bennett M. Shapiro. "The Existential Decision of a Sperm," *Cell* 49, no. 3 (May 1987): 293–94, esp. 293.

37. Lennart Nilsson, "A Portrait of the Sperm," in *The Functional Anatomy of the Spermatozoan*, ed. Bjorn A. Afzelius (New York: Pergamon, 1975), 79–82.

38. Ludwik Fleck, *Genesis and Development of a Scientific Fact*, ed. Thaddeus J. Trenn and Rober K. Merton (Chicago: University of Chicago Press, 1979), 38.

39. Jay M. Baltz carried out the research I describe when he was a graduate student in the Thomas C. Jenkins Department of Biophysics at Johns Hopkins University.

40. Far less is known about the physiology of sperm than comparable female substances, which some feminists claim is no accident. Greater scientific scrutiny of female reproduction has long enabled the burden of birth control to be placed on women. In this case, the researchers' discovery did not depend on development of any new technology. The experiments made use of glass pipettes, a manometer, and a simple microscope, all of which have been available for more than one hundred years.

41. Jay Baltz and Richard A. Cone, "What Force Is Needed to Tether a Sperm?" (abstract for Society for the Study of Reproduction, 1985), and "Flagellar Torque on the Head Determines the Force Needed to Tether a Sperm" (abstract for Biophysical Society, 1986).

42. Jay M. Baltz, David F. Katz, and Richard A. Cone, "The Mechanics of the Sperm-Egg Interaction at the Zona Pellucida," *Biophysical Journal* 54, no. 4 (October 1988): 643–54. Lab members were somewhat familiar with work on metaphors in the biology of female reproduction. Richard Cone, who runs the lab, is my husband, and he talked with them about my earlier research on the subject from time to time. Even though my current research focuses on biological imagery and I heard about the lab's work from my husband every day, I myself did not recognize the role of imagery in the sperm research until many weeks after the period of research and writing I describe. Therefore, I assume that any awareness the lab members may have had about how underlying metaphor might be guiding this particular research was fairly inchoate.

43. Ibid., 643, 650.

44. Schatten and Schatten (n. 29 above), 51.

45. Ibid., 52.

46. Surprisingly, in an article intended for a general audience, the authors do not point out that these are sea urchin sperm and note that human sperm do not shoot out filaments at all.

47. Schatten and Schatten, 53.

48. Paul M. Wassarman, "Fertilization in Mammals," *Scientific American* 259, no. 6 (December 1988): 78–84, esp. 78, 84.

49. Ibid., 78.

50. Ibid., 79.

51. Ibid., 78.

52. Since receptor molecules are relatively *immotile* and the ligands that bind to them relatively *motile*, one might imagine the egg being called the receptor and the sperm the ligand. But the molecules in question on egg and sperm are immotile molecules. It is the sperm as a *cell* that has motility, and the egg as a cell that has relative immotility.

53. Wassarman, 78–79.

54. Paul M. Wassarman, "The Biology and Chemistry of Fertilization," *Science* 235, no. 4788 (January 30, 1987): 553–60, esp. 554.

55. Ibid., 557.

56. Ibid., 557–58. This finding throws into question Schatten and Schatten's description (n. 29 above) of the sperm, its tail beating, diving down into the egg.

57. Deborah R. Gordon, "Tenacious Assumptions in Western Medicine," in *Biomedicine Examined*, ed. Margaret Lock and Deborah Gordon (Dordrecht: Kluwer, 1988), 19–56, esp. 26.

58. Wassarman, "The Biology and Chemistry of Fertilization," 558.

59. Baltz, Katz, and Cone (n. 42 above), 643, 650.

60. Schatten and Schatten, 53.

61. Wassarman, "The Biology and Chemistry of Fertilization," 557.

62. Mary Ellman, *Thinking about Women* (New York: Harcourt Brace Jovanovich, 1968), 140; Nina Auerbach, *Women and the Demon* (Cambridge, Mass.: Harvard University Press, 1982), esp. 186.

63. Kenneth Alan Adams, "Arachnophobia: Love American Style," *Journal of Psychoanalytic Anthropology* 4, no. 2 (1981): 157–97.

64. William Ray Arney and Bernard Bergen, *Medicine and the Management of Living* (Chicago: University of Chicago Press, 1984).

65. J. F. Hartman, R. B. Gwatkin, and C. F. Hutchison, "Early Contact Interactions between Mammalian Gametes *In Vitro*," *Proceedings of the National Academy of Sciences* (*U.S.*) 69, no. 10 (1972): 2767–69.

66. Arney and Bergen, 68.

67. Ruth Hubbard, "Have Only Men Evolved?" (n. 12 above), 51–52.

68. David Harvey, personal communication, November 1989.

69. Rosalind Petchesky, "Fetal Images: The Power of Visual Culture in the Politics of Reproduction," *Feminist Studies* 13, no. 2 (Summer 1987): 263–92, esp. 272.

70. Rita Arditti, Renate Klein, and Shelley Minden, *Test-Tube Women* (London: Pandora, 1984); Ellen Goodman, "Whose Right to Life?" *Baltimore Sun* (November 17, 1987); Tamar Lewin, "Courts Acting to Force Care of the Unborn," *New York Times* (November 23, 1987), A1 and B10; Susan Irwin and Brigitte Jordan, "Knowledge, Practice, and Power: Court Ordered Cesarean Sections," *Medical Anthropology Quarterly* 1, no. 3 (September 1987): 319–34.

71. Thanks to Elizabeth Fee and David Spain, who in February 1989 and April 1989, respectively, made points related to this.

■ NATIONAL COUNCIL OF TEACHERS OF
ENGLISH/CONFERENCE ON COLLEGE
COMPOSITION AND COMMUNICATION

Resolution on the Students' Right to Their Own Language

The National Council of Teachers of English (NCTE) is an organization of 60,000 members devoted to advancing the best practices for language learning and literacy development. Through the resources on its Web site and the several conferences held around the country each year, NCTE offers language arts teachers from kindergarten through college many opportunities for professional development. In addition, the organization has drafted a variety of position statements that reflect the values and beliefs of its members. At the 1974 Annual Business Meeting held in New Orleans, the members of the NCTE and its constituent group, the Conference on College Composition and Communication (CCCC), adopted a resolution granting that all student dialects are of equal value. In the fall of 1974, this resolution was published in the journal *College Composition and Communication*. The resolution was reaffirmed by members in 2003 at the Conference on College Composition and Communication in San Francisco.

We affirm the students' right to their own patterns and varieties of language — the dialects of their nurture or whatever dialects in which they find their own identity and style. Language scholars long ago denied that the myth of a standard American dialect has any validity. The claim that any one dialect is unacceptable amounts to an attempt of one social group to exert its dominance over another. Such a claim leads to false advice for speakers and writers, and immoral advice for humans. A nation proud of its diverse heritage and its cultural and racial variety will preserve its heritage of dialects. We affirm strongly that teachers must have the experiences and training that will enable them to respect diversity and uphold the right of students to their own language.

■ THE ONION ───────────────────────────────────

National Museum of the Middle Class
Opens in Schaumburg, IL

The Onion is a parodic newspaper founded in 1988 by two undergraduates at the University of Wisconsin. After leaving college, one of the founders, Tim Keck, founded and now publishes *The Stranger*, an alternative weekly newspaper in Seattle. Mimicking the style of traditional newspapers, *The Onion* features satirical articles and editorials that report on national and international current events with sections on politics, education, sports, and entertainment. On several occasions, readers have mistaken the fictional stories in the newspaper for real news stories. The article "National Museum of the Middle Class Opens in Schaumburg, IL" was published in the issue from November 3, 2004.

■ ■ ■

SCHAUMBURG, IL — The Museum of the Middle Class, featuring historical and anthropological exhibits addressing the socioeconomic category that once existed between the upper and lower classes, opened to the public Monday.

"The splendid and intriguing middle class may be gone, but it will never be forgotten," said Harold Greeley, curator of the exhibit titled "Where The Streets Had Trees' Names." "From their weekend barbecues at homes with backyards to their outdated belief in social mobility, the middle class will forever be remembered as an important part of American history."

Museum guests expressed delight over the traditions and peculiarities of the middle class, a group once so prevalent that entire TV networks were programmed to satisfy its hunger for sitcoms.

"It's fascinating to think that these people once drove the same streets as we do today," said Natasha Ohman, a multimillionaire whose husband's grandfather invented the trigger-safety lock on handguns. "I enjoyed learning how the middle class lived, what their customs were, and what sorts of

A waitress from Chicago learns what the middle class was.

diversions and entertainment they enjoyed. Being part of this middle class must have been fascinating!"

During the modern industrial age, the middle class grew steadily, reaching its heyday in the 1950s, when its numbers soared into the tens of millions. According to a study commissioned by the U.S. Census Bureau, middle-class people inhabited great swaths of North America, with settlements in the Great Plains, the Rocky Mountains, the Pacific Northwest, and even the nation's urban centers.

"No one predicted the disappearance of the middle class," said Dr. Bradford Elsby, a history professor at the University of Pennsylvania. "The danger of eliminating workers' unions, which had protected the middle class from its natural predators for years, was severely underestimated. We believe that removal of the social safety net, combined with rapid political-climate changes, made life very difficult for the middle class, and eventually eradicated it altogether."

One of the 15 permanent exhibits, titled "Working for 'the Weekend,'" examines the routines of middle-class wage-earners, who labored for roughly eight hours a day, five days a week. In return, they were afforded leisure time on Saturdays and Sundays. According to many anthropologists, these "weekends" were often spent taking "day trips," eating at chain family restaurants, or watching "baseball" with the nuclear family.

"Unlike members of the lower class, middle-class people earned enough money in five days to take two days off to 'hang out,'" said Benson Watercross, who took a private jet from his home in Aspen to visit the museum. "Their adequate wages provided a level of comfort and stability, and allowed them to enjoy diversions or purchase goods, thereby briefly escaping the mundanity."

Many museum visitors found the worldview of the middle class — with its reliance on education, stable employment, and ample pensions — difficult to comprehend.

Thirty-five Booker T. Washington Junior High School seventh-graders, chosen from among 5,600 students who asked to attend the school's

Several members of the upper class learn how people without yachts used to pass the time.

annual field trip, visited the museum Tuesday. Rico Chavez, a 14-year-old from the inner-city Chicago school, said he was skeptical of one exhibit in particular.

"They expect us to believe this is how people lived 10 years ago?" Chavez asked. "That 'Safe, Decent Public Schools' part was total science fiction. No metal detectors, no cops or dogs, and whole classes devoted to art and music? Look, I may have flunked a couple grades, but I'm not that stupid."

Others among the 99 percent of U.S. citizens who make less than $28,000 per year shared Chavez's sense of disbelief.

"Frankly, I think they're selling us a load of baloney," said laid-off textile worker Elsie Johnson, who visited the museum Tuesday with her five asthmatic children. "They expect us to believe the *government* used to help pay for college? Come on. The funniest exhibit I saw was 'Visiting the Family Doctor.' Imagine being able to choose your own doctor and see him without a four-hour wait in the emergency room. Gimme a friggin' break!"

While some were incredulous, others described the Museum of the Middle Class as "a trip down memory lane." William Harrison, a retired social worker with middle-class heritage, said he was moved to tears by several of the exhibits.

"You wouldn't know it to look at me, but my parents were middle class," Harrison said. "Even though my family fell into poverty, I cherish those roots. Seeing that section on middle-class eating habits really brought it all back: the Tuna Helper, the Capri Sun, and the cookie dough in tubes. Oh, and the 2-percent milk and reduced-cholesterol butter spread! I was thankful for the chance to rediscover my past, even if the middle class *is* gone forever."

The Museum of the Middle Class was funded primarily by the Ford Foundation, the charitable arm of the Ford automotive company, which sold cars to the middle class for nearly 100 years.

■ MARY LOUISE PRATT

Arts of the Contact Zone

Mary Louise Pratt (b. 1948) is a Silver Professor and professor of Spanish and Portuguese Languages and Literatures at New York University. She served as president of the Modern Language Association in 2003 and has received numerous awards, including fellowships from the Guggenheim Foundation and the National Endowment for the Arts. Pratt is well known for her research in contact zones, which are defined as spaces where people from different and oppositional cultures interact, and her theory of contact zones has been highly influential in conceptualizing interactions in a wide range of contexts. Pratt first presented "Arts of the Contact Zone" as a keynote address at the Modern Language Association Literacy Conference in Pittsburgh in 1990. It was published in the journal *Profession* in 1991, and portions of the article were later developed in Pratt's book *Imperial Eyes: Travel Writing and Transculturation* (1992).

■ ■ ■

Whenever the subject of literacy comes up, what often pops first into my mind is a conversation I overheard eight years ago between my son Sam and his best friend, Willie, aged six and seven, respectively: "Why don't you trade me Many Trails for Carl Yats . . . Yesits . . . Ya-strum-scrum." "That's not how you say it, dummy, it's Carl Yes . . . Yes . . . oh, I don't know." Sam and Willie had just discovered baseball cards. Many Trails was their decoding, with the help of first-grade English phonics, of the name Manny Trillo. The name they were quite rightly stumped on was Carl Yastrzemski. That was the first time I remembered seeing them put their incipient literacy to their own use, and I was of course thrilled.

Sam and Willie learned a lot about phonics that year by trying to decipher surnames on baseball cards, and a lot about cities, states, heights, weights, places of birth, stages of life. In the years that followed, I watched Sam apply his arithmetic skills to working out batting averages and subtracting retirement years from rookie years; I watched him develop senses of patterning and order by arranging and rearranging his cards for hours on end, and aesthetic judgment by comparing different photos, different series, layouts, and color schemes. American geography and history took shape in his mind through baseball cards. Much of his social life revolved around trading them, and he learned about exchange, fairness, trust, the importance of processes as opposed to results, what it means to get cheated, taken advantage of, even robbed. Baseball cards were the medium of his economic life too. Nowhere better to learn the power and arbitrariness of money, the absolute divorce between use value and exchange value, notions of long- and short-term investment, the possibility of personal values that are independent of market values.

Baseball cards meant baseball card shows, where there was much to be learned about adult worlds as well. And baseball cards opened the door to baseball books, shelves and shelves of encyclopedias, magazines, histories, biographies, novels, books of jokes, anecdotes, cartoons, even poems. Sam learned the history of American racism and the struggle against it through baseball; he saw the Depression and two world wars from behind home plate. He learned the meaning of commodified labor, what it means for one's body and talents to be owned and dispensed by another. He knows something about Japan, Taiwan, Cuba, and Central America and how men and boys do things there. Through the history and experience of baseball stadiums he thought about architecture, light, wind, topography, meteorology, the dynamics of public space. He learned the meaning of expertise, of knowing about something well enough that you can start a conversation with a stranger and feel sure of holding your own. Even with an adult — especially with an adult. Throughout his preadolescent years, baseball history was Sam's luminous point of contact with grown-ups, his lifeline to caring. And, of course, all this time he was also playing baseball, struggling his way through the stages of the local Little League system, lucky enough to be a pretty good player, loving the game and coming to know deeply his strengths and weaknesses.

Literacy began for Sam with the newly pronounceable names on the picture cards and brought him what has been easily the broadest, most varied, most enduring, and most integrated experience of his thirteen-year life. Like many parents, I was delighted to see schooling give Sam the tools with which to find and open all these doors. At the same time I found it unforgivable that schooling itself gave him nothing remotely as meaningful to do, let alone anything that would actually take him beyond the referential, masculinist ethos of baseball and its lore.

However, I was not invited here to speak as a parent, nor as an expert on literacy. I was asked to speak as an MLA [Modern Language Association] member working in the elite academy. In that capacity my contribution is undoubtedly supposed to be abstract, irrelevant, and anchored outside the real world. I wouldn't dream of disappointing anyone. I propose immediately to head back several centuries to a text that has a few points in common with baseball cards and raises thoughts about what Tony Sarmiento, in his comments to the conference, called new visions of literacy. In 1908 a Peruvianist named Richard Pietschmann was exploring in the Danish Royal Archive in Copenhagen and came across a manuscript. It was dated in the city of Cuzco in Peru, in the year 1613, some forty years after the final fall of the Inca empire to the Spanish and signed with an unmistakably Andean indigenous name: Felipe Guaman Poma de Ayala. Written in a mixture of Quechua and ungrammatical, expressive Spanish, the manuscript was a letter addressed by an unknown but apparently literate Andean to King Philip III of Spain. What stunned Pietschmann was that the letter was twelve hundred pages long. There were almost eight hundred pages of written text and four hundred of captioned line drawings. It was titled *The First New Chronicle and Good Government*. No one knew (or knows) how the manuscript got to the library in Copenhagen or how long it had been there. No one, it appeared, had ever bothered to read it or figured out how. Quechua was not thought of as a written language in 1908, nor Andean culture as a literate culture.

Pietschmann prepared a paper on his find, which he presented in London in 1912, a year after the rediscovery of Machu Picchu by Hiram Bingham. Reception, by an international congress of Americanists, was apparently confused. It took twenty-five years for a facsimile edition of the work to appear in Paris. It was not till the late 1970s, as positivist reading habits gave way to interpretive studies and colonial elitisms to postcolonial pluralisms, that Western scholars found ways of reading Guaman Poma's *New Chronicle and Good Government* as the extraordinary intercultural tour de force that it was. The letter got there, only 350 years too late, a miracle and a terrible tragedy.

I propose to say a few more words about this erstwhile unreadable text, in order to lay out some thoughts about writing and literacy in what I like to call the *contact zones*. I use this term to refer to social spaces where cultures meet, clash, and grapple with each other, often in contexts of highly asymmetrical relations of power, such as colonialism, slavery, or their aftermaths as they are lived out in many parts of the world today. Eventually I will use the term to reconsider the models of community that many of us rely on in teaching and theorizing and that are under challenge today. But first a little more about Guaman Poma's giant letter to Philip III.

Insofar as anything is known about him at all, Guaman Poma exemplified the sociocultural complexities produced by conquest and empire. He was an indigenous Andean who claimed noble Inca descent and who had adopted (at least in some sense) Christianity. He may have worked in the Spanish colonial administration as an interpreter, scribe, or assistant to a Spanish tax collector — as a mediator, in short. He says he learned to write from his half brother, a mestizo whose Spanish father had given him access to religious education.

Guaman Poma's letter to the king is written in two languages (Spanish and Quechua) and two parts. The first is called the *Nueva corónica*, "New Chronicle." The title is important. The chronicle of course was the main writing apparatus through which the Spanish presented their American conquests to themselves. It constituted one of the main official discourses. In writing a "new chronicle," Guaman Poma took over the official Spanish genre for his own ends. Those ends were, roughly, to construct a new picture of the world, a picture of a Christian world with Andean rather than European peoples at the center of it — Cuzco, not Jerusalem. In the *New Chronicle* Guaman Poma begins by rewriting the Christian history of the world from Adam and Eve (Fig. 1), incorporating the Amerindians into it as offspring of one of the sons of Noah. He identifies five ages of Christian history that he links in parallel with the five ages of canonical Andean history — separate but equal trajectories that diverge with Noah and

FIGURE 1   Adam and Eve

reintersect not with Columbus but with Saint Bartholomew, claimed to
have preceded Columbus in the Americas. In a couple of hundred pages,
Guaman Poma constructs a veritable encyclopedia of Inca and pre-Inca
history, customs, laws, social forms, public offices, and dynastic leaders.
The depictions resemble European manners and customs description, but
also reproduce the meticulous detail with which knowledge in Inca society
was stored on *quipus* and in the oral memories of elders.

Guaman Poma's *New Chronicle* is an instance of what I have proposed
to call an *autoethnographic* text, by which I mean a text in which people
undertake to describe themselves in ways that engage with representations
others have made of them. Thus if ethnographic texts are those in which
European metropolitan subjects represent to themselves their others (usually their conquered others), autoethnographic texts are representations
that the so-defined others construct *in response to* or in dialogue with
those texts. Autoethnographic texts are not, then, what are usually thought
of as autochthonous forms of expression or self-representation (as the
Andean *quipus* were). Rather they involve a selective collaboration with

and appropriation of idioms of the metropolis or the conqueror. These are merged or infiltrated to varying degrees with indigenous idioms to create self-representations intended to intervene in metropolitan modes of understanding. Autoethnographic works are often addressed to both metropolitan audiences and the speaker's own community. Their reception is thus highly indeterminate. Such texts often constitute a marginalized group's point of entry into the dominant circuits of print culture. It is interesting to think, for example, of American slave autobiography in its autoethnographic dimensions, which in some respects distinguish it from Euramerican autobiographical tradition. The concept might help explain why some of the earliest published writing by Chicanas took the form of folkloric manners and customs sketches written in English and published in English-language newspapers or folklore magazines (see Treviño). Autoethnographic representation often involves concrete collaborations between people, as between literate ex-slaves and abolitionist intellectuals, or between Guaman Poma and the Inca elders who were his informants. Often, as in Guaman Poma, it involves more than one language. In recent decades autoethnography, critique, and resistance have reconnected with writing in a contemporary creation of the contact zone, the *testimonio*.

Guaman Poma's *New Chronicle* ends with a revisionist account of the Spanish conquest, which, he argues, should have been a peaceful encounter of equals with the potential for benefiting both, but for the mindless greed of the Spanish. He parodies Spanish history. Following contact with the Incas, he writes, "In all Castille, there was a great commotion. All day and at night in their dreams the Spaniards were saying, 'Yndias, yndias, oro, plata, oro, plata del Piru'" ("Indies, Indies, gold, silver, gold, silver from Peru") (Fig. 2). The Spanish, he writes, brought nothing of value to share with the Andeans, nothing "but armor and guns con la codicia de oro, plata oro y plata, yndias, a las Yndias, Piru" ("with the lust for gold, silver, gold and silver, Indies, the Indies, Peru") (372). I quote these words as an example of a conquered subject using the conqueror's language to construct a parodic, oppositional representation of the conqueror's own speech. Guaman Poma mirrors back to the Spanish (in their language, which is alien to him) an image of themselves that they often suppress and will therefore surely recognize. Such are the dynamics of language, writing, and representation in contact zones.

The second half of the epistle continues the critique. It is titled *Buengobierno y justicia*, "Good Government and Justice," and combines a description of colonial society in the Andean region with a passionate denunciation of Spanish exploitation and abuse. (These, at the time he was writing, were decimating the population of the Andes at a genocidal rate. In fact, the potential loss of the labor force became a main cause for reform of the system.) Guaman Poma's most implacable hostility is invoked by the clergy, followed by the dreaded *corregidores*, or colonial overseers (Fig. 3). He also praises good works, Christian habits, and just men where he finds them, and offers at length his views as to what constitutes

FIGURE 2   Conquista. Meeting of Spaniard and Inca. The Inca says in Quechua, "You eat this gold?" Spaniard replies in Spanish, "We eat this gold."

"good government and justice." The Indies, he argues, should be administered through a collaboration of Inca and Spanish elites. The epistle ends with an imaginary question-and-answer session in which, in a reversal of hierarchy, the king is depicted asking Guaman Poma questions about how to reform the empire — a dialogue imagined across the many lines that divide the Andean scribe from the imperial monarch, and in which the subordinated subject single-handedly gives himself authority in the colonizer's language and verbal repertoire. In a way, it worked — this extraordinary text did get written — but in a way it did not, for the letter never reached its addressee.

To grasp the import of Guaman Poma's project, one needs to keep in mind that the Incas had no system of writing. Their huge empire is said to be the only known instance of a full-blown bureaucratic state society built and administered without writing. Guaman Poma constructs his text by appropriating and adapting pieces of the representational repertoire of the invaders. He does not simply imitate or reproduce it; he selects and adapts it along Andean lines to express (bilingually, mind you) Andean interests

FIGURE 3   Corregidor de minas. Catalog of Spanish Abuses of Indigenous Labor Force.

and aspirations. Ethnographers have used the term *transculturation* to describe processes whereby members of subordinated or marginal groups select and invent from materials transmitted by a dominant or metropolitan culture. The term, originally coined by Cuban sociologist Fernando Ortiz in the 1940s, aimed to replace overly reductive concepts of acculturation and assimilation used to characterize culture under conquest. While subordinate peoples do not usually control what emanates from the dominant culture, they do determine to varying extents what gets absorbed into their own and what it gets used for. Transculturation, like autoethnography, is a phenomenon of the contact zone.

As scholars have realized only relatively recently, the transcultural character of Guaman Poma's text is intricately apparent in its visual as well as its written component. The genre of the four hundred line drawings is European — there seems to have been no tradition of representational drawing among the Incas — but in their execution they deploy specifically Andean systems of spatial symbolism that express Andean values and aspirations.[1]

In Figure 1, for instance, Adam is depicted on the left-hand side below the sun, while Eve is on the right-hand side below the moon, and slightly lower than Adam. The two are divided by the diagonal of Adam's digging stick. In Andean spatial symbolism, the diagonal descending from the sun marks the basic line of power and authority dividing upper from lower, male from female, dominant from subordinate. In Figure 2, the Inca appears in the same position as Adam, with the Spaniard opposite, and the two at the same height. In Figure 3, depicting Spanish abuses of power, the symbolic pattern is reversed. The Spaniard is in a high position indicating dominance, but on the "wrong" (right-hand) side. The diagonals of his lance and that of the servant doing the flogging mark out a line of illegitimate, though real, power. The Andean figures continue to occupy the left-hand side of the picture, but clearly as victims. Guaman Poma wrote that the Spanish conquest had produced *"un mundo al reves,"* "a world in reverse."

In sum, Guaman Poma's text is truly a product of the contact zone. If one thinks of cultures, or literatures, as discrete, coherently structured, monolingual edifices, Guaman Poma's text, and indeed any autoethnographic work, appears anomalous or chaotic — as it apparently did to the European scholars Pietschmann spoke to in 1912. If one does not think of cultures this way, then Guaman Poma's text is simply heterogeneous, as the Andean region was itself and remains today. Such a text is heterogeneous on the reception end as well as the production end: it will read very differently to people in different positions in the contact zone. Because it deploys European and Andean systems of meaning making, the letter necessarily means differently to bilingual Spanish-Quechua speakers and to monolingual speakers in either language; the drawings mean differently to monocultural readers, Spanish or Andean, and to bicultural readers responding to the Andean symbolic structures embodied in European genres.

In the Andes in the early 1600s there existed a literate public with considerable intercultural competence and degrees of bilingualism. Unfortunately, such a community did not exist in the Spanish court with which Guaman Poma was trying to make contact. It is interesting to note that in the same year Guaman Poma sent off his letter, a text by another Peruvian was adopted in official circles in Spain as the canonical Christian mediation between the Spanish conquest and Inca history. It was another huge encyclopedic work, titled the *Royal Commentaries of the Incas,* written, tellingly, by a mestizo, Inca Garcilaso de la Vega. Like the mestizo half brother who taught Guaman Poma to read and write, Inca Garcilaso was the son of an Inca princess and a Spanish official, and had lived in Spain since he was seventeen. Though he too spoke Quechua, his book is written in eloquent, standard Spanish, without illustrations. While Guaman Poma's life's work sat somewhere unread, the *Royal Commentaries* was edited and reedited in Spain and the New World, a mediation that coded the Andean past and present in ways thought unthreatening to colonial hierarchy.[2] The textual hierarchy persists; the *Royal Commentaries* today remains a staple item on Ph.D. reading lists in Spanish, while the *New Chronicle and Good Government*, despite the ready availability of several fine editions, is not. However, though Guaman Poma's text did not reach its destination, the transcultural currents of expression it exemplifies continued to evolve in the Andes, as they still do, less in writing than in storytelling, ritual, song, dance-drama, painting and sculpture, dress, textile art, forms of governance, religious belief, and many other vernacular art forms. All express the effects of long-term contact and intractable, unequal conflict.

Autoethnography, transculturation, critique, collaboration, bilingualism, mediation, parody, denunciation, imaginary dialogue, vernacular expression — these are some of the literate arts of the contact zone. Miscomprehension, incomprehension, dead letters, unread masterpieces, absolute heterogeneity of meaning — these are some of the perils of writing in the contact zone. They all live among us today in the transnationalized metropolis of the United States and are becoming more widely visible, more pressing, and, like Guaman Poma's text, more decipherable to those who once would have ignored them in defense of a stable, centered sense of knowledge and reality.

Contact and Community

The idea of the contact zone is intended in part to contrast with ideas of community that underlie much of the thinking about language, communication, and culture that gets done in the academy. A couple of years ago, thinking about the linguistic theories I knew, I tried to make sense of a utopian quality that often seemed to characterize social analyses of language by the academy. Languages were seen as living in "speech communities," and these tended to be theorized as discrete, self-defined, coherent entities, held together by a homogeneous competence or grammar shared identically and equally among all the members. This abstract idea of the speech community seemed to reflect, among other things, the utopian way modern nations conceive of themselves as what Benedict Anderson calls "imagined communities."[3] In a book of that title, Anderson observes that with the possible exception of what he calls "primordial villages," human communities exist as *imagined* entities in which people "will never know most of their fellow-members, meet them or even hear of them, yet in the mind of each lives the image of their communion." "Communities are distinguished," he goes on to say, "not by their falsity/genuineness, but by *the style in which they are imagined*" (15; emphasis mine). Anderson proposes three features that characterize the style in which the modern nation is imagined. First, it is imagined as *limited*, by "finite, if elastic, boundaries"; second, it is imagined as *sovereign*; and, third, it is imagined as *fraternal*, "a deep, horizontal comradeship" for which millions of people are prepared "not so much to kill as willingly to die" (15). As the image suggests, the nation-community is embodied metonymically in the finite, sovereign, fraternal figure of the citizen-soldier.

Anderson argues that European bourgeoisies were distinguished by their ability to "achieve solidarity on an essentially imagined basis" (74) on a scale far greater than that of elites of other times and places. Writing and literacy play a central role in this argument. Anderson maintains, as have others, that the main instrument that made bourgeois nation-building projects possible was print capitalism. The commercial circulation of books in the various European vernaculars, he argues, was what first created the invisible networks that would eventually constitute the literate elites and those they ruled as nations. (Estimates are that 180 million books were put into circulation in Europe between the years 1500 and 1600 alone.)

Now obviously this style of imagining of modern nations, as Anderson describes it, is strongly utopian, embodying values like equality, fraternity, liberty, which the societies often profess but systematically fail to realize. The prototype of the modern nation as imagined community was, it seemed to me, mirrored in ways people thought about language and the speech community. Many commentators have pointed out how modern views of language as code and competence assume a unified and homogeneous social world in which language exists as a shared patrimony — as a device, precisely, for imagining community. An image of a universally shared literacy is also part of the picture. The prototypical manifestation of language is generally taken to be the speech of individual adult native speakers face-to-face (as in Saussure's famous diagram) in monolingual, even monodialectal situations — in short, the most homogeneous case linguistically and socially. The same goes for written communication. Now one could certainly imagine a theory that assumed different things — that argued, for instance, that the most revealing speech situation for understanding language was one involving a gathering of people each of whom spoke two languages and understood a third and held only one language in common with any of the others. It depends on what workings of language you want to see or want to see first, on what you choose to define as normative.

In keeping with autonomous, fraternal models of community, analyses of language use commonly assume that principles of cooperation and shared understanding are normally in effect. Descriptions of interactions between people in conversation, classrooms, medical and bureaucratic settings, readily take it for granted that the situation is governed by a single set of rules or norms shared by all participants. The analysis focuses then on how those rules produce or fail to produce an orderly, coherent exchange. Models involving games and moves are often used to describe interactions. Despite whatever conflicts or systematic social differences might be in play, it is assumed that all participants are engaged in the same game and that the game is the same for all players. Often it is. But of course it often is not, as, for example, when speakers are from different classes or cultures, or one party is exercising authority and another is submitting to it or questioning it. Last year one of my children moved to a new elementary school that had more open classrooms and more flexible curricula than the conventional school he started out in. A few days into the term, we asked him what it was like at the new school. "Well," he said, "they're a lot nicer, and they have a lot less rules. But know *why* they're nicer?" "Why?" I asked. "So you'll obey all the rules they don't have," he replied. This is a very coherent analysis with considerable elegance and explanatory power, but probably not the one his teacher would have given.

When linguistic (or literate) interaction is described in terms of orderliness, games, moves, or scripts, usually only legitimate moves are actually named as part of the system, where legitimacy is defined from the point of view of the party in authority — regardless of what other parties might see themselves as doing. Teacher-pupil language, for example, tends to be described almost entirely from the point of view of the teacher and teaching, not from the point of view of pupils and pupiling (the word doesn't even exist, though the thing certainly does). If a classroom is analyzed as a social world unified and homogenized with respect to the teacher, whatever students do other than what the teacher specifies is invisible or anomalous to the analysis. This can be true in practice as well. On several occasions my fourth grader, the one busy obeying all the rules they didn't have, was given writing assignments that took the form of answering a series of questions to build up a paragraph. These questions often asked him to identify with the interests of those in power over him — parents, teachers, doctors, public authorities. He invariably sought ways to resist or subvert these assignments. One assignment, for instance, called for imagining "a helpful invention." The students were asked to write single-sentence responses to the following questions:

What kind of invention would help you?
How would it help you?
Why would you need it?
What would it look like?
Would other people be able to use it also?
What would be an invention to help your teacher?
What would be an invention to help your parents?

Manuel's reply read as follows:

A grate adventchin

Some inventchins are GRATE!!!!!!!!!!! My inventchin would be a shot that would put every thing you learn at school in your brain. It would help me by letting me graduate right now!! I would need it because it would let me play with my friends, go on vacachin and, do fun a lot more. It would look like a regular shot. Ather peaple would use to. This inventchin would help my teacher parents get away from a lot of work. I think a shot like this would be GRATE!

Despite the spelling, the assignment received the usual star to indicate the task had been fulfilled in an acceptable way. No recognition was available, however, of the humor, the attempt to be critical or contestatory, to parody the structures of authority. On that score, Manuel's luck was only slightly better than Guaman Poma's. What is the place of unsolicited oppositional discourse, parody, resistance, critique in the imagined classroom community? Are teachers supposed to feel that their teaching has been most successful when they have eliminated such things and unified the social world, probably in their own image? Who wins when we do that? Who loses?

Such questions may be hypothetical, because in the United States in the 1990s, many teachers find themselves less and less able to do that even if they want to. The composition of the national collectivity is changing and so are the styles, as Anderson put it, in which it is being imagined. In the 1980s in many nation-states, imagined national syntheses that had retained hegemonic force began to dissolve. Internal social groups with histories and lifeways different from the official ones began insisting on those histories and lifeways *as part of their citizenship*, as the very mode of their membership in the national collectivity. In their dialogues with dominant institutions, many groups began asserting a rhetoric of belonging that made demands beyond those of representation and basic rights granted from above. In universities we started to hear, "I don't just want you to let me be here, I want to belong here; this institution should belong to me as much as it does to anyone else." Institutions have responded with, among other things, rhetorics of diversity and multiculturalism whose import at this moment is up for grabs across the ideological spectrum.

These shifts are being lived out by everyone working in education today, and everyone is challenged by them in one way or another. Those of us committed to educational democracy are particularly challenged as that notion finds itself besieged on the public agenda. Many of those who govern us display, openly, their interest in a quiescent, ignorant, manipulable electorate. Even as an ideal, the concept of an enlightened citizenry seems to have disappeared from the national imagination. A couple of years ago the university where I work went through an intense and wrenching debate over a narrowly defined Western-culture requirement that had been instituted there in 1980. It kept boiling down to a debate over the ideas of national patrimony, cultural citizenship, and imagined community. In the end, the requirement was transformed into a much more broadly defined course called Cultures, Ideas, Values.[4] In the context of the change, a new course was designed that centered on the Americas and the multiple cultural histories (including European ones) that have intersected here. As you can imagine, the course attracted a very diverse student body. The classroom functioned not like a homogeneous community or a horizontal alliance but like a contact zone. Every single text we read stood in specific historical relationships to the students in the class, but the range and variety of historical relationships in play were enormous.

Everybody had a stake in nearly everything we read, but the range and kind of stakes varied widely.

It was the most exciting teaching we had ever done, and also the hardest. We were struck, for example, at how anomalous the formal lecture became in a contact zone (who can forget Atahuallpa throwing down the Bible because it would not speak to him?). The lecturer's traditional (imagined) task — unifying the world in the class's eyes by means of a monologue that rings equally coherent, revealing, and true for all, forging an ad hoc community, homogeneous with respect to one's own words — this task became not only impossible but anomalous and unimaginable. Instead, one had to work in the knowledge that whatever one said was going to be systematically received in radically heterogeneous ways that we were neither able nor entitled to prescribe.

The very nature of the course put ideas and identities on the line. All the students in the class had the experience, for example, of hearing their culture discussed and objectified in ways that horrified them; all the students saw their roots traced back to legacies of both glory and shame; all the students experienced face-to-face the ignorance and incomprehension, and occasionally the hostility, of others. In the absence of community values and the hope of synthesis, it was easy to forget the positives; the fact, for instance, that kinds of marginalization once taken for granted were gone. Virtually every student was having the experience of seeing the world described with him or her in it. Along with rage, incomprehension, and pain, there were exhilarating moments of wonder and revelation, mutual understanding, and new wisdom — the joys of the contact zone. The sufferings and revelations were, at different moments to be sure, experienced by every student. No one was excluded, and no one was safe.

The fact that no one was safe made all of us involved in the course appreciate the importance of what we came to call "safe houses." We used the term to refer to social and intellectual spaces where groups can constitute themselves as horizontal, homogeneous, sovereign communities with high degrees of trust, shared understandings, temporary protection from legacies of oppression. This is why, as we realized, multicultural curricula should not seek to replace ethnic or women's studies, for example. Where there are legacies of subordination, groups need places for healing and mutual recognition, safe houses in which to construct shared understandings, knowledges, claims on the world that they can then bring into the contact zone.

Meanwhile, our job in the Americas course remains to figure out how to make that crossroads the best site for learning that it can be. We are looking for the pedagogical arts of the contact zone. These will include, we are sure, exercises in storytelling and in identifying with the ideas, interests, histories, and attitudes of others; experiments in transculturation and collaborative work and in the arts of critique, parody, and comparison (including unseemly comparisons between elite and vernacular cultural forms); the redemption of the oral; ways for people to engage with suppressed aspects of history (including their own histories), ways to move *into and out of* rhetorics of authenticity; ground rules for communication across lines of difference and hierarchy that go beyond politeness but maintain mutual respect; a systematic approach to the all-important concept of *cultural mediation*. These arts were in play in every room at the extraordinary Pittsburgh conference on literacy. I learned a lot about them there, and I am thankful.

NOTES

1. For an introduction in English to these and other aspects of Guaman Poma's work, see Rolena Adorno. Adorno and Mercedes Lopez-Baralt pioneered the study of Andean symbolic systems in Guaman Poma.

2. It is far from clear that the *Royal Commentaries* was as benign as the Spanish seemed to assume. The book certainly played a role in maintaining the identity and aspirations of indigenous elites in the Andes. In the mid-eighteenth century, a new edition of the *Royal Commentaries* was suppressed by Spanish authorities because its preface included a prophecy by Sir Walter Raleigh that the English would invade Peru and restore the Inca monarchy.

3. The discussion of community here is summarized from my essay "Linguistic Utopias."

4. For information about this program and the contents of courses taught in it, write Program in Cultures, Ideas, Values (CIV), Stanford Univ., Stanford, CA 94305.

WORKS CITED

Adorno, Rolena. *Guaman Poma de Ayala: Writing and Resistance in Colonial Peru*. Austin: U of Texas P, 1986.

Anderson, Benedict. *Imagined Communities: Reflections on the Origins and Spread of Nationalism*. London: Verso, 1984.

Garcilaso de la Vega, El Inca. *Royal Commentaries of the Incas*. 1613. Austin: U of Texas P, 1966.

Guaman Poma de Ayala, Felipe. *El primer nueva corónica y buen gobierno*. Manuscript. Ed. John Murra and Rolena Adorno. Mexico: Siglo XXI, 1980.

Pratt, Mary Louise. "Linguistic Utopias." *The Linguistics of Writing*. Ed. Nigel Fabb et al. Manchester: Manchester UP, 1987. 48–66.

Treviño, Gloria. "Cultural Ambivalence in Early Chicano Prose Fiction." Diss. Stanford U, 1985.

■ ANANDI RAMAMURTHY

Constructions of Illusion:
Photography and Commodity Culture

Anandi Ramamurthy is a senior lecturer in film and media studies at the University of Central Lancashire in England and a registered researcher for the British Film Institute. Her research focuses on advertising images of Africans and Asians from the British colonies, more specifically the cultural and economic impact of these racist advertisements. In addition, she analyzes representations of postcolonialism and immigration in film. Her article "Constructions of Illusion: Photography and Commodity Culture" was originally published in the collection *Photography: A Critical Introduction* (2000).

Introduction

The Photograph as Commodity

To the late twentieth century, commodity relations rule our lives to such an extent that we are often unaware of them as a specific set of historical, social and economic relations which human beings have constructed. The photograph is both a cultural tool which has been commodified as well as a tool that has been used to express commodity culture through advertisements and other marketing material. Tagg has described the development of photography as "a model of capitalist growth in the nineteenth century" (Tagg 1988: 37).

Like any cultural and technical development, the development of photography has been influenced by its social and economic context. The rise of commodity culture in the nineteenth century was a key influence on the way in which this technology was developed and used. John Tagg's essay provides just one example of the way in which photographic genres were affected by capitalism. He discusses the demand for photographic portraits by the rising middle and the lower-middle classes, keen for objects symbolic of high social status. The photographic portraits were affordable in price, yet were reminiscent of aristocratic social ascendancy signified by "having one's portrait done." Tagg describes how the daguerreotype and later the *"cartes-de-visite"* established an industry that had a vast clientele and was ruled by this clientele's "taste and acceptance of the conventional devices and genres of official art" (Tagg 1988: 50). The commodification of the photograph dulled the possible creativity of the new technology, by the desire to reproduce a set of conventions already established within painted portraiture.

If we look at other photographic genres, we can also observe the way in which commodity culture has affected their development. Photojournalism for instance, like other journalism, is primarily concerned with the selling of newspapers, rather than the conveyance of "news." For this reason, news photos, as Susan Sontag has noted, have been concerned with the production of "spectacle" (Sontag 1979). Just as photographic genres have been affected by commerce, so has the development of photographic technology. The "Instamatic" for instance was clearly developed in order to expand camera use and camera ownership. In turn, this technology limited the kind of photographs people could take (Slater 1983).

Were this chapter to discuss the commodification of photography in detail, it would be difficult to limit it, and it would most likely encroach on the subject area of every chapter in this book. Therefore this chapter will concentrate on the way photography has been used in representing commodity culture. In this sense, it will be as much about the decoding of visual commercial messages as about photography. Although the focus is on the specific qualities of photography in the production of commercial messages, photography forms part of a broader system of visual communication including painting, printing, as well as the broadcast media.

Photographs to Represent Commodity Culture

The use of photography within advertising and marketing does not constitute a particular genre. In fact, this area of photography borrows from all established genres, depending on particular marketing needs. Within the traditional "history of photography," commercial photography has been ignored, despite the fact that photography produced for advertising and marketing constitutes the largest quantity of photographic production. One possible reason for the lack of documentation and history-writing in this area is that commercial photography has not sought to stretch the medium of photography. One of the key characteristics of photography within advertising and marketing is its parasitism. It borrows and mimics from every genre of photographic and cultural practice to enhance and alter the meaning of lifeless objects — commodities.

Commodities are in fact objects — often inert — that have been imbued with all kinds of social characteristics in the marketplace. Marx called this process the fetishism of commodities, since in the marketplace (which means every place where things have been bought and sold) the social character of people's labor was no longer apparent and it was the products of their labor instead that interacted and were prominent. Advertising, in its turn, imbues these products with meanings which have no relation to the production processes of these objects. Advertising is a cultural form which is integrally linked to capitalism, and constitutes part of the system of production and consumption. Raymond Williams has discussed this relationship and the development of advertising in his essay "Advertising the Magic System" (Williams 1980). Thomas Richards, in a discussion of Victorian advertisements, describes commodity culture as the "culture of capitalism" (Richards 1990: 1–16). As Robert Goldman points out, "ads offer a unique window for observing how commodity interests conceptualise social relations" (Goldman 1992: 2). The representation of social relations in advertising has also been discussed in other texts on the history and study of advertising (Leiss et al. 1986; Myers 1986).

Photographs have played an important role in the production of signs, that have invested products with what Marxists have described as false meanings. They have also played an important role in the representation of commodity culture — namely, the culture of capitalism — as natural and eternal. (For a discussion on this, see Barthes 1977a.) In this way photographs in advertisements are a key tool for the making of ideology.

Breadth of Usage

The range of contexts within which photographs are used to sell products or services is so enormous that we are almost unaware of the medium of photography and the language which has been created to convey commercial messages. Photographs for commerce appear on everything from the glossy, high-quality billboard and magazine advertisements, to small, cheap flyers on estate agents' blurbs. Between these two areas there is a breadth of usage, including the mundane images in mail-order information and catalogues, the seemingly matter-of-fact, but high-quality documentary-style images of company annual reports, the varied quality of commodity packaging, and of course the photography on marketing materials such as calendars, produced by companies to enhance their status. While there are a number of critiques on advertising imagery, these tend not to be concerned with the photograph in particular. Other areas of commercial photographic production have received relatively no critical attention from scholars. If any history or literature has been written, it has tended to be commissioned by the companies themselves, or their associates, such as *Thirsty Work: Ten Years of Heineken Advertising* and *Some Examples of Benson Advertising*. These publications have also been unconcerned with the photographic aspect. More recently, articles such as Carol Squiers' "The Corporate Year in Pictures" have begun to provide an analysis to some of this photography (Squiers 1992).

Much of the discussion will focus on advertising, partly because it is an area rich for discussion, but also because it will enable us to consider some of the literature which critiques this photography. Through a closer look at ads we can understand the ideological significance of them and other commercial photographs in our lives as well as the hegemony of commodity culture. By analyzing a run-of-the-mill advertisement, we can understand how advertisements are constructed and act ideologically to support commodity culture, and can also see how photographs are employed in the making of ideology.

Case Study: Elizabeth Taylor's Passion — The Commodification of Human Relations

The main photograph in the advertisement is a rather soft focus dreamy image of the head and shoulders of Elizabeth Taylor, who appears to be wearing nothing but some diamond studded jewellery. Bright lights (perhaps stage lights) reflect off the jewelery and Taylor herself to present an image which is one of stardom. From our own cultural history we know that Liz Taylor has been associated with heroines such as Cleopatra — a passionate, determined, and arresting woman.

A crystal clear photograph of the bottle has been inserted into the main photograph on the right-hand side. The juxtaposition of bottle and Elizabeth Taylor's face in the advertisement obviously encourages their association. Purples and pinks within both images also affiliate the two images. The historical and cultural associations which we make with Liz Taylor through her film career are associated here with a bottle of scented liquid. Interestingly, under the bottle of perfume is written "Elizabeth Taylor's Passion." This lifeless bottle of liquid appears to have been given a human quality. There is another possibility of meaning too — the bottle is not her passion, despite the use of the possessive, but is the object of her passion. This notion is also enhanced by the glass object which Elizabeth Taylor appears to hold. It is the glass stopper from the perfume bottle. Liz Taylor has obviously opened the bottle and unleashed "passion," as though it is a quantifiable thing which can be bottled and unleashed in this way! Whether we interpret the perfume as containing Elizabeth Taylor's passion or being the object of her passion, the metamorphosis of the commodity as in some way human is complete. In the first instance it contains a human quality; in the second, passion — a human emotion, which occurs between people — takes place here, between a person and thing. The photographic montage is crucial in this creation of meaning. There is another statement in the advertisement which makes it resonate with further meanings: "Be touched by the fragrance that touches the woman." Here, we are invited to join in an experience in which stars have taken part. Yet, we are not simply coaxed into consumption by suggestions of glamour and beauty which Taylor may represent for us. The suggestion is also that she is *the* woman, imbued with qualities of womanliness. The image of Liz Taylor is of course one of standard femininity; she is even looking upwards, suggesting subservience. Her passivity is also increased by the way she holds the bottle stopper. She hardly seems to hold it at all. We cannot imagine those hands actually pulling open the bottle. One easy avenue offered to us in the search to be not just Elizabeth Taylor, but also womanly, is to use Passion. The commodification of human relations is one of the most pervasive influences of modern advertising, and photography plays an important role in creating images expressive of human emotions and relations which are used to give products superficial or "false" meanings. The pervasive nature of advertisements and the power of the photographic image not only leads us to be unaware of a process, which, when considered rationally, appears absurd, but also enhances these surface meanings above those of other product meanings which may exist through manufacture. What does it cost to produce the perfume? How much were the factory workers who produced and packaged Passion paid? Were they allowed to join a union? What were the health and safety conditions for the workers like? Was Passion tested on animals, and did it lead to animal suffering? Only eight cents out of every dollar in the cosmetics industry goes towards buying ingredients. Even this one piece of information can make us realize how little the advertisement tells us about the products in production. At the same time the ads provide an alluring image, the constructed meanings of which are enhanced by photographic realism, creating a culture in which it appears natural not even to want to know the context of production. These constructed meanings are not simply illusions; rather "they accurately portray social relations which are illusory" (Goldman 1992: 35).

The Grammar of the Ad

The Photographic Message

The photographic message, as Roland Barthes wrote, is made up of both a denoted message and a connoted message (Barthes 1977b). By the denoted message Barthes meant the literal reality which the photograph portrayed. In the case of the ad for Passion (see case study above), this would be the image of Liz Taylor and the perfume bottle. The second, connoted, message is one which he described as making use of social and historical references. The connoted message is the inferred message. It is symbolic. It is a message with a code — i.e., Liz Taylor signifies beauty, passion, feminity, nobility, and mystique. When we look at the documentary photograph, the denoted image appears dominant. We believe the photograph to be "fact," although, as Tagg has pointed out, it is impossible to have a simple 'denoted' message — all messages are constructed (Tagg 1988: 1–5). All photos are simulations and record moments discontinuous with normal time, and documentary images are highly coded both by the photographer's perspective and the privileging of certain moments, and also by the newspaper captioning of an image. The image for use in advertising, however, is different, in that we know from the start that it is highly structure. In the discussion on passion, I have already mentioned how the photograph of Elizabeth Taylor does not show her holding the bottle stopper properly. It is obviously a constructed and coded image. The play of light and the soft focus used in her portrait are also constructions, here used to convey romance. The use of soft focus in photography has often been used to signify romance and also femininity, as Pollock has mentioned in her reading of a Levi's advertisement (Pollock 1990: 215–216). The commercial photograph is not therefore perceived as primarily documenting real life. We are therefore unconsciously aware when reading the image that the connoted message is the crucial one.

However, while we know these images to be highly constructed, we are often unaware of the ways in which meaning is framed within them. The framing and structural devices which advertisers use are so well established that we read them unwittingly. Robert Goldman has described the classic advertising format as that of "the mortise and frame" (Goldman 1992: 61–85). He intends us to understand framing as the process of "selection, emphasis and presentation," and describes how all photographs are framed in production. In the ad for Passion, the photograph of Liz Taylor, for example, has been framed in such a way as to exclude any clothed part of her body, in order to increase its sexuality. A mortise, as Goldman notes, is a joiners' term for the joining of two pieces of wood together by making a cavity in one, into which a second piece is inserted. In the production of advertisements, the mortise in the small boxed image which usually contains the image of the product (e.g., the bottle of perfume). The photograph of the product is usually in a clear 'showroom' style, which suggests that it is purely documentary, but its frontal angle is one that we would never see in real life. This clear and stark style in itself sets it apart from the larger and usually more atmospheric photographic image, while they are structurally associated in the advertisement. Through this device, advertisers encourage us to combine the meaning of two separate and often seemingly incompatible messages. In the ad for Passion, the image of Liz Taylor and her human qualities of being a passionate woman are transferred to a bottle of perfume; i.e., a material thing is given human value and a human emotion is defined materially. Judith Williamson also discusses the association of two separate images in advertisements in her book *Decoding Advertisements*. She makes the important point that the process of association is one that actively involves the viewer in the production of meaning. She describes the viewer's role in producing meaning as "advertising work" (Williamson 1978: 15–19).

While it is useful to consider the form separately, Judith Williamson has also noted that it is impossible to divide the form and content entirely, since there is content in the form also. Most scholars considering questions of representation use methods first discussed in linguistics to decode visual signs (Williamson 1978: 17):

> A sign is quite simply a thing — whether object, word or thing — which has a particular meaning to a person or group of people. It is neither the thing nor the meaning alone, but the two together.
>
> The sign consists of the signifier, the material object, and the signified, which is its meaning. These are only divided for analytical purposes; in practice a sign is always thing-plus-meaning.

In the ad for Passion, Liz Taylor is the signifier of passion, which is the meaning signified. Through the structure of the ad, the perfume bottle also acts as a signifier of passion, although it does not actually have such a meaning. It is the "work" we do in reading the grammar of the ad — in reading its structure of form — that leads to the connection between the two signifiers being made.

The Transfer of Meaning

In his essay "Encoding/Decoding," Stuart Hall has considered our involvement in the production of meaning in more detail (Hall 1993). He discusses how images are first "encoded" by the producer, and then "decoded" by the viewer. The transfer of meaning in this process only works if there are compatible systems of signs and symbols which the encoder and decoder use within their cultural life. However, our background — i.e., our gender, class, ethnic origin, sexuality, religion, etc. — all affect our interpretation of signs and symbols. For this reason, Hall points to the fact that messages are not always read as they were intended to be. He suggests that there are three possible readings of an image: a dominant or preferred reading, a negotiated reading, and an oppositional one. The dominant reading would comply with the meaning intended by the producer of the image. The importance of readers interpreting images as they were intended is obviously crucial for commercial messages, and is one of the reasons why advertisers use the various framing devices which have been discussed above. Hall describes the negotiated reading as one which only partly conforms to the intended, dominant meaning. Finally the oppositional reading is one which is in total conflict with the meaning intended by the image-producer. A feminist interpretation of the advertisement for passion, which challenged the notion of "womanliness" presented by the ad, could be viewed as oppositional. Examples of ordinary people producing oppositional readings through graffiti have been collected by Jill Posner in *Spray It Loud* (Posner 1982). In *Reading Ads Socially*, Robert Goldman cites an example of a cigarette advertisement which was misinterpreted by many readers to create an oppositional meaning. In 1986, Kent cigarettes launched an ad campaign which depicted two people flying a kite on a page. In order to involve the viewer in the advertisement, the advertiser emptied the figures of content so that the reader could literally place themselves in the ad. Viewers, however, interpreted the silhouetted figures as ghosts because of the health warnings about smoking to which we have been accustomed (Goldman 1992: 80–81). The question of reception brings in to doubt the notion of global advertising which companies such as Coca-Cola and Benetton have tried to create. Can there really be worldwide advertising campaigns? People across the world will surely find different symbolic meanings in the same signifiers.

The Creation of Meaning in Photographic Styles

All photographs will be viewed by different people in different ways, whether in commercial contexts or not. The same photograph can also mean different things in different contexts. The commercial context, for example, can change the meaning of an image, just as different styles of photography will carry different messages. Let us look at an advertisement which does not use a style of photography normally associated with advertising. Because advertisers have traditionally been concerned with creating glamorous, fantasy worlds of desire for their products, they have tended to shy away from the stark, grainy, black and white type of imagery traditionally associated with documentary images and photojournalism, and have gone instead for glossy, high-color photography. Yet, at times of company crisis, or when companies have wanted to deliberately foster an image of no-nonsense frankness, they have used black and white imagery. In 1990, a short while after Nelson Mandela was released from jail by the South African authorities, the Anglo-American Corporation of South Africa brought out an advertisement entitled "Do we sometimes wish we had not fought to have Black trade unions recognized?" Underneath this title was a documentary photograph of a Black South African miner, in a

A crowd of miners demonstrates at the headquarters of the Chamber of Mines, the organisation of South African mine owners.

South African miners demonstrating outside the offices of the Organization of South African Mine Owners, (*Independent*, 26 August 1987). This photograph was used, torn from the newspaper page as it is here, by the Anglo-American Corporation of South Africa in their advertisement DO WE SOMETIMES WISH WE HAD NOT FOUGHT TO HAVE BLACK TRADE UNIONS RECOGNIZED? (*Published in the* Guardian, *2 April 1990.*)

show of victory (above). At a moment when Anglo-American foresaw massive economic and political change, they attempted to distance themselves from the apartheid regime. Yet Anglo-American was by far the largest company in South Africa, "with a new total grip over large sectors of the apartheid economy."[1] While presenting this advertisement to the public, De Beers — Anglo's sister company, in which they had a 35 percent stake — also cancelled their recognition agreement with the NUM at the Premier Diamond Mines, despite 90 percent of workers belonging to the union. The frank and honest style of address which black and white provided hid the reality for black workers in South Africa. The miner depicted was in fact celebrating his victory against Anglo-American in 1987. Here, at another moment of crisis, Anglo-American have appropriated this image of resistance. The parasitism of advertising enables it to use and discard any style and content for its own ends. Anglo-American are no longer interested in fostering this image (they declined permission to have the advertisement reproduced here). There is an added irony in Anglo-American's use of this image, since it is not strictly speaking a documentary image at all, but a montage of two images to capture the mood of the strike as the *Independent* saw it.

Black and white imagery has been used in other company contexts at moments of crisis. Carol Squiers has discussed the way in which they have been used in annual reports. Black and white, she notes, "looks more modest and costs less to print." As Arnold Saks, a corporate designer, said: "There's an honesty about black and white, a reality. . . . Black and white is the only reality" (Squiers 1992: 208). The symbolic value of using or not using a photograph has also been important for advertisers. Kathy Myers has explored the moments when advertisers have chosen to use and not use photographic images in an attempt to find symbols of ecological awareness (Myers 1990).

Hegemony in Photographic Representation

Commercial photography constantly borrows ideas and images from the wider cultural domain. It is clear that when we point the camera we frame it in a thousand and one ways through our own cultural conditioning. Photographs, like other cultural products, have therefore tended to perpetuate ideas which are dominant in society. Commercial photographs, because of their profuse nature and because they have never sought to challenge the status quo within society (since they are only produced to sell products), have also aided in the construction and perpetuation of stereotypes, to the point at which they have appeared natural and eternal (see Barthes 1977a; Williamson 1978, part 2). Through commercial photography we can therefore explore hegemonic constructs of, for example, race, gender, and class.

Photomontage — Concealing Social Relations
One of the key ways in which commercial photography has sought to determine particular readings of images and products has been through photomontage. Advertisements are in fact simple photomontages produced for commercial purposes, although most books on the technique seem to ignore this expansive area. While left photographers like Heartfield use photomontage to make invisible social relations visible, advertisers have used montage to conceal "reality." One of the peculiar advantages of photomontage, as John Berger wrote in his essay "The Political Uses of Photomontage," is the fact that "everything which has been cut out keeps its familiar photographic appearance. We are still looking first at things and only afterwards at symbols" (Berger 1972b; 1985). This creates a sense of naturalness about an image or message which is in fact constructed. An early example of the photomontage naturalizing social relations has been

discussed by Sally Stein, who considers "the reception of photography within the larger matrix of socially organized communication," and looks at the rise of Taylor's ideas of "scientific management" in the factory, and the way these ideas were also applied to domestic work (Stein 1981: 42–44). She also notes how expensive it was to have photomechanical reproductions within a book in the early part of the century.

Yet in Mrs. Christine Frederick's 1913 tract, *The New Housekeeping*, there were eight pages of glossy photographic images. This must have impressed the average reader. In her chapter on the new efficiency as applied to cooking, an image was provided which affirmed this ideology as the answer to women's work. The image consisted of a line drawing of an open card file, organized into types of dishes, and an example of a recipe card with a photograph of an elaborate lamb dish (see page 613). Despite Frederick's interest in precision, the card, which would logically be delineated by a black rectangular frame, does not match the dimensions of the file, nor does it contain practical information such as cost, number of servings, etc., which Frederick suggests in her text. As Stein points out, however, most readers must have overlooked this point when confronted with this luscious photographic image, which they would have accepted at face value.

> Because the page is not clearly divided between the file in one half and the recipe card in the other but instead flows uninterruptedly between drawing below, text of recipe, and photograph of the final dish, the meticulous organization of the file alone seems responsible for the full flowering of the dish.
> As a symbolic representation of modern house work, what you have in short order is a strict hierarchy, with an emblem of the family feast at its pinnacle.
>
> — STEIN 1981: 43

The more down-to-earth questions of time and money are ignored and almost banished. In response to those who believed that her reading was too contrived, Stein wrote: "If it seems that I am reading too much into this composite image, one need only note the title of Frederick's subsequent publication — *Meals that Cook Themselves*" (Stein 1992).

There are two key issues we can draw from Stein's analysis. Firstly, the example highlights the power of the photographic image to foster desire. While a rather ordinary image of a cake may have impressed an early twentieth-century audience, in the late twentieth century we are also mesmerized and impressed by the use of the latest technology, and it is still used to seduce us. Digital image-making is probably the field which is most effectively used today to capture our attention. We can see this clearly within TV commercials, such as the recent advertisements for Guinness and Holsten Pils lager. Spellbinding technology is also used within print advertisements, especially for photographic equipment. Ektakron film, for example, used a close-up of a bird's beak in 1989 to stun the viewer and the possible detail that could be achieved by using this film. The impact of the latest technology makes us forget the context of production, and the immediacy of the image makes the surface reality seem more real.

CROWN ROAST OF LAMB WITH PEAS AND STEAMED WAFFLE POTATOES

Select parts from two loins of lamb containing from seven to eleven ribs in each. Scrape the flesh from the bone between the ribs, as far down as the lean meat and trim off the back-bone. Keep the ribs on the outside, shape each piece in a semi-circle and sew together to form a crown. Tie securely. Cover each chop bone with a thin strip of salt pork to prevent burning. Dredge with flour, sprinkle with salt and pepper, and roast for an hour and a half until tender throughout. Remove the cubes of fat and replace with paper frills. Serve on a hot platter, with green peas in the centre of the crown, and steamed waffle potatoes around the base.

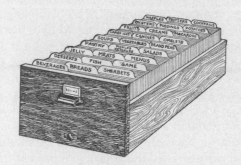

Specimen recipe card with illustration, from
Filing Cook Book
The New Housekeeping Filing Cook Book

Illustration from Mrs. Christine Frederick's *The New Housekeeping*, 1913.

Concealing Labor Relations

The second issue that Stein's analysis elucidates is the power of photo-montage in the commercial context to conceal labor relations. Judith Williamson has also discussed this with regard to a Lancia car advertisement from around 1978. The image depicts the Lancia Beta in an Italian vineyard. It shows a man who appears to be the owner, standing on the far side of the car with his back towards us, looking over a vineyard in which a number of peasants are working happily. In the distance, on a hill, is an old castle (this image is illustrated in Williamson 1979).

Williamson asks a series of questions:

> Who made this car? Has it just emerged new and gleaming from the soil, its finished form as much a product of nature as the grapes on the vine? . . . Who are these peasants? Have they made the car out in this most Italian field? . . . How can a car even exist in these feudal relations, how can such a contradiction be carried off? . . . What is this, if not a complete slipping over of the capitalist mode of production, as we survey a set of feudal class relations represented by the surveying gaze of possession, the look of the landlord with his back to us?
>
> — WILLIAMSON 1979: 53

Williamson also notes how the feudal Italian owner's gaze does not encompass both care (the product of industrial capitalism) and the owner's field of vision (the relations of Italian feudalism). She discusses the structure of the advertisement in order to understand why we don't question the contradictions of the image. The ad uses the traditional grammar of car advertisements with the showroom-effect camera angle, which intersects with the representation of "Italianness." The positioning of the car seems so casual that the man leaning against it could have just stopped to have a break and look at this Italian view. Maybe he is not Italian? Perhaps he will drive off and leave the "most Italian" scene behind. The narrative of chance on the horizontal axis of the photograph naturalises the vertical axis of Italian castle feudal relations and commodity ownership.

Contemporary advertisements also provide examples of the romanticized and non-industrial working environments. Hovis and other wholemeal bread producers have often used the image of the family bakery. Whisky distillers have also used this image to represent their brand as one which has been produced with special attention and one that has the experience of time behind it. . . .

Gendered Representations

Much of the literature which considers racist and sexist imagery, whilst using commercial photography for examples, has tended to discuss broader cultural readings rather than the commercial or photographic context. This section will discuss gendered representations.

The stereotypical and highly coded representations of women in popular culture have been given attention by many critics (Berger 1972a; Winship 1987a, 1987b; Williamson 1978). One of the key criticisms has been

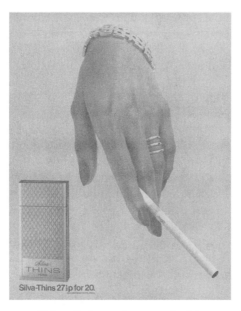

Silva-Thins 27½p for 20.

Women's hands have traditionally been photographed in ways that make them appear passive and decorative.

the way in which ads always represent women as objects to be surveyed. This has tended to increase the representation of women as objects to be surveyed. This has tended to increase the representation of women as both passive and objects of sexual desire. Erving Goffman has explored the body language used to represent men and women in his book *Gender Advertisements* to show how women in particular have been photographed for advertisements in ways that perpetuate gender roles (Goffman 1979). It is important to remember that the photographer always surveys his or her subject and personally selects what is believed to be worth photographing. The photographic process can also, therefore, exacerbate the voyeuristic gaze.

To understand the way in which men's and women's bodies are codified, we can look at the representation of hands in advertisements (see Winship 1987a). While male hands are often represented as active in advertising, female hands are usually represented as passive and decorative. In the Passion advertisement described earlier, for example, Liz Taylor did not even seem to be holding the bottle stopper properly; her hands were simply represented decoratively. In the ad below the female hand appears passive, with the cigarette only propped lightly between her fingers. It is also the woman's body — represented by fragments of her body here — that are highlighted as objects of sexual pleasure through the bright red nail polish. Today this coding continues, even in advertisements which appear to represent a degree of partnership. An advertisement for

Donna Karan perfume shows the male hands still taking the key role in an embrace. The man's arms practically cross the whole double-page spread. In contrast, the woman's hands simply curve upwards to touch his arms gently. Her action and pose do not enable her to play an equally active role in the embrace.

The fragmentation of the body — particularly women's bodies — is a feature of recent commercial photography. It makes the body more easily commodified and, with that, desire is also more easily packaged. In a content analysis of lipstick ads, Robert Goldman has pointed out that while most lipstick ads in 1946 depicted the whole body of a woman, by 1977 most ads only showed a part of the body (see ad on page 617). In this way beauty too is fragmented and commodified into ideal "types" of lips, noses, eyes, etc. One of the most famous examples of this fragmentation is the early 1980s advertisement for Pretty Polly tights, which depicted a woman's legs appearing out of an egg. This objectification and fragmentation of a woman's body received criticism at the time, with graffiti that read "born kicking." As Pollock indicates, it was only "after Picasso had visually hacked up the body, [that] we have been gradually accustomed to the cutting up of specifically feminine bodies: indeed, their cut-up-ness has come to be seen as a sign of that femininity." Significantly, Pollack adds that this "came to be naturalized by *photographic* representation in film, advertising, and pornography, all of which are discourses about desire that utilize the dialectic of fantasy and reality effects associated with the hegemonic modes of photographic representation" (Pollack 1990: 218; my emphasis).

Fashion Photography

So far I have concentrated on photographs within advertising, yet we cannot allow this area to subsume all discussion on photographs for commerce. Here, it is worth considering the genre of fashion photography, since this area of commercial photography has been particularly targeted with regard to discussions on the construction of femininity and gendered representations.

In *The Face of Fashion*, Jennifer Craik provides an historical account of the techniques of fashion photography from early photographic pictorialism of the nineteenth century, through the gendered constructions of the 1920s and 1930s which increasingly represented women as commodities, to the increasing dominance of the fashion photographer in the 1960s and the influence of filmatic techniques which led to clothes becoming more and more incidental within the fashion photograph. Craik also draws our attention to the increasing eroticism of 1970s and 1980s fashion photography. Most importantly she notes that the conventions of fashion photography are "neither fixed nor purposeful" (Craik 1994: 114). It is perhaps for this reason that critical literature on the genre as a whole is sparse. Most

Revlon introduces a new lipstick.

Revlon introduces a new lip conditioner.

Revlon introduces a new lipgloss.

Revlon introduces Formula 2.

Revlon introduces the great new lipstick and lipgloss in one.

Conditions. Colours. And shines.

Revlon Formula 2. New from the Revlon Research Group.

The commodification and fragmentation of women's bodies is a common feature of contemporary commercial photography.

of what has been written does not provide a critique of the genre as a whole, but tends to consider the constructions of gender and sexuality within these images. Femininity, as Craik notes, "became co-extensive with the fashion photograph" by the 1930s. The heightened sexuality of the fashion image in the 1970s and 1980s, with the work of photographers such as Helmut Newton, has been discussed by Rosetta Brooks (Brooks 1992: 17–24).

The way in which women read fashion images of women has also been explored (see Evans and Thornton 1989: ch. 5). As Berger commented: "Men look at women. Women watch themselves being looked at" (Berger 1972a: 47). As far as the photographic quality of the spreads are concerned, these have tended to be discussed in books, often commissioned by commercial enterprises such as *Vogue*, which eulogize these images and their relationship to "Art" photography. In this process the work of individual photographers has been discussed, rather than the genre itself. It is worth noting that even in their discussions of the fashion image and sexuality, that Brooks, as well as Evans and Thornton, discussed the issue through key examples of work by particular photographers. Their essays provide critical case studies of fashion images from the 1960s, 1970s, and 1980s by photographers such as Helmut Newton, Guy Bourdin, and Deborah Turbeville. In marking out fashion photography as an area for discussion, it seems clear that the glossy images which are mostly discussed contrast to the fashion photographs of the average mail-order catalogue, which could be described as fashion illustration.

Several signs or features of the fashion image which have been pointed out by various writers are worth considering together in order to understand the genre. Firstly, the transitory nature of fashion has impacted on the fashion image. Evans and Thornton have discussed this in terms of the ability of the fashion image to take "extraordinary liberties" and get away with images which are unduly violent, pornographic, or outrageous. Polly Devlin has pointed out the contradictory nature of the fashion image's transitoriness, by their aim to be both timely and timeless: "Its subject is a product with built-in obsolescence, and the result may be an amusing, ephemeral picture or a monumental statement" (Devlin 1979: 113).

There are other contradictions apparent within the fashion image. Rosetta Brooks has suggested that in fashion photography "we see the typical instead of the unique moment or event." Yet, at the same time as producing the typical, fashion photographers have aimed to construct a sense of what is original and unique within a particular fashion. They have also tried to produce images which stand their ground beyond the transitory space of the magazine and the transitory nature of fashion, and for example enter the gallery or the coffee-table book. The *Vogue Book of Fashion Photography* and the major Victoria and Albert Museum exhibition and its accompanying catalogue *Appearances: Fashion Photography since 1945* are testament to this conflict (Devlin 1979: Harrison 1991). Both provide a good collection of images of the classical fashion photograph, although the historical essays tend to be uncritical of the genre. It is clear that there are tensions in the relationship between fashion photography and both advertising photography and "Art" photography. The fashion image attempts to stand aloof from the undiluted commercial context of advertising, since most fashion spreads are commissioned by magazines which are not directly selling clothes. Yet the undeniable commercial angle has separated it from the "Art" photograph, despite the inevitable commercial context of the latter.

The relationship of the fashion spread to magazines rather than the manufacturers also emphasises the importance of the images' ability to project "a look, an image, a world" (Evans and Thornton 1989: 82). Their aim is not simply to highlight clothes, but rather to create identities. This construction has affected all fashion images, including those now produced by manufacturers. As Steve Edwards wrote, with regards to the *Next Directory*:

> As we flip the pages multiple identities whiz past our eyes. Distance and depth collapse into the intricate and exquisite surface of the image. What is there now to prevent us switching back and forth between these marvelous identities" She: now sipping tea on the lawn of the country seat, bathed in golden light, "well-dressed, well-bred," in that "endless summer." Now the belle of the southern states, young and raw, perhaps with an illicit negro lover. Now

the cultured woman, on her travels through Europe in search of adventure.
He: from the big city gentleman, to the rugged biker, to the fictions of Havana.
These are the worlds that the photograph has to offer. . . . Our only choice
is between its choices, we have no choice but to consume . . . or so the argument goes.

— EDWARDS 1989: 5

In constructing these identities, fashion photography also allows us to
view the social attitudes of a period.

In creating worlds of illusion, fashion photography has been influenced by all other areas of photographic practice. Early portrait photography and the *carte-devisite* had already established ways of photographing
people in fashionable or dramatic clothing, which were adopted by early
fashion photographers (Ewing 1991: 6–10). Fashion photographers such
as André Barre, Irving Penn, and Erwin Blumenfeld have also been influenced by Surrealism. The power of photojournalism and documentary
photography in the 1930s also affected fashion images, especially as photographers moved between the genres. Yet, the concentration on what is
contrived and stylized rather than the "captured" moment, so revered in
documentary, continues to set it apart. Films have also influenced fashion
photography, both in terms of content and the creation of looks and styles
and the way in which we are able to read what would otherwise appear
as fragmentary and disjointed image sequences in the fashion spread. In
creating images and "looks," the fashion photograph — in its attempts to
always find something new, different, glamorous, and often "exotic" — has
also been influenced by the increasing experience of international travel.
In the following case study we will therefore explore fashion and travel
images together. This should indicate the impossibility of considering
various commercial image-making forms in isolation. We live in a world
dominated by lifestyle culture, whose conventions are "neither fixed nor
purposeful."

Case Study: Tourism, Fashion and "the Other"

In this case study we will consider a particular hegemonic construction
from the nineteenth century — that of the exotic/primitive "Other" — and
explore the way in which it has been exploited in the commercial world.
Some of the most dominant ideological and photographic constructs were
developed during the nineteenth century, a period of European imperial
expansion. This history has affected the representation of black people in
all forms of photographic practice (see Gupta 1986; Bailey 1988; *Ten/8* 16;
Ten/8 2(3)). During the nineteenth century, the camera joined the gun in
the process of colonization. The camera was used to record and define
those who were colonized according to the interests of the West. This
unequal relationship of power between the white photographer and the

colonized subject has been discussed by many (Bate 1993; Schildkrout 1991; Prochaska 1991; Freedman 1990; Edwards 1992). These early anthropological and geographical photographers were sometimes paid employees of companies who organized campaigns to explore new markets. Emile Torday, for example — an anthropologist who used photography as a research aid — was paid by the Belgian Kasai Company to explore the Congo.

This history of photography is integrally linked to colonial and economic exploitation. A sense of submission, exoticism, and the "primitive" were key feelings, which these photographers documented and catalogued. Through these images, the European photographer and viewer could perceive their own superiority. Europe was defined as "the norm" upon which all other cultures should be judged. That which was different was disempowered by its very "Otherness."

During the period, the sense of "Otherness" and exoticism was not only captured "in the field" but was also exploited by photographers working in commercial enterprises. Malek Alloula has documented the genre of exotic/erotic colonial postcards which were sent by French colonists back to France. In his book *The Colonial Harem* he discusses images of Algerian women taken by French studio photographers in Algeria (Alloula 1987). In the confines of the studio, French photographers constructed visions of exoticism which suited their own colonial fantasies and those of the European consumers of these images. The paid Algerian models could only remain silent to the colonizers' abuse of their bodies. These images encapsulate Edward Said's description of Flaubert's Egyptian courtesan:

> She never spoke of herself, she never represented her emotions, her presence or history. He spoke for and represented her. He was foreign, comparatively wealthy, male, and these were historical facts of domination that allowed him not only to possess Kuchuk Hanem physically but to speak for her and tell his readers in what way she was typically oriental.
>
> — Said 1985: 6

The dominance of photographs of women in these commercial images is not by chance. Colonial power could be more emphatically represented through gendered relations — the white, wealthy male photographer versus the non-white, poor female subject. These images, bought and sold in their thousands, reflect the commodification of women's bodies generally in society. They are also part of the development of postcard culture which enabled the consumption of photographs by millions. The production of exotic postcards also brought photographs of the "Empire" and the non-European world into every European home. It was not only the photographs of non-European women which were sold: landscape photographs, which constructed Europe as developed and the non-European world as under-developed, were also popular (Prochaska 1991). These colonial visions continue to pervade contemporary travel photography, not only through postcards, but also in travel brochures and tourist ephemera.

Tourism

Today, many areas of commercial photography exploit exoticism and "Otherness," along with the ingredient of glamour to invite and entice viewers and consumers. In this way, some of the ideological constructs of colonial domination have become so naturalized that we hardly notice them. In the tourist industry, images of exoticized women and children in traditional garb are used to encourage travel through tourist brochures, posters, and TV campaigns. With submissive smiles and half-hidden faces these images, echoing those discussed by Alloula, continue to construct the East as the submissive female and the West as the authoritative male (see page 622). The non-European world is represented as a playground for the West. The bombardment of these images denies the reality of re-sourcefulness and intense physical work which actually constitutes most women's lives in the Third World. In the 1970s, Paul Wombell commented on this construct in a photomontage, which contrasted the fantasy tourist world with the reality for many Asian women workers in Britain. In many tourist advertisements, the image of work is so glamorized that we cannot perceive the reality.

The dominant photographic language of the tourist brochure has also affected how tourists construct their own photographs. These snapshots tend to reinforce the constructed and commodified experience of travel: what is photographed is that which is different and out of the ordinary. Most tourist snapshots also use a vocabulary of photographic practice which is embedded in power relations. Let us look at the photographs by Western tourists in the non-Western world. Tourism within Europe produces a slightly different set of relations. In the non-Western world, the majority of tourists who travel abroad are Western. Automatically a relationship of economic power is established, both generally and in terms of camera ownership.

While Don Slater (1983) has discussed the contradictory way in which the expansion of camera ownership has not led to new or challenging photographic practices in the non-Western world, this contradiction between ownership and practice is less evident. Tourists, having already consumed an array of exotic and glamorized photographs of the place before arrival, search out these very images and sites to visit and photograph in order to feel that their trip is complete. While many of the experiences revolve around architectural monuments, the desire to consume exotic/anthropological images of people has found a new trade, which has its parallel in the earlier studio-anthropological photography. In many tourist locations — in India, Morocco, and Algeria, for example — men and women sit in elaborate garb which the tourist can recognize as traditional and, more importantly, exotic. These people wait for those willing to pay to have their photograph taken with them. Tourism creates its own culture for consumption. Just like the model in the studio, he or she is also paid by the photographer to conform to an image which has already been constructed. Alternatively, at other sites, the tourist can dress up as part of the exotic

"Morocco," 1990. The "East" is still represented as an exotic and erotic playground for the "West."

experience, and photograph themselves (see page 623). The trade in these new "anthropological" images may have expanded to include the unknown snapshooter, but their purpose is not to encourage an understanding of a culture, but rather to commodify and consume yet another aspect of a place through the photographic image — the people.

Fashion

In fashion photography the consumption of "Other" worlds is domesticated through the familiar context of the fashion magazine and the more-often-than-not white model. In some cases it is hard to know where one genre ends and the other begins. Within fashion, the ordinary is made to appear extraordinary, and vice versa. Fashion photography, as I have already mentioned, is blatantly concerned with the constructed photograph.

Tourist Photograph. This photograph was taken in a carpet shop where tourists could dress up and role-play in a mock Bedouin tent.

It is also concerned with what is exotic, dramatic, glamorous, and different. Therefore, it is easy to see how some photographers have moved between areas of anthropological and fashion photography. Irving Penn's *Worlds in a Small Room* are a series of constructed images of peoples from around the world, whom Penn photographed while on assignments for *Vogue* (Penn 1974). In these images the genres of fashion and visual anthropology seem to collapse. The images tell us little about the people, but say a lot about Penn's construction of these people as primitive and exotic. As with the fashion shoot, these images are contrived and stylized, and Penn is at pains to find what is extraordinary and to create the dramatic. The isolated space of the studio removes the subjects from their own time and space, in a similar way to the French colonial postcards discussed above, and gives the photographer free rein to create every aspect

Arabia Behind the Veil (British *Marie Claire*, September 1988)

of the image. Interestingly, Penn described this studio space as "a sort of neutral area" (Penn 1974: 9). Yet, as we look through his book and peruse the photographs of Penn constructing his shots, the unequal relationship of power makes a mockery of the notion of neutrality.

The latent relationship between fashion and popular anthropological photography explains why the fashion magazine *Marie Claire* could include articles about ethnography without losing the tone of the fashion magazine. In their first issue, the article "Arabia Behind the Veil" represented the jewellery and make-up of Arab women in a series of plates, like fashion ideas (see above and opposite). If we look closely at the images it is clear that the photographer has used just two or three models and dressed them differently to represent a series of styles, just like a fashion shoot.

women, then, adopted the veil with the same intention as the Arab women of today: as a shield against the visual aggression and intrusion of men. The most well-documented, archaic function of the veil, therefore, remains simply to protect and preserve.

Sustaining a certain ambiguity of identity is vital in the battle against destructive forces. Moslems often change their names when they enter a strange village or when they fall ill, to avoid tempting fate (understandably making the administration of health centres unduly complicated); and people here do not kiss due to the belief that an open mouth allows bad spirits to enter and the soul to escape. Veiling, make-up and name-changing are all different methods of separating the individual from the malevolent forces, whether human or spiritual, of the outside world.

There is a rigidly drawn division in Arabia between public life, at work, and private life, at home. This is hard for the outward-looking Westerner to grasp, but maintaining the extreme seclusion of the domestic sphere has, particularly in Saudi, developed over the centuries and become a kind of congenital male obsession. A woman who emerges from the confines of the home unveiled goes beyond inviting the advances of strangers: she is in fact, exposing the most vehemently guarded element, prize even, of private life.

Moslems are burdened with an inescapable pressure that comes from constant social surveillance. Each individual is considered responsible for the actions of his neighbours, so a form of sacred citizen's arrest exists whereby people can successfully become their brother's keeper. In Riyadh, even driving through an amber light might lead to the person being followed, detained and denounced by a complete stranger.

It may seem like a distorted view of independence, but the veil can actually serve to release women from the stress of such intense vigilance; behind the thick black curtain, many Arab women feel liberated by their anonymity.

And the veil does not in itself prevent women from educating themselves or working and can actually co-exist with a surprising amount of freedom. For instance, in a region to the east of Yemen, women – even though they accept the veil – still practise the custom of 'temporary mar-

> **Maintaining the extreme seclusion of the domestic sphere has developed over the centuries to become a kind of congenital male obsession**

Arabia Behind the Veil — *cont'd*

In fashion photography we can see the continued use of the "harem" image, for example, as the site of colonial fantasy and as being oppositional to the white "norm." In the November 1988 issue of *Company* magazine, a fashion spread titled "Arabesque: Rock the Casbah — This is Evening Wear to Smoulder in" features nonwhite women in brocaded clothes, sitting and lying indoors on heavily ornamented fabrics, while pining over black and white photographs of men. The photographs of the women are bathed in an orangey, rich light. By contrasting color and black and white photography, the men seem to appear more distant and further unobtainable. The representation of sexuality here is of an unhealthy obsession. In contrast, the fashion spread following it, "Cold Comfort," features a white couple together, in a relationship of relative equality. Blue and brown predominate, in contrast to the previous spread, and the much more standard photographic lighting contrasts with the previous yellow haze, to present images which seem much more matter-of-fact, like the denim clothing advertised. Here, however, matter-of-factness acts to represent Europe as rational in opposition to the irrational East.

In *Marie Claire*'s June 1994 issue, another pair of fashion spreads also provides an example of the oppositional way in which East and West are presented, not just through content, but also through photographic codes. In "Indian Summer," the image of an exotic woman in physical and sexual abandon predominates the pages, as in the previous spread and the colonial postcards already discussed. The pages of this photo-story are almost like a film sequence with rapid cuts. As in the last "Orientalist" sequence, this woman is alone, but the themes of physical and sexual desire are paramount. Many of the shots use wide angles to enhance their depth and, along with rich oranges and blues, it gives the sequence a heightened sense of physicality. The spread which follows this, entitled "The Golden Age of Hollywood," contrasts by representing white men and women together, in relative harmony. This sequence is much more about glamour than "Cold Comfort," yet here again the notion of rationality is also encouraged by the style of clothing as well as the standard photographic lens used. There is also an almost colonial feel to this fashion spread, through the sepia tones of the photographs and the 1930s styling. The other important difference between the two fashion spreads is that, while the latter concentrates on the clothing, the former concentrates on atmosphere. The context of these images within the fashion magazine leaves the predominantly white women as the surveyors of "Other" women.

While I have discussed the use of colonial and exotic photographic messages in tourist and fashion photography separately, within the recent dominance of lifestyle culture there is little difference between these forms. Sisley's photo "magazine" from Spring/Summer 1990 makes this clear. The subject of this fashion label's photo magazine was a Moroccan caravan tour. Along with the series of travel photographs of a European man and woman, presumably in Sisley clothes, is the male traveller's diary. There is no written information on the clothes, and they are clearly not the main subject of the photographs, which concentrate on building up an atmosphere of unhindered travel. It is not just the fashion advertiser that has manipulated "the exotic" into a lifestyle and a fashion statement. Fashion magazines such as *Elle* and *Vogue* have done the same. *Elle*'s fashion spread from November 1987 entitled "Weave a Winter's Tale of Fashion's Bright New Folklore" was shot in Peru, and combines photographs of the season's clothes with tourist brochure images (see page 627). The main text is of a travel diary, with a subtext of photo titles that combine tourist descriptions and clothing details that include prices. Here, Peru is turned into the flavor of the month for fashion influence and tourism, which are not distinguished between in layout and photographic format. In a similar vein, *Vogue* focused on Egypt in their May 1989 issue.

Tourism and fashion marketing collide in this feature. (British *Elle*, November 1987).

   Images and photographs for both these magazines are the key to their commercial success. Here, there is also no distinct line between the advertisement and editorial photograph. What is clear, however, is the dominance of commercial interest in all these photographic images, which are contrived and stylized and are "positioned on a threshold between two worlds: the consumer public and a mythic elite created in the utopia of the photograph as well as in the reality of a social group maintained by the fashion industry" (Brooks 1992: 18–19).

The Context of the Image

Don Slater has criticized the semiotic critique of advertisements (characterized by writers such as Roland Barthes and Judith Williamson) for taking as assumed precisely what needs to be explained — "the relations and practices within which discourses are formed and operated" (Slater 1983: 258). Barthes' and Williamson's readings of advertisements have only provided a very limited social and historical context. Often even simple pieces of information, such as the magazine from which the images have been extracted and the date of advertisements, have not been mentioned. Liz Wells has commented on some of the limitations of *Decoding Advertisements*, especially Williamson's lack of consideration of multiple readings (Wells 1992).

While scholars have devoted some space to the understanding of a broad cultural context, the exploration of political and economic contexts is more rare. The vast array of commercial messages has also made their contextualization increasingly difficult. It would be impossible to contextualize them all. Information about processes of production are not always easily available, and this increases the reality of consumption over that of production:

> What commodities fail to communicate to consumers is information about
> the process of production. Unlike goods in earlier societies, they do not bear
> the signature of their makers, whose motives and actions we might access
> because we knew who they were. . . . The real and full meaning of production
> is hidden beneath the empty appearance in exchange. Only once the real mean-
> ing has been systematically emptied out of commodities does advertising then
> refill this void with its own symbols. Production empties. Advertising fills.
> The real is hidden by the imaginary.
>
> — JHALLY 1990: 50

To decode photographs and advertising images more effectively, it is essential for us to understand their context. Let us take, for example, Williamson's reading of the Lancia car advertisement (1979). Would a discussion of Lancia manufacturing and car production in the late 1970s reveal more about the image?

Since the founding of the Lancia firm in 1907, Lancia had been known for their production of quality cars for gentlemen, as one writer described it. With increasing conglomeration in all industries throughout the twentieth century, Lancia, as a family firm, ran into trouble and was eventually taken over by Fiat in 1969 (Weernink 1979). The Beta saloon was the first car to be produced by Lancia after the merger. First, which was known for producing smaller, cheaper cars, needed to distinguish the Beta from its own cars. Style and quality needed to be suggested, and "Lancia — the Most Italian Car" was the slogan used to enhance the sense of stylishness of the Lancia range generally. It is this slogan which has been visualised in the 1979 advertisement discussed by Williamson.

Apart from asserting a sense of style and quality, why has Lancia chosen to represent any form of labor relations in the advertisement? Most car advertisements of this period tended to talk about the car itself and its features — for example, its economical use of petrol or the size of its boot. This advertisement does not discuss the car's actual features at all. In the late 1970s strikes took place in many major industries in Britain and Europe. In September 1978, for example, the Ford car workers at Dagenham went on strike for nine weeks. Car manufacturers generally must have wanted to maintain an image of good industrial relations. The illusion of the contented happy peasant worker in the vineyards depicted by the ad discussed earlier glosses over the general unrest that was present during this period. Finally, the image of the peasant worker could carry another function. During the mid-1970s, the car industry began to introduce microprocessors into production for increased automation. The peasant workers depicted in the ad, outside of industrial production, also acted to represent Lancia has a quality "hand-crafted," "gentleman's" car.

Image Worlds

Let us look at an example of marketing photography, where an understanding of the context within which images are produced helps us to perceive the extent to which commercial interests affect photographic practice. David Nye, in *Image Words*, gives us a detailed exploration of the context of production, dissemination, and historical setting of General Electric's photographs between 1900 and 1930 (Nye 1985). As Nye notes, commercial photographers do not strive for uniqueness (as does the artist photographer), but rather for a solidity of a predictable character. In spite of their documentary appearance, Nye notes the contrast between the images produced by a socially concerned documentary photographer and a commercial photographer, even when the subject is the same. He compares two photographs of Southern textile mills, one by Lewis Hine, the other by a photographer working for General Electric. While Hine emphasises the people and children in the mills who work in potentially dangerous environments, the commercial photographer's image stresses machinery, electrification, and technical progress (Nye 1985: 55–56).

Nye also notes how, by the beginning of the twentieth century, the management of General Electric discovered the need to address four distinct groups — engineers, blue collar workers, managers, and consumers. Their desire to say different things to different groups affected the production of images for the company's various publications. While the *General Electric Review* (a company-sponsored scientific journal) used photographs which emphasized the machines, the publications for workers employed images which concentrated on the idea of the corporation as community.

Nye not only notes the varying sorts of photographs for different publications, but also the changing production of images over time. While images from 1880 to 1910 expressed a sense of relationship between workers and

Schenectady *Works News* **General Electric** (2 November 1923). Images which represented individual workers engrossed in a piece of interesting work dominated the cover of *Works News* during the 1920s. It did not represent the reality for most workers, but presented images which gave a certain dignity and harmony during a period fraught with conflicts.

managers (they were often photographed together), images after this date present a picture of a workforce which was much more highly controlled by management. Nye details how by the 1920s General Electric had 82,000 workers in their employment, in contrast to 6,000 in 1885. The burgeoning workforce made management's role more important, and the artisanal skills of the previous era had also all but disappeared. Labor unrest began to increase during the 1910s. In 1917, partly in response to these conflicts, General Electric began to publish a magazine called *Works News* which was distributed to all blue collar workers twice a month. The paper did not address the general workforce, but was tailored to each site. The covers of the magazine produced a new kind of photographic image not previously used by the company. They featured individual skilled workers photographed from head to toe and engrossed in a piece of interesting work. This kind of image was repeated on the cover of nearly every issue of *Works News* (see page 630), and did not represent the reality for most of General Electric's employees; but, since these workers were individualized and isolated, the generalization was only implicit. These kinds of images hardly existed inside the magazine, which concentrated instead on the workers — as a community which went on holiday, played in sports teams, and participated in other forms of recreation. The style of the cover photographs had a history in Lewis Hine's work a decade earlier. He had aimed to represent and give dignity to "real men" in difficult work. In adopting this style, the General Electric photographers were simply using it as a representational strategy to define the image world of the General Electric plant. It is only through an appreciation of the context of the image that we can understand the intent in the production of images by Hine and the General Electric photographer as different, and can therefore appreciate the different meanings of the image. The production of meaning is a process: As Marx noted in *Grundrisse*:

> It is not only the object that production creates for consumption . . . [It] also gives consumption its precise nature, its character, its finish. . . . Hunger is hunger, but the hunger that is satisfied by cooked meat eaten with a knife and fork is a different hunger from that which bolts down raw meat with the aid of hand nail and tooth. Production thus produces not only the object but also the manner of consumption, not only objectively but also subjectively.
>
> — Marx quoted in Slater 1983: 247

NOTES

1. As stated in anti-Apartheid campaign literature of the time.

BIBLIOGRAPHY

Key Texts

Alloula, Malek (1987) *The Colonial Harem*, Manchester: Manchester University Press.
Back, L. and Quaade, V. (1993) "Dream Utopias, Nightmare Realities: Imagining Race and Culture within the World of Benetton," *Third Text 22*.
Barthes, Roland (1977a) "The Rhetoric of the Image" in *Image, Music, Text*, London: Fontana.
Berger, John (1972a) *Ways of Seeing*, London: BBC.
Brooks, Rosetta (1992) "Fashion Photography" in J. Ash and E. Wilson (eds.) *Chic Thrills: A Fashion Reader*, London: Pandora.
Craik, Jennifer (1994) "Soft Focus: Techniques of Fashion Photography" in *The Face of Fashion*, London: Routledge.
Evans, C. and Thornton, M. (1989) *Women and Fashion: A New Look*, London: Quartet.
Goldman, Robert (1992) *Reading Ads Socially*, London: Routledge.
Myers, Kathy (1990) "Selling Green" in C. Squiers (ed.) *The Critical Image: Essays on Contemporary Photography*, Seattle: Bay Press.

Nye, David (1985) *Image Worlds: Corporate Identities at General Electric 1890–1930*, Cambridge, MA: MIT Press.

Slater, Don (1983) "Marketing Mass Photography" in P. Davis and H. Walton (eds.) *Language, Image, Media*, Oxford: Blackwell.

Squiers, Carol (1992) "The Corporate Year in Pictures" in R. Bolton (ed.) *The Contest of Meaning: Critical Histories of Photography*, Cambridge, MA: MIT Press.

Stein, Sally (1981) "The Composite Photographic Image and the Composition of Consumer Ideology," *Art Journal*, Spring 1981.

Tagg, John (1988) "A Democracy of the Image: Photographic Portraiture and Commodity Production" in *The Burden of Representation: Essays on Photographies and Histories*, Basingstoke: Macmillan.

Williamson, Judith (1978) *Decoding Advertisements: Ideology and Meaning in Advertising*, London: Marion Boyars.

—— (1979) "Great History that Photographs Mislaid" in Photography Workshop (ed.) *Photography/Politics One*, London: Comedia.

Winship, Janice (1987a) "Handling Sex" in R. Betterton (ed.) *Looking On: Images of Femininity in the Visual Arts and Media*, London: Pandora.

Other References

Bacher, Fred (1992) "The Popular Condition: Fear and Clothing in LA," *The Humanist*, September/October.

Bailey, David (1988) "Re-thinking Black Representations" *Ten/8* 31.

—— (1989) "People of the World" in P. Wombell (ed.) *The Globe: Representing the World*, York, Impressions Gallery.

Baker, Lindsay (1991) "Taking Advertising to its Limit," *Times* 22 July, p. 29.

Barthes, Roland (1977b) "The Photographic Message" in S. Heath (ed.) *Image, Music, Text*, London: Fontana.

Bate, David (1993) "Photography and the Colonial Vision," *Third Text* 22.

Belussi, Fiorenza (1987) *Benetton: Information Technology in Production and Distribution: A Case Study of the Innovative Potential of Traditional Sectors*, SPRU, University of Sussex.

Benetton (1993) *Global Vision: Untied Colors of Benetton*, Tokyo: Robundo.

Benson, S. H. (nd) *Some Examples of Benson Advertising*. S. H. Benson Firm.

Berger, John (1972b) "The Political Uses of Photomontage" in *Selected Essays and Articles, the Look of Things*, Harmondsworth: Penguin.

Devlin, Polly (1979) *Vogue Book of Fashion Photography*, London: Conde Nast.

Edwards, Elizabeth (ed.) (1992) *Anthropology and Photography 7860–7920*, New Haven: Yale University Press.

Edwards, Steve (1989) "The Snapshooters of History," *Ten/8* 32.

Ewing, William (1991) "Perfect Surface" in *The Idealizing Vision: The Art of Fashion Photography*, New York: Aperture.

Freedman, Jim (1990) "Bringing it all Back Home: A Commentary on Into the Heart of Africa," *Museum Quarterly*, February.

Goffman, Erving (1979) *Gender Advertisements*, London: Macmillan.

Graham, Judith (1989) "Benetton 'Colors' the Race Issue" *Advertising Age*.

Gupta, Sunil (1986) "Northern Media, Southern Lives" in *Photography Workshop* (ed.) *Photography/Politics: Two*, London: Comedia.

Hall, Stuart (1993) "Encoding/Decoding" in S. Durring (ed.) *The Cultural Studies Reader*, London: Routledge (first published in 1980).

Harrison, Martin (1991) *Appearances: Fashion Photography Since 1945*, London: V & A.

Jhally, Sut (1990) *Codes of Advertising*, London: Routledge.

Leiss, W., Kline, S., and Jhally, S. (1986) *Social Communication in Advertising*, Toronto: Methuen.

Mayle, Peter (1983) *Thirsty Work: Ten Years of Heineken Advertising*. London: Macmillan.

Mitter, Swasti (1986) "Flexibility and Control: The Case of Benetton" in *Common Fate Common Bond; Women in the Global Economy*, London: Pluto.

Morris, Roderick C. (1992) "The Best Possible Taste," *Spectator*, 15 February.

Myers, Kathy (1986) *Understains: Sense and Seduction in Advertising*, London: Comedia.

Penn, Irving (1974) *Worlds in a Small Room*, London: Studio Vista.

Phizacklea, Annie (1990) "The Benetton Model" in *Unpackaging the Fashion Industry: Gender, Racism and Class in Production*, London: Routledge.

Pollock, Griselda (1990) "Missing Women — Re-Thinking Early Thoughts on Images of Women" in C. Squiers (ed.) *The Critical Image: Essays on Contemporary Photography*, Seattle: Bay Press.

Posner, Jill (1982) *Spray it Loud*, London: Routledge.

Prochaska, David (1991) "Fantasia of the Phototheque: French Postcard Views of Senegal," *African Arts*, October.

Richards, Thomas (1990) *Commodity Culture in Victorian Britain*, London: Verso.

Said, Edward (1985) *Orientalism*, London: Penguin (first published in 1978).

Savan, Leslie (1990) "Logo-rrhea," *voice*, 24 November, New York.

Schildkrout, Enid (1991) "The Spectacle of Africa Through the Lens of Herbert Lang," *African Arts*, October.

Sontag, Susan (1979) *On Photography*, Harmondsworth: Penguin.

Stein, Sally (1992) "The Graphic Ordering of Desire: Modernization of a Middle-Class Women's Magazine 1919–1939" in R. Bolton (ed.) *The Contest of Meaning: Critical Histories of Photography*, Cambridge, MA: MIT Press.

Ten/8 16 "Black Image — Staying On."

Ten/8 2(3) "Critical Decade — Black British Photography in the '80s."

Weernink, Wim (1979) *La Lancia: 70 Years of Excellence*, London: Motor Racing Publications.

Wells, Liz (1992) "Judith Williamson, Decoding Advertisements" in *Reading into Cultural Studies*, London: Routledge.

Williams, Raymond (1980) "Advertising the Magic System" in *Problems in Materialism and Culture*, London: Verso.

Winship, Janice (1987b) *Inside Women's Magazines*, London: Pandora.

■ EDWARD SAID

States

Born in Jerusalem, Palestine, Edward Said (1935–2003) lived as a child in both Palestine and Egypt until 1948, when, after the establishment of the State of Israel, his family was driven out of Palestine and became refugees in Egypt. Said's parents later sent him to a boarding school in the United States, where he continued to live until his death. Even when he is not writing directly about the fate of the Palestinian people, it is difficult to separate Said's writing from the politics of his experience as an Arab, especially a Palestinian. Said's work as a literary scholar — he was University Professor of English and Comparative Literature at Columbia University — is also shaped by what he calls "the experience of dislocation, exile, migration, and empire," which predisposed him to identify and articulate moments of alienation. Indeed, nowhere perhaps is Said's writing more powerful than in its attempt to chronicle the experience of exile and the feeling of perpetual loss that attends it. The essay "States" is excerpted from Said's book *After the Last Sky: Palestinian Lives* (1986), a collaborative project with Swiss photographer Jean Mohr.

Caught in a meager, anonymous space outside a drab Arab city, outside a refugee camp, outside the crushing time of one disaster after another, a wedding party stands, surprised, sad, slightly uncomfortable [below]. Palestinians — the telltale mixture of styles and attitudes is so evidently theirs — near Tripoli in northern Lebanon. A few months after this picture was taken their camp was ravaged by intra-Palestinian fighting. Cutting across the wedding party's path here is the ever-present Mercedes, emblazoned with its extra mark of authenticity, the proud *D* for *Deutschland*. A rare luxury in the West, the Mercedes — usually secondhand and smuggled in — is the commonest of cars in the Levant. It has become what horse, mule, and camel were, and then much more. Universal taxi, it is a symbol of modern technology domesticated, of the intrusion of the West into traditional life, of illicit trade. More important, the Mercedes is the all-purpose conveyance, something one uses for everything — funerals, weddings, births, proud display, leaving home, coming home, fixing, stealing, reselling, running away in, hiding in. But because Palestinians have no state of their own to shield them, the Mercedes, its provenance and destination obscure, seems like an intruder, a delegate of the forces that both dislocate and hem them in. "The earth is closing on us, pushing us through the last passage," writes the poet Mahmoud Darwish.

The paradox of mobility and insecurity. Wherever we Palestinians are, we are not in our Palestine, which no longer exists. You travel, from

Tripoli, Badawi Camp, May 1983

one end of the Arab world to the other, in Europe, Africa, the Americas, Australia, and there you find Palestinians like yourself who, like yourself, are subject to special laws, a special status, the markings of a force and violence not yours. Exiles at home as well as abroad, Palestinians also still inhabit the territory of former Palestine (Israel, the West Bank, Gaza), in sadly reduced circumstances. They are either "the Arabs of Judea and Samaria," or, in Israel, "non-Jews." Some are referred to as "present absentees." In Arab countries, except for Jordan, they are given special cards identifying them as "Palestinian refugees," and even where they are respectable engineers, teachers, business people, or technicians, they know that in the eyes of their host country they will always be aliens. Inevitably, photographs of Palestinians today include this fact and make it visible.

Memory adds to the unrelieved intensity of Palestinian exile. Palestine is central to the cultures of Islam, Christianity, and Judaism; Orient and Occident have turned it into a legend. There is no forgetting it, no way of overlooking it. The world news is often full of what has happened in Palestine-Israel, the latest Middle East crisis, the most recent Palestinian exploits. The sights, wares, and monuments of Palestine are the objects of commerce, war, pilgrimage, cults, the subjects of literature, art, song, fantasy. East and West, their high and their commercial cultures, have

Tel Sheva, 1979. A village of settled nomads near Bersheeba. Some years ago, these people still lived in a tent, under the desert sky. The carpet on the ground is the only reminder of that earlier period.

descended on Palestine. Bride and groom wear the ill-fitting nuptial costumes of Europe, yet behind and around them are the clothes and objects of their native land, natural to their friends and attendants. The happiness of the occasion is at odds with their lot as refugees with nowhere to go. The children playing nearby contrast starkly with the unappealing surroundings; the new husband's large workman's hands clash with his wife's delicate, obscuring white. When we cross from Palestine into other territories, even if we find ourselves decently in new places, the old ones loom behind us as tangible and unreal as reproduced memory or absent causes for our present state.

Sometimes the poignancy of resettlement stands out like bold script imposed on faint pencil traces. The fit between body and new setting is not good. The angles are wrong. Lines supposed to decorate a wall instead form an imperfectly assembled box in which we have been put. We perch on chairs uncertain whether to address or evade our interlocutor. This child is held out, and yet also held in. Men and women re-express the unattractiveness around them: The angle made across her face by the woman's robe duplicates the ghastly wall pattern, the man's crossed feet repeat and contradict the outward thrust of the chair leg. He seems unsettled, poised for departure. Now what? Now where? All at once it is our transience and impermanence that our visibility expresses, for we can be seen as figures forced to push on to another house, village, or region. Just as we once were taken from one "habitat" to a new one, we can be moved again.

Exile is a series of portraits without names, without contexts. Images that are largely unexplained, nameless, mute. I look at them without precise anecdotal knowledge, but their realistic exactness nevertheless makes a deeper impression than mere information. I cannot reach the actual people who were photographed, except through a European photographer who saw them for me. And I imagine that he, in turn, spoke to them through an interpreter. The one thing I know for sure, however, is that they treated him politely but as someone who came from, or perhaps acted at the direction of, those who put them where they so miserably are. There was the embarrassment of people uncertain why they were being looked at and recorded. Powerless to stop it.

When A. Z.'s father was dying, he called his children, one of whom is married to my sister, into his room for a last family gathering. A frail, very old man from Haifa, he had spent his last thirty-four years in Beirut in a state of agitated disbelief at the loss of his house and property. Now he murmured to his children the final faltering words of a penniless, helpless patriarch. "Hold on to the keys and the deed," he told them, pointing to a battered suitcase near his bed, a repository of the family estate salvaged from Palestine when Haifa's Arabs were expelled. These intimate mementos of a past irrevocably lost circulate among us, like the genealogies and fables of a wandering singer of tales. Photographs, dresses, objects severed from their original locale, the rituals of speech and custom: Much

Amman, 1984. A visit to the former mayor of Jerusalem and his wife, in exile in Jordan.

reproduced, enlarged, thematized, embroidered, and passed around, they are strands in the web of affiliations we Palestinians use to tie ourselves to our identity and to each other.

Sometimes these objects, heavy with memory — albums, rosary beads, shawls, little boxes — seem to me like encumbrances. We carry them about, hang them up on every new set of walls we shelter in, reflect lovingly

Ramallah, 1979. An everyday street scene, banal and reassuring. And yet, the tension is constant. A passing military jeep, a flying stone — the incident, the drama, can occur at any moment.

on them. Then we do not notice the bitterness, but it continues and grows nonetheless. Nor do we acknowledge the frozen immobility of our atti-tudes. In the end the past owns us. My father spent his life trying to escape these objects, "Jerusalem" chief among them — the actual place as much as its reproduced and manufactured self. Born in Jerusalem, as were his parents, grandparents, and all his family back in time to a distant vanishing point, he was a child of the Old City who traded with tourists in bits of the true cross and crowns of thorn. Yet he hated the place; for him, he often said, it meant death. Little of it remained with him except a fragmentary story or two, an odd coin or medal, one photograph of his father on horseback, and two small rugs. I never even saw a picture of my grandmother's face. But as he grew older, he reverted to old Jerusalemite expressions that I did not understand, never having heard them during the years of my youth.

Identity — who we are, where we come from, what we are — is difficult to maintain in exile. Most other people take their identity for granted. Not the Palestinian, who is required to show proofs of identity more or less constantly. It is not only that we are regarded as terrorists, but that our existence as native Arab inhabitants of Palestine, with primordial rights there (and not elsewhere), is either denied or challenged. And there is more. Such as it is, our existence is linked negatively to encomiums about Israel's democracy, achievements, excitement; in much Western rhetoric we have slipped into the place occupied by Nazis and anti-Semites; collectively, we can aspire to little except political anonymity and resettlement; we are known for no actual achievement, no characteristic worthy of esteem, except the effrontery of disrupting Middle East peace. Some Israeli settlers on the West Bank say: "The Palestinians can stay here, with no rights, as resident aliens." Other Israelis are less kind. We have no known Einsteins, no Chagall, no Freud or Rubinstein to protect us with a legacy of glorious achievements. We have had no Holocaust to protect us with the world's compassion. We are "other," and opposite, a flaw in the geometry of resettlement and exodus. Silence and discretion veil the hurt, slow the body searches, soothe the sting of loss.

A zone of recollected pleasure surrounds the few unchanged spots of Palestinian life in Palestine. The foodsellers and peddlers — itinerant vendors of cakes or corn — are still there for the casual eye to see, and they still provoke the appetite. They seem to travel not only from place to place, but from an earlier time to the present, carrying with them the same clientele — the young girls and boys, the homeward-bound cyclist, the loitering student or clerk — now as then. We buy their wares with the same surreptitiously found change (who can remember the unit? was it a piaster? fils? shilling?) spent on the same meager object, neither especially good nor especially well prepared. The luxurious pleasure of tasting the vendor's *simsim*, the round sesame cakes dipped in that tangy mixture of thyme and sumac, or his *durra*, boiled corn sprayed with salt, surpasses the mere act of eating and opens before us the altogether agreeable taste of food not connected with meals, with nourishment, with routine. But what a distance now actually separates me from the concreteness of that life. How easily traveled the photographs make it seem, and how possible to suspend the barriers keeping me from the scenes they portray.

For the land is further away than it has ever been. Born in Jerusalem in late 1935, I left mandatory Palestine permanently at the end of 1947. In the spring of 1948, my last cousin evacuated our family's house in West Jerusalem; Martin Buber subsequently lived there till his death, I have been told. I grew up in Egypt, then came to the United States as a student. In 1966 I visited Ramallah, part of the Jordanian West Bank, for a family wedding. My father, who was to die five years later, accompanied my sister and me. Since our visit, all the members of my family have resettled — in Jordan, in Lebanon, in the United States, and in Europe. As far as I know, I have no relatives who still live in what was once Palestine. Wars, revolutions, civil struggles have changed the countries I have lived in — Lebanon, Jordan, Egypt — beyond recognition. Until thirty-five years ago I could travel from Cairo to Beirut overland, through territories held or in other ways controlled by rival colonial powers. Now, although my mother lives in Beirut, I have not visited her since the Israeli invasion of 1982: Palestinians are no longer welcome there. The fact is that today I can neither return to the places of my youth, nor voyage freely in the countries and places that mean the most to me, nor feel safe from arrest or violence even in the countries I used to frequent but whose governments and policies have changed radically in recent times. There is little that is more unpleasant for me these days than the customs and police check upon entering an Arab country.

Consider the tremendous upheavals since 1948 each of which effectively destroyed the ecology of our previous existence. When I was born, we in Palestine felt ourselves to be part of a small community, presided over by the majority community and one or another of the outside powers holding sway over the territory. My family and I, for example, were members of a tiny Protestant group within a much larger Greek Orthodox Christian minority, within the larger Sunni Islam majority; the important outside power was Britain, with its great rival France a close second. But then after World War II Britain and France lost their hold, and for the first time we directly confronted the colonial legacy — inept rulers, divided populations, conflicting promises made to resident Arabs and mostly European Jews with incompatible claims. In 1948 Israel was established; Palestine was destroyed, and the great Palestinian dispossession began. In 1956 Egypt was invaded by Britain, France, and Israel, causing what was left of the large Levantine communities there (Italian, Greek, Jewish, Armenian, Syrian) to leave. The rise of Abdel Nasser fired all Arabs — especially Palestinians — with the hope of a revived Arab nationalism, but after the union of Syria with Egypt failed in 1961, the Arab cold war, as it has been called, began in earnest; Saudi Arabia versus Egypt, Jordan versus Syria, Syria versus Iraq. . . . A new population of refugees, migrant workers, and traveling political parties crisscrossed the Arab world. We Palestinians immersed ourselves in the politics of Baathism in Syria and Iraq, of Nasserism in Egypt, of the Arab Nationalist Movement in Lebanon.

The 1967 war was followed shortly after by the Arab oil boom. For the first time, Palestinian nationalism arose as an independent force in the Middle East. Never did our future seem more hopeful. In time, however, our appearance on the political scene stimulated, if it did not actually cause, a great many less healthy phenomena: fundamentalist Islam, Maronite nationalism, Jewish zealotry. The new consumer culture, the computerized economy, further exacerbated the startling disparities in the Arab world between rich and poor, old and new, privileged and disinherited. Then, starting in 1975, the Lebanese civil war pitted the various Lebanese sects, the Palestinians, and a number of Arab and foreign powers against each other. Beirut was destroyed as the intellectual and political nerve center of Arab life; for us, it was the end of our only important, relatively independent center of Palestinian nationalism, with the Palestinian Liberation Organization at its heart. Anwar Sadat recognized Israel, and Camp David further dismantled the region's alliances and disrupted its balance. After the Iranian revolution in 1979 came the Iran-Iraq war. Israel's 1982 invasion of Lebanon put more Palestinians on the move, as the massacres in the Palestinian refugee camps of Sabra and Shatila reduced the community still further. By the end of 1983, Palestinians were fighting each other, and Syria and Libya were directly involved, supporting Palestinian dissidents against PLO loyalists. With the irony typical of our political fate, however, in mid-1985 we were united together in Sabra and Shatila to fight off a hostile Shi'ite militia patronized by Syria.

The stability of geography and the continuity of land — these have completely disappeared from my life and the life of all Palestinians. If we are not stopped at borders, or herded into new camps, or denied reentry and residence, or barred from travel from one place to another, more of our land is taken, our lives are interfered with arbitrarily, our voices are prevented from reaching each other, our identity is confined to frightened little islands in an inhospitable environment of superior military force sanitized by the clinical jargon of pure administration. On the West Bank and in Gaza we confront several Zionist "master plans" — which, according to Meron Benvenisti, ex-deputy mayor of Jerusalem, are "explicitly sectarian." He continues:

> The criteria established to determine priorities of settlement regions are *"interconnection [havirah]"* between existing Jewish areas for the creation of [Jewish] settlement continuity" and *"separation [hayitz]"* to restrict uncontrolled Arab settlement and the prevention of Arab settlement blocs"; *"scarcity [hesech]"* refers to areas devoid of Jewish settlement." In these criteria "pure planning and political planning elements are included."
>
> — *The West Bank Data Project: A Survey of Israeli Policies*

Continuity for *them*, the dominant population; discontinuity for *us*, the dispossessed and dispersed.

The circle is completed, though, when we Palestinians acknowledge that much the same thesis is adhered to by Arab and other states where sizable Palestinian communities exist. There too we are in dispersed camps, regions, quarters, zones; but unlike their Israeli counterparts, these places are not the scientific product of "pure planning" or "political planning." The Baqa'a camp in Amman, the Palestinian quarter of Hawaly in Kuwait, are simply there.

All forms of Palestinian activity, all attempts at unity, are suspect. On the West Bank and Gaza, "development" (the systematic strengthening of Palestinian economic and social life) is forbidden, whereas "improvement" is tolerated so long as there isn't too much of it; so long as it doesn't become development. The colors of the Palestinian flag are outlawed by Israeli military law; Fathi Gabin of Gaza, an artist, was given a six-month prison sentence for using black, green, red, and white in one of his works. An exhibit of Palestinian culture at al-Najah University in Nablus earned the school a four-month closing. Since our history is forbidden, narratives are rare; the story of origins, of home, of nation is underground. When it appears it is broken, often wayward and meandering in the extreme, always coded, usually in outrageous forms — mock-epics, satires, sardonic parables, absurd rituals — that make little sense to an outsider. Thus Palestinian life is scattered, discontinuous, marked by the artificial and imposed arrangements of interrupted or confined space, by the dislocations and unsynchronized rhythms of disturbed time. Across our children's lives, in the open fields in which they play, lie the ruins of war, of a borrowed or imported industrial technology, of cast-off or abandoned forms. How odd the conjuncture, and yet for Palestinians, how fitting. For where no straight line leads from home to birthplace to school to maturity, all events are accidents, all progress is a digression, all residence is exile. We linger in nondescript places, neither here nor there; we peer through windows without glass, ride conveyances without movement or power. Resourcefulness and receptivity are the attitudes that serve best.

The difference between the new generation of Palestinians and that of 1948 is striking. Our parents bore on their faces the marks of disaster uncomprehended. Suddenly their past had been interrupted, their society obliterated, their existence radically impoverished. Refugees, all of them. Our children know no such past. Cars are equally for riding or, ruined, for playing in. Everything around them seems expendable, impermanent, unstable, especially where — as in Lebanon — Palestinian communities have been disastrously depleted or destroyed, where much of their life is undocumented, where they themselves are uncounted.

No Palestinian census exists. There is no line that can be drawn from one Palestinian to another that does not seem to interfere with the political designs of one or another state. While all of us live among "normal" people, people with complete lives, they seem to us hopelessly out of reach, with their countries, their familial continuity, their societies intact. How does a Palestinian father tell his son and daughter that Lebanon (Egypt, Syria, Jordan, New York) is where we are, but not where we are *from*? How does a mother confirm her intimate recollections of childhood in Palestine to her children, now that the facts, the places, even the names, are no longer allowed to exist?

So we borrow and we patch things together. Palestinians retain the inflections of Jaffa, of Hebron, of Jerusalem and other cities left behind, even as their dialect becomes that of Beirut, Detroit, or Paris. I have found

Bourj el-Shemali Camp, Tyre, South Lebanon, 1983. The car bears witness to a drama, circumstances unknown. The flowers: the month of May, it is spring. The children: wearing smart clothes, almost certainly donated by a charity. They are refugees — the children of refugees.

out much more about Palestine and met many more Palestinians than I ever did, or perhaps could have, in pre-1948 Palestine. For a long time I thought that this was so because I was a child then, somewhat sheltered, a member of a minority. But my experience is confirmed by my oldest and closest Palestinian friend, Ibrahim Abu-Lughod. Although he was more in and of pre-1948 Palestine — because older, more conscious and active — than I ever was, he too says that he is much more in contact with Palestinians

Bedouin Encampment Near Bersheeba, 1979

today than when he was in Palestine. He writes, "Thanks to modern technological progress, Palestinian families, and Palestinian society as a whole, have been able to forge very numerous human, social, and political links. By getting on a plane I can see the majority of my friends. It's because of this that our family has remained unified. I see all the members of my family at least once or twice a year. Being in Jaffa, I could never have seen relatives who lived in Gaza, for example." But Ibrahim does not celebrate this sociability: "I constantly experience the sense that something is missing for me. To compensate for this lack, I multiply and intensify human contacts."

Over the missing "something" are superimposed new realities. Plane travel and phone conversations nourish and connect the fortunate; the symbols of a universal pop culture enshroud the vulnerable.

Refugee Camp, Gaza, 1979. A boy of unknown age.

Tel Sheva, 1979. A group portrait, taken at the request of the children.

There can be no orderly sequence of time. You see it in our children who seem to have skipped a phase of growth or, more alarming, achieved an out-of-season maturity in one part of their body or mind while the rest remains childlike. None of us can forget the whispers and occasional proclamations that our children are "the population factor" — to be feared, and hence to be deported — or constitute special targets for death. I heard it said in Lebanon that Palestinian children in particular should be killed because each of them is a potential terrorist. Kill them before they kill you.

How rich our mutability, how easily we change (and are changed) from one thing to another, how unstable our place — and all because of the missing foundation of our existence, the lost ground of our origin, the broken link with our land and our past. There are no Palestinians. Who are the Palestinians? "The inhabitants of Judea and Samaria." Non-Jews. Terrorists. Troublemakers. DPs. Refugees. Names on a card. Numbers on a list. Praised in speeches — *el pueblo palestino, il popolo palestino, le peuple palestinien* — but treated as interruptions, intermittent presences. Gone from Jordan in 1970, now from Lebanon.

None of these departures and arrivals is clean, definitive. Some of us leave, others stay behind. Remnants, new arrivals, old residents. Two great images encapsulate our unresolved existence. One is the identity card (passport, travel document, laissez-passer), which is never Palestinian but always something else; it is the subject of our national poem, Mahmoud Darwish's "Bitaqit Hawia": "Record! I am an Arab/Without a name — without title/patient in a country/with people enraged." And the second is Emil Habiby's invention the Pessoptimist (*al-mutasha'il*), the protagonist of a disorderly and ingenious work of Kafkaesque fiction, which has become a kind of national epic. The Pessoptimist is being half here, half not here, part historical creature, part mythological invention, hopeful and hopeless, everyone's favorite obsession and scapegoat. Is Habiby's character fiction, or does his extravagant fantasy only begin to approximate the real? Is he a made-up figure or the true essence of our existence? Is Habiby's jamming-together of words — *mutafa'il* and *mutasha'im* into *mutasha'il*, which repeats the Palestinian habit of combining opposites like *la* ("no") and *na'am* ("yes") into *la'am* — a way of obliterating distinctions that do not apply to us, yet must be integrated into our lives?

Emil Habiby is a craggy, uncompromisingly complex, and fearsomely ironic man from Haifa, son of a Christian family, Communist party stalwart, longtime Knesset member, journalist, editor. His novel about the Pessoptimist (whose first name, incidentally, is Said) is chaotic because it mixes time, characters, and places; fiction, allegory, history, and flat statement, without any thread to guide the reader through its complexities. It is the best work of Palestinian writing yet produced, precisely because the most seemingly disorganized and ironic. In it we encounter characters whose names are of particular significance to Palestinians: The name of Yuaad, the work's female lead, means "it shall be repeated," a reference to the string of defeats that mark our history, and the fatalistic formulae that color our discourse. One of the other characters is Isam al-Bathanjani — Isam the Eggplant, a lawyer who is not very helpful to Said but who keeps turning up just the same. So it is with eggplants in Palestine. My family — my father in particular — has always been attached to eggplants from Battir, and during the many years since any of us had Battiri eggplants the

Bersheeba, 1979. Near a Bedouin encampment, a little kitchen garden — and its scarecrow of bits and pieces.

seal of approval on good eggplants was that "they're almost as good as the Battiris."

Today when I recall the tiresome paeans to Battiris, or when in London and Paris I see the same Jaffa oranges or Gaza vegetables grown in the *bayarat* ("orchards") and fields of my youth, but now marketed by Israeli export companies, the contrast between the inarticulate rich *thereness* of what we once knew and the systematic export of the produce into the hungry mouths of Europe strikes me with its unkind political message. The land and the peasants are bound together through work whose products seem always to have meant something to other people, to have been destined for consumption elsewhere. This observation holds force not just because the Carmel boxes and the carefully wrapped eggplants are emblems of the power that rules the sprawling fertility and enduring human labor of Palestine, but also because the discontinuity between me, out here, and the actuality there is so much more compelling now than my receding memories and experiences of Palestine.

Another, far more unusual, item concerning this vegetable appears in an article by Avigdor Feldman, "The New Order of the Military Government: State of Israel Against the Eggplant," which appeared in the journal *Koteret Rashit*, August 24, 1983. Laws 1015 and 1039, Feldman reports, stipulate that any Arab on the West Bank and Gaza who owns land must get written permission from the military governor before planting either a

Farm Using Refugee Labor, Gaza, 1979

new vegetable — for example, an eggplant — or fruit tree. Failure to get permission risks one the destruction of the tree or vegetable plus one year's imprisonment.

Exile again. The facts of my birth are so distant and strange as to be about someone I've heard of rather than someone I know. Nazareth — my mother's town. Jerusalem — my father's. The pictures I see display the same produce, presented in the same carelessly plentiful way, in the same rough wooden cases. The same people walk by, looking at the same posters and trinkets, concealing the same secrets, searching for the same profits, pleasures, and goals. The same as what? There is little that I can truly remember about Jerusalem and Nazareth, little that is specific, little that has the irreducible durability of tactile, visual, or auditory memories that concede nothing to time, little — and this is the "same" I referred to — that is not confused with pictures I have seen or scenes I have glimpsed elsewhere in the Arab world.

Palestine is exile, dispossession, the inaccurate memories of one place slipping into vague memories of another, a confused recovery of general wares, passive presences scattered around in the Arab environment. The story of Palestine cannot be told smoothly. Instead, the past, like the present, offers only occurrences and coincidences. Random. The man enters a quiet alley where he will pass cucumbers on his right, tomatoes on his left; a priest walks down the stairs, the boy dashes off, satchel under arm, other boys loiter, shopkeepers look out for business; carrying an airline bag, a man advances past a display of trinkets, a young man disappears around the corner, two boys idle aimlessly. Tomatoes, watermelons, arcades, cucumbers, posters, people, eggplants — not simply there, but represented by photographs as being there — saturated with meaning and memory, and still very far away. Look more closely and think through these possibilities: The poster is about Egypt. The trinkets are made in Korea or Hong Kong. The scenes are surveyed, enclosed, and surrounded by Israelis. European and Japanese tourists have more access to Jerusalem and Nazareth than I do. Slowly, our lives — like Palestine itself — dissolve into something else. We can't hold to the center for long.

Exile. At a recent conference in America featuring a "dialogue" between Israeli and Palestinian intellectuals with reconciliation high on the agenda, a man rises from the audience to pose a question. "I am a Palestinian, a peasant. Look at my hands. I was kicked out in 1948 and went to Lebanon. Then I was driven out, and went to Africa. Then to Europe. Then to here. Today [he pulls out an envelope] I received a paper telling me to leave this country. Would one of you scholars tell me please: Where am I supposed to go now?" No one had anything to tell him. He was an embarrassment, and I have no idea what in fact he did, what became of him. My shame.

Portrait of Om Kalsoum, Nazareth, 1979

The Palestinian's claims on Israel are generally unacknowledged, much less seen as directly connected to the founding of the state. On the Arabs there is an ambivalent Palestinian claim, recognized in Arab countries by countless words, gestures, threats, and promises. Palestine, after all, is the centerpiece of Arab nationalism. No Arab leader since World War II has failed to make Palestine a symbol of his country's nationalist foreign policy. Yet, despite the avowals, we have no way of knowing really how they — all the "theys" — feel about us. Our history has cost every one of our friends a great deal. It has gone on too long.

Let Ghassan Kanafani's novella *Men in the Sun* stand for the fear we have that unless we press "them" they will allow us to disappear, and the equal worry that if we press them they will either decry our hectoring presence, and quash it in their states, or turn us into easy symbols of their nationalism. Three refugees concealed in the belly of a tanker truck are being transported illegally across the border into Kuwait. As the driver converses with the guards, the men (Palestinians) die of suffocation — in the sun, forgotten. It is not the driver's forgetfulness that nags at him. It is their silence. "Why didn't you knock on the sides of the tank? Why didn't you bang the sides of the tank? Why? Why? Why?" Our fear to press.

The Palestinians as commodity. Producing ourselves much as the *masabih*, lamps, tapestries, baskets, embroideries, mother-of-pearl trinkets are produced. We turn ourselves into objects not for sale, but for scrutiny. People ask us, as if looking into an exhibit case, "What is it you Palestinians want?" — as if we can put our demands into a single neat

A snapshot, Jerusalem, 1979

A snapshot, Jerusalem, 1979

A Tourist Shop, Old City of Jerusalem, 1984. Customers are rare. Will they be American, Swiss, or Israeli?

Jerusalem, 1979

phrase. All of us speak of *awdah*, "return," but do we mean that literally, or do we mean "we must restore ourselves to ourselves"? The latter is the real point, I think, although I know many Palestinians who want their houses and their way of life back, exactly. But is there any place that fits us, together with our accumulated memories and experiences?

Do we exist? What proof do we have?

The further we get from the Palestine of our past, the more precarious our status, the more disrupted our being, the more intermittent our presence. When did we become "a people"? When did we stop being one? Or are we in the process of becoming one? What do those big questions have to do with our intimate relationships with each other and with others? We frequently end our letters with the mottoes "Palestinian love" or "Palestinian kisses." Are there really such things as Palestinian intimacy and embraces, or are they simply intimacy and embraces, experiences common to everyone, neither politically significant nor particular to a nation or a people?

The politics of such a question gets very close to our central dilemma: We all know that we are Arabs, and yet the concept, not to say the lived actuality, of Arabism — once the creed and the discourse of a proud Arab nation, free of imperialism, united, respected, powerful — is fast disappearing, cut up into the cautious defensiveness of relatively provincial Arab states, each with its own traditions — partly invented, partly real — each with its own nationality and restricted identity. In addition, Palestine has been replaced by an Israel whose aggressive sense of itself as the state of the Jewish people fuels the exclusivity of a national identity won and maintained to a great extent at our expense. We are not Jews, we have no place there except as resident aliens, we are outsiders. In the Arab states we are in a different position. There we are Arabs, but it is the process of nationalization that excludes us: Egypt is for and by Egyptians, Iraq is for and by Iraqis, in ways that cannot include Palestinians whose intense national revival is a separate phenomenon. Thus we are the same as other Arabs, and yet different. We cannot exist except as Arabs, even though "the Arabs" exist otherwise as Lebanese, Jordanians, Moroccans, Kuwaitis, and so forth.

Add to this the problems we have of sustaining ourselves as a collective unit and you then get a sense of how *abstract*, how very solitary and unique, we tend to feel.

Strip off the occasional assertiveness and stridency of the Palestinian stance and you may catch sight of a much more fugitive, but ultimately quite beautifully representative and subtle, sense of identity. It speaks in languages not yet fully formed, in settings not completely constituted, like the shy glance of a child holding her father's knee while she curiously and tentatively examines the stranger who photographs her. Her look conjures up the unappreciated fact of birth, that sudden, unprepared-for depositing of a small bundle of self on the fields of the Levant after which comes the trajectory of dispossession, military and political violence, and that constant, mysterious entanglement with monotheistic religion at its most profound — the Christian Incarnation and Resurrection, the Ascension to heaven of the Prophet Mohammed, the Covenant of Yahweh with his people — that is knotted definitively in Jerusalem, center of the world, *locus classicus* of Palestine, Israel, and Paradise.

A secular world of fatigue and miraculously renewed energies, the world of American cigarettes and an unending stream of small papers pulled out of miscellaneous notebooks or "blocnotes," written on with disposable pens, messages of things wanted, of people missing, of requests to the bureaucracy. The Palestinian predicament: finding an "official" place for yourself in a system that makes no allowances for you, which means endlessly improvising solutions for the problem of finding a missing loved one, of planning a trip, of entering a school, on whatever bit of paper is at hand. Constructed and deconstructed, ephemera are what we negotiate with, since we authorize no part of the world and only influence increasingly small bits of it. In any case, we keep going.

The striking thing about Palestinian prose and prose fiction is its formal instability: Our literature in a certain very narrow sense *is* the elusive, resistant reality it tries so often to represent. Most literary critics in Israel and the West focus on what is said in Palestinian writing, who is described, what the plot and contents deliver, their sociological and political meaning. But it is *form* that should be looked at. Particularly in fiction, the struggle to achieve form expresses the writer's efforts to construct a coherent scene, a narrative that might overcome the almost metaphysical

Village of Ramah, Galilee, 1979. A secular high school with students from thirty-six neighboring villages.

impossibility of representing the present. A typical Palestinian work will always be concerned with this peculiar problem, which is at once a problem of plot and an enactment of the writer's enterprise. In Kanafani's *Men in the Sun* much of the action takes place on the dusty streets of an Iraqi town where three Palestinian men must petition, plead, and bargain with "specialists" to smuggle them across the border into Kuwait.

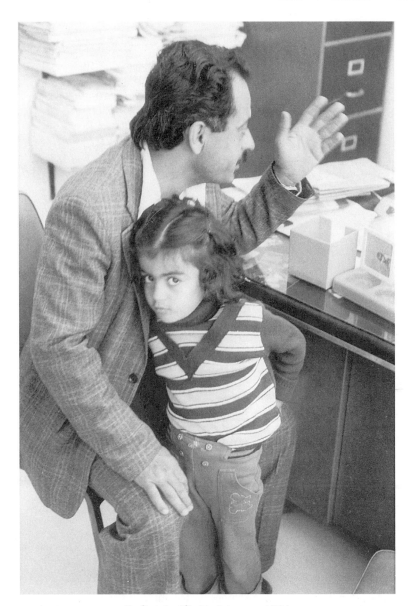

Pediatric Clinic, Amman, 1984

Impelled by exile and dislocation, the Palestinians need to carve a path for themselves in existence, which for them is by no means a given or stable reality. Like the history of the lands they left, their lives seem interrupted just before they could come to maturity and satisfaction; thus each man leaves behind family and responsibilities, to whose exigencies he must answer — unsuccessfully — here in the present. Kanafani's very sentences

Sidon, South Lebanon, 1983. A refugee writes out a message destined for her husband, a prisoner in the camp at Ansar.

express instability and fluctuation — the present tense is subject to echoes from the past, verbs of sight give way to verbs of sound or smell, and one sense interweaves with another — in an effort to defend against the harsh present and to protect some particularly cherished fragment of the past. Thus, the precarious actuality of these men in the sun reproduces the precarious status of the writer, each echoing the other.

Our characteristic mode, then, is not a narrative, in which scenes take place *seriatim*, but rather broken narratives, fragmentary compositions, and self-consciously staged testimonials, in which the narrative voice keeps stumbling over itself, its obligations, and its limitations.

Each Palestinian structure presents itself as a potential ruin. The theme of the formerly proud family house (village, city, camp) now wrecked, left behind, or owned by someone else, turns up everywhere in our literature and cultural heritage. Each new house is a substitute, supplanted in turn by yet another substitute. The names of these places extend all the way from the private (my friend Mohammed Tarbush expatiates nobly on the beauties of Beit Natif, a village near Bethlehem that was wiped out of existence by Israeli bulldozers in 1948; his widowed mother now lives in Jarash, Jordan, he in Paris) to the official, or institutionalized, sites of ruin — Deir Yassin, Tell el-Zaatar, Birim and Ikrit, Ein el-Hilwé, Sabra, Shatila, and more. Even "Palestine" itself is such a place and, curiously, already appears as a subject of elegy in journalism, essays, and literature of the early twentieth century. In the works of Halim Nassar, Ezzat Darwaza, Khallil Beidas, and Aref el-Aref, Palestine's destruction is predicted.

All cultures spin out a dialectic of self and other, the subject "I" who is native, authentic, at home, and the object "it" or "you," who is foreign, perhaps threatening, different, out there. From this dialectic comes the series of heroes and monsters, founding fathers and barbarians, prized masterpieces and despised opponents that express a culture from its deepest sense of national self-identity to its refined patriotism, and finally to its coarse jingoism, xenophobia, and exclusivist bias. For Palestinian culture, the odd thing is that its own identity is more frequently than not perceived as "other." "Palestine" is so charged with significance for others that Palestinians cannot perceive it as intimately theirs without a simultaneous sense of its urgent importance for others as well. "Ours" but not yet fully "ours." Before 1948, Palestine had a central agonistic meaning both for Arab nationalism and for the Zionist movement. After 1948, the parts of Palestine still inhabited by Arabs took on the additional label of the "non-Jewish" part of the Jewish state. Even a picture of an Arab town — like Nazareth where my mother was born and grew up — may express this alienating perspective. Because it is taken from outside Nazareth (in fact, from Upper Nazareth, a totally Jewish addition to the town, built on the surrounding hills), the photograph renders Palestine as "other." I never knew Nazareth, so this is my only image of it, an image of the "other," from the "outside," Upper Nazareth.

Thus the insider becomes the outsider. Not only have the interpositions between us and Palestine grown more formidable over time, but, to make matters worse, most of us pass our lives separated from each other. Yet we live in comradely communication despite the barriers. Today the

Camp at Ein el-Hilwé, Sidon, South Lebanon, 1983. Time passes: destruction, reconstruction, redestruction.

Palestinian genius expresses itself in crossings-over, in clearing hurdles, activities that do not lessen the alienation, discontinuity, and dispossession, but that dramatize and clarify them instead. We have remained; in the words of Tawfik Zayyad's famous poem, "The Twenty Impossibles," it would be easier "to catch fried fish in the Milky Way,/to plow the sea,/to teach the alligator speech" than to make us leave. To the Israelis, whose incomparable military and political power dominates us, we are at the periphery, the image that will not go away. Every assertion of our nonexistence, every attempt to spirit us away, every new effort to prove that we were never really there, simply raises the question of why so much denial of, and such energy expended on, what was not there? Could it be that even as alien outsiders we dog their military might with our obdurate moral claim, our insistence (like that of Bartleby the Scrivener) that "we would prefer not to," not to leave, not to abandon Palestine forever?

The proof of whatever small success we have had is not that we have regained a homeland, or acquired a new one; rather, it is that some Israelis have admitted the possibility of sharing a common space with us, in Palestine. The proposed modes of such a sharing are adventurous and utopian in the present context of hostility between Arabs and Jews, but on an intellectual level they are actual, and to some of us — on both sides — they make sense. Most Palestinians have their own special instance of the Israeli who reached out across the barricade most humanly. For some it is

Viewed from Upper Nazareth, Arab Nazareth, 1979

the intrepid Israeli lawyer defending Palestinian political prisoners, or trying to prevent land expropriations and collective punishment; for others it
is — the testimony of Salah Ta'amari, leader of the Palestinian prisoners
rounded up during the Israeli invasion and put in the Ansar prison camp,
comes to mind — an Israeli in a position of authority (prison guard or
army officer) who prevented some atrocity or showed some clear sign of
humanity and fellow feeling. For my part, removed from the terrible pressures of the scene, I think of all the Israeli (or non-Israeli) Jews whose
articulate witness to the injustice of their people against mine has marked
out a communal territory. The result has usually been a friendship whose
depth is directly proportional to the admiration I feel for their tenacity of
conscience and belief in the face of the most slanderous attacks. Surely
few have equaled the courage and principle of Israel Shahak, of Leah
Tsemal and Felicia Langer, of Noam Chomsky, of Izzy Stone, of Elmer
Berger, of Matti Peled, of so many others who stood up bravely during the
events in Lebanon.

There are few opportunities for us Palestinians, or us Palestinians *and*
Israelis, to learn anything about the world we live in that is *not* touched
by, indeed soaked in, the hostilities of our struggle. And if it isn't the
Palestinian-Zionist struggle, there are the pressures of religion, of every
conceivable ideology, of family, peers, and compatriots, each of them bearing down upon us, pushing, kneading, prodding every one of us from
childhood to maturity.

Rashidyé Camp, Tyre, South Lebanon, 1983. A local official collects messages from the relations of refugees for the International Red Cross.

In such an environment, learning itself is a chancy, hybrid activity, laced with the unresolvable antitheses of our age. The child is full of the curious hope and undirected energy that attract the curatorial powers of both church and state. Fortunately, here the spirit of the creative urge in all human activity asserts itself — neither church nor state can ultimately exhaust, or control, the possibilities latent in the classroom, playground, or family. An orderly row of chairs and tables, a disciplined recitation circle in a Catholic school with a nun in charge, are also places for the absorption of more knowledge and experience than authorities impart — places where the child explores here and there, his/her mind and body wandering in space and time despite the constraints in each. In a school

Kalandia (near Ramallah), 1967. A few days after the end of the June War: in the foreground, an Israeli officer, lost in thought. Behind the window, a young villager.

where the teacher is a devout Muslim, the child's propensity for disturbing or opposing the schemes of knowledge and discipline causes him/her to leave the table, disrupt the pattern, seek unthought-of possibilities. The tension between teachers and students remains, but better the tension than the peace of passivity, or the unresisting assent to authority.

The pressures of the here and now require an answer to the Palestinian crisis here and now. Whereas our interlocutors, our "others" — the Arab states, the United States, the USSR, Israel, our friends and enemies — have the luxury of a state in which institutions do their work undisturbed by the question of existence-or-not, we lead our lives under a sword of

Jerusalem, 1979. A dialogue between left-wing Israeli and Arab intellectuals.

Damocles, whose dry rhetorical form is the query "When are you Palestinians going to accept a solution?" — the implication being that if we don't, we'll disappear. This, then, is our midnight hour.

It is difficult to know how much the often stated, tediously reiterated worries about us, which include endless lectures on the need for a clear Palestinian statement of the desire for peace (as if we controlled the decisive factors!), are malicious provocation and how much genuine, if sympathetic, ignorance. I don't think any of us reacts as impatiently to such things as we did, say, five years ago. True, our collective situation is more precarious now than it was, but I detect a general turning inward among Palestinians, as if many of us feel the need to consolidate and collect the shards of Palestinian life still present and available to us. This is not quietism at all, nor is it resignation. Rather, it springs from the natural impulse to stand back when the headlong rush of events gets to be too much, perhaps, for us to savor life as life, to reflect at some distance from politics on where we came from and where we are, to regrasp, revise, recomprehend the tumultuous experiences at whose center, quite without our consent, we have been made to stand.

Jean Mohr's photograph of a small but clearly formed human group surrounded by a dense and layered reality expresses very well what we experience during that detachment from an ideologically saturated world. This image of four people seen at a distance near Ramallah, in the middle of and yet separated from thick foliage, stairs, several tiers of terraces and houses, a lone electricity pole off to the right, is for me a private, crystal-

Nazareth, 1979. A municipal kindergarten, looked after by nuns.

lized, almost Proustian evocation of Palestine. Memory: During the summer of 1942 — I was six — we rented a house in Ramallah. My father, I
recall, was ill with high blood pressure and recovering from a nervous
breakdown. I remember him as withdrawn and constantly smoking. My
mother took me to a variety show at the local Friends school. During the
second half I left the hall to go to the toilet, but for reasons I could not (and
still do not) grasp, the boy-scout usher would not let me back in. I recall
with ever-renewed poignancy the sudden sense of distance I experienced
from what was familiar and pleasant — my mother, friends, the show;
all at once the rift introduced into the cozy life I led taught me the meaning
of separation, of solitude, and of anguished boredom. There was nothing

Amman, 1984. Camp at Baqa'a, one of the oldest in Jordan. The YWCA looks after some of the kindergartens.

Jerusalem, 1984

to do but wait, although my mother did appear a little later to find out what had happened to me. We left immediately, but not before I furtively took a quick look back through the door window at the lighted stage. The telescoped vision of small figures assembled in a detached space has remained with me for over forty years, and it reappears in the adjusted and transformed center of Jean's 1983 picture. I never ventured anywhere near that part of Ramallah again. I would no more know it than I would the precise place of this photo; and yet I am sure it would be familiar, the way this one immediately seemed.

My private past is inscribed on the surface of this peaceful but somehow brooding pastoral scene in the contemporary West Bank. I am not the only one surveying the scene. There is the child on the left who looks on. There are also the Swiss photographer, compassionate, curious, silent, and of course the ever-present Israeli security services, who hold the West Bank and its population in the vise of occupation. As for those terraces and multiple levels: Do they serve the activities of daily life or are they the haunted stairs of a prison which, like Piranesi's, lead nowhere, confining their human captives? The dense mass of leaves, right and left, lend their bulk to the frame, but they too impinge on the slender life they surround, like memory or a history too complex to be sorted out, bigger than its subject, richer than any consciousness one might have of it.

The power grid recalls the Mercedes in Tripoli. Unassimilated, its modernity and power have been felt with considerable strength in our lives here and there throughout the Third World. Another childhood memory:

Near Senjel, a Village between Ramallah and Nablus, 1979

Driving through the Sinai from Egypt into Palestine, we would see the row of telephone and electricity pylons partnering the empty macadamized road that cut through an even emptier desert. Who are they, I would ask myself. What do they think when we are not here? When we stopped to stretch our legs, I would go up to a pole and look at its dull brown surface for some sign of life, identity, or awareness. Once I marked one with my initials EWS, hoping to find it again on the trip back. All of them looked exactly the same as we hurtled by. We never stopped. I never drove there again, nor can I now. Futile efforts to register my presence on the scene.

Intimate memory and contemporary social reality seem connected by the little passage between the child, absorbed in his private, silent sphere, and the three older people, who are the public world of adults, work, and community. It is a vacant, somewhat tenuously maintained space, however; sandy, pebbly, and weedy. All the force in the photograph moves dramatically from trees left to trees right, from the visible enclave of domesticity (stairs, houses, terrace) to the unseen larger world of power and authority beyond. I wonder whether the four people are in fact connected, or whether as a group they simply happen to be in the way of unseen forces totally indifferent to the dwelling and living space these people inhabit. This is also, then, a photograph of latent, of impending desolation, and once again I am depressed by the transience of Palestinian life, its vulnerability and all too easy dislocation. But another movement, another feeling, asserts itself in response, set in motion by the two strikingly marked openings in the buildings, openings that suggest rich, cool interiors which outsiders cannot penetrate. Let us enter.

■ MARJANE SATRAPI

The Veil

From *Persepolis: The Story of a Childhood*

Marjane Satrapi (b. 1969) was born and raised in Iran, but she was sent by her parents to study in Europe during the Islamic Revolution in 1979. "The Veil" is taken from *Persepolis: The Story of a Childhood* (2003), Satrapi's graphic novel about her early life in Tehran. This selection centers on how the new Islamic regime made it mandatory for all women to wear veils. *Persepolis* has been widely read and highly acclaimed; it was chosen by the Seattle Public Library as the "Seattle Reads" book in 2006. There is also a sequel to *Persepolis*, which describes Satrapi's later experiences in Europe and her eventual return to Iran. In 2007, Satrapi wrote and directed an animated version of her graphic novel, which won the Jury Grand Prize at the Cannes Film Festival. Although she now lives in France, Satrapi has claimed that "nowhere is my home any more."

■ ■ ■

THE VEIL

THIS IS ME WHEN I WAS 10 YEARS OLD. THIS WAS IN 1980.

AND THIS IS A CLASS PHOTO. I'M SITTING ON THE FAR LEFT SO YOU DON'T SEE ME. FROM LEFT TO RIGHT: GOLNAZ, MAHSHID, NARINE, MINNA.

IN 1979 A REVOLUTION TOOK PLACE. IT WAS LATER CALLED "THE ISLAMIC REVOLUTION".

THEN CAME 1980: THE YEAR IT BECAME OBLIGATORY TO WEAR THE VEIL AT SCHOOL.

WEAR THIS!

WE DIDN'T REALLY LIKE TO WEAR THE VEIL, ESPECIALLY SINCE WE DIDN'T UNDERSTAND WHY WE HAD TO.

IT'S TOO HOT OUT!

EXECUTION IN THE NAME OF FREEDOM.

GIVE ME MY VEIL BACK!

YOU'LL HAVE TO LICK MY FEET!

OOH! I'M THE MONSTER OF DARKNESS.

GIDDYAP!

EVERYWHERE IN THE STREETS THERE WERE DEMONSTRATIONS FOR AND AGAINST THE VEIL.

AT ONE OF THE DEMONSTRATIONS, A GERMAN JOURNALIST TOOK A PHOTO OF MY MOTHER.

I WAS REALLY PROUD OF HER. HER PHOTO WAS PUBLISHED IN ALL THE EUROPEAN NEWSPAPERS.

AND EVEN IN ONE MAGAZINE IN IRAN. MY MOTHER WAS REALLY SCARED.

HAVE YOU SEEN THIS?

DON'T WORRY, DARLING.

SHE DYED HER HAIR,

AND WORE DARK GLASSES FOR A LONG TIME.

I REALLY DIDN'T KNOW WHAT TO THINK ABOUT THE VEIL. DEEP DOWN I WAS VERY RELIGIOUS BUT AS A FAMILY WE WERE VERY MODERN AND AVANT-GARDE.

I WAS BORN WITH RELIGION.

AT THE AGE OF SIX I WAS ALREADY SURE I WAS THE LAST PROPHET. THIS WAS A FEW YEARS BEFORE THE REVOLUTION.

O'Celestial light!

BEFORE ME THERE HAD BEEN A FEW OTHERS.

A WOMAN?

I AM THE LAST PROPHET.

I WANTED TO BE A PROPHET...

BECAUSE OUR MAID DID NOT EAT WITH US.

BECAUSE MY FATHER HAD A CADILLAC.

AND, ABOVE ALL, BECAUSE MY GRANDMOTHER'S KNEES ALWAYS ACHED.

COME HERE MARJI! HELP ME TO STAND UP.

DON'T WORRY. SOON YOU WON'T HAVE ANY MORE PAIN. YOU'LL SEE.

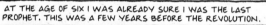

■ GIL SCOTT-HERON

The Revolution Will Not Be Televised

Gil Scott-Heron (b. 1949) is an American poet and musician. His spoken word poetry, which is accompanied by funk and jazz music, often discusses cultural and political topics. Scott-Heron's innovative combination of poetry and music has led to many considering him a pioneer of rap. The majority of Scott-Heron's work was released in the 1970s. In the 1980s, Scott-Heron was a vocal critic of Ronald Reagan. The poem "The Revolution Will Not Be Televised" first appeared on his album *Small Talk at 125th and Lenox* (1970). Throughout the poem, there are a number of cultural references, especially popular advertising slogans of the time. Scott-Heron's poem has been covered and sampled by numerous musicians, from Public Enemy to NOFX. Its title has been appropriated to critique contemporary culture, as well as to promote and sell commercial products (such as Apple computers).

■ ■ ■

You will not be able to stay home, brother.
You will not be able to plug in, turn on and cop out.
You will not be able to lose yourself on skag and skip,
Skip out for beer during commercials,
Because the revolution will not be televised.

The revolution will not be televised.
The revolution will not be brought to you by Xerox
In 4 parts without commercial interruptions.
The revolution will not show you pictures of Nixon
blowing a bugle and leading a charge by John
Mitchell, General Abrams and Spiro Agnew to eat
hog maws confiscated from a Harlem sanctuary.
The revolution will not be televised.

The revolution will not be brought to you by the
Schaefer Award Theatre and will not star Natalie
Woods and Steve McQueen or Bullwinkle and Julia.
The revolution will not give your mouth sex appeal.
The revolution will not get rid of the nubs.
The revolution will not make you look five pounds
thinner, because the revolution will not be televised, Brother.

There will be no pictures of you and Willie May
pushing that shopping cart down the block on the dead run,
or trying to slide that color television into a stolen ambulance.
NBC will not be able to predict the winner at 8:32
or report from 29 districts.
The revolution will not be televised.

There will be no pictures of pigs shooting down
brothers in the instant replay.
There will be no pictures of pigs shooting down
brothers in the instant replay.
There will be no pictures of Whitney Young being
run out of Harlem on a rail with a brand new process.
There will be no slow motion or still life of Roy
Wilkens strolling through Watts in a Red, Black and
Green liberation jumpsuit that he had been saving
For just the proper occasion.

Green Acres, The Beverly Hillbillies, and Hooterville
Junction will no longer be so damned relevant, and
women will not care if Dick finally gets down with
Jane on Search for Tomorrow because Black people
will be in the street looking for a brighter day.
The revolution will not be televised.

There will be no highlights on the eleven o'clock
news and no pictures of hairy armed women
liberationists and Jackie Onassis blowing her nose.
The theme song will not be written by Jim Webb,
Francis Scott Key, nor sung by Glen Campbell, Tom
Jones, Johnny Cash, Englebert Humperdink, or the Rare Earth.
The revolution will not be televised.

The revolution will not be right back after a message
bout a white tornado, white lightning, or white people.
You will not have to worry about a dove in your
bedroom, a tiger in your tank, or the giant in your toilet bowl.
The revolution will not go better with Coke.
The revolution will not fight the germs that may cause bad breath.
The revolution will put you in the driver's seat.

The revolution will not be televised, will not be televised,
will not be televised, will not be televised.
The revolution will be no re-run brothers;
The revolution will be live.

■ HAILE SELASSIE ───────────────────────────────

1963 Speech at the United Nations

Haile Selassie (1892–1975) was the last emperor of Ethopia, serving on
the throne from 1930 to 1974. After the Italian army invaded Ethiopia,
Selassie fled the country in order to address the League of Nations, asking
for the stronger countries of the world to protect the weaker ones. As a

result of his eloquent speech, he was named *Time*'s "Man of the Year" in 1936. Selassie was a strong supporter of the decolonialization of the countries of Africa and in 1963 founded the Organization of African Unity. That same year, he spoke to the United Nations, calling for peace and an end to racial discrimination and colonialism. Although he was extremely popular both in Ethiopia and abroad, Selassie was deposed in 1974 after a BBC documentary exposed widespread famine in the country. He died the following year, and there is much speculation as to whether or not he was killed by members of the new government. Selassie was considered by many Rastafarians to be the Messiah, and his 1963 speech at the United Nations was set to music by Bob Marley in his famous song "War."

"On the question of racial discrimination, the Addis Ababa summit conference taught, to those who will learn, this further lesson:

that until the philosophy which holds one race superior and another inferior is finally and permanently dicredited and abandoned;
that until there are no longer first class and second class citizens of any nation;
that until the color of a man's skin is of no more significance than the color of his eyes;
that until the basic human rights are equally guaranteed to all, without regard to race;
that until that day, the dream of lasting peace and world citizenship and the rule of international morality will remain but fleeting illusions, to be pursued but never attained.

And until the ignoble and unhappy regimes that hold our brothers in Angola, in Mozambique, and in South Africa in sub-human bondage have been toppled and destroyed; until bigotry and prejudice and malicious and inhuman self-interest have been replaced by understanding and tolerance and good-will; until all Africans stand and speak as free beings, equal in the eyes of all men, as they are in the eyes of Heaven; until that day, the African continent will not know peace.

We Africans will fight, if necessary, and we know that we shall win, as we are confident in the victory of good over evil.

The basis of racial discrimination and colonialism has been economic, and it is with economic weapons that these evils have been and can be overcome. In pursuance of resolutions adopted at the Addis Ababa summit conference, African states have undertaken certain measures in the economic field which, if adopted by all member states of the United Nations, would soon reduce intransigeance to reason.

I ask, today, for adherence to these measures by every nation represented here which is truly devoted to the principles enunciated in the charter.

We must act while we can, while the occasion exists to exert those legitimate pressures available to us lest time run out and resort be had to less happy means.

The great nations of the world would do well to remember that in the modern age even their own fates are not wholly in their hands.

Peace demands the united efforts of us all. Who can foresee what spark might ignite the fuse? The stake of each one of us is identical — life or death.

We all wish to live. We all seek a world in which men are freed of the burdens of ignorance, poverty, hunger and disease. And we shall all be hard-pressed to escape the deadly rain of nuclear fall-out should catastrophe overtake us.

The problems which confront us today are, equally, unprecedented. They have no counterparts in human experience. Men search the pages of history for solutions, for precedents, but there are none.

This then, is the ultimate challenge. Where are we to look for our survival, for the answers to the questions which have never before been posed? We must look, first, to the Almighty God, Who has raised man above the animals and endowed him with intelligence and reason. We must put our faith in Him, that He will not desert us or permit us to destroy humanity which He created in His image.

And we must look into ourselves, into the depth of our souls. We must become something we have never been and for which our education and experience and environment have ill-prepared us.

We must become bigger than we have been: more courageous, greater in spirit, larger in outlook. We must become members of a new race, overcoming petty prejudice, owing our ultimate allegiance not to nations but to our fellow men within the human community."

■ SANDRA SILBERSTEIN

From News to Entertainment:
Eyewitness Accounts

Sandra Silberstein is a professor of English at the University of Washington. She is an applied linguist who specializes in feminist theory and teaching English as a second language. In particular, Silberstein is interested in how people create meaning out of texts, especially public texts produced by the mass media. She is also the former editor of the journal for ESL teachers called *TESOL Quarterly*. "From News to Entertainment: Eyewitness Accounts" is a chapter from her book *War of Words: Language, Politics, and 9/11* (2002). She is currently working on a book titled *Contested Narratives: America and the O. J. Simpson Case*.

■ ■ ■

It's not just the story; everyone has great stories. You need to be a great storyteller.

— AARON BROWN, CNN ad for *NewsNight*

In the wake of 9/11, the media were alive with survivors' tales — stories that captured horrifying events and the fortitude of those who survived them. Like all stories, these would draw on common sense ("what any reasonable person would believe or feel or do in the same circumstance"[1]), but they would also speak to what it means to be an American. Storytelling, linguist Charlotte Linde tells us, can draw people together. It can "create group membership for [the speaker] and solidarity for [a] group."[2] Stories, by their nature, locate our very personal experiences within larger cultural norms and expectations. But for the televised narratives of September 11, the larger relevance was heavily constructed by reporters and the visual frames of the news media.

This chapter examines the role of television in creating September 11 narratives and in constructing social identities. There are two assumptions at work here in the discussion of identity, one more obvious than the other. The first is that identities are neither singular nor stable; that is, people have multiple identities, including, for example, being family members, professionals, religious (non)believers, (non)citizens. And these identities are not necessarily stable. Individuals can be seen as competent professionals at one moment and lose that identity in the next. (Consider the fate of Enron executives!) The second assumption is that identities are displayed, and thereby (re)constructed through interactions with others. One is identified as, for example, a news reporter or a reasonable person or an American on the basis of displaying recognizable features of these roles. The media can aid these displays and, in fact, (re)create collective identities. Viewers can be (re)made American through the televisual displays of the nation. All of this was at play in the aftermath of the trauma that was September 11 — the "Attack on America."

TV News

A brief introduction to the norms of television news coverage will be helpful here. In his analysis of news discourse, linguist Ron Scollon[3] distinguishes between the prerogatives of reporters and presenters (that is, newscasters) versus those he calls newsmakers. The former are given their authority by virtue of their role within an organizational framework. On the morning of September 11, newscaster Aaron Brown had recently assumed his organizational standing as one of CNN's principal anchors. According to *People* magazine, "Brown tailed a speeding New York City police car through red lights to his office to begin covering what he calls 'the biggest story of my life'."[4] But what was he to present?

"News," Anthony Bell tells us, "is what an authoritative source tells a journalist."[5] In contemporary coverage of major events, one often sees little of the event and a great deal of eyewitnesses and officials — Scollon's newsmakers. Newsmakers are delegated the floor (put in front of the camera) by the authority of the reporters. They may not "take the floor" on their own nor introduce their own topics. Typically, their role is to provide raw material for journalists' stories. But what happens when the material is still "raw" at airtime? The role of newsmakers is complicated in the context of the continuous, immediate, potentially unedited coverage of "Breaking News," as was the case on September 11. In such circumstances, the raw material can become the story. But we will see later that even in this "real-time" coverage, the framing by newscasters and the (tele)visual production of Breaking News manufactures a television narrative that is quite different from storytelling among friends.

A further complication for those who reported the events of September 11 is the increasing conflation of news and entertainment. Increasingly, news reports cover the emotional reactions of people (even reporters) to events, rather than the events themselves; that is, coverage is not so much about the occurrences themselves as it is narrations about them. This leads to an interesting reversal. Scollon notes that as journalists show more of their feelings, nonjournalists (eyewitnesses or "people on the street") are transformed discursively into "news-knowledgeable commentators."[6] As nonjournalists take on more of the style of the "authoritative, knowledgeable reporter," the reporters provide "entertainment" through emotion-laden commentary. Note the use of the term *entertainment* here does not imply that the content is necessarily enjoyable. This was certainly not the case on 9/11. But it contrasts with the senses of the term *news*.

Finally, Scollon notes that the primary social interaction displayed in news reporting is arguably not between reporters and viewers, but rather among journalists, as they produce a spectacle for the benefit of the viewers.

The Newscasters

Such were the television news conventions on 9/11 when Aaron Brown presented CNN reporter Richard Roth with one of the first eyewitness accounts of the day. Brown began with a display both of journalists' interactions and his reaction to the events. Following a report on shutting down airports and Disney World, he observes:

> Someone said to me a moment ago that before the day is over everything is going to be shut down, and that seems ta- to be where we're headed. Ah CNN's Richard Ross is on the, ah Richard Roth rather, is on the streets of New York and he can join us now. Richard, what can you tell us?

Brown enacts his institutional role by defining the situation and introducing the topic. In this instance the topic is rather broad ("What can you tell us?"), perhaps underscoring his lack of prior knowledge and the unedited immediacy of the coverage. We are watching a conversation between journalists.

With that delegation, Richard Roth (his organizational status displayed on screen: "Richard Roth/CNN New York") begins. He is literally standing on the street, and we see later what appears to be a line of people waiting for the opportunity to "report." Roth's introduction draws heavily on "entertainment." Terms that heighten emotion and intensify the description are highlighted below.

> Aaron, New Yorkers think they've seen everything but ah they'll never, they'll say they- they're **amazed** at what has happened, **stunned**. Right now behind me, what **normally** would be the World Trade Center is no more. A **huge** cloud of white smoke. And right now it's **like a war zone**. Thousands of New Yorkers **streaming** north. The mayor of New York City, Rudy Giuliani, has told everyone to get north of Canal Street. We're several miles north of it. Ah right now New Yorkers are trying to get out of Manhattan. There's a ferry on the west side going to New Jersey, it's really the only access out. The mayor advising ah that people should take the subways. We have seen **dozens** of emergency vehicles, **hundreds**. Firemen being bussed in, decamp- decontamination vans coming in, calls for blood donations, for New Yorkers, their faces their expressions — **stunned, amazed** right now. With us several of those people who witnessed some of the **carnage** today.

A Newsmaker Narrative

With that, Roth delegates the floor to person-on-the-street, Colleen. Before turning to Colleen's narrative it is worth reiterating a caution from the Introduction to this book. To analyze the mediated linguistic constructions of these events is not to minimize their horrific nature. And some readers may prefer not to read this graphic survivor narrative. My assumption is that language plays the central role in creating human societies. If citizens are to have any role in building a post-9/11 world, we need to examine the way in which our understandings are created and manipulated through language, in particular, how events are managed and manufactured through the mass media. In that spirit, Colleen's narrative will be examined with some care. Note that I have used pseudonyms for the three survivor narrators in this chapter, those who appeared in real time (Colleen, Mr. Gonzalez, and Mike Cartwright). Colleen's is produced in response to a question from CNN's Roth:

Tell us what you saw when you exited the subway station due to a lack of smoke, Colleen.

Roth's obvious misspeaking ("due to a lack of smoke") adds to the unedited immediacy as we watch Breaking News.

Um, it was very smoky and then we exited on Church Street out of the PATH train station. Um, I crossed over to Church and ah Fulton, and I was trying to get a cell phone. I was trying to get up the block, and I turned around and saw this tremendous fire. I thought it was a bomb, I couldn't see a plane. And I saw people jumping out of- off the building, many, many people just jumping. And in a panic, I had my bag and my cell phone and everything, and I was trying to find a phone because the cell phone wasn't working. Everybody was screaming, everybody was running, the cops are trying to maintain the calm. And in that haste people were stampeding. People started screaming that there was another plane coming, I didn't see the plane but I turned around and it just- the second building just exploded, and again all the debris was flying towards us. There was a woman on the ground with her baby, people were stampeding the baby. Myself and another man threw ourselves over the baby and pushed into the building. I got up and I just ran. And I ran towards City Hall. Then I said "oh God why am I running there?" And then I started to run towards the water. And then ah, I was by probably Spring Street, or- or- or I'm sorry Prince Street? I was at a pay phone and I heard the rumbeling [phonetic spelling]. I thought it was another bomb, I thought it was another building close to me. And then I just ah- ran from the pay phone. The man is grabbing me back telling me, "Stay here you're safe." I was like, "No way, I'm getting outta here. Go north." And then I ran into a shoe store because I wanted to call my husband, that's all I wanted to do. I wanted him to know I was alive because he knew I was in the World Trade. And um I got my office, and they connected me to my husband, and then we heard the second fall of the World Trade Center. And I- I'm astonished by the bombing. I just want to make a statement that these New York policemen and firemen, God bless them, they kept us calm, they tried so hard to keep us moving north. And it was just absolute, absolute horror, it was horror.

And when you look back there at what would be the Nor- the World Trade Center?

[
It's devastating,
I can't look back. My six-year-old just last week asked my husband and I to take him to the [voice breaking] observation deck, and it's gone. And you know what? Americans will persevere. And I don't think that we'll stoop to the level of these zealot, terrorist pigs. And we won't kill children, I hope, and mothers. But you know what? Whatever we have to do to eradicate the country or the world of this- of this vermin, I just hope Bush will do whatever is necessary to get rid of them. And I don't know, don't know what the root of, what they, of what the answer is
[
Al- alright thank you very much.

We will examine Colleen's narrative from several perspectives. First is its structure as a well-formed narrative. Live television doesn't permit the luxury of leaving poor interviews on the cutting-room floor. To some extent, Colleen likely demonstrated herself to be a competent storyteller before she was allowed on camera.

Linguist William Labov argues that fully formed oral narratives have six parts:[7]

1. *Abstract*: What is this story about?
2. *Orientation*: Who, when, where, what?
3. *Complicating action*: Then what happened?
4. *Evaluation*: So, what? Why is this interesting, or how do you feel about it?
5. *Result or resolution*: What finally happened?
6. *Coda*: That's it. I've finished and am bridging back to the present.

The abstract and the coda are considered optional. Evaluations can appear throughout a narrative, at each stage explaining and evaluating events and justifying tellability. Research shows that speakers who omit an orientation or evaluation are less favorably received, as was the case for working-class speakers with only a basic education in one European study.[8]

In contrast, Colleen's story is rich in orientation, detail, explanation, and evaluation. For readers who wish to examine its narrative structure in detail, it is presented in chart form in the Appendix to this chapter. Here it is worth noting that orienting statements indicating Colleen's location appear throughout her gripping narrative. Similarly, evaluative statements explaining her reasoning and feelings are also plentiful (e.g., "I was trying to get a cell phone"; "I thought it was a bomb"; "God bless them, they kept us calm").

We will see later what happens on live TV to a narrator with a less successful narrative structure. But for now we will remain with Colleen. Through her telling she establishes her identity on several fronts. Two of these work together: she is both a competent narrator and a competent person. As a narrator, she orients us more than once and evaluates the story continuously, alerting the listener to the significance of her actions.

Through her narrative construction, Colleen identifies herself as a competent person. In the midst of this crisis she has what one would need: her bag and her cell phone, and she's already discovered what everyone else in lower Manhattan will learn on that day: cell phone service was largely wiped out. People around her are "screaming," but she keeps her head. Her goals are clear: Colleen is simultaneously evaluating her decisions in terms of both her safety and her role as a responsible spouse. She must save herself and call her husband to let him know that she is safe. Colleen motivates her decisions in terms of one of these two imperatives. In fact Colleen's competence as a person is mirrored in the structure of her story, which can be understood in terms of these two complementary strands. Here is the story again. References to gaining safety have been bolded; references to reaching a telephone are underlined. Rhetorically and actually, both strands reach completion.

> Um, it was very smoky and then we exited on Church Street out of the PATH train station. Um, I crossed over to Church and ah Fulton, and I was trying to get a cell phone. **I was trying to get up the block**, and I turned around and saw this tremendous fire. I thought it was a bomb, I couldn't see a plane. And I saw people jumping out of- off the building, many, many people just jumping. And in a panic, I had my bag and my cell phone and everything, and I was trying to find a phone because the cell phone wasn't working. Everybody was screaming, everybody was running, the cops are trying to maintain the calm. And in that haste people were stampeding. People started screaming that there was another plane coming, I didn't see the plane but I turned around and it just- the second building just exploded, and again all the debris was flying towards us. There was a woman on the ground with her baby, people were stampeding the baby. Myself and another man threw ourselves over the baby and pushed into the building. I got up and I just ran. And I ran towards City Hall. Then I said "oh God why am I running there?" **And then I started to run towards the water.** And then ah, I was by probably Spring Street, or- or- or I'm sorry Prince Street? I was at a pay phone and I heard the rumbeling. I thought it was another bomb, I thought it was another building close to me. And then I just ah- ran from the pay phone. The man is grabbing me back telling me, "Stay here you're safe." I was like, "No way, I'm getting outta here. Go north." And then I ran into a shoe store because I wanted to call my husband, that's all I wanted to do. I wanted him to know I was alive because he knew I was in the World Trade. And um I got my office, and they connected me to my husband, and then we heard the second fall of the World Trade Center. And I- I'm astonished by the bombing. I just want to make a statement that these New York policemen and firemen, God bless them, they kept us calm, they tried so hard to keep us moving north. And it was just absolute, absolute horror, it was horror.

Gripping as these details are, the tellability of Colleen's story does not rest on her identity as a competent person alone. Colleen's narrative builds a sense of what it means to be human, to be a New Yorker, then an American, and a citizen of the world. Recall that storytelling can be used to create group membership for oneself and solidarity for a group. Stories locate one's very personal experience within cultural norms and expectations. In Colleen's world, people do the right thing. No normal person under normal circumstances would trample a baby. Colleen tells us that *in that haste* people were stampeding. And noticing that, Colleen and another man throw themselves over the baby. This is the only complicating action that is not followed by an evaluation, an explanation. In the absence of evaluation, doing the right thing becomes the default; it establishes a particular collective identity.

Colleen's narrative moves from individual to collective identity. She has already established herself as a New Yorker. She details the local geography and refers colloquially to "the World Trade." But she also creates solidarity with other New Yorkers, who, under God, do the right thing:

I just want to make a statement that these New York policemen and firemen, God bless them, they kept us calm, they tried so hard to keep us moving north.

Next, Colleen creates the listeners as Americans — a "we" who "persevere" don't "kill children and . . . mothers," and "do whatever is necessary" — this in contrast to "zealot, terrorist pigs" and "vermin" (certainly "them"). Here Colleen creates group membership for herself and solidarity for the group:

> And you know what? Americans will persevere. And I don't think that we'll stoop to the level of these zealot, terrorist pigs. And we won't kill children, I hope, and mothers. But you know what? Whatever we have to do to eradicate the country or the world of this- of this vermin . . .

Perhaps most significant, Colleen becomes an early media voice to rhetorically ratify George W. Bush as the commander in chief: "I just hope Bush will do whatever is necessary to get rid of them."

Colleen's presence on CNN renders her more than a storyteller. She has been delegated the role of newsmaker. Her gripping account certainly fulfills the "entertainment" imperative of contemporary news reports — again, not in the sense that these horrific images were enjoyable, but in the sense of a focus on the visual and on emotional reactions to events. Colleen is asked only two questions. The first is visual: "Tell us what you saw." The second requests an emotional reaction: "And when you look back there at what would be-used to be the World Trade Center?" In fact, this late focus on emotion elicits the only loss of composure in Colleen's lengthy description.

Throughout, however, Colleen constructs herself as another kind of newsmaker as well. Recall that Scollon argues that as journalists show more of their feelings, nonjournalists are transformed discursively into news-knowledgeable commentators. Nonjournalists take on more of the style of the authoritative, knowledgeable reporter. And Colleen takes this role seriously. Although Colleen makes a number of false starts, she makes only one apology: "And then ah, I was by probably Spring Street, or- or- or I'm sorry Prince Street." One can easily understand the need for self-correction, but the impulse to apologize is intriguing. Formal apology for slight inaccuracies would not seem to be required of her. Apologies display an expectation that one should produce a different behavior, in this case, greater accuracy. Arguably, Colleen's apology constructs her as a reporter for an audience that values accurate description of the local geography. This she provides. She begins by presenting her precise location and continues throughout to chart her course.

But, notwithstanding Colleen's journalistic instincts, she is not a newscaster; she has no institutional authority to speak. She has only been delegated the floor by a reporter who simultaneously delineates her topic: what she saw, how she feels. When Colleen begins to go beyond that, the hook takes her off the stage:

And I don't know, don't know what the root of, what they, of what the
answer is
[
    Al- alright thank you very much.

And Roth produces a closing frame:

> A lot of other New Yorkers here continuing the evacuation of lower Man-
> hattan. Back to you Aaron.

With that, Brown takes up the presenter role. He cohesively brackets the
story with a return to the theme of shutting things down and shares his
own reactions.

> Ah thank you Richard very much. Ah we told you a bit ago that the border,
> the U.S.-Mexican border was at a high state of alert- has been essentially
> closed down, shut down. We're now told that the U.S.-Canada border is also
> in a high state of alert. So essentially what officials are trying to do is seal off
> the country. So if anyone is either trying to get in or get out, ah it's gonna be a
> whole lot harder to do that. Ah, but what is possible and what is imaginable
> I guess changes on a day like this.

Clearly, a great deal of framing work has been done both by the newscasters and the newsmaker. But, in this respect, the description thus far is
only partial. Contemporary technology allows networks a great deal more
visual framing.

Manufacturing the News

During the course of Colleen's narrative, the screen is framed in complex
ways. Throughout, the CNN logo appears in the lower right-hand corner,
sometimes surmounting the word LIVE. On the left side, approximately
one-third of the way from the bottom of the screen is the heading BREAK-
ING NEWS appearing above the slogan AMERICA UNDER ATTACK.
Under these appear two levels of changing headlines. One is static; in the
transcript below, it is indicated in capital letters at the point that it first
appears. Below that, moving headlines sometimes appear. These are indicated below in lower-case letters at the point that they first appear.
Although the static heads (indicated in capitals) occasionally appear without moving titles, the reverse never occurs.

A further visual aspect of this construction is what fills the screen
while we hear Colleen's voice. We begin by seeing Colleen in a small box
next to a larger one that replays scenes of the World Trade Center attack
and the attendant chaos. Colleen momentarily fills the screen, and then,
for most of her narrative, we watch scenes occasionally labeled either "earlier" or "live." Colleen fills the screen momentarily at the end, then ends in
her small box. For much of her narrative, then, we are watching current or
prior footage of the event. Colleen's narrative becomes raw material after

all. In the course of its telling, it is manufactured to conform to the entertainment conventions of documentaries. She becomes a "voice over."

What is the effect of these multiple layers of information on the screen? One common linguistic theory of conversation is that people attribute logic to the statements made by others even if that logic isn't obvious. For example, people work hard to make sense of a statement, even if they've misheard it. This accounts for much humor, for example, the tirade by *Saturday Night Live*'s Emily Litella (Gilda Radner), who asked, "What's all this about violins in the street?" So one might assume that the titles framing Colleen's narrative invite a kind of active sense-making on the part of the viewer, even if these titles appear at random. They certainly allow (one could argue, invite) the construction of secondary narratives. In bracketed italics below, I indicate my own parallel narrative, a construction afforded me by CNN's framing.

MAJOR FEDERAL BUILDINGS EVALUATED IN WASHINGTON AREA

Plane believed to be an airliner crashes into Somerset County, Pennsylvania

Someone said to me a moment ago that before the day is over everything is going to be shut down, and that seems ta- to be where we're headed. Ah CNN's Richard Ross is on the, ah Richard Roth rather, is on the streets of New York and he can join us now. Richard, what can you tell us?

[*Everything's being shut down and buildings are being evacuated.*]

Part of Pentagon collapses after airliner reportedly crashes into military nerve center

Aaron, New Yorkers think they've seen everything but ah they'll never, they'll say they- they're amazed at what has happened, stunned. Right now behind me, what normally would be the World Trade Center is no more. A huge cloud of white smoke. And right now it's like a war zone. Thousands of New Yorkers streaming north. The mayor of New York City, Rudy Giuliani, has told everyone to get north of Canal Street. We're several miles north of it. Ah right now New Yorkers are trying to get out of Manhattan. There's a ferry on the west side going to New Jersey, it's really the only access out. The mayor advising ah that people should take the subways. We have seen dozens of emergency vehicles, hundreds.

[*Things are collapsing and crashing all around, not just in New York.*]

RICHARD ROTH

CNN NEW YORK then,

LOS ANGELES INTL. AIRPORT CLOSED

White House, Departments of Justice, State evacuated: Fires at Pentagon, National Mall

Firemen being bussed in, decamp- decontamination vans coming in, calls for blood donations, for New Yorkers, their faces their expressions — stunned, amazed right now. With us several of those people who witnessed some of the carnage today.

[*The symbols of our government are endangered, we are preparing for the worst, and everyone is stunned.*]

LOS ANGELES INTL. AIRPORT CLOSED

Tell us what you saw when you exited the subway station due to a lack of smoke, Colleen.

[Colleen in small box.] Um, it was very smoky and then we exited on Church Street out of the PATH train station. [Colleen in full screen.] Um, I crossed over to Church and ah Fulton,

[*Our transportation system — subways and planes — is under attack.*]

TERROR ATTACKS AGAINST TARGETS IN NEW YORK AND WASHINGTON

FAA halts all domestic air travel, diverts flights to Canada; first time in history

[Voice only] and I was trying to get a cell phone. I was trying to get up the block, and I turned around and saw this tremendous fire. I thought it was a bomb, I couldn't see a plane. And I saw people jumping out of- off the building, many, many people just jumping. And in a panic, I had my bag and my cell phone and everything, and I was trying to find a phone because the cell phone wasn't working. Everybody was screaming, everybody was running,

[*This has been an attack of real terror.*]

Lower Manhattan, United Nations evacuated; Philadelphia landmarks also emptied

the cops are trying to maintain the calm. And in that haste people were stampeding. People started screaming that there was another plane coming, I didn't see the plane but I turned around and it just- the second building just exploded, and again all the debris was flying towards us. There was a woman on the ground with her baby, people were stampeding the baby. Myself and another man threw ourselves over the baby and pushed into the building. I got up and I just ran.

[*Lower Manhattan is in chaos.*]

All Capital Hill buildings, U.S. Supreme Court evacuated

And I ran towards City Hall. Then I said "oh God why am I running there?" And then I started to run towards the water. And then ah, I was by probably Spring Street, or- or- or I'm sorry Prince Street? I was at a pay phone and I heard the rumbeling. I thought it was another bomb, I thought it was another building close to me. And then I just ah- ran from the pay phone. The man is grabbing me back

[*The city and national government buildings are in danger.*]

BOTH U.S. BORDERS ON HIGHEST STATE OF ALERT

telling me, "Stay here you're safe." I was like, "No way, I'm getting outta here. Go north." And then I ran into a shoe store because I wanted to call my husband, that's all I wanted to do.

[*We're in a high state of alert and nothing is safe.*]

10,000 emergency personnel scrambled to Trade Center fires, eventual collapse

I wanted him to know I was alive because he knew I was in the World Trade. And um I got my office, and they connected me to my husband, and then we heard the second fall of the World Trade Center. And I- I'm astonished by the bombing. I just want to make a statement that these New York policemen and firemen, God bless them, they kept us calm, they tried so hard to keep us moving north.

[*She is describing the collapse of the World Trade Center as it is announced and shown on the screen.*]

TERROR ATTACKS AGAINST TARGETS IN NEW YORK AND WASHINGTON

And it was just absolute, absolute horror, it was horror.

And when you look back there

[*New York and Washington are sights of terror and horror.*]

More than 150,000 people visit the World Trade Center on average day

at what would be the Nor- the World Trade Center?

It's devastating, I can't look back. My six-year-old just last week asked my husband and I to take him to the [crying] observation deck, and it's gone. And you know what? Americans will persevere. And I don't think that we'll stoop [Colleen on full screen] to the level of these zealot, terrorist pigs. [Colleen in box] And we won't kill children, I hope,

[*It may not be an average day today, but America will persevere.*]

TWO PLANES CRASH INTO TOWERS OF WORLD TRADE CENTER

and mothers. But you know what? Whatever we have to do to eradicate the country or the world of this- of this vermin, I just hope

[*We'll get the vermin who attacked the World Trade Center.*]

New York Police official calls scene "like war zone"

Bush will do whatever is necessary to get rid of them. And I don't know, don't know what the root of, what they, of what the answer is

                                    [
                                    Al-alright

thank you very much.

[*We are at war and Bush is the commander in chief.*]

A lot of other New Yorkers here [pan to man who appears to be waiting to speak] continuing the evacuation of lower Manhattan. Back to you Aaron.

Aaron: Ah thank you Richard very much. [Aaron appears.] Ah we told you a bit ago that the border,

AARON BROWN

CNN NEW YORK

the U.S.-Mexican border was at a high state of alert- has been essentially closed down, shut down. We're now told that the U.S.-Canada border is also in a high state of alert. So essentially what officials

All 24,000 Pentagon employees evacuated; part of building collapses in fire

are trying to do is seal off the country. So if anyone is either trying to get in or get out, ah it's gonna be a whole lot harder to do that. Ah, but what is possible and what is imaginable I guess changes on a day like this.

[*The Pentagon has been attacked and we are sealing off the country.*]

What are we to make of this very televisual narrative construction? On the one hand, we have a first-hand account by a person who has survived a quite terrible event. But through its presence on television, it contributes to constructing a new collective identity, a new "them" and "us," and to ratifying the results of a presidential election which was, until September 11, still very much contested in many people's minds. But the further framing of the narrative does a great deal more. Following the early morning of September 11, television networks showed the attack and collapse of the World Trade Center over and over again. And if viewers weren't alarmed enough, the unending headlines (really sublines) continually escalated the level of concern. These messages along with the voices of people who were "one of us," helped transform an attack into an act of war. With the construction of "us" came the inevitable "them" in a place once very far away. But the movement toward war and the televised geography lessons are the subject of later chapters.

A Truncated Narrative

By way of contrast, let's examine another interview, one that doesn't seem to go as well. Within an hour of Colleen's telling. Mr. Gonzalez, a maintenance worker at the World Trade Center was on the phone. Aaron Brown instructs him to "Tell me what happened." In Spanish-accented English, Mr. Gonzalez begins a narrative with apparently inadequate orientation and evaluation. Recall that the lack of these features in working-class narrators has been shown to earn low evaluations. In fact, Mr. Gonzalez is interrupted several times with requests for these features: an orientation ("how much time has elapsed") and an evaluation ("what did it *seem* like"). And, at a stage when these were sparse, the narrative is foreshortened. Activating his authority to delegate the floor, Brown brings the tale to an abrupt end: "Alright Mr. Gonzalez, let me stop you there."

In contrast to Colleen's transcript, the following does not document a synchronous performance, with interviewer and narrator working together to create a seamless description. Note that what is reproduced here is an excerpt. Mr. Gonzalez has seen truly horrific sights. To spare us some of those images, the transcript begins in the middle.

Mr. G: I went back in and ah- When I went back in, I saw people- I heard ah people that were stuck on an elevator, on a freight elevator, because all the elevators went down. And water was going in, and they were probably getting drowned. And we got a couple of pipes, and we opened the elevator, and we got the people out. I went back up, and I saw one of the officers for the Port Authority Police. I've been working there for twenty years, so I knew him very well. Ah my routine on the World Trade Center is to be in charge of the staircase and since there was no elevator service, I have the master key for all the, for all the ah ah ah staircase doors, so I went up with the police officer and a ah group of firemen. As we went up, there was a lot of people coming down. and while we got- it was very difficult to get up. When

Brown: Mr. Gonzalez

G: Ah huh

B: Mr. Gonzalez, how much time has taken- has elapsed here ah in in this, as you recount the events. Did it seem like hours, minutes, seconds what'd it seem like?

G: No it wasn't hours. It was

               [

B: But what'd it *seem* like?

G: well, there was a, there as a big time, like a gap. It

                        [

B: yeah

G: was a gap of time. I won't be able to tell you if it was 15 or 20 minutes,

                                 [

B: okay

G: but it was ah, it was a gap of time. We heard- while we were on the 33rd floor- I'm sorry on the 23rd floor, because we stopped there with the Fire Department, because their equipment was very heavy and they were out- they were breathing very hard. They took a break because they couldn't continue going up, so they wanted to take a break.

  B: yeah

  G: And ah, we have a person on a wheelchair that we were
    gonna bring down on a gurney, and a lady who was having
    problems with a heart attack, and um, and some other guy
    that was breathing hardly. We went a couple of floors up,
    while they were putting the person in the gurney, got up to
    the 39th floor, and we heard on the radio that ah the 65th
    floor collapsed. I heard it collapsed.
         [

  B: Alright, Mr. Gonzalez, let me stop
    you there, um and let me add you're a lucky man it seems
    like today. Thank you for joining us. Mike Cartwright, you
    were on the 64th floor, 65th floor?

Of course we can't know for certain why Mr. Gonzalez never reaches a
coda. So many features may have contributed to a foreshortening of his
tale. One can't help but wonder if his accented English contributes, as well
as the fact that he seems not to answer queries to Brown's satisfaction.
Perhaps the on-screen narrator waiting in the wings is judged to be more
telegenic than was Mr. Gonzalez on the phone.

News as Entertainment

The next narrator, Mike Cartwright, will have his own set of challenges in
matching his tale to the entertainment demands of television news. What
is particularly interesting in his interview are some of the questions. Below
are excerpts from the interview that surround questions.

  MC: Ah, it was packed. I mean it was a knot- a virtual traffic jam
    in the staircase ah, up and down, I guess. Um, it was very
    full.

  B: People screaming?

  MC: No, actually everyone maintained calm, ah really well. I was
    really impressed with that. Ah, I think, ah, for some people it
    brought back memories of the bombing, people who had
    been there before when that happened, but ah I was amazed
    really. Ah we got into the stairway. We were moving down
    when the Fire Department group were coming up. They'd
    say, you know, "Move to the left, everyone move to the left,"
    and everyone complied. A couple of people started crying a
    little bit, but you know we said, "We're gonna get outta here,
    we just gotta ah, just gotta focus and take it one step at a
    time."

  B: Was it noisy or was there screaming? Was there violence?
      [[

  MC: no it was ah   no

  B: Was it eerie?

MC: It- it was no fear- I mean it wasn't quiet. I mean people were talking in- in fact someone was laughing. I kept hearing that. I thought that was strange. But ah, it- it was pretty normal. I- er- we didn't know what was going on. I mean, all we knew was something major had happened. . . .

MC: The police were saying, "Don't look back, don't look back," and of course we made it about half a block, and I looked back, and I saw the other tower on fire, and I couldn't believe it and ah

B: Were you terrified? Were you terrified?

MC: Ah yes we're- when we were stuck in that stairway, I mean, we stopped every now, it- it started to get nervous. But we never had any fear of the building collapse. I mean, we had no idea what was going on, ah so um, but once I got out, and it's still sinking in the real full severity of it. I mean it's just an awful- awful thing.

B: That's true for everybody.

MC: Yep, so.

B: You're a lucky man.

MC: I am lucky I ah I thank God very much.

B: As well you might.

MC: Thank you.

B: Thank you very much, thank you.

Brown's "leading questions" attempt to get the speaker to focus on the entertainment aspects of the experience: feelings and emotions. He inquires whether people were screaming, if there was violence, if it was eerie, if the survivors were terrified. Not only were these not the case (was Brown disappointed that people weren't screaming?), but these were clearly not questions Mike Cartwright initially thought to address in building his informational narrative. Mike is a citizen turned reporter.

Mike is also a competent narrator. Below is the beginning of the interview. Note how skillfully he builds an orientation, even in the face of Brown's interruptions.

B: Thank you for joining us, Mike Cartwright. You were on the 64th floor, 65th floor?

MC: Sixty-fifth floor, yeah. That's where I work.

B: Tell me what happened?

MC: Well, I arrived at work early today.

B: What do you do?

MC: I work for the Port Authority

[

B: okay

MC: the Aviation Department, and ah I was just puttin' my stuff away, and all of a sudden we heard a loud crash, and ah the building started shaking. . . .

Evidence that Mike's narrative is well received by his interviewer comes from the closing. We noted above that television newsmakers have the floor by virtue of the authority of newscasters, who can take it away at any point. Recall Mr. Gonzalez's abrupt ending. In typical conversational closings,[9] speakers build a closing by taking several turns before talk ceases. One speaker makes a preclosing invitation by indicating that s/he has nothing more to say. If this is ratified and confirmed by both parties, a conversation ends. It's not the case that speakers say nothing other than Okay/Okay in closings, but with each turn, they indicate that they have no new information or topics to raise. If they do discover they have new business, the conversation continues. Here's a typical closing:

> A: Okay.
> B: Okay.
> A: Nice to talk to you.
> B: We'll do it again soon. Give my best to Sue.
> A: Will do.
> B: Thanks.
> A: Bye.
> B: Bye.

In the conversation/interview between Aaron Brown and Mike Cartwright, their closing follows a similar format, far different from the typical on-screen closing in which a newscaster simply announces that the conversation has ended ("Okay, thanks very much, back to you, Paul"). Perhaps because this is a real-time interview — one that meets the newscaster's approval — it is Mike who gets to the point of "passing," indicating no new topics. And, rather than closing immediately, Brown allows the full closing ritual to play out:

> MC: . . . and it's still sinking in the real full severity of it. I mean it's just an awful- awful thing.
> B: That's true for everybody.
> MC: Yep, so.
> B: You're a lucky man.
> MC: I am lucky I ah I thank God very much.
> B: As well you might.
> MC: Thank you.
> B: Thank you very much, thank you.

We have seen that in the unpredictable world of television interviews, the reporter on the street can encounter a range of speakers. Not all of them are as willing to participate as the narrators we've encountered thus far.

Not Playing

Television's tendency to turn tragedy into entertainment is not lost on the public, and it's not always greeted kindly, at least not by those who've just experienced trauma. Along with all the willing participants on 9/11, there were those who refused to play.

At one point early in CNN's coverage, the camera panned to a group of dust-covered survivors being led onto a bus. The camera moved in for a close-up as an off-camera interviewer (I) asked, "How did you get out?" The female interviewee (W) agreed to be a newsmaker/reporter, but drew the line at entertainment:

> W: The police officer told everybody to form a human chain. And we held on to each other, and he fl- flashed a light, and he directed everybody to building five. And we went out building five
>
> I: Did you see people bleeding?
>
> After what linguists call a false start ("Oh every body cou-see,"), W replied:
>
> W: You want blood, here's blood . . .
>
> She lifted her skirt to show a wounded leg and, with a wave of her hand, dismissed the reporter.

Live television news can be unnerving for both the newscaster and the newsmaker. And while citizens, by and large, know how to play, they are not always game.

Spinning the Image: The News Magazine

The unpredictable nature of live coverage explains why the television industry relies heavily on the highly edited news magazine format. This allows for carefully manufactured narratives, which can be cut and massaged until they are properly telegenic. At the same time, the immediacy of the interview format is maintained. Higher-status interviewees often prefer the control that this kind of coverage affords them.

Several networks featured interviews with Howard Lutnick in the early days after 9/11. Lutnick was the CEO of the world's largest bond firm, Cantor Fitzgerald, which had lost over 700 employees, including Lutnick's brother, in the World Trade Center. It was a tragically compelling story — one that news magazines were more than willing to tell repeatedly. Following is an excerpt from an interview with NBC *Dateline's* Bob McKuen. It begins with a shot of Cantor Fitzgerald's door closing and moves to digitalized scenes of workers in computerized cubicles. McKuen's voice-over announces:

> . . . You may not know its name, but one of those companies is called Cantor Fitzgerald. Cantor Fitzgerald dominates the bond market. Last year the firm did $50 trillion in business. But according to Chairman and CEO Howard Lutnick, what's made him most proud isn't his bottom line, but the kind of company it is.

Lutnick, now on screen, says:

> We are a family, we are the tightest group of people. We always have been a tight group of people, but you just don't know it — we did know it, but in this last couple of days, I mean, it's unbelievable.

As the camera pans debris of the World Trade Center and rescue workers, McKuen's voice is heard:

> And how long these past few days must have been for Howard Lutnick. In a catastrophe that's crushed an entire country, no one can have been hit harder than he has.

Lutnick on camera:

> We have lost every single person who was in the office. We don't know of any, not a single one person getting down from the 101st to the 105th floors where our offices were, not a single person.

As the interview continued, Lutnick's story is precisely "illustrated" by shots of the plane flying into the World Trade Center and the aftermath of the crash. This was the story of tragedy on a great scale. But it was also a story controlled and manufactured by both Lutnick and the media. From the perspective of the media, the news magazine format allowed them control and the ability to provide precise illustration of the tale. This was a far cry from the random shots that accompanied the real-time Breaking News coverage. The possibility of control served the interviewee as well. In the luxury of a sit-down interview, Lutnick was able to project an image of a fatherly CEO taking care of a family. In the course of these interviews, Lutnick promised to take care of that family. In the weeks that followed, he seemed to renege, then (in the face of mounting negative publicity) seems to have followed through. This was a survivor narrative played out elaborately in and by the media.

The Fully Manufactured Narrative: *Third Watch*

Finally, the media can fully manufacture a narrative — from the raw material of real people's experience, it can forge a composite story. This tactic was employed by the producers of TV's *Third Watch*, a series about rescue workers. It presented a show pieced together from the September 11 experiences of New York's men and women in uniform. In place of actors, the actual personnel were on camera. Multiple speakers produced a single narrative. The show began with a host explaining, "These are the people we portray on *Third Watch*, and this is the reason we portray them." Recall that the well-formed narrative begins with an *orientation* (Who, when, where, what?), moves to a *complicating action* (What happened?), and includes *evaluation* (What did you think? How did you feel?). As is evident in the brief transcript below, in the first moments of the hours-long show, composite versions of these elements had already been constructed. The names at the margins were shown on the screen, identifying the speakers.

Orientation + complicating action

Officer Mike Freeman:

Ah, on the 11th I had just finished my midnight tour so I left about ten after eight in the morning, 8:15. And it was just- normal day, you know, leave work, dry cleaners, post office that type of stuff, running a few errands. And I heard on the car radio that a small airplane had crashed into the World Trade Center.

Sgt. John Flynn:

I was on the New Jersey Turnpike, ah, the turnpike extension coming into Jersey when my wife called me. She goes, "Have you heard the news?" And as I'm answering the phone, I'm walking over and I can see the smoke coming out of- out of the North Tower.

Evaluation

Officer David Norman:

Initially we thought that it might have been a small aircraft or one of these stunt people, like the guy that landed on the Statue of Liberty. Ah, we really didn't know what we had.

Officer Edward McQuade:

I was totally unprepared for the magnitude of what I saw when I turned the news on. And I realized immediately, I said to him, "Look, I hate to cut you short, but," I said, "I think I'd better get to work."

Officer David Norman:

I get in my car and drove a couple blocks to where I could see the Trade Center. And from what I saw, I could tell that it was no small aircraft that hit that building.

Next complicating action

Sgt. John Sullivan:

So we had somebody close the HOV lane, had them close down the Brooklyn Battery Tunnel except for emergency vehicles, and start out some additional equipment.

Officer Kenny Winger:

Some guys just came running down. I said "Oh just jump in the back of the truck." I grabbed my bag, my uniforms, my gun-belt, got in the back of the truck. And I had everything . . . but my pants.

In its reporting of the events of September 11, television news offered a range of formats through which the public heard from those who survived the "Attack on America." All of these came to viewers through the powerful tools of audio/visual programming. From the immediate manufacturing of on-the-street survivor narratives to the production of news magazines to the construction of composite narratives, all of the tales provided by television were mediated accounts. They served to provide a nation with a shared tale of September 11.

Appendix: Colleen's Narrative Structure

Abstract	Tell us what you saw when you exited the subway station due to a lack of smoke, Colleen
Orientation	Um, it was very smoky and then we exited on Church Street out of the PATH train station. Um, I crossed over to Church and ah Fulton, and
Evaluation	I was trying to get a cell phone. I was trying to get up the block
Complicating action	and I turned around and saw this tremendous fire.
Evaluation	I thought it was a bomb,
Complicating action	I couldn't see a plane. And I saw people jumping out of- off the building, many, many people just jumping.
Evaluation	And in a panic, I had my bag and my cell phone and everything, and I was trying to find a phone because the cell phone wasn't working.
Complicating action	Everybody was screaming, everybody was running, the cops are trying to maintain the calm.
Evaluation	And in that haste
Complicating action	people were stampeding. People started screaming that there was another plane coming, I didn't see the plane but I turned around and it just- the second building just exploded, and again all the debris was flying towards us. There was a woman on the ground with her baby, people were stampeding the baby. Myself and another man threw ourselves over the baby and pushed into the building. I got up and I just ran.
Orientation	And I ran towards City Hall.
Evaluation	Then I said "oh God why am I running there?"
Orientation	And then I started to run towards the water. And then ah, I was by probably Spring Street, or- or- or I'm sorry Prince Street? I was at a pay phone
Complicating action	and I heard the rumbeling.
Evaluation	I thought it was another bomb, I thought it was another building close to me.
Complicating action	And then I just ah- ran from the pay phone. The man is grabbing me back telling me, "Stay here you're safe." I was like, "No way, I'm getting outta here. Go north." And then I ran into a shoe store

Evaluation	because I wanted to call my husband, that's all I wanted to do. I wanted him to know I was alive because he knew I was in the World Trade.
Complicating action	And um I got my office, and they connected me to my husband, and then we heard the second fall of the World Trade Center.
Evaluation	And I- I'm astonished by the bombing. I just want to make a statement that these New York policemen and firemen, God bless them, they kept us calm, they tried so hard to keep us moving north.
Coda	And it was just absolute, absolute horror, it was horror.

NOTES

1. Charlotte Linde, *Life Stories: The Creation of Coherence*, Oxford University Press, 1993. Linde builds on Livia Polanyi, *Telling the American Story: A Structural and Cultural Analysis of Conversational Storytelling*, Norwood, NJ: Ablex, 1985, p. 194.

2. Linde, p. 114.

3. Much of the description of television news coverage in this section follows from the work of linguist Ron Scollon, though he is obviously not responsible for the ways in which I appropriate this research. See Ron Scollon, *Mediated Discourse as Social Action: A Study of News Discourse*, London: Longman, 1998.

4. Michael A. Lipton and Diane Herbst, *People*, December 3, 2001.

5. Anthony Bell, *The Language of the News Media*, Oxford: Basil Blackwell, 1991, p. 191, as cited in Scollon, p. 216.

6. Scollon, pp. 261–2.

7. William Labov, *Language in the Inner City*, Philadelphia: University of Pennsylvania Press, 1972.

8. Ruth Wodak, "The Interaction between Judge and Defendant," in Teun van Dijk (Ed.), *Handbook of Discourse Analysis (Vol. 4)*, London: Academic Press, 1985. Cited in Michael Toolan, *Narrative: A Critical Linguistic Introduction*, Routledge, 1988, pp. 254–5.

9. This discussion of closings is based on the work of Emanuel A. Schegloff and Harvey Sacks, "Opening Up Closings," *Semantica* 7: 289–327, 1973. Readers can find an abridged version in Adam Jaworski and Nikolas Coupland, *The Discourse Reader*, London: Routledge, 1999.

I Has a Dream

I Has a Dream is an anti-Ebonics advertisement created for Atlanta's Black Professionals by Lee St. James, Creative Director for Austin Kelley Advertising. The provocative image portraying Martin Luther King Jr. turning his back on Ebonics was printed in poster format for display in schools. In addition, it was published in various newspapers, including the *New York Times* on October 9, 1998. Despite the prompting of some protest by a group of concerned linguists and educators, the advertisement was the Grand Prize winner of the Newspaper Association of America's ATHENA Award for best newspaper advertising.

■ ■ ■

Does this bother you? It should. We've spent over 400 years fighting for the right to have a voice. Is this how we'll use it? More importantly, is this how we'll teach our children to use it? If we expect more of them, we must not throw our hands in the air and agree with those who say our children cannot be taught. By now, you've probably heard about Ebonics (aka, black English). And if you think it's become a controversy because white America doesn't want us messing with their precious language, don't. White America couldn't care less what we do to segregate ourselves.

The fact is language is power. And we can't take that power away from our children with Ebonics. Would Dr. Martin Luther King,

Malcom X and all the others who paid the price of obtaining our voice with the currency of their lives embrace this? If you haven't used your voice lately, consider this an invitation.

SPEAK OUT AGAINST
EBONICS

Academic Bill of Rights

Students for Academic Freedom is an activist group that was founded by the controversial conservative writer David Horowitz after a study he conducted revealed that more college professors are Democrats than Republicans. According to Horowitz, this imbalance in favor of Democrats suggests that institutions of higher education seek to indoctrinate students with liberal ideology. The findings of this study from 2004 prompted the Students for Academic Freedom to draft the *Academic Bill of Rights* in order to "end the political abuse of the university and to restore integrity to the academic mission as a disinterested pursuit of knowledge." The American Association of University Professors, an organization of professors that dates back to 1915 and that has as its purpose advancing academic freedom in the university, opposes the *Academic Bill of Rights*.

I. The Mission of the University

The central purposes of a University are the pursuit of truth, the discovery of new knowledge through scholarship and research, the study and reasoned criticism of intellectual and cultural traditions, the teaching and general development of students to help them become creative individuals and productive citizens of a pluralistic democracy, and the transmission of knowledge and learning to a society at large. Free inquiry and free speech within the academic community are indispensable to the achievement of these goals. The freedom to teach and to learn depend upon the creation of appropriate conditions and opportunities on the campus as a whole as well as in the classrooms and lecture halls. These purposes reflect the values — pluralism, diversity, opportunity, critical intelligence, openness and fairness — that are the cornerstones of American society.

II. Academic Freedom

1. The Concept

Academic freedom and intellectual diversity are values indispensable to the American university. From its first formulation in the *General Report of the Committee on Academic Freedom and Tenure* of the American Association of University Professors, the concept of academic freedom has been premised on the idea that human knowledge is a never-ending pursuit of the truth, that there is no humanly accessible truth that is not in principle open to challenge, and that no party or intellectual faction has a monopoly on wisdom. Therefore, academic freedom is most likely to thrive in an environment of intellectual diversity that protects and fosters independence of thought and speech. In the words of the *General Report*, it is vital to protect "as the first condition of progress, [a] complete and unlimited freedom to *pursue* inquiry and publish its results."

Because free inquiry and its fruits are crucial to the democratic enterprise itself, academic freedom is a national value as well. In a historic 1967 decision (*Keyishian v. Board of Regents of the University of the State of New York*) the Supreme Court of the United States overturned a New York State loyalty provision for teachers with these words: "Our Nation is deeply committed to safeguarding academic freedom, [a] transcendent value to all of us and not merely to the teachers concerned." In *Sweezy v. New Hampshire*, (1957) the Court observed that the "essentiality of freedom in the community of American universities [was] almost self-evident."

2. The Practice
Academic freedom consists in protecting the intellectual independence of professors, researchers and students in the pursuit of knowledge and the expression of ideas from interference by legislators or authorities within the institution itself. This means that no political, ideological or religious orthodoxy will be imposed on professors and researchers through the hiring or tenure or termination process, or through any other administrative means by the academic institution. Nor shall legislatures impose any such orthodoxy through their control of the university budget.

This protection includes students. From the first statement on academic freedom, it has been recognized that intellectual independence means the protection of students — as well as faculty — from the imposition of any orthodoxy of a political, religious or ideological nature. The 1915 *General Report* admonished faculty to avoid "taking unfair advantage of the student's immaturity by indoctrinating him with the teacher's own opinions before the student has had an opportunity fairly to examine other opinions upon the matters in question, and before he has sufficient knowledge and ripeness of judgment to be entitled to form any definitive opinion of his own." In 1967, the AAUP's *Joint Statement on Rights and Freedoms of Students* reinforced and amplified this injunction by affirming the inseparability of "the freedom to teach and freedom to learn." In the words of the report, "Students should be free to take reasoned exception to the data or views offered in any course of study and to reserve judgment about matters of opinion."

Therefore, to secure the intellectual independence of faculty and students and to protect the principle of intellectual diversity, the following principles and procedures shall be observed.

These principles fully apply only to public universities and to private universities that present themselves as bound by the canons of academic freedom. Private institutions choosing to restrict academic freedom on the basis of creed have an obligation to be as explicit as is possible about the scope and nature of these restrictions.

1. All faculty shall be hired, fired, promoted and granted tenure on the basis of their competence and appropriate knowledge in the field of their expertise and, in the humanities, the social sciences, and the arts, with a view toward fostering a plurality of methodologies and perspectives. No faculty shall be hired or fired or denied promotion or tenure on the basis of his or her political or religious beliefs.

2. No faculty member will be excluded from tenure, search and hiring committees on the basis of their political or religious beliefs.

3. Students will be graded solely on the basis of their reasoned answers and appropriate knowledge of the subjects and disciplines they study, not on the basis of their political or religious beliefs.

4. Curricula and reading lists in the humanities and social sciences should reflect the uncertainty and unsettled character of all human knowledge in these areas by providing students with dissenting sources and viewpoints where appropriate. While teachers are and should be free to pursue their own findings and perspectives in presenting their views, they should consider and make their students aware of other viewpoints. Academic disciplines should welcome a diversity of approaches to unsettled questions.

5. Exposing students to the spectrum of significant scholarly viewpoints on the subjects examined in their courses is a major responsibility of faculty. Faculty will not use their courses for the purpose of political, ideological, religious or anti-religious indoctrination.

6. Selection of speakers, allocation of funds for speakers programs and other student activities will observe the principles of academic freedom and promote intellectual pluralism.

7. An environment conducive to the civil exchange of ideas being an essential component of a free university, the obstruction of invited campus speakers, destruction of campus literature or other effort to obstruct this exchange will not be tolerated.

8. Knowledge advances when individual scholars are left free to reach their own conclusions about which methods, facts, and theories have been validated by research. Academic institutions and professional societies formed to advance knowledge within an area of research, maintain the integrity of the research process, and organize the professional lives of related researchers serve as indispensable venues within which scholars circulate research findings and debate their interpretation. To perform these functions adequately, academic institutions and professional societies should maintain a posture of organizational neutrality with respect to the substantive disagreements that divide researchers on questions within, or outside, their fields of inquiry.

Op. cit., p. 50

■   AMERICAN ASSOCIATION OF UNIVERSITY PROFESSORS
Academic Bill of Rights

The statement that follows was approved for publication by the Association's Committee A on Academic Freedom and Tenure. Comments are welcome and should be addressed to the AAUP's Washington office.

The past year has witnessed repeated efforts to establish what has been called an "Academic Bill of Rights." Basing their views on data purporting to show that Democrats greatly outnumber Republicans in faculty positions, and citing official statements and principles of the American Association of University Professors, advocates of the Academic Bill of Rights would require universities to maintain political pluralism and diversity. This requirement is said to enforce the principle that "no political, ideological or religious orthodoxy should be imposed on professors and researchers through the hiring or tenure or termination process."[1] Although Committee A endorses this principle, which we shall call the "principle of neutrality," it believes that the Academic Bill of Rights is an improper and dangerous method for the principle's implementation. There are already mechanisms in place that protect this principle, and they work well. Not only is the Academic Bill of Rights redundant, but, ironically, it also infringes academic freedom in the very act of purporting to protect it.

A fundamental premise of academic freedom is that decisions concerning the quality of scholarship and teaching are to be made by reference to the standards of the academic profession, as interpreted and applied by the community of scholars who are qualified by expertise and training to establish such standards. The proposed Academic Bill of Rights directs universities to enact guidelines implementing the principle of neutrality, in particular by requiring that colleges and universities appoint faculty "with a view toward fostering a plurality of methodologies and perspectives."[2] The danger of such guidelines is that they invite diversity to be measured by political standards that diverge from the academic criteria of the scholarly profession. Measured in this way, diversity can easily become contradictory to academic ends. So, for example, no department of political theory ought to be obligated to establish "a plurality of methodologies

---

[1]This language derives from a Concurrent Resolution (H.Con.Res. 318) proposed in the House of Representatives by Jack Kingston during the 108th Congress. It also appears in a proposed amendment to Article I of Title 23 of the Colorado Revised Statutes, 24–125.5. Both pieces of legislation grow out of a version of the Academic Bill of Rights originally drafted by columnist David Horowitz. See http://studentsforacademicfreedom .org/.

[2]H.Con.Res. 318. We note, parenthetically, that, while this embrace of diversity may be reasonable in some circumstances, it may make little academic sense in other contexts, as, for example, when a department wishes to specialize in a particular disciplinary approach.

and perspectives" by appointing a professor of Nazi political philosophy, if that philosophy is not deemed a reasonable scholarly option within the discipline of political theory. No department of chemistry ought to be obligated to pursue "a plurality of methodologies and perspectives" by appointing a professor who teaches the phlogiston theory of heat, if that theory is not deemed a reasonable perspective within the discipline of chemistry.

These examples illustrate that the appropriate diversity of a university faculty must ultimately be conceived as a question of academic judgment, to be determined by the quality and range of pluralism deemed reasonable by relevant disciplinary standards, as interpreted and applied by college and university faculty. Advocates for the Academic Bill of Rights, however, make clear that they seek to enforce a kind of diversity that is instead determined by essentially political categories, like the number of Republicans or Democrats on a faculty, or the number of conservatives or liberals. Because there is in fact little correlation between these political categories and disciplinary standing, the assessment of faculty by such explicitly political criteria, whether used by faculty, university administration, or the state, would profoundly corrupt the academic integrity of universities. Indeed, it would violate the neutrality principle itself. For this reason, recent efforts to enact the Academic Bill of Rights pose a grave threat to fundamental principles of academic freedom.

The Academic Bill of Rights also seeks to enforce the principle that "faculty members will not use their courses or their position for the purpose of political, ideological, religious, or antireligious indoctrination."[3] Although Committee A endorses this principle, which we shall call the nonindoctrination principle, the Academic Bill of Rights is an inappropriate and dangerous means for its implementation. This is because the bill seeks to distinguish indoctrination from appropriate pedagogy by applying principles other than relevant scholarly standards, as interpreted and applied by the academic profession.

If a professor of constitutional law reads the examination of a student who contends that terrorist violence should be protected by the First Amendment because of its symbolic message, the determination of whether the examination should receive a high or a low grade must be made by reference to the scholarly standards of the law. The application of these standards properly distinguishes indoctrination from competent pedagogy. Similarly, if a professor of American literature reads the examination of a student that proposes a singular interpretation of *Moby Dick*, the determination of whether the examination should receive a high or a low grade must be made by reference to the scholarly standards of literary criticism. The student has no "right" to be rewarded for an opinion of *Moby Dick* that is independent of these scholarly standards. If students possessed such rights, all knowledge would be reduced to opinion, and education would be rendered superfluous.

[3]H.Con.Res. 318.

The Academic Bill of Rights seeks to transfer responsibility for the evaluation of student competence to college and university administrators or to the courts, apparently on the premise that faculty ought to be stripped of the authority to make such evaluative judgments. The bill justifies this premise by reference to "the uncertainty and unsettled character of all human knowledge."[4] This premise, however, is antithetical to the basic scholarly enterprise of the university, which is to establish and transmit knowledge. Although academic freedom rests on the principle that knowledge is mutable and open to revision, an Academic Bill of Rights that reduces all knowledge to uncertain and unsettled opinion, and which proclaims that all opinions are equally valid, negates an essential function of university education.

Some versions of the Academic Bill of Rights imply that faculty ought not to be trusted to exercise the pedagogical authority required to make evaluative judgments. A bill proposing an Academic Bill of Rights recently under discussion in Colorado, for example, provides:

> The general assembly further declares that intellectual independence means the protection of students as well as faculty from the imposition of any orthodoxy of a political, religious or ideological nature. To achieve the intellectual independence of students, teachers should not take unfair advantage of a student's immaturity by indoctrinating him with the teacher's own opinions before a student has had an opportunity fairly to examine other opinions upon the matters in question, and before a student has sufficient knowledge and ripeness of judgment to be entitled to form any definitive opinion of his own, and students should be free to take reasoned exception to the data or views offered in any course of study and to reserve judgment about matters of opinion.[5]

On the surface, this paragraph appears merely to restate important elements of AAUP policy.[6] In the context of that policy, this paragraph unambiguously means that the line between indoctrination and proper pedagogical authority is to be determined by reference to scholarly and professional standards, as interpreted and applied by the faculty itself. In the context of the proposed Colorado Academic Bill of Rights, by contrast, this paragraph means that the line between indoctrination and proper pedagogical authority is to be determined by college and university administrations or by courts. This distinction is fundamental.

A basic purpose of higher education is to endow students with the knowledge and capacity to exercise responsible and independent judgment. Faculty can fulfill this objective only if they possess the authority to guide and instruct students. AAUP policies have long justified this authority

---

[4]H.Con.Res. 318.

[5]Proposed amendment to Article I of Title 23 of the Colorado Revised Statutes, 24–125.5.

[6]See "Some Observations on Ideology, Competence, and Faculty Selections," *Academe: Bulletin of the AAUP* 72, no. 1 (January–February 1986): 1a–2a.

by reference to the scholarly expertise and professional training of faculty. College and university professors exercise this authority every time they grade or evaluate students. Although faculty would violate the indoctrination principle were they to evaluate their students in ways not justified by the scholarly and ethical standards of the profession, faculty could not teach at all if they were utterly denied the ability to exercise this authority.

The clear implication of AAUP policy, therefore, is that the question whether it is indoctrination for teachers of biology to regard the theory of "evolution" as an opinion about which students must be allowed "to reserve judgment" can be answered only by those who are expert in biology. The whole thrust of the proposed Colorado Academic Bill of Rights, by contrast, is to express distrust of faculty capacity to make such judgments, and to transfer the supervision of such determinations to a college or university administration or to courts. The proposed Colorado bill thus transforms decisions that should be grounded in professional competence and expertise into decisions that are based upon managerial, mechanical, or, even worse, overtly political criteria. The proposed Colorado bill also facilitates the constant supervision of everyday pedagogic decision making, a supervision that threatens altogether to undercut faculty authority in the classroom. It thus portends incalculable damage to basic principles of academic freedom.

Skepticism of professional knowledge, such as that which underlies the Academic Bill of Rights, is deep and corrosive. This is well illustrated by its requirement that "academic institutions . . . maintain a posture of organizational neutrality with respect to the substantive disagreements that divide researchers on questions within . . . their fields of inquiry."[7] The implications of this requirement are truly breathtaking. Academic institutions, from faculty in departments to research institutes, perform their work precisely by making judgments of quality, which necessarily require them to intervene in academic controversies. Only by making such judgments of quality can academic institutions separate serious work from mere opinion, responsible scholarship from mere polemic. Because the advancement of knowledge depends upon the capacity to make judgments of quality, the Academic Bill of Rights would prevent colleges and universities from achieving their most fundamental mission.

When carefully analyzed, therefore, the Academic Bill of Rights undermines the very academic freedom it claims to support. It threatens to impose administrative and legislative oversight on the professional judgment of faculty, to deprive professors of the authority necessary for teaching, and to prohibit academic institutions from making the decisions that are necessary for the advancement of knowledge. For these reasons, Committee A strongly condemns efforts to enact the Academic Bill of Rights.

[7]H.Con.Res. 318.

The AAUP has consistently held that academic freedom can be maintained only so long as faculty remain autonomous and self-governing. We do not mean to imply, of course, that academic professionals never make mistakes or act in improper or unethical ways. But the AAUP has long stood for the proposition that violations of professional standards, like the principles of neutrality or nonindoctrination, are best remedied by the supervision of faculty peers. It is the responsibility of the professoriate, in cooperation with administrative officers, to ensure compliance with professional standards. By repudiating this basic concept, the Academic Bill of Rights alters the meaning of the principles of neutrality and nonindoctrination in ways that contradict academic freedom as it has been advanced in standards and practices which the AAUP has long endorsed.

■ AMY TAN

Mother Tongue

Born in California to Chinese immigrants, Amy Tan (b. 1952) began her writing career as a technical and business writer. In her mid-thirties, Tan began writing fiction, but it wasn't until she visited China with her mother in 1987 that Tan found her identity as a fiction writer. The visit clarified not only Tan's often difficult relationship with her mother but also Tan's own cultural identities. About that visit, she writes: "I discovered how American I was. I also discovered how Chinese I was by the kind of family habits and routines that were so familiar. I discovered a sense of finally belonging to a period of history which I never felt with American history." This tension between cultures and between mothers and daughters became the basis for Tan's first novel, *The Joy Luck Club* (1989). That was followed by the novels *The Kitchen God's Wife* (1991), which also examined her family history; *The Hundred Secret Senses* (1995); *The Bonesetter's Daughter* (2001); and *Saving Fish from Drowning* (2005). "Mother Tongue" (1990), one of Tan's best-known essays, first appeared in *The Threepenny Review*, a literary magazine that publishes poetry, fiction, and literary essays.

■ ■ ■

I am not a scholar of English or literature. I cannot give you much more than personal opinions on the English language and its variations in this country or others.

I am a writer. And by that definition, I am someone who has always loved language. I am fascinated by language in daily life. I spend a great deal of my time thinking about the power of language — the way it can evoke an emotion, a visual image, a complex idea, or a simple truth. Language is the tool of my trade. And I use them all — all the Englishes I grew up with.

Recently, I was made keenly aware of the different Englishes I do use. I was giving a talk to a large group of people, the same talk I had already given to half a dozen other groups. The nature of the talk was about my writing, my life, and my book, *The Joy Luck Club*. The talk was going along well enough, until I remembered one major difference that made the whole talk sound wrong. My mother was in the room. And it was perhaps the first time she had heard me give a lengthy speech, using the kind of English I have never used with her. I was saying things like, "The intersection of memory upon imagination" and "There is an aspect of my fiction that relates to thus-and-thus" — a speech filled with carefully wrought grammatical phrases, burdened, it suddenly seemed to me, with nominalized forms, past perfect tenses, conditional phrases, all the forms of standard English that I had learned in school and through books, the forms of English I did not use at home with my mother.

Just last week, I was walking down the street with my mother, and I again found myself conscious of the English I was using, the English I do use with her. We were talking about the price of new and used furniture and I heard myself saying this: "Not waste money that way." My husband was with us as well, and he didn't notice any switch in my English. And then I realized why. It's because over the twenty years we've been together I've often used that same kind of English with him, and sometimes he even uses it with me. It has become our language of intimacy, a different sort of English that relates to family talk, the language I grew up with.

So you'll have some idea of what this family talk I heard sounds like, I'll quote what my mother said during a recent conversation which I videotaped and then transcribed. During this conversation, my mother was talking about a political gangster in Shanghai who had the same last name as her family's, Du, and how the gangster in his early years wanted to be adopted by her family, which was rich by comparison. Later, the gangster became more powerful, far richer than my mother's family, and one day showed up at my mother's wedding to pay his respects. Here's what she said in part:

"Du Yusong having business like fruit stand. Like off the street kind. He is Du like Du Zong — but not Tsung-ming Island people. The local people call putong, the river east side, he belong to that side local people. That man want to ask Du Zong father take him in like become own family. Du Zong father wasn't look down on him, but didn't take seriously, until that man big like become a mafia. Now important person, very hard to inviting him. Chinese way, came only to show respect, don't stay for dinner. Respect for making big celebration, he shows up. Mean gives lots of respect. Chinese custom. Chinese social life that way. If too important won't have to stay too long. He come to my wedding. I didn't see, I heard it. I gone to boy's side, they have YMCA dinner. Chinese age I was nineteen."

You should know that my mother's expressive command of English belies how much she actually understands. She reads the *Forbes* report, listens to *Wall Street Week*, converses daily with her stockbroker, reads all of Shirley MacLaine's books with ease — all kinds of things I can't begin to understand. Yet some of my friends tell me they understand 50 percent of what my mother says. Some say they understand 80 to 90 percent. Some say they understand none of it, as if she were speaking pure Chinese. But to me, my mother's English is perfectly clear, perfectly natural. It's my mother tongue. Her language, as I hear it, is vivid, direct, full of observation and imagery. That was the language that helped shape the way I saw things, expressed things, made sense of the world.

Lately, I've been giving more thought to the kind of English my mother speaks. Like others, I have described it to people as "broken" or "fractured" English. But I wince when I say that. It has always bothered me that I can think of no way to describe it other than "broken," as if it were damaged and needed to be fixed, as if it lacked a certain wholeness and soundness. I've heard other terms used, "limited English," for example. But they seem just as bad, as if everything is limited, including people's perceptions of the limited English speaker.

I know this for a fact, because when I was growing up, my mother's "limited" English limited my perception of her. I was ashamed of her English. I believed that her English reflected the quality of what she had to say. That is, because she expressed them imperfectly her thoughts were imperfect. And I had plenty of empirical evidence to support me: the fact that people in department stores, at banks, and at restaurants did not take her seriously, did not give her good service, pretended not to understand her, or even acted as if they did not hear her.

My mother has long realized the limitations of her English as well. When I was fifteen, she used to have me call people on the phone to pretend I was she. In this guise, I was forced to ask for information or even to complain and yell at people who had been rude to her. One time it was a call to her stockbroker in New York. She had cashed out her small portfolio and it just so happened we were going to go to New York the next week, our very first trip outside California. I had to get on the phone and say in an adolescent voice that was not very convincing, "This is Mrs. Tan."

And my mother was standing in the back whispering loudly, "Why he don't send me check, already two weeks late. So mad he lie to me, losing me money."

And then I said in perfect English, "Yes, I'm getting rather concerned. You had agreed to send the check two weeks ago, but it hasn't arrived."

Then she began to talk more loudly. "What he want, I come to New York tell him front of his boss, you cheating me?" And I was trying to calm her down, make her be quiet, while telling the stockbroker, "I can't tolerate any more excuses. If I don't receive the check immediately, I am going to have to speak to your manager when I'm in New York next week." And sure enough, the following week there we were in front of this astonished stockbroker, and I was sitting there red-faced and quiet, and my mother, the real Mrs. Tan, was shouting at his boss in her impeccable broken English.

We used a similar routine just five days ago, for a situation that was far less humorous. My mother had gone to the hospital for an appointment, to find out about a benign brain tumor a CAT scan had revealed a month ago. She said she had spoken very good English, her best English, no mistakes. Still, she said, the hospital did not apologize when they said they had lost the CAT scan and she had come for nothing. She said they did not seem to have any sympathy when she told them she was anxious to know the exact diagnosis, since her husband and son had both died of brain tumors. She said they would not give her any more information until the next time and she would have to make another appointment for that. So she said she would not leave until the doctor called her daughter. She wouldn't budge. And when the doctor finally called her daughter, me, who spoke in perfect English — lo and behold — we had assurances the CAT scan would be found, promises that a conference call on Monday would be held, and apologies for any suffering my mother had gone through for a most regrettable mistake.

I think my mother's English almost had an effect on limiting my possibilities in life as well. Sociologists and linguists probably will tell you that a person's developing language skills are more influenced by peers. But I do think that the language spoken in the family, especially in immigrant families which are more insular, plays a large role in shaping the language of the child. And I believe that it affected my results on achievement tests, I.Q. tests, and the SAT. While my English skills were never judged as poor, compared to math, English could not be considered my strong suit. In grade school I did moderately well, getting perhaps B's, sometimes B-pluses, in English and scoring perhaps in the sixtieth or seventieth percentile on achievement tests. But those scores were not good enough to override the opinion that my true abilities lay in math and science, because in those areas I achieved A's and scored in the ninetieth percentile or higher.

This was understandable. Math is precise; there is only one correct answer. Whereas, for me at least, the answers on English tests were always a judgment call, a matter of opinion and personal experience. Those tests were constructed around items like fill-in-the-blank sentence completion, such as, "Even though Tom was _____ , Mary thought he was _____ ." And the correct answer always seemed to be the most bland combinations of thoughts, for example, "Even though Tom was shy, Mary thought he was charming." with the grammatical structure "even though" limiting the correct answer to some sort of semantic opposites, so you wouldn't get answers like, "Even though Tom was foolish, Mary thought he was ridiculous." Well, according to my mother, there were very few limitations as to what Tom could have been and what Mary might have thought of him. So I never did well on tests like that.

The same was true with word analogies, pairs of words in which you were supposed to find some sort of logical, semantic relationship — for example, "*Sunset* is to *nightfall* as _____ is to _____ ." And here you would be presented with a list of four possible pairs, one of which showed the same kind of relationship: *red* is to *stoplight, bus* is to *arrival, chills* is to *fever, yawn* is to *boring*. Well, I could never think that way. I knew what the tests were asking, but I could not block out of my mind the images already created by the first pair, "*sunset* is to *nightfall*" — and I would see a burst of colors against a darkening sky, the moon rising, the lowering of a curtain of stars. And all the other pairs of words — *red, bus, stoplight, boring* — just threw up a mass of confusing images, making it impossible for me to sort out something as logical as saying: "A sunset precedes nightfall" is the same as "a chill precedes a fever." The only way I would have gotten that answer right would have been to imagine an associative situation, for example, my being disobedient and staying out past sunset, catching a chill at night, which turns into feverish pneumonia as punishment, which indeed did happen to me.

I have been thinking about all this lately, about my mother's English, about achievement tests. Because lately I've been asked, as a writer, why there are not more Asian Americans represented in American literature. Why are there few Asian Americans enrolled in creative writing programs? Why do so many Chinese students go into engineering? Well, these are broad sociological questions I can't begin to answer. But I have noticed in surveys — in fact, just last week — that Asian students, as a whole, always do significantly better on math achievement tests than in English. And this makes me think that there are other Asian American students whose English spoken in the home might also be described as "broken" or "limited." And perhaps they also have teachers who are steering them away from writing and into math and science, which is what happened to me.

Fortunately, I happen to be rebellious in nature and enjoy the challenge of disproving assumptions made about me. I became an English major my first year in college, after being enrolled as premed. I started writing nonfiction as a freelancer the week after I was told by my former boss that writing was my worst skill and I should hone my talents toward account management.

But it wasn't until 1985 that I finally began to write fiction. And at first I wrote using what I thought to be wittily crafted sentences, sentences that would finally prove I had mastery over the English language. Here's an example from the first draft of a story that later made its way into *The Joy Luck Club*, but without this line: "That was my mental quandary in its nascent state." A terrible line, which I can barely pronounce.

Fortunately, for reasons I won't get into today, I later decided I should envision a reader for the stories I would write. And the reader I decided upon was my mother, because these were stories about mothers. So with this reader in mind — and in fact she did read my early drafts — I began to write stories using all the Englishes I grew up with: the English I spoke to my mother, which for lack of a better term might be described as "simple"; the English she used with me, which for lack of a better term might be described as "broken"; my translation of her Chinese, which could certainly be described as "watered down"; and what I imagined to be her translation of her Chinese if she could speak in perfect English, her internal language, and for that I sought to preserve the essence, but neither an English nor a Chinese structure. I wanted to capture what language ability tests can never reveal: her intent, her passion, her imagery, the rhythms of her speech and the nature of her thoughts.

Apart from what any critic had to say about my writing, I knew I had succeeded where it counted when my mother finished reading my book and gave me her verdict: "So easy to read."

■ SUMMER SMITH TAYLOR

The Genre of the End Comment: Conventions in Teacher Responses to Student Writing

Summer Smith Taylor is an associate professor of English at Clemson University and cochair of the CCCC Committee on Assessment. At Clemson, she is director of the MA in Professional Communication and the Advanced Writing Program. Dr. Taylor studies writing assessment, especially the teaching and assessment of writing in engineering. Her most recent research study compares the intended meaning of engineering teachers' comments on student papers with the student writers' perceptions of their meaning. She has been published in many academic journals, and her article "The Genre of the End Comment," which originally appeared in *College Composition and Communication* in 1997, has been very influential within the field of rhetoric and composition. Using an empirical approach, Smith Taylor shows how teachers often write comments in a way that students have come to expect and that may, therefore, risk losing some of their impact.

■ ■ ■

A composition teacher finishes reading a student's paper and poises her pen over the blank space at the bottom of the final page.

> This is a very good essay. You used quotes well to support your argument and the discussion of the Cousteau museum was interesting and effective in developing your point. Your paper is well-organized and your argument is well-accommodated to your audience. Your equation of the slaughter of whales to the capture of dolphins for massive parks seems a bit extreme, though. Try not to stretch too much for startling examples. There are a few awkward sentence structures and your conclusion is a bit forced, but otherwise, this is well-done.

The teacher could have written anything, but she chose to script a statement that closely resembles not only her previous end comments, but also the end comments of other composition teachers. Why?

Part of the answer, at least, lies in genre. But the similarities between end comments cannot be ascribed to active regulation of the genre by the teaching community. Teachers usually do not receive formal training in commenting and rarely share their written comments with each other. End comments are not preserved in one location for perusal by members of the community. Teachers rarely read their comments more than once or twice, since comments are widely dispersed shortly after they are written. In addition, many teachers have probably considered changing their commenting strategies at least once during their teaching careers, and these changes would also seem to make a stable genre unlikely.

Yet faced with multiple student papers, the teacher nonetheless develops a pattern of response. And because other teachers face the same situation, they develop similar patterns. Over time, the teachers create a history of practice that, while always evolving, generates expectations for both readers and writers of end comments. In this way, a genre forms in response to "a recurrent rhetorical situation" (Miller 155), a situation which consists of the relationships between the teacher, students, their papers, and the educational institutions that sanction and encourage the interchange.

The teacher possesses the institutional power in the relationship and can use comments to motivate, educate, or chastise her students. But the student the paper, and the institution can also exert power over the teacher. The teacher may fear authority challenges from aggressive students who receive poor grades or who oppose the teacher's views on writing. Even the student with the most fragile self-esteem can hold a kind of power over the teacher if the teacher feels obligated to communicate gently with that student. And the student's paper is not without power in this rhetorical situation, since it can frustrate or mesmerize, persuade or offend the teacher. The educational institution also exerts power over the teacher's commenting by determining the focus of the teacher's curriculum, by rewarding or not rewarding the teacher for pedagogical innovations, and, in many cases, by requiring that the teacher return papers with comments within a specified period of time.

Rather than examining this complicated situation anew each time they write an end comment, teachers follow patterns that meet the needs of the situation. In Mikhail Bakhtin's theory of genre, these patterns are called primary and secondary speech genres. Primary speech genres are simple units of written or spoken discourse, such as apologies or greetings, that display "relatively stable" content, style, and structure each time they appear (Bakhtin 60). Secondary speech genres, such as novels, grant proposals, and end comments, are more complex units of discourse formed by "absorb[ing] and digest[ing] various primary genres" (62). Like primary genres, secondary speech genres display relatively stable content, style, and structure. If an end comment can be seen as a secondary speech genre, what are the relatively stable features that distinguish it from other types of discourse? What are the primary genres in the teacher's repertoire and according to what patterns do they combine to form end comments? Do the current generic conventions help teachers create effective comments? Would alternative ways of constructing comments be more appropriate?

Past research on commenting has generally focused not on these questions but on the discrepancy between teachers' commenting goals and the actual results of comments. Some researchers have argued that comments fail to achieve their pedagogical purposes because they are poorly written. Nancy Sommers, for example, argues that marginal and end comments often lack focus and specificity. Lil Brannon and Cy Knoblauch assert that comments reflect teachers' attempts to measure student writing against an ideal text, a practice which shifts authority over a text from the student writer to the teacher.[1] Others have researched the effect of comments on students' revisions. Melanie Sperling and Sarah Freedman, for example, found that one student consistently misinterpreted her teacher's marginal comments because the student did not share the teacher's knowledge and values regarding writing and revision. Larry Beason extended this research by identifying correlations between teachers' commenting aims and students' utilization of feedback. Still others have suggested that teachers should use alternative commenting methods, such as mentioning only the positive aspects of a piece of writing, in order to improve their responses (Zak).

But to address the problems with the average comment effectively, we first need to construct a better understanding of the nature of commenting as it is usually practiced. Robert Connors and Andrea Lunsford began this work in a 1993 article in which they outline some commenting patterns and tropes and identify some of the rhetorical principles that serve as the basis of teachers' evaluations. In the conclusion of their article, Connors and Lunsford issue a call to action. "Future studies," they write, should describe "in detail the topography we have only sketched in here . . . determining those genres and tropes of response we tend to privilege" (219). Such an effort, they argue, will help us understand our commenting roles and help new teachers enter our community. This study answers Connors and Lunsford's call for a better understanding of the genre of the end comment. My study was designed to identify the primary genres included in the teacher's repertoire, to determine the features of these primary genres, and to discover patterns of use of the repertoire to compose end comments. That is, I wanted to determine the range of options available to commenters and find out if commenters make similar choices when selecting from that repertoire, as Bakhtin's theory would predict. I also wanted to begin to assess the adequacy of commenting patterns for the task at hand.

First, I analyzed 208 end comments collected from ten teaching assistants at Penn State. The comments had been written in 1993 on papers produced by students in the university's first-year composition and rhetoric courses. The 208 comments were randomly selected so that the sample includes approximately the same number of end comments from papers that received grades of A, A–, B+, and so forth through D. A small number of papers that received the grade of F were also included in the sample. Then, to ensure that the results of this study would describe end comments written by teachers in a range of post-secondary institutions, I analyzed a second sample containing end comments written between 1983 and 1985 by teachers at universities of various sizes located in every region of the United States. I collected these comments from student papers originally gathered by Connors and Lunsford as part of a large-scale study of student errors and later used by them in the study of commenting described above. Connors and Lunsford constructed this sample randomly, as they explain:

> In response to a direct mail appeal to more than 1,500 teachers who had used or expressed interest in handbooks, we received . . . more than 21,500 papers from 300 teachers. . . . After stratifying our batches of papers by region, size of school, and type of school, we used the table of random numbers and the numbers that had been stamped on each paper as it came in to pull 3,000 papers. . . . Using the random number tables again, we pulled 300 papers. ("Frequency" 398–99)

From this representative sample of 300, I removed all papers which contained no end comment.[2] From the remaining 192, I randomly selected equal numbers of papers from each grade category as I had done with the Penn State sample. The national sample then included 105 end comments.

To begin my analysis, I read a set of comments and made a list of the types of remarks they included. I considered these topics, ranging from evaluations of the paper's organization to offers of assistance, the repertoire of primary genres from which teachers choose when composing end comments. To ensure that this repertoire included all primary genres used by teachers, I then read the entire set of comments, searching for additional primary genres. I found no additional genres, and therefore I am confident that I have identified the most commonly used primary genres. Then, I read all 313 comments again, recording the following for each: the primary genres it includes, the order in which those primary genres appear, and the grammatical subject and mood of each incarnation of a primary genre. Finally, I evaluated the comments and considered alternative patterns.

The Repertoire of Primary Genres

The study identified sixteen primary genres, falling into three groups: judging genres, reader response genres, and coaching genres.[3] (See Table 1.) A primary genre may consist of several sentences, a single sentence, or simply a phrase or fragment.

TABLE 1   Frequencies of Primary Genres in Sample

PRIMARY GENRE	TOTAL NUMBER IN SAMPLE
Judging Genres	
Evaluation of development	199
Evaluation of style	118
Evaluation of the entire paper	106
Evaluation of focus	105
Evaluation of effort	96
Evaluation of organization	88
Evaluation of rhetorical effectiveness	82
Evaluation of topic	63
Evaluation of correctness	52
Evaluation of audience accommodation	51
Evaluation of grade	48
Reader Response Genres	
Reading experience	67
Identification	43
Coaching Genres	
Suggestion for revision of current paper	155
Suggestion for future papers	88
Offer of assistance	37

Judging Genres

Not surprisingly, the majority of the primary genres in the teacher's commenting repertoire are tools for judging. Each of the eleven primary judging genres can express a positive or a negative message. (See Table 2 for the positive and negative frequencies of each judging genre.)

In the sample end comments, evaluations of focus, organization, development, and style are relatively equally distributed between positive and negative messages. But some primary genres are much more likely to express praise than criticism, while others demonstrate the opposite tendency.

For example, more than four out of five teacher evaluations of the entire paper are positive, despite the even distribution of grades across the sample. Teachers may be reluctant to write negative evaluations of an entire paper because they feel such statements would simply indicate global failure rather than pinpointing failings which can be corrected, or because they realize sweeping negativity could destroy a student's relatively fragile self-confidence. They may justify writing almost exclusively positive evaluations as a way to demonstrate fairness or sensitivity. Unfortunately, the positive-only convention in the evaluation of the paper genre is so strong that some teachers may write positive evaluations of the paper without actually believing them, simply to conform to the generic conventions. Of course, the positive evaluations range from high praise such as

TABLE 2   Positivity and Negativity of Judging Genres

JUDGING GENRE	POSITIVE	NEGATIVE
Evaluation of development	55%	45%
Evaluation of style	55%	45%
Evaluation of the entire paper	83%	17%
Evaluation of focus	43%	57%
Evaluation of effort	82%	18%
Evaluation of organization	62%	38%
Evaluation of rhetorical effectiveness	65%	35%
Evaluation of topic	84%	16%
Evaluation of correctness	5%	95%
Evaluation of audience accommodation	59%	41%
Justification of the grade	27%	73%

"This is an excellent paper!"[4] to mild praise with negative overtones such as "This is a pretty good narrative," and these variations allow the teacher to balance conformity with a measure of honesty. But when generic conventions become so strong that they lead teachers to make insincere statements, teachers' credibility and the effectiveness of the end comment may suffer.

Several other evaluative genres are also generally positive, but since they appear less frequently in end comments and evaluate a specific aspect of the student's paper, they often seem more sincere. One such primary genre is the evaluation of student effort. In this case, teachers usually make positive statements, perhaps to acknowledge the struggles of both strong and weak writers. For example, although one teacher found little else to praise in a particular paper, he or she commented "You worked hard on planning this paper — the outline was a good idea." Negative evaluations of effort seem to be a genre violation of a sort. They appear very rarely — only, it seems, when the teacher is sufficiently frustrated with the level of work represented by the paper to abandon worries about harming the student's self-esteem.[5] For example, one teacher wrote, "The poor quality of the ideas, style, and proofreading tells me that you didn't spend much time on this paper."

Approximately two-thirds of evaluations of rhetorical effectiveness, evaluations that address the persuasiveness of the writer's argument are positive. The genre generally appears in end comments written on A and B level papers. Teachers presumably consider other matters more urgent when commenting on average and below average papers. The audience accommodation primary genre, which explicitly discusses the extent to which the writer's strategies address the needs or attitudes of the writer's chosen audience, follows the same pattern in the Penn State sample as that of rhetorical effectiveness. No conclusions can be drawn about this primary genre from the national sample because only five of the 105 national comments include the genre. Perhaps the Penn State teachers use this primary genre more frequently than other teachers because the Penn State composition program emphasizes audience accommodation. The difference in frequency of the primary genre in the two samples may indicate the influence of the institutional setting and changing disciplinary emphases on commenting.

More than three-quarters of evaluations of topic are positive. In contrast to the rhetorical effectiveness and audience accommodation genres, evaluations of topic tend to appear only on papers graded C or below. Typically, these positive evaluations, such as "You've really got something interesting in this topic," highlight the interest or potential of the topic and seem designed to soften the negative evaluations that appear elsewhere in the comment. In fact, this primary genre may exist largely to help teachers fulfill the generic convention of including positive evaluations in end comments even when the student's paper is poor. These evaluations of topic could also provide encouragement for revision efforts.

Other judging genres, such as evaluation of correctness and justification of the grade, are selected from the repertoire primarily to convey negative messages. Naturally, teachers rarely mention correctness unless they perceive a problem. Justifications of the grade, which explicitly mention the reason for the letter grade assigned to the paper, are usually an attempt to forestall authority challenges, which occur most often when a student receives a low grade. For example, one teacher wrote "Though an interesting read, this paper does not fulfill the assignment and must receive a failing grade."

In summary, teachers select from eleven primary genres when evaluating a student's writing. Five have strong associations with praise and two with criticism, although teachers occasionally ignore the conventions. The remaining four genres are not tied to either positive or negative content.

Teachers also follow generic conventions for the phrasing of judging genres. For example, positive evaluations are frequently written as fragments, such as "nicely done" and "good paper." Eighty-six percent of all fragments in the sample express positive evaluations. Teachers are most likely to write fragments when evaluating the entire paper, organization, and style. Fragments provide no reasons for the praise and may give the impression of hastiness, thus weakening the praise.[6]

The primary judging genres also display patterns of grammatical subject. The teachers used "the paper" (or a variant such as "the organization" or "the style") as the grammatical subject of 46% of evaluative sentences. The use of "the paper" or a similar construction can lessen the impact of the evaluation by distancing it from the student. For example, a statement such as "You organized the second section well to bring out your main point" accords the student more credit than does a statement such as "The second section is well-organized to bring out the main point." Similarly, the use of "the paper" or a similar subject acts as a buffer between the student and criticism in negative statements. In other words, strict adherence to the generic convention of "the paper" or a variant as subject at times benefits the comment, but at other times harms it. The Penn State comments demonstrate three ways to alter the generic subject conventions to produce stronger and more personal comments in certain situations when "the paper" is less appropriate.

First, when expressing positive evaluations of focus, organization, development, the student's effort, audience accommodation, and topic, the Penn State teachers used "you" (meaning the student) as subject 58% of the time. This strategy heightens praise by acknowledging the student's active role in an achievement. When writing negative evaluations in these genres, the teachers conform to the "the paper" convention 63% of the time. Adherence to these local conventions is particularly obvious when a single sentence combines two primary genres, one of which carries a positive message and the other a negative message: "You make some good points, but this paper lacks a clear focus."

Second, when writing evaluations of correctness (100% negative in the Penn State sample), Penn State teachers used "there" as a pseudo-subject in 43% of the cases. For example, one teacher wrote "There are a lot of grammar errors in this paper." The use of "there" distances the criticism from the student writer even more than use of "the paper," and teachers may use it to protect the student from the stigma associated with correctness errors.

Third, 54% of the positive justifications of grades in the Penn State sample feature "I" (meaning the teacher) as subject. For example, "I gave your paper an A because you executed each aspect of the assignment well *and* wrote an especially strong conclusion." This technique heightens the praise by emphasizing that it comes from an expert, the instructor. It also allows the teacher to retain control over the discourse, even while acknowledging that the paper had an effect on him or her. (When negative, sentences justifying a grade in the Penn State sample conform to the "the paper" subject convention.)

Thus, rather than using "the paper" or a variant consistently in all situations, the Penn State commenters have developed other, no less consistent subject choice patterns for some situations when "the paper" is not the best subject. Such adaptations of the judging genres render them more flexible and responsive to actual contexts. Other features of the judging genres, most notably the strong tendency to write only positive versions of some genres and only negative versions of others, could benefit from similar adaptations. Evaluations of rhetorical effectiveness, audience accommodation, and topic seem particularly good examples of genres that could be effectively employed in their negative forms to point out common flaws in students' papers. Yet commenters generally write only positive versions of those genres. As commenters, we should strive to select from all available options to create the most effective response, rather than using only a portion of the options again and again regardless of situation.

Reader Response Genres

Evaluative genres form the bulk of the commenter's primary genre repertoire, but the repertoire also gives teachers other choices. The two reader response genres, for example, are tools for expressing the reactions of an active reader. Using these primary genres, a teacher can establish a more personal connection with the student and demonstrate the effects of words on readers.

The identification genre expresses the teacher's response to the student's personal experiences rather than to the student's writing. For example, a response to a paper that included a mention of the student's selection as a member of the baseball team included the following: "I have to congratulate you on your acceptance to the baseball team. I admire you because baseball will certainly require a large athletic commitment in addition to all the other academic pressures." Such attempts to break through the impersonality of the end comment and establish a connection with a student are unfortunately rare in the sample. The commenting situation — including the time constraints, the focus on assigning a grade, and the frequent similarities between papers in a set — works against recognizing the individuality of the student writer. Only one out of eight end comments in the sample includes the identification genre.

Statements in the reading experience genre are intended as representations of the thoughts the teacher had about the paper while reading it. For example, in an end comment for a paper about a swim meet, the teacher wrote: "Your narrative seems to lead up to the climax of the meet, but when we get to that point it's quite a let-down because you don't discuss the meet at all." By revealing the thoughts of a reader, such statements may remind students that their words have effects. The effects discussed are usually negative, such as confusion and disbelief, although the sample includes the occasional positive reading experience statement, such as "I am certainly convinced."

The reading experience genre often serves as evidence to support an evaluation. For example, one comment includes the following sequence of reading experience and evaluation of development: "I found myself wondering how somebody so unassuming and self-effacing can function as a role model. I don't understand how kids can know about him. You should have explained this point." The first two sentences in this example establish the teacher's confusion while reading, serving as a justification for the third sentence, which negatively evaluates the paper.

Examples of the reading experience genre are relatively rare in end comments, perhaps because they are more commonly written in the margin at the moment when the thought occurs to the teacher. Teachers may also be wary of using the genre to criticize a paper because it highlights the subjectivity of readers' responses. Statements of reading experience represent only the teacher's experience, often featuring "I" (meaning the teacher) as subject. They seem vulnerable to counter-arguments representing the reading experiences of peer reviewers or other readers. Some teachers give their statements more strength by aligning themselves with the student's audience, thus using an evaluation of audience accommodation to support the reading experience genre as in this comment: "I was confused by the sports terms you used, as non-sports-inclined members of your audience would also be." Such techniques may strengthen the effect of the reading experience genre.

Both reader response genres can serve as tools to remind students that their words affect readers. They also give the teacher a presence in the comment other than evaluator or writing coach, a presence reflected by the use of "I" as subject in almost two-thirds of these genres. The reader response genres, if used more frequently, could serve as an antidote to the usual impersonality of end comments.

Coaching Genres

In addition to evaluating and responding as a reader to students' papers, teachers also provide individualized instruction through end comments. For this purpose, the primary genre repertoire contains three coaching genres. The teacher can suggest ideas for revision of the current paper, suggest areas for improvement on future papers, or offer assistance to the student.

Suggestions (for current or future papers) can target either content or expression. Eighty-four percent of suggestions for revision of the current paper concern content issues, such as development, organization, and rhetorical effectiveness. Sixteen percent target expression, including correctness, clarity, and sentence structure. When suggesting areas to work on in future papers, teachers focused on content 35% of the time and expression 47% of the time. The other 18% request that the student put more effort into the next paper.[7]

Often, examples of the suggestion genres are merely veiled evaluations. For instance, one teacher wrote: "You could do some work on this essay to achieve smoother transitions and a tighter overall structure." According to my classification system, this statement is a suggestion for revision because it advises the student to "do some work on this essay." However, the main message of the statement is a negative evaluation of organization. Use of the suggestion genres to disguise evaluations may cause the student to view revision as punishment for mistakes, and may weaken the ethos of the teacher as coach. These evaluations-as-suggestions also provide few specifics to guide the student. In contrast, consider another suggestion for revision of organization from the sample: "Could you think of ways to continue the general text of the essay and integrate the examples in an overall reflexive or descriptive essay of Pittsburghese? In other words, could you group the specific examples to illustrate the more general points you made?" This suggestion follows a negative evaluation of the "list-like structure" of examples in the paper, and the suggestion naturally reinforces the negative evaluation. However, it also offers specific advice, and this advice is its main message.

The third coaching genre, the offer of assistance, gives students the opportunity to seek individualized instruction beyond that possible in an end comment. Most offers in the sample are related to suggestions and follow those suggestions in the comment. For example, the samples include the following offers: "Before you finalize your revision, show it to me" and "Stop by my office if you want to talk about these issues in your next paper." As these examples indicate, offers are highly standardized, usually including either "see me" or "stop by." They function in general as encouragement for the student to seek additional help, but can serve other, sometimes contradictory, purposes as well. For example, offers sometimes reveal the teacher's concern that the student will not understand the end comment, as in "I'd be happy to explain in more detail so see me if this hasn't made sense." Occasionally, on papers receiving grades below C, offers of assistance serve as warnings to the student, indicating the severity of the paper's faults and implying unpleasant consequences if the faults are not soon corrected with the teacher's help. For example a comment on a D paper includes the following offer: "You really should see me so we can try to do something about your punctuation problems before the next paper."

As for the phrasing of the coaching genres, whereas teachers generally use declarative sentences to express judging and reader response genres, they tend to use commands and questions to express coaching genres. Thirty-nine percent of suggestions for revision of the current paper and 85% of suggestions for future papers are stated in the imperative, such as "Be more aggressive in persuading your reader to agree with you next time." Teachers are also likely to use commands, such as "see me," in the offer of assistance genre. Sixty-eight percent of all offers of assistance occur in the form of a command.

The use of the imperative to suggest or make an offer is unusual in everyday conversation and most written genres. The high incidence of the command in the coaching genres supports Bakhtin's assertion that primary genres change when they are absorbed by secondary genres (62). In the case of the end comment, the alteration probably stems from the power relationships in the situation. The genres of suggestion and offer usually indicate an approach by the speaker/writer, placing the listener/reader in the powerful position of accepting or rejecting the proposition. The imperative mood allows the teacher to maintain at least outward control of the power in these situations.

The interrogatory mood also appears in the coaching genres. Over half of all questions in the sample convey suggestions for revision of the current paper. Most often, these statements are questions for further thought, attempts to push the student to think more deeply about a subject. For example, one teacher asked "What do you think about the political implications of your proposal?" But other suggestions simply take the form of questions in order to disguise a negative evaluation: "Wouldn't your argument be strengthened by mentioning the specific musicians?" This question and others like it clearly imply "yes" answers, conveying a strong negative evaluation along with the suggestion for revision. However, the question structure may encourage students to consider the suggestion by engaging them in a dialogue, even if it is a limited and unbalanced dialogue.[8]

Thus the content and phrasing of the coaching genres suggests that teachers use them to push students to improve their writing. But all three genres place the burden of action on students, who must take the suggestion or accept the offer of assistance. Students may be unwilling to do so because they are intimidated by the negative evaluations that lie just beneath the surface of most suggestions and offers, and by the teacher's display of power through commands. To minimize the intimidation and thus make the suggestions and offers more inviting to students, teachers should consider two techniques. First, provide specific guidance in suggestions, rather than simply restating an evaluation in question or command form. Second, rather than commanding students to accept offers of assistance, use a structure such as "If you stop by my office, we can practice with some examples to improve your sentence variety," which emphasizes the benefits of choosing to visit the teacher.

Patterns in the Secondary Genre

When composing an end comment, the teacher typically selects four or five primary genres (each consisting of a group of sentences, a single sentence, a phrase, or a fragment) from the repertoire. The resulting secondary genre usually begins with positive evaluation, moves to negative evaluation and coaching, and ends either with coaching or positive evaluation. This pattern is elongated or shortened depending upon the length of the comment and the quality of the student's paper.

Eighty-eight percent of end comments in the sample begin with a positive evaluation. Evaluations of the whole paper are especially common, appearing at the beginning of 23% of comments. In fact, if the teacher uses the genre at all, he or she is most likely to place it at the beginning of the end comment. Sixty-nine percent of evaluations of the entire paper appear in the opening position. On the other hand, judging genres that usually carry negative messages, such as evaluation of grammar and justification of the grade, almost never appear at the beginning of end comments. Coaching genres are also very rare in the opening position because they usually fail to convey the positive message required of an opening. Teachers may choose to begin comments positively for a variety of well-intentioned reasons. For example, teachers may imagine the student's feelings when receiving a judgment of his or her writing and then deliver the praise the student hopes for — even if the teacher considers the paper worthy of only an average grade. However, the sample end comments offer little evidence that the teachers respond to individualized understandings of each student; rather, they seem to identify with a generic student apprehension.

In addition to a tendency to identify with a generic student, other factors may cause teachers to begin comments positively. For example, some teachers may wish to demonstrate their fairness, believing that a positive opener will convince students that the teachers were not simply searching for papers' faults. Teachers who consider comments a tutoring or motivational opportunity might also hope to give the student a positive attitude towards the comment by beginning it positively.

These good intentions may motivate many teachers to write positive openers, but many others may write them simply to follow the generic rule, perhaps even expressing insincere or exaggerated praise in order to fulfill expectations. Although the persistent adherence to a ritual opening may seem benign, it may actually diminish the effectiveness of even the sincerest praise. If students do not read comments carefully, or at all, it may be because the comments take highly standardized forms. Students who recognize that the positive opening is a generic rule may ignore the meaning of all positive beginnings simply because they appear at the beginning. Students who receive a low paper grade or who have low confidence in their writing ability would be most likely to have this reaction. These students may view the teachers' negative evaluations as the "real" message of the end comment, the reason for the grade, and conclude that the aspects of writing evaluated negatively are more important to the teacher than those evaluated positively in the comment opener. Students who receive a high paper grade or who are confident in their writing ability may be less likely to discount praise due to its conventional placement in the comment, but the fact remains that recognition of the positive-first convention could affect all students' perceptions of end comments that begin positively and thus diminish the effects of positive openers.

To guard against a weakening of their positive evaluations, teachers should consider resisting the generic conventions of the end comment on certain occasions. For example, teachers could give a positive opening more significance by following it with related reader response or coaching statements, rather than moving directly to negative evaluations. If positively evaluating development, the teacher might, for example, briefly explain the effect of one of the student's examples on the teacher as reader. Or the teacher might suggest ways to strengthen certain examples in the paper using techniques the student used successfully with other examples. The positive portion of the comment would then have the same structure usually found in the negative portion, with evaluation followed by a reader response or coaching genre. This strategy would be especially appropriate when the teacher wished to accord the positive and negative evaluations in a comment equal importance, or when the teacher wished to recognize exceptional student effort or give a student extra encouragement.

In addition, teachers could strive to insert positive evaluations throughout comments, organizing the comment not around a positive-negative-positive structure, but around some other principle such as a series of main points. For example, a teacher could include both positive and negative statements about the focus of a student's paper, highlighting places where the student maintained a clear focus and places where that focus lapsed, before moving on to positive and negative statements about another aspect of the paper.

After the positive opening, the second primary genre is as likely to be positive as negative, except in shorter comments and those written on poor papers, in which the teacher usually begins to criticize the paper with the second primary genre. Teachers usually comment on the content of the paper in the second statement, perhaps in order to demonstrate that they have examined the student's ideas before (or at least concurrent with) passing a negative judgment on them. Twenty-three percent of second primary genres are evaluations of development, and 11% are evaluations of rhetorical effectiveness. By the third primary genre, 51% of teachers express negative evaluations, with evaluation of development still the most common primary genre (18%).[9] Thus, the turning point between positive and negative is conventionally the second or third primary genre in an end comment. Teachers often mark the turning points in this progression with words such as "however," "but," "although," and "while." These and other similar words, which occur 335 times in the 313 comments (an average of 1.07 per comment), imply a dismissal of preceding statements of praise. By integrating positive and negative statements as I have already suggested, teachers could minimize the dismissal of praise that tends to occur in the traditional structure.

When writing the fourth primary genre, teachers select another negative evaluation 33% of the time. But as the comment draws to a close, teachers are less and less likely to write negative evaluations. Comments usually close with coaching or positive evaluation genres, and the turn to these genres usually occurs in the fourth or fifth primary genre slot. Forty-two percent of fourth primary genres are coaching genres. Thus the conventional pairing of negative evaluation and coaching constitutes the second major component of the secondary genre, following the positive component at the beginning. In fact, if a comment includes a coaching genre (most often a suggestion for revision or for future papers), that genre almost always appears after the negative evaluations, as the fourth or fifth primary genre. This convention holds true even if the suggestion being made is unrelated to the negative evaluation it follows.

This convention follows a logical movement from problem to solution and is probably intended by most teachers to help the student. Placement of coaching after negative evaluations can indicate confidence in students' ability to improve their writing and can motivate students to work towards that improvement. However, in the context of the end comment, the coaching genres are so consistently paired with negative evaluations that they take on a negative association. Framed between positive evaluations, the negative statements and the coaching genres appear to be a single block of text. As a result, coaching genres (usually suggestions for revision or for future papers) may seem like punishment for the "mistakes" mentioned in the previous negative evaluations. Students may learn to expect suggestions as part of the negative block in an end comment, and may approach both negative evaluations and suggestions in the same frame of mind. Again, if students recognize the convention, it loses its effectiveness.

To reclaim the effectiveness of the coaching genres, teachers might consider resisting the generic conventions of the end comment by varying the placement of suggestions. For example, teachers could include suggestions for future papers that build on *positive* evaluations, reminding the student that improvement involves capitalizing on strengths as well as minimizing weaknesses. In addition, teachers could place coaching genres at the end of the comment, with a positive statement between the negative evaluations and the coaching genres. This genre resistance would help break the conventional association between suggestions and negative evaluations, allowing the coaching genres to receive status as separate genres, rather than appearing as adjuncts to negative evaluations.

Although some comments end with a coaching genre, most comments end with a positive evaluation. Fifty percent of fifth primary genres are positive evaluations, as are 51% of the rather rare sixth and seventh genres. This positive-last convention probably derives from the same impulses that cause the positive-first convention: empathy with the student, a desire to demonstrate fairness, an attempt to motivate, and, of course, an obligation to follow a generic rule. Because the positive-last convention is not as strong as the positive-first convention, a positive ending may seem more significant and credible to students who are aware of the conventions of end comments.

Putting It All Together

This study identified a complex set of commenting conventions, including a repertoire of primary genres and patterns of selecting from that repertoire to construct a product we recognize as an end comment. The following examples of end comments demonstrate how these choices work in practice. The first, taken from the national sample, was written on a "C" paper about child abuse.

> Nicely done. The basic five-paragraph format works well for you and the paper is well-organized as a result. But the second paragraph needs some attention to transitional elements and certainly you need to catch the mechanical errors throughout. Focus attention on these two elements in your next paper in order to get over the hump of competent writing. As always, if you have any questions, don't hesitate to see me.

This comment begins, like most end comments, with a positive evaluation of the entire paper (expressed all too typically as a fragment) and continues with a positive evaluation of organization. The third primary genre, an evaluation of style, is negative, as are most third-position genres in the samples. The teacher makes a second negative evaluation, this time of correctness, before making a suggestion for the student's next paper and offering assistance.

This comment could be improved if the teacher resisted some of the generic conventions. The teacher could express the opening positive evaluation of the paper as a complete sentence to render its conventionality less obvious. The teacher could also attribute praise more directly to the student by using "you" (rather than "the format" and "the paper") as subject of the positive evaluations. The teacher could change the order of the genres so that they do not fall into a neat division of positive and negative. Perhaps most importantly, the teacher could personalize the comment by referring to specifics of the paper's content, and by including a reader response genre to emphasize the teacher's position as reader and the effect of the paper on readers. This comment contains very little to connect it to any particular paper, student, or teacher; in other words, the teacher did not adapt the generic conventions to the situation surrounding this particular comment.

The second example, taken from the Penn State sample, was written on an "A" paper evaluating the life of Booker T. Washington.

> You've done an excellent job with this evaluation you found so difficult to write. You are especially strong at supporting your claims with examples and backing them up with appropriate outside sources.
>
> Ideally, you would spend a little more time establishing why you chose particular criteria (and not others). Remember in future writing that this is important.
>
> Also remember the importance of locating well-respected scholars in the field who support your position. Some claims in this evaluation might be seriously challenged because there is much controversy about Washington's "truthfulness" these days. Show knowledge of other supporters to help your defense.
>
> Great attention to sentence structure, transitions, and paragraph coherence, as well.

This comment, although quite different in tone and content from the first, also follows the patterns identified in this study. It begins, typically, with a positive evaluation of the entire paper, and continues, also typically, with an evaluation of development. Notice that first one aspect of development (examples and evidence) is evaluated positively, and then another aspect (explanation of criteria) is evaluated negatively. In accordance with the usual pattern, the teacher follows the negative evaluation with a coaching genre, making a two-sentence suggestion for future work. Instead of writing a positive ending at this point, as the pattern would predict, however, the teacher circles back to negativity with an evaluation of the rhetorical effectiveness of the student's argument. Then, the teacher again uses a suggestion, this time for revision of the current paper, to follow the negative evaluation. Finally, the comment closes with a positive evaluation of style conveyed, all too typically, with a sentence fragment.

While this comment conforms to the typical pattern, it also departs from the conventions in some beneficial ways. For example, the teacher begins with a positive evaluation of the whole paper, but personalizes it with a reference to the difficulty of writing the paper, information the teacher must have remembered from conversations with the student. This personalization helps render the positive opening less conventional and therefore makes it seem more sincere. The teacher also uses "you" as subject, especially when praising the student, further personalizing the comment and attributing the strengths of the paper directly to the student.

Of course, this comment could also be improved. The teacher could strengthen the positive evaluation of development (second sentence) and balance the positive and negative portions of the comment by adding a reader response genre at the end of the first paragraph to explain the reasons a particular example is persuasive. The teacher could also use a complete sentence to express the positive evaluation of style at the end of the comment, thus giving it more weight and reducing the impression of hastiness created by the fragment.

These two end comments demonstrate the generative range of the secondary genre patterns revealed by this study. The two comments vary in length and tone, and respond to papers with different grades. Yet both of them conform to the key patterns of the end comment genre. Nearly all patterns identified in both the primary genre repertoire and the secondary genre held true for both the national and the Penn State samples, indicating that most elements of the end comment genre are relatively stable across time and place.

The stability of the genre — the very feature that makes end comments recognizable and, perhaps, easier to write — may also reduce the educational effectiveness of the comment. The stronger a generic convention, the more it constrains teachers' choices, encouraging them to write statements that fulfill generic expectations and discouraging them from resisting the genre even when resistance would be rhetorically effective. Students who have noticed the similarities between end comments they have received may tend to dismiss the advice they are given as formulaic and conventional.

Teachers in the sample did sometimes resist generic conventions. And conventions were stronger in some cases, such as writing a positive evaluation of the entire paper, than in other cases. As teachers, we must heighten our awareness of the constraints of generic conventions and the danger they pose to end comments' effectiveness. I have suggested several ways to resist the conventions to combat the negative effects of stability, but teachers should experiment with other ways to resist as well, always being certain to match the resistance to the situation. The danger to the effectiveness of the end comment is its stability as a genre — we must be vigilant to ensure that our alterations do not become permanent, and therefore constraining, modifications.

Acknowledgments

I wish to thank Jack Selzer for his constant encouragement and his frequent and thorough comments on this article, Davida Charney for her support of my interest in empirical research and her comments on the article, and Don Bialostosky for enthusiastic and tolerant instruction in genre studies. Thanks also to Richard Straub and Richard E. Miller for their careful attention to the article and their useful comments. I am also grateful to ten teachers at Penn State for allowing me to study their end comments, and to Bob Connors and Andrea Lunsford for allowing me to include their collection of student papers in my sample. A version of this article was presented at the 1994 Penn State Conference on Rhetoric and Composition.

NOTES

1. For further discussion of assessment based on ideals, see Huot.

2. One hundred and eight of the papers had no end comment. Twenty-one of these had a checklist indicating the student's performance on a variety of criteria, and the other 87 had only marginal comments. For this study, I analyzed only teacher responses written as sentences or phrases at the end of a student paper or in a "comments" space on a cover sheet.

3. The sixteen primary genres could have been classified in any number of ways. I choose these groups after completing my analysis because they seemed the most useful for highlighting the overall movement in the secondary genre from evaluation to suggestion.

4. All quotations of genres in this article were taken verbatim from the sample.

5. Note that negatively evaluating effort is different from suggesting that a student somehow alter his or her effort in the future. Although suggestions often imply a negative evaluation of effort, that implication is not their main purpose. And many suggestions concerning effort are simply offers of advice about the writing process.

6. In a survey of her students, Claudia Keh found that students consider one-word comments least helpful because they provide no explanation of the praise or criticism.

7. In both suggestion genres, the Penn State teachers tended to target content, whereas the national teachers tended to target expression. Eighty-nine percent of Penn State teachers' revision suggestions concerned content. The commenters in the national sample also targeted content but showed a greater tendency than the Penn State teachers to make suggestions about expression. Twenty-nine percent of the national sample suggestions for revision address expression, compared to only 11% of those in the Penn State sample. When suggesting areas to work on in future papers, Penn State teachers again were more likely to target content (45%) than expression (36%). The national sample teachers targeted expression 75% of the time, mentioning content only 8% of the time. (The other 17% of the suggestions for future papers in the national sample, and 19% in the Penn State sample, focus on student effort.)

The tendency of the Penn State teachers to comment on content while the national sample teachers comment on expression may derive from changes in the composition community between the early 1980s (when the national sample teachers wrote their comments) and 1993 (when the Penn State teachers wrote theirs). Although only nine to eleven years separate the comments, during that time the discipline's focus on rhetoric strengthened, and correctness and expression began to be deemphasized. The difference between the two samples may also derive from the Penn State composition program's emphasis on audience and rhetoric, which may lead Penn State teachers to comment more frequently on content issues than most teachers.

8. Keh found that her students consider questions the most helpful form of commenting because of their interactive nature. Her students said questions push them to think about a teacher's query.

9. If they do not choose development, the national and Penn State teachers diverge in their choices for the third statement, with the Penn State teachers preferring to comment on content and the national teachers preferring expression. The Penn State teachers' second choice for the third slot is evaluation of focus, at 13%. Suggestions for revision of the content of the current paper constitute 11% of all third statements in the Penn State sample. Evaluations of audience accommodation and negative evaluations of topic are also frequent choices. The mixed selection for the third statement in the Penn State sample indicates that teachers select a genre to address the content-related faults of the paper at hand.

In contrast, if the national teachers did not choose evaluation of development for the third genre, they tended to choose genres that target expression. Fourteen percent of the end comments in the national sample use evaluation of correctness as their third statement, and 12% use evaluation of style. Another 14% of national third statements offer suggestions for improving expression. Thus, while the national sample matches the Penn State sample in negativity of the third genre and in the favorite choice for the spot, it displays a tendency to focus on expression, rather than content, that is consistent with patterns in the use of suggestion genres by teachers in the two samples. This distinction between the two samples may be due to changes in the composition community or to features of the Penn State program, as discussed in footnote seven.

WORKS CITED

Bakhtin, Mikhail. "The Problem of Speech Genres." *Speech Genres and Other Late Essays*. Ed. Caryl Emerson and Michael Holquist. Trans. Vern McGee. Austin: U of Texas P, 1986. 60–102.

Beason, Larry. "Feedback and Revision in Writing Across the Curriculum Classes." *RTE* 27 (1993): 395–422.

Brannon, Lil, and Cy Knoblauch. "On Students' Rights to Their Own Texts: A Model of Teacher Response." *CCC* 33 (1982): 157–66.

Connors, Robert, and Andrea Lunsford. "Frequency of Formal Errors in Current College Writing, or Ma and Pa Kettle Do Research." *CCC* 39 (1988): 395–409.

———. "Teachers' Rhetorical Comments on Student Papers." *CCC* 44 (1993): 200–23.

Huot, Brian. "The Literature of Direct Writing Assessment: Major Concerns and Prevailing Trends." *Review of Educational Research* 60 (1990): 237–63.

Keh, Claudia. "Feedback in the Writing Process: A Model and Methods for Implementation." *ELT Journal* 44 (1990): 294–304.

Miller, Carolyn. "Genre as Social Action." *Quarterly Journal of Speech* 70 (1984): 151–67.

Sommers, Nancy. "Responding to Student Writing." *CCC* (1982): 148–56.

Sperling, Melanie and Sarah Freedman. "A Good Girl Writes Like a Good Girl." *Written Communication* 4 (1987): 343–69.

Zak, Frances. "Exclusively Positive Responses to Student Writing." *Journal of Basic Writing* 9 (1990): 40–53.

Acknowledgments (continued from page vi)

Text

Patricia Bizzell. "Hybrid Academic Discourses: What, Why, How" by Patricia Bizzell. From *Composition Studies*, Volume 27, Number 2, Fall 1999. Reprinted by permission of the author.

The Black Panther Party. "Ten Point Plan." Reprinted by permission of the Dr. Huey P. Newton Foundation. (www.blackpanther.org)

Blue Scholars. "The Ave." Lyrics by Blue Scholars. Copyright © 2006. Reprinted by permission of Blue Scholars.

Barbara Ehrenreich. "Cultural Baggage." From the *New York Times Magazine*, April 5, 1992. Copyright © 1992 by Barbara Ehrenreich. Reprinted by permission.

Jeanne Fahnestock and Marie Secor. "Rhetorical Analysis." From *Discourse Studies in Composition*, edited by Ellen Barton and Gail Stygall. Copyright © 2002 by Hampton Press, Inc. Reprinted by permission of the publisher.

Stanley E. Fish. "How to Recognize a Poem When You See One." From *Is There a Text in This Class? The Authority of Interpretive Communities* by Stanley Fish, pp. 322–37 (Cambridge, Mass.: Harvard University Press). Copyright © 1980 by the President and Fellows of Harvard College. Reprinted by permission of the publisher.

Paulo Freire. "The 'Banking' Concept in Education." Chapter 2 from *The Pedagogy of the Oppressed* by Paulo Freire. Copyright © 1970, 1993 by Paulo Freire. Reprinted by permission of the publisher, The Continuum International Publishing Group.

Michel Foucault. "Panopticism." From *Discipline and Punish* by Michel Foucault. English translation copyright © 1977 by Alan Sheridan (New York: Pantheon). Originally published in French as Surveiler et Punir. Copyright © 1975 by Editions Gallimard. Reprinted by permission of Georges Borchardt, Inc., for Editions Gallimard.

Clifford Geertz. "Thick Description: Toward an Interpretive Theory of Culture." Chapter 1 from *The Interpretation of Cultures*. Copyright © 1973 by Basic Books. Reprinted by permission of Basic Books, Inc., a member of the Perseus Books Group.

Beverly Gross. "Bitch." From *Salmagundi Magazine*, Summer 1994. Copyright © 1994 by Beverly Gross. Reprinted by permission of the author.

Suheir Hammad. "First Writing Since." First published in *In Motion Magazine*, November 7, 2001. Reprinted by permission of the author.

E. D. Hirsch Jr. "Preface to *Cultural Literacy*." From *Cultural Literacy* by E. D. Hirsch Jr. Copyright © 1987 by Houghton Mifflin Company. Reprinted by permission of Houghton Mifflin Company. All rights reserved.

Langston Hughes. "Theme from English B." From *The Collected Poems of Langston Hughes* by Langston Hughes, edited by Arnold Rampersad with David Roessel, associate editor. Copyright ©1994 by the Estate of Langston Hughes. Reprinted by permission of Alfred A. Knopf, a division of Random House, Inc.

Ada María Isasi-Díaz. "Hispanic in America: Starting Points." Originally published in *Christianity in Crisis*, May 31, 1991. Copyright © 1991 Ada María Isasi-Díaz. Reprinted by permission of the author.

Martin Luther King Jr. "Letter from Birmingham Jail." Copyright © 1963 by Martin Luther King Jr. Renewed copyright © 1991 by Coretta Scott King. Reprinted by permission of The Heirs to the Estate of Martin Luther King Jr., c/o Writers House, Inc., as agents for the proprietors.

Jonathan Lethem. "The Ecstacy of Influence." From *Harper's Magazine*. Copyright © 2007 by Harper's Magazine. All rights reserved. Reprinted from the February issue by special permission.

James W. Loewen. "The Land of Opportunity." From *Lies My Teacher Told Me: Everything Your American History Textbook Got Wrong* by James W. Loewen. Copyright © 1996 by James W. Loewen. Reprinted by permission of The New Press. "Handicapped by History: The Process of Hero-Making." From *Lies My Teacher Told Me* by James W. Loewen. Copyright © 1997. Reprinted by permission of The New Press. (www.thenewpress.com)

Ronald Macaulay. "Extremely Interesting, Very Interesting, or Only Quite Interesting? Adverbs and Social Class." From the *Journal of Sociolinguistics*, Volume 6, Number 3, 2002: 398–417. Copyright © Blackwell Publishers, Ltd. Reprinted by permission of the author.

Emily Martin. "The Egg and the Sperm: How Science Has Constructed a Romance Based on Stereotypical Male-Female Roles." Originally published in *Journal of Women in Culture and Society*, Volume 16, Number 31, 1991. Copyright © 1991 by University of Chicago Press. Reprinted by permission of the publisher.